UNITED STATES

30°N

Los Angeles ◉

MEXICO

Oahu

Hawaii

HAWAII

15°N

Mexico City ◉

North Pacific Ocean

Clipperton

Kiritimati

Line Islands

0°

equator

I

ds

C O O K

Marquesas
Islands

Galapagos
Islands

ICAN
MOA

F R E N C H   P O L Y N E S I A

I
S
L
A
N
D
S

Tuamotu Archipelago

Society Islands

Tahiti

15°S

Rarotonga

Austral Islands

Gambier Islands

Pitcairn
Islands

h Pacific Ocean

30°S

Easter

THE PACIFIC ISLANDS

Reproduced with permission from the
Center for Pacific Islands Studies at the University of Hawai`i at Mānoa
by Manoa Mapworks, Inc.
Revised 1997.

155°W

140°W

W ── E

125°W

45°S

110°W

95°W

American
Anthropology in
Micronesia

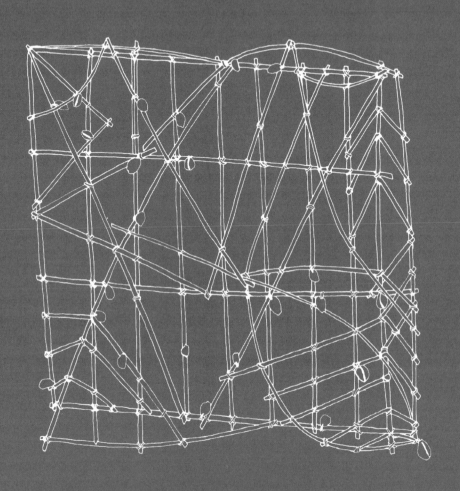

American Anthropology in Micronesia

Micronesia

An

Assessment

EDITED BY

Robert C. Kiste

Mac Marshall

UNIVERSITY OF HAWAI'I PRESS

HONOLULU

99 00 01 02 03 04   5 4 3 2 1

Library of Congress Cataloging-in-Publication Data

American anthropology in micronesia : an assessment / edited by Robert
C. Kiste and Mac Marshall.
p. cm.
Includes bibliographical references and index.
ISBN 0–8248–2017–7 (cloth : alk. paper)
1. Ethnology—Micronesia—Congresses.   2. Ethnologists—United
States—Congresses.   3. Micronesia—social life and customs—
Congresses.   I. Kiste, Robert C., 1936–   . II. Marshall, Mac.
GN669.A48   1998
306'.09965—21   98–29104
CIP

Maps and figures by Manoa Mapworks

Designed by Barbara Pope Design

Printed by The Maple-Vail Book Manufacturing Group

For Len and Hazel Mason
and
Norm and Tersa Meller

Contents

Illustrations

Tables in Text

Tables in Appendix 3

Preface

My own fascination with the Pacific Islands began in the mid-1950s when I spent two years in military service in what was then the Territory of Hawai'i. Later, at a small liberal arts college in Missouri, Lowell Holmes introduced me to anthropology, and his example suggested a career as an anthropologist specializing in the Pacific region. Holmes had recently completed his doctorate with a restudy of Margaret Mead's pioneering work in Sāmoa.

I finished my undergraduate education as an anthropology major at Indiana University, and at some point along the way, my interests began to focus on cultural change and applied anthropology in the Pacific Islands. Given those interests, two options for graduate school stood out above all others: the University of Oregon to study with Homer G. Barnett, and Stanford University to work with Felix Keesing. For a variety of reasons, I chose Oregon and Barnett.

My introduction to Micronesia occurred when I became a participant in Barnett's National Science Foundation–funded project on relocated communities in the Pacific, and was selected to work with the people who had been removed from Bikini Atoll in the Marshall Islands. I began my field research under tutelage of Leonard E. Mason of the University of Hawai'i who had previously worked with the Bikinians. As part of Barnett's research design, Mason introduced my wife, Valerie, and me to the Bikinians in June 1963. In the next year, and also as part of the Barnett project, Mason and I collaborated in research with the relocated Enewetak community, also in the Marshall Islands.

Back in Honolulu in late 1964, I first met Alex Spoehr when we compared notes about Marshallese ethnography. Later, while writing the report for Barnett's project (Kiste 1968) and my own dissertation at Oregon (Kiste 1967), I worked briefly with Ward H. Goodenough and David M. Schneider in Key West, Florida, in the training program for the initial wave of Peace Corps Volunteers destined for Micronesia in 1966. While the Florida encounter was brief, the opportunity to "talk shop" with two more of the vanguard of American anthropology in Micronesia was a heady experience for a student still struggling with a doctoral dissertation.

Another connection with Mason had enormous consequences for my own career. At a dinner at the Masons' home in 1964, I first met E. Adamson Hoebel and his wife, Irene, and in large measure, that encounter eventuated in my first faculty appointment as an Assistant Professor in the Department of Anthropology, University of Minnesota. Hoebel was departmental chairman at the time, and as a new faculty member I could not have asked for a better mentor. The Minnesota years were interrupted on two occasions by appointments as a visiting professor in the Department of Anthropology, University of Hawai'i, and by a further period of research in the Marshalls. I was also fortunate in that most of my twelve years at Minnesota were shared with Eugene Ogan. I benefited greatly from my discussions of anthropology and Oceania, particularly Melanesia, with Ogan, and we sustained our mutual interest in the Pacific at that northern outpost of American academia.

Because of my connections with five of the participants (Barnett, Goodenough, Mason, Schneider, and Spoehr) in the Coordinated Investigation of Micronesian Anthropology (CIMA), I have been keenly aware of the extent of American anthropology's involvement in the area. For reasons that should be apparent from this volume, it was perhaps inevitable that my sense of anthropology's presence in Micronesia was only intensified when I moved to the University of Hawai'i in 1978 to direct the Pacific Islands Studies Program, now the Center for Pacific Islands Studies (CPIS).

On December 7, 1991, a commemoration in Honolulu of the Japanese attack on Pearl Harbor was the first of many ceremonies around the Pacific to mark the fifty years that had elapsed since the events of World War II. Reflecting on such observances, it occurred to me that it would also be an appropriate time to assess the results of American anthropology's half century of involvement in Micronesia. I first raised the idea of a conference to accomplish this with Karen Nero and Glenn Petersen during the XVII Pacific Science Congress in Honolulu in 1991. Mac Marshall was soon involved in our delibera-

tions. Conference topics and contributors were identified through further discussions and correspondence with Marshall, Nero, and Petersen, and an initial
planning session was held at the 1993 annual meeting of the Association for
Social Anthropology in Oceania (asao) in Kailua-Kona, Hawai'i. By happen-
stance, most of the contributors were in Honolulu during the summer of 1993,
and a second planning session was held to design the conference program.
The eighteenth annual cpis conference, entitled "American Anthropology
and Micronesia," was held October 20–23, 1993, at the Tokai University facility
in Honolulu.

Thirteen invited papers were presented at the conference. Eleven were revised for publication and appear as chapters 1 through 11 of this volume. In
most cases, authors received feedback from their fellow contributors as well as
the editors, and revisions were substantial. A few chapters went through
second and sometimes third revisions.

Regrettably, other commitments and heavy workloads prevented two conference participants, Vicente Diaz, University of Guam, and Karen Peacock,
University of Hawai'i, from revising their papers. As a consequence, Diaz's
paper on the work of American anthropologists on Guam, "Reclaiming Culture
and History from a History of Culture in Guam," and Peacock's on anthropology and education in the US Trust Territory of the Pacific Islands, "Dick
and Jane Meet Emi and Tamag: Culture and the Classroom in Micronesia,"
are not among the chapters of this volume, but they are discussed in chapters
5 and 13 and are cited as unpublished works.

By intention and design, the anthropologists and others who were among
the initial researchers in Micronesia immediately after the war were not asked
to critique the results of their own labors. Instead, the last day of the conference was divided into two sessions that reviewed the proceedings of the
previous three days. In the morning session, three of the early researchers,
anthropologists Ward Goodenough and Leonard Mason and political scientist Norman Meller, reflected on their own experiences in Micronesia and commented on the thirteen papers. Subsequently, all three gave generously of
their time and contributed to the critique of papers as they were revised for
publication.

For the afternoon session, Vicente Diaz chaired a panel of Micronesians
who gave their views and assessments of the work and involvement of American anthropologists in Micronesia. The panel was composed of Resio Moses
of Pohnpei; Anne Hattori and Cecilia Perez of Guam; Faustina Rehuher and
Richard Salvador of Palau; and Joakim "JoJo" Peter of Chuuk. Other Micro-

nesians, mainly students, and other conference participants contributed to the discussions.

Registrations for the conference numbered around 150, and participants came from as far away as Guam in the west and several states on the US East Coast. Particularly welcome was a contingent of the old guard from trust territory days in Palau: Now living in Honolulu, Daniel and Shirley Peacock, and William Vitarelli, a resident of Maui, had served in education and other capacities in both Palau and Saipan. Also on hand were Roland and Maryanne Force who had conducted anthropological fieldwork in Palau in the early 1950s. Roland directed the Bishop Museum from 1962 to 1976 before moving to New York as director of the Museum of the American Indian. The Forces had recently returned to Honolulu, and the conference welcomed them back to the islands. Regrettably, Roland Force's retirement in Honolulu was of short duration. He died unexpectedly but of natural causes in 1996. Roland is missed by his many friends in Honolulu and elsewhere. Maryanne Force is editing the account of his years at the Museum of the American Indian that Roland had finished only a short time before his death.

Tokai University provided an excellent venue for the conference. The availability of meeting rooms, food service, lodgings, and parking under one roof facilitated discussion and interaction among participants. Tokai's location near the University of Hawai'i at Mānoa, Waikīkī and the Ala Moana Center, and downtown Honolulu makes for an attractive meeting place.

Lastly, concerning the production of the volume at hand: I had known Mac Marshall for about half of the time that American anthropology has been involved in Micronesia, but he and I had never collaborated on a project. In the four and a half years since the conference, Mac and I have worked with the contributors to revise their conference papers as chapters for this volume. Fortuitously, as editors we tended to focus on and notice different kinds of things, but at the same time our overall opinions concerning the separate chapters and the volume as a whole have been remarkably in accord. In short, our respective talents have complemented one another, and I could not have asked for a better collaborator and colleague.

It is my hope that this volume does justice to the efforts of the many anthropologists who have worked in Micronesia over the last half century, and that it contributes to the history of our discipline.

Robert C. Kiste

Acknowledgments

In the course of developing this volume, the editors have become indebted to numerous individuals. Violenda "Vi" Nakahara, Secretary, Center for Pacific Islands Studies, University of Hawai'i, has been of major assistance at all phases of the project. Most importantly, Vi prepared several versions of the manuscript as it went through the painstaking process of multiple revisions. Further, her superb management of the Center's front office and assistance with the administration of the Center's overall program made it possible for Kiste to devote much of his time over the last several years to this project. Joan Flannery, the Center's clerk-typist, gave a willing hand whenever it was needed. Daniel Foster's help with the name index is much appreciated.

Letitia "Tisha" Hickson, the Center's outreach coordinator, was largely responsible for the success of the 1993 conference that launched the entire endeavor, and she provided invaluable assistance to several of the contributors as they accessed source materials at the Pacific Collection, Hamilton Library, University of Hawai'i, from their home institutions. Tisha's efforts were well beyond the routine call to duty. Richard Kosaki, President, Tokai University at Hawai'i, and his staff, particularly Wanda Sako, provided an excellent site and support for the conference.

From the very beginning to the very end of the project, Karen Peacock, Curator, and Lynette Furuhashi, Librarian, Pacific Collection, were unstinting in their support. They were always available to ferret out odd pieces of needed information, locate the best photographs, or find others who knew what we needed to know. In the last category, Karen's father and mother, Daniel and Shirley Peacock, a long-time librarian and executive secretary, respectively, with the former US Trust Territory of the Pacific Islands, were enlisted as sources of information not found in any archival resource.

Of all the contributors to this volume, a special note of thanks must be extended to Don Rubinstein. He was quick to respond to all our inquiries, and he drew upon his resources at the University of Guam to locate additional necessary information.

At the National Academy of Sciences, Washington, D.C., Janice Goldblum was enthusiastic about the project and located documents pertaining to the planning of American anthropology's initial involvement in Micronesia; maps 1 and 2 dating from the late 1940s were made available through her good office.

Jane Eckelman, Manoa Mapworks, Honolulu, redrew maps 1, 2, and 3 from the originals. The endpaper maps, map 4 and figures 1 through 4 were designed by Eckelman, and her creative talents speak for themselves.

Mary Anne Fischer, Maryanne Force, Ward Goodenough, Richard Handler, Mike Levin, Leonard Mason, Mel Spiro, Hardy Spoehr, and Jack Tobin were generous in their time and efforts in the location and loan of photographs for publication.

David Givens, formerly with the American Anthropological Association, assisted our research in the Association's offices, and it was he who called our attention to the *International Directory of Anthropologists*, edited by Melville J. Herskovitz in 1950. That document proved invaluable and provided much of the material in chapter 1 concerning the historical context of American anthropology's involvement in Micronesia.

Kiste owes a special debt to Sitiveni Halapua, Director, Pacific Islands Development Program, East-West Center, who provided secluded office space where much of Kiste's work on this volume was accomplished.

At the University of Hawai'i Press, William Hamilton, Director, and Pamela Kelley, Acquisitions Editor for Pacific materials, were supportive and encouraging throughout the course of the project. We owe a special debt to Jan Rensel. As copy editor for the University of Hawai'i Press, her talents and attention to detail gave the manuscript that extra needed touch and improved the quality of the final product.

Lastly, we wish to thank the eleven authors who contributed to this volume. They were patient through the long editing process, and their cooperation and collegiality have been greatly appreciated.

Robert C. Kiste
Mac Marshall

Abbreviations

AAM	Association for Anthropology in Micronesia
ALS	Amyotrophic lateral sclerosis
ASA	Association for Social Anthropologists
ASAEO	Association for Social Anthropology in Eastern Oceania
ASAO	Association for Social Anthropology in Oceania
AWC	Atlas of World Cultures
BAE	Bureau of American Ethnology
BIA	Bureau of Indian Affairs
CAHA	Council of the Humanities Art gallery (Guam)
CCS	Cross-Cultural Survey
CIMA	Coordinated Investigation of Micronesian Anthropology
CNMI	Commonwealth of the Northern Mariana Islands
COM	Congress of Micronesia
CPIS	Center for Pacific Islands Studies (University of Hawai'i)
DCPP	Comparative Study of Cultural Change and Stability in Displaced Communities in the Pacific (University of Oregon)
EA	Ethnographic Atlas
FMAD	Foreign Morale Analysis Division
FSM	Federated States of Micronesia
HRAF	Human Relations Area Files
JIC	Justice Improvement Commission
MARC	Micronesian Area Research Center (University of Guam)
MPH	Master's of Public Health degree

NIH	National Institutes of Health
NIMH	National Institute of Mental Health
NRC	National Research Council
NSF	National Science Foundation
ONR	Office of Naval Research
UOG	University of Guam
PACE	Pacific Cratering Experiments (Enewetak Atoll)
PALI	Pacific and Asian Linguistics Institute (University of Hawaiʻi)
PD	Parkinsonism-dementia complex
PES	Philippine Ethnological Survey
PHA	Pacific History Association
PhD	Doctor of Philosophy
PIP	Pacific Islands Studies Program (University of Hawaiʻi)
PNG	Papua New Guinea
PSB	Pacific Science Board
RMI	Republic of the Marshall Islands
SCCS	Standard Cross-Cultural Sample
SCS	Soil Conservation Service
SIM	Scientific Investigation of Micronesia
SONA	School of Naval Administration (Stanford University)
SPC	South Pacific Commission
TAT	Thematic Apperception Test
TRIPP	Tri-Institutional Pacific Program
TTC	Trust Territory Code
TTR	Trust Territory Reports
UN	United Nations
UNTS	United Nations Treaty Series
UOG	University of Guam
UPNG	University of Papua New Guinea
US	United States
USCC	United States Commercial Company
USDOE	United States Department of Education
USP	University of the South Pacific (Fiji)
USPHS	United States Public Health Service
USTTPI	United States Trust Territory of the Pacific Islands
WES	World Ethnographic Sample
WRA	War Relocation Authority

Introduction

Robert C. Kiste and Mac Marshall

THIS VOLUME FOCUSES ON those Micronesian islands that have experienced American colonial rule: the Carolines, the Marshalls, and the Marianas. Not included in our purview are the contemporary Micronesian nations of Nauru and Kiribati, which lie geographically within what usually is called Micronesia but have rather different colonial histories. Over the past fifty years, the areas of Micronesia administered by the United States have shared a unique colonial experience that sets them apart from both their Micronesian neighbors and the rest of the Pacific (with the possible exception of American Samoa). The impact of American rule has been particularly great in the political arena, and Micronesia's massive economic dependency can be rivaled only by the territories of the French Pacific. In providing a separate analysis for "American Micronesia," we do not deny that culturally and historically it shares many characteristics with and has numerous linkages to other Micronesian and other Pacific islands. Indeed, such connections are considered in Robert C. Kiste's discussion of Micronesia as a culture area in chapter 13.

This volume also focuses on sociocultural anthropology and the several offshoots of the discipline that have developed in the last five decades. Explicitly not included here are prehistory, anthropological linguistics, and physical anthropology. The applied anthropology interests of the 1940s were played out primarily within the domain of sociocultural anthropology, and until recently that subfield has dominated research in Micronesia. Most major work in archaeology came later, with a substantial amount of research accomplished only in the past twenty years (see Rainbird 1994 for a recent summary; see also

1

appendix 2C). During the early postwar years a few anthropological linguists worked in Micronesia, but the large body of research on Micronesian languages completed subsequently has been done almost exclusively by linguists. For example, under the Pacific and Asian Linguistics Institute (PALI) project, several faculty members and graduate students in the University of Hawai'i Department of Linguistics have devoted extensive study to Micronesian languages. While a few researchers in the first group of American anthropologists to work in Micronesia after World War II represented physical anthropology, this area of inquiry has since been neglected compared to the other subfields (see appendix 2C).

In the 1940s, anthropological research in Micronesia provided a major impetus for a new and struggling academic discipline. Anthropology's practitioners in American universities and museums were relatively few in number, and research funds were scarce, particularly for overseas fieldwork. Most sociocultural research was conducted as salvage ethnography on American Indian reservations, often during the summer months; a tradition of extended periods of field research had yet to be established among North American anthropologists. Although the postwar involvement of anthropologists in Micronesia continued a variety of war-related applied projects, it also represented an entirely new venture. The opportunity for overseas fieldwork was without parallel in American anthropology, opening to English speakers a new part of the Pacific as a major research area. Collectively, the several different programs that constituted the effort in Micronesia represent the largest research initiative in the history of American anthropology.

American anthropological research in Micronesia can be divided into two phases. In the first, applied concerns dominated the World War II years and remained paramount through the 1950s. Most of the anthropologists at this time were funded or employed by various agencies of the US federal government, some in the direct hire of the US Trust Territory of the Pacific Islands (USTTPI). By the early 1960s the tide had clearly turned, and the second phase began. The last applied anthropologists became community development officers, took other positions in the administration, or ended their service in Micronesia. Thereafter most research was conducted by individuals as an academic endeavor, with practical applications of little or no concern.

With all of this in mind, each invited contributor to this book, based on their previously demonstrated expertise, was asked to review a particular subject area and assess how post–World War II anthropological research had affected the Micronesian people themselves, the US colonial administration, and the discipline of anthropology.

Kiste and Suzanne Falgout (chap. 1) describe the historical background of American anthropology's involvement in Micronesia, review the heyday of applied work there, outline the developments of the last twenty-five years, and discuss the shifting political milieu within which they occurred. As a historian, David Hanlon (chap. 2) analyzes the interplay between anthropology and history, particularly the recent convergence of the two fields. In the process of showing how American colonialism affected anthropologists' use of history, he calls into question the very existence of an entity called "Micronesia."

Each of the authors of chapters 3 through 8 examines the research conducted by American anthropologists in a specific topical area of sociocultural anthropology. Although in most cases they focus primarily on disciplinary concerns, they also consider connections between work done in the era of applied anthropology and research completed later when anthropology was pursued mainly for its own sake.

In chapter 3, William Alkire reviews research conducted by anthropologists on environmental and ecological topics. He summarizes a number of important anthropological and regional issues that have been clarified by this work, and examines different cultural adaptations that have evolved in Micronesian societies. These adaptations include certain forms of kinship, social organization, and related political institutions, which in turn are explored by Mac Marshall and Glenn Petersen in chapters 4 and 5. Marshall also touches on the integral relationship among social institutions, land tenure systems, and the ecological settings outlined by Alkire. In contrast to Hanlon, Marshall argues for "a common pool of ideas" that provides a framework of "Micronesian-ness." Similarly, Petersen holds that there are shared Micronesian political patterns, both traditionally and in the ways these societies have adjusted to colonialism and introduced political forms. He discusses how strategic interests and the politics of the colonial regime have affected both anthropology and the cultures and societies of the region.

Matters of ethnicity and identity are intertwined with political and other issues at all levels of the social and cultural worlds of Micronesians: local kin groups and communities, states within nations, and the new nations of the region. In chapter 6, Lin Poyer shows that anthropologists have sometimes used sociological concepts to discuss ethnicity, and that the language used in the discussion reflects whether or not ethnicity is viewed as a "social problem." Regional politics and other regional issues are considered, and the ques-

1993 Conference. Karen Nero, seated, talks with *Ward Goodenough* (back to camera); *Nancy Lewis, Department of Geography, University of Hawai'i; and William Alkire. In background, left to right, Leonard Mason* (back to camera), *Karen Peacock, Mac Marshall, Donald Rubinstein, and Robert Kiste. Photograph by Carolyn Yacoe.*

1993 Conference. Left to right: *Vicente Diaz, Micronesian Area Research Center, University of Guam; Resio Moses, Secretary of Foreign Affairs, Federated States of Micronesia; Faustina Rehuher, Director, Belau National Museum; Joakim Peter, Chuuk, student, University of Hawai'i. Photograph by Carolyn Yacoe.*

1993 Conference. Left to right: *Faustina Rehuher, Director, Belau National Museum; Richard Salvador, Palau, student, University of Hawai'i; Peter Black. Photograph by Carolyn Yacoe.*

1993 Conference. Left: *Tisha Hickson,*
Outreach Coordinator and Conference
Organizer, Center for Pacific Islands
Studies, University of Hawai'i; right:
Kathy Czar, Social Studies teacher,
Seabury School, Maui, Hawai'i.
Photograph by Carolyn Yacoe.

tions of ethnicity she discusses relate to Hanlon's doubts over whether "Micronesia" is a meaningful construct.

In chapters 7 and 8, Peter Black and Karen Nero analyze the influence of culture and personality studies as a common inspiration for further developments in psychological anthropology and for the anthropology of the arts in Micronesia. In following psychological anthropology's transformations from emic/etic analysis, to ethnoscience and cognitive anthropology, to ethnopsychology, Black shows that many of the central developments in psychological anthropology since World War II have grown directly out of research in Micronesia. Nero describes a great irony: she contends that some of the early anthropological work on the arts of Micronesia was far ahead of its time, but because this work was later ignored, studies of the arts of Micronesia generally have languished.

Chapters 9 through 11 return to applied concerns in more recent years and issues pertaining to the relevance of anthropology for the world of practical affairs. Francis X. Hezel (chap. 9) discusses the relative merits of sociological and anthropological conceptual frameworks for understanding social problems in contemporary Micronesia. After reviewing a series of such problems—youth misbehavior, alcohol abuse, suicide, child and spouse abuse—he concludes that anthropological approaches have been far more fruitful. In chapter 10, Don Rubinstein looks at research by medical anthropologists in the islands, and then examines the health and medical systems put in place by the American administration. Although he discusses a wide variety of such research, in the end Rubinstein claims that medical anthropology has been a rather minor player in the wider Micronesian health arena since the end of the war. From the perspective of a legal scholar, Edward C. King (chap. 11) gives a mixed review to anthropology's impact on the judicial system of the trust territory. While he acknowledges that the work of anthropologists helped shape the USTTPI legal system and the principles that system produced, he also notes that there was no formal mechanism by which the court could systematically draw on anthropological knowledge.

The last two chapters offer two different kinds of overviews. Marshall (chap. 12) provides background on the movement of American anthropology into Micronesia, sketching the social relations that existed among the different individuals and institutions involved. Then, tracing "academic lineages," he reveals the substantial impact of the postwar push in Micronesia on the more general development of Pacific anthropology. Finally, Marshall discusses the overall theoretical and practical contributions of the Micronesian research for anthropology as a discipline. In chapter 13, Kiste returns to the core question that gave rise to both the 1993 conference and this book: What has resulted from American anthropology's half century of involvement in Micronesia? In so doing he wrestles with the issue of Micronesia as a meaningful culture area, and lastly he offers some suggestions about the future direction of research in Micronesia.

In an effort to provide as thorough a record as possible of our subject matter we have included three appendixes to the volume. Appendix 1, prepared by Falgout and Kiste, provides cross-checked lists of the participants in the sequence of major anthropological research ventures that took place in Micronesia after the war. These ventures are described at some length in chapters 1 and 12.

Appendix 2, assembled by Marshall, lists Micronesia anthropology PhD dissertations accepted by US universities from 1945 to 1997. These are arranged alphabetically by author by decade, chronologically by university, and finally by island area and anthropological subfield.

Appendix 2 offers a springboard to consideration of the postwar development and impact of anthropology in Micronesia. It reveals that before 1960, eleven of the fourteen anthropology doctorates for dissertations about Micronesia were awarded by just two universities: Harvard and Yale. These two institutions had played central roles in the conception and launching of the Coordinated Investigation of Micronesian Anthropology (CIMA). Beginning in the 1960s, as some of the CIMA-sponsored researchers took up faculty positions elsewhere, they began to supervise a "second generation" of Micronesia researchers. By the 1970s many of these scholars had teaching positions of their own and mentored the next group of anthropologists. During this decade Micronesia anthropology PhDs were awarded by no fewer than two dozen universities, a pattern that declined only slightly during the 1980s. With the exception of Fred Reinman's dissertation and excavations on Guam (1965), Alex Spoehr's early work in the Northern Marianas (1957), Edward and Delila Giffords' research on Yap (Gifford and Gifford 1959), and Douglas Osborne's work on Palau (1966), archaeology has developed in Micronesia mostly in the 1980s (see appendix 2C). Appendix 2 also shows the overwhelming dominance of sociocultural anthropology in the islands—which may be seen as one result of the applied focus of CIMA and subsequent research developments.

Appendix 3 represents a more substantial contribution, which the editors solicited from Terence Hays, a New Guinea specialist. We were aware that, in connection with another project, Hays had done the background research necessary to report and analyze the representation of Micronesian anthropology in two different places: standard cross-cultural databases and samples, and introductory anthropology textbooks published over the past fifty years. Appendix 3 provides the results of his analysis along with his conclusions concerning the overall impact of Micronesian anthropology in these two arenas.

CHAPTER ONE

Anthropology and Micronesia: The Context

Robert C. Kiste and Suzanne Falgout

ON MONDAY, DECEMBER 8, 1941, the day after the Japanese attack on Pearl Harbor, George Peter Murdock called together the faculty and graduate student staff of the Cross-Cultural Survey, Institute of Human Relations, Yale University, and they began the task of assembling information on the former Japanese mandated islands in Micronesia. Items they collected included the ethnographies produced by the Südsee Expedition (1908–1910), directed by Georg Thilenius during the German colonial era (1899–1914), and other German records; a lesser quantity of material (Hatanaka 1979) from the period of Japanese rule (1914 to World War II); and American publications from the mid-nineteenth century to the present (Mason 1985a, 32). Although unforeseen at the time, the work at Yale was only the beginning of the largest research effort in the history of American anthropology and a major program in applied anthropology. This chapter outlines the context in which these and subsequent events unfolded.

THE SETTING

In the early 1940s, anthropology was still a relative newcomer on the American academic scene. The American Anthropological Association was just over forty years old, and its Fellows numbered about three hundred. About a dozen and a half departments offered a doctorate in anthropology, and six dominated the production of new PhDs. Of the 106 doctorates awarded in anthropology between 1939–1940 and 1945–1946, 87 came from six institutions: Harvard (24),

Columbia (19), Chicago (12), Pennsylvania (12), Yale (11), and the University of California, Berkeley (9). (*American Anthropological Association News Bulletin* 2 [Nov.] 1948). The Society for Applied Anthropology was just a fledgling organization, its inception predating the disaster at Pearl Harbor by only a few months.

The conceptual frameworks of anthropology were largely derived from the Boasian paradigm of historical particularism, with cultural relativism a basic tenet of the discipline. However, as discussed below, centrifugal forces were beginning to erode anthropology's four-field holistic approach into the sub-disciplines of cultural anthropology, linguistics, archaeology, and physical anthropology. As George Stocking has noted, cultural anthropology had only recently evolved from ethnology, and it was an American "cultural anthropology" as opposed to British "social anthropology" (1992, 147–159).

Cultural anthropology itself was a product of its North American origins and history. The vast majority of American anthropologists had conducted field research among Native American societies that had experienced severe disruptions. Traditional ways of life had been abruptly ended, and many Native Americans had been resettled on reservations, often far distant from their ancestral homelands. Cultural anthropology's research agenda was largely one of salvage ethnography. As the traditional past could not be directly observed, it was elicited from the memories of older informants. Ethnographies of the day resembled catalogues with standard entries to be filled: kinship, life crises, religion, folklore, settlement pattern, economics, and so on. The anthropologist's task was to describe these elements and traits and arrange them into culture complexes and culture areas.

Prior to World War II, the Pacific Islands had already achieved a position of prominence in anthropology because of the work of such figures as Raymond Firth in Tikopia, Bronislaw Malinowski in the Trobriands, and Margaret Mead in American Samoa and New Guinea. For a variety of reasons, particularly a paucity of research funds, fieldwork outside of the Americas was the exception rather than the rule. But given the small size of the profession in the United States at the time, the number of American anthropologists who reached the Pacific was greater than generally appreciated today. Evidence of this can be found in an *International Directory of Anthropologists* (Third Edition), published in 1950 under the editorship of Melville J. Herskovits. Fortunately for the concerns of this volume, the data were collected during the immediate postwar years, the period of the greatest intensity of American involvement in Micronesia.

Seventeen American cultural anthropologists had conducted research in the Pacific before the war, and another ten from the other three subfields had also worked in the region. The seventeen were almost evenly divided between Polynesia and Melanesia.[1] With two major exceptions (the research of Felix Keesing [F. Keesing and M. Keesing 1956] and Margaret Mead [1928] in the two Samoas), much of the work in Polynesia in the 1920s and 1930s was associated with the Bishop Museum and concerned the reconstruction of traditional cultures. As examples, one thinks of the work of Kenneth P. Emory in the Society Islands and Tuamotus (Emory 1940, 1975; Highland et al. 1967), E. S. C. and Willowdean Handy in several Polynesian locations, and Ralph Linton (1923, 1926) who collaborated with the Handys (Handy 1930) in the Marquesas. In contrast to their colleagues who worked in Polynesia, Margaret Mead (1935), Douglas L. Oliver (1955), Hortense Powdermaker (1933), and John Whiting (1941) conducted research in Melanesian societies that had suffered far less outside intervention. Other than Laura Thompson (1941), no American anthropologist had set foot in Micronesia, but her work on Guam during the late 1930s was a harbinger of future projects. Thompson was concerned with an acculturated people, the Chamorros of Guam, and her research was commissioned by the US Navy for applied purposes.

In the decade or so prior to World War II, interest in salvage ethnography was waning (after all, the results that could be achieved diminished with each passing year), and a "rising current of scientism in the late 1930s" had begun to challenge the Boasian program (Stocking 1992, 142). For some anthropologists, it had become an article of faith that their discipline was indeed a science more or less on par with the natural sciences. For example, Felix Keesing (1945) repeatedly referred to "the science" of anthropology in a volume entitled *The Science of Man in the World Crisis* edited by Ralph Linton during the war years.

Stocking has identified three developments within the "scientizing trend" in cultural anthropology, all three more integrative in purpose and design than Boasian ethnology: a psychological focus via the culture-and-personality movement that grew out of Ruth Benedict's configurationalism; a sociological line that stemmed in part from the functionalisms of Malinowski and A. R. Radcliffe-Brown but was broad enough to include Robert H. Lowie's and Murdock's interests in social organization; and a "techno-environmental" or materialist orientation that led to the cultural ecological and neo-evolutionary approaches of Julian Steward and Leslie White (Stocking 1992, 135–142). Several chapters in this volume analyze how research in Micronesia has reflected these trends. For example, Peter Black (chap. 7) outlines developments in psychological anthropology that were largely inspired by the culture-and-personality movement; Karen Nero (chap. 8) suggests that the same movement influenced some of the research on art forms; the contributions by Mac Marshall on kinship (chap. 4) and Glenn Petersen on political organization (chap. 5) reflect certain of the sociological interests; and William Alkire (chap. 3) discusses cultural ecology in Micronesia.

Other forces at work in the decade before World War II also shaped the transformation of anthropology. Social problems accompanying the Great Depression heightened the social consciousness of many scholars and demanded a more relevant anthropology. Reflecting the concern with contemporary social issues, the discipline shifted away from memory ethnography toward the study of culture change. The first studies of acculturation appeared in 1932 (Bee 1974, 94), and in their landmark memorandum on acculturation (1936), Robert Redfield, Ralph Linton, and Melville J. Herskovits attempted to set a new research agenda. Such stirrings were not confined to America; in Britain, Malinowski had begun to call for an anthropology of "the changing native" (1929, 1930).

However, the demand for relevancy was not new; the hope that anthropology might be of applied value had been expressed throughout much of the nineteenth century. Sir Edward B. Tylor ended his last major work, *Anthropology*, with the premise that "the study of man and civilization is not only a matter of scientific interest, but at once passes into the practical business of life . . . and . . . may guide us in our duty of leaving the world better than we found it" (1909, 439–440).

Also in the late nineteenth century, the US Congress began to sponsor geographic, geologic, and ethnographic research, in the rather vague hope that the results might be useful (Foster 1969, 196–197). As one consequence, the Bureau of American Ethnology (BAE) was created within the Smithsonian Institution in 1879. Major John Wesley Powell, the Bureau's first director, reported: "In pursuing these ethnographic investigations it has been the endeavor as far as possible to produce results that would be of practical value in the administration of Indian affairs" (1881, xi; quoted in Foster 1969, 197). In reality, the published BAE reports were largely descriptive, often esoteric, and mainly of interest to anthropologists, and Foster was correct in his assessment that "there is little evidence that they played any role in determining Indian policy" (Foster 1969, 197).

A second major attempt to use ethnographic information for the administration of dependent peoples followed the founding of the Bureau of American Ethnology by three decades. After the American acquisition of the Philippines in 1898, a Philippine Ethnological Survey (PES) was established within the Department of the Interior with Albert E. Jenks as director, and between 1906 and 1910, several anthropologists were commissioned to conduct ethnological research. Some excellent ethnographies resulted, but as in the case of the BAE reports, they were mainly of interest to other anthropologists and had no discernible impact on policy and administration (Foster 1969, 199; Kennard and Macgregor 1953, 832).

For a quarter century after the demise of the Philippine Ethnological Survey there was little if any tangible recognition that peoples with different and diverse cultural backgrounds presented any special administrative problems, and it appears that there were no organized attempts to apply anthropology. Indeed, anthropology's relativism would seem to have been out of step with the times. America was the great "melting pot." The process of assimilating minitories into the mainstream was assumed to be both inevitable and desirable. Given the historical context, it is understandable that after his work in the Philippines, Jenks returned to the University of Minnesota and developed an Americanization training program to hasten the process of assimilation (Foster 1969, 199).

Some change occurred with Franklin Delano Roosevelt's administration, the advent of the New Deal, and the appointment of John Collier as Commissioner of the Bureau of Indian Affairs (BIA) in 1934. For the first time, organized research projects were designed to address specific problems of administration. The intent of the Indian Reorganization Act of the same year was to bring local self-government to the reservations, and Collier formed an Applied Anthropology Unit within the Bureau to investigate existing patterns of leadership and informal government among Native Americans. A BIA Education Division was also created to research the many problems of Indian education.

Collier's influence extended beyond the Bureau. In the mid-1930s, the Technical Cooperation–Bureau of Indian Affairs unit within the Soil Conservation Service (SCS), Department of Agriculture, employed anthropologists and other specialists to investigate a variety of problems related to resource utilization and federal policies pertaining to Indian lands. Anthropologists also conducted SCS studies of rural populations elsewhere in the nation (Kennard and Macgregor 1953, 832–836).

After her own experience conducting educational research for the Bureau of Indian Affairs, Laura Thompson, Collier's colleague and spouse, became the first American anthropologist to work in Micronesia (Thompson 1991, 81–87; 101–108). In the late 1930s, on assignment with the US Navy, Thompson conducted research on Guam to advise the navy regarding educational and other policies for its administration of the indigenous Chamorro people. Her work was the first applied anthropological effort sponsored by the US Navy in Micronesia, and as noted, it foreshadowed future developments.

APPLIED ANTHROPOLOGY AND WORLD WAR II

No sooner had the applied anthropology of the 1930s gained momentum than World War II broke out. An unprecedented number of professional anthropologists and some of their graduate students were soon engaged in the war effort, in a broad range of applied tasks. A special school opened in 1942 at Columbia University, charged with training military officers for duty in occupied areas including Micronesia (Bashkow 1991). Another such school was later opened at Princeton University. Survival training courses were mounted for men likely to be stranded in unfamiliar environments, and the techniques of descriptive linguistics were instrumental in the development of the army's language training programs. Additional programs were designed to interpret the behavior of American allies, and yet others to help civilians cope with wartime conditions at home.

Of particular importance for subsequent developments in applied anthropology, including those in Micronesia, were two wartime projects, both involving Alexander Leighton. Early in the war, the War Relocation Authority (WRA), the agency responsible for the relocation of the West Coast Japanese-Americans, employed anthropologists and other social scientists to carry out ongoing analyses of problems involved with the administration of the internment camps. Leighton and several colleagues worked at one such camp in Poston, Arizona.

In early 1944, Leighton and some of the Poston team formed the nucleus of the Foreign Morale Analysis Division (FMAD). Its task was to gain an understanding of Japanese cultural, social, and psychological characteristics. The Foreign Morale Analysis Division pioneered the variety of analysis known as "study of culture at a distance," tackling such issues as the strength of Japanese morale, the design of effective propaganda, attitudes toward authority and the emperor, and the postwar administration of Japan. Ruth Benedict's *Chrysanthemum and the Sword* (1946) is the best known FMAD-derived publication. From his Poston and FMAD experience, Leighton (1945, 1949) outlined some general principles regarding the application of anthropological research that influenced later developments in the US Trust Territory of the Pacific Islands (USTTPI).

As Murdock foresaw, the need for reliable information on Japan's former League of Nations Mandated Territory in Micronesia became especially acute with the outbreak of the war. For many years beforehand, the Japanese had hidden the area behind a "bamboo curtain," providing only the cursory information required by the League of Nations and severely restricting foreigners' access to Micronesia (Peattie 1988). The flow of even this minimal information was cut off when Japan withdrew from the League in 1935. In a real sense, American forces in Micronesia would fight a war in a largely unknown territory.

By 1943, the initiative launched by Murdock at Yale had produced tangible results. Now a commander in the US Navy, Murdock supervised the production of military handbooks for the postwar naval administration of Japanese Micronesia. Over the next two years, four handbooks were published, on the Marshall Islands, East Caroline Islands, West Caroline Islands, and Mandated Mariana Islands (US Navy, Office of the Chief of Naval Operations 1944a, 1944b, 1944c, 1944d). The handbooks were well received, and both the anthropologists involved and the navy were pleased with their collaborative effort.

At war's end, a state of euphoria, confidence, and optimism prevailed in America, and anthropologists shared the general mood of the nation. In contrast to later times and other conflicts, there was little uncertainty about the moral objective. A great fight against the evils of fascism, the "good war" had been won. While there were some dissenting voices, for most anthropologists, the applied work of the 1930s and their war experience strengthened an optimism about the usefulness of anthropology and its future relationship with the federal government, both civilian and military.

IMMEDIATE POSTWAR MICRONESIA

At the close of World War II, the US Navy occupied the former Japanese mandated area and had the temporary responsibility for its administration. American interest in Micronesia had been manifest throughout the nineteenth century, culminating in the annexation of Guam at the end of the Spanish-American War. At that time, as Petersen (chap. 5) discusses, America had also considered taking over the remainder of the Marianas and the Carolines.

Once the United States obtained possession of Micronesia at the end of

World War II, however, there was no doubt that it intended to retain control over the islands. At the same time, there were no definite plans for the future, and the issue of control became the source of lively and often bitter debate in Washington, D.C. The Department of War (later Defense) and many members of Congress favored outright annexation, while the Departments of State and the Interior argued that it would be embarrassing for America to acquire new territory as a result of the war. The three departments squabbled over which would ultimately gain control, and within the military, the army challenged the navy's stewardship (Richard 1957c, 3–8).

From 1944 until approval of the United Nations Trusteeship Agreement on July 18, 1947, Micronesia was administered by a navy military government. Theoretically, the navy followed a "hands-off" approach to the administration of the islands. A December 1945 policy statement decreed that the inhabitants of the occupied territories should be "encouraged and assisted to assume as much as possible the management of their own affairs and the conduct of their government" (Meller 1969, 26). The "hands-off" policy was in part a necessity (Falgout 1995, 103): Because postwar demobilization had reduced manpower and logistic support, the navy lacked the resources for extensive and direct rule of any kind. At the same time they attempted to introduce the beginnings of democratic institutions at the community level (locally elected councils and magistrates), and made modest attempts to initiate universal systems of health care and education. They simply assumed that the introduction of American-style institutions was desirable. While consequences may not have been thought out, and initial efforts were small in scale, an American agenda had been set in place, and the consequences would be extensive.

The status of a "strategic trust" within the framework of the United Nations (UN) provided a compromise solution that justified the American presence in Micronesia. The United States could use the islands for defense while avoiding outright annexation of new territory. In testimony before the US Senate Committee on Foreign Relations in 1947, General Dwight D. Eisenhower was quite explicit about American interests. He noted that many of the islands "are nothing but sandspits. They are of very little economic value. Our sole interest in them is security" (quoted in Leibowitz 1989, 487).

With the beginning of the UN trusteeship in 1947, the navy was instructed to form a civil administration, but little changed. The navy remained in control, and many of the same navy officers remained in place, shedding their uniforms for civilian garb. (They did not, however, relinquish their commissions as naval officers.) Meanwhile, the infighting continued in Washington, and in the end, President Truman made the final decision. In 1951, the administration of the trust territory became the responsibility of the Department of the Interior (Kiste 1986, 127).

But the vestiges of military control were not so easily dispelled. The Cold War with the Soviet bloc was soon to emerge, and from the very outset of American rule, the United States had pursued a policy of strategic denial. Access to Micronesia was denied to other nations and most outsiders. Aside from members of the administration and the military, even American citizens needed permission to enter the area. Those few who did gain access were mainly anthropologists, other researchers, visiting congressmen, government bureaucrats, or others on official business. Such restrictions continued to apply throughout the 1950s, and as recently as the early 1960s a security clearance was required of would-be visitors. During the same period, the navy also strictly controlled entries to and departures from Guam.

Initially, it appears that political and strategic concerns also kept all of American Micronesia outside the mainstream of events in the larger Pacific region. The case in point was the South Pacific Commission (spc), formed in 1947 by the region's six colonial powers: Australia, France, the Netherlands, New Zealand, the United Kingdom, and the United States. The commission was created as a solely advisory body to the colonial administrations; its founding charter, the Canberra Agreement, included such areas as education, health, and general social and economic development, "but political questions were excluded" (T. R. Smith 1972, 13). Some of the oral history surrounding spc origins suggests that the United States was primarily responsible for this restriction, while other accounts give credit to France and the United Kingdom. Whatever the case, it is certain that the United States did not want the other metropolitan powers interfering with its strategic concerns north of the equator. In his history of the South Pacific Commission published on the occasion of its twenty-fifth anniversary, T. R. Smith, the commission's third secretary-general (1958–1963), indicated that "neither France nor Britain nor the United States was willing to give away any of her rights to decide the political future of her dependent territories" (1972, 47). In any event, Guam and the US Trust Territory of the Pacific Islands were not included within spc boundaries until after responsibility for both territories was transferred to the Department of the Interior in 1951 (1972, 64).

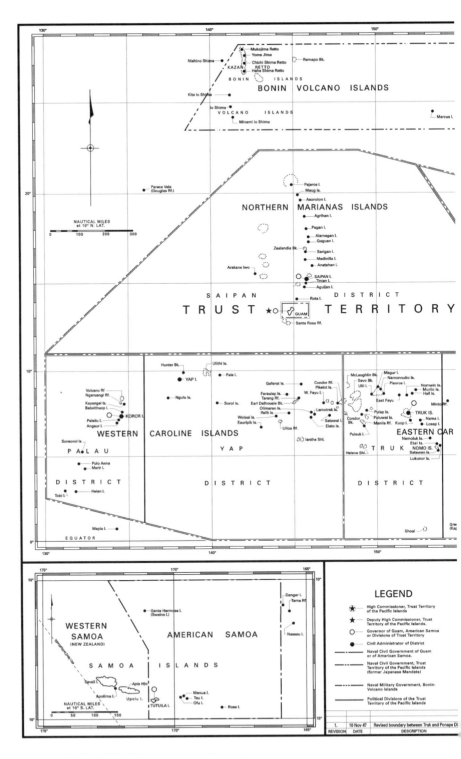

Map 1. US Naval Island Governments, September 1947
Early map of the US Trust Territory of the Pacific Islands. It reflects that the
Office of the High Commissioner was located in Honolulu at the time. Other
island entities under naval administration are indicated. Original map
courtesy of the Naval Academy of Science.

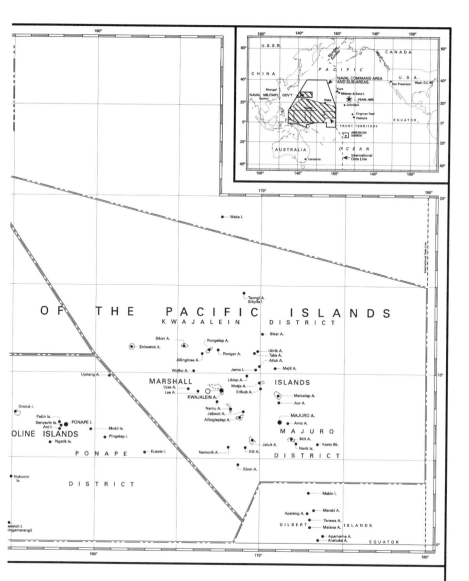

PACIFIC OCEAN AREA
U.S. NAVAL ISLAND GOVERNMENTS
INCLUDING TRUST TERRITORY OF THE PACIFIC ISLANDS;
GUAM, AMERICAN SAMOA, JOHNSTON, WAKE,
KURE, MIDWAY, SAND, BONIN AND VOLCANO IS-
LANDS AND KINGMAN REEF

3 SEPT. 1947

AUTHORITY

(a) Guam placed under Naval jurisdiction by Executive Order 108A, dated 23 Dec 1898.

(b) American Samoa placed under jurisdiction of the Secretary of the Navy by Executive Order (unnumbered), dated 19 Feb 1900. Swains Island included by joint resolution of Congress approved 4 March 1925.

(c) Midway Island placed under jurisdiction by Executive Order 199A, dated 20 Jan 1903.

(d) Johnston, Sand and Wake Islands and Kingman Reef placed under Naval Jurisdiction by Executive Order 6935, dated 29 Dec 1934.

(e) Kure Island placed under Naval jurisdiction by Executive Order 7299. dated 20 Feb 1936.

(f) Bonin-Volcano Islands placed under Naval jurisdiction of Joint Chiefs of Staaff paper 1231, approved 30 Jan 1945.

(g) Trust Territory of the Pacific Islands placed under civil administration of the Secretary of the Navy by Executive Order 9873, dated 18 July 1947.

U.S.NAVY DEPT BUREAU OF YARDS & DOCKS DRAWING NO. 454,616

A-12679

APPLIED ANTHROPOLOGY IN MICRONESIA

Immediately after the war and with navy authorization from none other than Admiral Chester A. Nimitz, Commander in Chief, Pacific Fleet and Pacific Ocean Area, the University of Hawai'i conducted a brief reconnaissance of Micronesia. During a three-week period beginning in mid-December 1945, anthropologist John Embree, botanist Harold St. John, geographer Raymond Murphy, and zoologist Harvey Fisher visited the Marshalls, Kosrae, Pingelap, Guam, and Palau (Embree 1946b). The university expressed a continued interest in the area, and in the summer of 1946, three teams from the departments of zoology and bacteriology, botany, and agriculture conducted surveys in the Marshalls, Chuuk, and Pohnpei (Quigg 1987, 16).

Embree was soon to leave Hawai'i for interests in Southeast Asia, but he was replaced in the department of anthropology by Leonard Mason in January 1947. In the same month, political scientist Norman Meller joined the university's faculty. As a navy language and intelligence officer, he had been involved in the disposition of the Japanese civilian population on Saipan after the American invasion in 1944. Ironically, Meller was initially hired as director of the Territory of Hawai'i's Legislative Reference Bureau, which was part of the university, not because of his experience in Micronesia but for his political science expertise.

In the coming years, Mason and Meller were to shape much of the university's interests in Micronesia and the rest of the Pacific. In 1950, Mason chaired the committee that created the master of arts degree in Pacific Islands studies, and the Pacific Islands Studies Program. The latter was rechristened the Center for Pacific Islands Studies when it became part of the new School of Hawaiian, Asian, and Pacific Studies in 1987. (For a history of Pacific Islands studies at the University of Hawai'i, see Quigg 1987.)[2]

By the early 1950s, American anthropology had been involved in Micronesia for a decade. This was an era in which a series of anthropological projects were organized to meet practical ends. Following Murdock's Yale project, the School of Naval Administration (SONA) was opened at Stanford University in early 1946 to train naval officers to serve as administrators in American Samoa and Guam as well as in the trust territory. As SONA associate director, anthropologist Felix Keesing designed and directed the five-month course. The School of Naval Administration emphasized training in cross-cultural awareness and skills, and the curriculum included basic cultural anthropology and a number of Pacific-related topics. Between April 1946 and

August 1947, three SONA classes graduated over one hundred ninety officers (Barnett 1956, 12–13, 91, 176; Richard 1957a, 137–171).

Coterminous with the School of Naval Administration, and also under navy sponsorship, the US Commercial Company (USCC) conducted an economic survey of Micronesia. Douglas Oliver, a Harvard University anthropologist, served as project director, and from May to August 1946, four anthropologists, William Bascom, Edward T. Hall, Leonard Mason, and Carl Pelzer, and an anthropologically oriented sociologist, John Useem, were among almost two dozen specialists who conducted field research in Micronesia (Oliver 1971, xi–xii). Except for Thompson's earlier work on Guam, this was the first intensive field research conducted by American anthropologists in Micronesia. As part of their assessments of postwar economic conditions, authors of the USCC reports included substantial ethnographic data. They provided baseline information for subsequent research, and like the navy handbooks, they were valued by administrators because of their immediate practical use.

In her history of the navy's administration of the trust territory, Dorothy Richard wrote that "the completed [USCC] reports, arranged in twenty volumes, and representing a $160,000 investment were forwarded to the Cinc Pac Flt [Commander in Chief, Pacific Fleet] on May 21, 1947" (Richard 1957b, 427–428). Unfortunately, these materials were not published. Apparently, there was some confusion over publication rights (Fosberg, personal communication 1989), and there was a claim that the navy had suppressed publication because it was criticized for a lack of attention to Micronesia's economic recovery (Mason 1973). (However, as Hanlon points out in chapter 2, descriptions of devastated societies served to justify the neglect of indigenous history and to promote an agenda for Americanization.) In the end, copies of the reports were filed with the Library of Congress. A summary report edited by Douglas Oliver, which contained specific recommendations to improve Micronesia's economy, was published by Harvard (1951) and later reprinted by the University of Hawai'i Press (1971).

Few USCC recommendations were acted on by the US Naval Administration (Mason 1973). According to its official history, the navy was pleased with the results of the USCC survey, but "long term problems of native administration demanded more extensive investigation and study of many facets of Micronesian culture" (Richard 1957c, 571).

Murdock and Oliver also played instrumental roles in shaping the next anthropological effort in Micronesia. In response to continued requests for assistance by the navy, the Pacific Science Board (PSB) was established as a

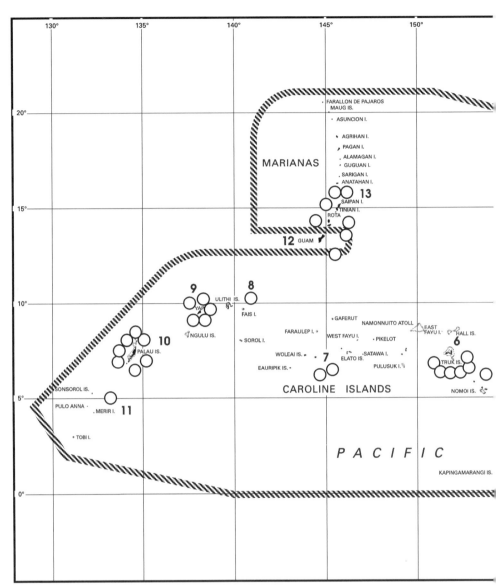

Map 2. Cima Map, 1947

Map developed by the US Navy during the planning stage of the cima project. Leonard Mason (University of Hawai'i) managed the Honolulu end of the project, but did not conduct fieldwork under cima auspices. William C. Canup (Harvard University) and Katherine Luomala (University of Hawai'i) withdrew and never participated in the project. Original map courtesy of the National Academy of Sciences.

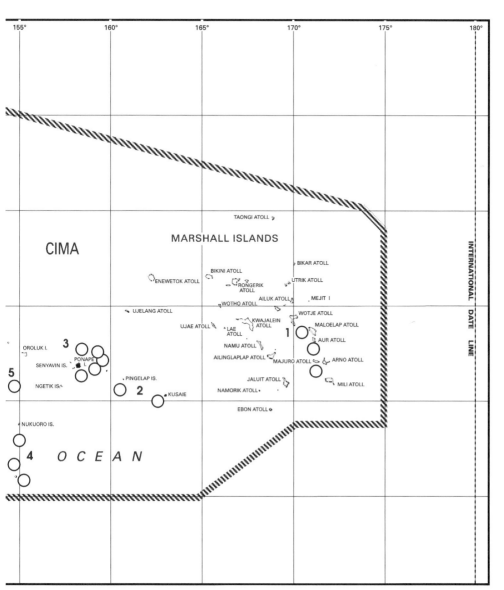

CIMA MAP

committee of the National Research Council (NRC) in late 1946. The Pacific Science Board was to promote research, advise government, and encourage international cooperation with regard to Pacific science. Murdock was among the board's eleven members, and Oliver served as a consultant (Richard 1957c, 571–575). The board's Honolulu Committee was headed by Leonard Mason, the recent hire at the University of Hawai'i who had been part of the work at Yale as well as a member of the USCC research effort.

In January 1947, the Pacific Science Board became the administering agency for the Coordinated Investigation of Micronesian Anthropology (CIMA), with Murdock as project director. Funding was provided by the Office of Naval Research (ONR), the Viking Fund, and participating institutions. Between July 1947 and January 1949, 41 CIMA researchers (25 cultural anthropologists, 4 physical anthropologists, 4 linguists, 3 geographers, 2 sociologists, 2 physicians, and 1 botanist) representing twenty universities and museums were divided into teams and assigned to conduct field research in different parts of Micronesia (see appendix 1).[3]

In some respects, the Coordinated Investigation of Micronesian Anthropology resembled the earlier BAE and PES research efforts; it was assumed, or hoped, that ethnographic data would be of value for the administration of dependent peoples. In Micronesia, the German Südsee Expedition between 1908 and 1910 had been a similar effort, but most of the results of that investigation were published long after Germany had lost the islands to Japan in 1914 and thus were of no administrative use. While some anthropological work was done by individual Japanese researchers (Hatanaka 1979), there was no organized research program comparable to the Südsee Expedition or CIMA efforts during the Japanese colonial era between the two world wars.

While the objective was basic research, there has been some debate about the extent to which CIMA research topics were determined because they were of particular interest to the navy. In his examination of David M. Schneider's CIMA-sponsored research on Yap, Ira Bashkow reviewed the larger context in which Pacific anthropology was situated in the immediate postwar period and reported that "two broad scientific constituencies were offering competing visions of the future of scientific research in Micronesia" (1991, 182). He characterized one of these as "an emergent network of academic veterans of the war agencies, based for the most part in major East Coast universities, which Murdock drew together behind Oliver's plan for a centrally coordinated investigation." The Oliver plan was drafted in the summer of 1945, and it called for a postwar " 'organization for systematic scientific exploration,' which 'besides possessing intrinsic scientific value,' would 'assist powerfully in the administration and development of the area' "(Bashkow 1991, 182).

Bashkow characterized the Murdock forces as "an upstart group" in Pacific science with "formidable connections in Washington," which "encountered significant opposition from a second, much older, scientific constituency," which had long been connected to the Pacific Science Association and institutions on the West Coast. He identified the leaders of the second group as Herbert Gregory and E. S. C. Handy of the Bishop Museum and Felix Keesing of Stanford University (and formerly of the University of Hawai'i) (Bashkow 1991, 183). Bashkow suggested that their approach was akin to that of the Boasian "historical" ethnographers who saw the utmost urgency for salvage ethnography and were alarmed at the "sociological" and "applied" angle of Murdock's agenda. (It is clear, however, from his chapter in _The Science of Man in the World Crisis_ [1945] and his later SONA involvement that Keesing would not have been alarmed at efforts to apply anthropology.)

While the Harvard and Yale group eventually prevailed and the battle between East and West Coast constituencies may have been real in the corridors of power in Washington, D.C., the actual consequences for research in Micronesia may have been less than Bashkow implied. In Hawai'i, as Honolulu CIMA officer, Leonard Mason saw little tangible evidence that there was any significant impact for policies guiding CIMA implementation. Homer G. Barnett, a CIMA researcher in Palau and the first civilian USTTPI staff anthropologist, reported: "Each study was the result of a proposal by the men who did the work; and while it was anticipated that the resulting information would be useful to the administration, this was not the primary consideration dictating the inclusion of projects in the program" (1956, 35). George Foster later suggested that the freedom to select research topics "was undoubtedly responsible for the eminence of the anthropologists who flocked to the Pacific; a list of their names reads like an anthropological Who's Who" (1969, 208).[4]

Barnett and Foster painted an unambiguous picture of a free hand for researchers, but reality was more complicated. Bashkow reported that the agreement between the Pacific Science Board and the navy was also clear: "in emphasizing 'the importance of the freedom of science,' it reserved to CIMA participants the right to study what they might and to report on any matters not 'affecting national defense' " (1991, 185–186). At the same time, Bashkow noted, there was "an unmistakable attempt to give positive direction to research, which was differentially realized in different CIMA expeditions." Further, in an apparent quote from Murdock, funds were "allocated to projects roughly in proportion to their correspondence with administrative needs and priorities." Bashkow indicated that in some instances Murdock "provided compelling specification of the 'administrative uses' he had in mind" (1991, 186). For example, Murdock identified the matrilineal system of land tenure in the Marshalls, resettlement problems in the Marianas, and depopulation on Yap as concerns that represented major administrative problems. Despite this, the results were mixed. None of the CIMA research in the Marshalls focused on land tenure. Resettlement problems in the Marianas were researched by a geographer who responded to a "research imperative" (Bashkow 1991, 186). Bashkow has documentary evidence that some pressure was put on the CIMA team on Yap to address the depopulation problem (1991, 212). However, Douglas Oliver, who was in charge of the team, recalls today that the interest in depopulation was a natural outgrowth of a long-standing concern dating back to the Japanese era, rather than a response to any kind of pressure from authorities (Oliver, personal communication 1995).

Optimism about the applications of anthropology continued, however; while he was not an unbiased observer, Murdock wrote that the cooperation between civilian anthropologists and the navy "might well serve as a model for the collaboration of lay scientists and government agencies in a political democracy" (Richard 1957c, 582).

As a result of CIMA and navy requests for continuing research, funding from the Office of Naval Research was extended to launch the Scientific Investigation of Micronesia (SIM), a program of studies in the physical, biological, and life sciences. During the 1949–1951 period, thirty-one investigators conducted research in anthropology, botany, forestry, geography, geology, marine ecology, and vertebrate ecology. At the request of the South Pacific Commission, which was conducting research on the economic development of low islands elsewhere in the Pacific, the major SIM activity was the Coral Atoll Project, an ecological survey of Arno Atoll in the Marshall Islands. In the summer of 1950, Mason and one of his graduate students, Jack Tobin, were among thirteen SIM team members on Arno. Five other anthropologists, Edwin G. Burrows, Kenneth Emory, Ann Fischer, Alex Spoehr, and Harry Uyehara, were engaged in other facets of the SIM project in the US Trust Territory of the Pacific, and Ward H. Goodenough conducted research in the Gilbert Islands (Richard 1957c, 585–593).[5]

Another CIMA offshoot was the appointment of applied anthropologists at the district and territorial levels of the USTTPI administration. Difficulties had been encountered with the utilization of the CIMA material. The distribu-

CIMA research team in Honolulu en route to Micronesia, 1947.
Photograph courtesy of Ward Goodenough.
Front row, left to right:

Saul Riesenberg
Melford Spiro
William Lessa
Rupert Murrill
Ward Goodenough
Back row, left to right:

Frank LeBar
Raymond Murphy
Alice Joseph
unknown woman
Veronica Murray
George P. Murdock
Joseph Weckler
Conrad Bentzen

Homer G. Barnett, CIMA researcher, Palau, 1947. Photograph courtesy of George Spindler.

Conference of Staff, District, and Assistant Anthropologists, Guam, 1956. Left to right: *Shigeru Kaneshiro, Francis Defngin, Gustave Weilbacher, Frank Mahony, Jack Tobin, Tion Bikajle. Photograph courtesy of Jack Tobin.*

Conference of Staff, District, and Assistant Anthropologists, Guam, 1956. Left to right: *Frank Mahony, Tion Bikajle, Jack Tobin, Francis Defngin, John deYoung, Shigeru Kaneshiro* (front), *Gustave Weilbacher* (back), *Richard Emerick. Photograph courtesy of Jack Tobin.*

*Former Assistant Anthropologist
Francis Defngin at United Nations,
1963.* Left to right: *John De Jongh,
US Office of Territories; Sydney Yates,
Head, US Delegation to Trusteeship
Council; Francis Defngin; Adlai
Stevenson, US Ambassador to the
United Nations; Andrew Roboman,
Yapese chief; Vincente Santos, Advisor
to US Delegation. Trust Territory
Archives (Photo 3375.01), Pacific
Collection, University of Hawaiʻi
Library.*

tion of reports was limited to a few typescript copies, and some reports were a long time in preparation. Of equal if not greater concern, and like the earlier BAE and PES publications, the language of the CIMA reports "was oriented toward the professional social scientist rather than the lay administrator" (J. Fischer 1979, 239), and materials collected had been used by the administration largely on an informal basis, usually at the initiative of the individual CIMA participants (Mason 1973). As a consequence, anthropologists were engaged to interpret CIMA findings.

The first of these was Thomas Gladwin, appointed as the anthropological field consultant (later known as district anthropologist) on Chuuk where he had been a CIMA researcher. Following Gladwin, Philip Drucker was made staff anthropologist attached to the High Commissioner's Office, then located in Honolulu. Within a short time, Gladwin took up an administrative post; he was replaced on Chuuk, and eventually, an anthropologist was hired for each of the territory's six districts. A notice on the front page of the April 1950 _American Anthropological Association News Bulletin_ read:

> NAVAL OPERATIONS has again requested NRC to supply Anthropological Field Consultants for positions with the Civil Administration Units on the Marshall Islands, at Yap and at Ponape. This Trust Territory employment is paid at an annual rate of $3,650.00. Quarters for dependents are not presently available. Appointees will be expected to devote about two-thirds of their time to local problems where the application of anthropological knowledge will aid the Administration. The remainder is to be devoted to personal research. Opportunities exist for advanced graduate students of some maturity to do original work.

Among the first hires in 1950 were Jack Tobin (Marshalls), Shigeru Kaneshiro (Palau, Rota, Yap), Frank Mahony (Chuuk and Pohnpei), and Francis Mahoney (Palau and Yap).

The anthropology positions were continued with the transfer of the administration to the Department of the Interior in 1951. In all, a total of eleven men served as district anthropologists. In addition to those above, the others were John "Jack" Fischer (Chuuk and Pohnpei), Alfred Whiting (Pohnpei), Richard Emerick (Pohnpei), Harry Uyehara (Palau), Robert McKnight (Palau), and Robert Solenberger (Saipan). Ten of the eleven began their work in Micronesia as graduate students. However, Gladwin and Francis Mahoney had had CIMA experience. Tobin was a SIM participant. Uyehara was the most experienced of all having been a participant in the USCC, CIMA, and SIM projects. The others received their introduction to Micronesia when they took their positions as district anthropologists.

At some point, the district anthropologists began to employ Micronesian assistants, who by the late 1950s were known as assistant anthropologists. A total of five were employed in four USTTPI districts: Tion Bikajle (Marshalls), Gustave Weilbacher and Pensile Lawrence (Pohnpei), Francis Defngin (Yap), and Adalbert Obak (Palau). Another Palauan, a certain M. Emesiochl, is listed as a coauthor of one publication (1960) with McKnight and Obak, and he is described as "an aspiring student on anthropology from Palau." (No assistant anthropologist served in Chuuk or the Northern Marianas.) The assistant anthropologists received informal training in anthropology, learned how to conduct interviews and censuses, assisted with routine office chores, and attended the conferences that brought together all of the anthropologists employed by the trust territory. Perhaps most importantly, they helped the district anthropologists achieve a better understanding of the peoples and cultures of their several districts (Tobin, personal communication 1995). Several of the items that appeared in the Anthropological Working Papers series published by the US Trust Territory of the Pacific were coauthored by the anthropologists and their assistants, and in a couple of instances, the assistant anthropologists were the sole authors.

Homer G. Barnett was the first staff anthropologist hired under the Department of the Interior, and he had three successors: Saul Riesenberg, Allan Smith, and John deYoung. (Barnett and Riesenberg had both been CIMA researchers.) Influenced by Leighton, Barnett was particularly concerned to clearly define the roles and responsibilities of the anthropologists and to have these understood by the administration. This topic was also a lively part of discussions at Trust Territory Anthropologists Conferences held in 1952 and 1957 (USTTPI Archives 1952, 1957).

In Barnett's view, the anthropologist was a technical or scientific specialist who was to be a neutral intermediary link as an interpreter between the administration and the islanders. The anthropologist was to advise on the implementation of projects, evaluate the success of programs, and conduct research of theoretical interest to anthropology or practical importance to the administration. Administrative and technical services were to be kept separate. As a technician, the anthropologist was not a policymaker; rather, he devised the means by which administrative ends might be achieved. Indeed, "Means and Ends," the title of one chapter in his *Anthropology in Administration* (1956), conveys the essence of Barnett's model.

Few anthropologists today would feel comfortable with such a mandate for applied work, and the examples Barnett gives in his book (1956), his lectures at the University of Oregon in the early 1960s, and the accounts of others who were involved indicate that it was difficult, if not impossible, to actually work in the manner he envisaged. Some difficulties were rooted in the very nature of the job description while others grew from the changing conditions of the trust territory.

Interior Department budgets for the territory's administration were parsimonious at best and relatively constant from fiscal year 1952 through fiscal year 1965. Actual budgets ranged from a low of $4,271,000 in 1952 to a high of $6,304,000 in 1962 (Leibowitz 1989, 495). Circumstances during the Interior Department administration of the territory were actually far worse than these small numbers indicate. When the navy withdrew, communication, air and sea transportation, and other support services were reduced. These services had been funded separately in the navy's budget, so that the navy had requested only a small additional budget for their Civil Administration in Micronesia. Yet, when the Department of the Interior submitted to Congress a budget request that included costs to cover these former navy services as well as administrative costs, Congress complained that the navy had needed less, and decreased the amount of funds awarded accordingly (Oliver, personal communication 1995). The navy's withdrawal also meant a reduction in very broadly trained and capable personnel. The Interior Department personnel who replaced them had virtually no training or experience in Micronesia. To these inexperienced and otherwise harried administrators, anthropologists were often viewed as luxuries, to be used only for administrative purposes.

Jack Fischer's (1979) account as well as Suzanne Falgout's (1990, 1995) research of the personal records of district anthropologists in the USTTPI archives reveal the frustrations and difficulties experienced on both sides. Not uncommonly, anthropologists were expected to serve as unofficial ombudsmen, field trip officers, troubleshooters, and representatives of the administration in a variety of other capacities, including the implementation of policies with which they sometimes sharply disagreed. Although their job descriptions specified that perhaps one-third of their time was to be allotted for their own research, such opportunities were seldom, if ever, realized.

Matters of personality were also important. Some of the anthropologists got along well with their nonanthropological colleagues and through their informal relationships had considerable influence on the administration. Robert Gibson, the trust territory's first civilian director of education under the Department of the Interior, was particularly receptive to anthropological perspectives, as were educators William Vitarelli and Daniel Peacock who served under him. Vitarelli, a Columbia University-trained sociologist, became well known for his community-based work in Palau, including the Modekngei School, which emphasizes self-reliance and the maintenance of Palauan culture. Peacock shared many of the same perspectives. After his initial assignment in Palau, he served in the High Commissioner's Office on Saipan where he was able to influence educational policy. Edward Furber, the first chief justice of the USTTPI Supreme Court, was another trust territory hand who was more than sympathetic toward anthropology, and as Edward C. King (chap. 11) makes evident, Furber's judicial decisions reflected substantial anthropological input. Men such as Gibson, Peacock, Vitarelli, and Furber were well-known figures in the trust territory, and undoubtedly there were other administrators who saw some utility and value in anthropological knowledge. In chapter 11, King discusses the ways in which anthropology influenced his own legal career in Micronesia.

However, as Jack Fischer's (1979) account makes painfully clear, mutual animosity frequently characterized the relations between anthropologists and administrators. In particular, anthropologists encountered difficulty when some administrators failed to understand that their research strategy involved a close and confidential relationship with informants and participant observation. Furthermore, John Whiting (n.d.) reported that anthropologists' suggestions about administrative practices were often disliked and sometimes even feared by those expatriates who saw it important to "keep these natives where they belong." Several arguments over the confidentiality of sources resulted in the addition of Section 342 to the USTTPI Code, which made conversations between anthropologists and informants privileged information (with the exception of those regarding murder or manslaughter) (USTTPI Archives 1955). In some cases, anthropologists took unusual measures to ensure that their fieldnotes did not fall into the wrong hands (J. Fischer n.d.; Marksbury, personal communication 1988).

To some, the experience of applied anthropology in the trust territory during the 1950s was disappointing. Of the eleven who served as district anthropologists, six eventually completed their doctorates, but they did so more slowly than their peers at home. Because of the burden of day-to-day administrative assignments and a working environment that was not conducive, and sometimes hostile, to academic pursuits, most produced little published research of general anthropological interest during their tenure in Micronesia. Only four went on to have academic careers (J. Fischer 1979, 246).[6]

The last of the staff anthropologists, John deYoung, initiated the above-mentioned series of Anthropological Working Papers, but it was of short duration (1957–1961). DeYoung also rescued a number of valuable anthropological reports on land tenure, and they appeared under his editorship in 1958. During the latter part of his tenure as staff anthropologist, deYoung moved increasingly into administration, and he was not replaced when he left the position in 1961. By the early 1960s, only one of the former district anthropologists was still employed by the USTTPI administration. Robert McKnight was a community development officer in the High Commissioner's Office, which had been relocated to Saipan in 1962. With the demise of the district anthropologists, the assistant anthropologists turned, or often returned, to other professions in education and community development.[7] In addition to the employment of anthropologists by the trust territory in the 1950s, a modest amount of anthropological work in Micronesia was sponsored by the Tri-Institutional Pacific Program (TRIPP). Funded by the Carnegie Foundation, this program was directed by some familiar names: Alex Spoehr, George P. Murdock, and Leonard Mason, representing their respective institutions, the Bishop Museum, Yale University, and the University of Hawai'i. Included was the research of Roland and Maryanne Force and Douglas Osborne in Palau, Leonard Mason's continued work with the Bikinians in the Marshalls, and Bernd Lambert's work in the Gilbert Islands. The Tri-Institutional Pacific Program also funded the research of political scientist Norman Meller on the Guam and Marshall Islands legislatures (Quigg 1987, 27–32; Spoehr 1966).

Somewhat ironically, Goodenough's book *Cooperation in Change* (1963) appeared shortly after the applied anthropology program in the trust territory had ended. The irony is that, according to the folklore of anthropology in Micronesia, this volume was originally conceived as a handbook for community development workers in the trust territory with USTTPI sponsorship. Such was not the case; the trust territory was not involved. Rather, at the suggestion of Alexander Leighton, *Cooperation in Change* was commissioned by the Russell Sage Foundation. Initially, it was to be a manual presenting the practical principles of what to do and not to do in development work. Once into the project, Goodenough realized that such items already existed. As a consequence, he shifted his purpose to that of providing a theoretical understanding of the processes involved in social and cultural change, particularly where change is initiated with the cooperation of the people involved. In doing this, Goodenough drew heavily on his own anthropological field experiences in Chuuk, the Gilbert Islands, and New Britain (Goodenough, personal communication 1994).

Cooperation in Change has been one of the more widely read books of its kind. It has influenced many individuals who have worked in applied capacities in the trust territory, including several generations of Peace Corps Volunteers, as well as many others elsewhere in the Pacific and the world. The contributions of Francis X. Hezel, Don Rubinstein, and Ed King to this volume (chaps. 9, 10, and 11) offer some reflections on both the application of anthropology and the lack of its use in the trust territory over the last fifty years. Lin Poyer (chap. 6) also notes that *Cooperation in Change* has been important for conceptual frameworks related to ethnicity and identity.

The postwar years of navy rule and the decade of the 1950s have been characterized as an era of "benign neglect in Micronesia." As long as its strategic interests were met, the United States had no other major concern with the area. While some improvements in health and education occurred and the foundations of district legislatures were laid, the minuscule budgets available precluded any significant economic development. The USTTPI administration was little more than a caretaker operation, and plans for the future were nonexistent or vague at best. For some parts of Micronesia, however, it is difficult to describe this era as benign. For example, it was during this time that the American nuclear weapons test program was conducted in the northern Marshall Islands (S. Firth 1987; Hines 1962), and the Northern Marianas were cordoned off by the Central Intelligence Agency for the training of the Nationalist Chinese military. Benign or malign, the combination of a caretaker administration, the policy of strategic denial, and the anthropological presence has led some observers to charge that the era was one in which the United States maintained it own "ethnographic zoo" (Heine 1974, xv).

A NEW ERA

The decade of the 1960s marked a major turning point for Micronesia. The era of large-scale organized anthropological ventures in the territory drew to a close. There were a few more projects: The Displaced Communities in the Pacific Project (DCPP) at the University of Oregon, directed by Homer G. Barnett, was funded from 1962 to 1967 by the National Science Foundation. Although it included the USTTPI communities of Bikini (Kiste 1974), Enewetak (Kiste 1987), and Kapingamarangi (Lieber 1968a), the project focused not on

Micronesia as such but on the whole Pacific. In 1967, Leonard Mason directed a summer field study program in Majuro, teaming four University of Hawai'i anthropology graduate students with four Marshallese researchers for training in fieldwork techniques (Mason 1967a). Under the direction of Stephen T. Boggs, a similar project was undertaken the following year on Chuuk (Boggs 1969). For several years beginning in 1966, anthropologists were instrumental in the design and implementation of training programs specially developed for Peace Corps Volunteers headed for Micronesia. Several experienced Micronesian hands were involved, including Frank Mahony and Jack Tobin in charge of training on Moloka'i in Hawai'i, and Ward Goodenough coordinating operations in Florida.

Otherwise, in contrast to earlier times, anthropology as practiced in Micronesia became an individualized activity. Most research became "anthropology for anthropology's sake" conducted by individuals with financial support from the National Institutes of Health, the National Science Foundation, and other funding sources. Many new faces appeared on the scene, some of whom were students of those who had been involved with the Coordinated Investigation of Micronesian Anthropology. Dozens of doctoral dissertations have been produced since the 1960s (see appendix 2), and the number of American anthropologists with primary research interests in Micronesia has multiplied. As individuals, a few have occasionally taken on short-term applied projects of one kind or another, but their work has been scattered and is largely known only from anecdotal accounts.

Anthropological research in Micronesia also received a boost from the founding of the Association for Social Anthropology in Oceania (ASAO) in 1967.[8] While it is concerned with the entire Pacific, several Micronesian specialists were instrumental in the initial organization of the association, and Micronesianists' interests have been well represented on the ASAO Board and among its officers ever since. Launched in 1970 with *Adoption in Eastern Oceania,* edited by Vern Carroll, the ASAO Monograph Series has provided a prestigious publishing outlet in which Micronesianist scholars have been prominent. One ASAO volume, *Exiles and Migrants in Oceania,* edited by Michael D. Lieber (1977a), linked DCPP, ASAO, and Micronesian interests.

The change in the nature of anthropological activity in Micronesia during the 1960s occurred with and partly as a consequence of a major shift in American policy toward the trust territory. In 1961, a UN visiting mission was extremely critical of the American stewardship of the territory. In response, the Kennedy administration doubled the USTTPI annual budget. An intensive Americanization of Micronesia was launched, a development that has created massive social and economic dependency. While the actual impact of the infamous Solomon Report on American policy remains debated (Nevin 1977, 124–128), that 1962 report gave a clear signal that the United States intended to shape Micronesia's future in ways compatible with its own perceived strategic interests (US Survey Mission 1962).

What began under Kennedy escalated and ran amok during the Johnson administration. Annual USTTPI budgets continued to soar, and the Peace Corps was only one of many new initiatives. American territories (in both the Pacific and the Caribbean) were included within the framework of Johnson's "Great Society," and during its heyday there were over one hundred sixty separate US government programs operating in the trust territory. By the mid-1980s, the territory's annual budget exceeded $110 million, and federal programs accounted for at least another $35 million (Kiste 1993, 71).

Many of the programs were inappropriate for small island communities and proved corrosive to Micronesian cultures and societies. An American-style educational system became the trust territory's largest industry. Government bureaucracy grew by leaps and bounds. Urbanization proceeded at a rapid pace as islanders abandoned their home communities for urban areas where they sought employment, education, entertainment, medical care, and other fruits of Uncle Sam's apparent largesse. In the end, Micronesia's dependency has come to rival, and perhaps outstrip, even that of the French territories in the Pacific.

The UN mission's criticism in 1961 also precipitated movement in the political arena. On several occasions in the 1950s, leaders from the districts had been called together to advise the administration. By 1961, it was evident that they had taken to heart American notions about democracy and self-determination, and they lobbied for a territory-wide legislature. As a result, the Congress of Micronesia (COM) was formed in 1965. Once organized, COM leaders were quick to act. In the following year, they petitioned President Johnson to establish a commission to explore the trust territory's political future. The request went unanswered, and in 1967, the Congress of Micronesia created its own Micronesian Political Status Commission (Kiste 1986, 131). In the process, Norman Meller, University of Hawai'i political scientist, was asked for advice, guidance, and training, and his *Congress of Micronesia* (1969) provides a detailed account of the creation of the Congress and the range of alternative future statuses it considered. Meller (1985) was later involved as an advisor when the constitution for a self-governing Micronesia was designed. Petersen (chap. 5) comments on Meller's contributions.

Anthropologists were not involved in the development of the Congress of Micronesia, and whatever influence they may have had at an earlier time, they played no measurable role in shaping the massive changes that began in the 1960s. Anthropological input was not sought. Indeed, there was some feeling that anthropologists were obstructionists and opposed to change. Washington turned to other sources for advice and planning. A master plan designed for the trust territory by a large Washington, D.C., planning firm dismissed anthropologists as being primarily concerned with the preservation of the exotic. It evidenced absolutely no understanding of the integral relationships between people, kin groups, communities, and land and landholdings. Planners viewed outer-island communities as an anathema to development in general and recommended "a policy of carefully planned inducements designed to speed up the concentration of population on a relatively few of the major islands" (Nathan Associates 1966, 96). In short, it recommended the depopulation of the outer islands.

NEW POLITICAL STATUSES

The negotiations that began in 1969 concerning the future political status of the US Trust Territory of the Pacific were also shaped by America's involvement in Vietnam and a concomitant plan to establish a defense perimeter in the western Pacific Islands. Initially, the United States considered commonwealth as the only viable alternative to continued trusteeship. Such a status was tantamount to incorporation into the United States and would have given America control of the islands for strategic and almost any other purpose. That alternative was rejected by some Micronesian leaders in favor of what was then a yet-to-be-defined arrangement of free association.

During 1971 and 1972, the United States agreed to discuss free association, but independence was never entertained as a serious option by Washington. Meanwhile, the disclosure of American priorities encouraged existing sentiments for fragmentation by framing some islands within the territory as "haves" and some as "have nots." The "haves" were three in number: In the east, the missile test range at Kwajalein Atoll gave the Marshalls high strategic value. In the west, the Northern Marianas and Palau represented the coveted western defense perimeter. With the enhanced bargaining power derived from their strategic locations, the three "haves" set out to negotiate their separate political and financial fortunes. Having less to offer, the four "have nots" (Chuuk, Kosrae, Pohnpei, and Yap) were given little option but to remain together in what was to become the Federated States of Micronesia (FSM).

The hurried pace of change and the accompanying Americanization of Micronesia were sources of consternation to many anthropologists, but more than anything else, the imposition of American strategic interests on the political status negotiations caused an outpouring of criticism from many observers, both within and outside the profession. Many anthropologists shared the opposition to the war in Vietnam and the activities of American intelligence agencies elsewhere. The backlash against involvement of the defense and intelligence communities was widespread. In Micronesia, Thomas Gladwin was one of the more vocal critics. He claimed to regret his earlier work with the administration, declared himself a nonanthropologist, and became an advocate of Micronesian independence. Gladwin was not alone, and others, particularly younger anthropologists, joined his condemnation of the role that anthropology played in the 1940s and 1950s. In their view, anthropologists had been at best naive and unwitting collaborators of an effort to perpetuate the subordination of Micronesians. The debate among anthropologists and other interested observers was epitomized by an exchange between Roger Gale (a graduate student in political science) and Leonard Mason at the annual meeting of the Society for Applied Anthropology in 1973 (Gale 1973; Mason 1973). Justified or not, activities undertaken in the immediate postwar years were judged by the concerns and values of the Vietnam era.

The lamentations within anthropology were of little consequence. In 1975, the Northern Marianas voted for commonwealth status, and in the following year, congressional and presidential approval created the Commonwealth of the Northern Mariana Islands (CNMI). The people of the Northern Marianas became American citizens and the Commonwealth of the Northern Mariana Islands became part of the United States.

In 1983, voter majorities in the Federated States of Micronesia, the Marshall Islands, and Palau each approved Compacts of Free Association with the United States. In brief, the compacts define a relationship in which the island states grant the United States a number of strategic prerogatives in exchange for self-government (including both internal and external affairs), generous financial support, and the provision of certain services. The islanders are citizens of their own freely associated states, and while they do not enjoy American citizenship, they have the right to enter and work in the United States. Among the more important strategic prerogatives, the United States has the responsibility for defense, the right of strategic denial, and the right to establish bases and conduct military operations in the islands. The United States ultimately decides what constitutes a matter of defense. In 1985, the compacts for the Federated States and the Marshalls were ratified by the US Congress. In the following year, President Reagan declared the compacts to be in effect, and by 1990, UN approval had been achieved. Both new governments became members of the United Nations in 1991.

The history of Palau has been quite different. As in the case of the Federated States and the Marshalls, Palau's compact required approval by only a simple majority of the voters. Until 1993, however, Palau's nuclear-free constitution conflicted with the strategic provisions in the compact that allow the presence of nuclear weapons, and any attempt to override the constitution required the approval of three-fourths of Palauan voters. In the decade that began with the initial plebiscite in 1983, seven plebiscites failed to achieve the necessary votes to override the constitution.

The issue was resolved in 1993. Palauans altered their constitution, and the compact was approved by a simple majority in November of that year. The approval of the US Congress and President Clinton soon followed and the last vestige of the US Trust Territory of the Pacific ceased to exist. Palau became a freely associated state on October 1, 1994, a full quarter century after negotiations over the trust territory's future political status began in 1969.

UNSETTLED FUTURES

The new political statuses have had their disappointments and difficulties. For example, there is a widespread feeling in the Northern Marianas that the federal government is "colonialist in its basic mentality to the Commonwealth," is insensitive to island needs, and interferes far too much in local affairs (Tenorio 1989, 2). In contrast with the freely associated states, the Commonwealth does not control a two-hundred-mile Exclusive Economic Zone of its own, is limited in its participation in regional affairs, and cannot negotiate treaties and other arrangements with other states in the region. In short, the autonomy of the Northern Marianas is limited, and there is some sentiment that the commonwealth arrangement should be renegotiated. Any such hope would appear somewhat quixotic. The view in Washington is clear and simple: the Commonwealth of the Northern Mariana Islands is part of the United States and its people are American citizens.

The Federated States of Micronesia and the Marshall Islands have encoun-

*Hotel and shopping complex, Saipan,
Commonwealth of the Northern
Marianas, 1996. Photograph by
Robert Kiste.*

*Upscale shopping facility for tourists,
Saipan, Commonwealth of the
Northern Marianas, 1996. Photograph
by Robert Kiste.*

Japanese tourists, mother and child,
Tumon Bay, Guam, 1998. Photograph
by Floyd Takeuchi, Editor, Hawai'i
Business Magazine.

tered some difficulties with the status of free association, and Palau can antic-
ipate some of the same. The arrangement is not well understood in the international community. The strategic provisions of the Compacts of Free Association have clouded the status of the freely associated states and caused
debate about their sovereignty and independence (S. Firth 1989; Michal 1993).
The debate has largely been diffused as the Federated States and the Marshalls
have gained membership in the South Pacific Forum, joined the United
Nations, and established diplomatic relations with dozens of nations around
the world.

Perhaps the greatest challenges to the Federated States and the Marshalls
are the magnitude of their economic dependency and their rapidly growing
populations. With durations of fifteen years, their compacts are set to expire
in the year 2001. While it is impossible to determine the exact amount of the
financial packages, the figure commonly quoted for the Federated States and
the Marshalls together is $2.5 billion (*Washington Pacific Report* 1986). How-
ever, the subsidies are "front-loaded" and decline in five-year increments over
the compact period. In the beginning, it was assumed that investments for
development during the early years of the compact would assure greater economic self-sufficiency by the turn of the century.

Performance has lagged far behind hopes and expectations, however, and
rapid population growth has only increased anxieties about the future. The
FSM and Marshall Islands populations are among the fastest growing in the
world, and they are now estimated at approximately 105,700 and 54,700 respectively (South Pacific Commission 1995). (The number of Marshallese has
quadrupled since World War II.) It is projected that both will double within
the next twenty to twenty-five years (South Pacific Commission 1993). FSM
and Marshall Islands citizens have begun to migrate to the United States,
Guam, and the Northern Marianas, and this trend is anticipated to increase in
future years.

Palau is in a privileged position. The implementation of its Compact of Free
Association is relatively new, and it can learn from the experiences of the
other two freely associated states in Micronesia. It can also look at the often
negative consequences of the massive development schemes fueled by external
investment, especially in the tourist industry, that have engulfed Guam and
the Northern Marianas in recent years (Kiste 1994). There are indications that
Palau's entry to the international arena has been made somewhat easier by the
examples of the Federated States and the Marshall Islands. Palau gained UN
membership in December 1994, and it became a member of the South Pacific
Forum in September 1995.

IN RETROSPECT

Approximately a half century has passed since American anthropologists became involved in Micronesia. Those who pioneered the work of the 1940s could not have imagined the Micronesia of today. The past three decades in particular have witnessed phenomenal change in all sectors of society and culture. Islands once remote and difficult to reach are now instantly accessible by telephone, facsimile, and jet airplane, and in a few places, Micronesians get their daily dose of CNN News. Once rural and subsistence-based societies have become largely urbanized with cash economies dependent on external sources of funding. Thousands of Micronesians have attended universities in the United States, and American-style political structures appear to be firmly in place. The US Trust Territory of the Pacific is now but a memory.

The subject matter of the anthropology of fifty years ago has also radically altered, or in some instances, disappeared completely. Indeed, the discipline itself has also been transformed. Prior to World War II, anthropology was still struggling to create a niche for itself in American academia. It is now difficult to conceive of a time when anthropologists had only begun to discover the phenomenon of acculturation or when a classic such as Benedict's *Patterns of Culture* (1934) was still new.

Applied anthropology was also a relatively new endeavor in the early 1940s. Margaret Mead commented on how World War II served as the catalyst that "made it possible for organized groups of anthropologists to take the initiative of wholehearted participation in the war effort" (1979, 146). She recounted how the later ambiguities of the Korean War, the witch-hunting era of McCarthyism in America, and most important of all, Vietnam, had changed the moral climate of the nation and caused many anthropologists to withdraw from contact with federal programs related to military and defense interests, including technical assistance, which itself had become suspect (Mead 1979, 147).

The debates over the uses of anthropology have been both healthy and necessary for the discipline. Certainly, anthropology is a much more self-critical and self-reflective endeavor today than formerly. With regard to the applications of anthropology in Micronesia, much that was of concern is now moot at best. For a variety of reasons, the new governments in Micronesia see little or no need to seek anthropological opinion. In the case of the freely associated states, in marked contrast to the past, proposals for anthropological research must now be reviewed and approved by the Micronesian governments themselves.

In retrospect, judging from the entire range of anthropological work in

Micronesia, the CIMA project had the greatest overall impact on the discipline. It placed the largest number of researchers in the field, and in turn, they became mentors of subsequent generations of anthropologists who worked in the area (see Marshall, chap. 12). As one consequence, an area of the world once little known in the English-language anthropological literature is now among the best known (see Kiste, chap. 13, and Hays, appendix 3).

Like Micronesia itself, anthropology, both pure and applied, has grown much more complex and has experienced a population explosion of its own. With its proliferation into numerous subdisciplines and specializations, as the chapters in this volume reflect, today's anthropology would not be recognized by those who launched its involvement with Micronesia a half century ago.

NOTES

The authors wish to thank several individuals who read and provided useful suggestions for the preparation of this chapter: William Alkire, Ward Goodenough, Leonard Mason, Norman Meller, Douglas Oliver, and Jack Tobin.

1. Of the seventeen American cultural anthropologists who conducted field research in the Pacific prior to World War II, four worked in two culture areas: Willowdean Handy was in several locations in Polynesia (the Samoas, Marquesas, Societies, Tonga, Cook Islands, and New Zealand) and Melanesia (Fiji); Gordon Macgregor worked in four Polynesian islands (Tonga, Samoa, Rotuma, and Tokelau) and two places in Melanesia (Fiji and the Solomon Islands); Margaret Mead was in both Polynesia (American Samoa) and Melanesia (Papua New Guinea); and Laura Thompson worked in both Melanesia (Fiji) and Micronesia (Guam). Seven others conducted research in Polynesia only: E. S. C. Handy (the Samoas, Hawai'i, Marquesas, Societies and New Zealand); Edwin G. Burrows (Wallis and Futuna); Kenneth Emory (Hawai'i, Society Islands; Tuamotus); Felix Keesing (Western Samoa and New Zealand); Ralph Linton (Marquesas); Edwin Loeb (Niue); and Alfred Metraux (Easter Island). The remaining six worked only in Melanesia: George Devereux (Papua New Guinea); Buell Quain (Fiji); Clellan S. Ford (Fiji); Douglas Oliver (Solomon Islands); Hortense Powdermaker (New Ireland); and John Whiting (Papua New Guinea). See *International Directory of Anthropologists* (1950), edited by Melville J. Herskovits.

2. Ironically, given its geographical location, the expression of interest immediately after World War II, and the founding of the Pacific Islands Studies Program (PIP) in 1950, the University of Hawai'i provided little or no tangible support for decades. Leonard Mason was the first director and served in that capacity for most of the program's first fifteen years (1950–1965). Norman Meller followed as director for most of the next decade (1965–1975).

A grant from the Rockefeller Foundation in 1957 helped to establish the Pacific

Collection, Hamilton Library. Beginning with the 1972–1973 academic year, the Pacific Islands Studies Program received its first US Department of Education (USDOE) Title VI grant in support of a Pacific Islands language and area studies program. Title VI funding has been continuous since that initial award. Substantial administrative support and funding for Pacific Islands Studies from the university did not occur until the 1980s. As indicated, the Pacific program became the Center for Pacific Islands Studies (CPIS) in 1987. At about the same time, it and other USDOE-supported language and area studies programs became designated as National Resource Centers. The Center for Pacific Islands Studies is the only such Center in the United States devoted to the Pacific Islands region.

Concerning support from the University of Hawai'i, it should be recalled that in the early years of the Pacific program, the university was a small territorial institution. In 1950, the faculty and staff numbered under 500 and student enrollments were around 5,000. There were very few graduate programs, and the doctorate in anthropology was not authorized until 1962. University support for Pacific Islands Studies was long in coming; there was some sentiment that when compared to Asia, Pacific Island countries were small and relatively insignificant. The region's intellectual importance to anthropology, literature, and the natural sciences was largely unappreciated.

3. In her account of the CIMA project, naval historian Dorothy E. Richard incorrectly indicated that there were 42 CIMA scientists—35 anthropologists, 4 linguists, and 3 geographers (1957c, 576–577)—but her table of CIMA participants lists 43 individuals. The actual number was 41 because 2 of those included in Richard's table, William C. Canup and Katherine Luomala, withdrew and never participated.

4. Foster was commenting with the benefit of two decades of hindsight. Most of the CIMA researchers were graduate students or anthropologists at the beginning of their professional lives. While opinions will necessarily differ, perhaps a dozen or so of the young researchers of the late 1940s who "flocked to the Pacific" under the auspices of CIMA went on to be identified with Micronesia and achieve real distinction in their anthropological careers.

5. In addition to the ambitious CIMA and SIM research programs, anthropologists located in Honolulu (they were few in number, perhaps a half dozen in all) were being called on for assistance concerning policies and problems in both the US Trust Territory of the Pacific and Guam. In 1948, Sir Peter Buck and Leonard Mason were consulted regarding the plight of the people of Bikini Atoll in the northern Marshalls who had been relocated in 1946 when their ancestral homeland was selected as a nuclear test site. In 1948, Mason was commissioned to conduct a study of the Bikinians and their problems on Rongerik Atoll. Also during the late 1940s, Mason was part of a four-man team who conducted the Management Survey of the trust territory to assist with the development of budget plans by the US Department of the Interior. Between 1947 and 1951, Mason and Kenneth Emory of the Bishop Museum served on the Advisory Committee on Education for Guam and the US Trust Territory of the Pacific.

6. However, in assessing the overall outcome of the applied work of the 1950s, it must be recalled that the district anthropologists were novice field-workers when they took up their positions, and the staff anthropologist, who could have provided advice and counsel, was stationed at the High Commissioner's Office in faraway Honolulu before it was moved to Guam in 1954 (Van Cleve 1974, 140). Like Hawai'i, Guam was not part of the trust territory, and its location at the extreme western edge of Micronesia kept the staff anthropologist at some distance from the men in most of the districts. By the time the High Commissioner's Office was relocated to Saipan in 1962, the applied anthropology program had been ended, and in any event, Saipan's location north of Guam was no improvement.

With today's frequent jet travel and telecommunications, it is easy to forget that locations and distances were of much greater importance in the 1950s. At that time, there were no direct flights from Honolulu to any part of the trust territory. Rather, one had to fly from Honolulu via Wake Island (for refueling) to Guam, and then find transport eastward to most of the trust territory. Transportation across the territory between Guam and points east was achieved by surface vessel or twice-weekly flights of a sixteen-passenger seaplane. Competition for seats on the aircraft was fierce, and not uncommonly, ticketed passengers were bumped to make room for high-ranking officials and others with political influence and clout. Weight limitations often meant that letters and packages posted by air were delayed and left behind. The USTTPI districts were not linked with one another or with the High Commissioner's Office by reliable phone service, and radio communication was not dependable.

7. There were striking parallels between the experiences of American anthropologists in Micronesia and their German predecessors some four decades earlier. In an unpublished paper, "A Glance on Augustin Krämer," Dietrick Schleip (n.d.) reports that Thilenius had given priority to topics of administrative importance, and includes a quote that appears to be a directive from Thilenius indicating that researchers were "to give prominence to colonial needs (dwellings, population, death-rate, etc.)." At the same time, in a familiar-sounding complaint that the colonial government did not make use of ethnographic knowledge, Krämer wrote: "The government has no working plan; nowhere is [there] any method of social and economic development. This is the consequence of their low opinion of scientific research." (The source for the Thilenius quote is given as "Thilenius 1908, 2," but the 1908 publication is not listed in Schleip's bibliography. The source for the Krämer quote is given as "Krämer diary of the HSE, HMV, 27. Dec.1909." HMV is identified as the Hamburgiseches Museum für Völkerkunde; HSE is not identified by Schleip.)

8. Initially, ASAO was founded as the Association for Social Anthropology in Eastern Oceania (ASAEO). Its first newsletter in May 1967 reported on a symposium on adoption and fosterage that had been held the previous March at the University of California, Santa Cruz, and it noted that "we discussed as well wider questions of social anthropology in the Pacific."

One major conclusion reached at the symposium was that the intensification of modern social anthropology research in the Pacific has not so far been sufficiently systematic: we have gone out as individuals or in small team projects, largely out of touch with our colleagues, and have pursued diverse research interests and published the results in scattered bits and pieces. Organized comparative studies like those on politics and kinship that brought African social anthropology into focus have so far been lacking.

What, then, to do about it? We decided to form this association, as a means of organizing research, disseminating information, and arranging recurring symposia on topics in Oceanic social anthropology.

It appears that the founders feared that their interests would be overwhelmed by the increasing amount of research being conducted in mainland New Guinea, and so it was excluded from the organization. In the same edition of the newsletter, the rationale for the scope of ASAEO was explained:

Our primary scope includes, in area, insular Melanesia, Micronesia, and Polynesia; and in subject, social anthropology. Our relegation of New Guinea to the periphery is not aimed at excluding our colleagues working in this area or at denying the many ethnographic and theoretical concerns we share. Rather, it reflects our recognition of the different strategies entailed in New Guinea research, and of the great advances achieved in recent years toward the sort of organization and systematic comparison we hope ourselves to attain.

Within three years, there was a change of heart. The fifth newsletter, issued in March 1970, reported the ratification of a constitution including the following provision:

The name of the organization has been changed to the Association for Social Anthropology in Oceania (ASAO), deleting the "Eastern" to accord our new scope, which includes New Guinea.

In 1971, the short-lived Association for Anthropology in Micronesia (AAM) was formed with the hope of fostering closer ties between anthropological researchers and Micronesians (Mason, personal communication 1995). The Micronesian Area Research Center, University of Guam, served as the organization's secretariat, and Volumes 1 and 2 (three issues each) of the AAM newsletter were published in 1972 and 1973. An important exchange between Leonard Mason and Roger Gale about the nature of American anthropology's involvement in Micronesia appeared in the second issue of Volume 2 (see Petersen, chap. 5). There was not enough interest to sustain both ASAO and AAM, and the latter died after the second year of the newsletter's publication. Copies of the AAM Newsletter are on file at the Pacific Collection, Hamilton Library.

CHAPTER TWO

Magellan's Chroniclers?
American Anthropology's History in Micronesia

David Hanlon

MY TITLE, "Magellan's Chroniclers," comes in plural form from the two words that open William Alkire's *An Introduction to the Peoples and Cultures of Micronesia* (1977). I use the phrase to introduce my own examination of the relationship between history and American anthropology in the area called "Micronesia"—a relationship deeply affected by a tradition of colonialism that began in literary form with the words written down by Magellan's chronicler, Antonio Pigafetta, on the sighting of Guam or Guahan on March 6, 1521. I begin my exploration of American anthropology in Micronesia by diverting first to other words written down in London not so long ago. I have read that in 1968 the following question was inscribed on the stall door of a men's room in the London School of Economics: "Is Raymond Firth real or just a figment of the Tikopian imagination?" (Comaroff and Comaroff 1992, 9). Would it be too irreverent to adjust that question to read: "Are Ward Goodenough, Leonard Mason, and Norman Meller real or just figments of Micronesian imaginations?" Or is an inquiry into the practice of American anthropology in the Caroline, Mariana, and Marshall Islands more appropriately served by a question that asks whether Micronesia is a figment of American and other colonial ethnographies?

I use these inversions of a seemingly frivolous query to begin a deeper consideration of American anthropology's history in the area called Micronesia and some of the very fundamental issues it raises. In addressing American anthropology's history in Micronesia, I am concerned not so much with charting the historical record—the "facts," if you will—of anthropological practice as with reflecting on anthropologists' understanding of history and their application of that understanding to the study of Micronesian societies. In the pursuit of this task, I seek to do four things: (1) to comment briefly on the more than century-old relationship between history and anthropology; (2) to characterize the still relatively recent convergence of these two academic disciplines as revealed in some of the more recent works by anthropologists in Micronesia; (3) to show how American colonialism affected anthropologists' use of history in earlier ethnographic studies produced between the immediate post–World War II period and the mid-1970s; and (4) to offer a few comments on what a fuller, more developed history of American anthropology in Micronesia might include. What I am advancing through this last item is a cross-cultural history that involves the people of the area called Micronesia as something more and other than objects of social science inquiry.

DUELING DISCIPLINES?

Much has been written about the uneasiness with which the disciplines of anthropology and history have regarded one another.[1] Anthropologists' early preoccupation with social totality and universal traits, and the structures and functions through which they might be gleaned, contrasted sharply with historians' focus on fragmentary evidence, "the complexity of causes, unforeseen consequences, and the small chances that make great events" (Dening 1980, 41). Anthropologists authenticated their findings by the direct observation that fieldwork provided, while historians retreated to archives to discover what they could of times and peoples past. Some forms of anthropological practice were decidedly antihistorical. Representing British functionalism's pronounced disregard for history and for those schools of diffusionist and evolutionist thought touched by a consciousness of the past, A. R. Radcliffe-Brown (1952) asserted that history explained nothing at all. French structuralists argued somewhat less vociferously that the pasts of nonwestern peoples were either unknowable or unimportant in the larger scheme of social science investigation. Claude Lèvi-Strauss (1963) dismissed history as a vehicle neither desirable nor possible for the study of primitive cultures. For him, the cultures of primitive peoples centered about the play of universal values as revealed in the organizing structures of those cultures.

A pronounced indifference toward nonwestern peoples' histories was not confined to certain schools of anthropological thought. Conventional historians' lack of interest in anything that was not written down and that did not involve war, trade, treaties, or the politics of European nations tended to reinforce the distance between the two disciplines. Hugh Trevor-Roper, the British imperial historian, insisted that only the history of Europeans in Africa was worthwhile and discernible; "the rest," he wrote, "is largely darkness, like the history of pre-European, pre-Columbian America. And darkness is not a subject for history." He went on to argue that historians should not amuse themselves with the "unrewarding gyrations of barbarous tribes in picturesque but irrelevant corners of the globe" (quoted in Krech 1991, 345).

The wariness with which anthropology and history regarded each other should not be overemphasized, however; there was approach as well as avoidance. For example, E. B. Tylor (1958 [1871]) was not opposed to history, but thought it should be more scientific. For Tylor, a more scientific theory would overcome the whim, arbitrary impulse, chance, and vagaries that historians saw in the past. By becoming more rigorous and scientific, history might then contribute significantly to that grandest, most sweeping of intellectual paradigms: evolution. A sense of history also showed in A. L. Kroeber's (1939) examination of culture traits across time and space, while Franz Boas (1940) advocated strong attention to history in his emphasis on cultural particularism. And E. E. Evans-Pritchard (1940, 1962) recognized the rituals of kingship among the Nuer of Africa as being both a product and source of history. There existed, in short, other schools of anthropological practice that were conscious of the proposition that the study of change over time invited a discourse with historians.

For a time ethnohistory, in its recognition of nonwestern pasts, offered an empirical, positivist, and culturally sensitive middle ground on which historians and anthropologists might meet to study the dimensions of culture contact and culture change. Greg Dening has described early ethnohistory as the "bastard child of history and anthropology, born out of the snobbish reluctance of historians to be interested in anyone who was not white and did not wear a crown, and born too out of the intransigent belief of anthropologists that to understand anyone they must be alive, in remote places of the world and in dire danger of disappearing" (1980, 35). This brand of ethnohistory, however, failed to satisfy most historians who remained skeptical about the use of myth and legend, and most anthropologists who saw it as not dealing vigorously enough with such vital topics as kinship, exchange, social organization, and status rivalry. To be effective, the convergence of history and anthropology would have to be something more than ethnohistory, something that evidenced an awareness of process, complexity, negotiation, and the imperfect, incomplete accommodations between local interests and foreign intrusion.

I understand that when the relationship between history and anthropology is raised, anthropologists are quick to ask: "Which anthropology?" Historians respond similarly: "Which history?" As the discipline of anthropology sought to escape the limitations of evolutionist, structuralist, and functionalist paradigms that either were ahistorical or reduced history to a simple matter of change over time, historians also looked beyond their empirically focused concerns for causality, sequence, personality, and event explained through the positivist tradition of European thought. For historians, the turn toward anthropology and culture resulted from a growing awareness that communities existed with distinctive rituals, beliefs, and practices not easily accommodated by sweeping regional studies or considerations of base and superstructure. To chart history's discovery of anthropology would take a long, deep intellectual history—one that included the development of the Annales School, with its initial attention to temporally deep, geographically wide studies of social and economic topics; the challenges raised to conventional Marxist analysis by Marxist historian E. P. Thompson's use of culture; and the profound influence of Clifford Geertz's symbolic anthropology on the whole subfield of historical practice—cultural history—that focuses on the European past.

Historians such as Robert Darnton and Natalie Zemon Davis now scrutinize European societies in the same way many anthropologists study nonwestern cultures. The descriptions tend to be thick, with particular attention to the deeper meanings behind the public performance of symbol-laden rituals and practices. Cultural history, at least for Europe, represents a subversive kind of historical sociology, a history that seeks to counter the hegemony of the privileged classes in and over the study of the past. History, however, is not made in a vacuum independent of the forces about which it writes. The discovery of the hidden histories of heretofore forgotten groups of people in European society has brought with it a consideration of power and its effects on both the course of events, and the recording and remembering of them. Antonio Gramsci (1971) reminded us that history is made in the struggle among diverse life worlds coexisting in a given time and place; holding competing ideologies affected by and involving matters of class, gender, race, ethnicity, and language; and striving for space within a dominant hegemonic order. In short, cultural historians, like anthropologists, have come to accept the notion of culture as a domain in which different groups of people contend for power in both practical and symbolic ways.

Beyond the Euro-American world, cultural history becomes an even more complicated inquiry better described as ethnographic history or even historical anthropology. Anthropology's rapprochement with history in the Pacific results primarily from the work of Marshall Sahlins and Greg Dening. Sahlins borrows heavily from French structuralism and from Annales historian Fernand Braudel. Attempting to reconcile structure and event in a theory of history centering around the death of Captain Cook in Hawai'i, Sahlins (1981) explored the interplay between prescriptive structures of cultural understanding and behavior, and the challenge posed to them by the unscripted, spontaneous nature of historical circumstance. The result of such a conjuncture is both reproduction and transformation accommodating change within an established but flexible and resilient cultural order. Sahlins argued that the anthropological experience of culture explodes the practice of history; "Suddenly," he wrote, "there are all kinds of new things to consider" (1985, 72). More oriented toward symbol than structure, Dening (1978) proposed a cross-cultural approach to history that recognizes the problems of meaning, and how the communication of cultural knowledge through words, gestures, symbols, and rituals is transmitted, received, interpreted, and changed across beaches and other boundaries. As Sahlins would have anthropologists become historians, Dening (1988) argued for an ethnography of strangers as well as natives, and a recognition that, in a new and different sense, all history is essentially ethnohistory because of the ways that different cultures give distinctive styles and purposes to their expressions of historical consciousness.

MICROHISTORIES IN MICRONESIA

Recent anthropology in American Micronesia evidences a consciousness of history and, more particularly, reflects the convergence of the two disciplines over the last two decades.[2] Sahlins' brand of structural history is manifest in Richard Parmentier's (1987) work on the Palauan past. Like Sahlins, Parmentier believes that history is locally ordered and culturally determined. In his view, the Palauan past is revealed through physical signs that serve as historical markers of events deemed significant, memorable, and thus historical. The texts or sources of the Palauan past include not just the writings of outside visitors, but stones, hillsides, geographical configurations, and the physical layout of Palauan villages whose spatial configuration and distinctive architectural features offer a diagram of Palau's deep political history. James Peoples (1985), in his work on Kosrae, argued against the persisting and false dichotomy between traditional and modern culture. He saw not just the nature of

economic activity but the more general issue of history on the island as resulting from the complex interplay of local and foreign forces. Thus, Peoples'
work provides a caution against the imposition of inappropriate or incomplete theoretical constructions (in this case modernization and dependency
theory) that limit history to the actions of outsider forces, agents, and systems. In different ways, Parmentier and Peoples have argued that the determinants of the Palauan and Kosraean past are firmly rooted in Palau and Kosrae,
respectively.

It is not difficult to lose sight of islands and islanders amidst the sweep of
world capitalism, the spread of Christianity, the imposition of colonial rule,
or the violence of world war. Dening posited that there has yet to be written a
history of religious conversion in the Pacific that pays enough ethnographic
attention to affected beliefs and symbol transfer (1980, 199). That may well be,
but I have always thought Peter Black's work on Christianity in Tobi (1978)
contained the core of a fine cross-cultural history of religious change in its
efforts to look at Tobian understandings of the missionary Fr. Elias,[3] his
words, his work, and the history that preceded him. Mac and Leslie Marshall
(1975, 1976, 1990) combined fieldwork with archival research to produce an
interesting sociocultural history of alcohol use and abuse in Chuuk,[4] while
Juliana Flinn (1992a) and Catherine Lutz (1988) gave considerable attention to
history and colonial policy in their studies dealing respectively with mobility
and migration on Pulap, and emotional meanings on Ifaluk. I suspect that we
will soon be treated to a very different, much more localized and culturally
nuanced history of world war in a volume being put together by Lin Poyer,
Laurence Carucci, and Suzanne Falgout.[5]

Not all anthropologists who have addressed history in their work are certain about how knowable island pasts really are. Glenn Petersen (1990a), more
of a deconstructionist than he realizes, has cautioned us, as have E. H. Carr
(1961) and Benedetto Croce (1923), that history is also very much about the
present in which it is produced or constructed. For Petersen, the deeper
dimensions of the Pohnpeian past are mirrored only faintly and in very general patterns that address contemporary political concerns. Whatever its real
or actual past may be, Nan Madol, the megalithic site of human-made islets,
stone structures, and canals located just off the southeastern coast of Pohnpei
proper, provides first and foremost not a history text but a lesson about power
and government.

A greater sensitivity to local pasts invites consideration of what history
might mean and how it is used in different island settings. For instance, Poyer

(1984, 1993) has written of local or indigenous conceptions of history and their effect on the formulation of cultural identity. She discussed how local accounts of the 1837 massacre of the adult male population of Ngatik or Sapwuahfik inform and reveal that island people's sense of themselves today. Following the massacre came an influx of whites, Pohnpeians, and other islanders who reached the atoll and intermarried with the surviving population of Sapwuahfik women. Such tragedy and its aftermath would seem on the surface to be the ingredients for a torturous and total redefinition of identity. Foreign intrusion meant violence, death, and cultural disruption, but also brought Christianity, material goods, and even blood ties with Americans. These latter developments, argued Poyer, constitute an integral part of the remembered history of the 1837 massacre, and help distinguish the people of Sapwuahfik in their own minds and in positive ways from those of nearby islands and atolls.

Anthropologists' recent work with Micronesian pasts, I would contend, is not only relevant to questions of identity, but it also encourages the realization that history and the doing or construction of history are locally ordered and culturally determined as to purpose, mode of expression, and significance. In another publication (1992), Poyer again expounded on the different significance attached to historical properties by local people and outside cultural experts. The artifacts and battle sites of World War II on the atoll of Toiwa or Maloelap in the Marshalls hold far less cultural and even historical importance for that island's people than sites associated with the past activities of their ancestors and deities. Different definitions of historical significance, Poyer found, hold important implications for the study of history across cultures. Similarly, Karen Nero (1992d), examining the events surrounding the 1866 death of Scottish trader Andrew Cheyne in Palau, explained how local versions of an event are developed and maintained for hegemonic purposes. The question then becomes not the binary opposition between local and foreign accounts, but the admission of the plurality of local accounts whose differences reflect the identity and interests of their historians or advocates.

In examining the more recent coming together of the two disciplines in the field of Micronesian studies, I do not mean to suggest that anthropology's relationship with history is a short one, only dating from the mid-1970s or so. Far from it. I would argue that most American anthropologists working in the area called Micronesia have had a degree of consciousness about the past. Alkire's work (1978) strikes me as infused with a strong though subtle sense of history in its attention to the influences of environment on human activity over time. He wrote of the ecological inventories of coral isolates, clusters, and complexes, and of the ways in which the interplay of atoll resources, population pressures, and natural disasters can promote over time a host of coping strategies. These range from war to more constructive social practices including cooperation, exchange, temporary migration, and the imposition of restrictions or taboos designed to insure effective resource management. In considering the environment, there is of course the ocean. Thomas Gladwin's *East Is a Big Bird* (1970) is a history of sorts that locates navigation and ocean-going voyages squarely within the contexts of Puluwatan history. Gladwin wrote of a people, surrounded by a sustaining but sometimes hostile ocean, who live by sailing. Their ability to sail and navigate has provided Puluwat people with new ideas, skills, and technologies, and with networks of social, political and economic ties essential to their survival. Puluwat's past, then, and Gladwin's consciousness of it are inextricably linked to the ocean and to that island people's ability to sail upon it.

In concluding this section of my inquiry, I need to make two points. First, I do not mean to suggest that American anthropology's more recent consideration of history in Micronesia is without problems. I will turn to these problems toward the close of this chapter. The strength of the works cited above lie in their attention to and consideration of local histories, and in their gentle, respectful struggle with an understanding of history in Micronesia employed by an earlier generation of anthropologists. The most significant contribution of this recent, more historically nuanced anthropology may well be its inadvertent displacement or decentering of academic histories and professional ethnographies in favor of more local expressions and reflections regarding culture and history by people called Micronesians.

Second, I wish to reiterate my view that American anthropology's consideration of history is by no means a recent development. History was never a totally alien element, completely absent from American anthropologists' construction of Micronesian societies. The forces that affected and constrained anthropologists' sense of history in Micronesia in the first decades of America's presence were war and the colonial rule that followed it.

Colonialism, by its very nature, stands hostile and oblivious to indigenous versions and visions of local pasts. Histories that revisit precolonial times loom as potentially threatening and ultimately subversive to colonial agendas predicated on possession, control, and exploitation. The war that first brought or, in Guam's case, returned American rule to the islands called Micronesia proved near total in its destruction; it destroyed lives, devastated landscapes, and buried for a while a consciousness of the islands' deeper pasts. The rubble and ashes of war seemed to create a new ground zero, with the promise that all history was to be made in the change to come—change that was considered inevitable, desirable, and necessary, change to be dictated and directed by Americans. Later American anthropologists would rediscover a history that could serve as preface, background, or introduction to their ethnographic work, but it would be a history of colonialism in the region, other people's colonialism. I turn next to a consideration of World War II and the immediate postwar years, and the ways in which local histories of Micronesian islands and atolls were largely denied or dismissed in the interests of military administration and American rule.

THE HISTORY OF WAR-DEVASTATED ETHNOLOGY

As it had in 1899 and 1914, war brought a change in the colonial administrations of Micronesia.[6] Unlike the Spanish-American conflict or World War I, whose major battlegrounds lay elsewhere, the struggle for supremacy in the Pacific between Japan and the United States had some of its most violent encounters among the islands. People who had never before heard of Micronesia became familiar with such names as Tarawa, Kwajalein, Truk (now Chuuk), Saipan, Guam, Angaur, and Peleliu. Referring directly to the battles fought on Micronesian islands, Fletcher Pratt, author of *The Marines' War,* wrote that "never in the history of human conflict had so much been thrown by so many at so few" (1948, 144). With 36,000 shells dropped on it, Kwajalein endured the most concentrated bombing of the Pacific war. Other Micronesian islands experienced similar devastation. Saipan was invaded on June 15, 1944, by 127,000 American troops supported by 535 ships (Gale 1979, 144). Caught between the armies of the two major combatants and surrounded by a Japanese and Korean civilian population of more than 11,000, some 2,300 Chamorros and 900 Carolinians struggled to survive in a home that had become a strange and dangerous land. The battle for Saipan created, in the words of Japanese colonial historian Mark Peattie (1988, 285), "unbounded horror." By the time the fighting ceased, a defoliated, potted, ravaged landscape stood in place of once prosperous, productive islands. Douglas Oliver's (1961, 371) general characterization of World War II in the Pacific as "catastrophically disturbing" the lives of island peoples spoke directly to local experiences of global war in Micronesia.

Written texts that seek to describe war and its effects can carry, in their own ways, themes that are destructive and dangerous. Homi Bhabha (1990), Patrick Brantlinger (1988), Mary Louise Pratt (1992), and Edward Said (1979), among others, have pointed out the subliminal, politically charged messages that can lie embedded in the simplest, most seemingly straightforward narratives. While not meaning to deny or diminish the tragedy of war, I argue that representations of war-devastated societies in Micronesia ultimately helped legitimate in more public and international arenas an agenda for change that served American interests. In the process, these representations also worked to suppress a consciousness of both the precolonial and colonial periods of the Micronesian past.

Published in 1957, Lt. Col. Dorothy Richard's three-volume history looms as the officially commissioned record and canon on the United States Navy's occupation and administration of Micronesia from 1944 to 1952. Its sheer physical size, the extensive detail embedded in its essentially narrative, chronological structure, and the inclusion of numerous tables, figures, charts, lists, and reproductions of primary documents give Richard's history an intimidating quality. The geographical foci of her text are the Mariana and Marshall Islands, where the earliest and heaviest American fighting took place and where wartime relief efforts and postwar administrative concerns proved most prominent. She described most of the Marshall Islands as totally devastated by the effects of the war and cited accounts from American landing forces that characterized the people as "ill, dazed, hungry and clad in tatters. Even the sails of their canoes were threadbare. . . . Their economy was ruined and they had no trade goods nor money. Their diet was barely a subsistence one. There was no market for their copra and their coconut trees were deteriorating from lack of care" (Richard 1957a, 339).

Other Micronesian island groups touched directly by combat are represented in similar language. In the logic of Richard's text, and the photographs that accompanied it, the destructive effects of the war on Micronesian islands and atolls necessitated the wholesale reconstruction of these island societies, a major effort that would have a particularly American character to it.

Americans, wrote Richard, expected that their role as liberators would secure a welcome reception and an extended period of goodwill from grateful, needy, debilitated local populations (1957a, 341). But their expectations of appreciation, cooperation, humility, and gratitude on the part of islanders were bound to go unrealized. The earliest US naval officials in the area acknowledged the alienation of island peoples toward a nation whose bombs, bullets, and blockades had caused injury or death to many of their friends and rela-

Relics of earlier colonial regimes in Micronesia. Remains of Spanish wall and German Catholic church tower, Pohnpei. Trust Territory Archives (Photo 2375.02), Pacific Collection, University of Hawai'i Library.

Devastation of Peleliu Island, Palau, after the American invasion, 1944. Photograph courtesy of the Belau National Museum.

US Marine questioning Saipanese
during invasion of Saipan, June 1944.
US Marine Corps photograph,
National Archives.

Fais Islanders gathered to salute the
American flag early in US Navy
occupation of Micronesia, January
1945. US Navy photograph, National
Archives.

Islander giving information to US Marine officer during US Pacific Fleet task force evacuation of Japanese garrison, Woleai Atoll. Japanese and US Navy officers observing the transaction. September 1945. US Marine Corps photograph National Archives.

Marshallese children examining American magazines, Majuro, Marshall Islands, 1945. US Navy photograph, National Archives.

tives. John Useem (1945a), a sociologist working with the military government, noted that Micronesians did not regard Americans as liberators who had saved them from an awful fate; rather, they understood the US invasion of their islands most immediately in terms of the disruption it had caused in their lives. An oral history of the period from Enewetak describes the people of that atoll as impressed by US military might, but distressed by the attitudes and behaviors of their new overlords (L. Carucci 1989). Americans were seen as powerful, intelligent, wealthy conquerors who had little need for the people of Enewetak. The American homeland came to be regarded as the "source of a force" to be celebrated and feared, a force that was ultimately indifferent to and disruptive of Marshallese society. Conquest and philanthropy, then, were not the compatible combination Americans thought them to be. Apparently unimpressed by the distinctions that separated the United States from the United Nations, one elderly Palauan woman said to a member of an early UN Visiting Mission, "The next time you have a war, please don't have it here" (Nero 1989, 144).

Described as disturbed and devastated by a world war fought on their islands and atolls, Micronesians, it was argued, had no alternative but to change. That view was propounded in wartime histories, in the comments of military administrators during the immediate postwar period, and in the earliest writings of American anthropologists in the area. Useem (1946a) wrote of how the total devastation of war had created for Micronesians an unprecedented crisis in which they were completely powerless. John Embree, a University of Hawai'i anthropologist working in the area during the first year of military government, described the Micronesians' situation as a "dramatic example of the helplessness of the individual in the conflict of nations" (1946b, 1). He went on to describe Micronesians as people without a country and with no voice in the development of policies and decisions that would govern their lives. To him, life in Micronesia looked more constricted in 1946 than it had been in 1936. Representations of Micronesians as devastated, destitute, and powerless provided considerable license for an agenda of change that looked only to the future, not the past.

As discussed in other chapters of this volume, anthropologists were enlisted to serve this agenda of change by advising on the administration of the native peoples. Homer G. Barnett and George Peter Murdock had considerable influence in shaping the application of anthropology in Micronesia. Such an application was by no means a singular event. In his book *Anthropology in Administration,* Barnett noted: "In modern times, practically every nation with expanding frontiers has supported inquiries into the customs of native peoples in areas of projected or accomplished occupation.... Colonization programs, if they have not been dedicated to the destruction of indigenous populations, have necessitated a knowledge of local custom" (1956, 2).

As outgoing president of the Society for Applied Anthropology in May 1948, Murdock spoke of the scientific justification of American democracy. He claimed that American democracy's ultimate strength resided in the fact that it stood as the only form of government in harmony with the essential nature of culture change.[7] The policy of a democratic nation charged with the administration of a dependent people, thought Murdock, should be governed by an awareness of the inevitability and unpredictability of culture change, and democratic safeguards had to be maintained to insure that political change would be orderly, adaptive, and progressive. Murdock said that his chief hope for the Micronesian peoples was that they might escape the chaos, bewilderment, helplessness, and stagnation that had been the fate of American Indians. To his way of thinking, the US naval administration should concern itself with the maintenance of democratic safeguards, the provision of essential social services, and the implementation of appropriate measures designed to "prevent actions by the natives which all competent authorities recognize will be to their ultimate disadvantage and which future generations of natives will certainly regret" (1948a, 3–4).

And who would gain from the application of anthropology to military rule in Micronesia? Aside from the obvious benefits to the administration, there were said to be real advantages to the colonized population itself. In an address before the Royal Anthropological Institute in 1900, W. H. Flower proclaimed that the administration of native peoples was ultimately for their own good and in their own best interests: "A knowledge of their [other races'] special characters and relations to one another has a more practical object than a mere satisfaction of scientific curiosity; it is a knowledge upon which the happiness and prosperity, or the reverse, of millions of our fellow-creatures may depend" (quoted in Barnett 1956, 1).

The social sciences' inquiry into human societies and the general condition of humankind would also be aided by work in Micronesia, it was said. Oliver wrote of the scientific progress served by a study of human variability and the possibility that Micronesians might possess traits of ultimate value for all humankind (1951, 83). Micronesian findings, once filtered through appropriate theoretical schemes, could then be compared with data from other areas of the world (Useem 1947, 3). The ultimate benefit of this global comparison of ethnographic research would be a better identification and understanding of the many common denominators found in all human societies. Direct benefit would also accrue to the discipline of anthropology and some of the larger issues with which it was concerned. Embree (1946a) justified specific research in Micronesia as contributing to a better understanding of Polynesian origins, cultural diffusion, culture contact, and culture change.

The anthropologists working with the military government and later the US naval administration sanctioned by the UN Trusteeship Agreement with the United States saw themselves as arbiters between indigenous peoples disturbed deeply by war, and the naked, not always sympathetic face of American military power in the islands. Nicholas Thomas (1994) has written against a perception of colonialism as monolithic in its character, purposes, personalities, and efficacy. He has argued for a recognition of colonialism that is more sophisticated, localized, and also nuanced to the diverse, often conflicting agendas and approaches advanced by different groups of a single colonizing nation. To read Useem's descriptions (1945a, 1946a, 1946b) of the frustration, impatience, provincialism, and racism that often marked military governance in the islands, or to examine the records of the frequently intense debates between anthropologists and administrators in the first years of civilian administration, is to understand something of how American colonialism struggled with itself over the character and paradox of its presence in the islands.[8] My interest lies not with a condemnation of applied anthropology, but with what I see as applied anthropology's initially tacit acceptance of the assertion that a better history in Micronesia began in 1944 with the arrival of American military forces (see Petersen, chap. 5). This assertion was reinforced in many ways by the findings of several major anthropological studies of the islands undertaken in the immediate postwar period, most particularly, the United States Commercial Company's (USCC) economic survey of Micronesia and the Coordinated Investigation of Micronesian Anthropology (CIMA) project.

Carried out in 1946 and directed by the anthropologist Douglas Oliver, the USCC economic survey of Micronesia brought to bear the considerable resources and interests of various federal agencies including the Departments of State, Commerce, Agriculture, Navy, and Interior (Oliver 1951). The USCC survey identified and collected all sources of recorded information about Micronesia. The excavation of this knowledge included the translation of foreign language materials secured from foreign archives and the redrawing of existing maps using aerial photography and other techniques developed during the war. A list of research topics and objectives was assembled that, in essence, realigned and redefined Micronesian life in terms of the priorities, objectives, and categories of analysis of an alien social order. Noticeably absent in this list of research topics was any consideration of history or any real expression of a historical consciousness. The categorization of island life was in and of itself an aggressive act. It did not so much describe or represent authentically as change and reorder through listing and description. The omission of history from the index of this project, if unintended, nonetheless proved convenient.

The end product of the USCC investigations—twenty volumes of reports and one hundred forty article-length publications—contributed to the possession and remaking of Micronesia. Previously colonized by Spain, Germany, and Japan, and designated by a Greek term that emphasized a lack of size as its distinguishing, essential feature, this area of islands was rediscovered and reinterpreted by American specialists using terms, categories, and methods of analysis no less alien or distorting than earlier colonial renderings.

The CIMA project, like the USCC survey, was commissioned to support military rule in the islands.[9] Mason (1967b) characterized the CIMA effort "as a massive ethnology salvage program." Murdock viewed it as the largest and probably best equipped expeditionary survey in the history of modern anthropology (Richard 1957c, 582). According to Richard (1957c, 390), the CIMA mandate was to identify trends in the local development of governments and to point out incipient conflicts and socially disruptive patterns for correction.

The published research that resulted from the CIMA project was formidable and extensive; its final bibliography records thirty-two full reports and over one hundred articles and other publications on Micronesian kinship, political organization, cognitive measurements, economic exchange patterns, and general ethnography (Bowen 1963). Anyone who has read Foucault (1979, 1980) on the intimate link between knowledge and power, and the nation state's use of varied institutions and disciplinary technologies to create a docile collective social body that could be subjected, studied, used and transformed for its presumed betterment, might shudder a little to read the statement of purpose, found on the inside front covers of all CIMA final reports. Having acknowledged financial assistance from the Office of Naval Research and the National Academy of Sciences, that statement continues: "Studies in anthropology as well as human and economic geography were carried out in cooperation with universities, museums and research institutions under this project of the Pacific Science Board of the National Research Council, aided by financial assistance from the Viking Fund and other private sources" (Ritzenthaler 1949).

The extensive body of literature generated by the CIMA project did not result in a total denial of the past. There were ethnographic studies that included histories, but these were histories of colonialism, of colonial policies that excluded the people of the islands or that characterized their responses to colonial realities in careful, measured, and generic language. Alex Spoehr's book *Saipan: The Ethnology of a War-Devastated Island* (1954), for example, contains a rather extensive account of the historical antecedents of what was then contemporary Saipan. Spoehr devoted more than one hundred pages to the discovery and conquest of Saipan, the formation in very general terms of a hybridized Chamorro culture as a result of Spanish conquest and colonization, the eventual resettlement of the island in the early nineteenth century, the German and Japanese colonial periods, and finally the holocaust that was World War II. His work demonstrates how the interplay between colonialism and war limited anthropologists' conception of history in the islands to essentially colonial history; this limitation would endure for some time.

Other CIMA studies emphasized cultural survival through effective local strategies including appropriation, manipulation, and selective acculturation. In his study of postwar Palau, Useem (1945b) identified indigenous resistance to the Japanese colonial regime which had persisted throughout Japan's rule and intensified considerably during the last year of the war. Rather than cultural collapse, Useem saw the adaptability of a people and the persistence of a viable cultural identity that allowed for survival even in the face of a world war. Useem's vision of a vital society was later seconded by Arthur Vidich (1949) in his study of the historical patterns of Palauan factionalism and the ways that factions both confounded and manipulated different colonial regimes. In Useem's observations and Vidich's study, then, there was a sense of history that stood in marked contrast to other ethnographic descriptions of islanders as only victims of war, subjects of change, and people without a documentable past.

The work of Useem and Vidich foreshadowed a body of later ethnographic studies that included prefatory histories stressing selectivity, adaptability, and appropriation in Micronesian responses to foreign and colonial influences (Alkire 1965a; Bowers 1950; Force 1960; Gladwin and Sarason 1953; Hughes 1970; Hughes and Lingenfelter 1974; Joseph and Murray 1951; Labby 1976a; Lessa 1950a, 1962a, 1966a; Lingenfelter 1975; Riesenberg 1968; Schaefer 1976; Spoehr 1949a). These histories, offered as background or introduction to ethnographic inquiries, did not really address the messy entanglements and complexities of local negotiations and compromises with colonial institutions, policies, and practices. Rather, more often than not, they gave license for particular studies of some cultural institution or practice in a setting that inadvertently reasserted a timeless, ethnographic present free from the west and its attendant forces of colonialism and Christianity.

War and colonialism thus blinkered anthropologists' understandings of the depth and dimensions of the islands' pasts. Lost in most of the history that eventuated from the CIMA project was an awareness or acknowledgment of Micronesians as agents, actors, negotiators, appropriators, and manipulators. Missing from the prefatory histories of anthropologists' work was an admission that the islanders were involved in the making of their pasts—that they were people who had dealt with past colonial regimes, survived war, and were now coping with yet another colonial order that thought of itself as distinct and different, and not really colonial at all.

THE POSSIBILITIES OF LOCAL AND COUNTER-ETHNOGRAPHIES

I have considered something of American anthropology's changing sense of history from the immediate postwar period through the first two decades of the trusteeship to more contemporary times. I turn now to what a history of American anthropology in Micronesia might include, considering first the possibility of local or counter-ethnographies carried out by the people called Micronesians. The question is this: Were American anthropologists, whether engaged in applied efforts or later more independent research, the only ethnographers at work in Micronesia? I think not.

Useem wrote of Micronesians as ethnographers, endeavoring to discover the patterns of American behavior (1946a, 6). This effort gave way, he claimed, to a resignation that Americans were pro-native, but beyond understanding and unpredictable. Barnett (n.d.a) had a somewhat different view of Micronesians' abilities as ethnographers. In a piece entitled "American–Micronesian Relations," he contended that Micronesians rather than Americans had more frequent and productive opportunities to observe the other in matters pertaining to the intimate details of everyday life and work habits. Their motivation lay in their status as a subordinate group of people driven by the necessity of survival to understand as much as possible about those who had such incredible power over their lives. Barnett went on to argue that the success or failure of the trust territory government hinged on the images individually and privately presented by Americans to an observant and critical Micronesian audience. Vicente Diaz has pointed out to me that there exists in

Barnett's words a not-so-subtle argument for more and better American anthropology in the area. There also, I think, lies embedded in Barnett's statement a recognition of local counter-ethnographies done by Micronesians on Americans—counter-ethnographies that constitute distinctive, particular inquiries into the colonizer's culture; that seek to know in order to cope; and that in playful, subversive ways reflect colonial anthropology back on itself.

I have a story from the island of Pohnpei in the year 1910 that underscores the likelihood and possibilities of counter-ethnographies in the area called Micronesia. It concerns a meeting between the German ethnographer, Paul Hambruch, and a Pohnpeian priest/sorcerer by the name of Wasekelung.[10] Hambruch was, of course, a member of the German Südsee Expedition, which conducted research in Micronesia from 1908 to 1910. The Südsee Expedition was an exercise in salvage anthropology dedicated to capturing the last remnants of cultures assumed to be on the brink of inevitable extinction (Berg 1988). The desperation of the moment inspired Hambruch and other members of the expedition to write histories that, interestingly, revealed something of the interaction between triumphant colonial cultures and local declining ones. Hambruch's three-volume study (1932, 1936) of Pohnpeian history and culture has proved a vital source for later generations of anthropologists and researchers. John "Jack" Fischer, for example, borrowed heavily from Hambruch for his section on the history of Pohnpei in his *The Eastern Carolines* (1957a).

I have said something of Hambruch and the contexts of his presence on the island. What of Wasekelung? Among the people of the chiefdom of Kiti, which stretched along the eastern and southern areas of the larger island of Pohnpei, Wasekelung, in the first years of the twentieth century, stood as a revered priest and historian and a feared sorcerer. He played an instrumental role in the war between Kiti and Madolenihmw that was fought at Nahlapenlohd in 1852; he predicted the great typhoon of 1905 that devastated the island; and he served as an informant for Hambruch in his ethnographic research on the island. Wasekelung's meetings with Hambruch were arranged by the now better known and published Pohnpeian historian, Luelen Bernart, and took place at Bernart's residence at Rehntu in an area of Kiti called Wone. The story that I retell involved the issue of cannibalism.

In his research, Hambruch encountered numerous stories about the prior existence of a cannibalistic people on the island.[11] Reflecting the stories told Hambruch, an account from Bernart's *The Book of Luelen* describes these cannibals, called *liet*, as wild, frightening, ugly, unclean, lazy people who did not like to work; they "ate the flesh of animals and the flesh of humans. They were very cruel. There was no love in them" (1977, 12). At Rehntu, the German ethnographer asked the old sorcerer about the existence of cannibals or *liet* on Pohnpei. Wasekelung replied that there had indeed been such people in a time long past, but that they had been driven from the island. Hambruch then asked Wasekelung if he knew where the cannibals went. Wasekelung replied quickly and with a seemingly serious demeanor, "New Guinea, sir."

Hambruch (1936, II, text 51, 123) chose not to record Wasekelung's answer, but used instead an account provided by two other reputable historians from the south of the island, the brothers Louis and Warren Kehoe, which identified Pohnpei's *liet* or cannibals as having fled the island for areas to the west referred to as *Pai'izi* or, in more modern Pohnpeian orthography, *Peidi*. I cannot say why Hambruch chose to ignore Wasekelung's answer; he might have interpreted it as a sign of ignorance, or perhaps he detected a subtle mocking or derisive quality to the old sorcerer's reply. The flight of cannibals from Pohnpei may have been a troubling story for Hambruch because it co-opted for modern-day Pohnpeians a ground that German colonizers thought belonged to them, a ground that distinguished clearly between who was wild, frightening, ugly, unclean, lazy, cannibalistic and who was not; between who was civilized and who was not.

In the Wone area, the story is told and retold with a considerable amount of delight and laughter. For the people of Wone today, and I suspect in Wasekelung's time, the issue is not the exact location to which Pohnpei's cannibals fled; it is something else. I read Wasekelung's comments as a counter-ethnography that recognizes Hambruch's intrusion, his peculiar interest in important sensitive knowledge to which he had no right, and the awkward situation created by a direct, aggressive, alien manner of questioning. In Wasekelung's naming of New Guinea as the place to which Pohnpei's cannibals fled, there also exists a local acknowledgment of the larger imperial contexts of German colonialism and ethnography in the Pacific. Wasekelung understood New Guinea to be a German colony. By identifying New Guinea as the retreat of Pohnpei's cannibals, the old historian had implicated German ethnographic inquiry in a larger imperial process that was exploitative and racist.

I wish to tell another story that speaks to the possibilities of counter-ethnographies. Glenn Petersen and I were both on Pohnpei in the summer of

1983 doing research—Glenn in Awak and I in Wone. I had completed an inventory of colonial properties on the island about two years before. Glenn was interested in visiting some of the sites I had surveyed, particularly the German cemetery and the mass grave of fifteen Sokehs warriors executed for their role in the 1910 rebellion against German colonial rule. The German cemetery lies near the old Kolonia Town Dump—an appropriate place for a cemetery full of colonizers some might say—in a specific area of Kolonia that Pohnpeians refer to today as Yakiba. The word "Yakiba," itself another colonial artifact of sorts, comes from the Japanese and reminds any and all that the old town dump rested on the site of what was once the Japanese crematorium. After visiting the cemetery and its well-tended graves, we walked a quarter of a mile back toward the center of town and then turned left onto a badly rutted side road that traversed a small projection of land called Kumwonlaid. The mass grave of the Sokehs rebels is along the side of that road. Kumwonlaid, I am told, was formerly the location of a special shrine or *pei* dedicated to Inas, an ancestral goddess of the Sounkawad clan. I am unsure of German intentions, but the selection of the execution and mass burial site at Kumwonlaid would have impressed some Pohnpeians as other than arbitrary since many of the fifteen men executed were members of the Sounkawad clan.

Sometime just prior to our visit, the grave had been cleared by a team of young men employed by the Community Development Office with funds provided through the US Congress' Community Education and Training Act of 1968. A low rock wall, reinforced with poured concrete, bordered the grave. As Glenn and I observed and discussed the site, a man, Epensio Eperiam, happened by. I know Epensio; he is a friend and former colleague of mine. We shared an office at the Community College of Micronesia on Pohnpei in the late 1970s, he as a carpenter and I as a teacher of English as a second language. Epensio inquired about our presence in the area and then about our interest in the grave site. A member of the Sounkawad clan, Epensio's interest in our presence was something more than just idle curiosity. In the course of our conversation, Glenn remarked that the site seemed somehow less than fitting for the men who lay buried there. He thought the people of Pohnpei should construct a larger, more impressive marker to memorialize their heroic ancestors. Translated from Pohnpeian, Epensio's response to Glenn was "Why should we build it? You killed them."

In Epensio Eperiam's response lay, I think, an ethnographic statement about other versions of the past and the different meanings attached to them.

We obviously viewed the rebellion and the ways in which it should be remembered in a manner reflecting our politics and sense of history. The issue for Epensio was not about memorials, but rather about ultimate culpability and the appropriateness of sensitive and personal memories made public. For Epensio, a simply marked grave for his clansmen may have been enough in a world where the activities of humans comprised but a part of the island's past. His understanding of the rebellion seemed to reflect more locally rooted and entangled matters that defied a simple narration of the event as colonial resistance. Perhaps there was also his awareness that Inas, the ancestral goddess of the Sounkawad clan, disapproved of alien markers on land consecrated to her. The fact that Epensio referred to Glenn and me as *kumwail,* the Pohnpeian plural form of the word "you" designating three or more people, suggests that the distinctions we use to separate ourselves nationally, professionally, and ethnically hold less significance than we believe, or are understood and categorized differently by Islander ethnographers and historians. Is there more that binds rather than distinguishes German ethnographers and American researchers? A good cross-cultural history of American anthropology in Micronesia should seek to answer this and related questions.

MICRONESIANISM AND FUTURE HISTORIES

We should not overlook the more immediate and practical but nonetheless important dimensions involved in the practice of American anthropology and its history. A good cross-cultural history of American anthropology in Micronesia would also recognize that ethnographies and field notes will themselves become histories and historical documents over time. In this sense, Frederic Maitland (1936) may have been right in his oft-cited comment that anthropology must become history or risk becoming nothing at all. There is also the involvement and intervention of American anthropologists in the lives of the people among whom they have labored. There can be few twentieth-century histories of a Caroline, Mariana, or Marshall island that would not include mention of the anthropologists who lived, worked, and wrote on that island.

A good cross-cultural history of American anthropology in Micronesia would also take into consideration the ways in which Islanders have read and will continue to read and react to the ethnographies written about them. I wonder what Palauans think of a work that describes becoming Palauan as an imperfect, incomplete process that leaves many socially stunted and childlike, "even though they may have grandchildren of their own" (Barnett 1960, 10). I wonder how the people of Yap respond to an ethnographic portrait that describes them as a difficult, uncooperative, dishonest, quarrelsome, and arrogant people (Lessa 1950b, 17). I wonder, too, how students from the islands called Micronesia will react to one scholar's caution that ethnohistoric sources on the islands "must be restricted to those already skilled in the anthropology of the area" and who thus know how to evaluate and interpret them (Lessa 1962a, 374). I wonder, finally, what the answer will be when young people, after reading Edward Said (1979), inquire about the existence of a "Micronesianism"?

Most people in and around academia are familiar with Said's ideas on Orientalism, that pronounced, long-standing, politically purposeful tendency in western scholarship to take real cultures located in diverse, historically specific situations, and reduce them to an essentialized, timeless mass represented through exotic stereotypes that serve metropolitan programs of domination and rule. Orientalism is created in and by the texts of western scholarly discourse. The greater power and wealth of the west allows it not only to create a vision of others, but to assert and perpetuate that vision as well. Inhabitants of the area under study are rendered silent, powerless, and hence vulnerable, by the authority and expertise of those who represent them.

In the epilogue to *History and Tradition in Melanesia*, Roger Keesing and Margaret Jolly (1992) wrote of a Melanesia that endures as a category impervious to the tides of evidence that erode its foundations. The term "Melanesia" is, they argued, a self-perpetuating, self-reinforcing form of discourse that typifies the area and its people in terms of big men, pigs, shells, the centrality of exchange, the decentralized character of politics, and extreme linguistic diversity. Cannot the same argument with only slightly adjusted characterizations be made for the term "Micronesia"? I find it difficult to argue that Micronesia is anything but a colonial construct located, bounded, defined, and described by a series of different colonial regimes whose efforts were self-serving and exploitative. Witness the dissolution of the Congress of Micronesia into four separate governing entities. To speak, then, of Micronesia would seem to continue the game, thus giving credence to a nonentity and testament to the local variant of Orientalism that I have called Micronesianism.

Micronesianism, to me, seems a quiet conversation with its informing features in the colonialism that has prevailed over the region for more than a hundred years. It still speaks of a small group of isolated, resource-poor islands, located in a strategically important area of the world, left badly disturbed and in need of change by the forces of war. Micronesianism I hear as a hurried, persisting, less than convincing conversation about the necessity to develop these islands and their people in ways that we Americans see as appropriate and desirable for both them and us. Micronesianism, I hope, is a conversation that will fade to a whisper and later become a memory as the realization grows that there has always been far more to the islands' past than colonialism.

It seems to me that American anthropology, in the particularism of its ethnographies, has always possessed the power to subvert the idea of Micronesia. Why it has not challenged the idea more aggressively and publicly is a topic for further reflection. Some would argue that the answer lies in the essential nature of ethnography. John and Jean Comaroff noted that ethnography by its very practice makes objects of the people it studies (1992, 11–12). It cannot be otherwise because of the distance that separates the subjects of a text from its audience; because of the inequities of a world system that privileges ethnographic descriptions over the voices or self-representations of those being described; and because of the inherent reductionism involved in attempting to totalize a given topic within the limitations of a bound book. In another publication, the Comaroffs also addressed the issue of whether or not ethnography is inevitably an intrusion of the other (1991, xiii). They were ultimately optimistic on this point. Based on their work in South Africa, these scholars argued that if anthropology has been an instrument of colonizing culture in the past, there remains the possibility of it becoming a vehicle for liberation in the present.

If "liberation" is a problematic term for some of us, perhaps we can pose a more modest question for the time being. What have been the benefits of anthropological research and practice to the people called Micronesians? A consideration of this question would contribute, I think, to a good cross-cultural history of American anthropology and, at the same time, begin a dialogical ethnography that includes the people called Micronesians as more than informants or subjects of investigation. Such a development would allow the disciplines of anthropology and history to continue an already existing, mutually beneficial collaboration, and offer those of us engaged in the professional study of history and culture in the area called Micronesia the opportunity to become something more than Magellan's chroniclers.

NOTES

I am grateful for the very meticulous and helpful editing done by Robert Kiste and Mac Marshall, the coeditors of this volume. Finally, I would like to acknowledge the constructive criticisms of Francis Hezel, Lin Poyer, and many of the conference participants on my earlier draft.

1. I have relied on the following sources in my survey of the historical relationship and interaction between anthropology and history: Krech 1991; Biersack 1991; Carrier 1992; Dening 1980; L. Hunt 1989; and Peel 1993. For a consideration of some of the more practical differences that separate anthropology and history, see Cohn 1987.

2. I have written before on American anthropology's use of history in Micronesia (Hanlon 1989). Some material in this section draws from this earlier article.

3. Black mistakenly identified Fr. Elias as Fr. Marino in his 1978 article (Peter Black, personal communication 1993).

4. See also Marshall 1979a.

5. Consult, too, the related articles by L. Carucci (1989), Falgout (1989), and Poyer (1989) in *The Pacific Theater: Island Representations of World War II.*

6. Portions of this section draw from Hanlon 1994.

7. The full title of Murdock's speech is "How Shall We Administer Our Pacific Trust Territory?" A copy of this unpublished address can be found in the Hawaiian and Pacific Collection of the University of Hawai'i's Hamilton Library in Honolulu.

8. Some examples of the debates between administrators and anthropologists are contained in the microfilmed archives of the United States Trust Territory of the Pacific Islands (USTTPI). Four relevant cases are cited in the bibliography (USTTPI Archives 1950–1960, 1952, 1952–1959, 1953).

9. For histories of the CIMA project, see Barnett 1956; Gladwin 1954; and Murdock 1951.

10. My information on Wasekelung and his meeting with Hambruch comes from an interview with the now deceased Sohn Hadley on Mwudok island off Wone on June 9, 1983. According to Hadley, Wasekelung was a member of the Dipwenmen Pwetepwet clan, held the high priestly title of Nahnapas Kiti in his old age, and was unmarried as befitted his status as a priest and sorcerer. Wasekelung's connection to the people of Mwudok stemmed from the fact that his sister, called Khatenwei, was married to Sohn Hadley's great, great uncle, Johnny. At the time of our conversation Sohn Hadley was the section chief or *soumas en kousapw* for Mwudok; his title was "Soulik en Mwudok." Notes from my meeting with Sohn Hadley remain in my possession. Additional reference to Wasekelung can be found in Hanlon 1992a.

11. Mention of the previous existence of cannibals on Pohnpei is found in several accounts from Pohnpeian historians recorded and transcribed by Hambruch during

his six months of research on the island (see Hambruch 1932, I, text 1, p. 336; Hambruch 1936, II, text 53, 123; Hambruch 1936, III, text 80b, p. 271, and text 51, p. 379). It later became commonplace among Pohnpeians to identify New Guinea as the land to which Pohnpei's cannibals fled. For a different interpretation of cannibals on Pohnpei, see Petersen 1990a, 13.

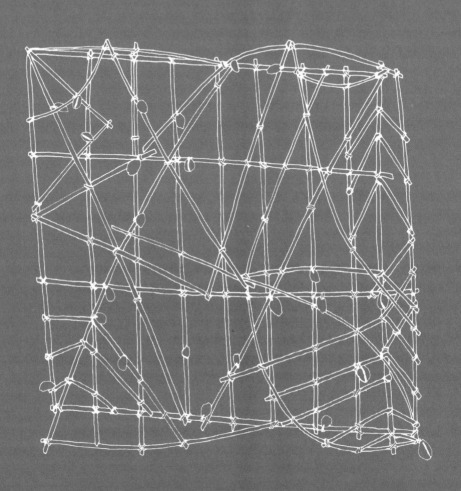

CHAPTER THREE

Cultural Ecology and Ecological Anthropology in Micronesia

William H. Alkire

ECOLOGICAL STUDIES IN ANTHROPOLOGY are generally concerned with the interrelationship of environment, subsistence activities, and society (Steward 1955, 30–42; Heider 1972, 207). Although a significant amount of research on these topics has been undertaken in Micronesia (some of it dating from the mid-1940s), preparing this chapter has only reinforced my long-standing impression that most of the methodology and tenets of cultural ecology and ecological anthropology have derived from work carried out in other cultural and geographic contexts. Many of those propositions, of course, have been tested or applied to Micronesian cases, but few if any insights derived from this work have influenced the wider discipline—at least when compared with the rather significant influence competing propositions of Polynesian and Melanesian origin have had. This and other kinds of Micronesian research have largely gone unnoticed by the discipline at large for a number of reasons, ranging from the political history of the region to shifts in academic interest. Several of these possibilities are discussed below and summarized at the end of the chapter.

THE EARLY YEARS: ENVIRONMENT AND ECONOMY

Since "the relationship between environment, subsistence, and society has been one of the constant and chief concerns of anthropology" (Heider 1972, 207), it is not surprising that this topic was a research focus for several anthropologists who arrived in Micronesia at the end of World War II. It is even less

*Leonard Mason
with Jibaj, Bikini
elder, Kili Island,
July 1963. Photo by
Robert Kiste.*

surprising when we consider two other circumstances. First, one of the more important theoretical paradigms of American anthropology during the 1930s (before the continuity of research was interrupted by the war) and the early 1950s (when extensive research programs resumed) was a paradigm that emphasized culture–environment linkages. The theoretical emphasis of this period might be characterized as evolving from culture areas to cultural ecology (Herskovits 1930; Kroeber 1939; Steward 1946–1950; Steward 1955). And second, the first anthropologists to enter Micronesia in 1944 and 1945 were affiliated with the US naval government, the US Commercial Company (USCC), or both. These individuals were charged with answering some very immediate, practical, and material questions—many of which were concerned with survival and the environment (which often had been severely disturbed by the war). Specifically at issue were how to jump-start a war-devastated local economy and how to resettle or repatriate large numbers of Japanese and Micronesian war-relocated people. It is clear that from 1944 onward through the US naval period and into the early years of the Department of Interior administration in Micronesia, anthropological theory was closely linked to practical and administrative action.

During the spring and summer of 1946 Douglas L. Oliver directed the research program of the USCC, which involved more than twenty researchers from anthropology, sociology, economics, agriculture, botany, entomology, geology, soil sciences, water resources, and nutrition (Oliver 1951; Bryan 1967). The breadth of this program and the interdisciplinary cooperation among these researchers, as reflected in their final reports, fostered an approach that later developed into a more specifically labeled ecological perspective. Five of the twenty USCC reports were written by anthropologists (Mason 1969a, 85). William Bascom (1946) reported on Ponape (now Pohnpei) and laid the groundwork for his later publications which emphasized the interconnection between agricultural production and the sociopolitical order of the island (Bascom 1948, 1949, 1965). Edward T. Hall, in collaboration with a geographer, provided a report on Truk (now Chuuk) (Hall and Pelzer 1946). John Useem (1946c, viii), who "led the first American civil affairs officers team ashore" on Palau (Belau), was chosen to provide a three-part report on Yap, Palau, and the "lesser islands of the western Carolines" (i.e., Ulithi, Fais, Sonsorol, Tobi, and Pulo Anna). Useem, like Bascom, emphasized a functional interrelationship between household economic activities and social organization. In the context of the present chapter, however, the two USCC reports by Leonard E. Mason (1946, 1947) were the most significant, because that research marked the beginning of Mason's lifelong career interest in the interaction of environment and culture in Micronesia. This is attested to not only by his publications, but also by his influence as a teacher of several generations of anthropologists trained at the University of Hawai'i.

Mason's work in the 1940s and 1950s served to keep anthropologists abreast of the contributions geographers were making to Micronesian research (Mason, Tobin, and Wade 1950; Mason 1951, 1952, 1958a). Foremost among these at the time was Raymond Murphy (1948, 1949, 1950), whose work highlighted the important contrasts which existed between 'high' (volcanic) and 'low' (coral) islands and the concomitant variations in land tenure practices. The USCC research reflected practical and administrative concerns and provided a baseline for the more intensive research programs of Coordinated Investigation of Micronesian Anthropology (CIMA), Scientific Investigation of Micronesia (SIM), Tri-Institutional Pacific Program (TRIPP), and the Displaced Communities in the Pacific Project (DCPP) which followed (Bryan 1967; Mason 1969a, 85–86). Much of this later research was broader in scope and theoretical

orientation, but environment, subsistence economics, adaptation, and resettlement were themes of continuing importance (e.g., Bentzen 1949; Weckler 1949;
Tolerton and Rauch 1949; Mason, Tobin, and Wade 1950; Bowers 1950; Emerick
1960; Lundsgaarde 1966; Lieber 1968a, 1968b; Severance 1976, 1979).

CULTURE CHANGE AND CULTURAL ECOLOGY

The aftereffects of World War II and the advent of the Cold War significantly
influenced Micronesian research during the 1950s and early 1960s. Both the
US naval government and later the Interior Department required people to
obtain a security clearance before they were granted entry to the region. This
had the effect of making Micronesia (including Guam) an exclusive research
ground for US citizens and residents. The American anthropologists who
chose (and were given permission) to work in the area soon found that the
wartime disruptions, relocations, and social changes precipitated by the postwar change in government and economic reorganization favored studies of
culture change over any of the other theoretical approaches of that time. Although both historical particularist or diffusionist research (with its synchronic
emphasis, e.g., Riesenberg 1950) and structural-functional studies that stressed
social solidarity (e.g., Schneider 1949) were undertaken, they soon were largely
abandoned in favor of studies that specifically addressed the topic of change.
In the 1950s a number of publications by geographers and anthropologists
dealt with various aspects of this topic. For example, Mason (1950, 1954) and
Neal Bowers (1950) discussed the effects of population relocations; Edward E.
Hunt, Jr. and his coauthors (1949, 1954) and William Stevens (1950) drew
attention to issues of demographic fluctuations; and Roland Force (1958) produced an in-depth study of culture change. Of these, Mason was the one who
most emphasized the importance of environment and geography, especially in
regard to the carrying capacities of the Marshall Islands (1947, 1950, 1951, 1952).

By the mid-1950s Mason had become interested in the cultural ecological
methodology of Julian Steward (1955, 30–42). Soon thereafter Mason deepened
his general commitment to an environmentally based research strategy by pursuing postdoctoral studies at Yale, where he worked with ecologist and con-
servationist Paul Sears (Mason, personal communication 1993). Yale, of course,
was an institution with a long-standing interest in both Polynesian and
Micronesian research (as seen by its participation in TRIPP and support for
the work of Murdock [1948b, 1948c], Goodenough [1951], Gladwin and Sarason [1953], Wiens [1962], and LeBar [1964]). Subsequently, in both his teach-

ing (especially his graduate seminar on Pacific Islands at the University of Hawai'i) and in his publications (1957, 1959a), Mason employed an explicitly "ecologic" methodology. Steward's influence, of course, was becoming widespread in the discipline at that time, including elsewhere in Pacific studies. Marshall Sahlins (1958), for example, had suggested that the variation in social stratification among the traditional societies of Polynesia was related to the environmental differences of the respective islands.

Benjamin Orlove (1980) argued that the first phase of cultural ecological theory derived jointly from the work of Steward (1955) and Leslie White (1959). In Micronesian research, however, White's direct influence has been negligible. The linkage of cultural ecology and cultural evolution is part of Steward's definition: "Cultural ecology is the study of the processes by which a society adapts to its environment. Its principal problem is to determine whether these adaptations initiate internal social transformations of evolutionary change" (1968, 337). Although White (1949, 1959) was also—and foremost—a neoevolutionist, the kind of ecological work that derived from his influence was concerned with energy flows, and therefore emphasized balance and homeostasis (Rappaport 1968). It should not surprise us, then, that White was largely ignored in the Micronesian context since those who adopted the cultural ecological paradigm were looking for a theory that would explain change and differentiation rather than continuity and balance.

Three other publications which appeared (or began to appear) in the 1950s were equally influential in shaping environmental and ecological approaches to the study of Oceania. The first was the *Atoll Research Bulletin* founded by botanists F. Raymond Fosberg and Marie-Helene Sachet. From its inception this periodical has provided an important outlet for the publication of articles and notes on the ecology of coral islands throughout the world and for the exchange of ideas among botanists, biologists, and anthropologists who have worked in Micronesia (e.g., Mason, Tobin, and Wade 1950; Stone 1951; Mason 1952; Tobin 1952; Mason and Uyehara 1953; Spoehr 1953; Murai 1954; Niering 1956; Doran 1961; Neas 1961; Falanruw 1971; Marshall 1975a). The second publication was a Wenner-Gren–sponsored volume, *Man's Role in Changing the Face of the Earth* (W. Thomas 1956), which similarly advocated cooperation and exchange of ideas among anthropologists (such as Spoehr 1956), ecologists, biologists, geographers, historians, and sociologists. And the third publication was an article by Ward H. Goodenough (1957a) in which he encouraged researchers to expand their evolutionary approaches and interests in a way that would aid in reconstructing ancestral Malayo-Polynesian cultural forms.

Contemporaneous with these publications, some administrative changes were also occurring within Micronesia. As discussed by Robert C. Kiste and Suzanne Falgout (chap. 1), the US Trust Territory of the Pacific Islands (USTTPI) emerged with a structure that employed anthropologists at both the staff and district levels (Barnett 1956, 86–109), and the district anthropologists were assigned the task of collecting a range of information dealing with local culture–environment concerns, especially as these might relate to subsistence needs.

Many stresses had been placed on local Micronesian communities by the disruptions of World War II and the subsequent change in colonial administration. Foremost among these were problems of resettlement, land ownership (both government and private), and land redistribution. The district anthropologists were asked to assemble data on both traditional and extant local land tenure. From this work was published a volume edited by the staff anthropologist (deYoung 1958) which supplemented earlier preliminary statements and reports of limited distribution. Jack Tobin, John "Jack" Fischer, Richard Emerick, Francis Mahoney, and Shigeru Kaneshiro all contributed chapters to this book. Two of the earlier CIMA reports had also focused on this topic (Tolerton and Rauch 1949; Weckler 1949), and land tenure has been an anthropological favorite ever since (Spoehr 1949a; Doran 1961; Defngin 1966; Kiste 1967; Mason 1967a, 1977; Wilson 1968; Lieber 1968b, 1974, 1979; J. Johnson 1969; McGrath and Wilson 1971; Rynkiewich 1972a; Alkire 1974a; Pollock 1974; J. Smith 1974; Marksbury 1979; Parker 1985; Damas 1994). These studies have highlighted both uniformities and contrasts in the ways Micronesians have adapted to their habitats: (1) Pie-slice subdivisions are typical of high islands in contrast to strip parcels on atoll islets; On both types of island, the larger sociopolitical divisions are analogous in form and function to the smaller land parcels (or estates); (2) Thus a universal conceptual unity inalienably ties people (kin groups) to land (their estates) in Micronesia (see Marshall, chap. 4 and Petersen, chap. 5); (3) The tenure system generally guarantees that all people have access to land of every important subsistence category (including reef and sea areas); (4) Each tenure system is inherently flexible (or processual [Parker 1985]) to accommodate shortages that might follow from demographic shifts or environmental disaster (Goodenough 1955); And lastly, (5) it is often the case that landholdings on high islands are more localized (regionally restricted) than those of atoll residents, whose patterns of kinship, marriage, and adoption frequently give them access to widely dispersed parcels. This last point has relevance for several other ecologically interesting ethnographic issues—for example, interisland marriage, adoption, communication, and migration. These studies of land tenure subsequently led researchers to direct similar attention to reef, lagoon, and sea tenure (Alkire 1965a; Nakayama and Ramp 1974; Johannes 1981; Goodwin 1983).

By the mid-1960s, security clearances for entry or travel in the region were no longer required. Soon thereafter a number of non-Americans began to undertake research in Micronesia. Foremost among these was a new generation of Japanese scholars—the Japanese, of course, had conducted extensive research during their period of colonial control (Hatanaka 1979). Land and sea tenure (as well as ethnoscience, discussed below) were among their favorite research topics (Shimizu 1982; Ushijima 1982, 1987; Ruddle and Akimichi 1984; Sudo 1984; Akimichi 1986). Some of these studies anticipated the later interest of American researchers in cognitive conceptualizations of land and sea.

Maritime adaptation, navigation, and technology were additional environmentally related topics addressed by researchers in the 1950s and 1960s (Goodenough 1953; Gladwin 1958; Davenport 1960; Alkire 1965a). These were topics long established in both the Micronesian (Thilenius 1914–1938) and wider Pacific anthropological literature (Haddon and Hornell 1936). The 1950s–1960s research, and that which followed, clearly established the important roles played by marine technologies in subsistence and long-term regional adaptation. It soon became clear that these technologies were most highly developed on the low islands (Alkire 1970, 1978, 1980; Gladwin 1970; Lewis 1971, 1973; Riesenberg 1972; McCoy 1973; Goodenough 1986). Interisland travel was more important to (and frequent among) coral island communities than among the larger and more resource-secure, high-island communities. Thus it seems somewhat ironic that the great contemporary fame of Mau Piailug, a navigator from the Micronesian coral island of Satawal, is associated in the popular mind with the Polynesian high islands of Hawai'i and Tahiti (Finney 1979, 59ff).

William Lessa (1950b, 1950c) was the first postwar anthropologist who detailed the existence of traditional interisland social and economic networks in Micronesia. In my own work during the 1960s and 1970s, I discussed their wider adaptive significance (Alkire 1965a, 1970, 1978). In the Central Carolines, exchange networks operated (and in many ways continue to operate) on at least three different levels. The widest system *(sawei)* linked the high island of Yap to a score of outlying coral islands reaching some six hundred miles from Ulithi to Satawal. More limited regional exchange networks (such as the *hú* between Lamotrek, Elato, and Satawal) tied smaller sets of islands to one another, while the smallest exchange systems linked communities on different islets dispersed around the lagoon of a single atoll (e.g., the *chúlifeimag* of Woleai). These systems facilitated a regularized exchange of goods and people between participating units, and since they were found in an area of the Carolines extremely vulnerable to typhoon damage, they functioned to guarantee survival (Alkire 1965a; Nason 1967). Comparable (although structurally different) exchange systems linked the dry islands of the northern Marshalls with those of the wetter south. This rainfall differential gave the southern islands a relatively reliable resource base and a superior position in a polity more centralized than any that ever developed in the Carolines (Spoehr 1949a; Mason 1954, 1959a; Tobin 1952, 1967).

David M. Schneider (1957a) and Lessa (1964) have also commented on the cultural and social consequences of natural disasters in Micronesia. But of equal interest are the adaptive problems that have followed from human-initiated disasters (Marshall 1979b). These, too, were researched during the period under discussion, frequently using cultural ecological models. Foremost among these were the cases of the forcibly resettled populations of Bikini and Enewetak, which are among the best documented in all anthropological literature (MacMillan 1947; Drucker 1950; Mason 1950, 1954, 1957, 1958a, 1958b; Tobin 1954a, 1955, 1967; Kiste 1967, 1968, 1974; L. Carucci 1980). The initial government optimism associated with both of these forced migrations soon dissipated when it became clear that the Bikinians could not easily adjust to the physical limitations of first Rongerik and later Kili, nor could they easily overcome their deep attachment to their ancestral lands (Kiste 1974, 97, 107–125). The Enewetak islanders encountered difficulties nearly as severe in trying to adjust to Ujelang, which is a significantly smaller atoll than the one they had to abandon (Tobin 1955, 1967). All of these researchers have discussed the adaptational problems and social and cultural changes that accompanied and followed relocation.

Subsistence cultivation, nutrition, health, and demography were also topics with environmental dimensions that attracted the interest of both practical and theoretical—government and independent—researchers during the 1950s, 1960s, and early 1970s (Murai 1954; Stone 1951; Hunt et al. 1954; Hunt et al. 1965; Lessa 1955; MacKenzie and Bikajle 1960; McKnight et al. 1960; Barrau 1961, 1965; Lessa and Myers 1962; McKnight and Obak 1964; Mahony and Lawrence 1964; Lawrence et al. 1964; Defngin 1964; Hainline 1964, Underwood [née Hainline] 1969; Pollock et al. 1972; Morton 1973). Of special interest, however, are the number of cultural ecology–oriented comparative and evolutionary studies that began to appear. These explored the evolutionary side of the Stewardian approach and served to attract the attention of a number of ethnoarchaeologists.

Again Mason was in the vanguard of the movement. In his *Humanités* article (1959a, 111), Mason compared the environments of seven Micronesian atolls, emphasizing the limitations on productivity from the perspective of Liebig's Law of the Minimum. He suggested a functional relationship "between suprafamilial authority and the economic processes of production and distribution" (1959a, 88). Among the seven atolls of his study, Arno and Onotoa fell at opposite ends of a continuum: "Chieftainship is elaborated most in the very culture best supported by economic abundance [Arno], and the one least endowed by Nature [Onotoa] is the only group in the series without chiefs" (1959a, 117). Published at nearly the same time as Mason's study was my comparison derived from the then available ethnographic literature, examining the relationships among environment, subsistence activities, and patterns of residence on eight Micronesian islands—four high and four low (Alkire 1960). The most important conclusions reached in my study were that, given the high rainfall of this region, differences between high and low islands were less important than commonly suggested (within the Polynesian literature, for example [Sahlins 1958]), and that types or patterns of settlement were correlated with the specific agricultural emphasis of each society. I further suggested that multicrop agriculture (primarily arboriculture), associated with matrilocality, tended to evolve with population growth into root and tuber monocropping and patrilocality (Alkire 1960, 144). Later, more detailed research and wider comparisons in the region have suggested a much more complex developmental history. Kenneth Knudson, for example, found that flexibility in social organization was actually the "rule" so that fluctuations in available resources could be accommodated more easily and efficiently. Resource fluctuations were frequent because environmental stresses were common throughout the region (1970, 270–271). This is a conclusion similar to that reached by Mason (1959a) and suggested by Goodenough (1956a).

Authors of a number of other publications have dealt with similar themes. Botanist Jacques Barrau proposed (primarily for Polynesia) an evolution from extensive, shifting (swidden) cultivation to semipermanent (intensive) lowland taro cultivation (1961, 18). This pattern, in fact, paralleled one also advanced for Melanesia (Clarke 1966). David Labby (1976a) provided the most detailed argument for these propositions in Micronesia based on his work in Yap. The social, economic, and political structures of that island, he believed, evolved (as populations grew and land and resources became more scarce) from shifting, upland cultivation and large matrilineal-matrilocal units to intensive, localized, lowland cultivation and small patrilocal estates. This analysis is based on a historical materialist argument in conjunction with an ideational (or symbolic) perspective. Somewhat earlier, for another area of Micronesia, Goodenough (1956a) had also proposed an evolutionary argument that linked land shortages and agricultural intensification to changes in kin group organization.

Regarding the Yap case, however, Rosalind Hunter-Anderson (1982), an ethnoarchaeologist, labeled the argument (which in the absence of any archaeological evidence had been based solely on ethnographic observations) the "Alkire-Barrau-Labby model." She believed it was seriously flawed and offered an alternative model based on an archaeological survey of Yapese settlement patterns. Her conclusion was that "yam gardening in the interior hills of Yap ('slash-and-burn') represent[ed] one of the last stages of intensification, not one of the first" (Hunter-Anderson 1982, 96). Her argument was closely reasoned, but any final choice between the competing theories, and decision about their applicability to specific islands, will only be possible after more intensive excavations have been carried out.

Ross Cordy is another archaeologist who employed a cultural ecological strategy in his Micronesian work. He stated that his intent was similar to that explicated in Sahlins' (1958) ethnohistorical analysis of Polynesian stratification (Cordy 1980, 1). Cordy proposed a covariance between population size and social stratification in Micronesia. His ecological and evolutionary arguments drew on ethnographic, demographic, and archaeological data (e.g., Alkire 1965a, 1978; Ayres et al. 1981; Hainline 1964, 1965; Hunter-Anderson 1982; Kiste 1974; Lingenfelter 1975; Nason 1970). His analysis found a "strong positive correlation between social stratification and population size within a polity" and "supports the hypothesis of the evolutionary success *in their specific environments*, of polities with more social strata" (Cordy 1986, 137–141 [his italics]).

A number of theoretical and methodological issues that have subsequently influenced cultural ecological research in Micronesia were raised by participants in two Honolulu conferences, separated by about a decade. The first was the 1961 Tenth Pacific Science Congress and its symposium, "Man's Place in the Island Ecosystem," chaired by Raymond Fosberg (1963). The second, held in late 1972, was an East-West Center conference on Pacific Atoll Populations convened by Vern Carroll (1975a).

At the Pacific Science Congress, Andrew Vayda and Roy Rappaport drew attention to the impact of "insularity upon the differentiation of one culture from another" (1963, 131). They were mainly interested in highlighting the effects isolation might have on the "founding or establishment of new cultures," and suggested that culture change in such situations might be analogous to the "founder principle" in genetics. They referred to some Micronesian data in developing this theory (Mason 1950, 1957, 1958b), but for the most part focused on Polynesian cases, including Sahlins' (1958) comparative study of Polynesian ranking, wherein he emphasized high and low island contrasts. Vayda and Rappaport concluded that reconstructing early population movements must take into account the probable inventory of traits carried by colonists and not posit conclusions about cultural differentiation based exclusively on the environmental contrasts between high and low islands. However, their work also raised the problem of how closely cultural anthropological theories might parallel or draw on bio-anthropological theories.

The East-West Center conference, on the other hand, directed the attention of researchers to the problems of accurately reconstructing pre- and early-contact population numbers and evaluating the dynamics of population growth and decline within atoll communities. A number of the Micronesian case studies presented by contributors dealt with the frequent population fluctuations of the region and the relationship these might have on cultural and institutional configurations (Alkire 1972a; Nason 1975; Rynkiewich 1972b; Marshall 1975b).

Some of the cultural ecological implications of the questions raised at these two conferences were examined in a subsequent comparison of ten Micronesian and Polynesian coral islands and archipelagoes (Alkire 1978). The study not only followed up on Vayda and Rappaport's theme of "insularity," but it also reassessed some of the generalizations that had appeared in the literature (Sahlins 1958, xii, 245–246, 252–253) concerning any "distinctive atoll type." It concluded that many of the cultural and structural features within these coral island societies varied fairly consistently with changes in the degree of isolation, frequency, or intensity of environmental stress, and density or size of population. By way of generalization, three contrasting adaptive types (rather than a single one) were proposed: isolates, clusters, and complexes. Using a technique that had become common in the work of cultural geographers and general systems ecologists, some of the data were summarized in rather elementary systems diagrams (Alkire 1978, 15, 93, 110, 135).

A final theoretical trend of the 1960s and 1970s with cultural ecological implications involved the advent of ethnoscience and the publication of increasing numbers of studies in ethnogeography, ethnobotany, ethnozoology, and ethnoecology (Frake 1962, 55). Many of the major contributions of ethnoscience might more appropriately be discussed in a review of cognitive studies, but this subdiscipline does overlap in some important ways with cultural ecology, specifically in regard to local conceptualizations of the environment and its components.

Ethnoscience as a research strategy weds Boasian particularistic ethnography with cognitive studies. Its objective is to identify, in each ethnographic case, "the principles by which a people classify their universe" (Sturtevant 1964, 100). Most of these studies, however, are not limited to a simple statement of principles, but rather offer multifarious classifications and encyclopedic lists. The intent is exhaustive and the result often exhausting—for field-worker, informant, and reader alike. A number of the early analyses of Micronesian subsistence and gardening practices (sometimes written or coauthored by Micronesians trained by district anthropologists) are constructed around "native" systems of classification (e.g., McKnight et al. 1960; Kim and Defngin 1960; Defngin 1964; Lawrence et al. 1964; McKnight and Obak 1964). Many ethnographies include some information of this kind (e.g., Dahlquist 1972; Lingenfelter 1975; Damas 1994), but several of the analyses from the late 1960s onward can be identified more specifically as "ethnoscience," that is, as primarily concerned with indigenous categories and domains of the environment, subsistence practices, and exploitative or adaptive technology (Goodenough 1966a; Alkire 1968, 1970, 1974b, 1982; Gladwin 1970; Mahony 1970; Riesenberg 1972; Helfman and Randall 1973; Johannes 1981). Some of the postwar Japanese anthropologists who have worked in the region have also published in this genre (Akimichi 1979, 1981, 1987; Aoyagi 1982; Shimizu 1982; Ushijima 1990). The cognitive dimensions of some of these studies have occasionally been mentioned by others (e.g., Frake 1985; Gell 1985).

ECOLOGICAL ANTHROPOLOGY

Orlove has labeled the second theoretical phase of ecological research in anthropology the era of "neofunctional and neoevolutionary" studies (1980, 235–239). Here he referred to an "energy" approach, derived from Leslie White's work (1949, 1959), which has since been elaborated and modified by Sahlins and Service (1960). John Bennett had earlier named the approach "cultural ecosystemicism" (1976, 165). Following Emilio Moran (1979, 42–63), I prefer the simpler label, "ecological anthropology."

In Oceanic research, Raymond Fosberg, the botanist who chaired the "Man's Place in the Island Ecosystem" symposium, spurred an interest in such concepts as ecosystems, entropy, and energetics (1963, 1–6). Among Oceanic anthropologists Vayda and Rappaport made the call explicit: "[there exist] both the possibility and the desirability of a single science of ecology with laws and principles that apply to man as they do to other species" (1968, 492). One serious shortcoming of cultural ecology, they went on to write, was its emphasis "on cultural factors as something apart from the kinds of factors influencing the relation of nonhuman organisms to their environments" (Vayda and Rappaport 1968, 492). Of course at that time Rappaport's *Pigs for the Ancestors* (1968) was the most influential publication in this genre. This trend, then, amounted to something more than merely promoting the use of biological analogies to help clarify cultural principles. Rather, it was a proposal to fully integrate human systems into a larger physical and biological web. The approach soon led to the application of general systems theory and systems diagrams (not a completely novel idea, as noted by Mead [1972, 8]), which permitted data to be presented more parsimoniously (if not more clearly) (Odum 1971). Unfortunately, Vayda and Rappaport's work (1968, 495) and general systems theory had either a stated or an implied preference for homeostatic models. This, like the biological models or analogies, ran counter to the cultural ecologists' focus on change and evolution. Some of the anthropological and geographic models using systems diagrams were designed to illustrate carrying capacity (Bayliss-Smith 1974, 1990; Alkire 1978, 15). Others, although synchronic "snapshots," did attempt to depict change by emphasizing that an ecosystem's boundary was always expandable; thus the diagrams could be extended to depict a general or "total" system or contracted to focus on any subsystem within it (Alkire 1978, 93, 110, 135; Bayliss-Smith 1982). Although Kiste (1974) did not use any general systems theory diagrams (or an energetics perspective), his narrative case study of Bikini clearly showed the dynamics of a population adapting to an expanding ecosystem—one that began on an isolated atoll and step by step became (at least perceptually) incorporated into a "world system."

However, it should also be noted that Fosberg's concept of system entropy implied dynamism and change, not homeostasis (1963, 3–5). William Clarke (1971) used this concept to great advantage in proposing an evolutionary sequence for the intensification of highland New Guinea agriculture (from multicropping and diversity to monocropping and simplicity), but the approach has had little impact within Micronesia. In fact, any impact of an energetics-focused ecology within Micronesian research has been largely

*Traditional housing and dress, outer
islands, Yap District, 1950s. US Trust
Territory Archives (Photo 3058.06),
Pacific Collection, University of
Hawai'i Library.*

Surround method of fishing, Eauripik Atoll, 1970s. Photograph by Michael Levin, US Census Bureau.

Marshallese sailing canoes, Ujelang Atoll, Marshall Islands, 1964. Photograph by Robert Kiste.

Yap Islander, field trip vessel, unloading copra in Palau, 1970s. Trust Territory Archives (Photo 2238.02), Pacific Collection, University of Hawai'i Library.

Outboard motor boats, Wééné Island, Chuuk, 1995. Photograph by Mac Marshall.

*Airline of the Marshall Islands service
to outer islands, Kili Island, Marshall
Islands, 1986. Photograph by Leonard
Mason.*

indirect or secondary. There are no Micronesian case studies similar to the detailed Melanesian accounts by Rappaport (1968, 1971) or Clarke (1971); in part, this may be because anthropologists had long emphasized that Micronesian societies were set within more extensive or "open systems" (see below). Energetics analyses are more easily constructed if communities are bounded and isolated—circumstances that often prevailed in Melanesia at that time. Micronesian data, however, have been reanalyzed by others using the energetics models of general systems theory. Most conspicuous in this regard is Howard Odum's analysis of energy flows on Lamotrek Atoll (1971, 104–105). Odum, of course, is not an anthropologist but a general systems theorist and "environmental engineer." In his book *Environment, Power, and Society* he attempted to demonstrate that "some of the bewildering complexity of our world disappears" when systems "are considered in energy terms" (Odum 1971, vii). Most sociocultural anthropologists are justifiably uncomfortable when they look at his diagrams and note that all cultural practices are submerged in a complex of energy circuits, loops, storage cells, switches, and heat sinks. And the ordinary reader might question whether his diagrams have really simplified "the bewildering complexity of our world." Nevertheless, one positive contribution that both general systems theory and Raymond Fosberg made to ecological anthropology and Micronesian studies was to refocus attention on the importance of system boundaries. The cultural ecological research on inter-island exchange networks had exposed the fiction of the "outer reef boundary" for most Micronesian islands. Clifford Geertz (1963), during his cultural ecology phase, had demonstrated the utility of an expansive perspective in his analysis of the impact of Dutch colonial policy on Indonesia: the system boundaries for the Indonesians expanded as their production was incorporated into the modern world (Geertz 1963, 48; see also R. F. Murphy 1967, 17–23). The indigenous trading and communication networks of many Micronesians (facilitated by their highly developed sailing and navigational technology) meant that via their own world view (or ethnoecological perspective) they had defined themselves as participants in a system that extended far beyond their individual islands and atolls (see, e.g., Alkire 1965a, 1977, 1980). It can be argued that on a number of Micronesian islands, whether high or low, the adaptive responses to changes in the social and natural environment brought about by colonial intervention and control derived from and expanded on traditional ethnoecological conceptualizations (Alkire 1981, 1984a, 1987, 1993a; Petersen 1979, 1986a, 1992a).

One final body of work that should be mentioned in this review is that of human behavioral ecology (a.k.a. evolutionary ecology, biosociology, human ethology, sociobiology, or socioecology): "Its central problem is to discover the ways in which the behavior of modern humans reflects our species' history of natural selection" (Cronk 1991, 251). At first glance this may seem peripheral to the sociocultural focus of this chapter, but since all ecological anthropologists refer to biological and psychological "imperatives," problems of life maintenance, and reproduction of the species (Orlove 1980, 20–21; A. Johnson 1982), all publications addressing these issues within Micronesia are undoubtedly relevant.

Among the biological anthropologists who have worked in Micronesia, Jane Underwood (née Hainline) and Michael Levin have focused on demographic questions of ecological importance (Hainline 1964, 1965; J. Underwood 1969, 1973; Levin 1976; Gorenflo and Levin 1989, 1991, 1994). Underwood's main work has shown how regional settlement patterns and cultural boundaries have influenced the genetic character of Yap's population. Her research has also led her to question the importance of induced abortions in the demographic history of Yap. Abortion was a cultural practice that an earlier team of physical and sociocultural anthropologists had proposed contributed to a rapid population decline on that island (Hunt et al. 1949, 1954). Underwood (1973) concluded that introduced diseases played a far greater role in this decline than any cultural practices.

Levin's (1976) analysis of the demography and history of the small and densely settled atoll of Eauripik emphasized that fish were as important a resource in maintaining that density as were agricultural products—again the ecosystem boundary must not stop at the water's edge.

Of equal interest in Levin's detailed study of Eauripik, however, was his identification of two population subsets on this tiny atoll, one he called center residents and the other periphery residents. He found that periphery residents were the more common participants in the cyclical migration pattern that had established two overseas Eauripik communities, one on Woleai and the other on Yap (see also Alkire 1993b).

Underwood and Levin have thus used their demographic and biological anthropological expertise to demonstrate the extent to which cultural practices have influenced the physical and genetic characteristics of the respective populations they have studied. Laura Betzig and Paul Turke have also published on this topic (Betzig et al. 1989), but as sociobiologists they are also interested in demonstrating how particular cultural practices on Ifaluk are governed by biological imperatives—imperatives that have developed in the course of human evolutionary history. In their various publications they have proposed that patterns of food redistribution, childbearing, mothering, adoption, and marriage all have sociobiological dimensions (Betzig 1988a, 1988b, 1988c; Betzig and Turke 1986a, 1986b; Betzig et al. 1988). To my knowledge no mainstream cultural ecologist, ecological anthropologist, or sociocultural anthropologist has yet critiqued this perspective of their Micronesian work, although Henry Sharpe (1986, 155–156) and Turke (1986, 156–157) have exchanged words about the basic theory.

Finally, a number of archaeologists and biologists have also focused their attention on issues associated with the ecology of marine exploitation in Micronesia (e.g., Bates and Abbott 1958; Reinman 1965, 1967; Davidson 1971; Ayres et al. 1981; Johannes 1981, 1985; Leach and Ward 1981; Fujimura and Alkire 1984; Hunter-Anderson and Zan 1985). This work has served to both raise and answer questions about cycles of exploitation, land and sea linkages, and production intensification associated with the growth and decline of local populations. In many cases, especially on the atolls, the sole remaining evidence of past dietary patterns is found in middens of shells and fish and sea mammal bones.

CURRENT TRENDS

By the 1980s, ecological anthropology was being criticized not only for its homeostatic emphasis but also for its focus on general systems flow charts within which it was difficult to identify regulating hierarchies or explain individual choice. It was criticized for devaluing culture: "The natural environment is always, and necessarily *mediated* by the cognitive capacities and 'culture' of the human members of a social system" (Bargatzky 1984, 404 [his emphasis]). "Cultural ecology should be first and foremost *cultural* or *social* ecology, or it misrepresents biology and distorts our understanding of culture, society, and their evolution" (Bargatzky 1984, 406 [his emphasis]). This reads like a call to return to Steward's approach, that is, to an ecological perspective that emphasizes the interaction of environment, subsistence practices, and other cultural forms, rather than a drift toward biological reductionism (A. Johnson 1982).

Orlove, too, suggested that greater attention should be paid to decision-making models and the individual's role in selecting among options (1980, 245–249). He foresaw the replacement of a homeostatic neofunctional ecology by diachronic studies that focused on mechanisms of change, and proposed calling this "processual ecology." He specifically mentioned Steward in this regard: "The questioning of the neofunctionalist approach has led to an ability to study productive activities, settlement patterns, and the like without attempting to show how they maintain human populations in equilibrium with their environments. In this way the processual approach and Stewardian cultural ecology may be seen to share some approaches" (Orlove 1980, 249).

At about the same time, however, in a review of demographic theory, Kenneth Weiss made the following point: "If the triumph of nineteenth century science was to show that nature is better viewed in terms of processes than of types, then that of the twentieth century has been to show repeatedly that the laws of nature are inextricably the laws of chance" (1976, 352).

This search for a set of principles to rejuvenate the research strategy of cultural ecology resonates with a similar search in biological evolutionary theory. In the latter case Stephen Jay Gould concluded that research had to take into account three principles: natural selection, contingency, and *rules of structure* [my emphasis] (Gould 1983, 1986; Rose 1983). There are clear parallels here with the proposals made for revitalizing cultural ecology. The forces of natural selection and chance (contingency) are always conditioned by rules of structure—what exists or will come to exist, has been or will be limited by preexisting forms or structures. "*Ecological factors never operate in a cultural vacuum* nor do the enduring patterns of language, kinship, and cultural values that every individual inherits prevent adaptation to a material environment" (Netting 1986, 101 [my emphasis]).

Some work within Micronesia has reflected the principles of this revised strategy (Alkire 1988; Petersen 1993b, n.d.). Notable in this regard are James Peoples' recent proposals concerning Micronesian political evolution: "There is no environmental determinism in [my] argument: had the Nuclear Micronesian cultural heritage been different, different political systems would have evolved in the islands. People interact with their environments, and these interactions depend on their cultural heritage as well as on the environment itself" (1992, 14). The "evolution and rules of form" perspective is one that has also revitalized Micronesian historical reconstructions (Hanlon 1988) and has potential relevance for undertaking research on how Micronesia has been incorporated into a world socioeconomic system (cf. E. Wolf 1982).

Nevertheless, from the mid-1980s into the early 1990s cultural ecology as a sociocultural research strategy has largely been supplanted by other theoretical and topical interests—cognitive, symbolic, and political. This trend, of course, has been true for the discipline at large. Thus the Micronesian ecological research that has occurred during these more recent years has primarily been done by sociobiologists (cited above), archaeologists, paleoanthropologists, demographers, and geographers (Craib 1981; Hunter-Anderson and Zan 1985; Hunter-Anderson 1990; Kurashina and Clayshulte 1983; Cordy 1983, 1986; Ayres 1990; Ayres et al. 1981; Yen 1990; F. Thomas 1993; Williamson and Sabath 1982, 1984; Gorenflo and Levin 1989, 1991, 1994). However, the possibility yet exists in sociocultural anthropology for a melding of interests along Gouldian lines, so that studies of adaptation and change that take account of the limiting effects of preexisting (cultural or cognitive) structures and "rules of form" will be done.

GENERALIZATIONS AND CONCLUSIONS

This review of ecological and environmental research carried out by anthropologists in Micronesia during the last fifty years has shown that a number of important anthropological and regional issues have been addressed and clarified, specifically:

Classification systems devised for or applied to Pacific Islands now recognize the complex character of the tropical Pacific environment. Classifications that focus on a single variable, such as "high and low" or "wet and dry," are incomplete and misleading. Degrees of isolation and vulnerability to natural disasters and resource fluctuations are equally important to the long-term survival of Micronesian populations.

An understanding of the processes involved in small island demographic change, especially as they relate to patterns of marriage, divorce, adoption, and kin group formation, is especially important in the study of island communities. Rapid and significant population fluctuations are frequently experienced on many islands in this region of the Pacific.

Complex systems of land tenure and resource inventories are typical of most areas of Micronesia. Populations are often dense and available resources can fluctuate rapidly. Therefore, survival depends not only on rules but also on an accepted flexibility in their application. Multicrop cultivation and multispecies marine exploitation are also favored in order to minimize possible food shortages.

Exchange networks, especially interisland systems, have played a crucial role in helping people successfully adapt to the coral island environments of Micronesia. These networks aid in the redistribution of resources and population. In some instances hierarchical and centralized sociopolitical systems have developed from them.

Studies of the processual sequences associated with land and marine subsistence intensification in Micronesia can contribute important insights in building and revising general theories of adaptation and cultural evolution for Oceania. Theories based exclusively on Polynesian and/or Melanesian data will prove incomplete.

The processes of readaptation as experienced by forcibly relocated coral island populations have been extensively documented in Micronesia. The Bikini-to-Kili and Enewetak-to-Ujelang cases highlight a number of pivotal variables that must be taken into account when predicting long-term survival on coral islands. Coral island environments are not uncritically interchangeable.

Research in Micronesia has demonstrated a strong conceptual linkage between the fundamental social units of society and the land they occupy. The basic principles that serve to organize social and political life have conceptual correlates in many other domains of life, ranging from the cosmological to the technical. In this regard one can say that the Micronesians themselves emphasize an ecological unity with their environment.

Ecologically oriented anthropological research in Micronesia reached its height in the 1960s and 1970s. The findings of this research, however, seem never to have made much impression on the discipline as a whole. The region remains largely unmentioned in texts specifically aimed at courses in cultural ecology or ecological anthropology (Vayda 1969; Cohen 1974; Bennett 1976; Hardesty 1977; Moran 1979; Netting 1986). In only one such text does the region receive even passing mention (Jochim 1981, 188). Similarly, during the last twenty-five years, in only one of four major reviews of cultural ecological research (Heider 1972; Netting 1974; Vayda and McCay 1975; Orlove 1980) is there any mention of the Micronesian work discussed above—and in that case (Orlove 1980) the single anthropologist cited (Labby) is submerged in a sea of geographers and biologists. Some Micronesian findings, however, have been cited in more specialized contexts, for example, archaeoastronomy (Aveni 1981), cultural geography (Bayliss-Smith 1990), and the application of graph theory to anthropology (Hage and Harary 1983, 1991). However, Micronesian cultural ecology has probably not been singled out for special shunning, since Micronesian research of any kind is rarely mentioned in introductory textbooks or cited by disciplinary colleagues (see appendix 3).

There are probably a number of reasons for this seeming disciplinary neglect. One of the more enduring, I think, derives from real and perceived "spheres" of political influence. Early in the century when anthropological field studies of Oceanic societies began (e.g., Malinowski 1922; Mead 1928), Micronesia was under German colonial control. Transportation to and within the region was more difficult than in the neighboring British, French, and American areas of administration. The great German South Seas Expedition of 1908–1910, in fact, had to depend on its own ship (Thilenius 1914–1938). Researchers from Australia, Britain, New Zealand, and the United States therefore tended to focus on Polynesia and Melanesia as field sites, both for logistic reasons and because most islands in these two regions were administered by their own governments. In 1914, Micronesia was transferred from the German to the Japanese political sphere. The political climate leading up to World War II made it even more difficult for foreign researchers to gain access to the region, and since most of the extant literature was in Spanish, German, and Japanese, it is understandable that pre–World War II English-language anthropologists (and their students) focused on Polynesia or Melanesia when they thought of the Pacific. But since World War II, as this volume makes clear, Micronesia has been drawn into the American political sphere and the English-language anthropological literature.

This being the case, why has its overall impact on the discipline been so slight? I believe politics continues to offer a partial explanation—politics both in the sense just mentioned and in the sense discussed by Glenn Petersen (chap. 5). In many instances scientific research in Micronesia, including anthropology, was a victim of Cold War politics. Security clearances and travel restrictions hindered research for the first fifteen years after World War II, preventing all foreign researchers and discouraging many American anthropologists from working in the region. Even after these restrictions were removed, it is my impression (based on twenty-five years of residence and work outside the United States) that most non-American colleagues and students continue to view Micronesia as wholly within the "American sphere of influence." The new political statuses of the various Micronesian states are beginning to alter this academic worldview; an increasing number of Japanese scholars and an occasional Australian (e.g., Connell 1983, 1986), have recently worked there.

Turning more specifically to the modest impact Micronesia has had in cultural ecology and ecological anthropology, academic and economic explanations may also be relevant. Among the early academic centers promoting these research topics, only the University of Hawai'i (with Leonard Mason) had a focus that included Micronesia, and in the 1950s it had no PhD program in anthropology to support such research. During the 1960s more money and expanded doctoral programs appeared, but by then Pacific research interests had shifted to what was then the "new frontier" of interior New Guinea. Although many of the outlying Micronesian islands were remote, none had been isolated from outside economic and political influence in the same way as highlands New Guinea. Furthermore, the theoretical focus of ecological anthropology, which was gaining ascendancy over cultural ecology, preferred bounded systems where energy flows could be more accurately or easily measured. Again New Guinea, with more than eight hundred different ethnolinguistic groups, had advantages over Micronesia where even remote communities had long histories of interaction with others through exchange and sociopolitical networks.

Researchers also seemed to find Micronesia less interesting than Polynesia in the study of cultural evolution, even though the emerging theories emphasized environmental circumscription as a prime mover (e.g., Carneiro 1970). But since the historical and archaeological record (meager as it was) revealed that the Micronesia polities were considerably smaller and less centralized or "statelike" than those of Polynesia, they were of less interest to these theorists. Before many of these suppositions could be fully explored, research money again became in short supply. However, these realities notwithstanding, the most important explanation for the limited contemporary interest in cultural ecological studies undoubtedly relates to a shift in theoretical focus within the discipline. Sociocultural anthropology has largely turned away from an "etic" perspective, where emphasis is placed on empirical and material explanations, toward an "emic" approach that emphasizes interpretive and ideational explanations of cultural phenomena and behavior (Harris 1979). Given this shift, can we expect any future environmentally oriented sociocultural research in Micronesia? I believe the future holds some promise in this regard for two reasons.

First, there is the already mentioned promise of a revitalized culture-centered approach to the study of adaptation. Second, there is a realization that the discipline has something to contribute to help solve a number of environmentally based problems currently faced by the peoples and cultures of the region: "One might have expected that as the environmental crisis deepened there would be contributions from the field of anthropological ecology. Equally, it might have been expected that a field so deeply concerned with the study of kinship and related problems might have contributed to the whole question of population control" (Mead 1972, 12).

As this chapter has perhaps made clear, anthropologists and ecologists who have worked in Micronesia have researched these very issues. Many of the studies reviewed above have examined issues of resource utilization and conservation, intensification of subsistence production, sustainability, population growth, decline and relocation, the nature and transformations of local technologies, and the process of incorporation into world systems (e.g., deYoung 1961; Falanruw 1971; Nakayama and Ramp 1974; McCoy 1974; Marshall 1979c; Severance 1980; L. Marshall and M. Marshall 1982; Lessa 1983; R. Stephenson 1987; Johannes 1985; Alkire 1987, 1993a; Petersen 1992c). It seems appropriate that any revitalization of culture-and-environment studies involving a more culture-centered ecological approach should also return to the kinds of research problems that were preeminent in the work of the first generation of anthropologists to enter Micronesia after World War II—those of the USCC and CIMA projects, and of the trust territory government.

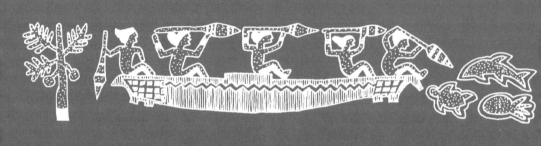

CHAPTER FOUR

"Partial Connections":
Kinship and Social Organization in Micronesia

Mac Marshall

ACCORDING TO RECENT WORK by Marilyn Strathern (1991), Papua New Guinea highlands societies can be seen as variants of each other as a result of people's communications and contacts with one another. In these communications, Highlanders draw from a pool of ideas that is always expanding and contracting, as new ideas are substituted for old and circulate among the interlinked societies. Though she discussed what she calls a "kind of conventional repertoire," Strathern rejected the idea of a regional highlands culture in which every society is "a variation on the same theme" (1991, 72–73), emphasizing instead the "partial connections" that exist among different populations over time. Thus there is a set of social and cultural themes drawn from a common but ever-changing store of ideas, variously combined and recombined in different societies over time.

Like the societies of the Papua New Guinea highlands, Micronesian societies may be thought of as "complex parts and uneven outgrowths of one another. If they are connected, they are only partially so" (Strathern 1991, 54). I use Strathern's perspective to examine kinship and social organization in Micronesia. I focus on the *general* set of themes from which local social forms developed rather than try to specify each and every different combination that developed over time as ideas and objects moved among the different Micronesian populations. While I see Micronesian societies as "partially connected" in Strathern's sense, it seems clear that over the years Micronesians have drawn on a conventional cultural repertoire—a common pool of ideas (including similar colonial experiences)—as they crafted the different sociocultural systems that exist from island to island today.

In this chapter I address seven intersecting topics or themes that allow for a discussion of significant debates in the literature on kinship and social organization. This also permits an evaluation of the theoretical and methodological contributions to the wider discipline by anthropologists who have worked in Micronesia. The seven major topics are: (1) siblingship; (2) systems of kinship and descent; (3) adoption, fosterage, and ritual kinship; (4) the links among kinship, land, and food; (5) marriage systems and practices; (6) incest taboos; and (7) postmarital residence rules. In organizing my contribution in this way, certain closely related and relevant topics necessarily will receive only passing mention, and some subjects will not be discussed at all.[1]

THE CONVENTIONAL MICRONESIAN CULTURAL AND SOCIAL REPERTOIRE

At a very general level it is possible to identify a conventional repertoire that provides a framework of "Micronesian-ness." This repertoire is found throughout the Caroline Islands, the Marshall Islands, and Palau, but it is not represented in the contemporary Marianas (with the exceptions of the Carolinian population on Saipan and the communities of recent immigrants from elsewhere in Micronesia that are now established on Guam and Saipan). As is well known, Chamorro culture was radically altered during the Spanish conquest in the seventeenth century, thus moving it away from the conventional repertoire of Micronesian culture.[2]

From the perspective of kinship and social organization several elements make up the conventional Micronesian repertoire, though these elements may have developed into particular specific forms from one island to the next. Throughout Micronesia, islands were divided into what usually are called districts in the literature, and these districts are major components of local social organization. Districts are named geographical entities occupied by members of named, ranked, nonlocalized, exogamous matriclans. The ranking of these clans is based on their putative order of settlement on the island and subsequent victories or defeats in interisland warfare, and their hereditary leaders hold positions in the traditional political order. These clans are divided into localized, property-holding matrilineages in most cases, with the following exceptions: the contemporary Chamorro (Spoehr 1954) and contemporary Kosraens (Ritter 1980, 770);[3] on the two Polynesian outliers of Nukuoro and

Kapingamarangi (Carroll 1966; Lieber 1968b); on Yap (Labby 1976a; Schneider 1984); and on Pingelap (Damas 1979, 1981; Schneider 1980) and Mokil (Weckler 1953). The Chamorro, Kosraens, Nukuoro, and Kapingamarangi have cognatic systems of descent; Mokil is patrilineal; and Yap and Pingelap are reported to have double descent, although this remains a matter of debate (see further discussion below).

Hence Micronesian social organization is usually constructed around matrilineages composed of descent lines that typically form the basis for residential groups. These residential groups more often than not take the form of matrilocal extended families. Members of Micronesian matrilineages own property and titles in common; have their own internal political organization ("lineage chiefs") based on seniority traced through lines of women; and continue to operate as major units of contemporary social, economic, and political life in most of the islands.

Another element in the conventional Micronesian repertoire is the centrality of sibling relations and their dominance over spousal and parental ties. Related to this is the ubiquity of adoption and fosterage throughout Micronesia—especially involving the children of one's siblings.

Finally, systems of land and sea tenure (which provide access to the major sources of traditional foods) are remarkably similar across Micronesia (again with the exception of post–Spanish occupation Chamorro society), and these systems reflect the dominant structural role played by matrilineal descent groups in most people's lives.

The various elements of conventional Micronesian society and culture have developed into distinctive local forms from one island or island group to the next, and each will be addressed in more detail in the discussion to follow.

SIBLINGSHIP

I have chosen to examine siblingship first because in many respects the other matters to be discussed in this chapter flow from it. As is the case in most Pacific Island societies, siblingship is a—perhaps *the*—general organizing principle of traditional Micronesian kinship and social organization, in substantial part because of the centrality of matriliny in this area. As David M. Schneider showed years ago, matrilineal descent groups rely on the interdependence of brothers and sisters for their viability, a reliance that contrasts with patrilineal descent groups who "can afford to lose a considerable degree of control over their female members" (1961a, 11). This interdependence among uterine or classificatory cross siblings also affects processes of lineage fission: "In a matrilineal descent group no male can found a new segment unless he is able to pair off with one or more sisters or other matrilineal kinswomen . . . and no female can found a new segment without a male from her own group" (1961a, 26). Siblingship is thus basic to other aspects of Micronesian kinship and social organization.

Throughout Micronesia siblings are viewed and view themselves as the closest of kin. For example, interdictions against incest or even the slightest hint of sexuality (including talk about sexual matters) are usually stricter for cross-sex siblings than for any other kin. But while they do not share sex, siblings do share land, food, and material possessions with one another, and same-sex siblings—especially sisters—often reside together after marriage. Siblings are the most frequent adopters of one another's children, and also routinely foster each other's offspring. Siblings usually own land together, not only as members of a common matrilineage, but also as coheirs of land from their father. In fact, where property matters are concerned, in much of Micronesia members of a matrilineage are viewed as 'siblings.'

The earliest clear statement of the importance of siblingship in Micronesian kinship and social organization was Ward H. Goodenough's classic *Property, Kin, and Community on Truk* (1951), a theoretically innovative and ethnographically rich book that has had wide influence in our discipline. He noted, "The nucleus of each lineage, and often its entire membership, is composed of the matrilineal descendents of a group of real or classificatory siblings who founded it as a major corporation" (Goodenough 1951, 70). Goodenough went on to observe that "the organization of a lineage is based on that of a group of own siblings," and that "in a corporate sense, therefore, all the members of a lineage are regarded as siblings. The kinship terms for siblings are used to designate the membership collectively when comparing its activities and responsibilities with those of such non-members as the fathers or spouses of the lineage personnel" (1951, 73). In addition, the political organization of authority and responsibility within the lineage is "expressed in the sibling relationship" (1951, 73). Thus we see that in Chuuk siblingship lies at the core of traditional kinship and social organization, including the ownership and allocation of rights to land and other property.

Similarly, on Bikini in the Marshall Islands sets of siblings form the core of the *bwij* or matrilineage, and real siblings think of themselves "as a *bwij* founded by their mother" (Kiste 1974, 48). For Palau, DeVerne Reed Smith argued that sets of brothers and sisters articulate internal lineage *(telungalek)* structure; serve "as the primary unit of relationship to other lineages via alliances that are created by and expressed through mutual exchanges based on marriage and/or adoption" (1981, 225–226); and share rights to Palauan valuables and land. While Yapese kinship and social organization is quite different from that found in most other parts of Micronesia, David Labby observed that 'siblings' are "those who shared rights in land with ego" (1976a, 49) and that this included ego's mother's brother, who acted in some ways as a 'father', but who was also classified by a special sibling term *wa'ayengin.* Although ego's mother's brother "was a 'parent' in the same sense as ego's mother, he was also a 'sibling' who shared a claim to land. The special sibling term appears to precisely mark the conjunction of these two roles" (Labby 1976a, 50).

While siblings are ranked by relative age within a sibling set, siblings within one generation—especially same-sex siblings—are also conceptually equated. One way this can be seen is in the strong generational influence in Micronesian kinship terminologies (discussed below in the section on Systems of Kinship and Descent). For instance, anyone ego's 'parent' calls 'sibling' (who is thus in ego's parent's sibling set) is a 'parent' to ego and a potential source of land and other property; anyone who shares land with ego is a 'sibling'; and anyone ego's 'child' calls 'sibling' is a 'child' of ego's and a potential heir to ego's property. Although apparently in precolonial times in Micronesia cross-sex siblings did not usually coreside after puberty, Alex Spoehr reported that coresident adult Marshallese siblings of either sex, together with their spouses and children, formed a typical stage in the developmental cycle of household groups on Majuro in the late 1940s (1949a, 113–114). Even so, in most of Micronesia, at least until quite recently, coresidence of postpubertal cross-sex siblings was unusual. For example, in the Carolines such brothers and sisters seldom slept in the same dwelling. Of Palau, Richard Parmentier wrote, "Restriction on the proximity of brother and sister compels these women to establish dwellings, called 'houses of senior women' *(blil a ourrot),* independent from those of male relatives holding the title" (1984, 659). On Ifaluk, "formerly, when unmarried youths slept in the men's house, brother and sister did not sleep under the same roof; but now that the men's houses are no longer used as bachelors' dormitories, and the young men sleep in their own homesteads, an unmarried man and his sister often sleep in the same dwelling" (Burrows and Spiro 1957, 144). A similar behavioral shift seems to have occurred on Romónum Island, Chuuk, in relatively recent times: "One change in residential practice was clear. . . . In 1947 I knew of no instance in which an adult brother and sister (uterine or classificatory) were domiciled together under the same roof. Informants agreed that such an arrangement was taboo. In 1964 there were several cases in which uterine and lineage brothers and sisters were so housed" (Goodenough 1974a, 85). Although modern conditions may have begun to break down the traditional residential separation of brothers and sisters in parts of Micronesia, cross-sex siblings typically continue to be constrained by respect or mild avoidance behaviors and sometimes both (see, e.g., Kiste and Rynkiewich 1976, 218; Sudo 1985).

Sibling ties provide both the prototypes for other relationships and the basic units out of which many other social groups are constructed. For example, Mac Marshall (1981a) and Juliana Flinn (1985a) have shown for Chuuk Lagoon and the surrounding atolls that "the strongest, most intimate, and most intense relationships are those between siblings" (Flinn 1985a, 68). Marshall (1981a) illustrated how sets of siblings serve as the "building blocks" of social organization in these islands in regards to property relations, marital alliances, and cultural notions of 'kinship.' Flinn reinforced this with her data from Pulap, adding, "Notions about sisters and brothers are linked with gender identity. Being male and female dovetails with being a male or female member of a descent group, a brother or sister" (1992a, 60). In an examination of the intersection among biogenetic kinship, friendship, and other created kin ties (e.g., adoption and clientship), Marshall (1977) demonstrated that the most intensive interpersonal relationships for people in Chuuk State are those among uterine, adoptive, and created siblings *(pwiipwi)*. Once again, biological (especially uterine) siblingship provides a prototype for other significant social relationships and cultural identities.

While the scholarly focus on siblingship in Oceania extends beyond Micronesia to Polynesia and Melanesia (e.g., Marshall 1981b), the research contributions from Micronesia in this arena have been significant. All of this work has helped to draw anthropologists' attention to siblingship as a basic ordering principle of social relations on a par with descent and affinity. It has also contributed to an examination of the similarities and differences between kinship and friendship.

SYSTEMS OF KINSHIP AND DESCENT

Insofar as labels have any utility for describing the complexity of dynamic social systems, the kinship systems of Micronesia are predominantly generational. However, because most of Micronesia also is characterized by matrilineal descent, the majority of kinship terminological systems reflect the principle of lineality as well as those of age, sex, and generation. The result is a patchwork of systems, in keeping with David Aberle's finding that "over 70 per cent of all matrilineal systems for which there is information have either Crow or Iroquois cousin terms. The bulk of the remainder have Hawaiian cousin terms" (1961, 717).

Apparently throughout the Marshall Islands there is a terminological system that differs from a straight generation (Hawaiian) type in two ways: (1) opposite-sex cross cousins are distinguished from parallel cousins and from same-sex cross cousins; and (2) a special term is used to designate mother's brother who, in turn, uses a special term for his sister's children (Spoehr 1949b, 108–109; cf. Kiste 1974, 46–47; Kiste and Rynkiewich 1976, 217; Rynkiewich 1984, 115). The resulting "Iroquois" terminology "can be regarded as a variant form [of a Hawaiian system] rather than as a completely separate and distinct type. The special avuncular and nepotic terms produce the effect of an overlay of lineage features on a generation base and reflect the importance of the maternal lineage as a social unit" (Spoehr 1949b, 109). This lack of a "pure" system in the Marshall Islands is characteristic of all of the Micronesian cases reviewed.

On Pohnpei, a Crow system of kinship terminology is employed but may be fading away, according to Glenn Petersen (1982a, 140). While a Crow variant is alive and well on Chuuk and many of the surrounding atolls (see, e.g., Flinn 1992a, 61; Goodenough 1951; Marshall 1972a), it is subject to at least occasional situational variability with an "alternative" Hawaiian pattern (see below). Elsewhere in the Carolinian atolls some version of what Marshall (1978) has dubbed "the Hawaiian Crow" seems to operate as the system of kinship terminology. This is explicit for Namonuito (J. Thomas 1977, 513), Lamotrek (Alkire 1965a, 52–53), Satawal (Sudo 1987, 89, 93, 99), Ifaluk (Burrows and Spiro 1957, 140–142), and Ulithi (Lessa 1966a).

Palau represents another "partial connection" to this set. For example, Roland and Maryanne Force mentioned "the presence of bifurcate collateral avuncular terminology coexisting in a system which exhibited Hawaiian cousin terminology" as "the most notable terminological inconsistency" (1972, 62; see also 68ff). And in one of his early papers on Yapese kinship, Schneider referred to Yap's Crow-type cousin terminology, which he saw as one of "a host of strains" because it existed "in the presence of patrilineal kin groups" (1953, 234). These various systems of kinship terminology nicely illustrate Strathern's "partial connections" in that they seem to be "complex parts and uneven outgrowths of one another" (Strathern 1991, 54).[4]

It is important to emphasize that these terminological systems are in flux and may change over time. Philip Ritter reported that traditionally the pattern on Kosrae was Hawaiian (1980, 763), although it is no longer so today. Force and Force discussed such changes for Palau at some length (1972, 61ff). For Micronesia, though, the example of such fluctuation that is of greatest theoretical interest to kinship studies is the identification of "situational variability" in the use of two different patterns of kinship terminology on Romónum, Chuuk.

In brief: Marc Swartz worked on Romónum several years after Ward Goodenough completed his initial study there, and Swartz (1960) reported that in certain circumstances a father's sister's son (FZS) was like a 'same sex sibling' and in other situations he was like a 'father.' This "dual classification of a kinsman" meant that sometimes Romónum people were using Hawaiian cousin terminology, and at other times they were using Crow terminology. The conundrum is clear: How could one community have two different systems of kinship terminology?

Swartz (1962) followed up his first article with a longer piece in which he explained this dual classification via the "situational determinant" of a father's sister's son's weak inheritance claims to a potential lineage's property. He did this by showing both structural and psychological bases for an FZS to be an ideal recruit for a descent line's labor force. In 1964, Goodenough returned to Romónum after seventeen years and he—like Swartz—was confronted by "what appeared to be a change in the use of kinship terminology" (1974a, 85). Goodenough pursued this issue at some length and while he confirmed that the Crow pattern he had recorded in the late 1940s was a reality, "it was also apparent that considerations affecting individuals could produce Hawaiian patterns of usage as well" (1974a, 88). He found that one such consideration was adoption: "Adopted persons . . . grow up looking upon the members of their adopted mother's lineage as lineage mates and regarding their siblings by adoption as siblings. In many cases the adopting mother is already a member of the child's lineage, for example, the child's mother's sister, but often she is the child's father's sister. In the latter case, the child's paternal cross-cousins become lineage mates by adoption and 'siblings' instead of 'parents' " (1974a, 90).

While Goodenough left this matter somewhat up in the air, I suggest that the likely answer to such dual classifications of kin is that kinship systems are a good deal less fixed and rigid than anthropologists customarily think. With this in mind, Goodenough himself provided a key clue at an earlier point in his article. After noting that the system of kinship classification operating on

Romónum in 1947 was of a Crow type, he stated, "The conceptual model of the system, however, remained one of 'generation' and 'Hawaiian' type" (1974a, 77). I have already suggested that the pool of ideas on which Micronesians traditionally drew in constructing their kinship terminologies included a generational emphasis and a bias toward matriliny. Thus in the Marshall Islands, and on many Carolinian atolls, we find systems that are essentially Hawaiian *except* that they terminologically mark the relationship between mother's brother and sister's child. It should come as no great surprise, then, that one "complex variant" to emerge from this pool is the contextual alternation between Crow and Hawaiian patterns on Romónum when certain situational variables come into play.

As I have already noted above, matrilineal descent groups (clans, subclans, lineages, and descent lines) figure importantly throughout most of this area. Nevertheless, matriliny is not found everywhere, and in some places it is found with a twist.

We know that Kosrae used to have matrilineal clans (which are now extinct) and contemporary Kosraens have a bilateral system of descent (Ritter 1980, 763). The Marshall Islands, Pohnpei, Chuuk, and all of the atolls in Chuuk State and Yap State have matrilineal descent, as do the Saipan Carolinians. In what Joseph Weckler (1953) called this "matrilineal sea," however, are found some exceptions. These cluster in two areas: the atolls located in Pohnpei State, and the high islands of Palau and Yap.

Pohnpei State includes five inhabited outer islands: Nukuoro, Kapingamarangi, Sapwuahfik (Ngatik), Mwokilloa (Mokil), and Pingelap. Both Nukuoro and Kapingamarangi are Polynesian outliers, and like most other Polynesian societies they are characterized by nonunilineal (cognatic) descent. The other three atolls are culturally Micronesian, and they present a somewhat different (and somewhat muddier) picture.

Weckler (1949, 1953) asserted that at the time of his study in the late 1940s Mokil was patrilineal. In the absence of any subsequent data to the contrary, we must assume that this remains the case. David Damas (1979, 1981) argued that Pingelap has double descent, although this assertion has been challenged by Schneider (1980). While it continues to have matrilineal clans, Sapwuahfik has also seen some development toward patriliny (Fischer 1957a; Poyer 1993, 43, 177). All three of these islands have experienced special events that nearly eradicated their populations and consequently have seriously altered their traditional systems. On Mokil and Pingelap very few people survived the major typhoon of circa 1775, while Sapwuahfik's adult male population was totally

massacred by European and Pohnpeian raiders in 1837. The present population of that atoll is descended from the surviving Sapwuahfik women and
children and various foreign immigrants (Poyer 1993). Thus all three atolls
underwent a major demographic trauma, all three were at least partially resettled by immigrants, and the development of patriliny (or double descent)
postdates these demographic disasters.

Palau and Yap each present complex and somewhat disputed pictures. Force
and Force reported that "Palauans clearly recognized a bilateral network of
relationships. They not only recognized filiation as being bilateral, but further,
they had terms for descent traced through either the mother or the father"
(1972, 41–42). A bit later in their discussion they stated that "while lineage
membership in Palau was allowable through one's father, historically there were
no patrilineages. Lineages were based on matrilineal descent, and included
some members whose route to membership was through their fathers" (1972,
42). DeVerne Smith's (1983) later superb analysis of Palauan social structure
demonstrated that descent in Palau is clarified if one views it in the context of
land, siblingship, marriage, and adoption. She found that Palauans have
matrilineages and patrilines bound together and articulated through exchanges
of land and other valuables involving cross siblings, spouses, and adoption
transactions.

The current picture of Palauan descent in relationship to land estates,
adoption, and ties through both men and women bears considerable resemblance to (although it is by no means the same as) the descriptions available
for Yap. Schneider (1962) originally argued that Yapese had double descent,
but he has since renounced that position (Schneider 1969a, 1984). In significant
measure his change of view has come about as a consequence of research in
Yap by several of his students (Kirkpatrick and Broder 1976; Labby 1976a). The
revised view of Yap is that the *tabinau* is not a patrilineage (as Schneider had
originally claimed), but rather that it refers to the relationship between named
land estates and the people who have rights to those estates. The Yapese
genung is still accepted as a matrilineal clan (Schneider 1984, 81, 87), but with a
number of qualifications based on emic categories that encompass both kinship and descent (1984, 88ff). So, as with Palau, there seems to be a system of
descent that considers ties through women to be stronger, but in which relationships among persons and land are founded in a complex set of exchanges
—especially marriage exchanges (see, e.g., Labby 1976a).

Another significant contribution from Micronesian studies to theories of
kinship and descent concerns the importance of performance in establishing

kinship. In much of Micronesia, as in Hawai'i, "kinsmen are made as well as born" (Sahlins 1985, 28). Space does not permit a full exploration of this topic, so a few passing comments will have to suffice. Marshall's (1977) emphasis on the sharing of land, food, and nurturance in Chuuk and surrounding atolls as bases for creating kin stressed behavior over biology. Similarly, Schneider's (1984) reconsideration of the Yapese *tabinau* pointed to *doing* rather than *being* as the crucial distinction (1984, 72). Flinn (1992a) highlighted the same sorts of issues for establishing (or disestablishing) kinship on Pulap. DeVerne Smith (1981, 1983) also argued for the necessity of *actions* (in the form of exchanges) to validate kinship in Palau.

ADOPTION, FOSTERAGE, AND RITUAL KINSHIP

Over forty years ago Weckler (1953) published the first article devoted exclusively to adoption in a Micronesian society. It was followed soon thereafter by Ward Goodenough's suggestion that "adoption of the land-poor by kinsmen in land-rich groups is another device for solving the land distribution problem. . . . It is of special importance where the land-owning groups become unilinear" (1955, 81). Much of the significant work on this topic since then appeared in the 1970s, in two Association for Social Anthropology in Oceania (ASAO) volumes devoted to adoption and fosterage in Oceania (Brady 1976; Carroll 1970a).

Weckler pointed out that adoption practices are particularly common in the Pacific, and he noted that "nearly a third of the children born on Mokil since the prehistoric typhoon [circa 1775] have been adopted" (1953, 556). Among several motives Weckler gave for adoption "is the Mokil view that every man must have a sister and every woman a brother" (1953, 558), a motive that underscores the significance of cross-sex siblingship in Micronesia. Children are highly prized on Mokil, as they are throughout Micronesia, and Mokil married couples have a "universal desire" to have children. Weckler suggested that "the foremost motive" for adoption is childlessness, and he wrote that "*every* childless couple during the past 175 years has adopted one or more children if the marriage endured even a few years" (1953, 558). This observation anticipated a major debate that developed in the literature approximately a quarter of a century later over reasons for adoption.

Data from Romónum, Chuuk, suggested to Ruth Goodenough "that there are apparently no strongly operating factors to sustain such a high rate of adoption [a crude adoption rate of 10.9 percent] other than childlessness or the occasional orphaning of children" (1970, 316). In her article Goodenough provided a very sound basic description of adoption practices in Chuuk and a clear and well-supported analysis of the Romónum material. She concluded that adoption in Chuuk was primarily a consequence of childlessness brought on by sterility from venereal disease.

A few years later, Marshall (1976a) argued that this explanation did not appear to have general validity for communities throughout Chuuk State. He compared data from Namoluk with Ruth Goodenough's Romónum material and found that Namoluk had both a higher crude adoption rate and a higher rate of fertility. While he agreed that childlessness clearly was one factor in adoption and fosterage on these islands, he emphasized that sterility was not sufficient to account for the Namoluk case. Instead he "argued that the simplest and most inclusive explanation for the high rate of adoption and fosterage practiced in greater Trukese society is that adoption and fosterage represent part of a larger pattern of sharing among relatives." (1976a, 47). This explanation accounted for fosterage as well as adoption—something Goodenough's did not do.

Over the next several years a number of other anthropologists who worked in Micronesia engaged this solidarity-or-sterility debate over adoption. Drawing on his very rich demographic data from Kosrae, Ritter suggested that solidarity *and* sterility are necessary to any regional or cross-cultural explanation of adoption and fosterage: "If we consider all adoption, fosterage, and *kuhlacnsap* ['temporary child transfer'] relationships, sharing of resources among kin is clearly an important factor in maintaining the high rate of transfer of children, although sterility and sterile periods of the adult life cycles are also highly significant" (1981, 58). Although he supported the solidarity argument, Ritter cautioned that demographic factors should not be slighted in emphasizing adoption and fosterage as the sharing of resources among kin, and he made a case for viewing adoption and fosterage as a process with a multivariate explanation. He closed with a tentative hypothesis that "the rate of what we call true adoption is directly related to the rate of infertility in systems where vertical inheritance is common," and that "the more absolute the system of vertical inheritance, the greater the likelihood that . . . the frequency of true adoptions would be closely related to the frequency of childlessness" (1981, 60).

Like Ritter, Damas (1983) acknowledged the importance of both kinship factors (solidarity) and demographic considerations (sterility) in accounting for adoption on Pingelap Atoll, but Damas concluded that "both Marshall and Ritter have undervalued Goodenough's material" (1983, 340). Damas argued further "that there are places in Oceania, such as Pingelap and Romónum, where the rise and fall of adoption rates are highly sensitive to demographic changes, such as those caused by fluctuating fertility rates" (1983, 340).

Continuing the discussion of reasons for adoption and fosterage in Micronesia, Flinn reported that for Pulap Atoll in the Western Islands of Chuuk State "adoption follows a similar pattern [to that on Namoluk] of sharing among kin" and "strengthens internal solidarity through reinforcing this [sibling] bond" (1985b, 95). With 53 percent of children of elementary school age and below adopted, adoption on Pulap "invariably involves a bond between siblings, the most important of which is found among members of a matrilineal descent group" (1985b, 96). Besides strengthening ties between a matrilineal descent group and the offspring of its men, adoptions also sustain ties of kin solidarity between migrants and those who remain on Pulap. Flinn's study provided no support for Ruth Goodenough's sterility explanation.

All of these investigations taken together give a rich picture of adoption and fosterage in several Micronesian societies. It seems clear that both kinship solidarity and demographic fluctuations (e.g., rates of childlessness) play a role in these phenomena. Whether, as Ritter (1981) suggested, the relative role of such variables has to do with social structural factors, or whether, as Damas (1983) argued, there may be some subareal distinctions between the Eastern Carolines and islands further to the west, remains unresolved.

A partial solution to these puzzles might be found if one carried out a systematic analysis of the several other significant contributions to the literature on adoption and fosterage that exist for Micronesia, even though these studies do not directly address the solidarity-versus-sterility debate. In addition to Ruth Goodenough's (1970) chapter, the ASAO monograph edited by Vern Carroll (1970a) contains detailed examinations of adoption and fosterage in the two Polynesian outlier communities of Nukuoro (Carroll 1970b) and Kapingamarangi (Lieber 1970); the same volume also includes John "Jack" Fischer's (1970a) analysis of Pohnpeian adoption. The second ASAO monograph dealing with adoption and fosterage in Oceania (Brady 1976) provides even more coverage of Micronesia. Along with Marshall's (1976a) contribution, it contains chapters on Kosrae (Wilson 1976), Arno Atoll (Rynkiewich 1976), Yap (Kirkpatrick and Broder 1976), and Rota in the northern Marianas (J. Smith 1976). Rounding out the coverage of all major areas of Micronesia on this subject is the extensive treatment adoption receives in DeVerne Smith's book on Palau (1983, especially pp. 203–218) and in John Thomas' (1978) doctoral dissertation on Namonuito.

The general Micronesian emphasis on adoption has followed a special development in Chamorro culture on Saipan, apparently having been merged with the ritual kinship system known as *compadrazgo* which is widespread in Hispanicized societies. As already noted above, parents' siblings are the most common adopters in most Micronesian communities; the Chamorro pattern described below seems to represent a combination of this pattern with ritual coparenthood. Noting that every Saipanese Chamorro child has two sets of godparents—those of baptism and those of confirmation—Spoehr commented, "The Chamorros also exhibit a contrast with many Latin-American communities in that godparents are very often relatives—either siblings or first cousins of the parents—particularly those of the first child, at least one of whose godparents is often a sibling of father or mother. . . . There is no conscious attempt among the Chamorros to exclude close relatives from the *compadrazgo* relationship and to select instead non-relatives. Rather, the reverse is true" (1954, 311). Spoehr further observed that the Saipan Carolinians have also taken on the *compadrazgo* institution as part of Catholicism, and that "among Carolinians the *compaire* [term used between a child's natural parents and its godparents] relationship tends to reflect their sibling relationship, which is often important in day-to-day economic relationships" (1954, 315). It seems safe to conclude from Spoehr's description of *compadrazgo* on Saipan that this form of ritual kinship shares some things in common with broader patterns of Micronesian adoption. Perhaps the greatest difference, however, is that few (if any) godchildren go to reside with their godparents, whereas most adopted children live with their adoptive parents. Likewise, another difference between Chamorro ritual kinship and Micronesian adoption is that godchildren do not usually inherit land or other property from their godparents. Instead, the ritual kin relations operate in the moral and religious realm, and mutual obligations primarily concern life crisis events.

It is clear that adoption is a very common transaction in Micronesia, with typically half or more of all children being adopted. For Sapwuahfik (Ngatik), Lin Poyer referred to "the extensive adoption and fostering of children through a wide range of kin ties" (1991, 364). Robert C. Kiste wrote that "at least one-fourth of the Bikinians had been adopted as children, but my data are incomplete, and the number of adoptions was much greater" (1974, 51). William Alkire recorded that "on Lamotrek half of all the children in 1962–63 who were 16 years of age and below had been adopted. The percentage on Satawal was even higher: more than three-fourths of the children had adoptive parents"(1965a, 60).[5] And Don Rubinstein (1978) reported a truly astronomical rate of adoption for Fais in the Western Carolines, where 92 percent of the populace had been adopted as of 1977. He suggested that there is a Fais organization of sentiment that is "centrifugally structured . . . 'turned outward' from the immediate family," and that socialization on Fais "aims towards detaching the child from exclusive identification with the natural family" (1978, 7).

Given the focus on adoption in the United States in recent years, the increased prevalence of international adoptions, and growing concern about the psychological consequences of adoption for children, anthropological data on the subject such as those from Micronesia are of considerable practical importance in helping to understand a process that is much more common in the Pacific than in Europe and North America (see Modell 1994).

THE LINKS AMONG KINSHIP, LAND, AND FOOD

Over thirty-five years ago Schneider noted the conjunction of kinship, land, and food in Micronesian cultures: "The symbolic value of food throughout Micronesia is difficult to overestimate. It enters into every relationship, every crisis, almost every ritual, and it is the center of a complex of psychological concerns and anxieties that have not yet been clearly unraveled for any Micronesian culture, though its existence is clearly perceived and remarked on by almost every ethnographer" (1961b, 220). Perhaps partially in response to this observation, several anthropology doctoral dissertations subsequently completed in Micronesia had food as their central subject (Dahlquist 1972; Demory 1976; Pollock 1970; Severance 1976; Steager 1972). While the details of these studies will not be reported here, I will sketch the general ways that food is connected to land and kinship in Micronesian cultural systems.

Some years ago Martin Silverman (1971) developed an argument concerning the relationship between shared land and shared kinship which he called "the blood and mud hypothesis" of Oceanic kinship. This equation of land and kin is common in Micronesia. For example, describing Lamotrek, Alkire stated that "a *bwogat* is a group of land parcels. . . . In practice, though, a *bwogat* is more than land; it is also the people who live upon and control it" (1965a, 46). Further, "*bwogat,* in meaning, is interchangeably used for both the land and the people who own it" (1965a, 47).

While there is no question that this relationship is very important, food must be added as a crucial part of this symbolic nexus (yielding something that might be called the "blood, mud, and grub" hypothesis). Most, if not all, Micronesian peoples have elaborated the symbolic linkages among kinship, shared rights to land, and eating together the food products of shared land.

For example, in Chuuk, 'land' is commonly referred to as 'food' (*mwongo;* Marshall 1981a, 208; cf. Sudo 1984, 227), and on Yap "any man who feeds a man is, by that act, his son" (Schneider 1969a, 4). On Nukuoro, " 'relatives' are those with whom one shares rights in land" (Carroll 1968, 3–4). Michael D. Lieber has more fully explicated this concept of kinship for Kapingamarangi, and the ideas contained in this quotation from one of his articles may be taken as an outline of Micronesian attitudes on this subject:

> One naturally shares with kinsmen. . . . As an object of sharing, land sustains life substance. Children are fed from the land by their parents, and aged parents are fed from the land by their children. Siblings are fed from the land by one another. Land is shared not only with the living, but also with the dead. People are buried in the land on which they lived. Thus within the land and that which composes the land are the physical remains of the life substance which one shares with his ancestors and other relatives. (1974, 77)

This statement about relationships among land, food, and people helps us make sense of statements from elsewhere in Micronesia. For example, DeVerne Smith reported that on Palau, "I was often told, 'People come and go, but the land and the name of the land stays and never, never changes' " (1981, 244). Similarly, on Yap, there is a general formulation "which is contained in the exchange of a man's sexual 'labours' on the woman's reproductive 'land' for a woman's labours on his food-producing land, of a man's food-producing land for the woman's child-producing 'land.' The process by which the people of the clans reproduced and the process by which the land produced were totally bound up in each other" (Labby 1976b, 177–178; cf. Lingenfelter 1993, 154).

Although it has long been recognized that food carries a heavy symbolic meaning for Micronesians—far more than for peoples in many other parts of the world—the anthropological investigation of food in relation to kinship and land remains relatively undeveloped. One sign that this is beginning to change is Flinn's recent book (1992a) and her statement that "it is impossible to overestimate the symbolic value of food on Pulap and in Chuuk in general. The sharing of resources is typified by the sharing of food as an expression of solidarity. Food is prepared, distributed, and shared among kin, and thus defines who is kin. Nonkin do not participate in this process, and a participant is kin by definition . . . the primary way to sustain and validate kinship is through sharing food" (1992a, 56). Very clearly, on Pulap (and, I would argue, throughout Chuuk State), kin are those who share land and food, whether or not they share biogenetic ties (cf. Marshall 1977, 1981a, 38–39). As has been seen at several points in the discussion above, Micronesian kinship—like its Polynesian cousin—is difficult to separate from food and from the land on which food is grown. Kinship in Micronesian societies is comprised of intertwining ties among persons, land estates, food, and the interchanges among these.

Throughout most of Micronesia members of matrilineal descent groups share rights to land, with lineages normally serving as the property-holding groups. Most Micronesians also have certain kinds of rights to at least some of the lands of their father's kin group, and children frequently inherit land from their father at or near the time of his death. Food, as a product of shared land, represents the kin group's contribution or "presence" at various wider community activities, ranging from church-related events, to feasts marking major holidays (e.g., New Year), to weddings, funerals, and political installations. In Yap and Palau, food figures centrally in kin-group exchanges that join and reinforce the ties between spouses and cross-sex siblings (Labby 1976a; D. Smith 1983).

This symbolic equation among kinship, land, and food goes well beyond the borders of Micronesia to other parts of Oceania.[6] Kin are linked to one another as much through consumption of the life-sustaining products from shared lands as through common biogenetic connections. This is very different from the more narrow western notion of "real" kinship as an exclusively biological phenomenon.

There are various interesting ways in which this symbolic nexus involving land, food, and kinship is revealed to outsiders and brought home to Micronesians themselves. Edwin G. Burrows and Melford E. Spiro noted that the strength of the incest taboo between cross siblings is marked on Ifaluk by mild avoidance; this includes not eating food cooked over the same fire, or even sharing a cigarette—which involves ingesting a substance in a manner analogous to food and drink (1957, 144).[7] This same cross-sibling prohibition is found widely on the Carolinian atolls. For instance, Flinn noted that a woman should never "eat food or drink coconuts he [her 'brother'] has tasted, or smoke his cigarette. Some women are careful even with imported cups, reserving one solely for the use of their brothers" (1985a, 70). Interestingly, as people age on Pulap, the need for care and nurture from younger women becomes paramount instead of mutual support sustaining the descent line. Brother-sister avoidance patterns interfere with this necessity and thus become cumbersome. Changing the inter-generational brother-sister tie to a "father-daughter" one, however, combines in one relationship the support and nurture expected of fellow descent group members together with the rights and duties of the "parent-child" tie. The care and attention a "child" shows a "parent" now is available from within the descent group for both men and for women. Elderly men and younger descent group women can then comfortably reside together. (Flinn 1985a, 80).

Flinn's finding is another nice illustration of how situational determinants may affect kin terminology.

In the spirit of "partial connections," Yap provides another complex variant drawn from the common repertoire of kinship, land, and food, and the widespread emphasis on cross-siblingship in Micronesia—a variant that sheds some light on the brother-sister avoidance found on Pulap and Ifaluk. Schneider observed that "brother and sister are at once siblings and they are of opposite sex" (1969a, 12). This poses a conceptual problem for Yapese kinship because while "same things share, different things exchange":

> brother and sister are both same and different, and they therefore contain a contradiction which must be contained. If they are to remain both same (as siblings) and different (as opposite sex) then clear diacriticals are required to maintain the segregation of the contradictory elements. Since one focus of contradiction is land, and land is so fundamentally important in Yap culture, it is land rights that must be precisely controlled and contained. And so the *drilyun a yam,* the anniversary of the death of a man, is marked by giving food to the *m'fen;* thus the bond between brother and sister as siblings who share and as brother and sister where brother provides care and protection, is marked by the gift of food from the land they were both born of. (Schneider 1969a, 13)

I suggest that whereas on Yap the "clear diacriticals" necessary to mark the simultaneous closeness and distance between cross siblings are marked in land, on the Trukic-speaking Carolinian atolls these diacriticals are marked in another part of the "blood-mud-grub" triad, namely, in comestibles such as food, drink, and cigarettes. Were this to be followed out more systematically for all Micronesian societies (somewhat along lines of what D. Smith [1983] has accomplished for Palau), my guess is that it will be found impossible to fully describe Micronesian kinship without a concurrent consideration of the meanings of land and food in these societies.

MARRIAGE SYSTEMS AND PRACTICES

It is commonly understood in anthropology that "the institutionalization of very strong, lasting, or intense solidarities between husband and wife is not compatible with the maintenance of matrilineal descent groups" (Schneider 1961a, 16). This is because the bonds of descent (especially as they concern property rights) are potentially in conflict with the marital tie. Women, in particular, must give their primary loyalty to their descent groups rather than to their husbands if matrilineal descent groups are to be maintained (Schneider 1961a). Related to this is a need to specify and limit the husband's authority over his wife and children, and to delineate this (usually domestic) sphere clearly from the major areas of descent group interest (Schneider 1961a). This famous "matrilineal puzzle" (Richards 1950), and the emotional interest of a father in his own children, is a strain with which most Micronesian societies have had to contend (see, e.g., Spoehr 1949b, 110; Thomas 1980). One possible way to deal with the "matrilineal puzzle," which clearly organizes relations among male in-marrying affines, is prescriptive cross-cousin marriage (Schneider 1961a, 21).

Cross-cousin marriage appears to be or to have been permissible over wide areas of Micronesia, and it is clearly preferred in a number of societies. It seems to have been allowed throughout the Marshall Islands, although it was practiced to very different degrees from one island to another. For example, Kiste and Michael Rynkiewich (1976) showed that while Bikinians explicitly prefer bilateral cross-cousin marriage, and while approximately two-thirds of the marriages at the time of Kiste's research were between cross cousins, the people of Arno do not express any particular preference for such marriages, and only 1 percent of the marriages Rynkiewich recorded were of this type. Similarly, Spoehr found people on Majuro in the late 1940s allowed cross-cousin marriage but practiced it at a very low frequency—approximately 6 percent of the marriages in his sample (1949a, 197, 214). Nancy Pollock noted that cross-cousin marriage was considered ideal on Namu (1974, 104), but she provided no data on the frequency of such marriages there; the same is true for Ujelang (L. Carucci 1988, 6).

In the Carolines the richest data available for cross-cousin marriage are for

David Schneider and Yapese informant, Rumung Island, Yap, 1947. Photograph, cover of Harvard Alumni Magazine, April 1948, and courtesy of Richard Handler.

Ward Goodenough in Honolulu en route to Micronesia 1947. Photograph courtesy of Ward Goodenough.

Ward Goodenough and Boutau K. Efot, chief of Chorong and research assistant, Romónum Island, Chuuk, 1964–1965. Photograph courtesy of Ward Goodenough.

Namoluk Atoll in Chuuk State (Marshall 1972a, 1976b). As with the Bikinians, bilateral cross-cousin marriage is preferred and consciously arranged by Namoluk people, and approximately 60 percent of all marriages in the genealogies collected involved real or classificatory cross-cousins. Elsewhere on Carolinian atolls, Burrows and Spiro wrote that on Ifaluk "cross-cousin marriage is permitted, but not required, nor even especially preferred" (1957, 143). Reports of relatively high rates of cross-cousin marriage also exist for Lukunor (Borthwick 1977), Piis-Losap (Severance 1976), elsewhere in the Mortlocks (Marshall, field notes, 1970), and to a lesser extent on Namonuito (J. Thomas 1978). Finally, Alkire noted that cross-cousin marriage may once have been found among chiefly clans on Lamotrek (1965a, 56).

On the Carolinian high islands, Ward Goodenough stated that cross-cousin marriage was not allowed on Chuuk (1951, 120), although subsequent fieldwork elsewhere in Chuuk Lagoon has shown that such marriages did occur on some of the islands and that his statement should be taken to apply only to

Romónum. For instance, John Caughey (1977) found cross-cousin marriages on Wuumaan, and Marshall (field notes, 1976) found them in Peniyesene on Wééné. Ritter (1980) cited Ernst Sarfert's 1919 finding that bilateral cross-cousin marriage was permitted on Kosrae up until the early twentieth century, but Ritter suggested that such marriages were "relatively infrequent" and this practice has been considered inappropriate on Kosrae more recently, accompanying other profound changes in kinship and marriage patterns (1980, 762–763). On Pohnpei, where the demographic upset during the contact period was less pronounced, cross-cousin marriages are apparently allowed but not actively preferred:

> Ponapeans consider sexual intercourse with certain kinds of non-matrilineal relatives permissible or even sometimes desirable, especially between cross-cousins. Marriages between cross-cousins are spoken of as *pwopwoud nan peneinei* 'marriages in the family.' Some informants nevertheless disapprove of cross-cousin marriages on the grounds that they are usually arranged by the family to keep property together and that they ignore the natural romantic preferences of the couple. (Fischer, Ward, and Ward 1976, 201)

But in at least partial contradiction to this is Falgout's recent statement concerning

> the preferred type of traditional Pohnpei marriage, the "family marriage." This type of marriage occurs among cognatic cross-cousins, particularly among those residing in nearby communities, and results in a concentration of support and landholdings, and hence of status, *manaman* [respect, power and authority], and wealth. Family marriages were considered so desirable in the past that, occasionally, parents might even attempt to promise their unborn children (1993, 135).

On Palau cousin marriages between the offspring of brothers occasionally occurred in the past, but there was no preference for them, and at the time of the Forces' research they found there was "no question that today Palauans are uncomfortable at the thought of the offspring of siblings marrying" (Force and Force 1972, 94). This finding was reinforced by DeVerne Smith, who wrote that "one should never marry within the range of close blood. . . . When marriage occurs in the distant ranges of blood, it is possible to 'correct' the marriage by paying a valuable" (1983, 46, cf. 142–144). Sherwood "Woody" Lingenfelter mentioned caste endogamy and local village endogamy in Yap (1993, 151), but neither his work nor any other source for Yap indicates that cross-cousin marriage was practiced there. Given the severe depopulation that occurred on both Yap and Palau in the nineteenth century, I venture to speculate that cross-cousin marriage may once have been permitted in both societies, but that it "fell apart" in the face of the demographic disasters that people faced.

Several other Micronesian marriage practices are deserving of at least passing comment. Although DeVerne Smith stated unequivocally that in Palau "one should not marry the kin of former affines in sororate or levirate marriage" (1983, 143), such marriages were widely permitted, and even encouraged, in other parts of Micronesia. The most detailed information of this practice comes from Namoluk, where "every attempt is made to arrange a sororal or leviratic marriage following divorce or death of a spouse—especially if there are children—in order to maintain a previously established alliance" (Marshall 1976b, 192). Such marriages with real or classificatory siblings of former spouses constituted 53 percent of all remarriages (N = 547) contained in the Namoluk genealogies. Common on Lamotrek was what Alkire called "serial sororal polygyny": situations "where a man had married a girl [*sic*], divorced her, and then married the sister of this former wife. Similarly, a number of cases were noted in which a woman had divorced a man to marry his brother" (1965a, 55). Although their data do not show how prevalent the practice was, Burrows and Spiro found that on Ifaluk, "when a man dies, his brother may marry the widow. But this practise (the levirate), is not required or regarded as particularly praiseworthy" (1957, 145). Curiously, these authors said nothing about the presence or incidence of the sororate on Ifaluk.

For the Marshall Islands, Spoehr stated that the sororate and levirate, along with cross-cousin marriage, "are all encouraged and favored by the society, but they are not mandatory," and he suggested that they "do not even make up the majority of marriages" (1949a, 204). Spoehr went on to note that sororal and leviratic marriages "are limited to the sibling of the deceased spouse"; that they "are both regarded with favor"; and that "they are said to be particularly good if there are small children of the deceased spouse to be considered [compare with Namoluk]. I was told that sororate and levirate particularly held among chiefly families and was not so common among commoners. Whatever the custom once was, the incidence . . . is far from high today. I was able to record only three cases of the sororate and none of the levirate existing among current marriages, although I made special inquiry on this particular point" (1949a, 215). No numerical data were given on the incidence of sororal and leviratic marriages for any other of the Marshall Islands.

Ward Goodenough wrote that both of these kinds of secondary marriages

were practiced on Romónum in former times, but "the usage is said by informants to be less strongly adhered to today" (1951, 122). Sororal and leviratic
marriages apparently were required on Romónum unless the deceased
spouse's lineage released the surviving spouse from such obligation. I have
not located information concerning whether the sororate and levirate are or
were practiced on Kosrae, Pohnpei, or Yap.

Before conversion to Christianity, polygamy was allowed in most Micronesian societies, although it does not appear to ever have been very common
and often it seems to have been associated with high rank. For instance, Ward
Goodenough noted that "only six of the 397 marriages recorded in the
Romónum genealogies were polygynous and only one was polyandrous," and
he went on to observe that "polygyny is still practiced [in the late 1940s] to a
slight degree on Truk" (1951, 123) with particular reference to Fááychuuk.
Marshall (1972a) found a small number of polygynous and polyandrous
unions in the Namoluk genealogies, although multiple marriages were a thing
of the past there in the early 1970s when he did his research. For Ifaluk there is
only the passing statement that "polygyny, though said to be permissible, is
not practised" (Burrows and Spiro 1957, 145), with no comment about polyandry. Serial monogamy, with an average of over three marriages per adult,
was the rule on Lamotrek—at least "until recent missionary influence"—but
polygamy was not. After mentioning two instances of polygyny, one on
Lamotrek and one on Satawal, Alkire commented, "Other than these two
instances, and stories which make reference to sororal polygyny and fraternal
polyandry, there is no evidence that such multiple marriages were very
common" (1965a, 55).[8]

Of Palau, Force and Force stated, "Monogamy was the normative pattern
. . . but wealthy chiefs sometimes had additional spouses. Only they could
afford the expense of multiple spouses and the attendant economic obligations"(1972, 28). DeVerne Smith amplified this, noting that "polygyny traditionally was a right of rank," although "some wealthy *(merau)* men who were
not of high rank by birth were permitted to have two wives" (1983, 145; cf.
D. Smith 1981, 259). She also wrote that the Japanese discouraged this practice
(which they probably also did elsewhere in Micronesia, reinforcing the earlier
admonitions of Christian missionaries), and that it was "abolished in a 1948
edict issued by the chiefs of Yoldaob and Babeldaob" (1983, 145).

Some Micronesian communities practiced sibling-set marriage, where a
group of real or classificatory siblings from one descent group married a similar group from another. As with cross-cousin marriage, the sororate, and the

levirate, sibling-set marriages helped establish alliances between property hold-ing groups.[9] They also further reinforced ties among the siblings themselves.

Marshall presented data on sibling-set marriage for three communities in Chuuk State: Romónum Island, Peniyesene district on Wééné Island, and Namoluk Atoll (1981a, 215). These data show that between 55 percent and 68 percent of the marriages for the three samples were among sets of descent group siblings, and that between 21 percent and 40.5 percent of these involved siblings marrying into the same matrilineage.

Data on this form of preferred marriage are sparse for other areas of Micronesia, but whether this is a result of the absence of the practice or of a failure to look for such unions is not clear. A statement by Spoehr makes it appear that sibling-set marriages did not exist on Majuro in the late 1940s: "I looked for a case where a brother and sister married a sister and a brother . . . but was unable to find an instance"(1949a, 190). The situation for Palau is even more explicit: "Unlike in Truk . . . it would be highly unusual to have two females from the same lineage marry within the same unit. In a sense, this would be 'putting all one's eggs in the same basket' " (D. Smith 1981, 259). On the other hand, Jane Underwood (personal communication 1996) told me that "brother-sister exchange" marriages are found among members of Guam's Chamorro population.

INCEST TABOOS

Incest taboos have been a subject of enduring interest in anthropology, in part because they are thought to be universal—in some version—to human soci-eties. Ideas about the origin and presumed universality of the incest taboo continue to be a focus of theoretical debate in anthropology (e.g., Erickson 1989; Leavitt 1989, 1990; Roscoe 1994; A. Wolf 1993), yet who is covered by such rules (and why) remains a vexed issue. Material on incest rules in Micronesian societies feeds into this long-standing controversy in important ways, par-ticularly in its contributions concerning kinship as a cultural construction as opposed to biologically based theories of incest aversion. Micronesian data also provide important information on the relationships among incest, exog-amy, and demographic variables in small populations.

The single best source for data on Micronesian incest regulations is a spe-cial issue of *The Journal of the Polynesian Society* (Huntsman and McLean 1976). Along with articles on four Polynesian societies, it includes contribu-tions on Yap (Labby 1976b), Namoluk (Marshall 1976b), Pohnpei (Fischer,

Ward, and Ward 1976), and Arno and Bikini in the Marshall Islands (Kiste and Rynkiewich 1976). These articles make it clear that while it is important to retain an analytical distinction between incest and exogamy, rules and regulations governing sexual relations and who one may marry are closely interlinked in Micronesia. Incest regulations in Micronesia focus particularly on cross-sex siblings and the mother-child dyad, a finding that reinforces the earlier discussions above of the importance of matriliny and the centrality of sibling relations in these islands.

Labby (1976b) reported that for Yapese there were two kinds of incest: that among members of the same matrilineal clan *(ganong)*, and that among persons who had claims on the same land-estate *(tabinau)*. Of these, "the worst kind of incest was that between mother and child, or between brother and sister" (1976b, 172), all of whom are members of the same matrilineal clan. Clans are basic social units in Yap and clan membership forms an integral part of each individual's social identity. "The continuance of the clan was seen as depending upon the cultural rule of exogamy. To disobey that rule and commit incest was thought . . . to bring about the extinction of the clan itself" (1976b, 174). Similarly, incest among members of the same *tabinau* or land-estate, which passed from father to son, was viewed as destructive "self-consumption." Two members of the same land-estate group had to avoid sexual relations "because they would initiate an exchange which was basically inoperable. Marriage between two people of the same land-estate group would be like marriage between two persons of the same clan, that is, the land attempting to perpetuate itself and in this sense similarly 'cannibalistic.' Incest within the land-estate group thus threatened the process by which the value of the land-estate was maintained and enhanced over generations" (1976b, 177). From these observations, Labby concluded, it should be evident why mother-child or brother-sister incest was considered worse than that between father and daughter: "Mother and child and siblings were of the same clan as well as being members of the same land-estate. Were they to commit incest it could block both the proper reproduction of the clan *and* the proper transmission of the land-estate" (1976b, 177).

Marshall (1976b) noted that on Namoluk incest and endogamy are not linguistically distinguished; the local conception of incest is both a proscription on sexual relations and a prescription for exogamy. The Namoluk case directly raises the issue of whether there is a biological basis for the incest taboo: "Namoluk persons hold that incest can occur both between distant 'blood' relatives (members of the same matriclan) and between certain kin who are not linked by biogenetic ties at all" (1976b, 182). Closer biological kin comprise the *futuk* 'flesh and blood.' This grouping is made up of close uterine kin (members of the same subclan or matrilineage), who are related either as mother-child or as 'siblings.' Marshall describes the *futuk* as "the kernel of Namoluk kinship," with other categories of kin (more distant matrilineal relatives, patrilateral kin, and various sorts of created kin) forming a shell around this kernel.

As on Yap, there are degrees of incest on Namoluk: all such relationships are "bad," but incest within the *futuk* is worse than other kinds of incest. The key point here for anthropological theory is "that marriage and sexual relations are prohibited between persons *who treat each other* as 'parent', 'child' or 'sibling' " (Marshall 1976b, 184). Hence it is *behavior* rather than biology that is crucial in determining cases of incest for these people.

Pohnpeians have two common terms for the English word incest, which Jack Fischer, Roger Ward, and Martha Ward translated as "evil gazing" and "rotten corpse eater" (1976, 200). "Evil gazing" is the more general term, and it is extended to sexual relations and marriage (compare with Namoluk) "within the nuclear family other than between spouses, relations between anyone and parent's parent or sibling, between anyone and spouse's parent, between parallel cousins, and between members of a single matrilineage, matrilineal subclan or clan" (1976, 200). "Rotten corpse eater" is used to designate incest involving closer relationships—those within the nuclear family "and above all for brother-sister incest" (1976, 200). This lexical distinction suggests that Pohnpeians, like Yapese and the people of Namoluk, view some kinds of incest as worse than others. It also shows the emphasis that is placed on cross-sibling ties on Pohnpei as elsewhere in Micronesia.

Bikini and Arno atolls represent both chains (Ralik and Ratak) in the Marshall Islands, are ecologically distinct, and have populations of quite different sizes; and Bikini has historically been much more isolated than Arno. Thus the comparative study offered by Kiste and Rynkiewich (1976) is of particular value in providing us with examples of two quite different locations in the Marshalls regarding this subject.

Like the people of Namoluk, the small population of Bikinians prefer bilateral cross-cousin marriages, whereas those from Arno (which has five times the population) express no such preference (although cross-cousin marriages are allowed). Kiste and Rynkiewich explained this difference both as a consequence of the difference in size of the two atolls' populations, Bikini's relative isolation, and Arno's easy access to spouses from other nearby islands. These ecological and demographic differences also influence attitudes toward and the incidence of incest and exogamy. For example, in fourteen of the twenty cases of intraclan marriages recorded for Arno, only one spouse, or neither, was a member of an indigenous lineage, and "while the Arno people consider violations of clan exogamy to be 'wrong' or 'improper' and therefore theoretically 'forbidden', marriage and sexual intercourse between members of the same clan are not considered to be serious moral transgressions when only one of the partners is a member of a lineage indigenous to Arno" (1976, 221–222). On Bikini, by contrast, no cases of intraclan marriage had occurred, and "as each of the three clans is represented by a single lineage, the situation is similar to that found on Arno where no marriages have occurred among members of the same lineage" (1976, 223).[10]

Extending their basic argument for the differences they found between the two communities, Kiste and Rynkiewich concluded that both populations "have modified certain elements of Marshallese systems of kinship and marriage as they have responded to the ecological and demographic circumstances peculiar to their own home atolls and islands" (1976, 225). This has led the people of Arno to reject the rule of clan exogamy for the two largest clans, and to view breaches of clan exogamy as not very serious if committed by members of lineages indigenous to different atolls. On the other hand, the Bikinians, with a much more limited range of sexual and marital partners, have expanded the category of kinsmen with whom sex and marriage are appropriate, have developed a preferential cross-cousin marriage rule, and have accepted a relatively high frequency of improper marital unions.

There is scattered information on incest and exogamy restrictions for other Micronesian islands. Spoehr mentioned that there was "a strong feeling against sexual intercourse or marriage within the clan" on Majuro, and he recorded only one instance of intraclan marriage (1949a, 178–179). On Ifaluk, the incest taboo covers parents, siblings ("real and classificatory"), and clan members (Burrows and Spiro 1957, 301). A fact Burrows and Spiro recorded for Ifaluk concerning adoptive kin applies widely in Micronesia: "The *aivam* ['adoptee'] belongs to two kinship groups, his 'natural' as well as his adoptive. This means that he is subject not only to the incest taboos of his biological siblings, but to those of his adoptive siblings as well" (1957, 268). Ifaluk rules of exogamy also apply to cases of adoption along with the incest taboo: "Children adopted into a *kailang* ['matriclan'] other than their ancestral one may not marry members of either *kailang*" (1957, 125–126).

In the pioneering work on incest in Micronesia, Alfred Smith and John Kennedy (1960) compared the categories of relatives to whom incest taboos were extended in several closely related atolls in outer-island Yap State. Like Kiste and Rynkiewich (1976), they concluded that demographic and ecological factors accounted for the variability.

Smith and Kennedy found no variation in the extension of incest taboos to matrilineal relatives, with no cases of intraclan marriages on Woleai (Falalap and Falalis), Eauripik, and Lamotrek. However, they *did* find variability in the extension of incest taboos to non-clan relatives. Reportedly, neither Woleai nor Lamotrek had any marriages between consanguines of any sort, while on Eauripik there were "two instances of matrilateral cross cousin marriage, and two other marriages between persons who are more distant consanguineal relatives" (1960, 644).

Drawing on the published literature for Ifaluk, Smith and Kennedy concluded that Ifaluk was like Woleai and Lamotrek in having no cross-cousin marriage. In seeking to account for Eauripik's difference in allowing cross-cousin marriage, they mentioned a situation also found on Bikini and Namoluk, where cross-cousin marriages are preferred—that nearly half the population of Eauripik belonged to a single clan.[11] In their words:

> This explains why incest taboos are not extended bilaterally on Eauripik. If one spouse were always a member of the Woleai clan, an individual whose father is a member of the Woleai clan would marry a person who is also a member of the Woleai clan. Then the fact that the father and the spouse are members of the same clan would not mean, of course, that there is always a traceable relationship. There would always be an assumed relationship and sometimes a traceable one. This system, therefore, cannot maintain an aversion to marriage with the father's clan mates or relatives. This system is also conducive to the development of a preference for cross-cousin marriages. (1960, 646)

Along with this demographic consideration, Smith and Kennedy argued that an ecological difference (geographical isolation) helped account for marriage with consanguines on Eauripik. As with Bikini, Eauripik is relatively isolated (Bikini is eighty miles from its nearest neighbor, and Eauripik ninety miles). The problem with this ecological isolation explanation is that it does not account for cross-cousin marriage and island endogamy on Namoluk. Namoluk is *less* isolated (its nearest island neighbor is only thirty-five miles away), and yet 86 percent (820/949) of marriages in the genealogies took place between two Namoluk persons. Furthermore, Namoluk people have a high rate of cross-cousin marriage (nearly two-thirds of all marriages; see Marshall 1976b). Thus Namoluk (and Bikini, which has 66 percent cross-cousin marriages) is *far* above the few cases of cross-cousin marriage that Smith and Kennedy reported for Eauripik. From this it seems that the demographic argument may be a necessary but not sufficient explanation for variability in the extension of the incest taboo and the development of preferential cross-cousin marriage. Given the Namoluk example, the ecological argument (geographical isolation) does not seem to be supported.

The best account of demographic factors influencing incest and exogamy restrictions, and vice versa, is Ritter's (1980) discussion of how the bilateral extension of the incest taboo during Kosrae's severe depopulation in the nineteenth century led to an increase in incestuous marriages and affairs in one particular village nearly a century later. The bilateral extension of the incest taboo on Kosrae was associated with the extinction of matrilineal clans and was "both an *extension* of the rules [of exogamy] to first and second cross cousins and a *relaxation* of clan exogamy" (1980, 771). At that time, because of severe population loss, "the main problem that the Yewan area people and most other Kosraens faced was a lack of kin rather than a lack of appropriate nonkin to marry. Thus, the extension of the exogamy restriction to first and second cross cousins, consistent with the increasing emphasis on bilateral kinship, had little effect on the availability of marriage partners within the area" (1980, 764). As the repopulation of Kosrae occurred during the twentieth century, however, Yewan became increasingly inbred, such that in the early 1970s "nearly all of the individuals in Yewan under about 30 years of age are second cousins or closer. . . . Consequently, it has become extremely difficult for young Yewan Kosraens to find nonkin marital partners within the village" (1980, 764). Yewan people have tried to accommodate to this difficult situation in several ways, resulting in more village exogamy and a large increase in the number of unmarried young people; a third consequence of their dilemma, however, has been growth in the number of kin marriages—usually between second cousins. Ritter reported that second cousins commonly become lovers in the village as well. As Ritter noted (e.g., 1980, 763), all of this is consistent with the demographic argument advanced by Smith and Kennedy (1960), Kiste and Rynkiewich (1976), and Marshall (1975b): that cousin marriage is likely to occur in small, relatively isolated demes.

POSTMARITAL RESIDENCE RULES

When the subject of postmarital residence is brought to mind in anthropology, one thinks immediately of the famous debate between Goodenough (1956b) and Fischer (1958a) concerning the small island of Romónum in Chuuk Lagoon. Both men collected data on postmarital residence rules and choices on Romónum within three years of each other, yet they reached quite different conclusions about the classification of residence for this population of a few hundred people. This disagreement posed a significant quandary because at the time anthropologists were in the habit of classifying and labeling societies according to a variety of characteristics that were then compared statistically in cross-cultural samples. Such cross-cultural studies were complicated, or even rendered impossible, if the units of classification (e.g., the residential "types") were ambiguous. Fischer and Goodenough's disagreement also called into question the relevance of descent to the classification of residence.

Briefly, Goodenough found that 71 percent of Romónum's populace resided matrilocally and only 1.5 percent patrilocally, while Fischer reported that 58 percent resided matrilocally and 32 percent patrilocally. Using his own figures, Goodenough wrote, "we would not hesitate to classify Trukese society as essentially matrilocal," whereas with Fischer's data, "I would myself be inclined to classify Trukese society as bilocal" (Goodenough 1956b, 22). These two different sets of figures provided one of the earliest instances in which the issue of reliability in ethnographic reporting was raised and aired (cf. Caughey and Marshall 1989, 2–3; Heider 1988).

Noting and discussing two different problems—that of recognizing the patterns of residence in a society, and that of classifying the residence of individual couples—Goodenough (1956b) showed that the ethnographer needed more than simply census data to make accurate determinations of this sort. Fischer (1958a) set out to revise the general typology of residence rules then in use, with a goal of accounting for ambiguities of the sort highlighted by the Romónum material he and Goodenough had separately collected. Harry Raulet (1959) raised some caveats about Fischer's revised typology, to which Fischer (1959a) subsequently replied.

Prior to the Goodenough-Fischer debate, Fischer (1955) had published an article on avunculocal residence on the nearby atoll of Losap. Since the different classification of avunculocality turned out to be one of their major points of disagreement in the Romónum case, the Losap article is germane to this important theoretical controversy.

Aside from passing mention of "dominant" residence rules in various doctoral dissertations, there are relatively few other reports of postmarital residence rules in Micronesia. Alkire provided quite detailed data for Lamotrek, where he found that 67 percent of the populace resided matrilocally or uxorilocally (note Goodenough's report of 71 percent matrilocal on Romónum), 14 percent patrilocally or virilocally, and 17 percent resided with their adopters (Alkire 1965a, 48–49).[12] On the closely related atoll of Ifaluk, Burrows and Spiro included information showing that 68 percent of the married couples resided matrilocally, 10 percent patrilocally, and 20 percent heterolocally ("living in various other places") (1957, 132–133). And on the nearby island of Fais in the Western Carolines, according to Rubinstein, postmarital residence "is almost entirely virilocal, but about a third of all married couples have settled on the husband's adoptive estate, not his natal estate" (1978, 3). Thus even in closely related Carolinian societies the "dominant" residence rule varies considerably from island to island.

This variability is reinforced by studies of other places in Micronesia. Writing of the Marshall Islands, Spoehr commented, "It cannot be said that residence is prevailingly patrilocal, matrilocal, or neolocal. All forms occur" (1949b, 111). Likewise, Kiste indicated that on Bikini "there was no preferred rule of residence" and that "shifts in residence easily occurred" (1974, 70). At least traditionally in Palau "postmarital residence was initially patrivirilocal; at the death of the husband's father the couple either remained at the father's house . . . or moved to the husband's matrilineal house" (Parmentier 1984, 663). Residence has been virilocal on Kosrae since the 1920s or earlier (Ritter 1980, 764, 768).

In a thorough examination of principles of residence in domestic group formation (as opposed to postmarital residence as such) on Pingelap, Damas (1986) posited the principle of the solidarity of the father-son bond and "a somewhat weaker bond existing between brothers" to account for both virilocally oriented residence and the high frequency of nuclear family units. While there was a normative principle of virilocality on Pingelap, Damas analyzed a variety of data to show why it is not always realized in practice. The most prominent factor affecting achievement of the virilocal ideal was permanent emigration and circular migration of sons, and Damas (1986, 247) argued that "in addition to the cyclic changes in domestic unit formation and devolution, [these] powerful counter effects of emigration prevented a high degree of realization of the virilocal extended family as a residential unit." In his conclusions he suggested that "various factors will probably always operate to inhibit full realization of residential principles or norms" (1986, 251), and that analyses of residence probably ought to be confined to empirical data rather than normative abstract principles.

CONCLUSIONS

I have found little evidence that anthropological studies of kinship and social organization had a *direct* effect on colonial administration or policy during the trust territory period. While it is entirely possible that some of the more enlightened administrators read some of these works and incorporated their understandings into decisions they subsequently may have reached, it seems clear that this particular anthropological literature—unlike that, say, on land tenure, or on traditional political systems—has been of little practical import in Micronesia (see Petersen, chap. 5). Likewise, I doubt that these writings have had much effect on Micronesians themselves, save perhaps the few who may have found them helpful in completing college term papers.

But the impact of this scholarship on the discipline of anthropology has been very different. Data on kinship and social organization from Micronesia have played a central role in several significant anthropological debates and have been incorporated into the anthropological record in other important ways (e.g., into the Human Relations Area Files, which includes extensive materials on the Marshall Islands, Truk [Chuuk], Woleai, and Yap; see appendix 3). In part this has been because two leading figures in the anthropological study of kinship and social organization—Ward Goodenough and David Schneider —had their primary fieldwork experience in Micronesia. Not only in their ethnographically based books and articles, but also in broader theoretical treatises, these men have both publicized and highlighted data from the islands.

Probably the single most influential item from the published work on Micronesian kinship on the discipline of anthropology as a whole is Ward Goodenough's *Property, Kin, and Community on Truk* (1951). If one looks through the literature on kinship, one finds this book cited again and again (e.g., Fortes 1969; Keesing 1972; Stephens 1963). Goodenough's article on residence rules (1956b) also is very widely cited, mainly because the issues it addresses transcend the specifics of ethnographic location (see, e.g., Fortes 1969; Goody 1973; Heider 1988; Keegan and Maclachlan 1989; Keesing 1972). Many of Goodenough's other major works (e.g., Goodenough 1956c, 1965a,

1970), which are rooted in his ethnographic experiences in Chuuk and draw heavily on Micronesian material, have also had a profound impact on contemporary cultural anthropology (see Marshall and Caughey 1989 for a general discussion of this; see also Black, chap. 7).

David Schneider, like Ward Goodenough, has been a major player in postwar theoretical debates in anthropology—particularly in the realm of kinship. And like Goodenough, Schneider's more general theoretical work often has been heavily informed by his ethnographic experience in Micronesia. The volume he coedited on matrilineal kinship (Schneider and Gough 1961) is considered the "bible" on that topic, and one finds it referred to in many different sources (e.g., Joseph 1994; Keegan and Maclachlan 1989). One of its major illustrative chapters is based on material from Chuuk (Schneider 1961b), and the most widely quoted chapter in the volume uses many Micronesian examples (Schneider 1961a). Next to his iconoclastic work on American kinship, the book by Schneider that has found the widest readership in the discipline may be his *A Critique of the Study of Kinship* (1984). In this book, grounded fundamentally in his Yap material, Schneider argued that much of the anthropological research on kinship over more than the past century has been misguided and the analyses too simple to capture the full cultural complexity of the topic. Finally, Schneider's (1957b, 1962) early work on such topics as incest and double descent on Yap is often mentioned in more general discussions of these subjects (e.g., Fortes 1969; Shimizu 1991).

Adoption is a subject that has caught anthropologists' attention in the past two decades, and chapters in the major edited collections by Carroll (1970a) and Ivan Brady (1976), including those on Micronesian societies, are often cited by others when discussing adoption and fosterage as general phenomena or in other parts of the world (e.g., Carsten 1995; Eggan 1972; Guemple 1979; Lebra 1989; Modell 1994). The same is true of the chapters on siblingship in Micronesia contained in the ASAO monograph on that subject (Marshall 1981b). For example, John Moore (1988) made reference to Marshall's chapter on siblingship in Chuuk, and Charles Nuckolls (1993a) to DeVerne Smith's chapter on Palauan siblingship. The volume as a whole and various chapters within it receive attention from several contributors to Nuckolls' (1993b) edited collection, *Siblings in South Asia* (de Munck 1993; Pugh 1993; Weisner 1993), from Suad Joseph (1994) in her recent article about Lebanese siblings, and from Janet Carsten (1995) concerning relatedness among Malays in Pulau Langkawi.

Occasionally, other specific publications involving kinship and social organization in Micronesia have come in for extensive discussion in the wider disciplinary literature. Examples of this are the use Akitoshi Shimizu (1991) made of Labby's (1976a, 1976b) work on Yap, and the detailed treatment of Marshall's (1977) article on the nature of kinship in Chuuk in Brackette Williams' (1995) recent innovative look at the intersection of kinship, caste, race, and nationality.

In the material presented above I have sought to convey the idea that Micronesian kinship and social organization share a family resemblance, at the same time that they contain significant—occasionally even fundamental—differences. I have borrowed Marilyn Strathern's notion of "partial connections" as a way to discuss this. There are clear connections across Micronesia in such things as siblingship and adoption and fosterage, even as there are marked differences in descent systems, marriage practices, and postmarital residence rules. What is important, I think, is that there _does_ seem to be a conventional Micronesian social and cultural repertoire, although it must be recognized that some aspects of this repertoire are shared more widely in the Pacific than in Micronesia alone. Nevertheless, as I reread materials in preparing this chapter I was even more convinced that the time is ripe for synthetic scholarship in Micronesia. By this I certainly do not mean that the ethnographic record from these islands should be searched for a set of traits that might yield variations on a common theme, because I doubt that there is any single common theme that would encapsulate all of the sociocultural systems of Micronesia. Rather, in the search for anthropological partial truths, I believe that using a concept like "partial connections" can help us gain a better understanding of the _partial_ linkages and overlaps that exist.

NOTES

This chapter has benefited from helpful comments provided by William Alkire and Robert Kiste, for which I am most grateful.

1. For example, there is a very large literature on land and sea tenure in Micronesia. This literature is addressed only insofar as it bears specifically on the links among kinship, land, and food, and no attempt is made here to fully cover land tenure (a subject that would require a chapter in its own right). Similarly, there have been many interesting alterations in patterns of marriage in Micronesia as a consequence of migration and greater interisland and interareal contact (see, e.g., Marksbury 1993; Marshall 1975b; Ritter 1978–1979). These are not even mentioned below, where the focus is on traditional patterns of marriage.

2. And as is also well known, Guam and Saipan (and other locales in the Northern Marianas to a much lesser extent) today harbor significant immigrant populations from Asia and North America who have further altered social life and social forms on these islands.

3. Traditional Chamorro and Kosraen social organization was built around matrilineal clans (Ritter 1980; Spoehr 1954).

4. In fact, although he used different language to discuss these things, such "complex parts and uneven outgrowths" seem to have been in Goodenough's mind when he wrote his seminal article, "A Problem in Malayo-Polynesian Social Organization" (1955).

5. When Ken-ichi Sudo did his fieldwork on Satawal between 1978 and 1980, this had dropped to about 60 percent of all children under age 15 (1987, 97).

6. Writing of traditional Hawaiian culture, for example, Marshall Sahlins stated: "Parents and children are people of the same kind: they are composed of the same thing, whether by the reproduction of substance or its common consumption. It follows logically that a person whose food comes from a certain land—*'āina*—is a child—*kama*—of it, a *kama'āina*, just as those who are born to it. (In folk etymology, *'āina*, the 'land', is glossed as the 'feeding-place'.)" (1985, 28–29).

7. Sudo found a version of this taboo on Satawal, but on that island at least it applied differentially to males and females:

> *Yuun* is a verb meaning "to drink" or "to inhale", and this taboo strictly forbids sisters from touching anything their brothers have touched with their mouths. A sister is forever forbidden to handle any eating or cooking utensil which her brother has even once touched with his lips. Even if he has not touched the plate with his lips but has placed on the plate food which he has chewed, the plate and pot are taboo items. However, brothers are not forbidden to use their sisters' utensils or smoke their sisters' cigarettes (1985, 16).

8. Bill Alkire pointed out to me that in a matrilineal context, a man with more than one wife, where the wives were not sisters, would have to divide his time among three different land estates: his own (sister's), and those of his two or more wives. Hence constraints on the allocation of a man's labor may have been the most important limiting factor on such marriages.

9. Some, but by no means all, sibling-set marriages might also be cross-cousin marriages.

10. A similar situation pertained on Namoluk where no members of the same lineage *(eu futuk)* had married, although there had been five instances of intraclan marriage (Marshall 1976b, 185).

11. Kiste and Rynkiewich reported that 44 percent of the Bikini population (123/282) were members of one clan (1976, 215), and Marshall noted that 49 percent of the

Namoluk population belonged to a single clan (1976b, 195). Interestingly, in the time between 1951, when Smith gathered date for Lamotrek (Smith and Kennedy 1960, 644), and the time of Alkire's fieldwork there in 1962–1963, Mongalifach clan grew to 50 percent of the Lamotrek population (Alkire 1965a, 29). Marshall suggested that in such circumstances intraclan marriage will begin to occur (1976b, 195).

12. Alkire gave these as 68 percent, 12 percent, and 17 percent (1965a, 48), but a recheck of his calculations results in the slight correction reported here.

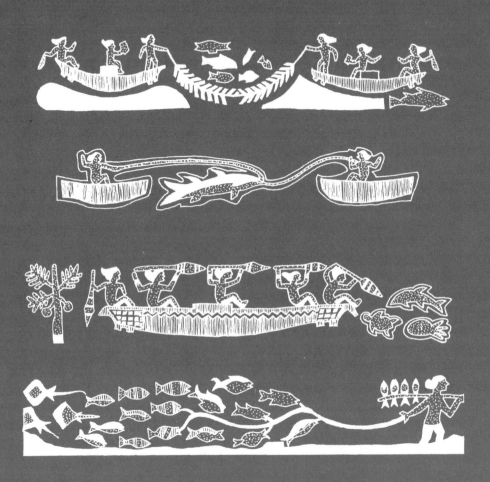

CHAPTER FIVE

Politics in Postwar Micronesia

Glenn Petersen

AMBIGUITY AND AMBIVALENCE PERVADE the American presence in the Western Pacific, Micronesians' responses to it, and the outlooks of anthropologists and others who have studied there.[1] Almost any generalization made about political events and processes there can be contradicted by another. Nonetheless, in this chapter I formulate several overarching points and observations:

1. that there are shared Micronesian political patterns, including leadership rooted in linked kin and territorial groupings, and political legitimacy grounded in elements of everyday experience;
2. that Micronesian societies are well prepared to deal with the world beyond the reef, by readily adopting foreign political forms in order to regain self-government, and by their own dual political structures hinging on distinctions between internal and external relations; and
3. that political anthropological studies of Micronesia have usually concerned the politics of the American presence as well as political processes indigenous to the islands.

THE SETTING

I begin by examining a topic often overlooked in considerations of the American presence in Micronesia: the wider geopolitical context. In his account of "America in Micronesia," Fred Kluge wrote of "America's accidental presence in the Pacific" (1991, 234), a telling phraseology that provides a highly fore-shortened perspective on America's history in the area. There is little about America's occupation of Micronesia that is novel, let alone accidental. To put the Western Pacific's strategic location in broader perspective, the Cold War, to which many attribute the American presence in the islands, was but the latest manifestation of a much longer historical process.

A lengthy history including the China trade, the whaling industry, disputes over guano islands, the Wilkes Expedition, and Congregationalist missions, should remind us that American interests in the Pacific intensified through-out the nineteenth century. By century's end, Hawai'i, American Samoa, Guam, and the Philippines had all been annexed or occupied. Serious consideration was given to including the Carolines and the other Marianas with the territo-rial booty acquired in the Spanish-American War (Millis 1989, 317, 381), and the navy had begun to formulate a set of minutely detailed contingency plans for the conquest of Micronesia, which were updated continuously until the United States finally invaded the islands during World War II (Miller 1991).

In the end, it was not so much the costs of conquering the islands that pro-voked the clamor for their outright annexation as it was a sense that earlier mistakes had been made and opportunities lost. American diplomatic insis-tence that no country should gain territory as a result of the war ultimately declared invalid the claims of those who called for undisputed American pos-session of Micronesia. The US military agreed to trusteeship only in the belief that its strategic provisions preserved American control over the islands in perpetuity.

In a survey of political geography, Martin Glassner argued that "in a real sense the United States acquired two separate empires consecutively: one con-tinental and the other (with one exception) insular" (1993, 285). Paraphrasing the old saw that the British empire was acquired in a fit of absentmindedness, he observed that "the empire of the United States was acquired enthusiasti-cally but administered absentmindedly." This "second American empire" dif-fered from other overseas colonial empires in that "it is never officially (and rarely unofficially) called an 'empire.' Nor are the individual units ever referred to as colonies" because "the United States is ambivalent at best and perhaps even embarrassed at having a colonial empire. . . . Few American citizens have been or are now aware of the empire" (1993, 285).

The politics of anthropology in post–World War II Micronesia were framed by this history and these assumptions; little was accidental about the Ameri-can presence in the islands. When control was ultimately assigned to the Interior Department, Micronesians found themselves in a position similar to that of American Indians, whose destinies were subject to the same changing administrative fashions, oscillating between poles of neglect and forced assimilation that can be traced back to the eighteenth century (cf. Kiste and Falgout, chap. 1).

It appears to me that American anthropologists' underlying familiarity with this history may explain some of the strains that have characterized their relations with both military and civilian administrations. Many were openly dubious of the politics of anthropology in Micronesia from the outset.

THE EARLY YEARS

The beginnings of American political anthropology in Micronesia may be dated to Laura Thompson's 1938–1939 Guam fieldwork, published as *Guam and Its People* (1941) by the American Council of the Institute of Pacific Relations, an eminently political organization. In his paper for the 1993 conference on American anthropology and Micronesia, Vicente Diaz placed Thompson's work on Guam "outside the realm of systematic anthropological research in Micronesia," and argued that it is treated as "an anomaly, an exception to the topic of anthropology, culture, history and Micronesia" (1993, 3–4). Diaz found, in general, that accounts of Chamorro history are little more than "occasions of western, especially American imperialism and notions of superiority as contrasted to Spanish tyranny" (1993, 4), and in particular, that Thompson stressed that the opportunity to do the *first* professional research on Guam was "more important" than her discovery of the arrogance and insensitivity of American military government on the island (Diaz 1993, 8). But neither her work in the 1940s nor her recent autobiography (Thompson 1991) seem to support these conclusions.

Thompson did not limit herself to a study of the internal dynamics of Guam's Chamorro society; she dealt explicitly with the politics of military occupation. Her criticisms of the navy's policies were so pointed, she once told me, that she was "blackballed" from ever returning. She feared the navy's history of cavalier administration in Guam would be repeated in the rest of Micronesia, and her 1944 article, "Guam: Study in Military Government," was meant as a warning of what might occur. Though others took up her critique as events unfolded in Micronesia, it seems only Thompson fully developed the point that the United States had *already* become a colonial power, and a rather lackluster one at that. The more common line was that the United States had no experience administering colonies and thus required the School of Naval Administration (SONA), staffed by anthropologists, to learn how to do so. Given the many years American forces had administered a small empire's worth of colonies, not to mention the occupations of Nicaragua, Haiti, and other satrapies, it is in retrospect rather remarkable that such claims were made.

Thompson argued that an effect of the military governor's "absolute authority" over Guam "was to cancel most of the native civil rights and the system of limited self-government which had grown up under Spanish rule. The Chamorros were reduced from full Spanish citizenship to indefinite status of 'wards' of the American Government" (1944, 149).[2] Thompson's concern on the eve of the navy's impending takeover in Micronesia was to point out the basic failures of American colonial administration: "The Guam record points to the dangers implicit in the increase of military government under the American flag and indicates the necessity of limiting such regimes to the smallest possible geographical area and of terminating them at the earliest possible date consistent with the needs of national defense" (1944, 153). She insisted that American policy should not only respect individual personality and "cultural diversity," but also "be aimed at encouraging and assisting native peoples toward the achievement of ultimate self-government" (1944, 153).

In another essay, Thompson delved more deeply into Chamorro history, writing of an "unrelenting native resistance" to the Spaniards, despite a "customary lack of political unity" (1946, 6). As a result of this struggle, she argued, the Chamorros had substantially modified the terms of the Spanish acculturation forced on them. While they lived in villages part of the time, they also managed to continue farming the hinterlands, thus "retaining ties to their ancestral lands (and all that this meant from the psycho-cultural point of view)." The Spanish were thus required to build on "what already existed and interfered relatively little with underlying native patterns of living" (1946, 7).[3] It appears to me that, Diaz's critique notwithstanding, Thompson both compared American administration unfavorably with Spanish rule and celebrated the Chamorros' relatively successful struggles to continue defining their own lives under the Spanish.

Yet another of Thompson's points also reappeared in subsequent years. She assailed the "internal rigidity of structure" and the "one-way flow of authority" that characterized Guam's naval government, insisting that these would prevent the "development of genuinely democratic political institutions or any real self-government" (Thompson 1946, 10–11). Thompson believed that this underlying political structure would make it impossible for individual administrators, no matter how well trained, to ameliorate conditions.

As a direct consequence of her disenchantment with American policy in Guam, Thompson foreshadowed the activities of a younger generation of Micronesianist anthropologists in the 1970s and 1980s. Diaz asked to what extent Thompson's work is typical, and "how it prefigures a whole tradition of American anthropology in Micronesia during and after the war when American anthropologists are employed by the US government" (1993, 11–13). In what follows I argue that her work was considerably more typical than critics of American anthropology in Micronesia have realized. Glenn Alcalay has found it "troubling that anthropologists—given their sociocultural training and supposed sensitivity about indigenous peoples—did not raise more of an objection concerning their role in aiding the colonial project in Micronesia" (1992, 186). In my own early work (Petersen 1971) I articulated similar views. But this perspective misapprehends the degree to which anthropologists in Micronesia were in fact aware of the contradictions of working there and took pains to communicate their concerns.

As the US military began to administer Palau and the Marianas, *Far Eastern Survey* and *Applied Anthropology* became venues for criticisms that were, if not always as direct as Thompson's, at least in harmony with her observations. Pieces by John Useem and John Embree, active duty naval officers at the time, were the first anthropological reports on postwar Micronesia.[4] These articles concerned the military administration of the islands and its consequences, and like Thompson's, illustrated both the nature of the research being done, and the close relationship between scholarship and advocacy that subsequently prevailed. Their work provides clear evidence that anthropologists in Micronesia have long been concerned not only with the study of political processes in the islands, but also with the politics of the American presence.

Useem accepted the widely shared assumption that the United States would permanently govern the islands, and went on to claim that it was inexperienced in "governing alien cultures" (1945b, 1; 1946b, 21). Because he thought it apparent that the islanders were incapable of "operating politically as an independent state," he saw no fundamental conflict between native and American interests (1945a, 101). Nevertheless, Useem was keenly sensitive to some fundamental contradictions inherent in America's position in the islands. He noted the "inner contradictions in the Americans' conception of their role": while the United States claimed to be liberating the islanders, it was simultaneously exercising needlessly stringent control over them (1946a, 42–43). Despite American claims about democracy and equality, most Americans in the islands viewed Micronesians as inferior (1946b, 23). Useem also queried whether administrative problems were due primarily to shortcomings of individual administrators or to the structure of colonial rule itself. After some equivocation, he suggested that a well-defined policy was of primary importance (1946a, 48–49), which was a fairly radical suggestion at the time. Elsewhere, Useem shared Thompson's outlook that the entire structure of colonial rule had to be changed (1945b).

Useem's views on the character of Micronesian sociopolitical life also raised basic themes that resurface in later work. For instance, he wrote of "native class structure with its preferential treatment of elite [*sic*]" and a Micronesian emphasis on social stratification, yet he also noted that "democratic processes are an inherent part of Micronesian society, [though] the means of expressing the collective will and the relationship of leaders to followers do not resemble Western ways" (1945a, 95; cf. 1945b, 2; 1946a, 40).

Useem was acutely conscious of acculturation issues and of the islanders' sophisticated responses to the pressures placed on them. He grasped that Micronesians had evolved a "dual social order": by means of "effective techniques for dealing with outsiders, they outwardly conformed but kept their ancestral ways in in-group relationships" (1946a, 47; cf. 1945b, 3). Ironically, he did not fully grasp the import of his own observation that because they were "old hands at playing the role of subordinates, Micronesians quickly developed the necessary techniques for getting along with their rulers" (1945a, 99). This may explain why he apparently believed that there was a "universal desire . . . to remain permanently under American jurisdiction" (1945a, 101).

Embree's published work on Micronesia focused almost entirely on the shortcomings of the American administration. Noting that the islanders had less freedom in 1946 than in 1936, and since the war was over, Embree asked whether continued paternalism was justified (1946a, 162). He decried navy restrictions on access to the islands, revealing that it had denied entry to, among others, an unnamed anthropologist (clearly Thompson) (1946a, 163). He saw in this behavior the beginnings of what has sometimes been called the "zoo" policy,[5] ostensibly intended to protect the islanders from unfortunate cultural influences. Embree insisted that German and Japanese policies had already transformed the area—and that "the clock cannot be turned back" (1946a, 163).

Embree maintained that both military and civil administrations were totally subordinate to military concerns (1949, 207–208). Military government officials, having absolute power, "often come to regard all attempts of people under their jurisdiction to better their condition as subversive" and this absolute power in time produces overwhelming attitudes of superiority (1949, 217–

218). But Embree did not excuse these administrators on the grounds that the United States lacked experience governing colonies. The US military, he noted, had already had "extensive experience" in the administration of civilian populations in Latin America and the Philippines, among other places (1949, 209). Like Thompson and Useem, Embree was eager to see anthropologists play a central role in the American administration of Micronesia to redress these wrongs.

Unfortunately, it was not long before anthropologists moved beyond such criticisms to open clashes among themselves. The critiques launched by Thompson, Useem, and Embree may in fact have been responses to the activities of some anthropologists who were involved in formulating military policy in Micronesia. George Peter Murdock, John Whiting, and Clellan S. Ford had left Yale for the US Navy's Office of Occupied Areas where they were apparently quite influential (Bashkow 1991). A memorandum outlining an administrative framework for postwar Micronesia was drafted "in language that leaves little doubt of Murdock's primary authorship" (Bashkow 1991, 181). Maintaining that the islands' "feudal," even "primitive political tradition" assured the failure of any attempt to "impose" representative government, the document concluded that "all in all, the interest of the inhabitants (and incidentally, the best interests of the United States) would be best served by establishing in most of these islands a strong but benevolent government—a government paternalistic in character, but one which ruled as indirectly as possible" (Richard 1957a, 18–19). The memo called for complete naval control over the area "on a permanent or at least semi-permanent basis" (Bashkow 1991, 180–181)—perhaps a quid pro quo for ensuring that anthropology would be granted an important part in formulating these paternalistic policies. The navy's initial offer of funding for anthropological research in Micronesia, drafted in part by Murdock, cited its " 'pressing need' for information relevant to island government," given "the obscurity of the native system of land tenure and the scarcity of knowledge concerning the political and social structure of native communities" (1991, 185).

Perhaps it was to safeguard anthropology's potential in Micronesia that Felix Keesing attempted to refute the charges leveled by Thompson, Useem, and Embree. As associate director of the School of Naval Administration at Stanford, Keesing (1947) insisted that the Guamanians enjoyed a large measure of self-government and that in Micronesia the navy was putting "far greater powers into native hands" than had the Japanese (1947, 63). He described the degree of self-government to "be allowed to such peoples"—

that is, "the so-called 'backward' sections of humanity"—as the most "ticklish" question facing those who were deciding what to allow. Keesing was confident that under the tutelage of the Americans being trained at the School of Naval Administration, Micronesians would soon be debating the ideals of freedom and democracy "about as vigorously as they are [discussed] among most Guamanians" (1947, 63). Keesing agreed that American military demands were the "paramount consideration" in formulating policy in the area, and that it was therefore best to keep the navy in charge of administering the islands (and perhaps keep his school in business). In time some degree of self-government might be achieved, but independence could never be expected (1947, 65).

Fearing that anthropology was in danger of being corrupted, Edward T. Hall, who worked in Micronesia with the US Commercial Company in 1946, pursued the issue in an article entitled "Military Government on Truk" (Hall 1950a). He described "how applied anthropology was practiced (and disregarded)" by chronicling a series of missteps taken by the military government as it attempted to reorganize local Trukese (now Chuukese) politics. He concluded that "it was difficult to convince the military that they would have to exercise great ingenuity in order to govern the Trukese or else accept the fact that the chiefs were still running things to suit themselves and paying mere lip service to the Americans" (1950a, 25, 28). He seemed certain that the Trukese had their own notions concerning the role of chiefs in island affairs, and that the military government was equally adamant that the Trukese learn to do things the American way.

Thomas Gladwin's (1950) response might be described as near apoplectic.[6] He feared that Hall's criticisms might prompt the military to stop employing anthropologists (he was at the time a high-ranking administrator in Truk and had been a Coordinated Investigation of Micronesian Anthropology [CIMA] researcher). He also wanted to explain, however, why efforts to alter Truk's political organization were not working as smoothly as they should have (1950, 18). Gladwin noted that Trukese chieftainship "was very different from the clearly defined and powerful institutions found in most of the other areas of Micronesia" (1950, 17). He thus touched on one of the more intractable problems in the study of Micronesia's indigenous political institutions: the relative degree of power and authority invested in chiefs and elites.

The profoundly contradictory character of this early work in applied political anthropology is highlighted by Gladwin's remark that the point of "reorganizing the political structure of Truk" was "to restore to the people their control over their native officials without at the same time making the system so diffuse that its usefulness to the administration would be gone" (1950, 19). The people were to be afforded control over their own leaders, but not to a degree that would in any way threaten American control. Absent was any recognition that previous colonial administrations had done exactly the same thing: attempted to integrate the local polities into a new system of indirect rule. Admitting that "the administration requires certain changes in the political structure of the society in order to accomplish its objectives," Gladwin went on to explain that those objectives were "simply to meet the needs of the people with the greatest economy of effort on their part and ours" (1950, 23). In retrospect, it is clear—and it was certainly clear to many of Gladwin's contemporaries in Micronesian applied anthropology—that America's primary objective in Micronesia was to occupy the area with the greatest economy of effort.

ETHNOGRAPHIC RESEARCH IN THE IMMEDIATE POSTWAR YEARS

Despite the extraordinarily productive labors of members of the Thilenius Expedition (1908–1910), Micronesia was still poorly understood in the mid-twentieth century. For example, Robert H. Lowie's *Primitive Society* (1921), which went into its fourth printing in 1953, portrayed a Micronesia we now find unrecognizable: The "nobility held undisputed sway, looking down with supreme scorn upon their serfs . . . who are completely subject to their master's caprice" (1921, 217). Lowie insisted that the liberating influences of missions and colonial administration had thus far been unable to wrest these benighted souls free of their absurd fealty (1921, 351–352). This outlook may shed some light on Murdock's assumptions about Micronesian feudalism and his political brief for benevolent paternalism in the islands.

While Murdock's ambitious plans for anthropology in Micronesia emphasized the utility of an applied program, scholars affiliated with the Pacific Science Association, such as E. S. C. Handy, Sir Peter H. Buck, Edwin Grant Burrows, and Felix Keesing, sought support for an alternative research project, one that "did not lend itself easily to producing results of any 'utility' to colonial administration." Handy "warned that Pacific research 'will assume a very different shape if Murdock picks it up and carries on with it,' and he 'emphatically' opposed suggestions 'that the future of research and administration in Pacific islands is to be largely a function of the U.S. Navy Department' " (Bashkow 1991, 183). These scholars wanted instead to free areal research from the traditional domination of whatever colonial power happened to reign at the moment, but they were ultimately thwarted by the strategic provisions of the trusteeship, which left the navy and its anthropologists in control (Bashkow 1991, 184–185).

Murdock's CIMA program attempted to respond to both "pure" and applied research imperatives. Its participants were able to select their own topics for research, but at the same time Murdock informed them that funding was being "allocated to projects roughly in proportion to their correspondence with administrative needs and priorities" (quoted in Bashkow 1991, 186). It appears that administrative needs asserted precedence. In supervising Harvard's Yap project, for instance, Douglas L. Oliver felt it necessary to remind David M. Schneider and his colleagues, midway through their work, that the navy funding made their own dissertation projects "secondary" to the studies of social organization and depopulation they were obligated to provide (Bashkow 1991, 220).

Nevertheless, the CIMA participants produced a wealth of high-quality ethnographic studies. I draw on this work to emphasize important, recurrent themes, and to relate these to postwar anthropology as a whole and to more specific issues deriving from the American presence in the area. These themes include the nature of traditional leadership, concepts of rank, the intersection of territorial and kinship-based patterns of social organization, survival of traditional political systems, interisland relations, and land tenure. Finding no overriding order inherent in this material, I have organized it arbitrarily, beginning with the smallest atolls, then moving from west to east in considering the larger islands, ending with Leonard E. Mason's comparative study of atoll political organization.

In what follows, I single out key areas that reflect the shared, commonly encountered concerns of those who undertook analyses of politics in Micronesian communities during the years immediately following World War II.[7] Edwin G. Burrows and Melford E. Spiro's *An Atoll Culture* (1970), first published in 1953, is an exemplary model of the genre. Simultaneously comprehensive and concise, it conveys the authors' respect and admiration for the people of Ifaluk.

The relevant portions of the Ifaluk book commence with a consideration of "property" and an attempt to clarify misunderstandings about its nature, undoubtedly a reflection of Murdock's concern for the navy's preoccupation with "native systems of land tenure" (Bashkow 1991, 185).[8] Although islanders referred to certain pieces of land as belonging to the chiefs, the authors explained, these parcels were equivalent to what was termed "public property in the U.S. Ifaluk's political economy should not be mistaken for feudalism" (Burrows and Spiro 1970, 146).[9] In trying to determine whether it was the clans (as opposed to individuals and lineages) that owned or controlled property, Burrows and Spiro first learned that the reefs and lagoon belonged to individual clans, but this was disputed later, when the island's five chiefs met together and decided that these areas belonged collectively to the chiefs (1970, 150). While it was determined that there were some small differences in the size of landholdings, no one was without land (1970, 169).

Variations, contradictions, and ambiguities were likewise found in the division and organization of labor. When asked whether a chief might successfully demand agricultural produce, for example, one man initially told them he could, but in another context the same man emphatically denied that this was so. Any division of labor was minimal, and certainly not organized around differences in rank. Indeed, the chiefs were among the island's most industrious men (Burrows and Spiro 1970, 160). Particularly noteworthy is Burrows and Spiro's discussion of how communal tasks were undertaken: there was "utter anarchy" (1970, 317). On the only occasions they were able to observe chiefs giving orders, a chief "did indeed give orders, but so did nearly everybody else." There was simply no way to determine, through observation, who was in charge. "Ifaluk still extends democracy to economic production," they concluded, explicitly contrasting life there with the American way (1970, 162–163). Women seemed to do more than their share of the drudge work, but were not "downtrodden," and managed their own affairs without supervision from the men (1970, 159). Under certain circumstances, women could even become chiefs (1970, 185).

The hierarchy of rank ran through every aspect of social life: "Rank is so highly valued and respected that it stands out as one of the master-values of this culture" (Burrows and Spiro 1970, 179). Even so, the only status divisions they could find—between chiefs and so-called commoners—were "part-time distinctions," visible only on formal occasions. Under ordinary circumstances, it was impossible to determine anyone's rank from personal interactions within social groups. Everyone attempted to act unostentatiously, and this effectively prevented humiliation of inferiors (1970, 179–180). There was one exception: chiefs were expected to make more gifts, and the highest chief was expected to give "lavishly" (1970, 173).

Rank, principally justified by clan and lineage seniority and the genealogical seniority of individuals within these groups, was paralleled by notions about territory: localities, specific places, and portions of places or buildings were also ranked (Burrows and Spiro 1970, 190). And although rank was rooted in clanship, it was conceptually merged with territoriality; chiefs had authority over localities as well as over their own kin groups (cf. Marshall, chap. 4). The specific character of this authority, however, was a source of considerable ambiguity and of conflicting reports from the people themselves—they could not agree on what it was (Burrows and Spiro 1970, 186–187).

Burrows and Spiro ended their chapter on "government" with the following comparison: "In form the government of Ifaluk is strictly aristocratic. In practice it is quite democratic, in the sense that every individual gets a chance to express his opinion and can make sure that it will be heard and considered by those in power. The government of the United States, in form, is strictly democratic. In practice, as all citizens seem to agree, it falls far short of that ideal" (1970, 198). They concluded that if democracy were the desired end, there was simply no need to change Ifaluk's traditional form of government (1970, 198–199).

In *Kapingamarangi: Social and Religious Life of a Polynesian Atoll* (1965), Kenneth P. Emory described a society much like Ifaluk, despite its Polynesian origins. Discussing land tenure, Emory stressed that all land was privately held and that there was a remarkable degree of equality among all the island's families (1965, 80, 92). He organized his discussion of Kapinga politics around a system of dual chieftainship, with sacred *(ariki)* and secular chiefs. The only "class" distinctions were between the sacred leaders and the rest of the people, and Emory noted that members of the sacred lineage did not think of themselves as superior to others (1965, 93). Virtues such as industriousness and humility were desired in all people, but were particularly expected of leaders (1965, 79, 98).

Emory's descriptions of actual social practices were not as extensive as those of Burrows and Spiro. However, he described council meetings attended by all of the island's mature (age thirty and older) men and women in which even the youngest were free to speak and there was no order of precedence in the speech-making (1965, 96, 101). The island's *ariki* was initially appointed as magistrate by the US administration and then elected to his position by the people. Earlier chiefs had served in similar roles for preceding colonial administrations, though at one point people had apparently become dissatisfied with their chief, and convinced the Japanese to replace him (1965, 94, 102).

In turning to William Lessa's Ulithi work, I focus particularly on the relationships among Yap, Ulithi, and the rest of the Central Carolines known collectively as "the Woleai." Lessa sought to reconstruct the system of voyages from the easternmost islands through Ulithi and on to Yap as it was reported to have functioned in its proto-contact glory days. He detailed the complexities of the system and discussed the relevance of changes in it for American administration in the islands.

At the heart of Lessa's analysis lay two key elements. First, the system included multiple, discrete, and yet thoroughly interrelated aspects, which he termed political (or tribute), land-ownership (the *sawei*), and magico-religious. Second, in the Ulithians' memory, the system as it had operated in its heyday conferred more benefits than costs on the atoll peoples. Lessa referred to this network of relationships variously as "the Yap Empire" (1950b), the "Yap sphere of authority" (1950c, 29), and "the political dominance . . . exercised by the people of Yap . . . over certain subject islands to the east" (1956, 67)—that is, he consistently characterized these arrangements in political terms. Nevertheless, he portrayed the system as resting on underpinnings that were not essentially political, but rather more concerned with notions of kin reciprocity and the bidirectional movement of important resources. For instance, in analyzing the flow of goods, he concluded that "the balance is really in favor of the tributary islands" (1950c, 43); and in describing certain forms of behavior required of outer islanders visiting Yap, he reported that because the same taboos were observed by the Yapese in similar circumstances, they were thus "impartial and not designed to maintain the superiority of any group" (1950c, 44). Moreover, in his portrayal of the *sawei,* he acknowledged that ownership of the land should not be taken too literally, given that Ulithians themselves "never referred to it as implying land ownership" (1950c, 41). Unfortunately, such terms as "tribute," "rent," "landlord-serf systems," and "caste" run throughout his work and have received far more attention than the caveats that appear beside them. Lessa asserted these conclusions with considerable assurance, but it is important to remember that his descriptions of interisland relations were in fact speculative reconstructions, that largely reflected the Ulithians' outlook and experience rather than the perspectives of the many peoples inhabiting atolls to the east of them.

Lessa made it clear that within the overall context of exchange relations, movement of material resources between high and low islands constituted the most frequent form of exchange and had the greatest impact on the course of islanders' daily lives. These economic aspects of the *sawei* system far overshadowed its religous and political attributes.

Lessa's early work on clans and lineages reflected some of the conceptual problems encountered by nearly all ethnographers working in the area. After finding distinctions between greater and lesser clans, and concluding that these distinctions were based on the size of their landholdings, he then acknowledged that some groups with "big" status "are really comparatively unimportant in the local scene" and that local political standing was often quite independent of a group's place in the *sawei* (1950c, 34).[10]

Lessa concluded that the old Yapese empire was disintegrating and that this was largely a good thing. He recommended that the American administration follow a laissez-faire policy because he thought a sudden break undesirable: a "slow break . . . would give schools and missions time to alter values and beliefs" (1950b, 18). Lessa's recommendations were based on the premise that "the natives are not prepared for immediate change," especially older people who were not eager to cut ties with Yap—time had to be allowed for "the old conservatives to die out" (1950b, 18). Ulithi would in time, however, serve as a "spearhead" for the coming "revolt" against Yap: "Agencies for the breakdown of the Yap empire already exist and operate. The American administration, wittingly or not, fosters accelerated efficacy of these agencies through missions, schools, trade, motorized transportation and democratic ideals. The trend is irreversible and plans to aid it should be made accordingly. This should be done discretely so as not to cause unpleasant reverberations" (1950b, 18).

John Useem found Palau simultaneously more modernized and more traditional than he had imagined. In his view Palauan society was much more vibrant and resilient than the American occupation forces were prepared for, and Palauans were not very interested in returning to any sort of idealized past. He believed them to be far more eager than other island peoples to retain a foreign presence in their islands because they had been successful at modifying their lives without undermining the cultural foundations of their society. This adaptability was, in turn, a consequence of what he saw as a high tolerance for variation within the society. The very character of Palauan society was traditionally a matter of dispute (1950, 142–143). Useem pointed, for instance, to "internal contradictions" in succession to leadership positions. In one case, "two rivals for the headship appeared, each with legitimate claims based on two different cultural traditions" (1945c, 582–583). Useem observed that "foreign governors, native political factions, and the personality of the office holder himself profoundly affect the actual role played by the chief. Hence, even within a given society the activities of the chiefs are not alike" (1948, 24). He also discussed competing stereotypes of Palauan chiefs: one strong and ruthless, the other devoted to using authority as a means of advancing conditions for the entire community. This disparity was reflected in contemporary disputes concerning the proper behavior of chiefs.

Useem was particularly interested in the nature of power, and his analyses of Palauan politics examined the array of checks and balances built into them. "Although power was distributed unequally and along hierarchical lines, it was not linear but circular. While chiefs outranked other title-holders, their right to rule was circumscribed" (1950, 144). Only in this context can we apprehend his remark that chiefs "were the personification of power" (1950, 144). He described chiefs as the senior ranking members of the society, and then argued that it was only under colonial rule that "the symbolic status of senior-ranking position was made into a functional one of 'chief,' who was assumed to be supreme within his jurisdiction in a manner like that of the sovereign in the homeland of the foreigners" (1952, 264).

At every turn, Useem argued, Palau's leaders were checked by their communities. No title-holder could act without the approval of the others; individual and clan rank, the latter theoretically immutable, were undergoing continual change; rules that apparently ordered succession did not guarantee anyone a position of authority (1952a, 268). In some areas even low-ranking clans and villages had the right to argue in councils and to exercise a veto. In other localities, criticism of the elite was supposedly a grave offense, but people commonly would "acquiesce to any orders given but actually . . . evade their execution while verbally simulating compliance" (1950, 144). Useem called these "negative defenses" and explained that they allowed for individual autonomy without undermining "the system of power itself" (1950, 144–145). In his 1945 articles, Useem described Palauan political organization in formal, almost abstract terms, but by the end of the decade he was much more concerned with the "actual" operation of political life—a shift not all those who worked in the area were either willing or able to make.

Useem's interest in power was leavened by the careful attention he paid to the effects of colonial rule on indigenous political structures and organization. He reported that these processes both weakened and strengthened the authority of traditional leaders (1945c, 575; 1950, 146), but as time passed he became increasingly convinced that a succession of foreign administrations had been determined to centralize the local polities in order to make them instruments of indirect rule. He described how the American military governor had assigned to the heads of Palau's two confederacies "duties of the heads of states. On the premise that ancestral customs were being reestablished, the governor delegated to these two officials more authority than they had ever possessed before, and the confederations were transformed into formal political states. The heads of the confederations were eager to capitalize on this rare opportunity to strengthen their control and proceeded to do so" (1952, 266).

In response to these long-term intrusions, the Palauans devised what Useem (1945c) termed a system of "in-facing" and "out-facing" chiefs. Later, however, he reframed this: "To shield the native leadership from foreign pressures and, in part, to carry out duties assigned by the foreigners, a dual power structure evolved. One political organization 'faced' the foreigners, while the other 'faced' the natives" (1952, 264–265). These parallel systems sometimes led to struggles for preeminence between those who operated within them, in a sense defeating the very purpose for which they were evolved (1945c, 579).[11]

Useem was conscientious in his generalizations. He cautioned that "Micronesia" was a foreign term that the Palauans did not use, nor did they consider themselves part of something called Micronesia. The many islands were traditionally autonomous; no "native empires" existed in the area (cf. Lessa's [1950b] use of the term "empire" with regard to Yap). Moreover, Useem warned against any attempts to apply his own analyses of Palauan political institutions to other regions or to generalize about Micronesian social organization: "To say that the chieftainship system prevails in the Carolines and the Marshalls gives little indication of the role of the chief in each society" (1948, 23). He did, nevertheless, go on to generalize about some of his earlier criticisms of the United States' role in the islands.

Useem was dubious about grafting American political forms onto Palauan society and saw little need for doing so, arguing that it was a mistake "to presume that there is no real democracy in Palau's traditional patterns" (1952, 277). He was especially skeptical that a colonial power ruling by fiat could even pretend to be in position to introduce democratic institutions. Palau's nominally hereditary rule did not mean that it was an autocratic society, and indeed, the form of democracy the United States introduced seemed to be "a manipulative symbol rather than a human value of worth" (1952, 279).[12] Useem's views matched those expressed by Burrows and Spiro.

Useem's Palauan work may be compared usefully with Homer G. Barnett's. Barnett saw many of the same contradictions, but often interpreted them differently. He found the Palauans quite comfortable with their colonial history, pointing out that, unlike the Pohnpeians, they had "never risen against their foreign overlords" (1960, 12). The "waywardness of human destiny produces an ambivalent attitude toward those who hold the reins of power"

(1960, 13). But he also saw in their dealings with these rulers a "residue of latent hostility" masked by "tact, politeness, and reserve" (1960, 13).

Barnett noted in Palauans a "deep sense of inferiority that their treatment by foreigners has reinforced" and concluded that "this attitude has impeded the efforts of Americans to instill democratic principles and promote their long-range objective of self-determination" (1960, 16–17). These comments call attention to the differences between Barnett's outlook and Useem's: Useem viewed the Palauans as successfully working around the imposition of foreign rule, while Barnett saw them as resigned to it.

Regarding the Palauan political style, Barnett and Useem were largely in accord. Barnett referred to the cooperative, joint character of authority and political initiative, and to the emphasis on deference: "Everyone is humble, poor and unimportant," despite their "obsession" with ambition (1960, 15). But Barnett significantly amplified our knowledge of a key factor Useem over-looked—the tensions between age and rank. "In Palau, age itself commands respect, but so does success; and often these two qualifications for esteem and authority do not coincide" (1960, 58). This was a result of the simultaneous existence of two levels of leadership and two classes of titles. One class of chiefs was relevant solely within clans, while the other operated within com-munities at large—that is, it was territorial in nature. Leadership could extend over large units or small segments of either kin groupings or territories. Some men—called *rupaks*—held both types of titles and could exercise authority beyond their kin group and immediate surroundings. In earlier times these leaders possessed "authoritarian power," but foreign rule had chipped away at it (1960, 58–59). Barnett perceived that sometimes relatively young men held higher-ranking titles than older men. A younger man with wisdom would defer to an older man with a high title. Older men with low titles, however, were in an awkward position since a high title was a sign of success; without such a title they were in an ambiguous, even "pathetic" position. "The diffi-culty is that the Palauan theory of social existence does not fit the facts of life" (Barnett 1960, 60). Moreover, since "Palauan reputations are based upon present activity, not on the memory of past glory, . . . a man cannot rest on his laurels; there are too many others who want to make a name for them-selves" (1960, 60). Such crosscutting spheres or realms of prestige are widely encountered in Micronesia and are in fact responsible for much of these societies' extraordinary political success.[13]

Ward H. Goodenough's *Property, Kin, and Community on Truk* (1951) is a complex work in which a discussion of Chuukese politics is rooted in an exegesis of corporate, land-owning kin groups. Goodenough explained that his focus on property relationships (i.e., land tenure) was a consequence of realizing that "the aspects of Trukese social structure described depended for their definition" on these relations (1951, 12). He acknowledged, nevertheless, that "important for the orientation of our study was the navy's sponsorship of the research and the interest it expressed in using the results to develop an informed administration in Micronesia" (1951, 12). Goodenough's long-term theoretical interests, reflected in the body of his work, were at least partly shaped by the requirement "that a report on land tenure so formulate the principles of native property law that an administrator would be equipped to assess claims and settle disputes" in such a manner "that the natives would feel that justice had been done in accordance with their principles" (1951, 12). In order to accomplish this he set out to produce what he likened to a "grammar of culture" (1951, 12). But Goodenough was also particularly concerned with the politics of status, a topic to which he would later return (1965a). Consequently, he paid considerably more attention to ways in which status positions were differentiated from one another than to either the relative downplaying of status differences or the tensions that arose when the differences were simultaneously exalted and diminished.

Goodenough noted the extremely fragmented Chuukese political scene, with local districts that were politically independent; the "district chiefship was the highest political office" (1951, 129).[14] The clans or lineages within a district were ranked according to the seniority of their alleged arrival in the area, and the district chief was the head of the senior kin group (1951, 136). One did not have to reside in a locality to be a member of it.[15] We see here the basic Micronesian intersection of clan and territory: the categories are both distinct and overlapping. Moreover, Goodenough observed that patrifiliation was of great importance in binding together matrilineages within these districts: "It is the patrilineal tie, coupled with territorial localization and cemented with the obligations of divided ownership, which makes a district a social as well as a territorial unit" (1951, 138–139).

Goodenough described Chuukese chieftainship as rather rigid in its patterns of succession, explaining that "chiefship is exercised . . . by the oldest man of the founding lineage" (1951, 142). The seniority of the ranking lineage meant that it held "residual title" to the district's land, and the "provisional title holders to territory . . . owe the chief periodic gifts of produce from the land" (1951, 142). If a lineage should fail in this obligation, "the chief has the right to

*Saul Riesenberg with unidentified
Micronesians, Pohnpei, 1963. Riesenberg Collection, Pacific Collection, University of Hawai'i Library.*

confiscate its holdings" (1951, 142).[16] On the other hand, a district chief had
"relatively little jurisdiction over members of his district. . . . A chief who
threw his weight around too much would find the rest of the district taking
sides against him in open feud. He would be killed, and his lineage would be
exterminated or driven out of the district" (1951, 142).[17]

In few works has a Micronesian political system been analyzed more
closely than in Saul Riesenberg's *The Native Polity of Ponape* (1968). His "salvage ethnography" approach led Riesenberg to reconstruct an idealized and
highly formal political structure, rather than to chart the dynamics of Pohn-

peian political organization as it actually functioned.[18] He was inclined to describe paramount chiefdoms as having been "organized on a feudal basis," to claim that the heads of the local chiefdoms or sections were "appointed by and formerly held their fiefs as vassals under the principal tribal chiefs," and to write that "in theory all the land formerly belonged ultimately to the [chiefs] who received tribute and whose rule was absolute" (1968, 8). Pohnpei's matriclans had no clan chiefs other than those who were heads of the paramount and local chiefdoms, while ranked matrilineages were headed by "the senior man of each." Riesenberg termed the subclans or lineages controlling the two parallel lines of titles "royal and noble classes" and reported that the ideal was for them to intermarry exclusively, so that "all high chiefs carried royal blood on one side and noble blood on the other" (1968, 14). Chiefly authority was underlain by one or more protective spirits or ancestral ghosts, whose anger at failures "to perform proper acts of fealty" would lead to retribution. Of the commoners Riesenberg concluded, "Their status corresponded much more closely to that of a feudal peasant than that of a slave" (1968, 15)—language hinting of a dialogue with Lowie, under whom he did his doctoral work.

In analyzing the complexities of the Pohnpeian title system, Riesenberg attempted to describe an ideal model equally applicable to all of the islands' paramount chiefdoms, despite the great variation among them that the historical data suggest. And although he discussed some of the historical dynamics of relationships among the paramount chiefdoms, he portrayed the chiefdoms as essentially fixed in size and status.

After elaborating on the formalities of the political system, Riesenberg acknowledged that "the actual state of affairs is, however, quite different" (1968, 34). Neither succession to the chieftainship nor advancement within the ranks was ever a certain matter, with exceptions in fact being the rule: "We have until now spoken as though promotions and succession in the title hierarchy were regulated mainly by the principle of clan seniority.... But a significant omission in this presentation remains, namely, the acquisition of titles through prestige competition" (1968, 76). While the leading clans tended to "monopolize" the higher titles, "it is clear that the majority of mature men must possess tribal titles and that among them must be a large number of commoners" (1968, 76). The status of those holding higher titles was "ascribed" and that of those holding lesser titles was "achieved." Achieved status was won largely through competitive contributions to feasts, the regular presentation of first fruits, the performance of "service" of various types, and warfare (1968, 76).

Riesenberg concluded that "Ponapean life seems to focus particularly on those activities we have labeled political." Their time and energy were devoted to interpersonal competition, and the extraordinary productivity of their agricultural system allowed them to direct "a great part of their energies into political channels." Their political system was thus in a "fluid state" but well balanced by an abhorrence of "self-aggrandizement." Despite his references to feudalism, Riesenberg recognized that "unilateral decisions are seldom made; lower title holders are consulted, public opinion is sounded, and deference is paid to the principle of a fair distribution of titles." The chiefs "seldom ran roughshod over their tenants, despite the native theory that they owned all the land" (1968, 110).

Riesenberg's monograph easily lends itself to the excesses of tendentious ethnology. Most descriptions of Pohnpei's polity draw from the more formalized aspects of his discussion and ignore details of the system's flexibility and its lack of any real dynamics resembling feudalism. Pohnpei possesses a complex system of ranked titles, but daily political life is not much different from that of most other high islands in the Carolines and is organized around the same basic political principles that seem to characterize all Micronesian societies.

In an article first published in 1959, Leonard Mason (1968) compared the resource bases and sociopolitical organizations of seven Micronesian atolls. Of these, only Arno appeared to have a political system in which authority over production and distribution extended beyond the family. Mason found that while family groupings were generally capable of producing enough to meet their own needs, they were less autonomous in other realms, and that reciprocity was not so much a matter of economic necessity as "a social recognition of the respective rights and obligations of participating families" (1968, 324–325).

Pointing to first-fruits ceremonies, Mason argued that ties between chiefs and the people were rooted in "the popular belief that the office of chief symbolizes the source of food, e.g. the land on which it was grown may have been settled originally by the chief's ancestors," though he specified that this carried no implication of rent or tribute (1968, 326 327).[19] The chief served as an intermediary with spirits who ensured the land's continuing bounty.[20] People may have been willing to delegate authority to a chief, but they also restrained his actions through informal pressure from the elders. Mason concluded that if a chief were to exercise much influence, he "must demonstrate the value of his services to the point where the community will be willing to share its limited produce with him," and that the extent of any suprafamilial authority depended on surplus production (1968, 326–327). "Chieftainship is elaborated most in the very cultures supported by economic abundance," while on the least productive islands the "economy cannot support the luxury of a chiefly superstructure" (1968, 328–329; cf. Sahlins 1958).

In the work of the mid to late 1940s we have found a wealth of ethnographic detail on the political organizations that operated within communities and linked them together. There were, of course, considerable differences in the perspectives of the anthropologists working in the area. Most were impressed with the political systems they encountered, and with the people they met. In nearly every case they found themselves describing two different phenomena: the formal qualities of these systems as described by older people —that is, "key informants" speaking of the past—and the actual flow of political life in thriving communities. Some thought these differences were largely due to changes wrought by contact and colonialism; others saw them as inherent in the nature of social life. Some were certain that democratic processes had to be introduced; others believed them to be already in place. Some were generally critical of the American administration, while others largely ignored the contemporary scene and focused their attention wholly on the ethnographic tasks at hand. In any case, these ethnographers preserved a marvelous record of some very fundamental similarities in Micronesian sociopolitical organization. Political legitimacy in Micronesia appears to have derived from everyday life experiences: birth order, caregiving, cultivation of the land, and the clash of personalities.

ADMINISTRATIVE ANTHROPOLOGY

In a letter to the *American Anthropologist,* John Embree (1950) launched a strong attack on the discipline in general, suggesting that the war had caused many social scientists to lose their objectivity regarding culture and to accept the "white man's burden." He called attention to "the wholehearted support of the United States Naval administration by a group of anthropologists on the general principle that such administration would be best for the Micronesians' own good" (1950, 430). He challenged, as reminiscent of nineteenth-century imperialism's worst cant, Murdock's (1948b) suggestion that Micronesian societies should be transformed into modern democracies, and argued that applied anthropology in the islands was based on an assumption that American culture was clearly "the best there is." These anthropologists' current role, Embree maintained, was to assure that the United States would be able to rule the area with a minimum of trouble, rather than to put themselves into service on behalf of those being ruled (1950, 431). John "Jack" Fischer—who had gone to the Carolines as a graduate student and in time became an administrator—responded to Embree, acknowledging that most American officials did have a highly ethnocentric notion of progress and were indeed intent on replacing Micronesian cultures with America's. But, Fischer pointed out, any anthropologist who tried to temper this general goal would quickly lose his job: "Secretly he may hope that the administration will gradually become more and more tolerant of the basic values of the administered. He may do his best toward this end, but in contemporary American society he can hardly shout his position from the housetops" (1951, 133).

Several years later, Fischer spelled out his objections to the American administration of Micronesia in more detail (1957a). His observations are particularly telling because he completed them in 1955, only two years after he finished serving as district island affairs officer, the second-ranking administrator on Pohnpei. He was troubled by the prevailing viewpoints concerning the nature of indigenous political institutions, and devoted considerable space to detailing the ways in which local leaders—chiefs—were responsive to and bound by the will of their communities (1957a, 185–186). While agreeing that the most "extreme difference in status between chiefs and commoners in the area today is found on Ponape," he stressed that on Pohnpei status was more often achieved than ascribed and that there was little in the way of class stratification. He also remarked on the relatively equal treatment accorded women (1957a, 195–196).

These findings shaped Fischer's consideration of "problems in the introduction of western political institutions and law," to which he devoted a large section of his monograph, *The Eastern Carolines* (1957a, 180–197). He noted a characteristic contradiction in the American attempt to create representative political institutions: despite claims that these bodies were legislatures, they served largely to provide for "promulgation of orders and laws received from the territorial government" and were in fact granted no legislative powers (1957a, 183–184). Fischer focused particularly on the interaction of traditional leaders with these new bodies, pointing out that despite efforts made to educate islanders about the supposed functions of these bodies, they did not view them as the Americans intended them to, that is, as institutions of a truly effective representative democracy. At the same time, Fischer noted: "In spite of the great powers of the traditional chiefs in theory, the island governments in many places in Micronesia before foreign contact were probably much more democratic in effect than reports sound" (1957a, 185).

Fischer was generally skeptical of American attempts to foster change in the islands (1979, 246). He argued that "rapid introduction of new political institutions with little outside supervision is not practical," explaining that "the less active intervention the less disturbance, both for good and for bad, will occur" (1957a, 189). Moreover, he was not sure that even the Americans' small and tightly closed administrative outposts in the islands were worthy of support. The Americans thought of themselves as not only superior but as having special rights. The Micronesians, on the other hand, concluding that whatever superiority existed was based on American military might, were not prepared to "concede that their own relative social and political inferiority [was] based on any inevitable or innate racial inferiority" (1957a, 196).

Homer G. Barnett's *Anthropology in Administration* (1956) illustrated many of the problems Fischer raised. Barnett demonstrated that basic confusion over the degree to which the anthropologists were to serve as administrators or as researchers kept them from doing either job very well. They simply never fit into the administrative system, despite all good intentions to the contrary; "the truth is that anthropologists and administrators do not, on the whole, get along well together" (1956, 49). Although Barnett was concerned primarily with the tasks anthropologists had undertaken, his study sheds light on the character of the administration in which they served. His insistence on the importance of the anthropologists' neutrality was matched by his commitment to the introduction of new political institutions (including legislatures, councils, and magistrates) and to seeing these prevail over local practices. This neutrality was in fact overridden by a thinly disguised advocacy; anthropologists were charged not only with providing "knowledge of the attitudes of the people governed" to "a democratic government such as the one the administration represented," but with instructing the Micronesian people in these "alien principles of self-government" and encouraging "development of leadership and responsibility in accordance with them" (1956, 5, 102). Anthropologists' participation was essential, Barnett explained, because "the democratic process which is being inculcated is so unfamiliar to the Micronesians that without check or guidance they cannot as yet be entrusted to regulate their own affairs in accordance with its principles" (1956, 5).

This perspective was manifest in a lengthy memorandum Barnett had directed to district administrators on the role of local "magistrates." The hoary problem of representative government in a colony, taken up by Useem and Fischer, was entirely overlooked in Barnett's discussion of these functionaries, who were popularly elected but nevertheless "in their official capacities . . . represent the [US] government" (1956, 140). The basic problem he outlined was that the magistrates, in dealing with issues that arose from "the injection of our ideas into their way of life," frequently found themselves in conflict with the chiefs. Even though this new system was not supposed to "deprive the Chief of any of the powers granted him by custom," there was considerable stress within communities because the administration had, "of course, admittedly and deliberately curtailed chiefly powers" (1956, 141). The solutions considered at the time consisted largely of enhancing the magistrates' prestige by providing them with salaries, uniforms, and badges (1956, 143).

Magistrates were seen as "errand boys and flunkies" by the administration and as "dummy figures" by the Micronesians (Barnett 1956, 142); legislative assemblies were not to be trusted running their own affairs; and traditional forms of self-rule were being curtailed. Administrative anthropology as described by Barnett appears to have been primarily concerned with figuring out how to Americanize Micronesia as effectively and efficiently as possible.

One of the last anthropologists to serve on the US Trust Territory of the Pacific Islands (USTTPI) staff, Robert McKnight presented a trenchant summary of the American impact on Micronesian life, noting at the outset that American and Micronesian accounts of what the United States wrought in the islands had been at odds with each other (1974, 37). It was no coincidence that his chapter was placed at the beginning of Daniel Hughes and Sherwood "Woody" Lingenfelter's *Political Development in Micronesia* (1974). In it McKnight argued that Americans tended to emphasize achievements, without necessarily slighting problems, but seldom questioning the appropriateness of the American development models applied in Micronesia.

McKnight called attention to a basic phenomenon that Useem had earlier recognized, the Palauans' tendency to create parallel political structures to deal with the colonial administration. Western observers, seeing that few hereditary leaders were elected to the newly-established political offices, believed that "Palauans had come to reject their traditional form of government," while a more reasonable interpretation, McKnight suggested, would have been that both sides chose "to ignore one another." The American tendency to disregard traditional leaders actually resulted in an appreciable increase in their status, which had fallen during the years when they had been put in the position of serving as yes-men for the Japanese (McKnight 1974, 42–43). This echoes a situation reported for other parts of Micronesia (e.g., Fischer 1974) and raises some doubt about the degree to which the administration ever seriously contemplated respecting local institutions. Moreover, McKnight argued, given the flexible nature of Palauan polities and the well-known Palauan interest in innovation, most traditional leaders had been forward-looking pacesetters. But the ineptitude of the American administration and the inappropriateness of the models it attempted to impose led many of these leaders to reverse "their political orientation, viewing their chiefly authority mainly as an instrument of conservatism rather than modernization" (McKnight 1974, 50). McKnight concluded that political development in the area was destroying the traditional leadership structure, without providing any equivalent to replace it. The traditional structure, which "combined a complex and highly representative form of community government with a positive drive for modernization," was "indeed failing and will, no doubt, eventually collapse" (1974, 52–53).

This applied anthropology episode did not last for long, and appears to have foundered partially on criticisms from the very anthropologists who participated in it—just as Gladwin had feared. It was largely concerned with implementing political change and was, by most accounts, not very successful; many of its failures seem to have derived from the contradictions inherent in the attempt to impose democracy on a colonized people. At about the same time that the USTTPI anthropology program was withering away, however, a few scholars were able to begin relatively unfettered research there.

TOWARD THE ETHNOGRAPHIC PRESENT

Roland Force's portrayals of political institutions and change in Palau are perhaps best understood in the context of the eerie ambivalence that characterized American politics in the 1950s, when he did his fieldwork. Force explained that trusteeship "guaranteed to residents of the Trust Territory human rights which are almost identical with those enjoyed by the citizens of the United States" and that "native welfare is the prime concern of trusteeship" (1960, 74). He wrote of the "countless" ways in which a "benevolent" administration "improved the welfare of Micronesian cultures" (1960, 93). But this rosy picture was contradicted by his descriptions of political changes the United States had forced on the Palauans. He spoke of "considerable functional distress," and "dysfunctional" conflicts between older and newer political systems (1960, 112, 122). He described the Palauans' "enurement to supersedure under directed cultural change" (1960, 135). Their situation was "a losing

Roland Force interviewing Charlie
Gibbons, Palau, TRIPP *project, 1954.*
Photograph courtesy of Maryanne
Force.

cause in a time of great change in which ultimate executive authority resides
in an administration which has actively introduced antithetical ideas of leadership and political representation, and in which traditional organs of social
control have suffered disintegration" (1960, 122).

Force's observations alternately reaffirmed and countered Useem's and Barnett's. With Maryanne Force, he emphasized the high degree of social stratification and chiefly power in Palau, making only passing reference to internal
flexibility and mobility (Force and Force 1972, 8, 13). They suggested that the
Trust Territory Code had actually restored power to the hereditary chiefs (1972,
113), even as they argued that Americanization undermined traditional ways.
Palauan political organization had undergone accelerated changes as a consequence of intense and deliberate American influences, despite United Nations

(UN) support for the development of representative institutions and preservation of traditional Micronesian cultures. The Palauans, Force and Force maintained, were torn between loyalty to these new ways and to "time-honored traditions of fealty," and caught between America's security mind-set and UN decolonization pressures (1965, 4, 10–11). It was as a consequence of such countervailing tendencies, they argued (1965, 10), that the dual set of Palauan political organizations had developed (in contrast to Useem's observation that this process had been underway throughout the colonial era, as a coping stratagem the Palauans had deliberately devised). The Forces concluded that profound changes were inevitable: "The ultimate result of the establishment of independence according to democratic principles of local representative government must be the replacement of traditional principles of self-government. The course is set. Micronesians have no recourse but to move forward" (1965, 11). Their underlying belief, which seems contrary to the data they presented, was that the United States had not tried to Americanize the Micronesians, but merely to introduce American democracy. Despite references to the possibility of independence, and their recognition that many Micronesians had no desire to become Americans, the Forces believed that cultural differences among Micronesian societies were so great that "a federated Micronesia seems absurd" and, moreover, that even a united Micronesia would ultimately be too small to stand alone (1965, 13–14). In the end, it seems almost as if the Forces were describing two entirely different scenes: they were able to analyze the destructive forces of American policy in Micronesia even as they denied them.

There may be a relationship between anthropologists' perceptions of indigenous social organization and their views concerning the relative merits of introducing American representative democracy. For instance, to the extent that Force and Force interpreted indigenous Palauan society as highly stratified and ruled by powerful chiefs, they praised the introduction and ultimate success of American patterns of government. Useem and Fischer, on the other hand, emphasized the basic democratic character of traditional Micronesian societies, and doubted the good such American institutions could bring to the Palauans and Pohnpeians.

William Alkire's work represented a return to the study of ongoing life in Micronesian societies, and he managed to avoid the almost obsessive concern with what the United States was doing that had characterized the era of applied anthropology. In *Introduction to the Peoples and Cultures of Micronesia* (1977), he surveyed political systems throughout the area, and in his Lamotrek monograph (1989a), first published in 1965, he explored the complex relationships between clan seniority and territorial chieftainship that lie at the heart of all Micronesian sociopolitical relationships.

Lamotrek had a range of chiefly roles, distributed among different descent groups and various status positions within particular kin groups (Alkire 1989a, 32–33). The atoll was divided into districts, each with its own chief. There was also an islandwide paramount chief. The chiefs' authority was rooted in genealogical seniority, and on the basis of this authority, "chiefly clans direct the activities of nonchiefly clans." The paramount chief was able "to direct the activities of all island residents regardless of clan affiliation" (1989a, 67). Chiefs' rights "derived from the multiple sources of kinship and territoriality" (1989a, 68). Alkire argued that the existence of various alternative rules governing key elements of social life were an indigenous means of dealing with population imbalances (1989a, 171). He demonstrated the dualistic organization of Lamotrek's sociopolitical organization (1989a, 71–72), and the development of a "chief for the foreigner" system that minimally disrupted traditional politics while enabling the islanders to deal effectively with colonial administrators (1989a, 163).

Sociopolitical organization on the atolls is not as simple as is often portrayed. While the demographically larger high island sociopolities elaborate these basic elements, Alkire's work shows that the basic patterns of duality, flexibility, and crosscutting kin and territorial organization are pan-Micronesian. These patterns are not mere adaptations to particular demographic and environmental conditions, as those engaged in hypothetical reconstructions of Micronesian social evolution would have it. Alkire's portrayal of Lamotrek decision-making processes also highlights both the participation of all those with interests in them and the role of Lamotrek's female paramount chief, demonstrating the inclusive character of island politics, despite their emphasis on hereditary access to status positions (1989a, 34–36).[21]

The basic sociopolitical patterns on Lamotrek nested within a larger system of traditional interisland links through Ulithi and on to Yap, and also integrated Lamotrek closely with nearby Elato and Satawal. Alkire demonstrated the complexity of these ties. Some magico-religious elements were eliminated when most islanders converted to Christianity, but the multistranded interisland ties continued to be essential to survival on the smaller islands and were actively cultivated and preserved. Despite manifest ideologies of superiority and inferiority, Central Carolinian interisland politics were not about domination and submission.

Robert C. Kiste's Bikini work adds several elements to our understanding of the region's polities. While stratification in the Marshalls Islands resembled that found elsewhere in Micronesia, the degree of authority lodged in the hierarchical levels seems to have been more pronounced. This may be due in part to the relatively early penetration of German copra operations, which made land far more valuable than it was elsewhere, but some aspects may predate European arrival. Kiste noted that "the principles of relative age and seniority of generation sometimes proved in conflict. As cultural norms did not specify either principle as having priority over the other for determining rank and succession, there was a structural ambiguity in the system" (1974, 52). This structural ambiguity is critical to making the region's societies— ostensibly organized around immutable hereditary rank—vital, flexible, and successful. There is a recurrent contradiction in matrilineal societies: an elder sister has younger brothers, some of whom are considerably older than her sons. Despite their genealogically junior status, these younger brothers often claim that seniority of generation takes precedence over seniority of line (as determined by the relative age of siblings) and assert their right to succeed. Disputes between mothers' brothers and sisters' sons are common. Resolutions may sometimes be clear-cut, but in most Micronesian societies ambiguous situations of this sort underlie political disputes. Roland Force (1960) pointed out for Palau that age and rank are in perpetual competition with each other, and Useem (1950) described competing, legitimate claims for titles there. This same ambiguity drives a recurring social dynamic in the Woleai (Alkire 1989a, 44–46), while a great many disputes over Pohnpeian succession hinge at least partly on this tension (Petersen 1982b). Micronesians are able to rely heavily on genealogical seniority as a principle of political organization precisely because it is offset by this structural ambiguity; indeed, an analysis of this same contradiction lies at the heart of Edmund Leach's exegesis in his classic *Political Systems of Highland Burma* (1965, 259–263).

Kiste's work illustrates another common issue. In the Bikini case "the traditional power of the chief had largely been eroded due to the alienation of once-chiefly land," while (with reference to the atoll's ostensible chief) "there is no doubt that his status as head of the community was enhanced when he was named magistrate and was recognized as such by the administration" (1974, 65). This situation occurred widely throughout the region. The influence of traders, missionaries, and colonial administrators both diminished and increased the status and authority of Micronesian leaders. Historians and ethnographers have repeatedly recorded this key lesson of the Micronesian experience:

there is no simple way to summarize the impact of large-scale external forces on the region's political organization. Authority vested in leaders may have been increased or decreased, or both may have occurred simultaneously, in different social spheres. Since Micronesians tend to emphasize both an ideology of powerful seniority and processes of democratic consensus making, as well as individual political skills, it is impossible to be sure what any society was like in the precontact era. Therefore, certainty about the kinds of changes that have occurred postcontact is equally problematic.[22]

Finally, Kiste called attention to the fragile nature of Micronesian unity, due to cultural differences and American encouragement of separatism. And though he believed that "as long as American defense interests were served, the Territory administration was allowed to operate in a policy vacuum," Kiste also argued that "it is apparent that the programs implemented in the 1960s were designed to both Americanize and make Micronesians dependent upon the United States so that the latter could maintain hegemony over the area" (1974, 196–197; see also Kiste 1983; 1986).

Kiste has not been alone in advancing the notion that there was no US "policy" in the area, given the highly contradictory character of official attitudes toward the trust territory. Other anthropologists working in Micronesia have called attention to these contradictory aspects of the American presence in the islands, noting that the United States wanted to preserve indigenous cultural institutions—and to thoroughly transform them. "Policy" is a problematic term: it may refer to a consciously developed, deliberately enacted plan, or it may simply be a way to summarize what has taken place. While it is difficult to demonstrate that the contradictions and generally chaotic nature of attempts to implement programs in Micronesia were planned, it is possible to describe what the United States has wrought in the islands—itself a matter of some debate—as American policy. From this view, American policy has been to "make Micronesians dependent upon the United States so that the latter could maintain hegemony over the area" (Kiste 1974, 196–197).

Woody Lingenfelter (1975) scrutinized the Yapese political system to a degree matched only by Riesenberg's Pohnpei work. Yapese authority was rooted in genealogy and land, with greater emphasis on the latter. The Yapese system of rank drew from genealogy, age, and success in competitive activities like feasting. Authority derived largely from land (1975, 92–93), yet this authority was tempered by checks and balances intended to curb abuses. Various tripartite and dualistic systems created structural balances; councils controlled chiefs within communities; alliances prevented chiefs and communities from accruing too much power within the wider polity (1975, 107, 114, 126, 176). A "Yapese fear of too much centralized power" had yielded effective techniques to place a "curb on the personal power of any high chief" (1975, 152, 176). Multiple, crosscutting sources of prestige—lodged in land estates, associations, sections, and chiefly titles—combined with a range of rivalries and spheres of competition to prompt "cutthroat political maneuvering." The "ongoing, dynamic" processes of ranking among villages meant that the entire political scene was continually contested and always in flux (1975, 92, 117–118, 134). Even the most obvious manifestation of Yapese social stratification, the "eating classes," were complex products of multiple factors, including age, rank, and land ownership. Moreover, their role seems to have been limited to public displays of status, not matters of responsible authority (1975, 95–97). Ultimately, only warfare provided the power that Yapese ideology otherwise denied the chiefs (1975, 175).

Chiefly authority did not bring much economic benefit. Lingenfelter gave many examples of chiefs returning more than they received and suggested that chiefs had to do so to retain their authority (1975, 144–145). In the system of tribute and *sawei* that linked Yap to the atolls, "the Carolinians invariably received greater economic benefits from the exchange than the Yapese" (1975, 153). Of course, this only represents the Yapese perspective on the matter.

As in the rest of Micronesia, Yap's political organization has undergone contradictory changes. The long population decline, along with population movements toward Colonia, meant that the society has lacked the human resources necessary to sustain certain political activities, and "traditional leadership is stripped of important authority and power" (Lingenfelter 1975, 16). While Japanese rule led to "the emasculation of island-wide leadership and authority," traditional leaders serving as magistrates recouped a great deal under the American administration (1975, 186, 191). Gradually, Yapese have taken over the newly introduced government and "the structure of the new political statuses so nearly duplicates the traditional structure that legitimacy is derived from traditional values" (1975, 201). Because legitimacy remains rooted in the land, and not in families, the traditional chiefly system itself has remained legitimate (1975, 196).

While Lingenfelter analyzed the traditional polity before detailing changes in it, Daniel Hughes focused his attention almost entirely on the nature of the changes in Pohnpei's political arena. More than any other anthropologist, Hughes sang the praises of "political development" and did not seem ambivalent about it. As a high school teacher at Xavier in Chuuk before doing graduate work in anthropology, he had helped train many of the Micronesian leaders who were moving into administrative and legislative positions in the USTTPI government, and he was proud of their accomplishments. Hughes demonstrated little awareness of tensions that existed on Pohnpei, even as he offered ample evidence of them. For example, he described the legislature established by the United States as having "legislative authority over the entire Ponape District," but he either did not mention or glossed over the fact that the district administrator and high commissioner could veto legislative measures without the possibility of being overridden (1969a, 35; 1969b, 279). Despite considerable evidence of arbitrariness in the actual governance of the trust territory, Hughes referred frequently to the ways in which the United States was introducing democracy to a people unfamiliar with it (1969a, 37; 1969b, 279).

Hughes saw that Pohnpeians distinguished between their traditional political units and the chartered municipalities. The traditional polities simply operated as parallel institutions of the sort that Useem and others had described for other parts of Micronesia. Hughes' accounts of a municipal councilman (1969a, 37; 1969b, 282) resonate with Useem's (1952) discussion of the out-facing chief. Hughes believed that a decline in the sacred character of the paramount chiefs, as portrayed by Riesenberg (who described an ideal type, not observed patterns of behavior), was "influenced by the egalitarian notions of the democratic system introduced by the Americans," and that "it seems probable that the egalitarian principles of democracy have influenced the present Ponapeian attitude toward the distribution of tribute" (1969b, 285, 289). On the other hand, Hughes dismissed the claims of American administrators "that the democratic system could not be meaningful on Ponape because the people would vote as their leaders told them to" (1972, 144). As he pointed out, if their leaders told them how to vote, Pohnpeians would simply say, "yes," and then proceed to do as they pleased; furthermore, had these leaders actually controlled the introduced system, it would have been fully staffed by their relatives (Hughes 1972, 143–144).[23]

GROWING TENSIONS

At the end of the 1960s the problems generated and the opportunities provided by the introduction of new political institutions into Micronesia received increased attention. World War II had marked the beginning of the end of colonialism, but "for much of Micronesia, however, the same strategic locale that once marked the islands for early colonization also contributed to a late decolonization" (Alkire 1977, 91). Two significant conferences on this topic were organized during this period at the Center for South Pacific Studies, University of California, Santa Cruz. The first, in 1969, "Political Modernization of Micronesia," included scholars with long-term involvement in Micronesian affairs and two Micronesians. The second, "Micronesian Realities: Political and Economic" (see F. Smith 1972), included seven Micronesians, some who were students, and some already established leaders. Nearly all of them subsequently came to play significant roles in charting Micronesia's future.

In my opinion the present moribund state of political anthropology in Micronesia can be partly explained by reference to these two conferences and the resultant volumes. Almost none of the work done by anthropologists during the preceding twenty-five years was acknowledged in them. During that time anthropologists had documented political norms, values, ideologies, and most significantly, real political action in a substantial number of thriving Micronesian societies. But the era was characterized by America's overwhelming presence, by its relentless insistence on the introduction of American political models, and by the Micronesians' awareness that it was only through adoption of American forms—if not true internalization of them—that they could convince the United States to accord them a degree of genuine self-determination. The United States, therefore, set the tone and the agenda of all political discussions as the drive to terminate the trusteeship increasingly dominated political activity in the islands. How Micronesians had done things in the past—or might prefer to do them in the present—was deemed irrelevant to discussions of what might be called for in the future. As a consequence, the most useful ethnographic work was (and has continued to be) ignored.

The Santa Cruz volumes reflected steadily growing tensions between Micronesians and Americans, fueled mainly by the Congress of Micronesia's (COM) increasing strength and frustration. Mason suggested that the Congress of Micronesia was the most effective Micronesian voice (1969b, 5), and Norman Meller termed it "the cutting edge of political change in Micronesia" (1969, 1). Though others were inclined to emphasize its initiation of future status negotiations, Meller was more impressed by the integrative role the Congress played in "promoting Micronesian unity" (1969, 8). Apparent unity, of course, enhanced the Micronesians' leverage in their status negotiations. Meller also noted a blossoming interest in independence (1969, 15), a topic developed further by a number of the Santa Cruz contributors, particularly Hans Wiliander (1972), who was a member of the Congress, and Robert Robbins (1969). This was a time when some Micronesian leaders became more openly critical, not just of particular USTTPI administrative decisions, but of American foreign policy in general. Kaleb Udui argued "that where a conflict has arisen between national self-interest and humanitarian idealism, as in Micronesia, the United States has always decided to give priority to the former at the expense of the latter" (1972, 16).

Political anthropology in Micronesia was eventually undone—or at least deemed irrelevant—by historical events. By the time self-determination had become an all-consuming issue, many Micronesian leaders perceived anthropologists as ambivalent and judged their work ambiguous. Though some anthropologists were sanguine about the likely benefits from changes they encountered, most were troubled by them. Their response, however, was to describe, explain, and marvel at older forms of social organization, forms that Micronesians tended to take for granted. Anthropology was considered important neither by the United States, intent on transforming the region, nor by the Micronesians, intent on developing solutions that would transfer power over their lives into their own hands. Little has changed in subsequent decades.

Having been snubbed by nearly everyone else, anthropologists proceeded with their own examination of politics in the area. The Hughes and Lingenfelter volume, *Political Development in Micronesia,* appeared in 1974. The idiosyncratic histories of the islands and the varying perspectives of the contributors led to a diverse set of case histories, and it is difficult to draw general conclusions from the volume.

Seeking to explain why the Pohnpei District Legislature received so little respect, Hughes pointed to "the unclear and uncertain definition of [its] nature and purpose" (1974, 109). As in his earlier work, he overlooked the possibility that the problem lay largely with the legislature's lack of real authority. Lingenfelter described events that were something of a victory for Yap's legislature, the role of which Yap legislators were able to define more clearly with the assistance of Peace Corps lawyers. "Once the colonial and local officials reached a mutual understanding of the authority and power" of the various political bodies, "the model furnished a very effective governing organization" (Lingenfelter 1974, 66). Lingenfelter's analysis derived in part from a contrast between Yap and Pohnpei, and he concluded that "in a multi-ethnic area like Micronesia a common 'model' of district governments is a colonial myth" (1974, 69–70).

The contributions by Michael Rynkiewich, James Nason, and Jack Fischer also provide some enlightening contrasts. In the Marshalls, "colonial policies, often rationalized as development, led to the destruction of the Arno political system, mainly through the dissolution of ties of reciprocal obligation between chiefs and commoners" (Rynkiewich 1974, 164). On Ettal, in the Mortlocks, people were from the outset concerned about retaining autonomy and were "eminently successful," having "managed to retain overall control of decision-making on internal affairs" (Nason 1974, 140). This resulted in significant changes in certain cultural features, "yet the essential qualities and elements of leadership as traditionally defined were continued intact" (1974, 140). And on Pohnpei, the lack of American interest in traditional leaders, as compared to Japanese attempts to co-opt them, "made the high chiefs practically immune to interference by higher authority," leaving them in position "to maintain their influence," which "[could not] be easily altered by governmental policy" (Fischer 1974, 175–176).

While the contributors to the two Santa Cruz volumes simply ignored anthropology's role, those included in the Hughes and Lingenfelter volume highlighted the essential problem anthropologists faced in Micronesia: Largely particularistic in orientation, they demonstrated how the course of events in each part of the trust territory had unfolded. But about overall experiences resulting from the intersection of an array of different societies and cultures with a haphazardly imposed colonial administration—one that lacked clear ideas of what it should do, beyond ensuring American control of the region—they had little to say.

Moreover, anthropologists were divided among themselves over the matter of Micronesian unity. Clearly, one lesson from the Hughes and Lingenfelter volume is that an almost infinite variety of developmental processes was underway in the area. Anthropologists had long called attention to antagonisms among some of the island populations and to the entirely artificial character of "Micronesia." In hindsight, their data suggested there was little to hold the region together. Nonetheless, the Congress of Micronesia believed that its best hope for successfully negotiating an end to American rule lay in presenting a united front. A strong surface current emphasized unity in the region, while a perhaps equally strong undercurrent worked against it.

Hughes and Lingenfelter's book represented the culmination of a long trend in the political anthropology of Micronesia, a point when scholars could still discuss the relative merits of development. By the time the next collective volume appeared, the outlook was different.

When Catherine Lutz's *Micronesia as a Strategic Colony* (1984a) appeared a decade later, the situation had greatly altered. With the exception of Lingenfelter's important monograph (1975), little new on Micronesian politics had been published. The terms of discussion had also changed almost entirely. The Lutz volume primarily gave voice to activists appalled at the terms on which trusteeship was being terminated. The anthropological contributions of Glenn Alcalay, William Alexander, Eulalia Harui-Walsh, Richard Marksbury, Mac and Leslie Marshall, Glenn Petersen, and Don Rubinstein not only drew on their firsthand field knowledge of the area but were motivated chiefly by a shared sense of indignation.

The most serious critique ever leveled at American anthropology in Micronesia was Roger Gale's "Anthropological Colonialism in Micronesia," presented at the 1973 meetings of the Society for Applied Anthropology. Gale, then coordinator for the Friends of Micronesia, previously had spent time teaching politics at the University of Guam.[24] His was a take-no-prisoners approach: he sought to demonstrate that anthropologists had performed as "political actors in disguise," using their scientific status "to cover their patently political involvement in matters outside the purview of scientific inquiry"—that is, as citizens of the United States their loyalties unquestioningly lay with their own government and its political priorities. "There has been virtually no criticism of the legitimacy of the colonial system nor has there been much self-conscious appraisal of anthropology's role in Micronesia" (Gale 1973, 3–4).

Gale claimed that anthropologists were charged with a range of tasks intended to alter indigenous political institutions, and that they did so willingly because of their assumptions that "progress and Americanization" were synonymous and that the American way was "more moral since it is conceived of as more 'democratic' and 'equalitarian' " (1973, 5–6). Micronesia, he concluded, provided "a case study of anthropology at its worst" (1973, 28). In retrospect, Gale's charges appear overblown and in many ways erroneous, but they underpin the outlook of many young anthropologists who did their research in the wake of the Vietnam War, a point illustrated by most of the contributions to the Lutz volume.[25]

NORMAN MELLER

Norman Meller's work is not strictly anthropological, but he is one of the few social scientists outside the discipline to have consistently done research in Micronesia, and his writings have long appeared alongside those of anthropologists. Meller has always shown respect for and sensitivity toward Micronesian cultures, and he is the only political scientist whose material regularly appears in Micronesianist anthropologists' bibliographies.

Moreover, unlike most anthropologists, Meller played a very significant role in the processes of change and development under examination here. He served in a number of advisory and consulting positions in the development of modern Micronesian political institutions, most notably in the 1965 creation of the Congress of Micronesia and in the organization of the 1975 Micronesian Constitutional Convention, about both of which he has written substantial monographs (Meller 1969; 1985). Given Meller's stature and applied work, many of the initiatives proposed and implemented in the islands were undoubtedly influenced by him.

Meller has always had particular respect for the Congress of Micronesia, although in some of his early pieces he seemed a bit concerned about the events that led to its creation, attributing the motivating forces to the "broad axe of anti-imperialist accusation" at the UN (1965, 245; 1970, 318). Initially, he was unsure about just how much authority the Congress would actually wield, noting that it might have limited or even no law-making powers, given the overwhelming power of the administration's veto. But he suggested that the Congress could play an important part in a process of political socialization (1970, 311; 1965, 245).[26] He celebrated the Congress as "the only organ of the central government responsible to the people" (1965, 246). He saw the creation of the Congress of Micronesia as "the single most important political change" since the United States began administering Micronesia, an event which "foreshadows a shift of political power from the American High Commissioner to the territory's Micronesian inhabitants and raises a potential challenge to the entire course of the area's administration" (1967, 457; 1970, 316). Acknowledging the fears within the districts that single-member district representation would threaten internal unity, he was certain that the Congress was proving itself the greatest integrating and unifying institution within Micronesia (1970, 335).

It was at just this same time, however, that Carl Heine argued quite the opposite: the Congress presented "a false sense of unity" and showed "a united

Senate, Congress of Micronesia, 1966.
Trust Territory Archives (Photo 3504.05),
Pacific Collection, University of Hawai'i
Library.

Left to right, front row:

Strik Yoma, Chief Clerk of Senate
Senator Olympio T. Borja
Senator Bailey Olter
Senator Jose R. Cruz
Senator Joseph Tamag
Janet Breeze, Journal Clerk

Back row:

Senator Roman Tmetuchl
Sergeant-at-Arms Victorino Guerrero
Senator Frank Nuan
Senator Tosiwo Nakayama
Senator John O. Ngiraked
Senator Issac Lanwi
Senator Amata Kabua
Senator Eliuel Pretrick
Senator Andon Amaraich

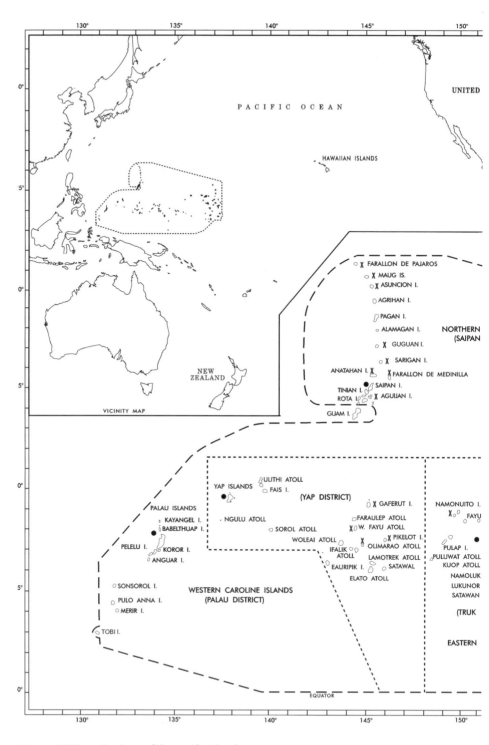

Map 3. US Trust Territory of the Pacific Islands
Map used by the Office of the High Commissioner between 1957 and 1967 before
Kosrae (Kusaie) became a separate administrative district. It regularly
appeared as the back cover of the Micronesian Reporter, a quarterly news
magazine published by the Office of the High Commissioner.

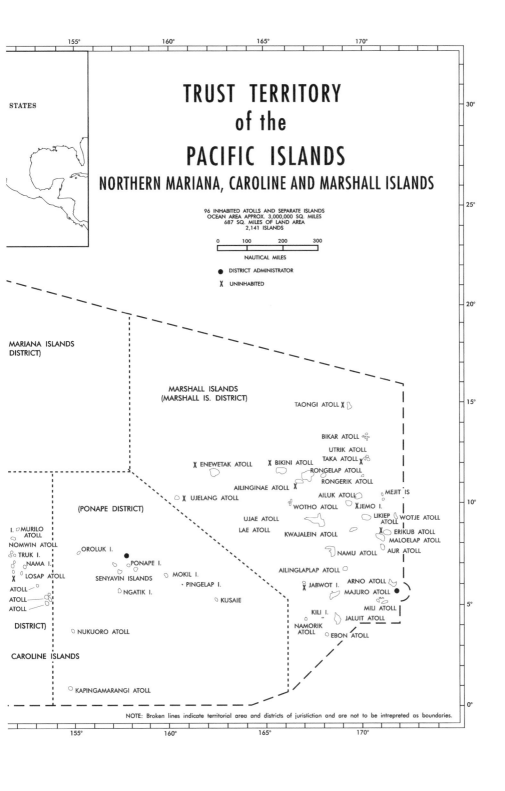

STATES

TRUST TERRITORY
of the
PACIFIC ISLANDS
NORTHERN MARIANA, CAROLINE AND MARSHALL ISLANDS

96 INHABITED ATOLLS AND SEPARATE ISLANDS
OCEAN AREA APPROX. 3,000,000 SQ. MILES
687 SQ. MILES OF LAND AREA
2,141 ISLANDS

0   100   200   300

NAUTICAL MILES

● DISTRICT ADMINISTRATOR

X UNINHABITED

30°

25°

20°

MARIANA ISLANDS
DISTRICT)

MARSHALL ISLANDS
(MARSHALL IS. DISTRICT)

15°

TAONGI ATOLL X

BIKAR ATOLL

UTRIK ATOLL
TAKA ATOLL X

X ENEWETAK ATOLL   X BIKINI ATOLL

RONGELAP ATOLL
RONGERIK ATOLL

AILINGINAE ATOLL X

AILUK ATOLL
MEJIT IS

X UJELANG ATOLL

WOTHO ATOLL   X JEMO I.

(PONAPE DISTRICT)

LIKIEP   WOTJE ATOLL
ATOLL

UJAE ATOLL

LAE ATOLL

X   ERIKUB ATOLL
MALOELAP ATOLL

10°

I.   MURILO
ATOLL

KWAJALEIN ATOLL

NAMU ATOLL   AUR ATOLL

NOMWIN ATOLL

OROLUK I.

TRUK I.

NAMA I.

AILINGLAPLAP ATOLL

X   LOSAP ATOLL

SENYAVIN ISLANDS

PONAPE I.

MOKIL I.

X JABWOT I.   ARNO ATOLL

ATOLL

· PINGELAP I.

MAJURO ATOLL   ●

ATOLL

NGATIK I.

ATOLL

KUSAIE

MILI ATOLL

5°

DISTRICT)

KILI I.

JALUIT ATOLL

NUKUORO ATOLL

NAMORIK
ATOLL   EBON ATOLL

CAROLINE ISLANDS

KAPINGAMARANGI ATOLL

0°

NOTE: Broken lines indicate territorial area and districts of jurisdiction and are not to be intrepreted as boundaries.

Norman Meller speaking at Congress of Micronesia, date uncertain. Trust Territory Archives (Photo 3500.01), Pacific Collection, University of Hawai'i Library.

1993 Conference. Left: *Norman Meller;* right: *Glenn Petersen. Photograph by Carolyn Yacoe.*

front only because it has a common foe—the American Administering Authority. Once that adversary is removed, the inherent feelings of regionalism will resurface" (1970, 203–204). Indeed, Meller recognized that in the process of considering a bicameral congress, equality of representation in the upper house (as opposed to proportional representation in the lower) would "safeguard district interests, reflecting the Micronesians' ethnocentrism" (1967, 459).

Meller's views on the ways in which traditional patterns of Micronesian social organization affected the process of political change are not entirely clear to me. His writings manifest an ambiguity and ambivalence that mirrors the attitudes of many anthropologists who have worked in the region. Perhaps these attitudes are occupational hazards of working in a colonial context during a decidedly postcolonial era. Meller acknowledged that there had existed "democratic processes concealed by formalism" and "consensus processes denying authority to any man or single group of men," but he also mentioned "autocracy once possessing absolute, arbitrary powers of life and death" (1970, 315, 317). Likewise, he cited processes through which colonial rule variously strengthened and weakened the positions of the chiefs (1970, 319–324). He argued that "traditional institutions have remained, the chiefs exerting political influence by directing their people how to vote" (1970, 327). He also took this position following the 1983 plebiscite in the Federated States of Micronesia (FSM) on its Compact of Free Association with the United States, a notion I have tried to rebut (Meller 1985; Petersen 1985, 31–34).

Finally, I cannot resist remarking on the prescience of one of Meller's passing observations: "It is probably only a matter of time as the Pacific islands move toward self-government before the USSR will seek to obtain access to land support in some strategic part of this world. Every move of these island peoples to govern themselves will then be scanned for evidences of subversion and their natural aspirations to political self-determination will pose overriding problems of security" (1965, 253–254).

Two decades later, as the US Senate considered the Compacts of Free Association with the Marshall Islands and the Federated States of Micronesia, Senator J. Bennett Johnston asked for—and received—the American negotiators' assurances that the terms of the compacts hedged Micronesian autonomy sufficiently to allow the United States to prevent Micronesians from having any sort of intercourse with the Soviet Union (US Senate 1984, 166–167). Meller's grasp of American patterns of political behavior has been as keen as his understanding of the Micronesian scene.

TOWARD THE END OF THE CENTURY

The most recent anthropological work with a political cast has been oriented more toward ethnographic than applied ends. William Alkire has linked the Central Carolinian atolls to Yap, and to relations among Yap's districts, helping to integrate the work of Lessa and Lingenfelter. As Lingenfelter (1975) demonstrated, Gagil district's status in Yap is explained by the wealth it accumulated through its authority over the outer islands. The *sawei* system gradually declined because colonial administrations provided services that replaced it, but with the growth of self-government in Yap, links between the atoll peoples and the Yapese have again become important. In order to circumvent traditional patterns of super- and subordination, however, the outer islanders shifted most of their interactions to the area around the administrative center (Alkire 1981; 1993b). This change underscores the persisting utility of these interisland ties. Likewise, Alkire's analysis of relations between the Saipan Carolinians and the atolls from whence they came shows how these links preserve a wide range of options for all concerned (1984b, 283).

Alkire has also continued to work on the ties between kinship and land, emphasizing that seniority and control over land "are two interrelated variables that are used to establish relative rank" (1984a, 6–7). This point is usefully juxtaposed to his observations about the perceptions of minority populations throughout Micronesia: "Ethnic and outer island minorities have deep-seated suspicions about any political change that concentrates power in the hands of a traditional opposition majority or in a center that has developed out of recent migration" (1984b, 283).

The complex interconnections among seniority, land, and rank contribute to these tensions. Emigrants have long been viewed as necessarily subordinate to the "host" or previously resident population. Micronesian politics are embedded in relationships framed in terms of the sequence of arrivals on a given island; as a result, minority populations who relocate to larger islands and urban centers are inherently vulnerable. Resources from beyond Micronesia that underwrite life there today are funneled through the national and state capitals and may merely reinforce, exaggerate, and exacerbate these inequities.

Micronesia's outer islanders have long had to deal with ideological subordination. In the past, however, they were equals in the actual patterns of resource exchange, as most analyses of the *sawei* have emphasized. But today they have become more dependent on cash salaries earned on the larger islands.

They are perceived as supplicants by the peoples of the urban centers. To overcome or counterbalance this trend in the Federated States of Micronesia, outer islanders are more inclined to extend their allegiance beyond state boundaries to the national government, where all three presidents have had outer-island backgrounds.[27]

In my own work I have analyzed the character of indigenous Micronesian societies and their responses to colonial pressures, explaining how the former shapes the latter. This research continues a long tradition running from Useem to Alkire (Petersen 1979, 1984). In examining the fissioning process in a Pohnpeian chiefdom (1982b), I illustrated the basic organizing principles of Pohnpeian local politics that are buried beneath the routines of daily life. They surface fully charged only when a crisis—in this case one of legitimacy—challenges the calm that otherwise seems to reign. These principles hinge on themes of decentralization and the primacy of local rule, expressed in a chief's observation that "one man cannot rule a thousand." The political struggles that drive these decentralizing tendencies spring from competing interpretations of the relationships between genealogical seniority and territoriality, and ensure continual uncertainty in matters of status and rank. This, in turn, provokes the constant prestige competition that keeps Pohnpeian society rich and thriving. Though Pohnpei appears to be among the most rigidly stratified societies in the region, it does not operate much differently than most other Micronesian societies. In particular, an emphasis on personal restraint *(kanengamah)* and concealment effectively deters attempts to accumulate centralized power (Petersen 1993a). Any doubt about the indigenous character of this dynamic is dispelled by consideration of Pohnpeian mythology. This is organized around competing versions of each story, and provides flexibility of interpretation as well as post hoc justification of nearly any political maneuver. At the same time, however, the myths share a single overriding theme: the absolute importance of political decentralization (Petersen 1990a).

The 1983 FSM plebiscite on free association with the United States and subsequent events showed that many Pohnpeians judge contemporary politics by these same organizing principles. Local autonomy—independence, if you will —is of great importance to them, and their political decisions reflect this. They analyze their alternatives in terms of their own traditions as well as those that have accompanied political forms introduced by the United States (Petersen 1985, 1986b, 1990b). This tendency is by no means exclusive to Pohnpei; at the 1990 Constitutional Convention, delegates from throughout the Federated States demonstrated that they share these concerns (Petersen 1993c, 1994).

Alkire's observation about the fears of Micronesia's minority peoples applies to many of the majority populations as well: continual factional opposition among regions within a culture area such as Chuuk Lagoon, or the big islands of Yap and Pohnpei, is both a product of fears about centralizing or aggrandizing tendencies (well documented by anthropologists) and a means for preventing these from becoming anything more than vague threats.

Even as anthropologists have recorded the changes pummeling Micronesians, they have chronicled Micronesians' success at surviving the difficulties caused by the ill will or ignorance of foreign colonial rulers. Today some of their problems are at least partly of their own making. Mac and Leslie Marshall's study of women's temperance in Chuuk portrayed a more recent trend, describing how these women "played an active political role as agents of change in instituting and maintaining prohibition from 1978 to the present" (1990, 2). They examined how these women's goals intersect with the influences of Christian denominations, incipient social classes, and a growing degree of self-government, in an attempt to shift political behavior beyond traditional gender and family expectations. But they also detailed the problems visited on Micronesian communities by an influx of cash-generated consumerism, the destruction of subsistence patterns that once gave shape and meaning to lives, and the relative inability of local initiative to forestall these larger, externally influenced disasters.[28]

Some of the more flagrant violators of Chuuk's prohibition law were legislators. The level of disregard these lawmakers demonstrated for the law does not bode well for the future of the representative democratic institutions supposedly established through America's political development efforts. And when government relies so heavily on taxes derived from imported luxury goods such as tobacco and alcohol, it is unlikely to show much interest in shaping an economy less dependent on cash and imports. Modern Micronesian politics are hostage to the area's consumerist economy. In the end, these conditions stand as a not very encouraging summary of all that introduced, induced, or forced political development has wrought.[29]

THE CURRENT DILEMMA

Contemporary anthropologists face a dilemma in Micronesia. Anthropology's greatest contribution has been the description and analysis of Micronesian social and cultural life, but these successes reinforce an unfortunate tendency to exoticize modern Micronesia. Even as a knowledge of long-standing social

patterns helps explain why various communities have responded so differently to colonial rule, anthropologists fail to appreciate fully the degree to
which they now need the assistance of economists, psychologists, political scientists, and social workers to help understand and interpret modern life in
the region.

Two key elements of Micronesian sociopolitical organization underlie all
other problems of analysis. First are the vague, shifting, and contradictory
links among descent, seniority, and land. These three factors, sometimes independent and in other cases interdependent, are always invoked to explain the
ties that bind communities together and the systems of ranking the authorities that govern them. The second element, which derives from the first, is
that ascribed seniority on the one hand, and ideas about individual competence as demonstrated through competitive performance on the other, form
competing bases for authority.

Relationships arranged around one or another permutation of these variables may be found in every Micronesian society, from the smallest atoll societies to the largest high island groupings. The contradictions and ambiguities
inherent in these systems provide the tensions and flux that give them their
viability. The same features that permitted adaptation to the vagaries of nature
in an area prone to drought, typhoons, and other natural calamities have provided Micronesians with the adaptability that has characterized their highly
successful responses in the colonial and postcolonial eras.

In the end, if anthropological studies of politics in postwar Micronesia
have achieved less, and garnered less recognition, than they might have, I think
this is at least partly because of Micronesians' successes. In the early years, anthropologists were impressed by the peoples they encountered, with their obvious capacities to run their own lives, and with their clearly articulated desires
to regain control over their societies. However, that was a time when, as
Fischer (1951) noted, criticism of the American way of life—which took for
granted America's right to rule Micronesia—was liable to result in unemploy-
ment. Eventually, these criticisms were more widely disseminated; they were
heard and given attention. Domestic opposition to the American presence in
Vietnam can be attributed in part to a point of view cultivated by anthropologists, which in turn arose partly out of the occupation and administration of
Micronesia. As intellectual opinion shifted more toward anti-imperialism,
anthropologists working in the trust territory found themselves in an awkward
position. As the tragedies of colonial history and underdevelopment became
more widely known and debated, anthropologists singing the praises of Micro-

nesians who endured in the face of these calamities were often looked on as apologists for colonialism. Political anthropology in Micronesia has always been somewhat out of synchrony with the rest of scholarship and public opinion. This may not be such a bad thing, and it has certainly provided anthropologists with a degree of independence.

NOTES

I thank Tisha Hickson and the Center for Pacific Islands Studies staff, and Sarah Sluss and the Baruch College Library staff, for providing me with research materials while I was abroad. In addition to the editors, William Alkire and Fran Hezel provided me with extremely helpful commentaries on the original draft of this chapter.

1. My views concerning US interests in Micronesia are largely in accord with E. H. Carr's (1964) critique of what international relations theorists call "the harmony of interests": I believe that American policy makers have had the Micronesians' best interests in mind only when these have not interfered with American interests. For this reason I doubt that our work will be of equal use to all concerned.

2. Political analysis such as this can easily become tendentious. In this chapter I let these authors speak in their own words, rather than presenting my interpretations of what they said.

3. Some of Thompson's conclusions here, as well as some of the details, are open to challenge, but my interest is in her overall historical perspective and its relation to later work in Micronesia.

4. John Useem has been described by Kiste and Falgout (chap. 1) as an anthropologically oriented sociologist, and accordingly, his research is discussed along with that of anthropologists who also worked in Palau.

5. Carl Heine (1974, 56, 146) made reference to "the concept of Micronesia as a 'zoo' or 'museum,'" terms often used to describe US Micronesian policy in the postwar years. However, Felix Keesing (1945, 392) used these terms in a context that predated the American occupation of Micronesia, suggesting that they did not originate there.

6. Roger Gale (1973, 26–27) cited an unpublished 1973 lecture at Stanford University in which Gladwin apparently reported that he had written this piece "at the request of the administration."

7. Because the various accounts do not agree in their use of the ethnographic present, I have opted to use the past tense for all of them; this should not necessarily be taken to mean that the institutions and patterns of behavior described have disappeared.

8. As Joan Vincent's history of political anthropology (1990) demonstrated, modern anthropology, since its mid-nineteenth century beginnings, has consistently been concerned with the nature of property.

9. Burrows and Spiro were obviously responding to Murdock's terminology.

10. Lessa's data on the organization of the *sawei* system in the Woleai, particularly in the eastern islands, are somewhat thin—much of the voyaging had ended long ago, and most of the rest had been terminated by the Germans and the Japanese. So tenuous were some of the accounts about Ulithi's relations with these islands that Lessa at one point (1950c, 48) reported that on infrequent trips to Chuuk, Ulithians would stay with the island's "paramount chief"—a position that did not exist.

11. The existence of such parallel systems, and the tensions between them, were also seen at the 1975 Micronesian Constitutional Convention and particularly at the 1990 Federated States of Micronesia (FSM) Constitutional Convention, where the issue of a formal Chamber of Chiefs as part of the national government proved among the most intractable problems the delegates faced (Petersen 1993c).

12. Daniel Hughes later spoke explicitly about grafting democracy onto Micronesian societies (see below), a notion Useem had taken pains to challenge.

13. Marc Swartz (1959) reported that in Chuuk, age was perceived as a detriment to leadership; this de-emphasis on age as an element of status was unique in Micronesia, I believe, if indeed it was anything more than a chance occurrence in Chuuk.

14. Goodenough declined to label these districts "villages" because of their dispersed settlement, a pattern found on most of the high islands in the Central and Eastern Carolines.

15. A central problem in my analysis of Pohnpeian chieftainship (1982b) was my initial misunderstanding of this simple fact: matrilineal succession to office does not at all necessarily conflict with patri-virilocal postmarital residence.

16. At the 1990 FSM Constitutional Convention, the Chuuk delegation was particularly worried by attempts to further strengthen the national government's power to enforce public health quarantines that could halt the flow of first-fruits offerings. This appears to reflect certain traditional concerns about property rights. Chuuk delegates also mounted considerable opposition to the proposed Chamber of Chiefs, partly from fears that it might freeze relative status rankings they preferred to keep fluid.

17. This differs from many other descriptions of Micronesian chieftainships, which speak on the one hand of the tremendous authority of the chiefs, and on the other of the complex means by which this authority was circumscribed. On Chuuk chiefs had little authority and if they abused it, they and their kin were subject to extreme sanctions, not modest social controls. Chuukese chiefs were expected to be humble, avoid arrogance, and engage in indirect remonstrances (Goodenough 1951, 143). While possession of *itang* knowledge and skills was an advantage (1951, 144), it appears that fewer skills were expected of these leaders than of those in many other islands, where there was much more competition for leadership. An inverse relationship may exist between the emphasis placed on lineage seniority and the skill levels expected of leaders.

18. For his doctoral research Riesenberg had prepared to undertake "salvage" work with the last few members of a Southern California Native American group when the

CIMA project provided an opportunity to travel to Micronesia. His research framework was clearly organized around this earlier model (see Kiste and Falgout, chap. 1).

19. In the recent *Kabua v. Kabua* case in the Marshalls, continuing complex links among land, chiefly succession, tribute, and related topics remained matters of critical importance.

20. The widespread connections among food, land, primacy of settlement, chiefs' ancestors, chiefs, feasting, and first fruits receives further discussion below.

21. Lamotrek is interesting in this regard because the emphasis on genealogy resulted in a woman's succeeding to the island's highest office.

22. Some islands, of course, have experienced less colonial interference than others, and probably have undergone fewer changes.

23. Elsewhere (Petersen 1985) I have documented Pohnpeians saying quite vociferously that their chiefs cannot tell them how to vote.

24. I worked with Gale at that time, lobbying members of the UN Trusteeship Council. We discussed this material at length and he cited my early work on this topic. The present chapter is, in one sense, a product of twenty years of further thoughts concerning the ideas Gale and I then held in common.

25. See Cynthia Enloe's *Bananas, Beaches and Bases* (1989, 46–48) for a strikingly parallel analysis of the American women sent to teach in the Philippines in the early years of the American occupation.

26. Compare Meller's awareness of the Congress of Micronesia's limited legislative powers, in the face of the administration's veto, with Hughes' disregard of this fundamental issue.

27. In a volume edited by Jocelyn Linnekin and Lin Poyer (1990a), Michael D. Lieber, Juliana Flinn, and Poyer each chronicled the struggles of atoll peoples, who must periodically visit or reside on Micronesia's larger islands, to deal with the problems presented to them by their minority status. Flinn's monograph (1992a) on the Pulapese community settled in Chuuk's capital and Poyer's (1993) on Sapwuahfik's relations with Pohnpei explore this dynamic in considerable detail.

28. Gender studies and feminism had not yet shaped anthropological consciousness in those early days, and there is not much discussion of gender and power. Nevertheless, the topic was occasionally raised, particularly in Palau. Useem, for instance, specified that clans owned the land while all other property was controlled by families; women controlled their families' wealth and were accorded political titles in the same manner as men (1945c, 570; 1952, 267). Barnett placed considerable emphasis on women's roles and achievements, citing the proverb, "Women are strong, men are weak" (1960, 18).

29. Cultural evolutionary theory has played a small but relevant part in Micronesia's political anthropology. Murdock thought he saw "small feudal states with an elaborate class structure" nearly everywhere in Micronesia and believed they were in the process of evolving in Chuuk and nearby islands. He thus claimed to have ob-

served " 'on the hoof,' so to speak, a process of state development and class formation" (1965, 245–247). As I have indicated, Murdock described Micronesian politics as feudal well before he ever traveled to the islands; his visit there did nothing to alter those views. With the conspicuous exception of Labby (1976a), most other evolutionary formulations have likewise misconstrued the ethnographic data by overestimating the rigidity of Micronesia's stratified systems, thereby reducing them to simplified abstractions (see, for example, Hunter-Anderson and Graves 1990; Bath and Athens 1990; Cordy 1993; cf. Petersen 1990c). A series of controlled comparisons of social evolution in Micronesia (influenced in part by Sahlins' early Polynesian work [1958]), beginning with Mason (1968) and Alkire (1960), have had somewhat more success. Subsequently, Kenneth Knudson (1970, 1990), Ross Cordy (1986) and James Peoples (1992) have pushed these analyses further, linking together ecological, technological, and political factors to explain the development of systems of stratification in Micronesia.

CHAPTER SIX

Ethnicity and Identity in Micronesia

Lin Poyer

IN THE LAST FIFTEEN YEARS, issues concerning ethnicity and personal and group identity have come to occupy an increasingly central place in anthropological theory. Ethnicity and identity studies have engaged a growing number of Pacific scholars, particularly those working in the new nations of Melanesia (e.g., Gewertz and Errington 1991; Keesing 1992; Larcom 1990; Pomponio 1992; Watson 1990; G. White 1991) and in such multiethnic societies as Hawai'i, New Zealand, and Fiji (e.g., Dominy 1990; Hanson 1989; Hazlehurst 1993; Lal 1986; Linnekin 1983). Indeed, studies from the Pacific Islands have contributed to a range of issues related to cultural identity (e.g., A. Howard 1990; M. Howard 1989a; Jolly 1992; Keesing 1991; Keesing and Tonkinson 1982; Linnekin 1990; Linnekin and Poyer 1990a; Trask 1991).

Illustrating this, the contributors to Jocelyn Linnekin and Lin Poyer's edited collection, *Cultural Identity and Ethnicity in the Pacific* (1990a), explicitly related work on Oceanic constructions of identity to general theoretical issues in the study of ethnicity. The volume presented Pacific examples of the cultural construction of community identities; chapter authors recognized that Pacific Islanders have different models of personal and group identity, that ethnicity is linked with history, and that analysis of these topics must include symbolic as well as material correlates of community identity. Three chapters deal with areas of Micronesia: Kapingamarangi and Pohnpei (Lieber 1990), Pulap and Chuuk (Flinn 1990), and Sapwuahfik (Poyer 1990).

The Micronesian studies in this recent volume on ethnicity theory reveal a line of thought that can be traced to post–World War II applied anthropologists concerned with "problems" of minorities in the region's population centers. Following the Coordinated Investigation of Micronesian Anthropology (CIMA), and overlapping with the work of district anthropologists, the 1950s and 1960s saw a new generation of researchers enter Micronesia. Like their predecessors, many were both problem-solving applied anthropologists *and* academic scholars; their writings began to link Micronesian ethnography more directly to contemporary topics in anthropological theory. Reflecting current developments in anthropology, the postwar decades saw applications of cognitive and cultural analyses to Micronesian cases. In recent years, symbolic approaches have intersected with history and political economy in the study of cultural similarities and differences (cf. Hanlon, chap. 2 and Petersen, chap. 5).

In this review, I describe the origins of American anthropology's study of Micronesian ethnicity in the postwar context and trace the development of studies of cultural identity through the 1990s. This chapter addresses two related intellectual issues: first, interaction among neighboring populations (the sociological study of ethnic relations), and second, internal and external perceptions of differences among populations (the cultural study of group identity).

Inquiries into the study of differences among peoples in Micronesia reveal systematic changes in the language used to write about them. As Micronesian studies kept pace with broader theoretical developments, writing about ethnic issues decreased for a time in favor of writing in terms of "culture." The subject of ethnicity spoke to differential power relations and entailed both political and economic analysis; it was thus appropriate for examinations of local policy and administrative issues. By contrast, "culture" spoke to a global professional scholarly audience for anthropological theory and, until recently, has had relatively minor practical spin-off. These paradigmatic shifts followed trends in anthropological theory, but also reflected the ever changing relations between Americans and Micronesians, as well as altered relations among Micronesians themselves.

BACKGROUND

To understand ethnicity in American Micronesia, it is necessary to begin well before World War II. How islanders constructed cultural sameness and difference—that is, ethnic distinctions—before the era of Spanish contact remains a matter for discussion and is largely unknowable. Yet it is clear that as soon as European concepts of ethnicity entered the Pacific, they interacted with local realities to produce new sensibilities about islander vs. non-islander identities, and about differences among islanders. Spanish and Germans, through formal colonial policy, and British, Americans, and others, through less formal interactions, constructed groupings of what they saw as similar island populations, naming them in accordance with their own purposes.[1] It is beyond the scope of this chapter to explore the seventeenth to nineteenth century constructions of ethnic groups through the interaction of indigenous and European categories. However, a brief discussion of the ethnic categories operative in Micronesia immediately before the American era—during the Japanese colonial order—seems appropriate.

During the initial years of its rule in Micronesia, Japan worked to build a civil administration that would place it alongside of the colonizing nations of Western Europe, including educational, medical, legal, and economic programs. Increasingly throughout the 1930s Japan encouraged immigration to Micronesia from elsewhere in its empire. Japanese, Okinawans, and islanders were ranked hierarchically, with Japanese holding the highest status (see Peattie 1988 on Japanese rule in Micronesia). Relations between Japanese officials and islanders were mostly formal and distant, marked by status differences even when conditioned by personal affection. The Japanese cultivated some groups and gave little attention to others. For example, Chamorros developed privileged relations with the Japanese in Yap, compared to those between Yapese and Japanese. Children of Japanese married to Micronesians formed another such privileged group.

As military construction began in the mid to late 1930s, Korean and Okinawan laborers joined the ethnic mix, and many people were relocated for war work or to free land for military use. The wartime organization of labor seems to have heightened the sense of ranking among ethnic groups. For example, barracks and work tasks were assigned by ethnicity, and, during the dark days of the war in Kosrae and Chuuk, scarce food was apportioned by ethnicity. With the vast influx of troops and foreign laborers, islanders were greatly outnumbered in the regions affected, creating a profound sense of being powerless minorities in their own homelands.

When the Allies conquered Japanese Micronesia, they repatriated most Asians, although some remained as a temporary workforce. In the postwar years, there were fewer American troops on most islands than there had been Japanese, and those Americans seemed to Micronesians less formal, demanding fewer signs of respect and encouraging fraternization. Islanders and American servicemen attended church together, worked together, and ate together.

But there was still a clear difference between the two, and regulations often restricted contact between ordinary soldiers and Micronesians. Ironically, the separation widened as the intimacy of shared war faded into the past. The American impulse toward egalitarianism, so visible during the war years, was replaced by a pattern of hierarchical relations familiar to the military, contributing to a widening gap between islander and American in the postwar years.[2] Under navy civil administration and then under the US Trust Territory of the Pacific Islands (USTTPI) government, separate residences, recreation sites, and pay scales became fixtures of the American colonial era. Nonetheless, most Micronesians continued to feel that Americans were more informal and egalitarian than the Japanese had been. And in the long run, the American system of dealing with diversity left its mark. When the American government withdrew from Micronesia in the 1980s, it left a legacy of competitive pluralism, the ethnic model most familiar in American public politics.

HOW ANTHROPOLOGISTS HAVE DISCUSSED DIVERSITY

In chapter 1, Robert C. Kiste and Suzanne Falgout describe the civil affairs handbooks for Micronesia that were designed to assist American officers in their relations with local peoples during and after the conquest of the islands (US Navy Department 1944a, 1944b, 1944c; see also Marshall and Nason 1975, 23). Each contains a section on "ethnic minorities." The administration's primary concern was that such groups represented potential problems. A brief review of these materials reveals the initial approach that American social scientists took to diversity in the islands.

In the Western Carolines handbook, for example, ethnic minorities are identified as small numbers of Okinawans, Koreans, and Chamorros. The handbook comments, "Although relations between the Chamorros and the Caroline Islanders have not always been cordial, it is doubtful whether any serious [negative] feeling exists today" (US Navy Department 1944a, 64). In the Eastern Carolines handbook, Okinawans and Koreans are "the only important minority groups"; neither "poses any serious minority problem" (US Navy Department 1944b, 55). The Marianas handbook notes that because of Japanese immigration, "all racial groups in the area which are not Japanese are ethnic minorities"—that is, Chamorros and Caroline Islanders. "Neither of these two groups presents any real minority problem," states the handbook, "although the Chamorros . . . have sometimes been restive under foreign rule and may harbor some resentment against the Japanese" (US Navy

Department 1944c, 58). The handbook also reports ethnic divisions among Okinawans, Koreans, and Formosans.

In part, this early postwar attitude toward "ethnic minorities" as potential problems derived from contemporary sociology and public policy issues in the United States; it also reflected the prior Japanese administration's interest in dealing with identified populations by using a similar ethnic model. Very quickly, though, the repatriation of the large number of Asian soldiers and war workers altered the demographic face of the region, and researchers in the 1950s shifted from a discussion of ethnic minorities—even when the situation might usefully have been described in these terms—to a concern with cultural differences.

In *The Eastern Carolines,* for example, John "Jack" Fischer referred to "peoples," "communities," and "cultures," as well as "culturally distinct communities," "local cultures," and "islander societies," rather than writing about ethnic groups. In giving a "Cultural Classification of the Islands of Truk and Ponape Districts" (1957a, 7–11), Fischer engaged in the familiar ethnological task of ordering populations according to how "closely" or "distantly" they are "related"—a metaphor that resonates with implications of ethnicity but is more characteristic of the anthropologist's than the sociologist's lexicon. In Fischer's discussion, characteristic of the scholarly writing of the time, the "most basic cultural division" of the area distinguished Micronesian and Polynesian. There was then a threefold "basic division" into Kusaie, Greater Ponape, and Greater Truk, each of which was further subdivided. Shared features were attributed to common historical origin, reflecting the familiar vision of spread and differentiation over time from an ancestral population. This vision of closeness/distance with regard to cultural histories and origins is "closely related" to linguistic research, which was also being renewed in Micronesia after the war. Both language and cultural traits (and, later, material and physical traits, through archaeology and physical anthropology) were mapped onto the islands to compare similarities and differences among populations.

Fischer and his colleagues laid the groundwork of modern Micronesian ethnology while simultaneously serving as applied anthropologists in the administration of the islands. Their writing moved between "ethnicity" discourse—in which intergroup relations were viewed as potential problems to be managed—and "culture" discourse, in which intergroup differences posed scholarly questions of affiliation. To an extent, the two sorts of writing had different purposes and different audiences. However, they also suggest an in-

Lin Poyer. Photograph courtesy of Lin Poyer.

Ann and Jack Fischer, Pohnpei, early 1950s. Photograph courtesy of Mary Anne Fischer.

teresting duality in anthropological writing, one discussed by recent critics of ethnography: that is, anthropologists have at times isolated academic writing in an imaginary, timeless universe, insulated from political and economic issues. As discussed elsewhere in this volume (chapters 1, 2, and 5), anthropologists working in Micronesia in the 1950s were very much a part of attempts to solve contemporary problems, and research into ethnicity was as much a part of these efforts at applied anthropology as research into cultural affiliation was part of scholarly ethnology.

In the years immediately after the war, certain "hot spots" emerged that were perceived to be caused by ethnic issues, and these set precedents for understanding future developments in terms of interethnic relations. Anthropologists were called on to assist with these hot spots. One of the navy's first postwar tasks in the islands was to repatriate those who had been relocated by Japanese labor requirements and other displacements. Taking people "back home" implied a link between ethnicity and territory (place), a concept partly shared by Micronesians, Americans, and Japanese. There was broad agreement on the idea of returning people to their point of origin. But the trouble caused by ethnic thinking cropped up then as now (e.g., in eastern Europe): at what point does relocation stop? If Okinawan farmers should be returned to Okinawa, and Nauruans who spent the war in Chuuk returned to Nauru, should Chamorros long resident on Yap go back to the Marianas? What about the Mokilese and Ngatikese who had lived on Pohnpei since German times? If Japanese soldiers were to be returned to Japan, what about Japanese civilians who had long-lasting marriages with Micronesian women? And what of their children, who were often Japanese citizens?

One of the first ethnicity-related problems the United States faced was how to handle Micronesian-Japanese marriages. The Japanese partners had no choice, being ordered to leave; however, their wives and children had to decide whether to go to Japan or stay in the islands. In most cases the women and children decided to remain (Fischer 1957a, 65). Such relocations caused lifelong heartache; wartime survivors today are still saddened by the postwar separations. Because most of the skilled laborers, commercial fishermen, and entrepreneurs were immigrants, the economic effects of their departure were also severe (Fischer 1957a, 65). Perceived primarily as a security issue, the decision as to who would leave became a de facto exercise in social identity, as part-Japanese or part-Okinawan islanders decided—or had it decided for them —whether they were Asians to be deported or locals to be aided in postwar recovery. Individuals tried to manage these categories to their own advantage, of course. For instance, Mr. Masataka Mori, a member of a well-known Japanese-Chuukese family, laid aside his Japanese Army uniform and identified himself as an islander in order to remain in the islands. Mr. Nobuyuki Suzuki (mother Chuukese, father Japanese) stayed in Chuuk, but his older brother went with their father to Japan; the two brothers were not reunited until decades later. Anthropologists were not called on to negotiate individual identities, but they were asked for advice on repatriation issues, and in some cases to assist with relocation.[3]

After the repatriation period of the late 1940s and early 1950s, district anthropologists employed by the USTTPI government and independent researchers alike investigated and assisted with local problems that were construed by Americans as ethnic in nature. The three most significant of these were Carolinians and Chamorros on Saipan, Chamorros on Yap, and the general matter of "mixed-blood" people.

In his ethnography of Saipan, based on research in the Marianas from 1949 to 1950 as part of the Scientific Investigation of Micronesia program, Alex Spoehr discussed ethnicity in much the same terms he might have used for American society. He described Chamorro culture as "a Hispanicized Oceanic hybrid," "a new culture," "a Spanish-indigenous growth, incorporating also important American Indian and Filipino traits" (Spoehr 1954; cf. Diaz 1994). The first Carolinian settlers arrived on Saipan in 1815, and others came later. "Probably because they are a minority," Spoehr wrote, "the Carolinians display greater unity and cohesion as a group and are very conscious of their ethnic separateness" (1954, 26; cf. Alkire 1984b for an update on Carolinians on Saipan). Spoehr concluded, "Chamorros and Carolinians get along amicably enough. . . . However, the Chamorros as a whole consider themselves as a superior group and the Carolinians as a less civilized and backward one" (1954, 27).

> The Carolinians, on the other hand, feel they are different from the Chamorros, but not necessarily inferior, and during my stay a number of Carolinians expressed mild resentment at the Chamorros who imputed inferiority to their groups. . . . Yet under the successive foreign administrations of Saipan, the greater degree of westernization of the Chamorros, their greater literacy, and their eagerness to borrow from the culture of the administering group have given them a preferred position. (1954, 27–28)

Evident here are two points that became central to studies of ethnicity: first, a recognition that foreign rulers used ethnic distinctions as a basis for differential treatment, and second, an awareness that continual interaction generated attitudes that maintained ethnic boundaries. In Spoehr's case, as in other writing of the postwar era, these scholarly perceptions were nested in practical issues addressing problems of intergroup relations.

Since World War II, virtually all studies of Chamorros, including those on Guam (e.g., Joseph and Murray 1951; Bowers 1950; Poehlman 1979; Souder-Jaffery 1992), have used concepts of ethnicity familiar from studies of the multiethnic American mainland. This parallels a common scholarly and public perception that Chamorros are "more acculturated" or "more western" than other Micronesians. Due in part to a longer history of contact with Europeans, this perception has also resulted from the distinct role Chamorros have played in colonial administrations throughout Micronesia in the Spanish, German, Japanese, and American eras. As Vicente Diaz has pointed out (1994), Chamorros have been set apart by scholars, by politicians, and by themselves from other Micronesians; one element of this distinctiveness is the perception of Chamorros as an ethnic group in the sense that the phrase is used in American politics.

Chamorros themselves were an "ethnic minority" on Yap, where they played a favored and important role in commerce and government during the Japanese era. They were called a "minority group" (along with Okinawan and Korean laborers) in the *Civil Affairs Handbook* (US Navy Department 1944a), which numbered Chamorros at 240 in Yap district and 214 in Palau district in 1937. After the war, Yap's indigenous leaders indicated to Americans that they wished the Chamorros to leave and, though many had been longtime residents, the administration did relocate them. Most were resettled on Tinian and Rota, where businessmen and entrepreneurs were expected to become farmers. Chamorros were unhappy with this situation, and for many years they complained to administration officials and district anthropologists about the difficulties of relocation (see, e.g., Bowers 1950).

Administrators, and to a lesser extent anthropologists, were interested in individuals who were descended from island women and European, or occasionally Japanese, men. (The attention to bloods "mixing" rarely extended to offspring of interisland marriages.) This interest in "mixed bloods" probably reflected American folk models of biogenetic kinship and questions about the role of "blood" in kinship, appearance, and behavior (see Schneider 1968).

Though Margaret Chave's (1950) report on "mixed-bloods" in the Marshalls is a rare example of work devoted explicitly to this topic, most anthropologists in the postwar years discussed the "admixture" of local populations with Europeans and Japanese. For example, in the Eastern Carolines Fischer noted that "there is the prospect that in the next few generations existing intrusive racial strains will be thoroughly mixed with the rest of the population, as they already are socially" (1957a, 18). Spoehr found racial admixture a useful explanatory concept in contrasting Saipan's ethnic groups: "One key to the status positions of Carolinians and Chamorros is found in the marriages with outlanders from other parts of the Pacific and of the world" (1954, 28). Chamorros married Spanish, Europeans, Americans, Filipinos, Japanese, and mixed-blood Micronesians. "Mixed blood islanders" from elsewhere in Micronesia married Chamorros on Saipan and Tinian; "full-blood islanders" married Carolinians (Spoehr 1954, 28).

With the exception of physical anthropology, and to a lesser extent archaeology, a discussion of "racial" characteristics of populations has not been a major theme in the anthropology of Micronesia. On the other hand, individuals of mixed European or Japanese descent frequently appeared in reports on local conditions during the postwar years, as some such families had achieved economic and political importance. To name some examples, prominent Micronesian families partially descended from foreigners include the Mori, Narrhun, and Irons families in Chuuk, the de Brums, Capelles, Heines, and Milnes in the Marshalls, and the Herrmans on Kosrae. However, nowhere in Micronesia did such "mixed-race" groups become established as a distinct, labeled social stratum, perhaps because of the continued importance of matrilineal affiliation in securing rights to land and other heritables.[4]

In general, these elite minorities survived the war fairly well and retained or regained economic power afterwards. Some, however, suffered for their foreign connections and were treated by Japanese military as suspected spies or as prisoners (here I include the Belgian Etscheit family on Pohnpei). Most non-Asian "mixed" or non-native residents were perceived as valuable to the US Navy administration, and no effort was made to relocate them after the war. As in Japanese times, they were often called on for advice or given responsible positions. Thus in some places a three-tiered ethnic division effectively operated early in the American era: Americans, "mixed-blood" or foreign brokers, and local islanders. Perhaps immediately after the war, the topic of descendants of European-Micronesian relationships was of considerable scholarly and practical interest because Americans were in the process of negotiating how they themselves would relate to Micronesians.

AMERICANS AND MICRONESIANS AS ETHNIC GROUPS

During the early US era, then, local populations were governed by administrators using American notions of ethnicity. Similarly, under the Japanese, Japanese ideas of ethnicity had held sway. American and Japanese ideas overlapped considerably; for example, both thought it appropriate to organize labor according to ethnicity. Unlike the Japanese, Americans did not explicitly rank ethnic groups, with the one very important exception of separate wage scales for Micronesian and American employees. However, de facto rankings were apparent in American practices, for example, the preferential hiring of Chamorros on Saipan and at first on Yap.

In the immediate postwar years, the administration regularly assessed Micronesian responses to Americans (see, e.g., a section entitled "Attitudes towards Americans" in Homer G. Barnett's 1948 "Cima Interim Report" for Palau [Barnett n.d.b]; the final report is Barnett 1949). Fischer mentioned the problem of "cultural differences" between Micronesians and Americans and noted "it is inevitable for a time at least that Americans should occupy the key power positions in the government" and that American personnel "tend to constitute a self-centered foreign colony"; both of these factors "tend to produce in the minds of both governing and governed the belief that American citizens have special rights for lenient treatment before the law" (1957a, 196).

Like Fischer and Barnett, others usually reported that Micronesians accepted American superiority. Researchers rarely included American-Micronesian relations as a natural object of their studies. Spoehr set Chamorro and Carolinian in the context of "the total community" of Saipan, including military personnel, who "lived and worked largely within the boundaries of the [spatially separate] military reservations" and encountered islanders through contacts that "were purposefully limited by the authorities" (1954, 98–99). Civil administrators had closer local relations, since their duties concerned Micronesians. "Each group [US administrators and Micronesians] has its own residence area, and there is spatial and social distance between the groups, but it is considerably less than was the case with purely military personnel" (1954, 99). Spoehr's work provides a rare glimpse of colonizers and colonized in the context of straightforward academic ethnography. Ward H. Goodenough presented socially isolated foreign administrators and change agents in a broader context (1963, 413–415).

Among those involved with governing Micronesia, individuals like Spoehr were in the minority in viewing Micronesians and Americans as part of a single social system. Most Americans saw the two as quite distinct, and a colonial mentality fostered the whole range of ethnic discriminations, from American-only bars to unequal wages for Micronesians and Americans filling the same jobs. In 1971, changes in job classifications were implemented to eliminate discrimination. Overall, however, the interaction between Americans and Micronesians, like that between Japanese and Micronesians, was one of inequality. And while the colonial hierarchy persisted in emphasizing the broad category of "Micronesian" subjects, islanders themselves both maintained complex nested identities determined by cultural and linguistic background, and began to explore the social and political ramifications of accepting an identity as Micronesian.

KINSHIP, COMMUNITY, CONTEXTS, TRANSACTIONS

As the Micronesian world began to change economically and politically in the years after the war, the world of anthropology was also being reshaped by theoretical innovations. In the late 1940s and 1950s a new group of researchers spent formative years of fieldwork in the region and used their Micronesian experiences to forge new tools for anthropological inquiry.

A contribution of lasting significance in this regard is Ward Goodenough's well-known *Property, Kin, and Community on Truk* (1951), which began a theoretically sophisticated inquiry into the concept of "community." Beyond politics and kinship, Chuukese communities were integrated by a tendency toward endogamy, father-son gifts, age groupings, daily association and recreation, and linguistic features. Chapters on identity in Goodenough's *Cooperation and Change* (1963) presaged important connections between psychological theories of identity and sociological and cultural theories of ethnicity. Goodenough highlighted important linkages among cultural identity, language, and the social order, especially lineage membership and land rights.

Goodenough's work on Chuuk generated much of his later contributions to anthropological theory and is discussed in other chapters of this volume (e.g., Marshall, chapters 4 and 12). It is sufficient here to mention the article, "Rethinking 'Status' and 'Role' " (Goodenough 1965a). The concept of social identities, the distinction of these from statuses, the attention to variability in when and how social identities are expressed, the duality of social interaction (considering both ego and alter)—all these are ideas critical to the study of self and ethnic identity that emerged in the 1980s. Goodenough's writings in the 1950s and 1960s helped to lay the foundation for the turn to emic analysis that has characterized the past three decades of cultural anthropology (Caughey and Marshall 1989).

The late 1960s and early 1970s saw many students conduct dissertation research in Micronesia, amassing data that fueled a series of publications. The symposia and publication of volumes of comparative ethnography by the Association for Social Anthropology in Oceania (ASAO) formed an important part of this next era of research which continues to the present.

The first ASAO volumes were published soon after the association was founded. _Adoption in Eastern Oceania,_ edited by Vern Carroll (1970a), included articles by Carroll (Nukuoro), Michael D. Lieber (Kapingamarangi and Pohnpei), Jack Fischer (Pohnpei), Ruth Goodenough (Chuuk), and a conclusion by Ward Goodenough. This volume laid the groundwork for further studies in ethnicity by posing such questions as what is adoption, what is kinship, and what is parenthood. These questions were preliminary to inquires into what is a community, and what is an ethnic group—which were addressed in later ASAO volumes and elsewhere by some of the same researchers. The fourth ASAO volume, _Transactions in Kinship: Adoption and Fosterage in Oceania,_ edited by Ivan Brady (1976), explored the nature of kinship, with descriptions of the cultural premises and behaviors related to the rights of parents, categories of fosterage and adoption, and ideas about kinship. The questions about who is a parent and who is a child foreshadowed yet another question: Who is a member of X ethnic group?

Carroll's _Pacific Atoll Populations_ (1975a) addressed, among other topics, how one defines membership in a population at the level of individual and community. Along with the work on kinship and adoption, this volume set the stage for a generation of research that connected Micronesian studies to broad trends in anthropological theory, linking studies of the self, concepts of "otherness," and symbolic processes of differentiation and affiliation. Several chapters explored the cultural expectations generating community and individual definitions of ethnic affiliation. Speaking of Nukuoro, for example, Carroll wrote that they "regard themselves as a distinct ethnic community not included in any larger ethnic grouping" (1975b, 9)—signaling a culturally centered approach to the question of how communities are to be distinguished, and to what end, without (yet) taking on the question of why the term "ethnic" is appropriate here.

Other chapters in this volume discussed the demography of Micronesian populations, and incidentally or centrally pursued Carroll's suggestions about identifying an ethnic population. Nason's (1975) discussion of Ettal Atoll included the cultural rules determining who was locally considered to be an Ettal person. He stated that rules for becoming an atoll citizen were the same for Ettal as those described by Mac Marshall (1975b) for Namoluk (the two islands are historically related). Indeed, by the end of this volume it is clear that some general processes of ethnic affiliation operated across much of Micronesia, with particular similarity among atoll communities.

Marshall's discussion of Namoluk treated questions of ethnic affiliation even more directly. Namoluk's modern population descended from immigrants; "this heterogeneity of background—at least ten islands of origin—is ignored by the islanders who maintain the fiction that Namoluk is an ethnically distinct population" (1975b, 165). The word "fiction" was unfortunate—as deconstructionism has become fashionable, scholars have come to view a biological model of ethnicity as no more "real" than any other cultural notion. But Marshall recognized that genealogical heterogeneity may be quite disconnected from whether a population perceives itself as a community, and that this is often the case in Chuuk State (1975b, 165). "Unlike demographers," Marshall writes,

> Namoluk informants do not make the assumption that it is possible to divide people into specific unambiguous categories. They find questions like "Where are you from?" and "Are you permanently away from your home island?" at best ambiguous, and at worst meaningless. Sometimes, a question asking which island an individual is from will elicit contradictory responses from different persons; some will say one island, some another, and some will answer honestly that they do not know. This is so even though all of these persons know where the individual in question was born, where he has land rights, and where he resides at the moment. Such contradictory answers do not show ignorance or perversity. Rather, they illustrate a flexibility, an alterability, and a built-in ambiguity that are essential parts of the Namoluk perception of a concept like 'citizen of such-and-such a place.' Let us explore this idea more fully. (1975b, 171–172)

And Marshall did so. He described how citizenship was determined by "a complex of factors that includes birth, residence, land rights, marriage, client-ship, adoption, and, sometimes, official government registration and employ-ment" (1975b, 172). While going on to analyze changing patterns of marriage and migration, Marshall thus set up what proved to be an interesting task for the next set of workers: to understand what community membership means when constructed so flexibly.

RELOCATED COMMUNITIES AND ETHNIC BOUNDARIES

The initiative to study relocated communities included some of the same people and drew on some of the same questions that were considered in the "population" research. The importance of ethnicity is evident in the Pacific Displaced Communities Project directed by Barnett, and in other research on relocation and migration (e.g., Emerick 1960 and Severance 1976 for Pohnpei; Ritter 1980 for Kosrae; Shewman 1981 for Palau; Flinn 1985b and Reafsnyder 1984 for Chuuk State; Kiste 1974 and 1985 for the Marshall Islands). While much of this work dealt with demographic and geographic issues, some writ-ers on relocation and migration discussed how populations constructed themselves, and accepted labels given by others, as a distinctive group.

Exiles and Migrants in Oceania, edited by Michael Lieber (1977a), dealt directly with community and individual identity, and indicated the role of colonial systems in establishing, fixing, and altering community boundaries. It included several chapters on American Micronesia. Robert McKnight began the case studies by countering the Nathan Report's claim that concentrated populations and increased mobility "can speed the replacement of local particularism with a cohesive Micronesia" (Nathan 1966, 100, quoted in McKnight 1977, 10). Instead, social science knowledge about ethnic bounda-ries suggested that "the kind of happy homogenization portrayed in the Nathan Report is, in fact, not possible in Micronesia" given the dominance of the colonial administration over the social system (McKnight 1977, 12). McKnight described boundary processes that maintained relocated Southwest Islanders on Palau as a distinct community. At least as if not more important than cul-tural differences among groups was the fact that each related to the colonial system separately and differently. (McKnight was another anthropologist involved in applied work who saw the links between the politics of ethnicity and the scholarship of culture theory). To discuss boundary maintenance, McKnight had to address the same topics raised earlier by Carroll (1975b), indicating that research interest in ethnic boundaries had not yet been exhausted: what makes a person Palauan or Southwest Islander?

McKnight concluded that relocation constrained by limited space would most likely lead to "cultural particularism *and* congestion with the emergence of rigid ethnic-class structures and accelerated intergroup tension" (1977, 32–33). The vision of possible futures for Micronesia—homogenization or balkanization?—surfaced as an important theme in scholarly writing about the status talks surrounding the termination of the US Trust Territory of the Pacific (see below).

In the conclusion to *Exiles and Migrants,* Lieber (1977b) described two types of "social macrosystems": one results in "ethnic boundary–dissolving" systems in which immigrants are absorbed into the host society's structure; the other produces boundary-maintaining systems, of which colonial systems are prime examples. In the former, attempts to retain ethnic identity create difficulties; in the long run, intermarriages and the incorporation of children into the host structure often dissolve boundaries in these systems. But colonial regimes create and freeze ethnic boundaries, beginning with the suppression of warfare. Missions and commercial interests also help maintain ethnic boundaries; and, of course, colonial regimes have forced or encouraged relocation, often accompanied by political and economic arrangements that maintain boundaries. Lieber (1977b, 355) focused on a fundamental question: What does it take to make a community? Like earlier ASAO volumes, *Exiles and Migrants* centered on a cultural systems approach, a concern with premises, models, categories and systems of ideas as well as behavior.

POLITICS AND IDENTITY

Social scientists working on political issues in the 1940s and 1950s were concerned about how Micronesians were to be governed. Later, the focus of concern shifted to how Micronesians would govern themselves. By the 1960s, researchers had begun to ask what it meant to be "Micronesian" at all. While Japanese and American administrators had permitted some local flexibility, they nonetheless lumped islanders into a single category ("tomin," "Kanaka," "Micronesians") vis-à-vis the colonial power. But as Hanlon discusses (chap. 2), the notion of "Micronesian-ness" was an invention of outsiders, and one that was not widely shared by the island peoples themselves.

Although Micronesians have at times accepted and even promoted a joint Micronesian identity, they have also maintained and even expanded the significance of local identities. Variations in custom and language have become reified and expressed as political movements under some circumstances. Indigenous nationalist movements elsewhere encouraged self-reflection, which was spurred on by Micronesian youth educated abroad, by politicians and others actively seeking to define a new Micronesian identity, by Peace Corps Volunteers and other activists, and by writers who promoted "the Micronesian way" and pan-Micronesian identity. These all called explicit attention to the question of how and to what extent local community identities were to be balanced with the national identities that were presumably developing (see Petersen, chap. 5).

The US Navy began attempts to build democracy by establishing local and regional precursors to the district legislatures established in the 1950s (Meller 1969, 47–58). Anthropologists on the scene saw that American political models would not readily transfer to Micronesia. Fischer, for example, pointed to one problem involved:

> Persons not thoroughly acquainted with the languages and cultures of the islanders often fail to realize the degree of difference between many of the islands and the feeling of separateness which accompanies these differences. Even where there is considerable cultural similarity, as among the five petty states of Ponape or among the islands of Truk Lagoon or of the Mortlock group, the people of these formerly independent communities do not all consider that their cultural similarity inevitably implies that they should be politically united. (1957a, 181)

Also, men were reluctant to take positions of leadership outside their own community (1957a, 182). The problem of finding adequate local leadership— in the administration's terms—and then controlling it, bedeviled district administrators throughout the American era.

Using educational programs and public relations techniques, Americans cultivated a new generation of leaders, with deliberate attention to creating a nation-minded worldview. Education at the public Pacific Islands Central School and the private Xavier High School deliberately integrated students from all districts. The hope was that as USTTPI-wide political structures developed, new politicians would emerge to fill the new roles. The drive to create an indigenous sense of "Micronesian-ness" included special commemorative days; a Micronesian anthem; public attention to affiliation with the United Nations (UN), such as the celebration of UN Day holidays; and educational materials identifying Micronesia as a unit.

Commencement, Outer Islands High School, Yap District, 1971. Trust Territory Archives (Photo 2703.01), Pacific Collection, University of Hawai'i Library.

Meeting of Trusteeship Council, United Nations.
UN Photograph, 1978.
Trust Territory Archives (Photo 3377.04), Pacific
Collection, University of Hawai'i Library.
Left to right:

Mitaro Danis, Chuuk District Administrator
Lazarus Salii, USTTPI Office of Planning Director
Adrian Winkel, High Commissioner
Juan A. Sablan, Deputy High Commissioner

Xavier High School,
Chuuk, late 1960s or
early 1970s. Trust
Territory Archives
(Photo 2968.15), Pacific
Collection University of
Hawai'i Library.

As the termination of the US Trust Territory of the Pacific became the focus of political negotiations, anthropologists familiar with the region published cautionary commentaries, often insisting on the continuing significance of local identities (Petersen deals with the main issues [chap. 5]). Leonard E. Mason compared the geopolitical territory of Micronesia to "a package of assorted goods" wrapped and tied by international agreements, Micronesian desires, the Congress of Micronesia, and geography: "Should the wrappings be torn and the cords parted in delivery [i.e., in the course of negotiations to end the trust territory], nothing could prevent the goods from spilling out and being lost" (1974, 204). Countering unification were the centrifugal forces of diversity in language, "social and cultural practices," district center–outer island contrasts, imbalances in natural resource distribution, and contested claims to power among elected representatives, traditional leaders, and others.

By the early 1970s it was clear that a pan-Micronesian identity was not coalescing. This was reflected in scholarly writings, as well as events in Micronesia. The "states" would not merge into a "nation." As Mason presciently noted,

> Behind the present facade of unity, peoples of the Trust Territory display a welter of opposing identities deeply rooted in Micronesia's geography, traditional cultures, and history of contact with the rest of the world. Only in recent years, when confronting the United States on political and economic issues, have some islanders come to regard themselves keenly as "Micronesians," employing a label that symbolizes their status as territorial citizens seeking emancipation. Otherwise, individuals will on occasion identify themselves as residents of a certain district—as Ponapean, Marshallese, or Palauan—but such denotations generally lack strong feeling and commitment to other members of the named reference group. In the face-to-face interaction of daily life, identities are colored with a greater emotion and sense of belonging to social groups that are distinctive in beliefs, sentiments, and behaviors. Examples are island villages, clans, lineages, kindreds, classes, and collectivities based on shared language, religion, occupation, or proprietary rights. (1974, 225)

Political recognition of differences came in the form of the split negotiations. As the trust territory broke up and smaller island groupings reinvented themselves as new nations, the pragmatics of politics could be considered "applied ethnicity." Constitutions were written and voting districts determined using a mixture of indigenous categories of identity and introduced models of democratic pluralism. The phenomenon of "ethnic voting" and the intersection of competitive ethnic politics with "the Micronesian way" form a story now being written, as much by political scientists as by anthropologists. A cautionary note needs to be sounded, however, as the former assume that island populations operate in the same way as ethnic groups in the United States—for example, through bloc voting (e.g., Schwalbenberg 1984; Ranney and Penniman 1985). While the use of ethnic concepts borrowed from American politics may provide some insights, the apparent similarity masks significant differences in the perceptions and organization of Micronesian populations and those of American ethnic blocs.

In his 1974 article, Mason reviewed the loosening ties among the USTTPI districts at that time. Negotiators for the Marianas, Marshalls, and Palau districts were convinced that internal diversity made political unity untenable. (Other differences—especially in economic resources—were also critical.) In addition, some populations within districts negotiated for political recognition of their distinctive status: Rota in the Marianas, Kosrae in Pohnpei District, the atolls east of Yap, and the Fááychuuk area of Chuuk. As each island group set forth its own political and economic agenda, scholars began to explore the non–Pan-Micronesian-ness of these populations. It seemed that a "Marshallese" or "Chuukese" identity might prove as difficult to discover as a "Micronesian" identity, and that the distinctiveness of each population's politics and culture was worthy of scrutiny. In 1974, Daniel Hughes and Sherwood Lingenfelter edited a volume in which the particularities of local politics throughout the region were analyzed, and subsequently Hughes and Stanley Laughlin (1982) also explored the developing political culture of the Federated States of Micronesia (FSM).

With regard to local politics, Pohnpei has received the most attention from anthropologists. In an important series of articles, Hughes examined the intersection of traditional and elected leadership there (1969a, 1969b, 1969c, 1970, 1972, 1974, 1982). Glenn Petersen's work on Pohnpei has contributed not only to the study of local and national (FSM) politics, but also to the ethnology of chiefdoms, the political economy of colonialism, and the ideology of independence, all in the course of exploring what is distinctive about being Pohnpeian (see, e.g., 1979, 1982b, 1984, 1985, 1989).

The incipient alienation of Pohnpeians from both FSM national government and other ethnic groups in Pohnpei State derived from a "tension" in "the intersecting realms of ethnicity and development" (Petersen 1989, 285). Whereas new nations are often built out of some felt unity, "in the Micronesian case . . . ethnicity divisions were heeded, or at least given lip-service, where they coincided with American interests and ignored where they did not. The Micronesians learned that, while some ethnic, regional, and cultural differences have political standing, others do not" (Petersen 1989, 286). The question of which differences will be accorded political validity lies at the heart of recent studies of ethnicity in the islands.

One common pattern often presented as an ethnic distinction is the political contest between central and outer islands. In chapter 5, Petersen writes that there is a long-standing tension in Micronesia between the centrifugal push of local independence, and minorities' (e.g., outer islanders') desire to be part of a larger unit to protect their own interests (Lessa 1950c; Mason 1975). Earlier Petersen indicated that in Pohnpei State, outer islanders and Pohnpeians have different philosophies of government and different strategies for political development, with the outer islanders preferring federation (1989, 305). William Alkire confirmed that, throughout Micronesia, "ethnic and outer island minorities have deep-seated suspicions about any political change that concentrates power in the hands of a traditional opposition majority or in a centre that has developed out of recent migration" (1984b, 283).

In his discussion of Carolinians in the Commonwealth of the Northern Marianas Islands (CNMI), Alkire provided a case that demonstrated the flexibility and strategic political potential of ethnicity. "For many years, the Carolinians on Saipan have perceived themselves as an oppressed minority, discriminated against by both the majority Chamorros and the various colonial authorities" (1984b, 273). In contrast to German and Japanese rulers, Americans were seen by the Carolinians as "potential protectors" who would guarantee their minority rights vis-à-vis Chamorros (1984b, 275). Worried that they would lose American protection as a minority and links with Carolinians elsewhere in the trust territory, the Saipan Carolinians "became greatly concerned" at Marianas moves to initiate separate negotiations with the United States in 1971 (1984b, 275). They were especially alarmed at the proposal to merge the Northern Marianas with Guam, which would make them even more of a minority among Chamorros. They preferred less local control, since "from their point of view, local self-government meant perpetuation of Chamorro rule" (1984b, 276). At the same time, ethnic politics stimulated a cultural revival; Carolinians on Saipan began to represent themselves as a more purely native culture, contrasted with Chamorros as an "amalgam" of various imported cultures (1984b, 281). The Chamorros' frequent claim that they were not "native" was thus turned against them (1984b, 281).

Such a renegotiation of ethnic identity can renew old ties while creating new ones. Carolinians on Saipan now connect with Carolinians on the atolls of Yap State of the Federated States of Micronesia. Alkire wrote that "the outer islanders who look to Saipan want to 'modernize'; the Saipan Carolinians who look to the outer islands want to 'traditionalize' "(1984b, 283). Similarly, Pulapese present themselves as "traditional" models for their neighbors in Chuuk State (Flinn 1990). In these cases, an identity once denigrated as backward and less modern has been inverted to make a political virtue of authenticity. Such examples show that ethnicity may be manipulated as a strategically flexible weapon—an attribute that has drawn renewed attention to ethnicity as a topic of theoretical interest.

ETHNICITY THEORY

In the decades since the war, the focus of research and analysis has shifted from local communities to the level of intercommunity and regional processes. The first two decades of American anthropology in Micronesia saw increased concern about global impacts on Micronesian communities, and challenged any notion about island communities as stable isolates. When migration, relocation, identity negotiation, and culture change were more closely examined, researchers realized that the same processes were omnipresent, perhaps with varying intensity at different points in time. The vision of Micronesian communities became more tentative, and more dynamic —both metaphorically and literally. This opened new research questions in Micronesia itself, and connected work there with developing cultural, interpretive, political, economic, and critical perspectives in anthropological theory.

The ASAO volumes of the 1970s examined ethnicity as process, as encounter with the colonial system, and as interpersonal dynamic. At that point, however, "ethnicity" as a theoretical concept was used in a relatively unproblematic way. By contrast, during the 1980s and 1990s theoretical work that dealt explicitly with ethnicity did so, in a sense, to debunk it—that is, to deconstruct it as an analytical category and reveal it as an ideology and a social formation that appears under specifiable historical conditions (for another contribution from Micronesian anthropology that offers a similar deconstructive process in kinship studies, see Schneider 1984). Thus the Linnekin and Poyer volume begins with the following premise:

that there are alternative schemes of conceptualizing cultural differences, based on different theories of the origin and meaning of human variability, and that these cultural propositions structure social behavior. (1990b, 1–2)

The authors distinguish cultural identity from "ethnicity," which is more narrowly defined as "a set of theories based on the proposition that people can be classified into mutually exclusive bounded groups" determined by origin (1990b, 2). This approach identifies "ethnicity" as a particular way of talking about human diversity, common to some but not all cultures, rather than as a universal analytical category. In the 1990s, the impact of this approach is evident throughout Pacific studies. In Micronesia, it is revealed in increasingly nuanced examinations of how self-identified groups reproduce and represent themselves as cultural communities.

An example of changes in ideas about ethnicity and identity in Micronesia is the work of Michael Lieber, which has spanned three decades of fieldwork and theoretical development. He has expanded his analysis of Kapingamarangi ethnicity from his initial description of the relocated community of Porakiet on Pohnpei (Lieber 1968a) to increasingly complex analyses of Kapinga-Pohnpei interaction, engaging theoretical and ethnographic aspects of social and community identity (Lieber 1977c, 1984, 1990). Other scholars who began to publish in the 1980s have continued to demonstrate these new approaches to ethnicity. For example, Flinn (1990, 1992a) discussed how Pulapese customs, formerly considered backward, have become a point of pride and a focus for community identity and action. Likewise, Poyer (1988a, 1988b, 1990, 1993) described the historical construction and contemporary maintenance of a distinctive identity for the people of Sapwuahfik.

After a hiatus of several decades, the terms "ethnicity" and "ethnic group" as analytical concepts have again come into common usage. However, the greater use of ethnicity in social analysis has been largely restricted to problem-focused research, notably in politics, demography, and social issues. In this regard, Micronesian ethnicity may even become relevant within American politics, as Guam and the Northern Marianas are part of the American political system, and as Micronesians from Guam and all parts of the former trust territory migrate to the mainland United States where "Pacific Islanders" form a kind of ethnic group (Barringer, Gardner, and Levin 1993). The impact of federal programs in the islands has also encouraged discussions of ethnicity in two other fields, education and language. Given the importance of bilingual education, these two fields have obvious relationships (Goetzfridt and Wuerch 1989). Another problem-oriented research area that has made use of ethnicity is demography. Demographic studies have become more sophisticated in Micronesia, at least partly in response to the need for more precise statistics for social policy planning (Gorenflo and Levin 1989, 1991; Levin 1976). Such studies allow population-based analyses of migration, economic development (Nason 1984), and social problems like suicide and crime (see Hezel, chap. 9 and Rubinstein, chap. 10). Usually, demographic studies classify participants according to their culture of origin, and reflect an interest in identifying the ethnicity of individuals. But since migration has greatly increased throughout the region, culture of origin may refer to ancestors rather than to upbringing. And the ever increasing number of American-Micronesian and interisland marriages adds to the demographic and cultural challenges. Once again there is concern over minorities in a host society, and on Guam in the 1990s, ethnicity—including "Micronesian" ethnicity—has become an important and emotional topic for research and public discussion (Rubinstein and Levin 1992).

Some current research bears certain similarities to the anthropological work of the 1940s and 1950s. Once again, there are potential "ethnic hot spots" in Micronesia, and anthropologists are among those seeking to understand them. As before, these are troublesome concerns that may have practical political and administrative implications (e.g., the Compact impact controversy on Guam). Other examples include tensions within the FSM polity (Petersen 1993c); migrant communities in Chuuk (Flinn 1992a; Reafsnyder 1984); outer islanders on Yap (Alkire 1993b); and FSM politics and ethnicity reflected in dance (Pinsker 1992; Petersen 1992b).

It is not within the purview of this chapter to discuss the large body of work in applied anthropology, which will be left to others. But it should be noted that those who study bilingual education and other practical problems in the new Micronesian nations have come full circle, their work now resembling in many ways that of the post–World War II American anthropologists, who organized research to investigate problems confronting the United States as it threw its colonial mantle over the islands. Like the first American anthropologists in the region, researchers who work on culturally appropriate education, language preservation, migration, and social programs often speak in the language of ethnicity, while being fully conversant with the discourse of culture. As in earlier decades, "problems" are concentrated in urban areas, in centers of commerce and politics, on densely populated islands where members of different island populations gather and interact. This makes ethnicity —what we might think of as the pragmatic political dimension of culture— salient in the practical world of anthropology, even as it is deconstructed in the realm of theory.

PROSPECTS FOR THE FUTURE

Future research into ethnicity and cultural identity in Micronesia is likely to continue the parallel interests discussed at the beginning of this chapter: the sociological study of ethnic relations, and the cultural study of group identity.

On one hand, political and economic studies of interaction among neighboring populations will continue to delineate the factors that lead to tension or accommodation, to different social outcomes and alternate forms of community organization. Examples of this work likely to carry on into the next century include research into internal migration and links between outer islands and political centers; relations between the United States and the newly independent nations; nation-building in these new states; the internal politics of the Federated States of Micronesia; the applicability of American law and sociocultural norms in the Northern Marianas and Guam; and emigrant Micronesian communities in the mainland United States, Hawai'i, and Guam. Such topics have a strong practical interest and will continue to engage anthropologists who seek to understand the complex sociopolitical expression of cultural differences.

On the other hand, symbolic, historical, and explicitly cultural studies will continue to explore the indigenous and external perceptions of similarities and differences among populations. Language, handicrafts, dance and song, the social organization of local communities, ideologies of descent and behavior, norms of interpersonal interaction, culturally valued economic exchanges—these (and other) elements of what makes "us" and "them" bear much further study. Studies discussed in this chapter have set a framework for understanding the social processes and cultural symbols that establish and maintain community identity. The framework can serve as a guideline for research that will produce a library of ethnographies exploring the uniqueness of each community, set in the context of surrounding and interacting communities.

In pursuing these parallel research tasks, anthropologists will interact, more than ever before, with people who have a voice in how their cultural selves are described and analyzed in the professional literature. In ethnicity studies such interaction is not only welcome, it is essential. In this field, "internal" and "external" voices contribute distinct and equally valuable information; felt senses of personal and cultural identity are data equal in value to objective demographic or economic information. Communities recognize and represent themselves through cultural symbols; they reproduce and maintain themselves in a regional context through social processes. The links between social and cultural studies in anthropology—their essential interdependence—are very clear in investigations of group identity.

NOTES

1. I thank Robert Kiste for reminding me of the ethnic implications of early European contact in the naming of islands. For example, naming the "Marshall Islands" created "Marshallese" as a population unit, which later came to be seen as an ethnic or cultural identity. As Hanlon discusses in chapter 2, the terms "Micronesia" and "Micronesian" themselves are problematic.

2. Mac Marshall pointed out this tension between American egalitarianism and military hierarchy, a theme evident in several issues and events of the postwar years (discussed below).

3. Information on the Mori and Suzuki families comes from interviews I conducted in Chuuk during 1990–1991, as part of a study of the ethnohistory and impact of World War II in Micronesia, funded by a National Endowment for the Humanities Interpretive Research Grant. Of course, anthropologists were also involved in relocations of Americans of Japanese ancestry in the United States (e.g., Spicer, Hansen, Luomala, and Opler 1969; R. Wax 1971). Here, too, administrators failed to distinguish among identity, ethnicity, and "race."

4. Mac Marshall has commented to me that, in contrast, children of Islander-European unions did form a distinct social stratum in colonial Papua New Guinea (see Burton-Bradley 1968).

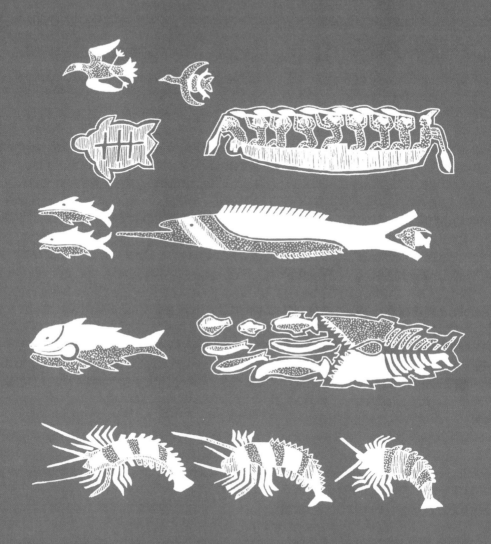

CHAPTER SEVEN

Psychological Anthropology and Its Discontents: Science and Rhetoric in Postwar Micronesia

Peter W. Black

TWO AWAKENINGS

Ifaluk Atoll is as good a place as any (and better than most) to begin considering the rather disconcerting question: What has been achieved by fifty years of research in psychological anthropology in Micronesia? After all, it is the location of the initial fieldwork of two of the most widely cited psychological anthropologists of their respective generations, Melford E. "Mel" Spiro and Catherine Lutz, ethnographers who have made Ifaluk infant bathing practices and Ifaluk emotion terms part of the common currency of the discipline. And 1947 is as good a year as any (and better than most) to use as an entry point. For this was not only the fieldwork year of the first contingent of Coordinated Investigation of Micronesian Anthropology (CIMA) researchers, including many who had special interests in personality and culture; it was also a year in which David Bidney could remark: "One of the outstanding characteristics of contemporary cultural anthropology is its serious concern with the study of the personality of the individuals participating in a given culture" (1949, 31). Furthermore, 1947 was the year when Laura Thompson republished her ethnography of Guam, a monograph that in several of its strategies for characterizing Chamorro culture (for example, its concern to describe childrearing practices) reveals the penetration of the ideas of the culture and personality school into the standard anthropological practice of the era.[1]

Mel Spiro and field assistant, Ifaluk
Atoll, 1947. Photograph courtesy of Mel
Spiro.

> *Early morning, Ifaluk, 1947. Mel Spiro, a Northwestern University grad-*
> *uate student, woke up yet again to the screams of his neighbors' babies being*
> *taken to bathe in the cold early morning ocean. Putting aside his annoy-*
> *ance, Spiro focused on the rage and terror he heard in those infantile*
> *screams, finding in them the beginnings of an answer to a question that*
> *had been troubling him: What was the source of the aggressive feelings that*
> *were so evident in the Ifaluk responses to the battery of projective tests he*
> *had been administering as well as in the folktales and other cultural mate-*
> *rials he had collected? This question was one of a pair; its mate was a ques-*
> *tion about how those feelings were managed. Where (if anywhere) in the*
> *eminently peaceful social life of Ifaluk was aggression expressed?*

Spiro's elegant solution to this puzzle requires no retelling here. Drawing on the Kardiner synthesis, it formed the basis for further refinements of the neo-Freudian paradigm, particularly in the development of the concept of "culturally constituted defense mechanisms." That analytic device, in turn, has been central to the exploration of the vision of culture and personality advanced by Spiro and others, a vision in which culture and personality is not a "specialty within anthropology but a distinctive theoretical approach to the various problems posed by the investigation of cultural and social systems" (Spiro 1978, 330).[2]

Fast forward to Ifaluk thirty years later. Once again a young American anthropologist was abruptly awakened on that remote (but by now anthropologically famous) atoll.

> *Night, Ifaluk, 1977. Catherine Lutz, a Harvard graduate student, awakened to the frightening realization that a man had entered her house. Once the excitement caused by her screams died away, Lutz reflected on the amused response of her Ifaluk neighbors to her initial reaction to the danger in which she had thought herself. Lutz heard in their laughter amusement at her misinterpretation of the situation and confirmation of her understanding that the island is a place of security, its people remarkably peaceable. In that laughter and in the special treatment people close to her offered over the next few days she also detected their pride in her "sensibleness" in being afraid. Her fear was funny because it was misplaced—there was no real danger—but it did confirm her hosts' evaluation of her as an intelligent (and intelligible) moral being.*

Rather than use the events as a window into the inner world of the Ifaluk, Lutz used them as a source of information on their cultural knowledge about such states. She also reflected on the panic with which she greeted that intruder, reading it as based in American cultural knowledge. This incident and others confirmed her developing understanding of how profoundly the ways Ifaluk people conceptualize emotions differ from the ways Americans, both academics and ordinary people, think (or at least talk) about such matters. Her discussion of these issues quickly brought Ifaluk folk psychology into the rapidly shifting framework for doing psychological anthropology. The clarity with which she set out an ethnopsychological perspective on Ifaluk emotions, free from anything smacking of psychodynamics, made her work a major factor in "culturizing" the psychological part of psychological anthropology.

It also helped to establish folk knowledge of persons as an important element in subsequent ethnographic research and analysis in Micronesia and beyond, especially that focused on issues of identity and history (Flinn 1992a; Larson 1989; Linnekin and Poyer 1990a; Poyer 1993). In this way ethnopsychology, too, has started to become, in the words of Spiro, "a distinctive theoretical approach to the various problems posed by the investigation of cultural and social systems" (1978, 330).[3]

THE VIEW FROM IFALUK

The dramatic differences in the analytic purposes to which Spiro and Lutz put their experiences tell us a good deal about the course of psychological anthropology, but so do the similarities in what they made of those experiences. These similarities and differences are good indicators of major continuities and discontinuities in the project of psychological anthropology as it has been pursued by American anthropologists in Micronesia over the last fifty years. I do not recount that history here in detail—although its organization into an early era of "Spiroesque" culture and personality research followed by a later "Lutzian" ethnopsychological period would not be a gross oversimplification. Equally, I do not present a comprehensive discussion of their theoretical and methodological differences, although later I discuss some of the implications of the fact that, despite such disagreements, their descriptions of the Ifaluk sociocultural world are remarkably similar, and their discussions of the islanders' psychocultural world are far more complementary than they are contradictory.

An assessment of the contributions of Micronesian psychological anthropology begins with Spiro and Lutz simply because doing so makes the point that work in Micronesia has greatly enriched the subdiscipline. If one takes a look at a selection of textbooks in psychological anthropology published over the last twenty-five years, one gets an idea of just how important Spiro's Ifaluk analyses have been. Robert Hunt's (1967) reader, Anthony Wallace's (1970) innovative and important essay, John Honigmann's (1973) textbook, Robert LeVine's (1973) breakthrough synthesis, Victor Barnouw's (1985) textbook, and Philip Bock's (1988) widely used and well-regarded revision all make significant use of one or more of Spiro's Ifaluk papers to further their arguments and illustrate their points.

And, of course, this is in addition to the impact of that work on other researchers, who mined it for useful ways to approach their own material.

One example among many can be found in William Lebra's 1982 article, in which the Ifaluk *alus* 'spirit' material is used to make sense of Okinawan religious beliefs.

Although her research is more recent, Lutz, too, has made a major contribution with her Ifaluk papers and book. In his 1988 psychological anthropology textbook, Bock described her work on Ifaluk emotion along with a discussion of Spiro's, as mentioned above, and in fine textbook fashion adjudicated their theoretical disagreements. Jay Dobbin also made extensive and well-reasoned use of both Ifaluk scholars in a project involving the analysis of spirit possession in Chuuk (1992; n.d.).

It is at the intersection where cognitive anthropology, psychology, and linguistics overlap, especially in studies of emotion, that Lutz has had the greatest impact. Geoffrey White and Anthony Marsella (1982) cited her 1980 dissertation in their discussion of emotion theory, and several papers at a 1981 Social Science Research Council psychological anthropology conference drew on her work (Shweder and LeVine 1984). Since that time her Ifaluk work has gained increasing notice. A few more instances will suffice. In 1987 both Roy D'Andrade (1987) and Nico Frijda (1987) published important analyses, each of which drew on different aspects of Lutz's material. Thomas Schweizer (1989) extensively cited her work in a paper designed to acquaint German-speaking sociologists with recent developments in naturalistic methodologies. Lutz has also been cited widely in several recent important collections (e.g., Stigler, Shweder, and Herdt 1990; Schwartz, White, and Lutz 1992; Borofsky 1993; and Kitayama and Markus 1994).[4]

Clearly, this brief overview reveals that research in Micronesia has made major contributions to psychological anthropology. Furthermore, the same point could be made with equal force had I chosen Chuuk as the starting point.[5] Therefore, if the question is, Has psychological anthropology gotten its money's worth out of research in Micronesia? the answer is an emphatic yes! And if one looks beyond anthropology and beyond Micronesia, one again sees significant impact. For example, despite the long-running tradition in psychological anthropology of complaining about neglect by psychologists (e.g., Schwartz 1992; Shweder 1984; Sargent and Smith 1949), Lutz's emotion work has drawn considerable attention in that discipline (e.g., Shaver, Wu, and Schwartz 1992). Also, Micronesian navigation has been noted by Jerome Bruner (1990) and Ulric Neisser (1976), both eminent cognitive psychologists —although the former referred to the works of Thomas Gladwin and Edward Hutchins only in passing and (illustrating the dangers of the rapid glance) had the Marshall Islanders sailing to and from their home on Puluwat Atoll (Bruner 1990, 36; see also Frake 1985, 256; Gladwin 1970, v).

Other types of psychologists also have been drawn to the literature of psychological anthropology in Micronesia. For example, Jaime Bulatao, a psychiatrist practicing in the Philippines, used material from Alice Joseph and Veronica Murray's 1951 report to characterize Filipino personality on the basis that the Chamorros and lowland Filipinos "are of the same racial stock" (Bulatao 1969, 300). In the same volume, Leslie Phillips and Juris Draguns held up Spiro's 1959 article as an exemplary illustration of what they called the role of culture in "deviant reaction" (1969, 23). Finally, Horatio Fabrega placed considerable reliance on Micronesian ethnographers (Spiro, Goodenough, Lutz, and Black) in his impressive demonstration of the utility of bringing together social psychiatry and ethnopsychology to further the understanding of schizophrenia (Fabrega 1989). The years of intensive research by anthropologists into psychological issues in Micronesia have, in this sense, paid off.

But what if the question is pursued beyond a narrow, self-referential, subdisciplinary frame? What does the "balance sheet" look like then? There are several sound reasons for approaching the question in this manner, the most persuasive of which has to do with the subject matter of psychological anthropology.

PSYCHOLOGICAL ANTHROPOLOGY AND OTHER MICRONESIAN DISCOURSES

Psychological anthropology, however conceived, deals with many of the most important and problematic features of human social life.[6] In one way or another these features are inevitably at issue in an enormous range of human activities. The outcome of ethnographic research in psychological anthropology, therefore, is relevant to other kinds of research and analysis in Micronesia, especially that centered on what has been called "experience near" dimensions of life. Given this, let us consider what can be said about the contribution of psychological anthropology in Micronesia to other Micronesian discourses.

My use of the term "Micronesian discourses" includes, but is not restricted to, anthropological subdisciplines attempting to comprehend (understand/ explain/interpret) Micronesian realities; it also covers other types of social scientific writing about (and especially by) Micronesians. In the final analysis, if psychological anthropology is to continue, it must offer something not just to itself but to others.

Scanning the education, mental health, suicide, substance abuse, and identity literatures of Micronesia reveals only traces of the work of psychological anthropology, even though its subject matter is obviously relevant to each of these areas. Furthermore, a good proportion of the instances in which its presence is detectable reveal only an indirect connection. The initial work has been picked up, made part of some general framework, and then cycled back out to Micronesia as part of that framework. For example, much of the educational literature (both anthropological and otherwise) has drawn on Gladwin's (1970) description and analysis of Puluwat cognitive styles, but his work has rarely been referenced directly; instead it has been mediated through the work of, for example, Michael Cole and his coauthors (1971) (see, e.g., Falgout and Levin 1992). In other instances only the vaguest of gestures has been made in the direction of that research tradition, as when personality traits read in the projective tests of particular populations at particular times have become part of a generalized and timeless Micronesian ethos or set of "values," with perhaps a nod in the direction of Spiro, Gladwin and Seymour Sarason, or Francis Mahoney. Likewise, the "interpersonal self" is a construct well represented in several of these literatures, but the ethnopsychological matrix out of which that concept has emerged is not. I do not wish to overstate the case; I *did* come across some direct references to psychological anthropology. Yet, overall, research in psychological anthropology in Micronesia seems to have had remarkably little impact on what can be called Micronesian Studies. Nor is psychological anthropology very visible in the writings of those few Micronesians carrying out social scientific research; in fact, I could find no social science produced by Micronesians which made much use of the literature written by psychological anthropologists. Those who came close to doing so included Eulalia Harui-Walsh (1984) whose paper on changing women's lifestyles on Ulithi cited the work of William Lessa and Marvin Spiegelman (1954); however, she drew on it only for normative statements on traditional female behavior and ignored their description and analysis of Ulithian personality (Harui-Walsh 1984, 86).

Gordon Jensen and Anthony Polloi's report (1984) on their gerontological research in Palau (in which oddly enough the subject population was defined as an "American minority population, the Palauans of Micronesia" [1984, 272]) used Homer G. Barnett's book (1979) for information about the traditional role of the elderly in Palau, but even though their article is replete with psychological terms and concepts, they made no reference to any of Barnett's psychological material. The report of their five-year follow-up study (Jensen and Polloi 1988) cited none of the literature from Palau, psychological or otherwise, with the exception of their own article mentioned above. In this study they were interested in cognitive functioning and used various tests to measure it, so one might have expected the extensive cognitive literature about Micronesia to surface; it did not.

However, that same cognitive literature does play a role in one of the most imaginative items in this genre. Arguing a maximalist case for Micronesia vis-à-vis the Law of the Sea negotiations, Masao Nakayama and Frederick L. Ramp based their claim on the navigation literature, using it to advance the case that Micronesians "feel toward their sea the way inhabitants of continental nations feel toward their land" (1974, iii).

It may well be that the absence of psychological anthropology from the social science writings of Micronesian scholars is related to the widely known distaste with which many Micronesians view the output of the culture and personality school when applied to their own societies. Nevertheless, the fact of that absence is disturbing.

The many social science literatures can seem like closed, nearly autistic, discourses that are in, of, and for themselves alone. As a collection of such discourses, "social science" (with the partial exception of economics) connects to very little outside itself. The situation persists despite the fact that social science proclaims itself to be more than just an ivory tower refuge for social scientists. This is a serious problem.

The specific story of the failure of psychological anthropology to contribute much to other Micronesian discourses is a useful ground for thinking about the more general problem of the isolation of the social sciences from one another and from other kinds of work. In exploring this ground, the first question has to be, What kind of discourse is the psychological anthropology of Micronesia? This preliminary classificatory exercise is necessary before it is possible to determine the potential utility of its statements for those working in other disciplines.

Perhaps psychological anthropology in Micronesia has been simply a series of unrelated maneuvers, heading off first in one direction and then another, responsive only to the political and social contexts within which projects are defined, research funded and carried out, and results published. If so, then despite the excellence of one or another study, the enterprise taken as a whole can have no intrinsic value. This is because the enterprise cannot be taken as a whole in any meaningful sense. If the psychological anthropology of Micronesia lacks definition and coherence, it lacks utility, and the blindness of other discourses to it is a nonproblem. If, on the other hand, it possesses coherence, then its possible utility remains open, the question of why it has not proven more useful retains its force, and the reasons for its neglect must be sought elsewhere. In the remainder of this chapter I move toward a point from which a judgment on this matter can be made. To reach that point, we must first look back to the origins of psychological anthropology in Micronesia and then consider the character of its development.

PREHISTORY

Oceania played a major role in the pre–World War II history of psychological anthropology. From the Torres Straits to Sāmoa, with stops at New Guinea, the Admiralties, the Marquesas, Dobu, and the Trobriands, the islands of the Pacific were home to many of its most important studies. Many of the features that by the outbreak of the war came to characterize American culture and personality studies emerged from these attempts to define and refine concepts and methods using data from Pacific island populations.[7]

But while the rest of Oceania was central to these developments, Micronesia played absolutely no role. Before World War II, its islands were *terra* perhaps even less *cognita* to psychological anthropologists than to the rest of the profession. And the war-inspired collection and translation of the existing literature revealed little, if any, material of direct use to those interested in the relationship of Micronesian cultures to Micronesian personalities. The major German sources contained only a rough-and-ready, commonsense, impressionistic psychology at work which produced statements largely free of careful descriptions or theoretically informed analyses. The *volkerpsychologie* of Wilhelm Wundt and Adolph Bastian, which perhaps could have provided the conceptual framework for such work, was nearly moribund by the time the Hamburg Ethnographic Expedition was written up (Thilenius 1914–1938). Nor did the Japanese publish much of any direct relevance.[8]

Even though they entered Micronesia without a database drawn from the literature, the first postwar researchers certainly did not come empty-handed. They came equipped with a powerful model of the relationship of personality and culture, a set of questions generated by that model, and a body of techniques for gathering information with which to address those questions.

BASIC PERSONALITY STRUCTURE

The anthropologists who brought the culture and personality approach to Micronesia were participants in a vigorous and flourishing intellectual enterprise which many of them considered to have the characteristics of a classic science. This was due in no small measure to a major theoretical statement by Abram Kardiner (1939). The Kardiner model seemed to offer a powerful framework for scientific research into the relationship of personality and culture. It acted as a kind of charter for the ethnographic investigation of personality in a variety of cultural settings, including Micronesia.

The central idea of Kardiner's neo-Freudian model was a construct called "Basic Personality Structure," defined as the set of personality features shared by members of a society. Basic Personality Structure was generated by shared childhood experiences, which were the outcome of socially standardized child-rearing techniques. These techniques, in turn, were determined by the cultural practices, called "Primary Institutions," most directly constrained by the group's environment. Out of shared childhood experience emerged shared, deeply seated propensities, dispositions, complexes—the Basic Personality Structure of that group. "Secondary Institutions," that is, cultural practices less tightly constrained by the group's environment, were seen to be shaped by the shared unconscious needs, fears, and drives that were part of that society's Basic Personality Structure. For this reason, Secondary Institutions were also referred to as "Projective Institutions."

Kardiner's theoretical apparatus seemed to solve one of the major conceptual difficulties facing American anthropology. Ever since Franz Boas had forcefully directed attention to the historical particularities of each people's culture, the problem of cultural integration had loomed forbiddingly large. How did one account for the wholeness, the coherence of a culture? Whence the pattern that made it more than a thing of shreds and patches? Various functionalisms (some more Panglossian than others), resurrected evolutionisms, and even the promotion of culture to superorganic status had not convincingly gone beyond Boas' inadequate reliance on habit and custom as the explanation for cultural coherence. Configurationism, Ruth Benedict's (1934) famous formulation, raised more questions than it answered. This is why Kardiner's work seemed such a genuine scientific breakthrough; Basic Personality Structure was what held society together. The institutions of a culture were integrated via its members' shared "nuclear complex."

Yet Basic Personality Structure, despite its advantages as an integrative mechanism, was merely a hypothetical construct. In the illustrative cases used to demonstrate the model, Kardiner and his group deduced Basic Personality Structure from ethnographic material and then used it to analyze that same material. A certain distressing circularity in the logic of this procedure was clearly evident even though the lack of circuits in the model itself was not seen as a problem in those precybernetic days. There was a clear need for empirical investigations to provide an independent measure of personality variables. Cora Du Bois (1944) took the first steps in this direction with her work in Alor, Indonesia, and the Micronesianists carried on from there, refining and developing the methodology. Following publication of Kardiner's first book came a sequence of classic ethnographic studies using projective tests to develop descriptions and assess ideas about shared and not-so-shared personality characteristics. The investment of CIMA and other early researchers in administering Rorschach, Thematic Apperception Test (TAT), and other projective tests makes great good sense when seen in this light, but much less in today's context.

CULTURE AND PERSONALITY IN THE SHADOWS

"From another time, almost another planet" is how George Spindler described what he called the "days of the *People of Alor,* [and] *Truk: Man in Paradise*" (personal communication 1993). That is fairly close to how most, if not all, anthropologists today view that time and its products, if they are even aware of them. Why this should be so is an interesting problem in intellectual history.

Culture and personality studies in anthropology, which in many ways culminated in *Truk: Man in Paradise,* can be seen as profoundly modern, embodying many of the senses of modernity against which postmodernism has invented itself. They thus present a large and inviting target for the kind of critique for which postmodernism has become notorious. The indictment could go something like this: "Blindly oblivious to their complicity in the creation of US colonial rule in Micronesia, they imposed western categories on the private worlds of people brought within their gaze by that power. They essentialized and generalized those inner worlds, suppressing and disauthenticating local diversity for their own purposes." Listen to Greg Dening on the Linton/Kardiner portrait of the Basic Personality Structure of the people they called Marquesans and he called Enata: "These abstractions are so removed from the actualities of Enata's life and so dependent on an agreed and sustained selectivity that 'Marquesan Culture' has become a free-floating concept, unattached to reality, an end in itself. It is like a painting or a poem in the possession of an art or literary critic. Its relation to what was or what happened is irrelevant. It belongs now as an item of exchange in an 'as if' world of discourse" (1980, 281).

Of the many anthropologists I asked to consider the question with which this chapter began, a surprising number gave responses that were quite emotional. Many senior anthropologists expressed bitterness, anger, or cynicism. They seemed to see their generation's work as under attack, an attack neither informed nor fair, and which if successful would sweep away much that is of value and leave in its place nothing of any great worth. Theodore "Ted" Schwartz spoke for many when he defended the "Herculean efforts [expended by the discipline] in bringing the diverse cultures of this planet under close observation and in the huge task of sorting, evaluating, and comprehending the data that have been accumulated" against the critique of what he named "new age anthropology" (1992, 346). In contrast with this was the eagerness of several younger scholars to deconstruct the early work, and to ask, in essence, "What went into the appallingly apolitical and ahistorical construction of Micronesia as an object of psychological inquiry?" Their clear inference was that political naiveté would be the most charitable possible answer.[9]

Many of those I approached betrayed a certain impatience and lack of sympathy with the project as it was outlined to them. Instead they seemed to hope that I would transform the inquiry from a rather straightforward inventory of scholarly impact within a delimited realm of anthropology into either a deconstruction of the early work with an all-too-predictable outcome, or a demonstration of the deeply anti-intellectual nihilism of hyper-relativistic postmodernism. Neither response, of course, is unique to the field of Micronesian psychological anthropology. Dening is an historian of Polynesia, after all, and Schwartz, an ethnographer of Melanesia. The whole enterprise of talking and writing about human life, especially as that life is lived in places far from scholarship's "home islands" seems to be increasingly characterized by such disputes. The disappearance of the early culture and personality studies from contemporary psychological anthropology is surely part of a larger movement in social thought. The story of that movement is particularly interesting in this context because it is occurring in the face of the fact that something very much like "science" has happened.

SCIENCE

That the CIMA and other early anthropologists viewed what they were doing as science may seem slightly quaint these days, but it has historical importance. For central to the view of anthropology-as-science is the belief that it is (or can be) both cumulative and self-correcting. It is my opinion that these two attributes were—and are—exhibited by the ethnographic research tradition (including that of psychological anthropology) established by the post–World War II researchers. If this is correct, then the widespread impression of discontinuity is revealed to be at least in part mistaken. Psychological anthropology in Micronesia begins to emerge as a phenomenon with at least two levels. On one level, that of the actual work itself, something we can reasonably label science can be seen. On the other level, where the general impression of the work is located, the science-like features of the research tradition receive little attention; discussion focuses on what various parties see as the faddish postures and cant of others.

The anthropological literature of Micronesia is notable for the number and quality of ethnographic disagreements it contains. Ward H. Goodenough and Jack Fischer on Chuukese residence rules, Marc Swartz and Goodenough on the classification of Chuukese kin terminology, Spiro and Lessa on Ifaluk sorcery, William Alkire and Goodenough on the number of Carolinian souls, Gladwin and Hutchins on how *etak* (a navigational technique) operates in Carolinian navigation—all are arguments over ethnographic material that demonstrate the operation of the self-correcting features of science (broadly defined). Given the lack of knowledge available at the beginning of the research trajectory, this is precisely what one would have expected of a developing science. In other words, this is how things were supposed to work.[10]

Further evidence that Micronesian ethnography has moved in a "scientific" fashion appears in the constructive use researchers have made of each other's work. This collaborative and cumulative dimension is especially evident in many of the accounts I have received. For example, Marc Swartz went to Chuuk for his dissertation research because it had "the background for the study of relations among kin that I wanted to make. I figured that Truk was ideal because there was Goodenough's social structure study and Gladwin's personality study" (personal communication 1993). Out of Swartz's research came several papers which, in turn, were drawn on by later researchers to advance their own analyses (e.g., McKnight 1960; Rubinstein 1983; Flinn 1992b).

Another example of this developmental process, illustrating the combination of strategic choice and fortuitous discovery typical of many narratives of scientific progress, was provided by the German anthropologist Lothar Kaeser (personal communication 1993). He dated his interest in Chuukese concepts of the soul (Kaeser 1977) and the body (Kaeser 1989) to his encounter as a frustrated junior high school teacher in Chuuk with a "termite-eaten" copy of Swartz's 1965 article in which Swartz "quotes a short passage from a chapter on super-ego orientation by Melford E. Spiro."

Spiro's passage seemed to be key to much of what Kaeser had seen but not understood in his classroom. Many things "were suddenly clear to me." And he was led to begin his careful study of the Chuukese "concept 'soul,' not only in its more religious aspects as the Chuukese 'spiritual double,' but also as what they call 'seat of emotions,' where not only emotions are located, but ideas and traits of character." Kaeser's experience is important because it illustrates the cumulative, if unpredictable, development of at least some anthropological understandings and because, among other things, his account directs attention to possible applied uses of those accumulating understandings. Of course, theory development can also come out of the use one researcher makes of the findings of another. Goodenough's account of how he was able to discover in Gladwin and Sarason the key to Chuukese religion illustrates this well (personal communication 1993).

Goodenough's substantial contributions to the scientific study of religion are built on and frequently illustrated by Chuukese ethnographic material which he has recorded over the years. His understanding of that material, in turn, is predicated on the findings of Gladwin and Sarason (1953). Goodenough makes a strong argument for setting aside belief in spiritual beings as a criterion for religion and adopting a functional definition.[11] At the basis of this position lies his understanding of how Kardiner-like shared unconscious needs, desires, and fears are dealt with in Chuukese society. Goodenough calls these "areas of concern" and they were disclosed to him (or at least confirmed) by the work of Gladwin and Sarason (1953). That work, especially the Rorschach interpretations, provided confirmation of Goodenough's insights into the emotional life of his informants and provided a matrix onto which he could map his understandings of their beliefs and rituals. By using the Rorschach results as an independent measure, in particular a list of ten traits described by Sarason (who had interpreted those protocols "blind"), Goodenough was able to avoid the kind of tautology into which Linton and Kardiner had fallen. And since those same concerns showed up in other areas of

Chuukese life—areas with no supernatural component—he could see no good reason for forcing the psycho-religious life of the Chuukese into the usual definition of religion. Goodenough did not want to "engage in the fruitless task of ramming the square pegs of other peoples' cultures in the round holes of our own" (1981a, 412).

"Square pegs and round holes"—if Kardiner's model was the charter for postwar culture and personality work in Micronesia, then this phrase of Goodenough's could serve as a motto for the later scholars who turned away from it. There is something a little ironic in this.

Goodenough has never turned his critique of what could be called "inappropriate eticism" onto Gladwin and Sarason's mapping of Chuukese inner worlds. Indeed he continues to draw on their analysis as he pursues his quest to establish a functional definition of religion—a definition he illustrates with Chuukese culture while also using it to illuminate that culture.[12] At the same time his analytic approach has given Micronesia strong claim to be the birthplace of contemporary cognitive anthropology.

The ethnopsychological perspective, which has largely replaced culture and personality, developed out of the cognitive turn in cultural anthropology, which itself had at least some roots in culture and personality studies. Much of this story played itself out in Micronesia. In important respects this also has been a story of "scientific progress" (as always, quite broadly defined). Ideas, methods, and data of the early era gave rise to insights and questions, which generated new ideas, methods, and data, which eventually led to the flourishing of a new research tradition. Here, however, one observes the major discontinuity remarked on not only by Spindler and others of his generation, but also by many of the younger scholars who followed them. It is as though the connections between the early work and the later work have become invisible. At this juncture it is appropriate to turn to the work of Thomas Gladwin, whose research career in Micronesia not only spans the perceived chasm but, in a curious fashion, exemplifies it.

COGNITION

Ward Goodenough is not the only ethnographer of Micronesia whose name is associated with the rise of cognitive anthropology. As Charles Frake pointed out (personal communication 1993), Thomas Gladwin also helped to set the stage. But there is a difference. Goodenough's Chuukese work has shown a steady continuity, a systematic working out of ideas and their implications over the decades as they are tested against new empirical observations. Glad-win, on the other hand, periodically engaged in a kind of auto-deconstruc-tion, abandoning one line of research for another. In 1961, anticipating the reflexive turn in anthropology by a good fifteen years, he published a harsh attack on the kind of work represented by *Truk: Man in Paradise*. Referring to what he called "the Freudian Bandwagon," he proclaimed that "we have sur-rendered our anthropological birthright to the clinicians, and received in return a methodology which is both limited in productivity and suspect in validity" (1961, 163). Of course, Gladwin's was not exactly a voice in the wil-derness on this issue. At the time he wrote this passage, an anti-Freudian and anti–culture and personality bandwagon was rolling at a quite respectable clip. For example, Alfred Lindsmith and Anselm Strauss (1950) and especially Bernice Kaplan (1961) published severe critiques, indicating that the psychol-ogists were not about to welcome anthropological projective testers into the fold. Gladwin's attack, though, remains memorable, not least because of his intimate involvement in the very enterprise that he was now belittling.[13] Yet, on closer inspection, it turns out that he did not completely abandon the in-sights gained by that now discarded approach; in fact, one of those insights became the central datum of the next phase of his work in Micronesia.

Two themes seem to run through much of the descriptive personality liter-ature from the early and middle period, in Chuuk as well as in Micronesia generally. One is a sharp focus on aggression (or the lack of it), and the other is a concern with future orientation (or the lack of it). I have already discussed the major contribution made by Spiro to the solution of the puzzle of Ifaluk aggression, a contribution that a number of researchers in Chuuk and else-where have drawn on. If aggression was said to be present but largely ex-pressed only in disguised and socially benign fashion, "future orientation," including such qualities as planning for the future and deferring present grat-ification, was said to be largely absent.

The absence of future orientation also emerges in descriptions written by nonanthropologists (e.g., Karig 1948 and Henning 1961) to introduce America's reading public to her newest natives. In this respect at least, both professional and casual describers of Chuukese personality agreed on what they were seeing. When one considers the events that preceded the arrival of the Americans in Chuuk, a sharp focus on certain aspects of the present at the expense of the future is perhaps understandable. After all, if the immediate past was any guide, then practically all a Chuukese could be certain of was that the future was uncertain. But anyone familiar with the long-term struggles between kin groups over land and titles characteristic of Chuuk and the rest of Micronesia can only view blanket claims of blindness to the future with scepticism. Perhaps Americans of this period, those in uniform as well as researchers and other visitors, by focusing so keenly on *individuals,* simply missed Chuukese interest in and planning for *group* futures. My guess is that whatever else was going on, stereotypes about Chuukese and other Micronesians were being created among Americans in Micronesia during this period.[14]

In any event, the widely shared perception that future orientation was lacking in Chuukese personality raised a number of difficulties. Not the least of these had to do with what is perhaps the most dramatic of Micronesian purposeful activities, the famous tradition of canoe voyaging. Gladwin began asking how it was that people could embark on what seemed inherently dangerous long-distance trips from one island to the next apparently without much planning or preparation and for such seemingly trivial reasons as a desire for tobacco. (But see Black 1984 for a reconsideration of tobacco famine as motivation.) That these voyages were traditionally undertaken without maps, sextants, or even compasses made them even more problematic. Out of his confrontation with this material, Gladwin produced a series of publications, at first addressing the relations between future orientation and Carolinian canoe voyaging, and then focusing more on problem solving and innovation as issues in the cognitive dimensions of the indigenous navigation system (Gladwin 1958, 1960, 1961, 1964). His *East Is a Big Bird* (1970) presented a book-length discussion of this fascinating material, based on new ethnographic research carried out on Puluwat Atoll. If *Truk: Man in Paradise* was one of the last of the culture and personality studies, then *East Is a Big Bird* marked the emergence of another research tradition—the very productive encounter of cognitive anthropologists and other cognitive scientists with a spectacular, nonwestern, nonliterate, intellectual edifice.

There is by now a substantial cognitive literature dealing with indigenous navigation in the Pacific. Nicholas Goetzfridt (1992) has recently published a useful bibliography. Several threads lead from that literature. One, of course, leads to the Polynesian canoe voyaging revival. Ben Finney (personal communication 1993), one of the central figures in this effort, reported that the awareness that long-distance voyaging using traditional techniques, skills, and knowledge still survived in Micronesia was an enormously encouraging demonstration of practical possibilities. Another important outgrowth of the navigation literature has been its significance in educational research and

Thomas Gladwin, CIMA project, Chuuk, 1947. Riesenberg Collection, Pacific Collection, University of Hawai'i Library.

Satawal canoe arrives at Okinawa for Expo '75. Trust Territory Archives (Photo 2638.04), Pacific Collection, University of Hawai'i Library.

Satawal canoe crew with High Com-
missioner Edward E. Johnston, Office of
the High Commissioner, Saipan, 1973.
Trust Territory Archives (Photo
2638.03), Pacific Collection, University
of Hawaiʻi Library.

planning. Paula Levin (personal communication 1993) pointed out that such an obviously complex and successful intellectual tradition, transmitted outside schools and without the benefit of the written word, stood as a challenge to those interested in improving classroom performance. For both of these applications Gladwin's research on Puluwat was seminal. My point here is that he glided over the fact that his Puluwat work drew on his earlier, equally important, work in the Chuuk Lagoon.

Even though the line of development from Gladwin's first book to his second (beginning with a concern about future orientation and ending with a focus on innovative thinking and problem solving) is quite clear to anyone reading the intervening articles, *Truk: Man in Paradise* does not play a visibly significant role in *East Is a Big Bird*. In the latter book personality traits of the Puluwat people are contrasted with those of the Lagoon Chuukese, but in quite an impressionistic fashion—with no reference to the source of the

Chuukese material in the careful ethnographic and projective research of two decades before.

Two points arise in this connection. The first is that inasmuch as the contrasts Gladwin drew between Puluwat and Chuukese personality are valid, then the many statements equating Puluwatese and Chuukese cognition raise serious questions. The rhetorical force of that equation is clear—it is to redraw the largely negative portrait painted earlier of Chuukese cognition. But to equate cognitive processes in two populations while at the same time sharply distinguishing personality processes requires more explanation than is given.[15] The second point raised by the lack of explicit attention given to *Truk: Man in Paradise* in *East Is a Big Bird* is one made earlier: Gladwin in his own work exemplifies both the continuity, and the blindness to that continuity, that is characteristic of the field as a whole. This is an important phenomenon.[16] It is most apparent in the heated discussions around the attempt to develop careful descriptions and analyses of Micronesian folk psychologies.

ETHNOPSYCHOLOGY

The ideas of both Goodenough and Gladwin were crucial for the emergence of the ethnopsychological perspective within anthropology, including Micronesian psychological anthropology. Thus, while Catherine Lutz's study of emotion is very much an outcome of her refusal to ram the square pegs of Ifaluk feelings into the round holes of western emotion theory, at the same time it shares a certain strategy with *East Is a Big Bird*. It is clear that in some respects Lutz performed the same operation on emotion that Gladwin did on thinking: problematizing the ordinary western way of conceptualizing a target psychological phenomenon on the basis of how it is conceived in the Caroline Islands and then challenging western academic psychology with the result.

Lutz and the others involved in ethnopsychological research and analysis in Micronesia (principally Caughey, Kaeser, and Black) were heirs to the culture and personality movement, but sought to go beyond it.[17] Lutz went to Ifaluk, as John Caughey (like Swartz before him) had earlier gone to Chuuk, because the CIMA researchers had provided careful descriptions of local personality. The assumption seems to have been that Ifaluk or Chuukese personality could be more or less "taken as it had been read" by Spiro on the one hand and Gladwin and Sarason on the other. Lutz reviewed the protocols from the projective testing Spiro had carried out and undertook TAT testing of her own. Caughey reviewed similar material from Gladwin and Sarason. Neither found this material particularly productive for the kinds of questions about folk psychological cultural knowledge that interested them (Lutz and Caughey, personal communications 1993). Nevertheless, just as Gladwin, without calling much attention to it, drew on his earlier culture and personality descriptions, so the later researchers have built into their models of Micronesian folk psychology actors who strongly resemble the people whose inner worlds were first described by the CIMA researchers. In my own continuing work on Tobian folk psychology and Tobian religion, for example, I have remained quite prepared to accept Spiro's Ifaluk ghost analysis as representing an important strong hypothesis about the inner experience of the Tobians (Black 1978, 1985, 1994). None of this ordinary and expectable activity would be worthy of comment were it not for the widespread impression of a sharp rupture in the history of psychological anthropology in Micronesia.

The conceptual contributions of the first generation of field-workers were even more important to the ethnopsychologists than the ethnographic descriptions. The ethnography was used as an almost unspoken or default baseline, while, as I pointed out above, the theoretical developments to which several of the early ethnographers had contributed so significantly provided key elements in the emergence of the ethnopsychological perspective. Gananath Obeyesekere has gone further (1990, 318–319 n.88). In the course of an acute questioning of the Hallowellian notion that the self is a cultural universal, he claimed that Lutz's ideal-typic version of Ifaluk ethnopsychology revealed "assumptions [which] are not in principle different from those underlying the very theories she criticizes" (1990, 319). Whatever the merits of this assertion, the impressive continuities between culture and personality studies and ethnopsychology are vividly apparent when a third, completely unrelated, perspective is brought into the equation—say, for example, sociobiology.

Laura Betzig and Santus Wichimai (1991) bring the latter point of view to bear on the ethnography of Ifaluk. The Ifaluk person who emerges in their analysis of conflict on the island seems as flat and culturally unspecific as the notorious "economic man" who strides through the analyses of rational choice theorists. The version of human nature that animates their Ifaluk brings into sharp relief the nuanced, passionate, and intensely social beings recognizable in the reports of both Lutz and Spiro.

Clearly the need is to take advantage of the complementarity of the two approaches. A close reading of Lutz's critique of Spiro's ghost analysis (1988, 207) reveals that the major differences lie in the choice of language. Lutz objected much more to the vocabulary with which Spiro represented the inner experience of the Ifaluk than to his interpretation of that experience.

This being the case, the possibilities offered by a combined—call it Hallo-wellian—perspective are well worth thinking about.

Fabrega, looking for material to illustrate the benefits of a cultural approach to schizophrenia, turned to Spiro's (1950a) paper and found rich descriptions of the conversations and behavior of a suicidal psychotic, but not much about the ethnopsychological context (Fabrega 1989). He also examined my essay on an attempted suicide (Black 1985), in which I presented an extended ethnopsychological treatment of the event but very little information about the internal experience of the person threatening to kill himself. Two separate but related perspectives led to two partial views. A rounded and thorough approach to understanding the experience of either of these two unsettled (and unsettling) Micronesians might have been available had those two partial views been combined.[18]

CONTEXT AND CONTINUITY

If, in both its ethnographic and theoretical dimensions, ethnopsychology in Micronesia emerged from (developed out of, built on) culture and personality studies, why all the heat? What are all those mutual denunciations doing in a discourse that exhibits so much continuity? The short answer to this question appears to lie not in the history of psychological anthropology in Micronesia but in the postwar political and social history of the United States. The rupture is not so much between culture and personality and ethno-psychology as between the World War II and the Vietnam eras.

There is no point in belaboring the obvious differences in the contexts within which the two generations did their work. Our two wars were very different, as was the America we first imagined and then contrasted with what we found in Micronesia, which itself was a very different place or set of places in the 1960s and 1970s than it had been in the 1940s and 1950s. But that contextual difference is the reason, when all is said and done, for the rhetoric of discontinuity.

The rhetoric has pointed toward a progressively decentered enterprise, with its categories destabilized and its practice undone. But the rhetoric has far outrun the reality: psychological anthropology, at least as it has been enacted in Micronesia, has retained its coherence. Furthermore, its self-correcting and cumulative qualities (obscured by the rhetoric as they may be) earn for it a cautious confidence.

This, then, is what the psychological anthropology of Micronesia has to offer other Micronesian discourses: a multidecade research effort which to its practitioners looks far more discontinuous than it is in fact. An enormous mass of empirical material has been gathered, large amounts of which remain available for reanalysis. A substantial body of literature has been created which addresses the cultural dimensions of motivation, affect, and cognition from a variety of perspectives and in a substantial number of Micronesian societies.[19] Ideas and methods have been tried out and refined, issues clarified, and questions sharpened. These are the attributes of a kind of science.[20]

TWO SUGGESTIONS

If the classification of this enterprise as a science is correct, then the fact that it is mostly ignored by other Micronesian discourses remains to be explained. By pointing out that the ideas, findings, and methods of psychological anthropology are ignored, I do not mean to claim that they should be uncritically accepted. It is possible that what it has to offer is of no value, and other disciplines are simply saving themselves the trouble of dealing with a mass of unproductive material. But this has not been demonstrated; indeed an accounting of this nature has rarely even been attempted. Such a judgment could only arise out of a serious encounter with psychological anthropology; what my survey of cognate literatures revealed was precisely that no encounters of any kind seem to have taken place.

The next steps in working out why that encounter never occurred would be to follow up on leads discovered in the course of this project. Since I have completed what I set out to do in this chapter, those leads will have to remain, in that classic social science phrase, "suggestions for further research." I will close, then, by briefly indicating two of them.

It is undoubtedly the case that, in Jay Dobbin's words, those doing psychological anthropology in Micronesia are an "esoteric coterie" and that may be part of the reason their work has had little direct "impact on Micronesia— either in education, health care, public policy or in the training of the educated elite" (personal communication 1993). He offered several suggestions to make sure that it "trickles down," as he put it. Implicit in his comments is the insight that psychological anthropology in Micronesia exists in a form that prevents outsiders from gaining access to it. What ends and whose goals are being served by this situation? Is it the case that a self-corrective and cumulative discourse *must* be inaccessible to outsiders? Would it be possible to produce out of the resources of psychological anthropology a body of what

Dobbin called mid-level literature, somewhere between scholarly monographs and Sunday supplements? Such a literature, he pointed out, would be of very great interest to human services personnel in Micronesia. A good model for this type of literature can be found in the *Micronesian Counselor,* a series of nontechnical papers on contemporary social problems produced by the Micronesian Seminar and edited by Francis X. Hezel. One line of investigation would be to determine just why such a large proportion of the neglect discussed in this chapter is self-inflicted.

The other place to look for the causes of the blindness to psychological anthropology is in the other discourses themselves. In his masterful account of the extension of mental health "services" to Micronesia, Albert "Britt" Robillard (1987) very convincingly demonstrated that the "needs" those services were created to meet were the needs of various agencies and institutions to mount such efforts. The mental health needs of the Micronesian societies were part of the taken-for-granted construction of those societies as under-developed versions of "modern" societies. As in so much else, the need for services was demonstrated by the very fact that there were no services. In all these efforts, psychological anthropology did not put in a single appearance. This absence was unbroken up to and during the training of Micronesian mental health workers in the concepts of elementary psychology (since it was "known" that psychological knowledge was absent from Micronesia).

And although at first sight this appears very strange, reading Robillard makes it clear that, given the purposes and assumptions of the effort, it would have been pointless for those designing the projects to have included psychological anthropology. After all, what useful information does it possess about budget levels, staffing patterns, career paths in professional psychology, and various other bureaucratic imperatives? In other words, the failure of psychological anthropology in Micronesia to have any impact on other discourses may be partially attributable to the fact that there really is nothing to be communicated despite their apparently overlapping subject matters.

No doubt a number of other "hypotheses" could be posed to account for the lack of meaningful encounters between psychological anthropology and other Micronesian discourses. Is the isolation of psychological anthropology in Micronesia self-imposed? Is it perhaps the outcome of a dynamic in which communication about "manifest" subject matter held in common is overwhelmed by latent and more powerful processes? Or is it the result of some other process altogether? In the end, the answers must await future analysis. My goal here was to discover if psychological anthropology had the necessary internal coherence to be a useful partner in exchanges with other discourses. My conclusion is that it does. Despite its considerable rhetorical disarray, psychological anthropology in Micronesia stands revealed, at least for now, as a specimen of scientific discourse.

NOTES

I wish to thank Robert C. Kiste for inviting me to write this chapter and for his suggestions during the course of its preparation. While preparing it I cast a wide net, contacting approximately seventy-five individuals who I thought might have something useful to contribute to the topic. The following is a list of those who responded with recollections, opinions, ideas, or suggestions: Kevin Avruch, Erika Bourguignon, Rainer Buschmann, John Caughey, Vincent Crapanzano, Jay Dobbin, Suzanne Falgout, Ben Finney, Charles Frake, Eleanor Gerber, Byron Good, Ward Goodenough, Alan Howard, Edward Hutchins, Dwight Huthwaite, Evelyn Jacob, Lothar Kaeser, Bernie and Bill Keldermanns, John Kirkpatrick, Weston LaBarre, Stephen Leavitt, Paula Levin, Catherine Lutz, James MacMurray, Mary McCutcheon, Don Rubinstein, Thomas Schweizer, Craig Severance, George Spindler, Mel Spiro, George Stocking, Marc Swartz, Geoffrey White, and Thomas Williams. Each of these people generously took time to respond and I thank them. I also thank my wife, Barbara Webster Black, who helped greatly with both the conceptual and the production sides of this project. Letitia Hickson of the Center for Pacific Islands Studies dealt with my many e-mail queries; Maureen Connors of George Mason University's Fenwick Library and Karen Peacock of Hamilton Library at the University of Hawai'i helped with the bibliographic end of things, for all of which I am grateful. The Program for Cultural Studies at the East-West Center provided a hospitable home away from home during crucial stages of the writing. Lastly, I wish to thank Mac Marshall for his very thorough (and very needed) editorial suggestions and Fran Hezel and Suzanne Falgout for their written critiques of the first draft of this chapter.

Writing about Micronesians seems more complicated than ever these days. And writing about people writing about Micronesians is yet more complex. Postmodernism (which during its heyday possessed a certain hegemonic quality, so that even those who did not wish to write in its vein often found themselves writing against it) may be breaking up, but it is far from clear what will take its place. Here I attempt to avoid the kind of naively Whiggish approach that James Clifford (1988) so rightly warned against without getting completely bogged down in displaying social and political contexts.

1. Given that she carried out her ethnographic research before the war, Thompson can be considered the first to bring a culture and personality perspective to bear on Micronesian material. The first to do so after World War II may well have been Edward T. Hall who, after being demobilized in 1945, spent a brief period as a postdoc-

toral student in sociology at Columbia University before going out to Chuuk to work for the navy for a few months. In his autobiography he discussed the Kardiner-Linton seminar at Columbia before relating how, once he arrived in Chuuk, people started bringing him their dreams for his interpretation (Hall 1992, 167). As nearly as I can make out, this would have been in 1946, several months before the arrival of the CIMA researchers. Hall coauthored the US Commercial Company (USCC) report on Chuuk with Karl Pelzer (1946). Even though that document and the other USCC reports (Useem 1946c; Mason 1947; and Bascom 1946) focused on economic factors, they all took some pains to discuss personality variables.

2. In a retrospective essay published in 1978, Spiro recounted the intellectual odyssey that led him to Ifaluk and to his annoyance at and then interpretation of those infantile screams. His analysis of Ifaluk aggression, spirits, socialization practices, and other psycho-cultural matters appears in his dissertation (Spiro 1950b), in the ethnographic monograph he wrote with Burrows (Burrows and Spiro 1953), and in a series of papers (Spiro 1950a, 1951a, 1952, 1953a, 1959, 1961b). See his 1965a paper for the concept of culturally constituted defense mechanisms at work. For a very clear overview and analysis of Spiro's intellectual career, see Avruch 1990.

3. In her monograph on Ifaluk emotion (1988, 200), Lutz recounted the episode of the attempted rape that wasn't. That monograph, her dissertation (Lutz 1980), and the impressive series of papers that followed (Lutz 1981a, 1981b, 1982a, 1982b, 1983a, 1983b, 1984b, 1985, 1987; Lutz and LeVine 1983) constitute the most substantial ethnopsychological corpus produced so far in Micronesia or, as far as I am aware, anywhere else.

4. In Kitayama and Markus 1994, see especially the chapter by Anna Wierzbicka, which draws extensively on Lutz's Ifaluk language material.

5. See Goodenough 1993 for a snapshot discussion of the research tradition in Chuuk. Since Goodenough's work, as well as Gladwin's, Swartz's, Kaeser's, and Caughey's is discussed later in this chapter, I refrain here from generating another list of citations to demonstrate their impact on psychological anthropology at large. Taken as a whole, it has been enormous.

Among others whose psychologically oriented work contributed to the development of the subdisciplines, mention should certainly be made of John "Jack" Fischer in Pohnpei and Chuuk, and Ann Fischer in Chuuk.

6. Precisely how their field should be defined is a matter far from a unanimity among those who identify themselves as psychological anthropologists, let alone those who, like Richard Shweder, wish to subsume it within "cultural psychology" (1990). Its place within anthropology as a whole is put well by George Stocking who describes it as "rising above the mass of modern adjectival anthropologies, but not usually granted parity with the traditional 'four fields' within the disciplinary core" (1992, 312).

7. It is possible that this strongly insular orientation had unintended consequences. Spindler (personal communication 1993) raised the interesting issue of whether or not the types of communities (Pacific Islands and Native American reservations) in which

culture and personality studies developed had influenced that development. Perhaps they did give rise to a more "uniformitarian view of human nature and psychology than might otherwise have been the case" as he put it. Black's bibliography of Micronesian psychological anthropology also lists a number of surveys of psychological anthropology in Oceania (Black n.d.).

8. For the moribund state of *volkerpsychologie* see Woodruff Smith 1991. In any case, Richard Thurnwald's (1913) Pacific researches never got closer to Micronesia than New Guinea and the Solomons. I have not been able to determine whether Bastian's (1899) ethnology of Micronesia had any impact, or even whether it was translated.

I have come across only four short papers whose titles would have caught the eye of anyone scanning the Japanese scientific literature on the Mandated Territories for psychologically relevant materials: Kotondo Hasebe's "Manifestations of Chagrin Among Micronesians"(1942), Yasuo Hashiura's "Customs and Manners of Childbirth and Infant Care Among the South Sea Islanders" (1940), Hijikata Hisakatsu's "Education and Sex Training of Children on Satawal Island in Comparison With Palau" (Hijikata 1941), and K. Sonoda's "The Personality and Development of Boys on Ponape as Evaluated by Blood Type and Location of Whorls of Hair on the Head" (1938). Momoshige Miura and Masashi Murakami (1967) reported on work that was done in 1942 but not published until long after the war.

9. A truly dark view would point to a passage in the notorious Solomon Report in which Micronesian psychology assumes political importance. The authors of the report noted that the increased spending that they called for (spending which Kauders, MacMurray, and Hammond aptly characterize as "malignant generosity" [1982, 99]) was unlikely to set off a self-sustaining development process. Therefore, the report recommended that the all-essential plebiscite be held as soon as possible in order to take "advantage of the psychological impact of the capital investment program before some measure of disappointment is felt" (quoted in Alcalay 1992, 190).

10. Mac Marshall (1989) made a complementary point: the widespread agreement among those who have carried out ethnographic research in Micronesia is an indication that the concepts, methods, and techniques of cultural anthropology are relatively dependable lenses on a relatively stable external reality. His article also contains the references to the first two ethnographic disputes mentioned above; Avruch 1990 contains a discussion of the Lessa-Spiro argument; see Alkire 1989b, and Hutchins 1980 and 1983 for reviews of the final two. Alan Howard (personal communication 1993) accurately remarked that anthropology was being transformed from a place for "puzzles to be solved" to something much more inwardly focused. The disputes over Micronesian ethnography indicate that the puzzles are still "out there" for those interested in working on their solutions.

11. It is very interesting that the clearest statements of the two opposing positions on this issue (whether the definition of religion must necessarily include a reference to

belief in spiritual beings) are by Spiro and Goodenough, both of whom carried out their dissertation research in Micronesia, a region not noted for elaborate indigenous religious belief or practice.

Goodenough has recounted different aspects of the use he was able to make of the Gladwin and Sarason material in a number of places (1974b, 1981b, 1988a). Caughey and Marshall (1989) provide an account of Goodenough's intellectual biography.

12. Goodenough (1974b) expressed some uneasiness about using what he called "the vocabulary of ego psychology" in the description and analysis of Chuukese religious experience. Aware that Chuukese do not care for such language (personal communication 1993), he is searching for an alternative vocabulary. Two items, one a poem (1988b) and the other an extract from his field notes (n.d.), indicate directions his search may take.

13. Another well-known shift in Gladwin's position was his change from being an apologist for the US Trust Territory of the Pacific Islands (USTTPI) administration (Gladwin 1956) to being one of its severest critics (Gladwin n.d.). "The most fundamental fact of American policy toward the Micronesians is its inherent altruism" (Gladwin 1956, 61) is a statement that, even in the context of the 1950s, boggles the mind.

14. Also evident in the early literature (anthropological and otherwise) are bits and pieces of the fascinating story of the construction of American-Micronesian joint understandings and ways of interacting. Perhaps the TAT protocols collected by so many of the early researchers would be a good source for that history. Certainly the field journals of those ethnographers must contain much that is historically valuable. Ira Bashkow's (1991) splendid essay based on David Schneider's journal from Yap shows very clearly not just how the ethnographer groped his way toward an understanding of his situation but how the Yapese did, too. Hints of the same process are evident in the journal excerpts that Homer G. Barnett published (1979).

15. This is not to deny that there might be important continuities in the experience, organization, and knowledge of affect, motivation, cognition, and perception within and across cultural boundaries in Micronesia. Perhaps an exploration of these issues using George Devereux's (1951) ideas about areal culture, areal basic personality, and ethnicity would be productive.

16. Although Gladwin's neglect of his earlier work in a context in which it would seem to be highly significant is particularly impressive given the importance of those two monographs, he is not alone in this. For example, Spiro's 1993 paper is an essay on primary process thinking in which nothing from Ifaluk appears, not even the talk of the "psychotic personality in the south seas" he described in 1950.

17. Any thorough exploration of the connections between the culture and personality school and the ethnopsychologists would have to consider the influence of the ideas of A. I. Hallowell, who through his publications and students significantly influenced American psychological anthropology in Micronesia since it began. Like the

earlier researchers, the ethnopsychologists drew on Hallowell's ideas. But while his work with the Rorschach tests was central to culture and personality research, it was his discussion of the self and its behavioral environment on which the latter built.

The following snatch of dialogue reported by Shweder (1984, 14) reveals some of the implications of building on the ideas of this very influential scholar (the first speaker is Ted Schwartz, the second Mel Spiro):

> T.S.: "I think Hallowell used to believe that this cultural ideology of the self not only represents but actually comes to constitute culturally different self structures."
>
> M.S.: "I think he did believe that, but I don't agree with it."

18. Charles W. Nuckolls' important essay "Spiro and Lutz on Ifaluk: Toward a Synthesis of Cultural Cognition and Depth Psychology" (1996) appeared after I had finished this chapter. It represents a valiant attempt to reconcile cognitive and Freudian perspectives using material on Ifaluk ghosts and emotions. In my view its failure to achieve this goal arises in large part from its failure to draw on more of the ethnological and theoretical literature surrounding this topic—in short, the work of psychological anthropology of Micronesia.

19. I do not mention perception, the fourth of the classical psychological systems, because with the exception of a passage about Ifaluk perception in an article by Hallowell (1956), and papers on perception in navigation by Tomoya Akimichi (1985) and Hutchins and G. Hinton (1984), I found nothing to mention.

20. Of course there is no guarantee that this coherence will continue. Perhaps the rhetorical heat is evidence that it is being lost. David Hanlon (1989 and chap. 2 of this volume) has rightly pointed out that Micronesia has many of the characteristics of a nonentity; so does psychological anthropology. And just as the political integrity (such as it was) of the trust territory proved unequal to the stresses of negotiating a future relationship with the United States, so the scientific integrity (such as it is) of psychological anthropology may prove unequal to the stresses of negotiating its own present.

On the other hand, if, as Robin Fox is reported to have said, "anthropology has become like a lunatic asylum where the patients have taken over" (*Science* 1993, 1801), then psychological anthropology might find itself in a very strategic position, and the psychological anthropology of Micronesia might suddenly take center stage. For according to Gregory Bateson, the unintelligible gibberish of an extreme evangelical sect in Scotland was once "believed to be the language of the Pelew Islands" (1961, vii).

CHAPTER EIGHT

Missed Opportunities:
American Anthropological Studies of Micronesian Arts

Karen L. Nero

There seemed to be so little that could be called art,
and that little was so simple, tha' I remember thinking,
during those early days, "For a study of art, this is pretty poor picking."
EDWIN G. BURROWS, *FLOWER IN MY EAR*

FROM THEIR INCEPTION, American anthropological studies of the arts of Micronesia have suffered from problems of definition and analysis—obstacles that continue to this day. With the exception of the work of Edwin G. Burrows, however, these studies and conceptualizations of Micronesian arts were guided by existing paradigms. It is important to situate this research within the history of anthropology, and not fault the early anthropologists for failing to take into account theoretical advances that postdated their work.

Once Burrows started grappling with a definition of art that could incorporate the artistic complex he found on Ifaluk, whether or not it conformed to western expectations (1963, 6–11), he offered theoretical perspectives well ahead of his time. Although Burrows foreshadowed Jacques Maquet's (1971, 1986) later formulations of art and aesthetics, Burrows' contributions were not widely appreciated, nor did Maquet cite him. Burrow's study was published posthumously, and unlike some others among the Coordinated Investigation of Micronesian Anthropology (CIMA) and Scientific Investigation of Micronesia (SIM) anthropologists, Burrows had no students who followed him into the field. Had others incorporated his insights into their research, some of the negative developments in Micronesian arts under the American administration might have been avoided.

Few American anthropologists who worked in Micronesia wrote seriously on the arts. Of the roughly three hundred postwar writings on Micronesian arts, only about 60 percent were by academics, broadly defined to include cultural anthropologists, archaeologists, ethnomusicologists, art historians, and others. More than half of these publications were under ten pages. Only four PhD dissertations (L. Carucci 1980, LeBar 1951, Jernigan 1973, Montvel-Cohen 1982), seven master's theses (Bailey 1978, Brooks 1988, Gillespie 1977, Le Geyt 1986, Mulford 1980, Schmidt 1974, Yamaguchi 1967), and one bachelor's thesis (Iwata 1985) were written directly about the arts and ritual behavior. Many of the academic contributions on the arts appeared in territorial publications, local journals, or encyclopedias outside the mainstream of anthropology, and their impact on the anthropology of art was limited. The educational institutions established on Guam and in the former US Trust Territory of the Pacific Islands (USTTPI) never supported the arts in a manner comparable to the University of the South Pacific (USP) or the University of Papua New Guinea (UPNG). Only in the last two decades have US Historic Preservation and National Endowment for the Humanities funds been available to help support local agencies, museums, and galleries. However, applied activities undertaken by American anthropologists in Micronesia in the fields of the arts, museums, and education have had significant impacts, both positive and negative. Among the more positive impacts of the anthropological endeavor were the collegial relationships established with indigenous researchers, beginning in the early years of the colonial administration. Of all publications in the decade from 1954 to 1964, nearly 10 percent were written by Micronesians, a percentage that more than doubled in the decade from 1985-1995.

During the early period of the American administration, anthropological theory was ill equipped to deal with any art systems other than the plastic and visual arts of painting and sculpture. The areas of artistic creativity practiced within Micronesia—performance arts, tattoos, costumes, architecture, stone monuments, sculpture, religious effigies, and rock art—nearly all fall outside this limited western view of visual arts, narrowly defined. Micronesian aesthetics are even further removed from European sensibilities: the minimalist lines of its rare wooden sculpture; the force of its basalt architecture; the aesthetic attention paid to utilitarian objects such as bait boxes; or Micronesians' multisensory emphasis on the ephemeral arts of integrated chants, scents, and meditative movement—the composite impact of a line of dancers moving and chanting in unison, wearing hibiscus fiber skirts or geometrically woven *tur* cloths, their skin glistening with turmeric-spiced coconut oil, accented by garlands of rare shells and rustling coconut leaf decorations, crowned by richly scented floral wreathes. Many Micronesian artistic endeavors are transitory; their aesthetic emphasis is on the perfection of the performance rather than the creation of a lasting object. When perfection is achieved, the thrill of recognition in the audience fulfills local sensibilities, but translates poorly into academic discourse.

THE ANTHROPOLOGY OF ART

Traditionally, the study of arts has been marginalized within anthropology. It is arguable whether the anthropology of art would have been considered a separate field of study in the late 1940s when American ethnographers set out for the Micronesian islands. Under Franz Boas (1955 [1927]) the study of art and artifacts had been integral to an anthropological study of society, yet in the anti-Boasian backlash of the 1930s, cultural anthropologists' overriding concern with "material culture" was considered outdated. Following A. C. Haddon's studies of British New Guinea and Torres Straits Island art, including tattoo (1894, 1905, 1912), Raymond Firth (1936) and Gregory Bateson (1958 [1936]) led the Pacific in writing in-depth studies of art in two Pacific Islands societies. With these eminent exceptions, the few pre-1940s studies of Pacific art were comprehensive ethnological studies such as those of the Südsee Expedition, or associated with archaeology (e.g., Linton 1925), and their emphasis was firmly on the material and visual, perhaps implying that artistic production was situated in the past, not the present (Wendt 1983).

Claude Lévi-Strauss initially published on the relationships between social structure and the structure of artistic designs in 1955 (reprinted in 1970; see also Lévi-Strauss 1963). William Alkire (1970) pioneered the application of a structuralist approach to Micronesian societies, examining how Carolinian measurement systems operate across different cultural domains, from architecture to canoes. In 1978, Adrienne Kaeppler used a structuralist approach to study the Tongan arts. Only beginning in the 1970s would cross-cultural theories of aesthetics and art incorporate the disparate subjects and media used outside western art traditions. Using historical and cross-cultural examples (medieval Christian architecture and reliquaries, the Japanese tea ceremony, Zen sand-and-stone gardens), Maquet (1971) expanded the analyst's range of subjects and media of art through his concept of aesthetic locus—the variety of domains and media on which cultures may focus their aesthetic expression over time. Maquet also provided the useful analytical distinction between objects made for artistic purposes within a society ("art by destination") and those later assigned artistic status, often by outsider museums ("art by metamorphosis"). Prior to these theoretical advances, the basis for understanding Micronesian arts was limited.

Ethnographic studies of arts in relationship to society were predominantly conducted in Africa and New Guinea where the sculptural arts, while radically different from western sensibilities, were nevertheless more understandable, and were a major influence on European artists' "primitivism" movements (Rubin 1984). Following Marian Smith's 1961 edited volume, interest in cross-cultural studies of art and symbolism effloresced in the 1970s, and theoretical frameworks developed through which anthropologists could study a range of artistic productions within a society, their relationships to outside economic forces, and the structural relationships between society and the arts (Bloch 1974; Forge 1973; Graburn 1976, 1979; Jopling 1971; Maquet 1971; Ortner 1974; Otten 1971). An anthropological emphasis on performance (a major locus of the arts in Micronesia) did not come to the fore until the late 1980s (Turner 1986; Schechner and Appel 1990), paralleling a general anthropological concern at that time with practice. Indeed, in order for researchers to appreciate the valuation of textiles (female "soft" valuables) exchanged across the Caroline Islands, certain feminist and postcolonial advances of the 1980s and early 1990s had to occur (Weiner 1980, 1992; Weiner and Schneider 1989; Appadurai 1986; Kopytoff 1986).

Few would argue with Jeremy Coote and Anthony Shelton's assessment that the anthropology of art follows the theoretical lead of mainstream anthropology and, lacking a unified structure or even subject matter in itself, poaches on folklore and mythology (1992, 2–3). The study of art fared badly as the discipline split into topical specializations (e.g., economics, politics); art was marginalized either as only a reflection of society, or as part of a mystifying superstructure. When anthropologists moved beyond understandings of the arts as simply reflecting society, to studies of the ways arts force viewers to form new syntheses of information and stimulate change, they encountered a serious problem: they feared that the process of attempting to explain this power would devalue or contain it. This tension led Alfred Gell (1992, 42) to propose that the anthropology of art is impossible unless it is conducted from an attitude of methodological philistinism (analogous to the atheism he suggested is required to study religion), or achieved through its divorce from the anthropology of aesthetics (the equivalent of theology). Yet it is aesthetic power that lies at the core of the artistic experience (see Davenport 1986). Problems remain in using words to represent and analyze the contradictory and multivalent expressions in which artistic representations excel. In the 1990s, however, anthropological concerns with representation, performance, and indigenous constructions of history have reestablished the primacy of art within an integrated study of cultural production (Strathern 1990).

CIMA, SIM, AND THE EARLY ADMINISTRATION

American anthropologists' studies of art in Micronesia have been extremely limited, with even less impact on the general field. Of all the studies conducted by researchers involved in the CIMA and anthropology and administration in Micronesia, only John "Jack" Fischer's work (e.g., his 1961 article), is consistently cited and reprinted in anthologies on the anthropology of art (Jopling 1971; Otten 1971). Yet Fischer's "Art Styles as Cultural Cognitive Maps" (1961) is only incidentally about Micronesia, in that he included the Marshalls among the twenty-nine societies in his cross-cultural sample. Among the CIMA and SIM anthropologists, only Burrows, Frank LeBar, and William Lessa conducted studies that focused directly on art, however broadly defined. Lessa's work on Ulithian folktales (1961, 1962b, 1966b, 1980) is often considered to lie within the somewhat separate field of folklore. The most important contribution to the general field of anthropology of art is Burrow's *Flower in My Ear* (1963), based on his work on Ifaluk Atoll. Yet, as discussed in more detail below, this work has had less influence and recognition than it deserves. Just why were the arts so understudied in Micronesia? An answer to this question entails investigations into anthropology writ large, and the history of the earliest American anthropological studies in the region.

To begin with, we must certainly credit (or fault) the general trend in American anthropology away from a Boasian interest in material culture, as well as the impact of the publications from the German Südsee Expedition. For the ethnographers who set out for Micronesia in the late 1940s, the numerous volumes Georg Thilenius edited on the 1908–1910 German expeditions to the Marshall, Caroline, and Mariana Islands made it appear that a study of the arts and material culture had already been done and was therefore unnecessary (Damm 1935, 1938; Eilers 1934a, 1934b, 1936; Hambruch and Eilers 1936; Krämer 1919, 1926, 1929, 1932, 1935, 1937; Krämer and Nevermann 1938; Müller 1917; Sarfert 1919). Furthermore, the Südsee Expedition had contributed to the general removal, to European collections, of those sculptural forms most readily understandable as art. In contrast, the expedition's comprehensive coverage of other aspects of Micronesian societies—conducted near the beginning of local colonial administration of the islands, but postdating the effect of commercial traders—provided a wealth of data against which new studies of "acculturation" could be compared (see Poyer, chap. 6).

CIMA and SIM Studies

With all the anthropological power unleashed in Micronesia between the late 1940s and the 1960s, it is difficult to imagine that major theoretical advances would not have occurred if in-depth studies of the arts had been conducted. This is ironic when we consider that Burrows' breakthroughs went unrecognized. Was there a bias in the topics covered by anthropologists during this time? If so, this raises questions about whether such bias was externally influenced and how.

In his essay on David M. Schneider's early fieldwork on Yap, Ira Bashkow (1991) proposed a partial explanation for the selection of CIMA topics. As Robert C. Kiste and Suzanne Falgout discuss in chapter 1 of this volume, Bashkow documented a competition over the goals and methods to be used in Pacific research in the immediate postwar years. George Peter Murdock (an avowed anti-Boasian) was primarily interested in developing a " 'scientific anthropology,' based on the 'formulation and verification, on a large scale and by quantitative methods, of scientific generalizations of a universally human or cross-cultural character' " (Murdock, quoted in Bashkow 1991, 174). Murdock's interest in applied anthropology coincided with Douglas L. Oliver's plan "for the establishment of a 'post-hostilities organization for systematic scientific exploration,' which 'besides possessing intrinsic scientific value,' would 'assist powerfully in the administration and development of the area' " (Oliver, quoted in Bashkow 1991, 182).

Bashkow saw the Murdock and Oliver conceptualization of Micronesian research as opposed to that proposed by the Committee on Pacific Investigations led by Herbert Gregory, E. S. C. Handy, and Felix Keesing of the University of Hawai'i. He likened the latter to "Boasian 'historical' ethnographers of indigenous peoples of North America . . . [considering] the 'ethnographic salvage' of vanishing artifacts and traditions as a project of utmost urgency . . . an approach which did not lend itself easily to producing results of any 'utility' in colonial administration" (Bashkow 1991, 183). The debate within academia became somewhat irrelevant in 1946 when President Truman announced that the islands would be placed under the United Nations (UN) trusteeship system and that this "strategic" trusteeship would continue indefinitely under naval administration. This turn of events apparently tipped the scale in favor of Murdock, who had been closely affiliated with the navy since 1943.

As Kiste and Falgout have indicated (chap. 1), in 1948 the National Research Council established a Pacific Science Board (PSB) to coordinate Micronesian research that would be requested and funded by the navy. Although "the agreement between the Pacific Science Board and Navy . . . reserved to CIMA participants the right to study what they might. . . . There was an unmistakable attempt to give positive direction to research. . . . As a matter of policy, funds were 'allocated to projects roughly in proportion to their correspondence with administrative needs and priorities' " (Bashkow 1991, 185–186), with financial bonuses for prompt reports for administrative uses. The navy's formal request for proposals specified studies of "the native system of land tenure and . . . political and social structure of native communities" (quoted in Bashkow 1991, 185).

In recent discussions about this period with Leonard Mason (personal communications 1993), he discounted Bashkow's descriptions of institutional rivalry. Mason did not know of alternate proposals or animosity between the two groups. In fact the Pacific Science Board, headed by Harold Coolidge but run by Murdock, worked closely with the University of Hawai'i, hiring Mason half-time for six months as a coordinator for CIMA staff en route to Micronesia. Perhaps the academic compromise to which Bashkow alludes had been reached, or the conflict overstated. Certainly, Burrows' participation in both the CIMA and SIM expeditions argues for the more open interpretation. Already established as an anthropologist specializing in the study of arts, and with prior research experience in Oceania, Burrows proposed projects in the arts and general ethnography of Ifaluk, and was funded for the CIMA study in 1947–1948 and again in 1953 under the SIM Coral Atoll Project.

While Murdock's approach helped direct Micronesian research toward applied goals (which a study of art could little hope to achieve), this is clearly insufficient to explain the lack of American anthropological interest in Micronesian art. Once again, the situation must be put in historical perspective. After the German ethnographic efforts in the Pacific prior to World War II, little attention was paid to Pacific arts, and what literature existed on Micronesian arts was written in German or Japanese. The Bishop Museum had engaged in studies of Polynesian material culture (e.g., Buck 1927, 1930), but the public was largely unaware of Micronesian art works, other than a few pieces held in European collections and displayed in an occasional art text or catalog. The first general study of Pacific arts (Linton and Wingert 1946) included little on Micronesia. Maurice Leenhardt's 1950 text, the *Arts of the Oceanic Peoples,* even included Madagascar, but had nothing from Micronesia. Tibor Bodrogi (1959) wrote two pages on Micronesia in his study, *Oceanian Art.* The authors of *The Art of the South Sea Islands* featured only one paragraph on Micronesian art (Buhler, Barrow, and Mountford 1962). Even the general labels assigned to the Pacific—the South Pacific, the South Sea Islands—apparently ignored the fact that there are inhabited islands to the north of the equator. American anthropological studies in Micronesia did not overcome international perceptions. Not until 1979 were Micronesian arts highlighted in a Pacific art book, *Made in the South Pacific* (Price 1979). Most books on Pacific art continue to slight Micronesian arts, partly because the books are based on museum collections, which are limited.

Major Studies: Burrows, LeBar, Lessa

Edwin G. Burrows set out in 1947 specifically to study the arts on the small coral atoll of Ifaluk, only to encounter a serious problem: where was the art? Apparently nothing existed that remotely resembled what passes for art in western societies. An accomplished Pacific scholar who had already completed a study of the arts of Uvea in Western Polynesia (Burrows 1938), he was initially at a loss to understand Micronesian artistic production. He had selected Ifaluk because it had never had a resident missionary, as he believed that Christianity would have undermined the religious impetus for creation of navigational and weather effigies and wooden carvings. But even without missionary influence Burrows initially found little to study on Ifaluk:

> The stunted growth of art is apparently a matter of scant raw materials and a cramping tradition. As to raw materials, not only are metal work and ceramics debarred on an island with neither ore nor clay, but stonework is hardly worth while in crumbly coral, nor wood carving in perversely cross-grained coconut or spongy breadfruit wood. There is only a little good hardwood, and not much pigment for painting. It seems likely that houses were once more decorated and decorative than they are now. Some of the people told Fritz Sarfert, the German anthropologist who visited Ifaluk two years after the disastrous typhoon of 1907, that they were not going to bother any more with the carefully constructed old style of house, because all houses would only be washed out to sea anyway in the next big typhoon. (1963, 6)

Edwin G. Burrows (upper right) *participating in religious ceremony, Ifaluk Atoll, 1947. Photograph courtesy of Mel Spiro.*

Nevertheless, Burrows persevered and soon discovered to his delight that "there was no underdevelopment of art on Ifaluk" (1963, 7). He had just been looking in the wrong places. Once he turned his attention from the visual arts, "the artistic specialty of Ifaluk came into view—gesture song, combining the three arts of music, poetry and dance" (1963, 7). Thus began Burrows' pioneering study of the performing arts, far in advance of their eventual theoretical recognition in the late 1980s. After a brief preface introducing Ifaluk and the social functions of art, Burrows opened with a rare study of a major body art: tattoo. He also described in detail other forms of bodily adornment: facial and body painting with turmeric, the fragrant garlands favored especially by men, the rustling coconut leaf decorations, and the finely woven *tur* or 'loincloths' with their geometric patterns, worn on ceremonial occasions. All these body and costuming arts combined on Ifaluk to create a multisensory perception that incorporated the audience in the performers' experience.

Most important, Burrows attempted a definition of art that could encompass these performing arts and sensibilities, a definition that differed markedly from prevailing western models:

> What is meant here by art? As a tentative definition, art is any human activity or product (artifact) that emphasizes form beyond all requirements except those of a distinctive pleasure that the manufacture and contemplation of form can give. By form is meant a perceptible relation of parts to a whole. The distinctive pleasure it gives is here [c]alled the "esthetic experience." It is often called 'esthetic thrill'; but in the author's recollection it is a pervasive glow, spreading from the region of the diaphragm, and varying indefinitely in suddenness and intensity, hence not necessarily a thrill. No definition of art has yet proved entirely satisfactory. (1963, 11)

Burrows was only on Ifaluk for seven months during his first trip, forcing him to rely on a local translator, Totogoeitin. Yet the poetically rendered song texts, a combination of Burrows' and Totogoeitin's work, are impressive. When Burrows returned in 1953, the people of Ifaluk decided to share with him the women's song texts, which they had apparently withheld during his first visit.

Burrows' study supports Coote and Shelton's (1992) claim that the anthropology of art follows the theoretical mainstream of anthropology. The main emphasis of *Flower in My Ear* is revealed in its subtitle: *Art and Ethos of Ifaluk Atoll*. Burrows explicitly set out to prove "the thesis . . . that the function of art in Ifaluk, and by implication wherever else art and the rest of life are as closely intertwined as they are there, is to express the values and sentiments—the ethos—that dominate motivation in that community" (1963, 10).

Burrows' analysis was conceived securely within the dominant culture and personality paradigm of the period, and he was undoubtedly influenced by his coresearcher, Melford E. Spiro, who became one of its leading proponents (see Black, chap. 7). Together they published a general ethnography of Ifaluk (Burrows and Spiro 1953). In that volume the music, poetry, and dance of Ifaluk are presented in a series of chapters on contrasting sentiments: rank and kindliness, seafaring and homecoming, zeal and skill. Yet in his final analysis, Burrows admits:

> If some of the values or sentiments that appear important from general observation of life on the atoll are not clearly expressed in the songs, then this method is so far inadequate. Actually, such unexpressed or inadequately expressed sentiments are not hard to find. (1963, 428)

It is not possible to offer a final outline of the ethos of Ifaluk.... Nevertheless, the song texts reveal enough to make similar attempts well worth while in other cultures that retain vigorous arts of their own, whether the dominant forms be song and dance, as on Ifaluk, or some other forms. (1963, 430)

Burrows contrasted American and Ifaluk arts and the relative degrees to which individuals participate in their creation. He suggested that the nearly universal participation by men, women, and children on Ifaluk was a more democratic form of art than the aristocratic American forms generally reserved to acknowledged experts. The personal participation by all members of the community, and their uniform costumes and body decorations, supported an egalitarian ethos. This emphasis on the truly democratic nature of Micronesian arts, rather than an elitist hierarchy, if carried to its logical extreme, could have helped break down the unfortunate arts/handicrafts distinction which is discussed below. Burrows called into question perceived contrasts between Micronesian hierarchies and American egalitarianism, which he emphasized in his closing statement: "They have the advantages of democracy; we have those of aristocracy" (1963, 431).

Burrows also analyzed the ways in which the Ifaluk used artistic media to critique earlier colonial power relations—an analysis far ahead of his time for the Pacific (see, however, Lips 1937; cf. Petersen, chap. 5). Burrows recorded a number of songs that ridiculed the Yapese and Germans, but songs critiquing Americans may have been untranslated, and some of their nuances unappreciated (Burrows 1963, 417). It is unfortunate that *Flower in My Ear* was Burrows' last work and that no students further developed his insights.

An anthropological focus on more pressing administrative issues did not indicate that the anthropologists themselves were not interested in the arts. In fact, the possibility of studying the contemporary production of "traditional crafts" prompted the selection of Romónum as the site for the CIMA study within Truk (now Chuuk) (Goodenough 1968, 13). Frank LeBar, one of the team members from Yale University, conducted a comprehensive survey of material culture (1951, 1964) and also made a collection for Yale's Peabody Museum. LeBar's emphasis was on technology, and he comprehensively cataloged Chuukese material production, including brief descriptions of artifacts no longer being produced such as the double model "spirit" canoe. The ethnographic team found that the production of traditional crafts had seriously declined in Chuuk, even on one of the two islands still noted for its crafts in 1947. Boats more suitable for outboard motors were replacing outrigger canoes, although Goodenough was able to purchase a canoe specially constructed for the University Museum of Pennsylvania during their stay. Only a few women still practiced weaving, but others retained the skills and taught some of the younger women in response to the anthropologists' commissioning of Chuukese textiles—a positive impact of anthropological interest in Micronesian crafts, and the collection of artifacts for US museums.

William Lessa (1961, 1980) focused on the verbal arts in his extensive studies of Ulithian oral narratives. Not only did he record, analyze, and transcribe or translate volumes of oral narratives, legends, and histories, but he also discussed the various forms of dance and the circumstances of their performance. In a Boasian vein, Lessa's primary concern was to record the Ulithian oral heritage so that it would not be lost—emphasizing the necessity of salvage operations to preserve the arts—and to add these previously unpublished tales to the existing pool of knowledge on Oceanic folktales. He was only secondarily interested in the relationships of oral literature to anthropological issues of social and political organization, technology, religion, and values (1961, 1–2), yet his background discussions are rich in ethnographic detail and analysis. Regional perspectives on relationships among neighboring islands were promoted by Lessa's comparison of motifs and tale types across the Pacific, such as how Gatschapar's control of Motikitik's fishhook demonstrates and maintains Ulithi's political dominance over Fais (Lessa 1961, 116). His salvage approach to oral histories produced an invaluable body of literature and sources for contemporary analysis (cf. Mauricio 1992 for a discussion of Pohnpeian oral historical studies). Lessa also grappled with the relationships of the oral narratives to history, commenting on the lack of historical interest he perceived in the stories, and the narrative absence of certain events of interest to Europeans (i.e., the arrival of the Portuguese; cf. Hanlon, chap. 2). While Lessa's focus on preservation implied a reification of culture within the past, he specifically connected the ways that Yapese and Ulithians use myths to charter contemporary relationships. Nevertheless, the contrast between his approach and Burrows' is striking. Burrows situated his studies in contemporary performance and bodily adornment—in hindsight one wishes there had been more dialogue between these two ethnographers.

Fundamentally, the American studies of Micronesian arts were flawed. Both Burrows' and Lessa's work provided a strong basis for further analytical development, but this was not forthcoming. The technological emphasis of LeBar's study overshadowed any considerations of the meanings of the arts within society: one searches in vain for identification of design motifs and their meanings. It seems that the right questions were not asked, or if asked, not answered. Lessa's concern to salvage the Ulithian oral heritage precluded more contemporary perspectives. Burrows' important contributions—recognition of the multimedia genre of artistic performance; documentation of an Ifaluk aesthetic sense different from that of the west but equally valid; and discussion of the democratic nature of Ifaluk art—were less influential in the anthropology of art than they deserved to be. And despite his insights, Burrows primarily treated the arts within a western theoretical framework so as to test western understandings of social processes, rather than using the arts to reveal indigenous aesthetic and artistic understandings.

Occasional and Overview Studies

Most of the early CIMA and SIM anthropologists focused their inquiries outside the arts, yet a number included brief descriptions of music and dance or artistic production within their ethnographies, or produced occasional articles in popular and academic journals or small regional publications. Burrows' analysis of music in psychological terms was continued by Fischer and Marc Swartz's (1960) examination of Pohnpeian and Chuukese love songs. They analyzed the related sentiments of aggression and masochism expressed in the song texts collected from the two island groups between 1949 and 1953, after providing a brief sociocultural background of the two societies and the occasions on which the songs were sung. Songs, rather than psychological tests, were used expressly as a sociopsychological index on the grounds that they were less threatening and distorting. Limiting their analysis to one dimension, the authors examined the hypothesis that Chuukese expressed more masochism, and Pohnpeians more aggression–self-confidence, and they related this to the relatively weaker social position of Chuukese men with regard to Chuukese women. At about this time Fischer (1959b) also studied meter in Carolinian oral narratives.

In a classic documentary essay on Caroline Island belt weaving, Saul Riesenberg and Anna Gayton (1952) analyzed a collection of Pohnpeian and Kosraean weavings in the (then) Lowie Museum of Anthropology at the University of California, Berkeley, and an heirloom piece, dated approximately 1870, owned by Riesenberg. Most of the study collection consisted of the mundane plain and full-stripe weave that had been readily available for sale or trade in the late 1800s; many of the pieces had been purchased in San Francisco from The Old Curiosity Shop, which in turn had purchased the items from sailors. Riesenberg and Gayton's article is technical in nature, and describes the range of Eastern Carolinian textile techniques, including shell bead embellishment and the knotted warp techniques of the finest Pohnpei and Kosrae weavings. It also addresses issues such as the origins and spread of backstrap loom weaving techniques in the Pacific. Unfortunately, any insights that could have been gained from ethnographic research with the weavers, or with those who remembered wearing or exchanging the pieces, were unavailable.

Mason's (1959b, 1964) contributions on Micronesian cultures to the *Encyclopedia of World Art* remain the most comprehensive and insightful overviews that we have of Micronesian arts. In a broadly comparative framework, he analyzed Micronesian aesthetic emphases on geometric and nonrepresentational designs, the ways artists capture the dynamics of number and rhythm by varying design combinations, and the relationships among tattooing, plaiting, weaving, and incised wood carving, predating Roger Green's (1979) analysis of the replication of Lapita designs across different media. Mason tackled issues of regional styles and influences from neighboring areas. He provided richly detailed discussions of the relationships between artistic styles of the several Micronesian cultures, and the ways in which each differentially develops widespread Micronesian characteristics. Although Mason worked only with the visual arts, he nevertheless included the many loci of Micronesian visual and three-dimensional arts—tattoo, textiles, mundane and religious carvings, and architecture—moving beyond the normative range of sculpture, paintings, or drawings generally considered at that time. While this study provided an excellent overview to the general public, its publication in the encyclopedia perhaps diminished its impact within anthropological circles.

During the first period of research on Micronesian arts under the German administration, except for the occasional article by an art collector (Beasley 1914) or the anonymous contribution to a local periodical (*Guam Recorder* 1939), all publications were substantial studies of the material culture of the region by professional ethnographers (Thilenius 1914–1938). During the American administration, academics continued to dominate publications on Micronesian arts, but rather than major studies, two-thirds of all publications during the decades from 1955–1974 were under ten pages in length. Many of these appeared in small regional outlets such as the *Micronesian Reporter,* the *Guam Recorder,* and *Micronesica.* For instance, Robert Ritzenthaler (1954) published an excellent study of Palauan bead money through the Milwaukee Public Museum, describing its various named categories and the oral histories surrounding its origins. Roland and Maryanne Force (1959) added an analysis of

*Leonard Mason and Marshallese mat
weaver, Arno Atoll, SIM project, 1950.
Photograph courtesy of Leonard
Mason.*

the materials from which the various beads were made, drawing comparisons to bracelets found in the Philippines. In turn, their work was followed up by Inez de Beauclair's (1962a, 1962b, 1963) studies of glass beads and bracelets on both Yap and Palau.

As Kiste and Falgout have described (chap. 1), a number of American anthropologists were employed as district anthropologists. Just as Burrows had collaborated closely with Totogoeitin and other Ifaluk assistants, these anthropologists worked closely with local mentors. Despite the conflicts and tensions inherent in either representing or dealing with a colonial administration, strong working relationships were established, and the long-term influences of these relationships were substantial. Many of the articles and USTTPI publications from this period were coauthored with local counterparts—9 percent in the decade from 1956–1965, and 13 percent during the decade from 1966–1975. This positive impact of the anthropological endeavor in Micronesia —the close working relationships of anthropologists with indigenous counterparts and coauthored publications—should be highlighted, as it was unusual in anthropological publications of that time period. For example, Robert McKnight, jointly with Adalbert Obak, wrote a series of articles on Palauan art forms. In addition to two items on Palauan and USTTPI "handicrafts" (McKnight 1962, 1964a), Obak and McKnight published on Palauan proverbs (1966) and kites (1964, 1969). McKnight also wrote on Palauan rock paintings, shell inlay, storyboards, and folklore (1964b, 1964c, 1967), as well as on jewelry from Nan Madol in Pohnpei (1964d). These were mostly local USTTPI publications, not articles in major anthropological journals. The laudable practice of publishing in locally accessible media undercut their possibly wider contribution to the discipline. It may also have promoted the view of the appropriate role of art as preserving and strengthening traditions from the past, rather than making meaning of contemporary events (see Dark 1993, 222).

APPLIED CONTRIBUTIONS

Any attempt to understand anthropological contributions to perceptions of the arts in Micronesia must include the applied projects in cultural preservation, most of which never entered the academic record, and many of which were initiated by indigenous leaders with the assistance of American expatriates and anthropologists. Prime examples are the museums and cultural centers established in each of the former district centers. Nearly all the museums have been hampered by a paucity of historic items and the loss of items from their collections, and the deterioration of museum buildings. The collections were small to begin with, and as elsewhere in the Pacific, most of the eighteenth and nineteenth century pieces of any value were gone. Some had been given or sold to or otherwise acquired by visiting ethnographers, sailors, traders, or missionaries and sent to European and American museums; others had been destroyed by natural processes or during World War II battles. Only the Palau Museum (now the Belau National Museum) has managed to stay in continual operation in one location since its founding in 1955 by Palauans Indalecio Rudimch, Francisco Morei, Alphonso Oiterong, and CIMA and later District Anthropologist Francis M. Mahoney. The directors were actively supported by leaders of the Palauan community and another district anthropologist, Robert McKnight. This museum has sponsored a large number of publications, including several on the museum and its exhibits (*Micronesian Reporter* 1956, 1959; Palau Museum 1973, 1976; McKnight 1962; Craddock and Craddock 1967; Sengebau et al. 1969; Owen 1972, 1974, 1978; Barizo 1979a, 1979b; Ramon 1975; Rehuher 1980, 1993; Belau National Museum 1989). Raphael Uag, curator and founder of the Yap Museum, has also contributed to the ethnographic record with his recounting of Yap's founding legends (Uag and Molinski 1969a, 1969b). Pensile Lawrence, who worked closely with Saul Riesenberg, curated the Ponape Museum. Mary Lanwi and Alfred Capelle were among the Marshallese instrumental in establishing the Alele Museum on Majuro. A Chuuk Museum was originally opened at the airport and later relocated to the town under the direction of the Historic Preservation Office. The late Teddy John opened the Kosrae Museum in that island's oldest building, across from the Lelu ruins. The Guam Museum, originally founded in 1932, is the region's oldest museum (Baird 1954; Glenn 1975). Like others established in Micronesia beginning in the 1950s, it suffered through numerous relocations and periods of inactivity. Throughout the region Micronesians and anthropologists have worked closely together to establish and maintain these museums.

Other applied examples include the construction of meeting houses as community centers and museums. Anthropologist Homer G. Barnett helped obtain South Pacific Commission (SPC) funding to construct the *Kebtot el Bai* 'Twin Meeting House' in the center of Koror in the 1950s (Barnett 1951). Conceived as a community center, the Twin Bai was expressly designed to bring together Palau's many village communities in constructing a meeting house for all of Palau. This project was innovative in many ways. The *bai* was not constructed on an existing meeting house site, which would have had much more localized meanings. The orientation of its gables was also unusual: the Twin Meeting House was not in fact a set of two *bai*, with gables at each end, like those of the highest chiefly councils. Rather, the "two" gable-ended buildings were joined into one, the four gables facing four different directions, representing the four ranking villages of Palau. The *bai* specifically incorporated stories from villages throughout Palau to underscore its unifying purpose. The *bai* was neither reserved for the use of chiefly councils, nor were the debates within its walls unknown to the public—in fact, except for the portion used as a museum (and for the sale of handicrafts), there were no walls, another significant innovation. This was indeed a community meeting house, where men's, women's, and mixed groups met. The Twin Meeting House served as a focal point of pan-Palauan identity and self-esteem until it was destroyed in a typhoon in 1967.

The Palauan chiefly meeting house *Bai ra Ngesechel ar Cherchar* was then constructed, according to tradition, in Ngeremlengui, the "older brother" village of Koror, before it was erected on the grounds of the Palau Museum (another "new" site which could transcend localized polities). Dedicated in 1969, its construction was fully documented by the Palauan chiefs and artists working under the direction of master artist Laurence Otaor (Sengebau et al. 1969), and by American archaeologist Douglas Osborne and other members of the American expatriate community in Palau. The stories depicted on the interior tie-beams were recounted in a small museum publication (University of Guam Gallery of Art 1973). This was one of two *bai* destroyed by arson in Koror during the confrontations surrounding Palau's nuclear-free constitution and its agreement of free association with the United States.

It is this interactive nature of art in society which would later come to the fore of anthropological studies. The two meeting house examples give an idea of the importance of their construction as cultural and architectural innovations, and of the self-conscious attempts to use art to mediate and draw together members of different communities, as well as their potential for being a very traditional target of intervillage disputes. Similar examples undoubtedly exist in the other islands of Micronesia, but very few of the "applied" projects such as the construction of the two *bai* ever entered into the academic record. In the early decades, as at present, many anthropologists working in Micronesia contributed to community projects in the islands, much as they would contribute to communities while living in the United States. What was the synergy among the anthropologist, the indigenous artists, and community members? To what extent was the design of the innovative Twin *Bai* and the conception of its use as a pan-Palauan meeting house, museum, and handicraft center the work of Palauans, or of the anthropologist? Too often these important questions were left unanswered, indeed were not even conceived or stated. The above synopses are based on oral histories and the rare document and photograph. Barnett did not write an academic article on the *Kebtot el Bai,* and the depth of his involvement, other than that suggested by his documented proposal for spc support, is unclear. Critics have charged that museums are primarily "western" institutions imposed in the Pacific. This perspective may unduly emphasize the contributions of anthropologists and expatriates; it certainly denies indigenous agency.

Anthropologists were only one of the outside influences affecting the directions of the arts during the USTTPI administration—other expatriates, including other islanders, probably wielded far greater influence. Just as the Yapese had helped construct many of the stone roads and platforms in Palau during the time of the stone money quarrying, and brought these ideas back to Yap, Palauans continued to learn Yapese and Chuukese songs and dances, Pohnpeians incorporated the dances of visiting traders, and all islanders mimicked the military cadence of visiting soldiers. Other songs and dances were received as gifts and tribute. Such cross-fertilization of the arts continued throughout Micronesia during the American administration, although perhaps initially dampened as peoples were repatriated to their home islands after the displacements of World War II. But opportunities for cross-cultural exchanges soon reopened. In the early years of the trusteeship, the Angaur phosphate mine in Palau continued to employ other Micronesian workers, and a number of songs and dances commemorate the lonely periods workers spent away from their loved ones. Prior to the establishment of secondary schools throughout the islands, the brightest students of each island group were sent to the Pacific Islands Central School and Xavier High School on Chuuk and Pohnpei, fostering cross-cultural Micronesian exchanges. Later, as Micronesians were incorporated into the USTTPI administration, entire families shifted between districts. Significant roles were also played by expatriate educators and artists such as Sandra Vitarelli Hobson, whose work helped revitalize pottery making in Palau (Hobson 1970).

Peace Corps volunteers, who were sent to the islands beginning in 1966 and learned Micronesian languages and cultures while living closely with Micronesian families, also deserve special mention. They were often tapped to assist in handicraft production and sales projects, to assist children's summer camps with their end-of-season productions, and even to join in traditional dances. One of the more popular of the ubiquitous Micronesian T-shirts (another important and unstudied island "expressive art" form) sold at the Yap

Co-op depicted a line of loincloth-clad dancers, one of whom was white. Popular author Fred Kluge, who was a Peace Corps volunteer when he served as editor of the *Micronesian Reporter* from 1967 to 1969, actively promoted Micronesian writers (Kluge 1969). A number of the former volunteers continued to live in or visit the islands after completing their contracts, and published numerous articles in local journals and news media, including the expanding *Glimpses of Micronesia and the Western Pacific* magazine which featured color photographic images as well as texts.

MISSED PERCEPTIONS

In the absence of later theoretical breakthroughs or close attention to Burrows' insights, one side effect of the work of early anthropologists and administrators was the unquestioned incorporation of western categories for understanding art, specifically the analytical distinction between "arts" and "crafts" (the title of Goodenough's 1968 article). This is unfortunate because of the uncritical designation (and implicit denigration) of Micronesian artistic productions as "handicrafts."

Generally speaking, in the west "the arts" are held to embody the "high tradition" of European production. The visual arts include sculpture and painting. Both media and technological skill are relevant to the categorization—generally it is oil painting, rather than watercolor, that qualifies. A finely crafted statue, preferably of bronze or marble, is preferred over wood. The "soft" textiles certainly do not qualify as "arts." In the performing arts, the emphasis is on the symphony or chamber orchestra, opera rather than mundane popular music, established theatrical productions over impromptu clowning. In the same vein, ballet is opposed to popular "folk" dances. In each case the distinction is based on a combination of form, technological skill, and genre. There is a contrast between the "high" arts of the aristocracy and the "low" mundane arts of the populace.

In medium, style, and substance, the popular productions of ordinary people, of the "working class," and of women, are thus excluded. (Women produce predominantly in "soft" media and in Europe were prevented from participating in many of the "high" arts). By extension, when these same criteria are applied uncritically across cultures, the artistic productions of women, and of other societies, become "crafts." Westerners value indigenous productions for the technical skill evident in their manufacture (the material culture emphasis of "natural history" museums), or for their esoteric power which is incorporated as a part of western culture through the collection of "curiosities" for museums (e.g., Stocking 1985; Clifford 1988, 1990). But these "handicrafts" only became Micronesian "art" through metamorphosis within the museum setting.

By the 1960s and 1970s one of Micronesia's critical practical problems was how to develop the economy. Hotly debated questions persist to this day: Did the Americans really want the islands to achieve economic independence, which would give them better leverage in political negotiations with the United States? Was economic independence possible, and according to whose definitions of resources? Could Micronesians ever earn as much from handicraft production as from the wages offered in the burgeoning government bureaucracies? Could their handicrafts compete with the much lower priced basketry and shell articles offered from the neighboring Philippines? Was true economic development ever envisioned by the USTTPI officials and their Washington bosses? (See Petersen, chap. 5, for a critical assessment of this topic.)

The US administration did not initially appreciate the economic (or perhaps artistic) value of Micronesian handicrafts. Palauan storyboard carvers, trained under the Japanese, reported that the US Commercial Company bought many boards from the carvers. They later found the boards drifting back to the dock after apparently being dumped at sea. Some carvers reused the wood to carve more boards for sale (Adelbai and Koontz 1989, 24). How did this experience affect less pragmatic carvers? By the 1960s and 1970s handicrafts were identified as a major product that Micronesians could develop for sale and export. The USTTPI government brought in UN advisors to provide short-term assistance (Yoffee 1979), and handicraft outlets were opened by community action agencies, aging centers, and women's organizations. The USTTPI Office of Economic Development considered how to implement handicraft production and sales (Udui 1971, 1979), and booklets and pamphlets on Micronesian handicrafts were prepared (Wells 1982). This was in line with SPC initiative to support handicraft production for sale (McBean 1976). The central dilemma of handcrafted art was apparently never confronted: Unless a significant number of workers were underemployed or demand for the product rose (say, as a result of its being recategorized as collectable "ethnic" art in western terms), thus raising the price producers could charge, they would not be able to earn from handicrafts what they could make for an equivalent amount of time as wage earners. The scale of production required to produce low-cost handicrafts at a volume sufficient for a reasonable return demonstrates the problem. Mainly because of his interest in carving, Guamanian carver Aguon produced coconut-shell ladles with hand-carved handles held in place by handmade *pago* fiber rope—at the rate of perhaps fifty per week. When offered a Japanese contract for 4,000–5,000 carved ladles per week he had to turn it down: "It's too hard to find somebody to help do this kind of work" (Aguon, quoted in O'Connor 1989, 23).

While "art" was used to describe Palauan carvings (Udui 1966), for the most part Micronesian artistic productions were classified as handicrafts. The Wells booklet (1982) is, in retrospect, quite naive. The "handicrafts of Micronesia," as found in the Wells collection, included the entire range of production from the ceremonial (and heirloom) Marshallese bordered mats to the pairs of *tangantangan* seed dolls quickly fabricated for sale to the Japanese.

Was this truly to be economic development? Was the cheap sale of hand-crafted items, some of which were important artistic items of traditional wealth or religious significance, to be equated with objects hastily assembled for sale to tourists? One UN expert suggested that the Carolinian navigational effigies could easily be prepared for sale to tourists at low cost—they would be sure to bring a good profit since the materials required were so few (but how many stingrays would have to be killed?). This, and other suggestions, were ignored, and any local commentary went unrecorded. There are indications that many Micronesians actively resisted the definition of important wealth items as "handicrafts," such as the Fais chiefs' decision not to allow the most intricately woven ceremonial *machiy* 'ceremonial cloths' to leave the island (Rubinstein 1987). But other islanders were pleased to have access to ready cash for items no longer valued. In the 1970s large pieces of Yapese stone money were broken down to manufacture small hand-sized pieces for sale (Graburn 1976 provides an overview of common processes of miniaturization and commodification toward an outside market). Full-size pieces were sold to tourists and departing members of the US administration, Coast Guard, Loran, and other support services. Early anthropologists routinely collected pieces of stone money for overseas museums. In the late 1980s, a tourist on one of the Carolinian atolls was offered a weather effigy for $20, and one of the pre-O'Keefe pieces of stone money was offered for sale at the Yap Treasures of the Islands Handicraft Store for $100. In this case an anthropologist interceded, notifying the historic preservation officer who explained to the owner that under Yapese law, such items could no longer be sold to outsiders or leave the island without a special permit.

Perhaps it was inevitable, given the applied nature of the early anthropological endeavor, and the uncritical acceptance of western conceptualization of the artistic productions of nonwestern societies as crafts, that Micronesian artistic productions would be offered for sale to the envisioned expatriate or tourist market. It logically follows the earlier practice of collecting native handmade items valued as technological examples or curiosities to be housed in natural history rather than art museums. As is common throughout the Pacific (N. Thomas 1991), islanders and their visitors mediated social relationships via an exchange of valued articles, and bartered mundane articles, food, and supplies. However, the entangled objects bridged disparate value systems that were incompletely understood on both sides. To commemorate their stay, visiting dignitaries and friends were freely offered many culturally important pieces, such as the inlaid carved serving bowl and money container given by Koror's Ibedul to Captain Wilson in 1783 (Keate 1788), or the carved beams Ruluked cut from the Ngebuked *bai* in 1862 to offer his departing friend (Semper 1982 [1873]). A number of these gifts are now in the British Museum of Mankind or German museums. Islanders had less control over the appropriation of other valued articles: Palauans still attempt to trace pieces of Palauan bead money that anthropologist Johan Kubary extracted as fines in 1871 (Kubary 1873, 189; these are now perhaps in the collections of German museums). Palauans apparently did not expect these moneys to be permanently alienated as most pieces circulate and cannot be held long by one individual or clan. The permanent removal of some of these wealth items into European collections contradicted the normal meanings of the transactions. Such valuables were important concentrators of wealth and power within the indigenous systems, and their exchanges were governed by strict conventions. Few western recipients were aware of the protocols governing their continued circulation, or the importance of retaining the social histories which gave them value (see Appadurai 1986, and Tapsell 1997 for a Māori perspective). A nineteenth century Kosraean *tol* 'man's sash' was recently gifted back to Kosrae, where it is on display at the Kosrae Museum, but this is a rare occurrence. Indigenous systems were transformed when pieces became reconceptualized in western terms as items that could be transferred and then come under full inalienable ownership. It has taken years, and countless losses, to begin to establish which articles should remain in Micronesia as part of the cultural heritage. Pieces of Yapese stone money once given or traded to visitors are now prohibited by law from leaving the island, and the weather effigy figures of Carolinian navigators, the most ornate *machiy*, and items of religious value are now generally protected from alienation, as are other forms of indigenous currency.

But there are new religious, economic, and political influences on islander values, and intergenerational relationships are also shifting, and at times disrupting, what might have been the expected transmission of knowledge and prized objects.

I do not wish to overstate the critique. Not all of the pieces sold as handicrafts fell into highly valued categories. Some weavings are mundane. Some, such as some contemporary Marshallese, Chuukese, and Pohnpeian trays and baskets, are made expressly for sale to outsiders and are based on crafts introduced by the Japanese or by other islanders. Other arts have been transformed: local Palauan histories were originally depicted on low-relief carved cross beams of the *bai*. When German anthropologist Augustin Krämer and his wife left Palau in 1910, some of their Palauan friends carved a separate "story" board for them depicting their accommodations at *Dngeronger Bai* (Krämer 1929). These "storyboards" were then developed for the tourist industry under the tutelage of Japanese anthropologist Hijikata Hisakatsu (Nero 1992a). Since then artists have capitalized on "handicraft" production, defined new markets, and expanded artistic styles in the process (Jernigan 1973; D. Smith 1975; Lockhart 1983a, 1983b, 1985; Adelbai 1985). While the carvings still tell stories, only some maintain the low-relief style. Others are three-dimensional sculptures, and most today highlight natural wood tones (enhanced by shoe polish) rather than the paintings on the *bai* beams. Palauan storyboards and three-dimensional carvings now form a flourishing genre with a range of offerings including quality carvings that secure high prices, and low-cost imports from the Philippines for those of undiscerning taste.

Other items have a value on the market that is derived both from the skill of their production and the cultural interest they provoke: Marshallese navigational instruction aids have been transformed into stick charts with shell "islands" clearly labeled (Hines 1952; de Brum 1961; Brandt 1963; Davenport 1964; Bryan 1978). Chuukese "lovesticks" are a favorite of tourists, Peace Corps volunteers, and anthropologists (*Micronesian Reporter* 1958). However, important questions remain unstated, unexamined. What is the meaning, for the artist and for the purchaser, of a Palauan legend board, or a contemporary Marshallese navigational stick chart? Does the piece continue to present history or a moral admonition, or represent the rich navigational knowledge of indigenous sailors, heightening and supporting appreciation of another culture? Or is it just a pleasing wall decoration, complete with a "quaint" story to tell friends upon returning home? Is esoteric knowledge transferred? To what extent does the selection of "cultural" themes support the teaching of traditional knowledge and skills to young artists? What is the effect of a studied emphasis on the past? With rare exceptions (D. Smith 1975; Nason 1984; Bailey 1985; Nero 1992a), contemporary transformations of traditional arts are understudied.

Unfortunately, a major impact of the American administration on the arts of Micronesia was their designation as handicrafts rather than arts, and as objects for sale at low cost. In retrospect we could wish there had been a more enlightened perception of those finely made textiles and ritual items that are objects of wealth and power in indigenous societies. But it would be unfair to lay the full blame on anthropologists for the designation of important arts as handicrafts, and for their subsequent devaluation and transformation to the status of tourist art (or for the opposite reification of ordinary daily productions beyond their local importance). This was the prevailing academic and lay understanding of arts at the time, and later theoretical insights were not then available. To this day, distinctions between Pacific arts and handicrafts remain unchallenged. The opinion of one of France's senior diplomats, expressed to Robert Kiste, Don Rubinstein, and Terence Wesley-Smith at a recent Pacific meeting, still captures most peoples' perceptions: "In the Pacific, there is no art; it is all handicraft" (Kiste, personal communication 1994). Could anthropologists have redefined the world's understanding of artistic production, and avoided devaluation and loss of important artistic traditions? If so, could they have avoided the reification and ritualization of these items in an entirely new set of tournaments of value—the international art market (Appadurai 1986)? The cross-cultural senses of aesthetics, and areas of aesthetic locus, were so widely divergent that this is questionable. There was a tendency to hope that simply because anthropologists were involved in the overall administration—regardless of their intensions or actual level of control—colonization would somehow have proceeded in a culturally and socially sensitive way.

THE 1960S AND 1970S FLORESCENCE

The involvement of colonial government and anthropologists did, however, result in some benefit to the arts in Micronesia. One positive spin-off of the drive to produce handicrafts for sale was governmental support for local fairs and festivals. And American anthropologists interacted in positive ways with local scholars to encourage a new generation of writers, artists, and researchers in the region.

Festivals, Fairs, and Art Shows

The first Palau art show was held in 1959, followed by a USTTPI-wide economic fair in 1960 (*Micronesian Reporter* 1959, 1960). The organization of the fairs depended to an extent on the energies of local organizers, but by the late 1960s UN Day was celebrated with some regularity in each of the district centers during the month of July. Local groups competed in dance and sporting competitions, and handicrafts were offered for sale. These fairs often occasioned behind-the-scenes influence from American anthropologists. Mac Marshall reports that for one fair he persuaded the old men of Namoluk to teach the young boys stick dances, which they later performed not only in the UN festivities but also for tourists at the Chuuk Continental Hotel, and for later political events. These dances thus remained in the contemporary Namoluk repertoire, rather than dying with the elders (Marshall, personal communication 1994).

The first Micronesian-wide Arts Festival was held in 1969. It attracted 345 entries, and the show traveled throughout the district centers and to Guam and Kwajalein (Boeberitz and Ngiraibuuch 1969). While traditional themes dominated the categories of sculpture and weaving and textiles, other categories highlighted contemporary themes and media. The second festival, in 1970, limited participation to Micronesian citizens, who competed in the categories of carvings, other handicraft, mixed media, drawing, stitchery (basketry), weaving (and plaiting), painting, and children's art. However, the continuation of the festival into its third year, under the auspices of the leadership of the Society of Micronesia Arts and Crafts, was in doubt (Ashman 1970, 22). Documentation of these arts fairs is incomplete.

Exhibits dedicated to Micronesian arts have always been rare. In 1951, the USTTPI administration, then based in Honolulu, sponsored an exhibit, *Life and Art in Micronesia,* at the Honolulu Academy of Arts (Griffing 1951a, 1951b). The University of Guam (UOG) held its first Micronesian art exhibit in 1969 (Montvel-Cohen 1970a). In 1973, the UOG art gallery sponsored a display of Rechucher Charlie Gibbons' *Visions of Old Palau* (University of Guam Gallery of Art 1973). The Palau Museum hosted another Palau Arts show in 1976 (Palau Museum 1976). In US museums most items are in protective storage, but Micronesian pieces may occasionally be included in permanent exhibits or highlighted in temporary exhibits. In 1979 the National Gallery hosted a *Pacific Expressions* exhibit (*Horizon* 1979). The most spectacular and internationally known of Micronesia's rare sculptural arts, the Nukuoro wooden images, or the Mortlockese masks, have been depicted and written about primarily in art or museum exhibition publications (Buhler, Barrow, and Mountford 1962; Guiart 1963; Davidson 1968).

Writers, Artists, and Scholars

Many second-generation scholars are Micronesians who worked with or were influenced by the early American anthropologists. In turn, these Micronesian have had a significant influence on the current generation of anthropologists, both indigenous and outsider, working in the islands.

Some attempts were made to incorporate the arts in the educational curriculum (Baker and Tanaka 1973). For example, the USTTPI Education Department published at least two song books in Palauan (Ezekiel 1962, 1963). In general, however, Micronesian literature and arts received little institutional support from the US federal programs and the US–based educational system.

In the early 1960s the educational system was strengthened throughout the region with the construction of new elementary schools in the villages, the recruitment of American contract teachers (augmented in 1966 by a massive importation of Peace Corps teachers), and the construction of both district- and subdistrict-level high schools (D. Ramarui 1976). Tertiary education was originally limited to special-purpose training: the teachers' and nurses' training institutes, begun in the 1940s, and a vocational school, which in the 1970s grew into the Community College of Micronesia. The arts were peripheral to the training goals of these institutions. Certainly, there was never an emphasis on the creative arts, literature, music, and drama, comparable to that at the University of the South Pacific and University of Papua New Guinea.

But in the late 1960s Micronesian students became eligible to apply for the types of financial support available to US students for tertiary education (Pell grants, work-study programs), which allowed many Micronesian students to attend US colleges. By the 1970s these students began to return, bringing new skills, and an increased emphasis on the use of English as the common language among Micronesians. Regional newspapers and publications such as the *Micronesian Reporter* began to regularly feature indigenous writers—in English. Valentine Sengebau joined this publication as staff writer in 1975, soon becoming its "poet in residence" (Sengebau 1976). John Mangefel enlivened the USTTPI newsletter with satirical letters to his "cousin," and numerous other poets and short-story writers were featured in special publications. Alfred Capelle published what must be the first Micronesian novel in an indigenous language (Capelle 1978). Mark Skinner (n.d.) has begun the task of compiling a bibliography of contemporary Micronesian literature.

By the 1970s a new generation of researchers had joined in the study of island societies. Prominent among the "direct descendants," in an anthropological sense, is Palauan anthropologist Katharine Kesolei, who studied with Mason and others at the University of Hawai'i. Continuing in the genre of folklore studies, she published two volumes of *Palauan Legends* (1971, 1975), returning to the German style of bilingual presentation. Her study of the oral legends of Palau expanded Lessa's conceptualization of oral histories to include their significance in the understanding of contemporary societies. This work culminated in a three-volume *History of Palau* (Palau Community Action Agency 1976–1978). Kesolei's work began a close association in Micronesian studies between the performance and keeping of history, which has influenced later analyses of both art and history. In 1977, a similar project was undertaken in Pohnpei, with the publication of *The Book of Luelen* (Bernart 1977), an indigenous Pacific history jointly edited by Jack Fischer, Saul Riesenberg, and Marjorie Whiting (see Hanlon 1992b for a detailed analysis; see also Hanlon, chap. 2). David Ramarui, a Palauan educator, prepared a comprehensive and insightful review of *The Palauan Arts* (1980) for the USTTPI Omnibus Program for Social Studies and Cultural Heritage. To my knowledge this was the only book on the arts published under this US federal program.

New American scholars also appeared on the scene. In 1973, Earl Jernigan completed his PhD dissertation, *Lochukle* 'pictures that tell a story,' on Palauan artistic traditions of bas-relief carvings derived from the *bai* gable and its tie-beam carvings. Jernigan provided a detailed account of the history and technology of the *bai* and its place in Palauan political and social relationships. He then analyzed the flourishing storyboard art industry in Palau, beginning with the primary storyboard carvers of the period, those who had studied with Japanese anthropologist Hijikata, the different artistic schools each had started, and the social contexts of contemporary carvings. Writers working primarily on other topics offered occasional articles on the arts, such as analyses of contemporary tourist art (Mitchell 1975; D. Smith 1975). Peter Steager, using Maquet's concepts of "aesthetic locus," proposed that on Puluwat such locus was found in the range of carved "wooden objects, plaited and woven materials, decorative lashing, and body adornment" (1979, 352), and then proceeded to demonstrate their interrelationships. Canoes were a major component of the aesthetic locus of outer-island societies, and a number of articles address details of their construction as well as the meanings of their ornamentation (Gladwin 1970; Montvel-Cohen 1970b; Browning 1972).

During the 1960s and 1970s several ethnomusicologists, students of Barbara Smith of the University of Hawai'i, entered Micronesian studies. Osamu Yamaguchi (1967, 1968, 1969, 1973, 1980, 1985, 1993) made a comprehensive study of Palauan musical genres, and C. R. Kim Bailey (1978, 1985) studied Pohnpeian music. Yamaguchi's student Junko Iwata (1985, 1988) later worked in Yap, augmenting Lessa's translations and analyses and Burrows' (1958, n.d.) mainly unpublished studies of the music of Ifaluk. Sixtus Walleser (1979) translated Yapese songs, and Raymond Kennedy (1972, 1980a, 1980b) published overviews of Micronesian, Chamorro, and Pohnpeian music and dance (see also Tanabe 1980; Ishimori 1987). However, much of this rich literature—the special chants and songs composed about intercommunity visits, World War II, the Japanese and American administrations of the islands, as well as love songs, and chants commemorating historical events—remains in the indigenous languages and is rarely accessible to those outside of the language group. The Human Relations Area Files of Yale made some unofficial translations of the texts collected by members of the German Südsee Expedition. Various music archives exist in Micronesia (at radio stations and historic preservation offices) and abroad (Bishop Museum in Honolulu). Recently, translations have been made of significant studies from the Japanese administration (e.g., Tatar 1985; Hijikata 1993, 1995). The Hijikata volumes feature valuable studies of legends, artifacts, games, and dance, and a previously unpublished manuscript on Palauan songs (Hijikata 1995, 239–249), and both volumes open with plates of Hijikata's watercolors, sketches, and wood carvings of Palau.

MOVING INTO THE POSTCOLONIAL ERA

Pacific arts have flourished in the postcolonial era. Developments range from regional and local festivals, innovations in the performing arts, and major initiatives in cultural preservation, to a renewed interest in both written and oral literature.

Pacific Festivals of Arts

By far the most important recent impetus to the arts was the participation of the Federated States of Micronesia (FSM), the Marshall Islands, Palau, and the Commonwealth of the Northern Mariana Islands (CNMI) in the Pacific Festivals of Arts. The new Micronesian nations were invited to participate in the Fourth South Pacific Festival of Arts in Port Moresby in 1980, where the Papua New Guinea (PNG) National Museum invited the visiting delegations to set up their own displays and hosted an international exhibit of Pacific arts. Palau, the Federated States of Micronesia (Yap and Pohnpei), Guam, and the Northern Marianas sent large delegations, who were joined by representatives of the other islands (Marvich and Robb 1980). A Carolinian sailing canoe joined the 150-strong canoe regatta that opened the festival. Preparations for the festival sparked local events. The Palauan coordinating committee sponsored a Cultural Awareness Week and competitions to select festival performers and items for a museum display. Some of the wood carvers recreated historical styles of inlaid serving dishes, referring to Krämer's (1919, 1926, 1929) depictions of turn-of-the-century pieces. Palauan storyboard carvings, paintings, watercolors, and scientific illustrations were displayed in the PNG National Museum's central gallery, along with paintings and sculptures from Papua New Guinea and countries throughout the region. After their display at the festival (Rehuher 1980), these pieces became part of the permanent collections of the Belau National Museum, where they serve as a models for contemporary carvers.

The South Pacific nations' warm welcome to the Micronesian countries included a renaming of the festival the Pacific Festival of Arts in recognition of the inclusion of the islands north of the equator. The other participants' appreciation of the Micronesian performances and arts strengthened the delegates' recognition of their own cultural heritages, at the same time that the Micronesians were able to experience the vitality of contemporary Pacific artistic media and literature. Particularly influential were the performances of Papua New Guinea's two major theatre companies, the National Theatre Company and the Raun Raun Company, featuring works by indigenous playwrights, and those of the popular PNG music group Sanguma, which combined traditional and modern musical forms and instruments. The cross-Pacific ties and expanded access to regional organizations forged during the 1980 festival have continued.

The 1985 Festival scheduled for Kanaky (New Caledonia) was canceled for political reasons. The 1988 Festival in Townsville, Australia, was the first to host a cultural forum to discuss topics such as effective programs to retain indigenous languages and cultural identity in the face of influences of the global culture, land alienation, and the politics of family and state-level violence.

These serious, primarily indigenous academic deliberations continued at the 1988 Waigani Conference on the State of the Arts in the Pacific, held in Port Moresby. Among the practical issues addressed were indigenous property rights and copyrights that could protect island artists and performers in the global marketplace while recognizing indigenous protocols. Delegates also proposed that local legislation be sponsored to require builders, public and private, to contract a percentage of construction costs for local art works to ensure that new buildings fit within the cultural as well as physical landscape of increasingly urban Pacific port towns.

The 1992 Rarotonga Festival of Pacific Arts was one of the largest ever, with delegations from the Federated States of Micronesia, the Northern Marianas, Guam, and the Marshall Islands. As in earlier festivals, official video crews taped the performances, and many national delegations included video teams who prepared tapes for local television programs. Contemporary Pacific voyaging canoes were highlighted in a regatta, including an extremely fast Marshallese *walab* 'large canoe' constructed as part of a resurgence of interest in Pacific navigation and voyaging. The festival was the first to sponsor an anthology of contemporary Pacific literature (Crocombe et al. 1992).

Performance

Contemporary studies of Micronesian arts have paralleled both islander and theoretical interests in issues of performance. A recent volume on the arts and politics in the contemporary Pacific (Nero 1992b) was the result of a series of Association for Social Anthropology in Oceania (ASAO) conference sessions on the topic. These analyses were elicited from seasoned anthropologists who had knowledge of the arts, although their research had focused primarily on other topics. In a way, the contributions were serendipitous, for those invited to participate initially expressed some puzzlement at the topic. For too long, the arts have been considered "reflective" of social structure, but now the anthropologists were being asked to consider ways in which the arts are used to challenge perceptions, stimulate change, and criticize or parody the status quo (Nero 1992a).

The lively ASAO symposium that developed emphasized contemporary performances and productions rather than the reification of past artistic traditions, and analyzed the ways in which people today use artistic traditions to reframe important political issues and force their audiences to reconsider the issues at hand. Nero (1992a) traced the artistic conceptualization of a key

Stick dance, Eauripik Atoll, 1970s. Photograph by Michael Levin.

Bechiyal Cultural Center, Yap, 1995. Photograph by Mac Marshall.

Bai *at Belau National Museum, 1995. Photograph by Mac Marshall.*

Palauan cultural symbol, the Breadfruit Tree, from a depiction of its spreading branches on a turn-of-the-century chiefly meeting house *bai* gable, to its substitution by a nuclear bomb explosion in a recent oil painting of a Palauan *bai,* and the transition of storyboard art to campaign billboards. Eve Pinsker (1992) analyzed the ways in which dance performances are used to simultaneously transmit both local and national identities. Glenn Petersen (1992b) demonstrated how and why a series of dance performances held shortly after Pohnpei rejected the compact of free association between the United States and the Federated States of Micronesia simultaneously celebrated local autonomy and asserted defiance against colonial and postcolonial authorities. Juliana Flinn (1992c) considered the ways in which the Pulapese use dance to define themselves as the keepers of traditional ways in Chuuk State. Turning ascriptions of backwardness around, the Pulapese assert the importance of the role they play and their right to participate in contemporary Chuukese affairs.

Petersen, Pinsker, and Flinn focused once again on the gesture song complex of music, poetry, and dance identified by Burrows as Micronesia's major art form. For the most part, however, studies of Micronesian dance have been conducted by nonanthropologists (Browning 1970; B. Dean 1976; Poort 1975; Gillespie 1977; Baty-Smith 1989) or appear only in brief reports (Gordon 1979; Thompson 1957; Kennedy 1980a). Jean Brooks (1988) wrote a master's thesis on Yapese dance, and Bailey (1985) extended her ethnomusicological studies in Pohnpei to include contemporary transformations of Pohnpeian dance.

Skits and clowning have long been a mainstay of community gatherings, but the rare performances analogous to western theater have seldom been documented (R. Underwood 1985a). Performances of a Hawaiian play on Micronesian navigation were enthusiastically received throughout the region in the late 1980s. The various islands chose different ways to commemorate the centenary of the Catholic Church in Micronesia: the Yapese danced the history, Chuukese sang it, while both Pohnpeians and Palauans dramatized the arrival of early missionaries (Hezel 1988). The Palauan centenary was commemorated in a video and bilingual book (Hezel 1991). It is becoming increasingly difficult to separate the performing arts from their role in commemorating and keeping history. In 1990, David Hanlon and Nero organized a session on the alternate media of historic heritage for the Pacific History Association (PHA) meetings on Guam, with overwhelming response. "Alternate media" were those nonwritten forms such as dance, chants, poetry, oratory, oral histories, carvings, architecture, stone monuments, and other nontraditional performative and visual media used throughout the Pacific to maintain and transmit history to future generations. Several of the presentations were primarily oral and visual, in keeping with the topic, but others have been published (Poyer 1992; Hanlon 1992b; Diaz 1992).

Historic and Cultural Preservation

I credited Katharine Kesolei above for bringing oral traditions into the serious study of history in Micronesia, and for emphasizing their performative aspects. As Chair of the Palau Historic Preservation Advisory Council she is one of a number of indigenous scholars and administrators actively supporting and preserving the arts and cultural heritage in the region. The historic preservation offices have established a charitable foundation in the United States, the Micronesian Endowment for the Arts, to receive tax-free donations. Carmen Bigler is the historic preservation officer for the Marshall Islands. Both Kesolei

and Bigler were students of Mason's at the University of Hawai'i. Alfred
Capelle, linguist and author, is another University of Hawai'i and East-West
Center alumnus. He is active in Alele Museum, historic preservation, language,
and video projects. Mary Lanwi, who had been instrumental in the long drive
to establish the Alele Museum, continues to operate one of the region's most
successful handicraft cooperatives. Faustina Rehuher holds a master's degree
from the Center for Pacific Islands Studies, University of Hawai'i. She directs
the Belau National Museum, is one of the founders of the Palau Resource Institute, and is currently studying Palauan chants. She is a member of the Pacific
Arts Festival Board and has developed several exhibits of contemporary
Palauan arts. For years Carmen Chigiy and the late Andrew Kugfas, and
members of the Yap Cultural Preservation Board, working closely with the
Councils of Tamol and Pilung and government agencies, have directed a number of projects including the reconstruction of community meeting houses;
the forceful redirection of US historic preservation projects from archaeological excavations to documentation of cultural practices; and plans for a
new Yap Museum. Chuuk and Pohnpei have reopened their museums.
Chuukese Historic Preservation Officer Elvis O'Sonis has begun recording the
diverse oral histories of Chuuk's many island polities. FSM national archaeologist Dr. Rufino Mauricio has recently taken on additional responsibilities
as national historic preservation officer. He and Pohnpei Historic Preservation
Officer Emmensio Ephraim and their staffs continue to deal with the incon-
sistencies of local, state, and national interests in the preservation of historic
sites. The late Teddy John, former director of FSM Historic Preservation, and
his staff on Kosrae established the Kosrae Museum; today Berlin Sigrah and
his staff continue John's work.

These Micronesians have actively redefined the meaning of historic preservation in the islands, and in the process have influenced the direction of US
national policy. Native American, Hawaiian, and other American groups have
followed suit, helping redirect the US system away from its emphasis on physical historic sites and toward issues of cultural preservation.

A Eurocentric definition of history would hold that only written documents
may be analyzed as historic evidence, while everything before would be relegated to prehistory. Such a position is untenable in a region where historical
consciousness is finely tuned, and oral histories may reach 300–400 years into
the past. Throughout the two decades since the US historic preservation program was extended to the trust territory, Micronesians have constantly fought
to redefine the meanings of "history" and "preservation" to include living cul-

tural heritage and knowledge, not just the material remains of past habitation. Micronesians have also incorporated Japanese models of cultural preservation, such as the "Living Treasures" status now conferred on select Palauan historians. American anthropologists and archaeologists too numerous to list have worked closely with Micronesian officers and their advisory councils as consultants and trainers in these endeavors.

As Burrows (1963) noted, western definitions of art have been equally unsatisfactory. It is unlikely that the indigenous peoples used generic terms that we could gloss as "art" for the various visual and performing arts that were an important part of life on the islands. Theoretical advances expanding the western definition came too late and were little appreciated by people who had been told they had "no art" and then learned of the large collections of valued pieces from their islands in European and American museums. A number of Micronesians recognize that most of these fragile early pieces would not have survived the harsh island environments and World War II. Those few who are able to travel to British and German museums, and the larger numbers visiting American museums, appreciate the opportunity to see these items from the past. But even the idea of preservation, divorced from use in ongoing social practices, is an innovation.

An important component of the work of Micronesian historic preservation offices is the recording of oral histories, cultural practices, and performances on videos, supported by comprehensive training projects on video techniques by anthropologist Allan Burns. Videos and cassettes are used as both official and family records of contemporary events, and historic preservation offices, education departments, and community action agencies maintain official video crews and archives of the growing and largely untapped video and oral tape collections. Local archives now document and establish the necessary culturally sensitive protocols for their use. The Marshall Islands Historic Preservation Office runs a local television station of Marshallese cultural programs, and videos of Marshallese dancers at the festival are frequent favorites of Alele Museum visitors. Micronesian arts have been a frequent video subject, including the life and work of Rechucher Charlie Gibbons in the video *Kle-Belau* (Belau National Museum 1989), and another video on Micronesian tattoos (Yatar 1992). The Pohnpei Historic Preservation Office recently completed a historical video that features chants and dance performances in explaining the Nan Madol site (Micronesian Seminar 1995).

While the volume at hand is an analysis of the last fifty years of social and cultural anthropology in Micronesia, it must be acknowledged that archaeology has had a close association with museums in the region, and that archaeologists have written descriptions of Micronesian sculptures (see, e.g., Davidson 1968). In which field does the study of rock art lie (Henrickson 1968; Simmons 1970; F. Stephenson 1971; Schmidt 1974)? Most Micronesian pottery was created in the prehistorical era, but it is described by both cultural anthropologists and archaeologists (Bryan 1937; Spoehr 1957; de Beauclair 1960, 1966; Borthwick and Takayama 1977; Thompson 1987). Archaeologists Carolyn and Douglas Osborne were integrally involved in the construction of the Palau Museum Bai in 1969, as a way of documenting this important technological process. Marvin Montvel-Cohen's (1970b, 1982) research principally concerned the social contexts of Carolinian architecture and canoe building, but he was a practicing artist who also organized Micronesian art exhibits (Montvel-Cohen 1970a, 1988). Archaeologists have conducted most studies of Micronesia's spectacular stone ruins and architecture (Athens 1980a, 1980b; Cordy 1993). With the exception of Palau, it has been primarily archaeologists, Japanese and European scholars, and nonanthropologists who have studied the community meeting houses (LeBar 1951; Kobayashi 1978; Nakamura 1977; Asakawa 1980; Sudo 1980a, 1980b; Sugito 1982a, 1987; Montvel-Cohen 1982; Tiesler 1981; Webb 1975; Morgan 1988; cf. Nero and Graburn 1981). David Robinson (1983) presented a historical review of the Palauan *bai* and its decorative motifs in his contribution to a Pacific Arts Association symposium; from this series of four symposia, his was one of the rare publications on Micronesian arts.

Contemporary Festivals, Exhibits, and Exhibit Catalogs

Contemporary arts festivals and some shops and other commercial concerns in the islands display wooden carvings, posters, watercolors, and oil paintings by contemporary artists, some of whom were trained in the United States. The subjects of these works include visions of the historical past, contemporary portraits, scenes of the rich underwater life, expert botanical illustrations, as well as highly contemporary political messages. There are other outlets for artistic endeavor. Saipan sports artistic bus stops (J. Dean 1983), and nearly all of the constitutional referenda and Compact plebiscites held in Palau inspired colorful billboards which vied for attention through their clever manipulation of legends and historical events to provide contemporary commentaries (Nero 1992a).

Permanent and rotating exhibits are displayed at the Belau National Museum in Koror, the Chuuk Ethnographic Museum, the new museum in

Pohnpei, and the Alele Museum in Majuro. These include archaeological and historical pieces and early photographs. A few items are on display at the Bechiyal Cultural Center in Map on the island of Yap, and a new museum for Yap is being planned. Guam hosts the widest range of cultural displays. In addition to the Guam Museum, the ISLA Gallery at the University of Guam mounts rotating exhibits, such as Rubinstein's 1992 exhibit featuring Micronesian textiles. The Council of the Humanities Art (CAHA) gallery, banks, and even fast-food places host exhibits of Micronesian artifacts, and the numerous hotels commission and display paintings, sculptures, and textiles made by local artists (Nelson 1994).

In 1986 the University of Hawai'i Art Gallery held a comprehensive exhibit of Micronesian arts and published a catalog (Feldman and Rubinstein 1986) that helped redefine the aesthetics of the islands and the importance of textiles in Micronesian artistic productions (Rubinstein 1986). Micronesian textiles also featured in a 1992 exhibit of Austronesian textiles (Rubinstein 1992a) and in *The Wealth of the Pacific* exhibit in 1993 at the Phoebe M. Hearst Museum of Anthropology at the University of California. The catalog produced for the University of Hawai'i exhibit is currently the only book-length treatment of Micronesian arts, but Rubinstein and Jerome Feldman are at work on the first comprehensive book of Micronesian arts, which will include pieces in US and overseas museums. In 1988, ISLA Gallery at the University of Guam exhibited Micronesian artifacts in conjunction with the Micronesian archaeology conference (Montvel-Cohen 1988). But for the most part major volumes on Pacific art (Gathercole, Kaeppler, and Newton 1979; Brake, McNeish, and Simmons 1980; Corbin 1988) continue to neglect the arts of Micronesia or depict the same few pieces in western collections: a *tino* figure from Nukuoro, a Chuukese canoe prow ornament, a Palauan *dilukai* figure of the heraldic woman from premissionization *bai* gables, perhaps a Mortlockese *tepwpwaanu* mask.

Poetry and Songs

Literature is an understudied area of Micronesian artistic production. As the earlier work of Lessa, Kesolei, and others attests, the oral literature of Micronesia has always been a rich and vibrant part of contemporary enjoyment in the islands. Once Micronesians began using English as another language of composition, their works won wider recognition. *Xanadu,* the UOG literary magazine, began publication in 1966, and Xavier High School's *The Three*

Towers, along with territorial publications and news media, publish poetry in English. Skinner's bibliography includes approximately eight hundred works published since World War II by nearly four hundred indigenous and non-indigenous writers of the region—a corpus that is constantly expanding both within the region and in the Micronesian diaspora to the United States.

However, institutional support for contemporary publications and anthologies is still limited (Peck 1982). Hermana Ramarui's collected works (1984) was locally printed. Most other poems have been scattered in various media or were passed around by hand—especially during the long period of confrontation between Palau and the United States in the 1980s. Many recent Micronesian poems have political connotations (R. Underwood 1987). Several of Elicita Morei's poems have been published (see Morei 1992). Except for the Hermana Ramarui anthology, the largest recent collection of poems and stories from the region is the volume published for the Sixth Pacific Festival of Arts (Crocombe et al. 1992). Little critical attention has been focused on the works, and much more work is needed simply to collect the existing material. At the time of Skinner's assessment he concluded that "development and writing of literature has not gained an important place in the region" (n.d, 4). Hopefully, with the establishment of a master's program in Micronesian Studies at the University of Guam, the expansion of the Pacific Islands' literature program at the University of Hawai'i, and the increased participation of Micronesian students at the University of the South Pacific (which has an active program in Pacific literature and theater arts), students will now be able to build on the growing number of publications.

Anthropological texts devoted to the study of World War II in the Pacific often include translations of the occasional chant or song (Falgout 1989; Nero 1989; Lindstrom and White 1993). The highly evocative and multilayered meanings of these chants and songs undoubtedly contribute to difficulties of translation. An unpublished paper by Rubinstein (n.d.) permits a comparison with Burrows' (1963) earlier work on Ifaluk, demonstrating some of the changes that have taken place within the discipline. "And We Remain, Suffering" is a poignant analysis of one dance song as an oral history account of the ways in which the people of Fais experienced World War II. Rubinstein set his translation and the original text side-by-side in an appendix. He provided a background for the island of Fais and its experience of World War II before proceeding to a detailed analysis of the text, the circumstances of its composition, the genre of songs and their contemporary presentations, and the circumstances of the recording. In Rubinstein's depictions of the use of humor "as a rhetorical weapon of protest . . . aim[ed] both against the outsiders as well as themselves" (n.d., 6) we see displayed some of the ambivalence and colonial critiques that one could only infer from Burrows (see also Yamaguchi's 1993 study). Highly contextualized translations into English such as Rubinstein's paper will probably remain the exception until indigenous scholars join the endeavor. In the meantime the practice of some anthropologists in recording and archiving historical and contemporary chants and songs could be expanded.

There are several highly active areas of musical performance in Micronesia that have not been seriously studied, including that of the churches, and of the burgeoning local music industry. Contemporary Micronesian communities are filled with the sounds of church choirs, not only on Sundays, but during choir practices and services held throughout the week. Recordings of Micronesian artists, made in the Philippines and the United States, fill the airwaves with contemporary compositions, indigenous renditions of regional and global hits, even Yap Rap! The rhythmic structures of reggae, disco, and cha-cha are appropriated by Micronesian dancers, the texts transformed into local compositions. Flinn (1992c) has briefly touched on the elders' proactive use of music and dance to direct or redirect individual actions—lengthy dance performance practices held during times of limited food supplies. Similar examples of a grandmother drawing a fussy toddler into song come to mind, but this is a relatively unexplored area of the ways arts are used in socialization as well as socializing.

Textiles, Wealth, and Power

It is an unfortunate correlate of the arts and crafts dichotomization discussed above that textiles, nearly universally the domain of women, are categorized as crafts. In the process they are devalued. They fall into the "mundane" side of the spectrum, as perhaps technically well produced but somehow aesthetically inferior artifacts, no matter what the cultural significance of the genre within their home societies.

Women no longer continue many of the most important textile traditions of Micronesia. Men no longer weave the textile money of Yap. Few heirloom pieces remain in the islands. Such textiles were once important status markers of chiefly titles and lineages, used in rituals throughout the life cycle from the birth of a child to death and burial, but most importantly as wealth to support the political power of the lineage and transact dynastic marriages or to mark an ascension to chiefly title. Today no one continues to weave the most elaborate warp-tied, beaded and brocaded Kosraean and Pohnpeian textiles, or the finest Marshallese mats with their wide geometrically patterned brocade borders in rich earth tones. Only a few of the oldest women and men remember seeing them woven, or weaving them personally. The pieces of textile wealth of the Pacific, even today, remain for the most part protected from the gaze of outsiders. Highly valued by their producers, still circulated as wealth between political units, their sale may be prohibited. Even those that have made their way into museum collections are rarely exhibited because of their fragility, and the potential damage from the light, decreased humidity, and heat of a display atmosphere. Anthropologists seldom study textiles or their production, and their apparently mundane character often precludes close attention.

Ironically, outsider devaluation of textile arts has at times served to protect them (so we cannot entirely fault it). Early anthropologists often did not study women's work as seriously as men's for a number of reasons, including the indigenous withholding of information which Burrows encountered during his first visit to Ifaluk. Women, especially on the small Carolinian atolls, were rarely drawn into labor relations in the same ways men were, and thus remained free to continue existing practices. The women of the central and eastern Carolinian atolls continue to weave *tur* on backstrap looms, not only the heirloom *machiy* and the more mundane textiles of banana fiber and hibiscus, but *tur* of imported cotton in vibrant new colors. *Tur* continue to be used in exchanges with the Yapese of Gagil; and on the atolls they form an important part of "payments" to chiefs or between lineages for violations in custom, breaking taboos, and other offenses, and are required during funerals (Alkire, personal communication 1994). They remain the primary article of female clothing, marking "outer-island" identity when women visit Yap or Chuuk (Flinn 1992c), although the men today generally wear western shorts or *tur* of commercial cloth except for ritual ceremonial occasions. Throughout the years *tur* have been one of the major items sold and traded with outsiders, and they constitute a significant source of cash earnings.

Several studies have focused on Carolinian woven textiles (Mulford 1980; Sugito 1982b; Welborn and Bothmer 1977), plaiting (Bothmer 1988), and basketry (Kaeppler 1965; Mulford 1991). A European PhD student is currently researching contemporary exchanges of Carolinian *tur*. The most important study of Micronesian arts of the new generation is Rubinstein's 1987 analysis of the *machiy*. Yet it was serendipitous that this was written. Rubinstein reported that despite his lifelong interest in textiles, he paid little attention to those being woven on backstrap looms on the island of Fais where he studied the socialization of children. It was only after the curator of the Salem Peabody Museum sent him "photographs of a chiefly burial shroud from Fais that the Museum had received in 1803" that he spoke to the weavers. To his surprise, the women not only recognized and named the patterns, but described the principles of ordering the design units in a system of artistic production that had apparently remained unchanged for two centuries. This led Rubinstein to uncover the social and spatial relationships encoded not only in the ceremonial and mundane textiles, but analogously in village spatial patterning, and tattoo designs. This is the most comprehensive structural analysis of artistic production within a Micronesian society (cf. Alkire 1970), and provides a model of the value of extending such studies in other islands and art forms. In the University of Hawai'i Art Gallery exhibit and catalog, Rubinstein (1986) also extended the analysis of textiles and the social relationships they express throughout Micronesian societies, relating the textile designs to those found in tattoo, plaited materials, and social forms.

We need not, however, necessarily look only to the woven ritual textiles for such rich social analyses. Janet Keller's (1988) study of the everyday mats and carrying baskets of West Futuna, Vanuatu, reminds us that even mundane articles can carry heavy symbolic associations, and that these everyday items may be as important for the expression of cultural identity as the more symbolically loaded items of political exchange. Similarly, Annette Weiner's (1976, 1980) emphasis on the important economic role of Trobriand Island women's banana fiber bundles in the contemporary political economy, and her coedited volume (with Schneider 1989) analyzing the intersections between wealth, gender, and power, have focused academic attention on women's wealth and textile productions. Contemporary Micronesian artists throughout the region have turned to batiks as an important new commercial (Vitarelli 1986) and artistic medium (Nelson 1994).

THE POSITION OF GUAM IN MICRONESIAN ARTS

As Vicente Diaz (1993) and Kiste (chap. 13) have discussed, because of its separate colonial history, Guam differs from the other islands in many ways. At the 1993 conference on American anthropology and Micronesia in Honolulu, Micronesian discussants reported that for many people of Guam, any notion of themselves as Micronesian as opposed to Guamanian (which often incorporates the idea of being an American) is recent and often rejected. Throughout the past century the people of Guam have had a different relationship to the US government, and were in many ways more closely incorporated into American cultural institutions, than other peoples in Micronesia. Despite anthropologists' recent contributions to the study of Micronesian arts, and their continued assistance in training contemporary scholars both in the islands and in US institutions, the current generation is repeating the practices of past researchers in slighting Guam.

Similarly, for years Guam's presentations at the Pacific Festivals of Art were considered suspect by many island participants. It took Laura Souder's introduction to the syncretic Chamorro performances offered in 1988 to convince audiences that Pacific heritages, not just Guam's, are comprised of many different cultural components that have been incorporated into contemporary identities. The current paucity of studies of the arts on Guam is an unfortunate artifact of the ways in which academic endeavors have been defined. With the rotating exhibits at the ISLA Gallery at the University of Guam, the CAHA gallery, and in public buildings, and support for the occasional play as well as music concerts, the Guam art scene is undoubtedly the liveliest in the entire region, yet the least studied. The fault, of course, does not lie with the state of the arts in Guam, nor does it necessarily rest with the few resident anthropologists and academics, who are vitally involved in supporting and exhibiting such arts. Once again, the need to maintain and support the arts takes precedence over sitting back and writing academic articles on the process; one of Micronesia's enduring dilemmas is the limited numbers of trained people to do all the tasks required in the new countries and transforming territories. As much as we might hope for more of Robert Underwood's witty analyses (e.g., 1985b), his current position as Representative to the US Congress, charged with the difficult task of leading the US government to grant commonwealth status to Guam, is considered a higher priority.

ASSESSING THE INTERPLAY BETWEEN ANTHROPOLOGY AND THE ARTS IN MICRONESIA

The early CIMA and SIM anthropologists and the USTTPI administrative anthropologists directly contributed to the anthropological study of Micronesian arts, despite their primary research focus on other topics. Their applied projects and their training of both American and indigenous scholars also benefited the region. It is difficult to analyze American contributions to the study of Micronesian arts without acknowledging the work of archaeologists, ethnomusicologists, art historians, and academics of other disciplines and nationalities working there. Yet even with the assistance of these other academic disciplines, the arts of the region have been understudied and undersupported. As the availability of US funds declines, we can only hope that the private sector will continue to provide an impetus for contemporary expression.

A significant impact—both positive and negative—of the anthropological endeavor in Micronesia has been the collection of artifacts and art objects for museums abroad. Early German ethnographers pursued an aggressive collecting campaign. The more recent active role of anthropologists in collecting contemporary items for personal or museum collections in the United States has had some positive effects in that it has helped preserve the knowledge of artistic traditions (the commissioning of Chuukese textiles by LeBar discussed above, and the canoe Goodenough had made for the University Museum of Pennsylvania). In more recent years a number of people have made collections, including Mac Marshall and James Nason for the Burke Museum in Seattle, and Don Rubinstein for the Salem Peabody Museum. These collections were made within the ethical codes of the American Association for Museums in consultation with local artists and administrators, and will add to the recognition of Micronesian arts in the world at large.

Indigenous scholars have focused on their local communities in writing and producing their own teaching materials to replace the US–centered curricula available to the schools. It is understandable that their publications are localized. Again a dissonance between applied and academic trajectories remains, despite strong efforts by several anthropologists to incorporate indigenous scholars in professional meetings such as the ASAO, PHA, and regional conferences.

While institutional support for the arts may not necessarily be flourishing, Micronesian artists continue in the multiple genre they have always pursued —performance of dance/music/poetry, chanting of current events and past histories, oratory, singing, clowning, sculpture, architecture, the careful aesthetic attention to utilitarian objects, the weaving of items of wealth and power. To these must be added today's new media: contemporary oil paintings and watercolors, batik, posters and billboards, written literature, recorded music. It is unlikely that the arts of Micronesia are in danger, although a few genres such as tattoo are relatively dormant at present.

All considered, this analysis of the American anthropological study of Micronesian arts supports Coote and Shelton's (1992) claim that endeavors within the anthropology of art do not create theories relevant to the discipline at large but follow the general theoretical direction of the time. This is unfortunate, for Burrows' redefinition of art and his emphasis on performance could have advanced anthropological theory in general, not just the study of the arts. These insights went unrecognized, perhaps because they were couched within one of the dominant paradigms of the period. Let us hope that in the postcolonial era, with the leadership of the growing number of scholars who possess the deep cultural knowledge necessary to understand indigenous artistic systems in their own terms, such a rethinking of anthropological theory in the Pacific will yet be possible.

NOTE

An earlier version of this chapter was presented in 1993 at the conference on American anthropology and Micronesia sponsored by the Center for Pacific Islands Studies, University of Hawai'i. I would like to thank Robert Kiste for envisioning and sponsoring this very fruitful exchange of ideas, the many participants and members of the audience for their conference comments, and Letitia Hickson and the entire CPIS staff for their organization and support. Geoffrey White, Director of the Program for Cultural Studies at the East-West Center, offered me preconference visiting fellow status and support that made it possible to tap the wealth of the Pacific Collection, Hamilton Library, University of Hawai'i. The research on which this analysis is based has been supported by a number of sources over the past fifteen years, including NIMH Grant #5 T32 MH14640-04 0111 from the Institute for the Study of Social Change at University of California, Berkeley; the Palau Community Action Agency; the Micronesian Community Action Director's Organization; Koror State Government; the USTTPI Office of Aging; the University of California, Irvine, through the Robert Gumbiner Fund; NSF Grant #BN59023003; and the US Office of Historic Preservation. Leonard Mason, William Alkire, Mac Marshall, and Robert Kiste provided excellent editorial suggestions. Micronesian colleagues, friends, and members of my adoptive families in Palau and Kosrae are too numerous to mention; however I would like to especially thank and acknowledge the late Ngiraklang Malsol, Katharine Kesolei, Faustina Rehuher, Moses Sam, Kempis Mad, the late Andrew Kugfas, Carmen Chigiy, Laura Souder, Cammy Akapito and Elvis O'Sonis, Kodaro Gallen, Alfred Capelle, Mary Lanwi, Carmen Bigler, the late Teddy John, and Kemwel Tilfas for all they have taught me about their arts over the years. Errors of interpretation remain my own.

A full bibliography of all works on Micronesian arts referred to while researching this paper has been compiled and is available at the Center for Pacific Islands Studies, University of Hawai'i. For other bibliographies that include Micronesian arts, see Hanson and Hanson 1984 and McLean 1977, 1981.

CHAPTER NINE

American Anthropology's Contribution to Social Problems Research in Micronesia

Francis X. Hezel, SJ

SOCIAL CHANGE WAS NOT a major emphasis in the initial work of American anthropologists in Micronesia. Only two of the thirty-two reports that issued from the Coordinated Investigation of Micronesian Anthropology (CIMA) dealt with problems related to social change: the study of depopulation on Yap by Edward Hunt and others (1949), and Neal Bowers' dissertation on the resettlement in the Northern Marianas (1950). Having compiled and translated earlier ethnographic material on Micronesia from scattered sources as part of the war effort, American anthropologists were more concerned to develop a fuller picture of the various Micronesian cultures.

What we today would call social problems were still largely undiscovered at that time. Although some in the American academic community began addressing issues like rural poverty and racism as early as the 1930s, it was only in the affluent postwar years that many of the domestic problems with which we still struggle first surfaced. One need only think of the spate of books on youth gangs and delinquency that were published in the 1950s. As the afterglow of its wartime triumph faded, America turned its gaze inward in a serious attempt at social self-analysis. This was the era of David Riesman's *The Lonely Crowd* (1950), William Whyte's *The Organization Man* (1956), and Vance Packard's *The Hidden Persuaders* (1957) and *The Status Seekers* (1959). These works were the products of American sociology, under whose domain social problems research fell, at least during that period. Thus administrators looked to sociology rather than anthropology when similar problems were experienced in Micronesia a short while later.

Anthropology stood prepared to assist societies suffering the early pangs of modernization. From its birth, the discipline had seen its purpose as more than building up a fund of lore on exotic societies and formulating general principles that governed culture. Like any science, anthropology ought to have its practical applications, and these applications were expected to be of a higher order of altruism than merely assisting developed nations to better understand the people they ruled so as to better consolidate their colonial empires. On the basis of its understanding of cultural dynamics, anthropology was expected to be able to facilitate the introduction of technology to societies in need of help. The skills of anthropology could serve local people by identifying the least painful means of implementing policies of change and by easing the transition to modern technology—or at least those elements of it that were judged appropriate for the culture. Indeed, Ward H. Goodenough's *Cooperation in Change* (1963) and Edward Spicer's *Human Problems in Technological Change* (1952) are good examples of early efforts to put anthropological insights at the disposal of those working in community development. Other anthropologists, in the meantime, served as advisors to the American administration in the US Trust Territory of the Pacific Islands (USTTPI). They sought to help fashion government policies that were both forward-looking and culturally appropriate, but at times they were able to take a more direct role in shaping events. Men like Jack Tobin, Thomas Gladwin, and Leonard E. Mason, by exercising initiative in their positions as cross-cultural brokers, successfully intervened on occasion to resolve community problems (Barnett 1956, 113–114; Tobin 1954a; Mason 1950).

By the mid-1960s, as anthropology began showing a new emphasis on the study of culture change and a shift in research priorities toward problem-oriented research, a new generation of doctoral candidates descended on the islands to investigate social and political change. Not all the inquiry into this area was carried out by doctoral students, however. As discussed in chapter 1, two teams of Micronesian and American students, in a project cosponsored by the East-West Center and the University of Hawai'i, produced a pair of anthologies on social change: *The Laura Report* (1967a), edited by Leonard Mason, and *The Truk Report* (1969), edited by Stephen T. Boggs.

The founding of the Association for Social Anthropology in Oceania (ASAO) in the late 1960s proved to be another step in the growing engagement of anthropology with problems related to social change. Although the earliest volumes that issued from ASAO symposia were comparative studies of such Pacific-wide institutions as adoption and land tenure, later symposia generated volumes on transplanted island communities (Lieber 1977a) and political development in Micronesia (Hughes and Lingenfelter 1974). In addition, the association soon widened its membership to include nonanthropologists and Pacific Islanders themselves. Thus began a dialogue that eventually brought forth works focusing more directly on social issues in these island societies. I admit to being one of the principal beneficiaries of this dialogue and my writings on social problems through the years reflect the influence of my anthropologist colleagues.

The Micronesian Seminar, a pastoral-research institute established by the Catholic Church in 1972 to engage in community education, owes a great deal to the influence of anthropology. The Seminar was founded to foster public reflection on today's social realities, a goal it has attempted to realize by convening conferences and publishing papers. As director of the Micronesian Seminar from the beginning, I established lasting friendships with and drew inspiration from dozens of social scientists who had worked in Micronesia. These contacts and the anthropological insights they offered gave direction to much of my later research on suicide and other social problems.

THE STUDY OF SOCIAL PROBLEMS

After a decade of accelerated development initiated during the Kennedy Administration, by the early 1970s Micronesia found itself partitioned into "two worlds," as Mason (1975) pointed out in his seminal article, "The Many Faces of Micronesia." There was the world of the outer islands, easily recognizable to anthropologists of an earlier era but increasingly neglected by administrators and marked by social and economic stagnation. There was also the world of the towns or urban centers (formerly called "district centers") and their environs, the sites of most public services and the main targets of development plans. The expanding populations of the towns were exposed to a variety of social forces that could no longer be ignored. Wage employment in the Carolines and Marshalls doubled from 3,000 to 6,000 between 1962 and 1965, and it doubled again to 12,000 during the next ten years (Mason 1975). The high school education explosion of the 1960s, in which the number of graduates grew from a hundred a year to ten times that number, was soon to be followed by an enormous increase in the number of college-bound students, as US federal assistance grants were extended to Micronesia in 1973 (Hezel 1992, 216). Town populations grew everywhere in Micronesia as migrants followed the jobs and educational opportunities. The most extreme example was Ebeye, which had for years been a small bedroom community for those working on Kwajalein and their kin. The population of the island, which came to be known as the "slum of the Pacific," soon grew to 8,000 (G. Johnson 1984).

If this new world offered previously unimaginable opportunities for Micronesians, it had its pitfalls as well. For example, the new-found wealth of those who lived on Pohnpei made it possible to buy outboard engines for their paddling canoes, but it also supported the twenty-one bars in Kolonia Town (Mason 1975, 12). Everywhere in Micronesia there were gloomy reports of wanton violence by drunken youth, public disorder on payday weekends, senseless suicides, and general dismay among community members who did not know what to do about this chaos.

Superimposed on this was the picture of life in Micronesia as it had been in the early postwar years: taro planting and breadfruit picking, village celebrations with mounds of food, respect forms of behavior observed in the presence of chiefs. For all the changes that had occurred during the 1960s and earlier, the illusion persisted that in certain places or certain times nothing had been disturbed in the rhythm of island life.

In this context, anthropology was challenged to improve the lot of humankind and to select its research targets accordingly. Would it continue to roam the elysian fields of the outer-island communities, a world that was home to an ever-diminishing percentage of Micronesians, to do what an earlier generation had done? Or would it respond to the calls for help from the people it was studying and put its insights at their disposal? In fact, it did neither—or possibly a little bit of both. A full swing around is probably more than we have a right to expect of a discipline with theoretical concerns to be met, but anthropologists showed enough willingness in collaborating with others on the study of contemporary social problems to alter the ways these problems were seen and to enrich the understanding of Micronesian communities for the next two decades. Let us look at several social problems to see the influence of anthropology's practitioners and perspectives on each of them in turn.

THE YOUTH PROBLEM

During the 1970s many were concerned about what they perceived to be a growing problem of drinking and disorder among Micronesian youth. As incidents of youth misbehavior multiplied, a generation of young males seemed rootless and increasingly alienated from the values of their island societies. The problem was regarded as all the more threatening because it was feared that they would grow up to be a criminal element in society. The perception in some circles was that Micronesia was in danger of losing a whole generation of its disaffected youth. Writings on the problem (e.g., Fox 1971; Basilius 1973) were founded on the premises of the deviance theory that guided similar work in the United States. The thinking of that day was epitomized in Michael Kenney's book-length study, *Youth in Micronesia in the 1970's* (1976).

Three main causes of delinquency emerged in Kenney's study: breakdown of the traditional family, lack of structured activities for youth, and diminished social control (Kenney 1976, 75). By far the most attention was given to the second cause, particularly with respect to the lack of jobs available for young people. Reflecting the opinions of many he interviewed, Kenney's main thesis was that young people were restless and getting into trouble because they were bored. The common assessment was that they just did not have enough to do. Give them basketball courts, sports leagues, and especially some way of earning money, and watch the difference. The largest of the three sections of his study, complete with page after page of tables, was a survey of what could be done to increase employment opportunities for youth. Kenney's assumption, grounded in the classical definition of anomie, was that if youth were deprived of legitimate opportunities to realize economic aspirations, they would turn to other means.

"The breakdown of the family," Kenney's term for another of what he saw as the main causes of delinquency, was hard to pin down because it was a catchall phrase used to describe many different ills in the family. Generally, it seemed to refer to the failure of parents to offer proper guidance to their children, because they were either too busy working or had too many children or both. At times, however, the term "breakdown" seemed to describe the growing divorce rate and the number of broken families. In any case, the referent was the nuclear family and not the extended families, which were under assault by the forces of modernization. Kenney and other observers did not appreciate that extended kin groupings were at the heart of Micronesian social organization. The models and analytical tools used to describe the youth problem in Micronesia were no different from what they would have been in America.

Many of Kenney's informants called attention to what he called the "clash of cultures." No one had any doubt that rapid modernization had a big part to play in youth behavior. Some pointed to the fact that, in contrast to traditional societies, a rift was developing between youth and adults, with each operating in an entirely different sphere. Youth were being educated by a foreign system and were being increasingly socialized in a realm outside the control of the family. For these reasons, the values that adults embraced were no longer considered important by the youth. A values gap was developing between the generations.

Territorial planners made the same assumptions in their proposals to obtain US federal funds under the Juvenile Justice Act (e.g., USTTPI 1976). Juvenile delinquency (redefined to include young adults up to the age of thirty) was regarded by almost everyone as a "serious" or "very serious problem" (USTTPI 1976, 25). The causes given for this problem were quoted at length from Kenney's report. The major programs outlined in the plan to deal with delinquency followed two lines: first, to upgrade youth services in all islands so as to "keep the kids off the streets," as it were; second, to improve the justice system so that it might better handle youthful offenders.

When the Micronesian Seminar convened a large, territory-wide conference on youth in 1977, the search began once again for the causes of the youth problem. We took the position that people could not remedy the situation unless they understood the social forces that went into creating it. A sociocultural analysis of the youth situation in Micronesia was an imperative first step (Hezel 1977, 2).

The conference began with a review of the usual explanations of the youth problem: alcohol abuse, lack of jobs, failure in school, boredom caused by lack of recreational opportunities, communication gap between the generations, and family breakdown. This list, however, was merely used as a departure point for further analysis. Participants were asked why these "causes," many of which had also existed in the past, should be so devastating at the present time. Participants were then introduced to the processes of sociocultural change, which remained the main topic for most of the week-long conference. Under Mason's guidance, participants examined the workings of the traditional culture, reviewed the principal forces acting to bring about social change, and drew for themselves a picture of the "contact culture" that had resulted from these changes.

The conference gave special attention to the place youth held in traditional society in contrast to the changing world of the present. Three significant factors were seen as contributing to the ambiguities faced by modern youth. First, their roles were less sharply defined than they had been, and role conflicts had increased. Second, traditional recognition and rewards accorded to the young were less certain than before. Third, the authority system and social controls that formerly checked unacceptable behavior had eroded. More significantly, however, in this conference the problems of the young were discussed, perhaps for the first time, in the context of cultural change. However tentative and provisional, an attempt was made to show the relevance of the dynamics of cultural change to the problem at hand. The terms for defining the problem were no longer primarily those of American sociology but rather those of cultural anthropology. The point was repeatedly made that youth could not be understood apart from the family and the changes that had befallen it.

Having played a key role in placing the discussion of the "youth problem" in its proper cultural setting at the 1977 conference, anthropologists subsequently took the lead in exploring youth delinquency. Don Rubinstein, who had just completed his fieldwork on Fais, was awarded a grant by the Justice Improvement Commission (JIC) to conduct a study of the social aspects of delinquency. A 1980 conference, jointly sponsored by the Justice Improvement Commission, the Micronesian Area Research Center (MARC) of the University of Guam, and the Micronesian Seminar, discussed Rubinstein's preliminary report. The event was of considerable significance because it heralded a period of close collaboration between anthropologists and locally based institutions. Alan Howard, professor of anthropology at the University of Hawai'i, served as a discussant.

Rubinstein's report challenged the dubious assumptions of a "delinquent personality" and a "delinquent career" on which much of the discussion of delinquency in Micronesia had been based (1980a, 3–4). He found little evidence for either in the pattern of delinquent behavior that he studied. Delinquency was, in fact, "an assemblage of minor misbehaviors and misdemeanors, and a very infrequent number of violent crimes, nearly universally associated with alcohol use" (1980a, 61). Rubinstein concluded that "juvenile delinquency is neither a widespread nor a serious problem in Micronesia" (1980a, 61). Most violence was unintended and occurred almost by accident while young people were recreating. He also noted that young men who engaged in delinquent behavior eventually married and settled down to become responsible members of the community. Thus, he concluded, "delinquency in Micronesia should be seen as a developmental phase and not as the incipient stage of a deviant career" (1980a, 61).

Rubinstein pointed to three social disruptions that were producing confusion among Micronesian youth: education, social mobility, and family change. In taking on a large share of the socialization function, schools were alienating youth from their home communities. The growing mobility among villages and islands was also disrupting the normal processes whereby social order was maintained in small communities. Finally, in addressing the matter of parental neglect that had been mentioned in previous studies, Rubinstein took note of the breakdown of the family. He associated parental neglect not with divorce or problems in the nuclear family, but with the deterioration of the extended family and the shift of responsibility for the young to individual parents. He noted the passing of the multiparent family and the advent of the two-parent family, a theme that was to emerge again and again in later research.

Anthropologists and those using anthropological perspectives had swept aside most of the dire predictions that had prevailed in the previous decade. A careful examination of police records revealed that a great majority of all arrests were of the young (those under the age of twenty), and most of these were for minor offenses. Contrary to the prevailing myth of the day, a study by a group of Xavier High School seniors in 1975 showed that high school dropouts were not disproportionately represented in the arrests (Dengokl et al. 1975). Delinquency was not, therefore, the inevitable fate of those who left the school system early. Nor were instances of delinquency, including major felonies, reliable predictors of criminal careers. Most of those arrested for assault and even homicide in their youth later put such deeds behind them and matured to become respectable members of their communities.

Rubinstein found that delinquency among youth was greater in the towns and larger communities where traditional social controls had begun to break down. The smaller and more integrated the community, the less youth disruption occurred. Even with the weakening of some social restraints, cultural rules remained sufficiently operative to ensure that young Micronesians did not totally run wild. Delinquency, although undeniably troublesome to the community, was not the threat that it had once seemed to represent.

In 1983 and 1984, when government planners resumed efforts to work out strategies for dealing with youth, they showed an increased sensitivity to the cultural issues. Richard Shewman, who held a master's degree in anthropology and served as director of the Northern Marianas Criminal Justice Planning Agency, drew up a manual outlining procedures for a series of community-based youth workshops (Shewman 1983, 1984). In his manual, Shewman scrupulously refused to impose preconceived definitions of problems. Influenced by Paulo Freire (1970) and other Third-World developmentalists, Shewman attempted to engage youth in the search for what was right and wrong with their society. His community-based approach involved young people in a careful examination of the values of their community, with special attention to points of conflict between traditional and modern-day values. In his open-ended approach and emphasis on cultural values and norms, Shewman was guided by his own anthropological training and the lessons learned during the 1970s.

ALCOHOL ABUSE

Much of the mayhem caused by youth was attributed to the use of alcoholic beverages, which had been legally permitted in Micronesia only since 1960. Indeed, the USTTPI delinquency prevention plan for 1977 echoed an assertion that had been made repeatedly during the 1970s: "At least 90% of all juvenile arrests are for illegal possession and consumption of alcohol; or while under the influence of alcohol disturbing the peace, assault and battery, and vandalism; and burglary and larceny to get alcohol or money to purchase alcoholic beverages" (USTTPI 1976, 24–25). Almost all of the crimes committed by those under the age of eighteen, and the vast majority of those committed by older persons, were alcohol related. It was clear that alcohol abuse was a key factor in the antisocial behavior of young Micronesians. This sent research off in a new direction: alcohol abuse among the young in Micronesia.

Francis Mahoney's 1973 study of alcohol use in Micronesia was an initial step. Mahoney, an anthropologist who had written his master's thesis on the personality of Palauans, studied "the set of attitudes held toward youthful alcohol abuse" rather than the patterns of drunken behavior itself (Mahoney 1974, 3). Bringing to bear his cultural knowledge of Micronesia, Mahoney observed that young Micronesians were traditionally granted an extended period of "play time" that lasted until around the age of thirty. Until then they were considered mere apprentices and did not enjoy "decision-making responsibilities either at home or in the community" (Mahoney 1974, 6). In an earlier time, males in this age category would have been "young warriors," Mahoney noted. Thus, from a Micronesian viewpoint, the concept of "juvenile" might quite properly be extended through the twenties to the early thirties. The prime analogue for the drinking party, Mahoney suggested, was the outer-island all-male coconut toddy circle. This was a relaxing evening's entertainment that enhanced rather than threatened the social solidarity of the group. The men might tell salacious stories and dance and sing without inhibition, but

there was no violence or insulting talk. In this respect, the outer-island drinking party differed from its opposite number in the district center (Mahoney
1974, 28–29).

In his discussion of the social causes of alcohol abuse, Mahoney simply
recorded what he learned in interviews with Micronesians. Some of the
reasons given for youth drinking—such as poor law enforcement, an ineffec-
tive court system, failure of parents to discipline errant children, and poor
parental models—pointed to a failure of the mechanisms that were expected
to regulate the behavior of youth. Other common explanations suggested the
lack of other amusements and the failure of the education system to provide
marketable skills as sources of present-day frustration. A few of the reasons
Mahoney heard were particularly incisive from a cultural viewpoint. Some
Micronesians explained that young people drank as an opportunity to permit
"exhibitionistic tendencies to surface," including dancing and flirting with
girls, and to "have an excuse for anti-social conduct" (Mahoney 1974, 46–55).
In other words, drinking freed young people from cloying cultural restraints.

Mahoney tried to establish a link between alcohol consumption and the
rate of violent crime, both of which he found especially high in Yap, Palau,
and Chuuk. He suggested that these three island groups were "the last parts of
Micronesia to have sustained acculturative contact with the Western world"
(Mahoney 1974, 22). Given enough time, he suggested, these islands, too, would
adjust to intoxicating beverages as the other parts of Micronesia had rather
successfully done.

Mac Marshall, who had conducted fieldwork on Namoluk in 1969–1971
and returned to Chuuk in 1976, carried the research into alcohol abuse even
further with his monograph on youth drinking in Chuuk. In *Weekend Warriors* (1979a), Marshall attempted to show the continuity in basic behavior
patterns before and since intensive outside contact. Drunken brawling, he
argued, provided a modern-day substitute for traditional warfare. Whether or
not this thesis is accepted, Marshall's book offered a refreshing new outlook
on the problem of alcohol abuse. A later book, *Silent Voices Speak,* described
the attempts of the local people to control this problem (Marshall and Marshall 1990).

In many publications of the day, authors decried the use of alcohol without
offering any insight on why alcohol should be such a big part of the life of the
young. Marshall (1979a) took up the important question of what function
alcohol serves for Chuukese (and by extension, other Micronesians). One of
the main functions is that the act of drinking redefines the person culturally;

the drinker now stands in a special category and is no longer entirely account-able for his acts. The very act of drinking declares a "cultural time-out." Marshall went on to suggest, however, that the new status of the drinker has boundaries of its own. There are scripted behaviors for drinkers and limits to what even a drunk person can get away with. Marshall described drunken behavior by youth in considerable detail to show that it was largely ritualized, although not without real risk of violence. Marshall's contribution was to show what drinking meant within the cultural context of a single Micronesian society. Not only did he seek to understand why young males drank, but he also explored their behavior and the limits imposed on their behavior.

Building on the materials written by anthropologists, the Micronesian Seminar in 1981 convened a three-day workshop on alcohol use among youth that was attended by more than twenty Micronesians representing every part of the trust territory (Hezel 1981). Following the lead of Mahoney and Marshall, we proposed to examine how and why alcohol was utilized by young people in the different island societies of Micronesia. Rather than view alcohol use as nothing but a "symptom of personal maladjustment or social malaise" and consider how the islands might rid themselves of this menace, the workshop tried to regard alcohol as something embedded in the culture and sought to understand its cultural meaning and context (Hezel 1981, 7). The workshop raised the questions: What part does alcohol play in island society? How is it used and what purposes does it serve? The assumption underlying the workshop was that if Micronesians could be helped to develop a sounder and more explicit understanding of the function alcohol plays in the society, they would be better able to determine what would have to be done to alleviate the problem.

The workshop did little more than underscore and possibly synthesize what had already come out in the earlier writings of Mahoney and Marshall. The workshop report explained that drinking serves three main functions in most Micronesian societies. First, it permits young men to express themselves much more freely, particularly with respect to their negative feelings. If it is true that young people fight because they are drunk, it is equally true that many get drunk precisely in order to fight. Second, it accords some brief recognition—even through the fear and disruption they cause—to the young, who are not very often granted recognition. Third, it offers an escape from the routine and an adventure with a sense of thrill and a whiff of danger. The point is made throughout the brief report resulting from this workshop that alcohol use among the young is far more controlled—through social norms governing

Downtown Bar, Kolonia, Pohnpei,
1982. Photograph by Don Rubinstein.

Young boys enjoying Budweiser, Yap,
1982. Photograph by Don Rubinstein.

*Urbanization on Saipan, Common-
wealth of the Northern Marianas, 1996.
Photograph by Robert Kiste.*

both the context of drinking and the behavior of those indulging in alcohol—than might at first be apparent.

Thanks to the anthropological approach taken, alcohol abuse and juvenile delinquency began to be understood as behaviors that were not at bottom counter-cultural; instead, they seemed to reflect some of the key elements of Micronesian cultures. Viewed this way, they no longer appeared as the terrible scourges that they were once thought to be.

SUICIDE

By the mid-1970s, another social problem came to the fore: youth suicide. A 1976 article drew public attention to the problem for the first time (Hezel 1976). The number of suicides, previously only a handful a year, had begun to climb in the early 1970s and had reached more than twenty a year by 1974. The great majority of the victims were males between the ages of fifteen and thirty; indeed, suicide was the principal cause of death among this age group.

The data revealed that almost all suicides were precipitated by a clash between the victim and his family. What was confusing, however, was the apparently trivial nature of the incident that was said to be the immediate cause of the suicide. Young men were hanging themselves because they had been refused five dollars by their father or because there had been no food for them when they returned home hungry. While the weak self-image of the suicide victim was acknowledged, it was noted that self-esteem for Micronesians is not rooted so much in what one can achieve as in "maintaining satisfying personal relationships with those most important in one's life" (Hezel 1976, 12). Micronesians, after all, were not known to commit suicide because their business failed, because they were thrown out of school, or because they lost their jobs. It was suggested that if uncertain relations between young men and their families led to the growing frequency of suicide, perhaps this was because the family, like the larger community, had been weakened in recent years. The cultural upheaval of modernization was taking its toll on the family; its roles had been relegated to other institutions, and the effectiveness of the supporting role it once played for the young had been eroded.

Micronesian suicides exhibited remarkable differences from those in the United States and the rest of the western world. The clinical depression that was often linked with suicide elsewhere seemed to be missing in Micronesia. Moreover, rates in Micronesia were very high among the young but diminished among older age groups, while in the United States rates rose with age. Suicides in Micronesia seemed very much a response to a certain problem with one's family, or even a particular family member. There was no evidence of the existential angst, or the general sense of meaninglessness that is so often related to suicides in the west (Hezel 1984, 1985a, 1987a). Very few of the victims seemed "severely disturbed, emotionally troubled, or mentally imbalanced" (Rubinstein 1980b, 5). Thus the body of literature on suicide in the United States and Europe was of little help in understanding the sudden suicide epidemic that had erupted in Micronesia.

Not all Micronesians looked with a kindly eye on the interest that was being shown in suicide. Some resented the unfavorable publicity that the islands were receiving and the insinuation that Micronesian society was so disturbed that large numbers of its youth were choosing death over life. Others were unconvinced that suicide was a major problem. Suicide, they suggested, was an entirely permissible and time-honored strategy for correcting certain impossible situations, for instance, after one had disgraced his family by committing incest. In their view, suicide was not a vexing problem, but a solution to certain insoluble difficulties that arise within the family. Was suicide, then, endemic or epidemic? Was it, like youth drinking and delinquency, a cultural response that represented continuity with traditional values and practices? Or was it another of the social plagues that had followed westernization?

As the number of victims in every part of Micronesia mounted, Rubinstein, then a fellow at the East-West Center, undertook an epidemiological survey of the case data (Rubinstein 1980b, 1981, 1983). Meanwhile, I continued to gather case files on recent suicides, which by 1980 had reached forty a year in the Carolines and Marshalls. Whatever else might be said about suicide, and as many Micronesian leaders were forced to acknowledge, it was clear that the rate was escalating with painful rapidity. Suicides, which had numbered perhaps five or ten a year throughout Micronesia in the early 1960s, had grown as much as tenfold in some districts. The frequency of suicide in places like Chuuk was among the highest in the world, and the specific rate for males aged 16–25 was over 200 per hundred thousand (Rubinstein 1985, 1992b).

Rubinstein and I adopted an ethnographic field approach in our study. Together we organized a series of workshops in which we elicited the interpretations of young Chuukese adults and youth leaders. At one workshop, we were introduced to the Chuukese term *amwúnumwún*, which proved to offer a key insight into the psychodynamics of suicide (Rubinstein 1984). *Amwúnumwún* means to distance oneself from others as a way of giving vent to strong feelings when it is culturally inappropriate to directly display such sentiments. Negative feelings are usually exhibited through some form of self-abasement, ranging from isolating oneself and refusing to speak to others to taking one's own life. The strategy is one of withdrawal rather than confrontation and is in keeping with similar behaviors throughout Micronesia and Polynesia (Hezel 1987a, 286).

American mental health personnel commonly viewed suicide as "retroflective anger," anger directed inward by the victims on themselves (Hezel 1987b, 21). However, as Rubinstein and I pieced together a Chuukese interpretation of suicide, we began to understand the serious limitations of western psychological frameworks. Initially, we had understood suicide as an act of aggression, a vengeful and defiant final strike against the family. Chuukese survivors of suicide attempts, however, appeared genuinely shocked at this interpretation of their act and vigorously denied any revenge motivation. Gradually, we came to understand that suicide, although it was often an angry response, contained elements of a lingering melancholy love that was thought to be beyond repair this side of the grave. This sentiment was also echoed in the maudlin and self-abasing lyrics of the Chuukese love songs that were heard almost continuously on the radio. As a dramatization of the victim's sorrow, hurt, and frustration, suicide was a withdrawal from a painful situation.

In 1982, with a grant from the National Institute of Mental Health, Rubinstein began a three-year ethnographic study of Chuukese family life to gain further insight on suicide. In an attempt to accumulate better case data, he interviewed friends and families of victims for a second and third time. As data were gathered on long-standing tensions within the family, many of the suicides that had at first appeared shockingly impulsive took on an entirely different aura. To be sure, some suicides resulted from a single isolated family spat, but these were far fewer than we had originally thought. For example, one young man from Chuuk was believed to have committed suicide because his parents would not intercede on his behalf to get back his wife after she had left him. As new data were collected, it appeared that the young man himself had sent his wife away, a girl picked for him by his parents, because of a long conflict with them over other family matters. As a last poignant memorial of himself, on the night of his suicide, the young man left his footprint and signature in wet cement on the floor of the family meeting house (Hezel 1984, 197–198).

What is the cause of the suicide epidemic since the late 1960s? Following Durkheim's well-known model, many attributed it to anomie resulting from rapid modernization in Micronesia. Rubinstein, however, took exception to this view and argued that there was no direct correlation between suicide and urbanization and rapid transition toward American lifestyles (1980b, 3–4). He demonstrated that suicide was most prevalent in peri-urban areas rather than in the most heavily acculturated places (Rubinstein 1981, 1983). Outer islands, with their traditional lifestyle, and towns, where modernization had progressed the furthest, showed relatively low suicide rates. Suicide was a phenomenon that occurred most frequently in those places that were in the process of transition toward modernization (Rubinstein 1981, 5–6).

There was another reason not to posit a one-to-one linkage between suicide and modernization. Suicide is a culturally patterned response to certain conflict situations; it is a Micronesian solution to certain kinds of interpersonal disruption. The very fact that one chooses to commit suicide implies a commitment to traditional values and norms of conduct—the centrality of traditional family relationships, the importance of the old prohibitions about voicing negative feelings toward older kin, and the validity of the age-old strategy of withdrawal to avoid conflict. Even if victims had been exposed to some westernization, they affirmed basic Micronesian values through their decision to die (Hezel 1987a, 287).

If the suicide epidemic could not be blamed on a general malaise arising from rapid change, was it possible to identify a more specific cause or causes? Rubinstein and I were convinced that the suicide epidemic was related to the breakdown of the traditional Micronesian family, especially since suicide was usually occasioned by a family problem or quarrel. Like others, we had a sense that the Micronesian family was changing dramatically, but we were not sure just how. Serious intergenerational tensions were evident, but one might ask whether such tensions had not always existed in Micronesian societies. Rubinstein hypothesized that the disappearance of the men's houses or similar institutions that had once served to educate and train young men had radically altered youth socialization (Rubinstein 1983, 14–17). I wondered whether competing modern institutions such as the school had not lured young people away from their own families so that they were less well integrated into traditional extended kin groups (Hezel 1984).

Many longtime expatriate residents believed that the increase in suicide was due to family neglect. Perhaps parents who were busy with their jobs or pre-occupied with other things were not giving enough attention to their children today. Yet, the interviews and other cultural data that Rubinstein and I analyzed gave quite the opposite impression. Traditional family structures throughout Micronesia permitted what could be called a "comfortable distance" between parents and children (Hezel 1985a, 122). In the context of the extended family much of the responsibility for exercising authority and socializing young men fell to other older relatives. Recent changes had the effect of concentrating this responsibility more and more in the biological parents, as multiparent families were giving way to families with just two parents.

A 1984 conference on Pacific suicide, inspired by the work being carried out in Micronesia, and organized by Geoffrey White under the auspices of the East-West Center, offered an opportunity to look at Micronesian suicide against a wider background. Significantly, nearly all the participants at the conference were either anthropologists or persons who adopted an anthropological per-spective on the problem. Although the conference itself produced few new insights into the causes of the suicide epidemic in Micronesia, it afforded us the opportunity to discuss our understanding of the etiology of suicide with others who had some familiarity with the area. Most of these others were anthropologists who had conducted their fieldwork in Micronesia. Within a year or two of the conference, Rubinstein and I had elaborated our own hypotheses for the dramatic increase of suicide. These theories, and others that have been advanced to explain suicide elsewhere in the Pacific, were re-viewed in a recent article (Rubinstein 1992b).

I looked to the weakening of the extended family system as one of the main causes of the suicide problem. The older system provided multiple kin options and supports for children. If they experienced harsh treatment at the hand of one "parent," they could readily find another to mediate the conflict or pro-vide the needed support. In today's nuclearized family, the father and mother have been forced to assume increased responsibilities for their children, with a concomitant increase in tension between parents and their offspring. I argued that the monetization of the economy has largely been responsible for the breakdown of the lineage system. Cash income, especially from jobs, has offered individuals an alternate resource base, thereby weakening the land-based lineage system (Hezel 1987a, 1989).

While partly agreeing with my explanation, Rubinstein has offered a somewhat different view. He has principally focused on the disruption of the socialization process resulting from the weakening of lineage and village-level organization. The political and economic changes (among them monetization) that stem from rapid acculturation have brought about structural changes in the extended family. In this our interpretations agree. But where I identified the locus of the problem in the heightened tension between parents and children brought about by the demands of modern parenting, Rubinstein looked to broader difficulties in the socialization of the young. During the various stages of the traditional socialization process, Rubinstein argued, the tension that appeared at the end of each stage was resolved when the child was incorporated into a larger social circle. As the child grew older, he was exposed to socialization by a widening circle of kin. The erosion of social structures at the lineage and village level has impeded this process by removing many of the cultural supports for young males. Young men remain dependent on their parents for favors of food and money at a time when they would ordinarily have been supported by a wider kin group (Rubinstein 1992b).

While very similar in substance, despite differences in emphasis, both explanations have their shortcomings. Neither explains the phenomenon of "love suicides"—suicides seemingly precipitated by sexual jealousy or anger at spouse or girlfriend which have become rather common in Palau and the Marshalls in the last decade. Nevertheless, suicide research in Micronesia has marked an advance in the approach to social research. Previous work, utilizing sociological and psychological assumptions, tended to lay the blame for social problems like suicide on the disruption springing from social change. The assumption was that suicide was a manifestation of personal disintegration, which in turn was caused by the social dislocation and anomie resulting from rapid modernization. All woes could be ultimately laid at the doorstep of macrosocietal changes. Rarely did anyone attempt to discriminate among these changes and almost never did they try to trace the impact of changes on key social institutions like the family. Social change, as presented in many writings on the Pacific, was undifferentiated and unmediated. Somehow, by some magic, it worked its way into society and made its force felt on the lives of individuals (Hezel 1987b, 17–18). In the suicide research on Micronesia, guided by anthropological techniques and concepts, Rubinstein and I rejected a simple anomic explanation. Whatever the limitations of our work, we have attempted to delineate the effect of macrosocietal changes on institutions such as the family that have an immediate impact on the lives of individuals.

CHILD AND SPOUSE ABUSE

In 1985 the Micronesian Seminar, then based in Chuuk, undertook a provisional study of child abuse and neglect at the request of the Truk Office of Community Action (Hezel 1985b). Shortly after the completion of this project, the Micronesian Seminar was contracted by the Trust Territory Justice Improvement Commission on Saipan to do a broader study for all the Caroline and Marshall Islands (Marcus 1991). These studies were prompted by a growing concern in the United States for research that would support stronger legislation on what was perceived to be a serious problem. The rights of children in the family and the desire to protect children from parental abuse were becoming key domestic issues in developed countries. It was assumed that these issues were, or at least ought to be, as relevant in Micronesia.

Research into what might loosely be called "child abuse" began with Dennis T. P. "Tom" Keene's study of young female runaways in the Marshall Islands in January 1985. Keene, an anthropologist who earned his doctorate at the University of Hawai'i, chose as the subject of his study a highly visible subgroup in Majuro, young women known as *kokan* 'traders,' who had left their homes and lived wherever they could find shelter. These women, ranging in age from fifteen to their early twenties, drank alcohol, smoked, ran around with men, and often supported themselves by prostitution. Many were newcomers to Majuro. Most had dropped out of school and had experienced tension with their families that often culminated in the parents cutting off their daughters' hair to humiliate them or throwing them out of the house altogether. Keene (1992) suggested that the flagrant promiscuity of these girls could be viewed as a defiant response to their problems with their families.

The community survey that the Micronesian Seminar did in Chuuk, which was extended to other parts of Micronesia, a year later uncovered further evidence that all was not well with Micronesian families. Adjustments, of course, had to be made in the definition of "child abuse" and "child neglect" to take into account cultural norms in child-rearing practices. Even so, the survey revealed a surprisingly high incidence of abusive behavior. In some cases the family singled out one or two of the children and subjected them to especially shabby treatment, denying them food and other treats that were granted to the rest of the children. Sometimes the family might badger a child, hounding him or her over the most trivial of matters, until the child simply left home and found shelter with other relatives or friends. One man, who disliked his daughter from birth, willfully neglected her for years until he finally decided to be rid of her completely and sold her to a neighbor for five dollars (Hezel 1985b).

There also came to light sordid tales of what could only be called physical abuse of children, even by the relatively lax Micronesian standards. One woman threw her niece into a well when the girl would not do the washing. Other parents were reported to have used sticks and metal rods to beat children who had been trussed and suspended from a tree. Now and then there was a report of a father who, in a drunken rage, flung a baby onto the cement floor of his house or out a window (Marcus 1991). Sometimes after a drinking binge young fathers beat their wives and children, a practice that women might loathe but had to accept with resignation. In all the cases, however, the child beating was judged by others in the community as so notably frequent and severe as to constitute an abuse.

Of greater concern than the individual incidents of neglect and abuse uncovered in the study was the pattern that seemed to emerge in the family situations of neglected and abused children. Those most often maltreated were stepchildren or children who had been handed over to others for fosterage. A woman who has remarried and brings children from her previous marriage to the home of her new husband may face serious tensions. Sometimes the stepfather shows decidedly preferential treatment toward his own children, as when he provides chicken and other treats for his children but denies these same things to his stepchildren. Occasionally, however, it may work in reverse, as when the father, to prove his love for his new wife, favors her children at the expense of his own. In Palau, which has an exceptionally high rate of births out of wedlock, young mothers often turn their children over to their own parents for rearing. The grandparents, who seem resentful of this additional burden, may discriminate against their grandchildren so strongly that the children simply leave home, even if it means taking up the life of drifters. In Yap the paternal grandfather of a young boy balked at taking him into his house and caring for him, although this would have been expected of the man by custom. The grandfather, who reluctantly acquiesced in the end, beat the child so badly that the boy soon ran away to find refuge elsewhere (Marcus 1991).

If these studies indicate anything, it may be that the "safety net" that served to protect children in the traditional Micronesian family now has gaping holes. In the past, remarriage, whether after divorce or death of a spouse, held little uncertainty and anxiety for children because they found security among their own extended families. Similarly, the practice of allowing fosterage within the lineage circle, not to speak of adoption outside this kin group, was once commonly practiced and posed few problems for the children. That it seems to be problematic today may be just another indication of the fragmentation of larger kin groupings in favor of an increasingly nuclearized family.

The community surveys also revealed a surprisingly large number of cases of sexual abuse, given the strong cultural prohibition against incest in Micronesian societies. According to an unpublished report, the incidence of sexual abuse on Palau is about as high as on Guam (Shewman 1992). The incidence in other parts of Micronesia is impossible to determine because of the loose methodology used in the study, but the incomplete data suggest that the rates may be rather high. In most cases the incestuous relationship is perpetrated by a father, stepfather, or uncle, and the sexual abuse may continue for years before the girl runs away or marries. In another study of child maltreatment in the Marshalls, a researcher reported seven cases of sexual abuse on Ebeye over a three-year period, all of them involving children under the age of seven years (Opie 1991, 48). Many of the elaborate restrictions designed to maintain a respectful distance between father and daughter seem to have fallen into disuse in recent times. Whether this has been responsible for a rise in sexual abuse—if indeed there has been an increase—is still to be established.

Two other anthropologists, Karen Nero and Laurence Carucci, have looked into the issue of domestic violence. In her 1990 article on wife beating in Palau, Nero suggested that the seeming increase in the frequency and intensity of beatings may be explained in part by the nuclearization of the Palauan household today. The physical isolation of the nuclear family from a larger kin circle forces the married couple to spend much more time alone than they would have in the past, even as it keeps out "the elders whose very presence mediates against domestic violence" (Nero 1990, 87). According to Carucci (1990), much the same process may be occurring in the Marshalls; and something similar may be responsible for the severe spouse abuse in Chuuk. The relatives of a married woman, who formerly were expected to protect her from excessive beatings, are much more hesitant today to intervene in what they consider a domestic squabble to be settled by the husband and wife. The growing problem of wife beating, like many of the other issues discussed in this chapter, would seem to be attributable in great part to changes in the structure and functioning of the family.

DIRECTIONS FOR THE FUTURE

Research into social problems will probably continue to expand into new areas of contemporary Micronesian life. The mounting evidence that family changes are a key factor in many recent social problems suggests that a serious study of the evolution of the family in Micronesia is long overdue. In 1989 the Micronesian Seminar, financed by a grant from the Misereor Foundation in Germany, undertook a study of changes in the family on Pohnpei and Chuuk. Based on interviews with key informants, the study focused on the differences in the family between 1950 and the present. Although by no means an unqualified success, the project produced papers on changing features of the Pohnpeian and Chuukese family. The topics treated included resources, food distribution, family labor, child rearing, and adoption (Barnabas and Hezel 1993; Oneisom 1994).

Another potential area for research lies along the gender divide in Micronesia. The sexes seemingly face very different types and degrees of stress in their day-to-day lives, and they certainly manage this stress very differently. As discussed, young men in Micronesia are notoriously prone to release tension by getting drunk or, in some situations, even committing suicide. Young women, who are culturally denied those outlets, have one or two forms of release of their own. The most notable is spirit possession, in which the woman is possessed by the spirit of a dead relative and speaks with the spirit's voice. Because the woman is not held responsible for what comes from her mouth, she may freely express feelings about the conflict situation in the family that usually gives rise to her "illness." An analysis of spirit possession in Chuuk was recently presented (Hezel 1993), but this phenomenon has yet to be studied on other islands.

The question of whether males are under more stress than females in Micronesia was raised years ago by Gladwin. His ethnographic material on the Chuukese life cycle, and Seymour Sarason's psychological studies of Chuukese subjects, indicated that men seemed to bear greater social pressures and enjoy fewer supports than women (Gladwin and Sarason 1953). A recent epidemiological survey of serious mental illness in Micronesia, showing male rates to be three to four times higher than female rates, has raised the question once again (Hezel and Wylie 1992). A conclusive explanation for the disparity in rates of mental illness is not offered, but some possibilities are suggested: The disparity might be due to drug use, which is fairly common among males but rare among females, or a social environment that seems to protect women and punish males.

ANTHROPOLOGY'S LASTING LEGACY

American anthropology has played a key role in social problems research in Micronesia since the late 1970s, when field-workers first turned their attention to the social problems that had become increasingly apparent after more than a decade of rapid modernization. Largely as a result of their influence, the social models drawn from American and European sociology that had previously been used to analyze Micronesian societies were discarded as inadequate. Anthropologists and those with an anthropological orientation initiated a culture-specific approach to the problems studied, emphasizing the meanings and values given to behavior by the local cultures. This has yielded a more satisfying understanding of these social problems, as the work on delinquency, drinking, suicide, and child and spouse abuse attests. In the future the same anthropological methods will no doubt be applied to a number of other social issues in Micronesia, even as the involvement of anthropologists in this research promises to grow.

There is a final paradoxical lesson to be drawn from this research. The study of social problems from an anthropological perspective over the past two decades has revealed that while much change has occurred, there has, nevertheless, been considerable stability and continuity in Micronesian cultures. The epiphenomena of modernization such as Micronesia has undergone in recent years are alarming and seem to portend a total collapse of the culture. In fact, however, each of the social problems we have analyzed illustrates the remarkable persistence of basic cultural structures and values. The alcohol problem among youth, far from being an abandonment of all societal norms, can be viewed as a rather controlled strategy by youth to find expressive outlets in a society that mandates restraint. A close look at youth delinquency reveals the final triumph of socialization processes over free-spirited youth; for youth, no matter how wayward, return to the fold virtually without exception by the time they reach adulthood. Child abuse is not without damaging consequences, but it is also a vivid indication of the continued importance of food and material goods as a measure of love in a Micronesian society. Even suicide, perhaps the most destructive of all these social problems, testifies in its own way to the strength and perdurance of the culture. Suicide today is an assertion of traditional values—the sacredness of family ties and respect for the senior status of elders—even as it demonstrates the importance of the age-old strategies of withdrawal and self-abasement to display emotional pain.

The same structural changes, particularly in the extended family, that have brought about the problems surveyed in this chapter will probably create further problems in years to come. But we may expect that they will provoke less anxiety than the earlier set of problems, if only because they will be viewed more clearly in their cultural context and not as signs of the imminent ruin of the society. In this respect as in many others, social problems research in Micronesia has been changed by anthropology once and for all.

CHAPTER TEN

Staking Ground:
Medical Anthropology, Health,
and Medical Services in Micronesia

Donald H. Rubinstein

Anthropology has little to offer
[health care providers in Micronesia]
except to provide interesting bedtime reading.
DR. WILLIAM PECK,
QUOTED IN *MEDICAL MANUAL FOR THE PACIFIC ISLANDS.*

MICRONESIA HAS BEEN UNIQUELY fertile ground for American anthropology during the past fifty years.[1] Where else in the world has a small population and land base the size of Micronesia provided a field on which about a hundred doctoral dissertations and an uncounted number of master's theses in anthropology have been produced? As the chapters in this volume manifest, anthropologists of all subdisciplinary stripes have plowed this ground, from ecological to psychological anthropologists. My purpose here is to sort out the history and legacy of medical anthropology in Micronesia since World War II.

For the second half of this fifty-year period, medical anthropology has been a recognized specialty within American anthropology, and during the 1960s and 1970s medical anthropology was the fastest growing section within the American Anthropological Association (Logan and Hunt 1978, xi). Today medical anthropology is the largest topical subfield in American anthropology (Schensul 1993, 15). Yet medical anthropology has never had a prominent place in anthropological work in Micronesia, and health care providers in Micronesia have not found anthropological writings very useful, as reflected in the quotation that opens this chapter. The reasons, I suggest, lie in the institutional histories and politics that have defined health issues both within anthropology and within Micronesia.

I view medical anthropology here both as a conceptual territory with its own theoretical focus and scope, and as an institutional system operating over time among other systems with competing political claims and interests. My aim is to explore how health and sickness in Micronesia have served as a ground on which various institutions, medical anthropology among them, have staked their claims.

FROM MEDICAL SPIRITS TO STATE HOSPITALS

Consider an image from Frank Mahony's study of Truk (now Chuuk) medicine (1970). A corpse of someone slain in battle would be lashed upright to a breadfruit tree facing the direction of the hostile village. The corpse would be mutilated to make it look even more fearsome and horrific, the lips would be sliced off, the eyes gouged out, and various medicines and foods and fish such as shark and stingray would be placed in front of it to "make the spirit hot and angry" (Mahony 1970, 169). In the absence of a corpse, a fabricated image or a burning brand might be staked to a particular spot to achieve the same effect.

What was of concern here and in Chuuk medicine generally, according to Mahony, was the problem of social control in the relatively egalitarian society of Chuuk. Mahony argued that "where superordinate controls are weak, as in Truk, illness may be regarded as punishment for all sorts of anti-social behavior, and consequently all of medical theory has important functions in social control" (1970, 262–263). In brief, the Chuuk theory of medicine is organized around various 'spirit-powers.' Each 'spirit-power' is a conceptual bundle that links ideas about diagnosis and cause of illness, symptoms, medical formulae for treatment, and related aspects of sickness and healing. The most powerful 'spirit-powers' in Chuuk medicine are known as 'set-down spirits,' which are a form of sorcery used in warfare (1970, 168–171).

At the time Mahony studied Chuuk medicine in the 1960s, people still recalled the specific areas where these 'set-down spirits' dwelled, threatening harm to "unsuspecting sojourners" (Mahony 1970, 170). One such area full of 'set-down spirits' was on Wééné, in the saddle between two hills where the boundaries of Mwaan, Iras, Tunnuk, and Mechitiw villages come together, a scene of heavy fighting in the past. Today it is the site of the Chuuk State Hospital. Mahony noted that "difficulties that patients sometimes encounter in the hospital, most especially the birth of a deformed child, which is an almost unequivocal symptom of this spirit power, are often attributed to the action of these spirits" (1970, 171).

For the people of Chuuk and elsewhere in Micronesia, the state hospitals opened the field of health and sickness to a whole new array of issues. Planned and built entirely with American funds, the state hospitals established the primary physical and institutional structures for the extension of cosmopolitan medicine to Micronesia. What was most clearly at stake from early in the American administration was the ability of Micronesian leaders to solicit and steer outside funds and resources into the area of health care, as well as other areas such as education, which served as grounds for American-Micronesian flows of funding and development technologies. An early incident may be cited which, though trivial, prefigured the shape of many later exchanges on this topic.

The scene was the Sixth Annual Conference of Chuuk magistrates, convened in Truk District in July 1957 (Truk District 1957, 27–31). Representatives from the US Trust Territory of the Pacific Islands (USTTPI) headquarters addressed the island magistrates, who had recently been given a tour of what was at the time the new hospital. The American public health official then admonished the magistrates to supervise their island health aides, to see that the dispensaries were maintained in good condition and that the villages were kept clean, and to assist in collecting fees from patients using the district hospital. Clearly on the mind of the public health official was a notion of local community proprietorship of health, and the limited central resources for outlying communities. The Truk magistrates, however, had a far wider field of opportunities in mind. One magistrate requested that the hospital provide tin roofs for the island dispensaries. Both of the visiting health officials quickly turned down that request. Another magistrate then asked whether more patients could be sent to Guam and elsewhere for treatment. At that point the USTTPI officials called for a coffee break.

During another session in this meeting one magistrate strongly stated the need for construction of a new building. This must have been a frequent request from this particular magistrate because the American USTTPI official responded sardonically, saying "I would like to compliment [the magistrate] on his interest over a long period of time in this matter. When I first came here last year he was asking about the same thing." And another American official advised the magistrate, "You bring it up at every meeting . . . and don't let us forget it and [one] of these days we will get it because of your efforts." The magistrate has the last word, spoken in fine metaphor proper to

Chuuk orators. He said, "Like a chisel and hammer. [I am] the hammer and the Americans are the chisel."

In the forty years since that meeting, the stakes have grown much larger, and Micronesian negotiators and planners of their health care systems have become much more adroit at hammering for health services. Now at issue are Micronesian government negotiations for federal programs, block grants, and assistance packages worth tens of millions of dollars annually in health facilities and care (see, for example, RMI 1989). In this Micronesian trajectory from medical spirit-powers to multimillion-dollar hospital facilities, where has medical anthropology positioned itself?

AMERICAN MEDICINE AND AMERICAN ANTHROPOLOGY MEET MICRONESIA

Prior to the American era in Micronesia, islanders had little contact with Western medicine. Medical care other than local remedies was generally in the hands of missionaries (Tabrah 1982, 7).[2] Some of the missionaries were themselves physicians, such as the American Protestant missionary Luther Gulick on Pohnpei, whose curing powers strengthened his claims for the islanders' allegiance (Hanlon 1984). Even on Guam, only one Spanish physician, devoid of medicine and with only a few medical instruments, was present when American naval forces arrived in 1899 (Becker 1993, 1). During the period that the US Navy created American-style health services for Guam, the German colonial administration (1900–1914) established the first hospitals elsewhere in Micronesia, but these facilities were limited to the administrative centers and were quite inadequate for providing treatment to the island population (Tabrah 1982, 7). During the Japanese era, both government and private health care facilities were established in Japan's mandated territory. In addition to the government hospitals in Saipan, Yap, Pohnpei, Chuuk, Kosrae, Koror, Angaur, and Jaluit, the Japanese maintained leprosaria and tuberculosis sanitoria in the administrative centers.

During World War II, diseases in the Pacific were a matter of American concern because of the potential impact of parasitic and other infectious diseases on military personnel (Mumford and Mohr 1943; US Army 1944).[3] After the war, all health care services for Micronesians were the task of the US Navy. Micronesians at first received care only on an emergency basis as part of the naval military government from 1944 to 1947 (Tabrah 1982, 10). With the establishment of civil government in July 1947, the navy justified its continued presence in Micronesia partly by getting into the work of health and educa-

US Navy doctor, assisted by eleven-year-old Marshallese girl, administering inoculation to Marshallese man, Majuro, Marshall Islands, June 1944. US Navy photography, National Archives.

tion. One might draw a parallel with the American missionaries who a century earlier had opened schools and clinics to strengthen their position in the islands.

This is not to belittle, however, the real need for medical attention that the navy encountered among the islanders. Wartime dietary and living deprivations, forced relocation of island communities such as the Woleaians (Barnett 1956, 94–95), and inadequate medical care during the war had taken a severe toll on Micronesian health. Intestinal parasites, yaws, venereal diseases, tuberculosis, skin diseases, upper respiratory infections, and eye disease were all prevalent, much like the situation naval medical officers had found on Guam nearly fifty years earlier. When the navy commissioned the first comprehensive health survey in the former Japanese mandated islands of Micronesia in 1948–1950, investigators found the islanders to be in generally poor health, though already recovered significantly from the immediate postwar period (Tabrah 1982, 9–10).

American anthropologists who entered Micronesia in the late 1940s came at a historical moment when the islanders' health was a subject of foremost administrative concern. Heightening this was a widely held conceit among observers of the Pacific that islanders were "inherently soft populations, vulnerable to the diseases of the Europeans, and doomed because of a psychological inability to adapt to contact with a superior civilization" (Pirie 1972, 187). For decades westerners had forecast the extinction of the Pacific Islanders, and this theory had received support from eminent anthropological authorities (e.g., Pitt-Rivers 1927). The depopulation of Yap had become a matter of international concern during the Japanese Mandate period and had prompted numerous inquiries from the Mandates Commission to the Japanese delegates (SONA 1948, 59). The anthropologist William Lessa, noting a baby boom already underway in Ulithi in 1948, speculated whether it was due to "a new zest for living which seems to have been inspired by missionary influence," to improvements in health, or to the recent return of able-bodied men to the island (SONA 1948, 60).[4]

Unraveling the causes of depopulation became the first medically related research challenge for American anthropologists in Micronesia. Under auspices of the Coordinated Investigation of Micronesian Anthropology (CIMA), four Harvard graduate students with specialties in demography, physical anthropology, and cultural anthropology comprised the research team. They produced a general description of Yapese social life and customs, and gave particular attention to critical factors in depopulation (Hunt, Kidder, Schneider, and Stevens 1949). This first attempt to solve the depopulation mystery pointed to the combination of disturbed social conditions in Yap and an increased frequency of voluntary abortions among Yapese women. The researchers admitted, however, that the prevalence and impact of venereal disease was still "the main unknown factor" (Hunt et al. 1949, 218). Because the population of Yap soon showed signs of a postwar rebound and recovery, the question of depopulation quickly lost its medical urgency. Nonetheless, several papers appeared over the next few years, rehashing the abortion thesis (Hunt, Kidder, and Schneider 1954; Schneider 1955; cf. Lessa 1955). But it was not until further data on Yapese demography were collected in the 1960s and 1970s, and some of the earlier data reanalyzed, that researchers discarded the abortion thesis and confirmed that introduced venereal disease was indeed the culprit (J. Underwood 1973).

The implications of this work were considerable for medically untreated populations affected by sexually transmitted diseases. It demonstrated that while introduced diseases might have an impact on fertility and not mortality, the demographic effect could be equally devastating (Lessa and Myers 1962). For anthropology generally, this twenty-five-year series of research projects and publications represented a successful process of hypothesis testing and cumulative science (E. Hunt 1978). For Micronesia specifically, the work came too late to make a difference, but it heralded the importance of demographic techniques in solving anthropological puzzles. Problems of population demography and fertility have continued to attract anthropological attention in Micronesia (e.g., Carroll 1975a; Levin and Gorenflo 1994; Turke and Betzig 1985). The current issue is no longer one of health and survival, however; rather, the focus is more on cultural ecology and adaptation (see Alkire, chap. 3).

As with the studies of infectious diseases, initial American inquiries into matters of diet and nutrition were motivated by a concern for the well-being of their own military personnel. Prior to the war, the US War Department commissioned a study of Pacific Island foods (Merrill 1943) intended as a survival guide for pilots who might be stranded in the islands. After the war, American concerns focused on the impact of diet and nutrition on Micronesian health. Some islanders had experienced severe food shortages during the war, and garden lands on some islands were devastated. A nutrition expert, Elmer Alpert, took part in the US Commercial Company Survey in 1946. He noted protein deficiencies in islanders' diet but he found no evidence of severe malnutrition (Alpert 1946). A few years later a public health specialist, Mary Murai, did more thorough nutrition fieldwork in Majuro and Chuuk as part of the CIMA team. Murai concluded that the apparent nutritional deficiencies found by Alpert were attributable to wartime disruptions and the Japanese occupation rather than to aboriginal diet (Murai 1954; Murai et al. 1958).

Also among the CIMA team were two physicians, Alice Joseph and Veronica Murray, who examined the health and physique of both Chamorros and Carolinians on Saipan (Joseph and Murray 1951).[5] At the time of their study in the late 1940s the food supply was precarious. Large numbers of children were poorly nourished, and disease was widespread, especially conjunctivitis, skin infections, intestinal parasites, and respiratory problems. Combining their health data with ethnographic descriptions and historical material, Joseph and Murray concluded that the Carolinians had fared much better during the war than the Chamorros. The Carolinians apparently had benefited from their greater resourcefulness in local food production and use and their customary food redistribution along kinship lines (Joseph and Murray 1951, 105).

Reasoning that chronic illness tends to lower mental as well as physical ability, Joseph and Murray administered a battery of tests to the Saipanese, including measurements of intelligence and projective tests of personality. They also collected psychiatric case histories. Although the significance and validity of these tests (the Bender Gestalt and the Rorschach) are considered questionable today, Joseph and Murray's work was at that time the most thorough description of the physiological and psychological impact of the war on a Micronesian community (cf. Black, chap. 7).

These early research questions—the causes of Micronesian depopulation, the adequacy of Micronesian diets, and the extent of physical and mental trauma from the war—addressed urgent problems of population health and survival during the postwar recovery years. However, the agenda for anthropological attention to health was defined not only by practical postwar challenges but also by the health organizational environment created by the US Navy. The institutional charter for the navy's health and sanitation program was a detailed statement of "Public Health Rules and Regulations for the Trust Territory of the Pacific Islands" issued in November 1947, which in effect established the American model of an exclusive medical bureaucracy that monopolizes and regulates health care through a system of licensure (SONA 1948, 206, 282–292; cf. Last 1990). Article 2 of the 1947 statement decreed that "it shall be unlawful for any person . . . to practice medicine or other of the healing arts for a fee unless duly licensed . . . by the High Commissioner" (SONA 1948, 282–283). Although enforcement was probably moot, one may read into this statement the debarment of a variety of Micronesian medical technologies.

The attitude of the dominant medical subculture of the navy toward "island-style medicine" is captured in a few lines of advice in the 1948 handbook prepared by the navy for use in training and administration:

> The medical worker . . . in penetrating below the surface of island life in relation to his sanitary and medical problems, is likely to find himself still in a world of taboos, omens, spells, charms, and psychological mumbo jumbo. . . . The problem has arisen in virtually all such areas as to whether the practice of local-type medicine should be officially forbidden. Any comprehensive law on this matter would be impossible to enforce. . . . Some administrations, including American Samoa, declare public practice of local medicine illegal; but rarely can cases be pinned down. (SONA 1948, 214–215)

This section of the handbook concludes with the line, "As a field for research, island therapeutics has been so far almost untouched" (1948, 215). This is hardly surprising, in light of the pall of quasi-illegality and scorn that the dominant medical subculture cast over indigenous medical practice.

The naval government plan was built on the assumption that Micronesia was at best a medical blank slate, at worst a netherworld of medical voodoo. An early planning document (US Navy 1945) spelled out assumptions, such as the existence of widespread disease and malnutrition, and the absence of hygienic conditions, before these conditions had in fact been verified. The plan further assumed "minimal humanitarian medical care will be furnished civilians" and that the supervisory authority of the medical department would be supported through liaison with other departments such as welfare and security (US Navy 1945, 2). In the name of health, the medical plan served as a piece of the "charter for intervention" (N. Thomas 1990, 156) of the newly installed naval military government.[6] In January 1946, the US Navy commissioned the School of Medical Practitioners on Guam, designed as a four-year course with a curriculum "patterned closely after the wartime accelerated programs of the leading medical schools in the United States." Among the required introductory courses were American history and geography, and European history (US Naval Medical Center 1948, 1).[7]

So at the arrival of the first cohort of American anthropologists in the late 1940s, the institutional frame of American medicine had already been drawn, and island "culture" had been positioned as extraneous, or even worse, adversarial, to American medicine. Medical development in Micronesia meant replicating institutional features of American biomedicine, beginning with training as physician surrogates a cadre of medical officers—all males and preferably familiar with American history and geography—to serve as the backbone of the medical system.[8]

Aside from the urgent postwar questions of what was causing depopulation and whether Micronesians were adequately nourished, health as such had little place on the anthropological research agenda. When anthropologists moved into administration, health problems were a very small part of their routine, compared with issues like land tenure and the development of civil government. Neither the specific assignments of the early district and staff anthropologists, nor the general emphases in American anthropology of the period, would have inclined these anthropologists to study health problems. Judging from the writings of the first twenty years of American anthropology in Micronesia, it is fair to say that until the mid-1960s anthropologists had no impact on Micronesian health or health services, and indeed had little direct involvement in this field.[9]

MEDICAL ANTHROPOLOGY: CONCEPTUAL DOMAINS AND MICRONESIAN PRAXIS

In the foregoing I have referred to medical and health-related anthropology research in Micronesia, but I have not tried to define medical anthropology as a conceptual domain. Definitions of medical anthropology are as slippery as definitions of anthropology generally. Few writers are in complete agreement on the conceptual outer limits or the shared central core of medical anthropology. Medical anthropologists claim as part of their domain aspects of physical anthropology and human evolution, human growth and maturity throughout the life cycle, disease ecology and history, diet and nutrition, population migration, demography, cultural ecology, culture and personality studies, mental health, drug and substance use, folk medicine, alternative medical systems, and medical and health care systems. In a book subtitled *Principles of Medical Anthropology in Melanesia,* Robert Pulsford and John Cawte (1972) even included chapters on "building an economy" and "building a nation."[10]

Indeed many writers have contended that medical anthropology is the overarching perspective that links the cultural and biological paradigms in anthropology and brings the subdisciplines back together (e.g., Brown and Inhorn 1990, 191; Foster and Anderson 1978, 1; McElroy and Townsend 1979, 7). Later in this chapter I comment more critically on the way that the discourse of medical anthropology has expanded to subsume ever-widening fields of work.

Here I take a more limited view, because embracing a broad definition of medical anthropology—for example, any anthropological study that bears on the totality of health and well-being—would engulf numerous anthropological subfields. Our division of labor in this volume has given other writers the tasks of discussing cultural ecology, ecological anthropology, culture and personality, psychological anthropology, and social problems such as suicide, substance abuse, and chronic mental illness (see Alkire, chap. 3; Black, chap. 7; and Hezel, chap. 9). My focus is on medical anthropology as a "bridge between the health sciences and anthropology" (McElroy and Townsend 1979, xvii). Specifically, I am concerned with anthropological work directly relevant to illness, disease, and health care in Micronesia. I discuss three areas of work within medical anthropology: the health aspects of diet and nutrition, anthropological contributions to specific disease studies, and the study of indigenous medicine and curing.

Diet and Nutrition

The researchers who studied problems of diet and nutrition immediately after the end of the war in Micronesia were not themselves anthropologists. While they worked closely with anthropologists, their focus excluded much of the wider cultural and social aspects of food production and exchange. Anthropologists on the other hand have described in depth the cultural meanings of food in Micronesia, the symbolic and social uses of food in kinship relations and exchange, and the importance of food in competitive feasting and island politics.[11] However, the attention to food has included rather little in regard to the interplay of food and health.

The main exception to this statement is Barbara Demory's (1976) study of the problem of poorly nourished children on Pohnpei. When Demory visited Pohnpei in 1973, the island had just experienced a "drastic increase in the number of children hospitalized for protein-calorie malnutrition" (1976, 7) and she chose her dissertation topic at the suggestion of several Pohnpei doctors. Her initial survey of a sample of households revealed that poor nourishment and borderline malnutrition were common, and that any infectious disease such as influenza could push a child below the borderline and cause malnourishment. She also collected medical data from hospital records for the preceding five years, showing that cases of kwashiorkor, one of the most severe forms of protein-calorie malnutrition, averaged more than eight per year. These clinically diagnosed cases represented, Demory surmised, only "the tip of the iceberg" (1976, 50–51). Her study was designed to answer the question, Why are many young children underfed and poorly nourished on an island which has fertile resources and a consistent production of horticultural surplus? (1976, 12–13).

Demory examined nutritional intake and the effects of sanitation, medical care, parents' education, and other cultural factors affecting children's welfare. She studied family life and organization, the allocation of food and land within households, and the problems inherent in autonomous, dispersed households. She also compared the household subsistence economy and the political prestige economy in the ways that they differently absorbed the time and energy of men. Her conclusions about the reasons for poor nourishment of children on Pohnpei pointed toward the political economy of the island society. Demory contended that "traditional politics . . . are the essence of Ponapean life, and mundane family matters, such as child feeding, must remain in second place as men strive to increase and to maintain their prestige" (1976, 152). Although Demory stopped short of considering some of the wider forces impinging on Pohnpei families, her study of child malnutrition is probably the most thorough analysis of the political economy of a health issue in Micronesia.[12]

Another anthropological study of the impact of diet on children's health in Micronesia is the work of Leslie and Mac Marshall, who looked specifically at the relationships between infant feeding and infant illness in Chuuk. Their findings suggest that serious and life-threatening illness is more common among bottle-fed than breast-fed children (L. Marshall and M. Marshall 1980, 37). Their work also provides a historical perspective on the factors that "have shaped the course of infant feeding practices" in the study community (L. Marshall and M. Marshall 1979, 248). This consideration of the historical dimension contributes to the literature on bottle-feeding, in which longitudinal studies are "notably absent" (1979, 241).

Nancy Pollock has written more generally on historical changes in food habits on Guam (1986), and on the health risks of dietary change and choice in the Marshall Islands (1973, 1975). In a wide-ranging historical review of food habits in the central and eastern Pacific, Pollock (1992) discussed symbolic and social aspects of food in a number of Pacific Islands societies, including Micronesia. She considered the relationship between food and indigenous concepts of health, and speculated that Pacific Islanders may have evolved distinctive metabolic adaptations after several millennia of eating root and tree starch foods. In particular, Pollock looked at westernized diet among urban Pacific Islanders as a factor in the increasing prevalence of obesity, diabetes, hypertension, and heart disease.

One other body of work that bears broadly on the issue of diet and health is the long-term study of alcohol use in Chuuk (and more widely in Oceania), also by Mac and Leslie Marshall (e.g., M. Marshall and L. Marshall 1975, 1976, 1990; M. Marshall 1979a, 1990a, 1990b, 1991a). In this volume, Francis X. Hezel (chap. 9) discusses some of this work from the perspective of a social problems approach, and here I will add only brief comments from the perspective of medical anthropology. What makes the Marshalls' contribution especially significant in this regard is the combination of insights from historical, ethnographic, political economy, and epidemiological data. The work is very nearly unique in producing two book-length studies of alcohol on a single Micronesian island over the course of a decade, and in reassessing earlier conclusions in light of later research. More recently, Mac Marshall (1993a) has addressed policy implications of his alcohol studies for Micronesian governments as he did earlier (1982) with his work on alcohol in Papua New Guinea. In the broader field of medical anthropology that examines the cross-cultural use of alcohol and other drugs, this series of publications has a prominent place (see, e.g., Bennett and Cook 1990).

A much smaller anthropological literature exists on the use of tobacco, marijuana, and other psychoactive substances in Micronesia. The primary focus of most anthropologists' attention has been on social and cultural aspects of tobacco and marijuana use (e.g., Black 1984; Carucci 1987; Larson 1987) rather than on health considerations. Within this literature, Mac Marshall's writings (e.g., 1987, 1993b) have been unusual in their explicit attention to public health aspects of substance use. Marshall (1981c, 1991b) has described regional epidemiological trends in cigarette smoking and chronic disease in Micronesia and in Oceania generally. More recently, he and coworkers have assessed the frequency of gasoline sniffing among youth in Chuuk while calling attention to the paucity of data on this topic and the need for further research (Marshall et al. 1994).

Studies of Specific Diseases

The disease ecology of Micronesia presents a distinct picture shaped by unique geographic and demographic factors, mainly: the small land mass and extreme isolation of islands; the susceptibility of atoll populations to the recurrent effects of devastating typhoons, tsunami, and droughts; the difficulty of subsistence within severe natural limits to available resources; and the history of contacts with outside agents. Leslie Marshall's (1993) summary of the disease ecologies of Australia and Oceania provides a useful comparative framework for viewing Micronesia's disease profile. During the past half century Micronesian island communities have suffered outbreaks of numerous infectious diseases, including dengue fever, influenza, leprosy, measles, rubella, yaws, hepatitis A and B, poliomyelitis, venereal diseases, gastroenteritis, cholera, dysentery, and toxoplasmosis. Some Micronesian populations have also experienced a high prevalence of chronic diabetes mellitus, obesity, hypertension, chronic obstructive pulmonary disease, chronic degenerative neurological disease, achromatopsia (a hereditary disorder of the retina), and the effects of nuclear radiation.

Knowledge of local population structure and cultural behaviors has frequently proved useful in elucidating a disease etiology, and consequently anthropology has a place in studies of disease etiology and epidemiology (for a particularly instructive example, see Lindenbaum 1979). In this section I review several anthropological contributions to understanding specific disease challenges in Micronesia, and assess the role of anthropology in these efforts.

The importance of islands as naturally occurring experiments in disease ecology is evident in a series of studies of toxoplasmosis infection in Micronesia, to which Leslie and Mac Marshall contributed while conducting dissertation fieldwork on Namoluk in 1970–1971. Earlier medical studies (G. Wallace

1969) had indicated a much higher prevalence of toxoplasmosis on Woleai and Ifaluk in association with cats and rats, than on Eauripik where cats and rats were absent. Namoluk Atoll, where *Toxoplasma* antibodies were found to be present in 77 percent of the population sampled in 1970 (Wallace et al. 1972), presented natural laboratory conditions for determining whether cats, rats, or both were involved in the human infection. Although it was not established that *Toxoplasma* was causing human disease on Namoluk, the parasite can cause extensive damage to the central nervous system and eyes, especially of infants (Wallace et al. 1972, 482; M. Marshall 1972b, 30). Among the several small, uninhabited islets of Namoluk Atoll, rats and feral cats lived on one islet, while another islet contained rats but no cats. The main islet had humans, cats, rats, pigs, and chickens. The Marshalls collaborated on a seroepidemiological study that revealed the *Toxoplasma* parasite to be endemic on the two islets where cats were present, and absent on the islet without cats. Detailed observations of eating habits and community sanitation on Namoluk indicated that cats were the essential reservoir of *Toxoplasma* parasites infecting humans (Marshall 1972b).

The explosive epidemic of leprosy among Kapingamarangi (hereafter Kapinga) people living in both Kapingamarangi Atoll and Porakiet village in Pohnpei is another example of the distinctive disease ecologies of island populations. Leprosy entered the Kapinga population in the mid-1960s through contact with Pingelapese, among whom the disease had been hyperendemic since 1918 when it was introduced from Nauru. By the end of 1982, histologically confirmed leprosy cases among the Kapinga reached an incidence of 12.5 percent (Worth et al. 1984, 740). The spread of infection among individuals showed distinctive patterns in the two Kapinga communities, one a remote atoll where people continue to support themselves by subsistence activities, and the other an urban enclave within the state capital of Pohnpei. Michael D. and Esther Lieber (1987) interviewed all the identified patients and analyzed their history of contacts with known carriers of lepromatous leprosy. Their analysis demonstrated that the differentiating pattern of infection "replicates in detail patterns of personal mobility by age and gender and patterns of kinship and friendship" characteristic of the two communities (Lieber and Lieber 1987, 479). They also mapped the genealogical connections among the one hundred thirty-six histologically positive individuals and revealed patterns of co-occurrence of infection or non-infection, independent of social interaction. Their findings suggest a genetic basis for susceptibility or resistance to leprosy.

One baffling fact emerged from the analysis of personal contacts: in a small number of cases of histologically positive individuals, "no personal contact whatever with any lepromatous person was reported" (Lieber and Lieber 1987, 474). The Liebers' analysis points to pandanus floor mats as the most likely medium of indirect transmission of leprosy among the Kapinga. Frayed mats expose the user to thousands of tiny fiber needles, and these fibers evidently can puncture the skin, release and hold live bacteria, and then inoculate other individuals. To date, however, the mat hypothesis has been only partly confirmed through laboratory tests performed on mats obtained from lepromatous patients from Pohnpei (M. Lieber, personal communication 1995).

Certainly the single disease entity in Micronesia receiving the most intensive and systematic study has been degenerative neurological disease. The extraordinary incidence of this disease in people of several Mariana Islands was reportedly "one of the most isolated, sustained, complex, intensely studied epidemics of human neurodegenerative disease in history" (Monmaney 1990, 86). A review of the voluminous literature chronicling the multiple competing medical hypotheses and protracted investigations of neurological disease on Guam is well beyond the scope of this chapter; I limit this assessment to the role of medical anthropology within studies of such disease on Guam.[13]

The Chamorros of southern Guam, where the prevalence of neurological disease is hyperendemic, recognized two separate disorders as long ago as the early 1800s (Monmaney 1990, 94, 99). One is a progressive muscular atrophy known locally as *paralytico* or simply *lytico*. The other involves "a relentlessly progressive dementia" including memory deficit, difficulty with comprehension, and personality change (Rodgers-Johnson et al. 1986, 8). Chamorros refer to this disorder as *bodig*, after an afflicted man who ran a bodega, or as *rayput*, meaning 'laziness,' because sufferers tend toward depression and inactivity (Monmaney 1990, 89).

Although *lytico* was noted on death certificates in Guam as early as 1902 (Monmaney 1990, 88), the diagnosis "amyotrophic lateral sclerosis" (ALS) did not appear until 1931 (Garruto and Yanagihara 1991, 259). ALS is a fatal neuromuscular disease popularly known as Lou Gehrig's Disease. Worldwide it is found in low incidence, but navy physicians on Guam in the mid to late 1940s found that it occurred with an extraordinarily high frequency. Village epidemiological surveys discovered an incidence rate "50 to 100 times higher than that of the continental United States" (Garruto and Gajdusek 1984, 78). The initial publications describing this phenomenon appeared in the early 1950s (Koerner 1952; Arnold et al. 1953) and within a year, the first of a long succession of researchers arrived on Guam to tackle "the Guam riddle" (Monmaney 1990, 92).

Recognizing that Guam might hold the answer to ALS, the National Institutes of Health (NIH) established a clinic and research laboratory on Guam in 1956 and maintained it for three decades. Within the first five years, researchers discovered the high incidence of a second uniformly fatal neurological disease *(bodig),* a sort of dementia associated with a parkinsonism-like movement condition, which they labeled "parkinsonism-dementia complex" (PD) (Hirano, Kurland, Krooth, and Lessell 1961; Hirano, Malamud, and Kurland 1961). The two disorders occurred in high incidence among Chamorros both in southern Guam and on Rota but not on other Mariana Islands, and often co-occurred within the same sibling set and even within the same individual (Garruto and Gajdusek 1984, 78).

Studies in the 1950s and 1960s conclusively ruled out a genetic etiology or infectious agents as explanations for Guam's neurological diseases (Garruto and Yanagihara 1991, 262). As researchers concentrated on locating an environmental cause, anthropological studies of changes in Chamorro diet, food preparation practices, and interaction with the environment took on special relevance. Marjorie Whiting, a nutritionist who had conducted fieldwork on Pohnpei with her anthropologist-husband, spent a month in Umatac village as an ethnographer of Chamorro diet, medical remedies, and food practices. She was the first researcher to advance the hypothesis that cycad seeds might be the source of a neurotoxin causing the extraordinary incidence of ALS and PD (Monmaney 1990, 92; Whiting 1963). More recently, Jane Underwood (1992) analyzed seasonality in Guam births during the period 1945–1984 and found that Chamorro ALS and PD victims showed characteristic patterns of birth seasonality, which also differed from the pattern of the Guam population generally. The distinctive pattern of birth seasonality among disease victims corresponded with rainfall patterns that affect the population dynamics of potential insect vectors. Underwood's work thus indicates a probable role of an insect-borne virus in the complex etiology of this disease.

Ralph Garruto, a physical anthropologist also associated with the National Institutes of Health, has been a major proponent of an alternative hypothesis, developed by D. Carleton Gajdusek, chief scientist of the Laboratory of Central Nervous System Studies where Garruto has worked since the late 1970s. In over forty scientific papers published alone and with colleagues, Garruto has presented evidence supporting the hypothesis that Guam ALS-PD (and identical neurodegenerative disorders in isolated populations in Japan and West

New Guinea) is associated with an environmental deficiency of calcium and magnesium in garden soil and drinking water (see, for example, Garruto, Gajdusek, and Chen 1980; Garruto 1981, 1985, 1987, 1991; Garruto and Gajdusek 1984, 1985; Garruto, Yanagihara, and Gajdusek 1985; Garruto and Yanagihara 1991). According to this hypothesis, the low concentrations of these essential minerals provoke a defect in mineral metabolism in affected individuals that results in excessive deposition of calcium and aluminum and consequent cumulative damage to nerve tissue.

Garruto and his colleagues have monitored the postwar epidemiological decline of neurodegenerative disorders among Chamorros on Guam and they have proposed that the disappearance of high-incidence ALS and PD is "a consequence of increased acculturation and westernization, decreased isolation, known changes in dietary habits and local water supplies, and much less dependence on locally grown food" (Garruto, Yanagihara, and Gajdusek 1985, 196). They also conducted studies of ALS and PD in migrants and found that Chamorro migrants from Guam to the United States have an increased risk of developing the disease, and that long-term Filipino migrants to Guam have a similar increased risk after about two decades' residence on Guam (Garruto and Gajdusek 1984, 79–80). Although a conclusive answer to "the Guam riddle" has continued to elude researchers, the incidence of ALS on Guam has decreased to perhaps a hundredth of what it was.

Garruto's work has added an important chapter to knowledge of the subtle and complex links among environment, nutrition, and disease. Also, biomedical scientists have come to recognize the unique opportunities that places like Micronesia offer for studying disease etiology. Garruto has pointed out that occurrences of focal, endemic diseases in island populations and similarly isolated, homogeneous human groups are "important paradigms for solving etiological and epidemiological problems of widespread medical significance, with an ultimate goal towards treatment and prevention" (1991, 347; see also Garruto 1981). These studies have special significance to medical anthropology because they demonstrate "the necessity to integrate field and laboratory research in such a way that their complementarity and cross-fertilization result in the further refinement of our understanding of the disease process" (Garruto 1991, 367).

A review of anthropological contributions to specific disease studies in Micronesia suggests, however, that the integration of anthropological fieldwork and biomedical laboratory research has not occurred widely. The Marshalls' work on toxoplasmosis in Chuuk and the Liebers' work on leprosy in

Pohnpei appear as instances of a generally infrequent collaboration between university-based medical anthropologists and laboratory-based biomedical researchers on specific disease entities in Micronesia. In both projects the anthropologists contributed to hypothesis design and testing, in addition to providing local logistic support for collection of biomedical samples. However, the collaborations were episodic and did not produce continued cooperation between anthropologists and representatives of biomedicine.

I now turn to another topic, the study of nonwestern theories of medicine and ways of treating disease. Ethnographers have had a long-standing interest in what used to be called "primitive medicine." Medical anthropologists have "recaptured" this interest, given it the name "ethnomedicine" and made it a part of their specialty (Foster and Anderson 1978, 6).

Ethnomedical Studies in Micronesia

During the first twenty-five years of American anthropology in Micronesia, indigenous medicine received scant attention. Laura Thompson included a brief discussion of Chamorro healers and indigenous medicine in her classic ethnography of Guam (1947, 197–203). An article by Saul Riesenberg (1948) briefly described how Pohnpei medicines are acquired and administered, discussed sorcery and supernatural causes of disease, and listed about forty Pohnpei disease entities and their treatments. John "Jack" Fischer collected extensive field notes on medicine in both Chuuk and Pohnpei, according to Mahony (1970, 18), but very little was published (see Fischer 1970b, 219–227). Mac Marshall (1975a) noted the medical use of vascular plants, where known, in his study of the natural history of Namoluk Atoll. It is likely that many other anthropological field-workers in Micronesia collected notes on medical plants and treatments (e.g., Black 1968) but did not publish this material. Fischer made brief mention of Chuuk medicines in an article on totemism (Fischer 1957b), and he offered the suggestion that the reportedly high incidence of asthmatic attacks on Pohnpei could be psychosomatic reactions to violations of totemic food taboos (Fischer, Fischer, and Mahony 1959).

The 1970s saw the completion of two doctoral research projects that stand as the centerpieces of ethnomedical studies in Micronesia. Both projects, Frank Mahony's study in Chuuk and Roger Ward's on Pohnpei, are comprehensive examinations of Micronesian understandings of medicine, illness, and treatment.

Mahony's (1970) study of Chuuk medicine was the first attempt to understand how a Micronesian medical system is conceptually organized, and how this system functions within its society. Mahony had served nearly ten years as a district anthropologist in Micronesia, mainly in Truk District, beginning in 1950. Having witnessed a decade of significant cultural change—the universal conversion to Christianity, the incursion of a money economy, and new social and political forms—he was struck by the "remarkable vitality" of Chuuk medicine (1970, 10). For Mahony, this theory of medicine was a piece of culture that had come through the mill of change nearly intact. He believed that it was one of the "pure products" (Clifford 1988, 1) that could give him an opening into understanding Chuuk thought and the functioning of Chuuk society.

One of Mahony's professors at Stanford was Charles Frake, whose formative 1961 article on disease diagnosis among a Filipino Muslim group had stimulated a tide of interest in cognitive anthropology. Much of Mahony's interest was in revealing the underlying cognitive structure of Chuuk diagnosis and medical formulae. In this effort Mahony was one of the many graduate student field-workers in anthropology in the 1960s who went searching for neat taxonomic hierarchies and found apparently much messier and more tangled cognitive systems than their mentors had described. Mahony's dissertation is a richly detailed description of 'spirit-powers' as the conceptual units around which the Chuuk theory of medicine is organized. Each 'spirit power' has a particular medicine, or set of medical formulae, associated with it. These formulae are conceptual packages that include medical ingredients, medical techniques, and proscriptions against particular activities.

A second thrust of Mahony's work is a functional explanation of how Chuuk medical theory serves to maintain social control. The core of the theory is that improper social conduct angers the spirits, and "illness results when bad spirits, or good spirits who have been annoyed or angered, gain ascendancy over an individual" (Mahony 1970, 224). One group of spirits, for example, is "concerned with restraining, controlling and channeling the behavior and activities of women, either by threats to their own health, or to the health of their children. The spirits seem to be supporting established social authority which, of course, has always been in the hands of men" (1970, 246). Another group of spirits function to safeguard the "security of village and garden boundaries," while yet another group punishes people for taking advantage of others' hospitality (1970, 249–250).

In this line of analysis, Mahony's theoretical forebears are much more distant than the 1960s new wave of cognitive anthropologists who informed the first part of Mahony's work. This line of thought dates back to early function-alist arguments in anthropology, at least to the time of the anthropologist-physician W. H. R. Rivers who worked in Melanesia at the turn of the century. Rivers was perhaps the first "medical anthropologist" who was interested in sickness as a punishment by spirits for breaking social norms (Rivers 1924; Rubel and Hass 1990, 117). Other anthropologists working in Micronesia had also explored the linkages between supernatural sanctions, illness, and social control (e.g., Lessa 1956, 1962b; Schneider 1957b; Spiro 1952).

This functionalist interpretation of Chuuk spirit-medicine led Mahony to some interesting conclusions. He noted: "In view of the fact that missionaries are actively suppressing Trukese medical theory and they and others are dis-couraging Trukese from resorting to it, an increase in social disorder would seem to be a logical consequence.... Since medical theory has been under attack in Truk for over a generation, it is not surprising that lawlessness seems to be on the increase and to present a more serious problem than anywhere else in the United States Trust Territory" (1970, 263).

A second conclusion concerned a contrast between the functions of Chuuk and Pohnpei medicine. The Pohnpei medical system appears roughly similar to that of Chuuk. Sorcery is an important cause of illness in both societies. But on Pohnpei, Mahony argued, illness is interpreted as punishment for offenses against men in high-ranking positions. Pohnpei medical theory about supernatural sanctions, according to Mahony, does not function in everyday social settings as it does in Chuuk (1970, 254–255). He attributed this differ-ence to the contrast in political authority in the two societies. Pohnpei is orga-nized hierarchically, with lines of ranked and graded titles, and chiefs who exercise considerable judicial authority, while chiefs in Chuuk have very little political or judicial authority. This "controlled comparison" between the two medical systems lends support to Mahony's functionalist thesis that medicine works for social control, that "medicine is the law" (cf. Cawte 1974). As a gen-eral theory, Mahony suggested that "where superordinate controls are strong, as on Ponape, illness may be viewed as punishment for offenses against offi-cials of high status, but medical theory does not have significant functions in the control of ordinary behavior. Where superordinate controls are weak, as on Truk, illness may be regarded as punishment for all sorts of anti-social behavior, and consequently all medical theory has important functions in social control" (1970, 262–263).

Mahony's contribution to the medical anthropology of Micronesia was significant. Not only was this the first thorough description of a Micronesian medical system, but it was also an attempt to explain how Chuuk 'spirit-powers' provide the conceptual underpinning of the system, and how this theory of spirit powers functions sociologically as a means of social control. On the other hand, Mahony's work has little to say of practical value for public health or medical work in Micronesia. A careful reading of Mahony's dissertation might reveal some knowledge of use to biomedical practice in Chuuk, but this was certainly not Mahony's focus or intention, although in his earlier incarnation as a district anthropologist in Micronesia he had written and lectured about the practical contributions of anthropology to public health (Mahony 1959). Mahony sought to analyze Chuuk medicine primarily in terms of moral causes and cognitive structures, and his study of Chuuk medicine thus suffers from a weakness of ethnomedical studies generally: an orientation that privileges indigenous theories of magic and the psychological effects of spirit beliefs, over empirical diagnosis and the efficacy of treatment (Fortes 1976, xiv–xv; Rubel and Hass 1990, 119).

Mahony's ideas about the function of medical systems in maintaining social control invited a cross-cultural comparison of Micronesian systems, especially between Chuuk and Pohnpei. Fortunately, within several years, Roger Ward's (1977) dissertation on curing on Pohnpei appeared. It not only provided an opportunity to reassess Mahony's hypothesis about medical theory and social control, but it considerably extended the scope of inquiry. Writing nearly a decade after Mahony, Ward also had the advantage of a growing literature in medical anthropology.[14] Like Mahony, Ward was interested in how "medical behaviors and ideas form a system" of interrelated components (1977, 28). His contribution was to explain something of the process and actual operation of a Micronesian medical theory, and not only the cognitive structure of the theory.

Ward organized his explanation of Pohnpei medicine around a general framework of the "illness episode." He first described the Pohnpei classification of illnesses, and here a significant difference appears between Pohnpei and Chuuk. In Chuuk medicine, 'spirit-powers' seem to underlie all sickness, while on Pohnpei a clear division is understood between 'sicknesses of the body' which have natural or somatic causes, and 'bad sickness' which has a supernatural basis (1977, 56). Chuuk medical theory appears conceptually more unified according to this comparison. Ward found three distinct categories of Pohnpei illness: "spirit sickness, sorcery, and a large number of conditions attributed to neither spirits nor sorcery . . . called 'bodily' or true sickness, meaning that they are physical in origin" (1977, 104).

Ward's dissertation follows the course of an idealized illness episode on Pohnpei, exploring the process of diagnosis, how curers interpret symptoms and signs of illness, principles and procedures of therapy, the economics of medicine payments, and how medical knowledge is acquired and transmitted. He provided what may be the only ethnographic description of a sort of Micronesian psychotherapy, which is designed to calm the emotions in someone suffering from 'feeling bad sickness,' an emotional illness that resembles depression, is associated typically with marital difficulties, and is more prevalent in women (1977, 140–144).

Ward also offered an explanation, more nuanced than Mahony's, of the relationship between medical theory and social control. Ward argued first of all that a large part of Pohnpei medical theory is "not at all concerned with behavior" but rather with correct identification and effective treatment of medical conditions (1977, 238–239). The system is empirical-experimental and oriented toward outcomes, rather than moral-behavioral and oriented toward causation. Mahony had claimed that Chuuk medicine is concerned with everyday interpersonal relations while Pohnpei medicine fixes on hierarchic relations. Ward suggested otherwise: medical spirits are equal opportunity employers, they "do not discriminate on the basis of social position." Rather, medical theory in the two societies simply reflects the situation that on Pohnpei "vertical interactions are more frequent and more important than horizontal," while on Chuuk "the most important relationships . . . are egalitarian" (1977, 249).

The question of how a Micronesian medical system changes in response to outside pressure also received different treatment in the hands of these two anthropologists. Mahony's theoretical perspective from structural-functionalism was troubled by change. If "medicine is the law," as Mahony held, then as Chuuk medicine weakens, lawlessness is bound to increase. Ward's perspective was more flexible, and he showed how Pohnpei medicine had been able to incorporate Western medicine into its own diagnostic and therapeutic process. Pohnpei medicine was also in the process of expanding the domain of 'real' sickness and reinterpreting the supernatural sphere under the influence of Christianity, modern medicine, and the elimination of the scourges of yaws and filariasis since the end of the Pacific War (Ward 1977, 260–261). Ward found that "despite technological, social, and religious change, medical belief and much of medical practice in modern Ponape is still predominantly Ponapean" (1977, 280).

These two dissertations have been discussed at length here because both are substantial studies, provide extensive descriptions, and raise provocative theoretical questions about how ethnomedical systems are conceptually organized and function. However, their impact on either Micronesia or medical anthropology generally has been nil. Regrettably, neither Mahony nor Ward published any of the material from their dissertations, so their work is virtually unknown. Not surprising, there are no citations of their work in recent textbooks and edited collections in medical anthropology (e.g., Johnson and Sargent 1990; McElroy and Townsend 1989; Romanucci-Ross et al. 1991).

Mahony's and Ward's dissertations appeared during a period of anthropological fascination with ethnoscience generally, and with ethnomedical studies in particular. At this same time, several students at the University of Guam were conducting studies on traditional Chamorro curers. The most comprehensive of these is Patrick McMakin's (1975) master's thesis, later published as a long article (McMakin 1978). McMakin also produced a guide to medicinal plants on Guam (McMakin and Moore 1977; see also A. Moore 1974). Like Mahony, McMakin viewed traditional healing as the "most intact survival of a [precontact Chamorro] cultural activity" and he viewed traditional curers as "living representatives of a past way of life" (1978, 14). His descriptive case study of the medical practice and philosophy of a small sample of Chamorro curers centers around one elderly man whom McMakin described as a master curer and mystic personality. McMakin concluded that an underlying similarity is apparent in the medical system of this master curer and those of several other curers whom he interviewed on both Guam and Rota. Because the curers were not acquainted with each other and had not learned from a common instructor, McMakin argued that the "basic [ethnomedical] approach has been passed down intact from precontact times with only minor innovations" (1978, 59). McMakin based his conclusion on a common set of five general components of treatment, but he did not examine the conceptual underpinnings of the system to the extent that Mahony and Ward did. His concern with showing Chamorro indigenous curing to be a survival of ancient culture elided, in the same way as did Mahony's work, issues of change in the conceptual structure and practice of indigenous medicine. McMakin's research has provided a foundation for continuing studies of indigenous curing on Guam, such as Ann Marie Pobutsky's (1982, 1983) papers on women healers of Guam (complementing McMakin's emphasis on male healers), and a more recent article by Ann Workman, Linda Cruz-Ortiz, and Debbie Kaminga-Quinata (1994).

In a 1982 paper on the traditional classification and treatment of illness on

Woleai and Lamotrek, William Alkire focused on the conceptual principles underlying Micronesian ethnomedical practices. He demonstrated how these practices are organized around dualistic and quadripartite divisions and combinations: medicines and other prophylactic techniques require four-day regimens, medical formulae typically involve pairs of ingredients, and so forth (1982, 31, 37). Because the dual opposition of land and sea also underlies disease classification and treatment, "illnesses that have their origin on land are treated with medicines concocted from interior ingredients" and vice versa (1982, 40). In elucidating the conceptual associations that organize indigenous medical classification and treatment, Alkire has contributed to a further understanding of Micronesian systems of logic, building on his earlier work on systems of measurement (1970) and conceptions of social order (1972b).

These studies of Micronesian ethnomedical systems coincided with a rapidly expanding interest in medical anthropology within American anthropology. Ward submitted his dissertation in 1977, the same year that David Landy published his influential reader in medical anthropology. During the preceding year two major collections of medical anthropology papers had appeared based on anthropological conferences, one international (Grollig and Haley 1976) and one British (Loudon 1976). During the two years following Ward's dissertation, four more textbooks on medical anthropology were published in the United States (Foster and Anderson 1978; Logan and Hunt 1978; Todd and Ruffini 1979; McElroy and Townsend 1979). Clearly, medical anthropology was happening. In Micronesia, however, interest in medical anthropology declined after the 1970s. In particular, few anthropologists working in Micronesia gave much attention to issues of health status, health transition, or health services. The basic question is: Why was medical anthropology virtually ignored in Micronesia when it was growing elsewhere in American anthropology? The answer may be found in the institutional history and politics of medical anthropology.

FROM APPLIED TO MEDICAL ANTHROPOLOGY

As Robert C. Kiste and Suzanne Falgout point out (chap. 1), applied anthropology was in its infancy when the vanguard of American anthropologists entered Micronesia in 1946, and medical anthropology did not exist. Indeed, the Society for Applied Anthropology had been founded at Harvard only five years earlier, on the eve of the Pacific War (Partridge and Eddy 1978, 32). However, from its very beginning, applied anthropology claimed an interest in the area of health, especially in the international public health programs and the studies of American food habits that took place as part of the war effort. Anthropologists joined the efforts of the Institute of Inter-American Affairs in 1942 and the Institute of Social Anthropology in 1943, both targeted at public health problems in Latin America (Foster 1969, 23–25). Ten years later, the engagement of applied anthropology and public health led to the conception of a medical anthropology, which was foreshadowed in William Caudill's seminal article entitled "Applied Anthropology in Medicine" in 1953. The nascent field was not christened as "medical anthropology" until 1963.[15] The official birth of the field occurred in 1967 when the Steering Committee for the Organization of Medical Anthropology was formed at the annual meeting of the Society for Applied Anthropology. In its early years the organization pushed to achieve full professional status, and by 1972 it came of age as a legally incorporated society within the American Anthropological Association.[16]

What was at stake in the establishment of medical anthropology as a separate professional entity? Of what relevance was this to anthropology in Micronesia? The stakes were the two most precious academic commodities: employment and research funds. By the late 1960s, it seemed evident that anthropology was losing major ground in the competition for funding. For example, between 1958 and 1969 anthropology slipped from 53 percent to 22 percent of the social science budget of the National Science Foundation (NSF) (Larsen 1992, 64). Sociology had become a prime competitor, and in the area of medicine and health, sociology had already gotten a jump on anthropology. A Committee on Medical Sociology had been organized in 1955 and was formally recognized by the American Sociological Association in 1959, more than a decade before the Society for Medical Anthropology came into official existence (Olesen 1978, 13).

The 1960s were golden years for the social sciences in American universities, and anthropology departments expanded everywhere.[17] By the end of the decade, however, it was becoming distressingly clear that the academic job market was not expanding as quickly as the number of academic job seekers. By the mid-1970s the job market had begun to shrink dramatically, and estimates predicted that only about one-third of new PhDs in anthropology would find traditional employment in academia (D'Andrade et al. 1975). At the same time, and partly due to the social upheavals of the 1960s, there was a national shift toward applied social science (Larsen 1992, 70). Both factors shaped the direction of anthropology. Medical anthropology provided an avenue for anthropologists to become more marketable in new types of positions in the health professions (Nurge 1978, 388; Chrisman and Johnson 1990, 94).[18] Such employment for medical anthropologists meant a turn away from more traditional anthropological turf such as Micronesia. Since the late 1970s medical anthropology has attracted only a very few graduate students to Micronesia, despite the enormous professional growth of medical anthropology in the United States and the enormous growth of the health industry in Micronesia.

A few anthropologists, myself included, with established interests in Micronesia have made a professional shift toward more health-related research topics, such as suicide or alcohol. The shift was motivated partly by research opportunities within the broad field of health that enabled us to find fundable and practical projects and to remain involved in Micronesian anthropology. Mac Marshall exemplifies this shift and has in part attributed his turning point as an "alcohologist" to new research opportunities in an area of likely future growth (1990b, 363). Similar considerations led to my own turn toward health-related research on adolescent suicide in Micronesia and my "recredentialing" via the master's degree in public health (MPH). Juliana Flinn is also among the small cadre of anthropologists who hold a master's in public health. In the anthropological literature on Micronesian emigration, Flinn's 1987 article appears to be the only one that deals with medical and health issues. This article describes aspects of the support networks and coping strategies of Pulap women in the United States.

Very few anthropologists since about 1977, however, have looked at Micronesian traditional medicine, American-style medical services, disease, or the health effects of urbanization and changing life style, despite the many reports that identify "problem areas" and call for study (e.g., Coyne 1984; Thaman 1985).[19] Among the more urgent public health problems in Micronesia are the very high rates of infant mortality from perinatal infection, and the increasing prevalence of malnourished children in urban areas (FSM 1989; Kent 1992; Palafox 1991; RMI 1990, 1991; Taylor et al. 1989). In the Marshall Islands, the reduction of infant and child morbidity and mortality has been declared as the primary national health goal (RMI 1984, 21). The governments of both the Republic of the Marshall Islands and the Federated States of Micronesia have also identified the problem of tremendous population growth as a priority health issue (RMI 1984, 43–44; FSM 1991, 216–219). Yet the whole complex of child survival and the management of population growth remains unexamined in recent years by anthropologists in Micronesia. It is ironic that anthropologists who focused on matters of population and diet and nutrition when they first entered Micronesia in the immediate postwar years now overlook related issues even when island governments have declared them as concerns of the highest priority.

Graduate students in medical anthropology today look elsewhere than Micronesia, and I believe this trend will continue, as a matter of career opportunities, institutional support, and research funding. If a new graduate student wants to study, for example, the interplay of culture and chronic illness within a particular group of people, the student would be better advised for the sake of future employment to do fieldwork in Honolulu or Philadelphia than in Chuuk or Majuro.

NEW PLAYERS, BIGGER STAKES

To bring this discussion to a close, I want to direct attention back to the course of American-style medical services development and health research in Micronesia. My point here is that while anthropology was disengaging from the area of medicine in Micronesia, Micronesian health services were becoming a major growth industry, increasingly coupled to the US national health system, and other institutional players were staking an effective research interest in this area.

As discussed above, the development of Micronesian medical services along American organizational lines was set in motion under the US Naval administration. The USTTPI administration generally stayed the course of American-style development, though meager funding during the first decade or so meant slow growth. The developmental course was largely aimed at a health care system anchored to centralized hospital-based "high-tech" curative medicine rather than preventive medicine and a system of dispersed primary health care stations. As funding increased in the late 1960s, departments within the US federal government actually competed for control of the USTTPI Health Services: the Department of Health, Education, and Welfare sought to transfer this "prize" away from Interior.[20]

Increasing funds led to expanding health services, additional medical professionals working in Micronesia, and wider horizons for action. During this period the USTTPI Health Services Department sought to attract health research projects to work in Micronesia. A 1968 report by the USTTPI Health Services director states that "universities are now being invited to engage in worthy [health] research activities within the Territory" and the report mentions several projects then underway or planned by the US Communicable Disease Center (now called the Centers for Disease Control and Prevention), the School of Public Health at the University of California at Berkeley, the School of Public Health at the University of North Carolina, and the School of Public Health and Tropical Diseases at Tulane University (Peck 1968, 11).[21] Shortly thereafter, a group of researchers from the University of North Carolina conducted a study of the relationship between cardiovascular disease and modern lifestyle on Pohnpei, assisted by anthropologists Jack Fischer, Martha Ward, and Roger Ward (see M. Ward 1989 for an informal discussion of this project; evidently the research results were never published formally).

Even as the US Trust Territory of the Pacific Islands began to wind down in the late 1970s, American health planning legislation was extended to Micronesia and helped to ensure that post-territorial health development would conform to US organizational assumptions.[22] By the early 1980s a conglomeration of federal and international programs was available to the Micronesian governments, and some two hundred fifty of these programs, contracts, and grants were health-related (University of Hawai'i 1984). Many were carried out by health-profession schools in American universities. These linkages between Micronesian health services and American universities or federal agencies increasingly shaped health research priorities and opportunities in Micronesia. The system is one in which contracts and programs are commodities linking provider-bureaucracies in the United States with consumer-bureaucracies in Micronesia. Setting aside the larger question of who controls the resources, the trade serves the purposes of parties on both sides.[23]

The one university which by far has positioned itself most effectively within this system is the University of Hawai'i. During the past thirty years an estimated $40 million of grants and contracts for health-related research and training in the US-affiliated Pacific Islands has passed through the University of Hawai'i, funding a range of activities from the development of the Micronesian Peace Corps Health Syllabus to evaluation research on health services. Perhaps over 95 percent of all American university-based health research and training projects for Micronesia have been carried out at the University of Hawai'i, through its schools of medicine, nursing, and public health.[24] While the dominant position of the University of Hawai'i within this system reflects the technical capacity that it has established to provide these services, it also reflects the health professional schools' close relationship with congressional leaders and policy makers in Washington (and at the US Public Health Service [USPHS] Region IX office in San Francisco) on the one hand, and with the health service leadership in Micronesia on the other.[25]

I have described this system because it illustrates the sorts of political relations and institutional interests that have supported a major stake in Micronesian health services by a university-based public health department during the past twenty or thirty years. Had there been an effective application of medical anthropology within Micronesia during this period, it would likely have taken similar institutional shape, and would have involved the integration of medical anthropologists with other university-based and Micronesia-based health professionals working in partnership with the health services leadership in Micronesia. One might easily imagine such a collaboration having developed between the University of Hawai'i Department of Anthropology, which has had a major interest in medical anthropology, and the University of Hawai'i health professional schools, which have been big players in Micronesia. That these institutions never found common ground for mutual stakes in Micronesia is certainly a missed opportunity for medical anthropology.

Medical anthropology grew out of the cross-fertilization of anthropology and public health, both of which have had sizable stakes in Micronesia. Yet medical anthropology itself has covered little ground and has garnered little attention from health care providers in the islands. As American anthropology enters its second half-century in Micronesia, this situation seems unlikely to change.

NOTES

I am grateful to Maxine Becker for providing me with references and reprints from the Micronesian Health Archives, University of Guam College of Nursing and Allied Health; to Suzanne Falgout for bringing to my attention material from the Trust Territory Archives; to Karen Peacock for assistance in locating materials in the Pacific Collection, University of Hawai'i at Manoa; and to Roylinne Wada for providing information from the School of Public Health, University of Hawai'i. Usha Prasad and the editors of this volume provided useful suggestions on an earlier draft of this chapter.

The opening quotation for this chapter is from a medical manual designed as a practical primer for American health care providers and health educators working in Micronesia. William Peck MD, MPH, a longtime resident of Micronesia, first began his medical work on Guam in 1950, and served as director of public health on Guam and, beginning in June 1967, as director of health services for the US Trust Territory of the Pacific Islands. He lived on Tonowas Island in Chuuk Lagoon from 1972 to 1975, and during those years he organized and ran the MEDEX training program under the auspices of the University of Hawai'i. The quotation is excerpted from a lengthy section in which Peck advised American health workers in Micronesia to be guided by their own sensitivity and an open-minded approach, rather than attempt to glean from anthropological writings a set of cultural rules for appropriate conduct in Micronesia.

1. This chapter focuses on Guam and the islands of the former US Trust Territory of the Pacific Islands.

2. Useful summaries of the development of government medical services in Micronesia under Spanish, German, and Japanese colonial administrations are found in the military government and civil affairs handbooks (US Navy 1943, 73–74; US Navy 1944a, 109–111; US Navy 1944b, 97–98).

3. This central concern with the effects that diseases found in Micronesia might have on American military personnel is evident in the way the War Department categorized medical data from the islands: "Diseases of special military importance; Diseases of potential military importance; Serious diseases of nonmilitary importance but likely to affect small numbers of troops; Diseases causing high mortality rates among native populations; Miscellaneous communicable diseases" (US Army 1944, 10–16).

4. The notion that islanders were dying of malaise and needed the influence of an American missionary or doctor to give them a "new zest for living" was the theme of a popular postwar novel set in Ulithi (Divine 1950). The novel was rather loosely based on the "true story of wartime experiences" coauthored by a navy dermatologist and a navy chaplain stationed in Ulithi (Wees and Thornton 1950).

5. As with other members of the CIMA team, Joseph and Murray had been well briefed by anthropologists Peter H. Buck, Kenneth P. Emory, Felix Keesing, and Leonard E. Mason. Joseph, in addition, had previous fieldwork experience in Native American communities, had coauthored with Laura Thompson a book on the Hopi (Thompson and Joseph 1944), and had coauthored a book on the Papago (Joseph et al. 1949).

6. Nicholas Thomas' analysis of the creation of state power in early colonial Fiji is helpful in understanding how US naval authorities justified their administrative rule in postwar Micronesia. In Fiji, "the links between many features of native behaviour and the problem of depopulation potentially sanctioned administrative intervention in numerous aspects of indigenous life" (N. Thomas 1990, 156).

7. The name of the school was changed to the School of Medical Assistants on April 23, 1948 (US Naval Medical Center 1949). During the first semester students were required to take basic English, American geography, American history and government, and the history of "old Europe." Science and laboratory classes began in the second semester.

8. The view persists that island "cultures" are all more or less equivalent across Oceania in regard to the way they trouble Western medicine. See, for example, the University of Hawai'i *Medical Manual for the Pacific Islands* (Tabrah 1982). Micronesia serves to typify Oceania, and "culture" falls within the section "Problems Relating to Medical Care."

9. The literature from applied anthropology and personal accounts by anthropologists who were in Micronesia during this period make almost no mention of medical or health-related work (e.g., Fischer 1979; Gladwin 1950; Hall 1950a, 1950b, 1992; Keesing 1949; Macgregor 1955; Mason 1953; Spoehr 1951; Useem 1947). Homer G. Barnett (1956, 103, 137) gave examples, perhaps hypothetical, of anthropological assignments from this period: surveying community attitudes toward island health aides, or advising the government on how to overcome community resistance to vaccinations. Meeting together in Koror in 1957, district anthropologists pondered problems such as how to collect patient fees for health aide salaries, and how to bring women into medical care roles.

10. See also Hasan 1978 as an example of wide conceptual claims in medical anthropology. Although earlier formulations made claims for a "strong common core" within general medical anthropology (Todd and Ruffini 1979, 9), as the field has grown the problem of the "core" has vexed efforts at developing a common curriculum for graduate programs in medical anthropology. See, for example, Stephen Schensul's 1993 proposal and responses to it (Dressler et al. 1993; Gilbert 1993).

11. Barnett was one of the first anthropologists in Micronesia to point out the "mystic and semi-sacred quality" of food as a form of communion between people (1949, 56). See also the more extended treatments by Paul Dahlquist (1972), Nancy Pollock (1970), Craig Severance (1976), and Peter Steager (1972).

12. "Political economy in medical anthropology" and "critical medical anthropology" have since emerged as labels of a conceptual paradigm toward which Demory's work points. See, for example, Morsy 1990 and Singer 1986. Unfortunately, Demory never published her research findings (they exist only in the form of her doctoral dissertation), so her work is almost unknown to anyone other than Micronesian area specialists. One of the wider forces that Demory failed to consider is the twentieth century history of the relocation of Micronesian communities under colonial administration. The community that Demory sampled is comprised of many non–Pohnpei Islanders who were relocated to Pohnpei, and who thus were disadvantaged in their access to choice garden land (Glenn Petersen, personal communication 1993).

13. The National Institutes of Health published a bibliography of ALS-PD of Guam (Garruto et al. 1983). Monmaney 1990 gives a useful account of competing research hypotheses and results.

14. At the time that Mahony was writing his dissertation, there were no textbooks in medical anthropology, and only a few review articles addressed the newly named subfield (e.g., Scotch 1963). Mahony's readings were mainly in the anthropology of magic, witchcraft, and sorcery. The only citation of "medical anthropology" in Mahony's dissertation is Alland 1966.

15. George Foster and Barbara Anderson summarized the early publications that served to define the new field of medical anthropology during the decade 1953–1963 (1978, 3): Caudill's 1953 survey of the emerging interest of applied anthropology in the

health field; Norman Scotch's 1963 major survey article "Medical Anthropology"; and Benjamin Paul's 1963 discussion of "medical anthropologists" in an article entitled "Anthropological Perspectives on Medicine and Public Health."

16. See the *Medical Anthropology Newsletter,* published irregularly beginning in October 1968, for accounts of early efforts at institutionalizing and professionalizing medical anthropology, and establishing its separate identity from applied anthropology.

17. NSF funding levels in social science give an indication of the extraordinary growth of the social science "industry" in the 1960s. During the 1960s NSF social science funding increased 625 percent, compared with a 250 percent increase in the 1970s, and a less than 10 percent increase in the 1980s (Larsen 1992, 24).

18. Discursive claims in medical anthropology also expanded in the 1970s and proponents of medical anthropology subsumed an ever-widening domain of topics and perspectives. A countervailing discursive movement developed in the 1980s as practitioners of "clinically applied medical anthropology" sought to reclaim a core ground of biomedically relevant work within the increasingly fragmented and broadening field of medical anthropology. Tension continues between proponents of the biocultural paradigm and critics who argue for a broader approach informed by social relations and political economy. See, for example, the exchange between Andrea Wiley (1992, 1993) and Merrill Singer (1989a, 1989b, 1993); see also Leatherman et al. 1993.

19. I found only two graduate students who have conducted medical anthropology fieldwork in Micronesia since the 1970s. Both students' projects are recent, and at the time this chapter was going to press, neither had completed his dissertation or published his data. Glenn Alcalay (New School for Social Research) surveyed birth defects among Marshallese outer atoll children, to investigate the health effects of islanders' exposure to radioactive fallout from nuclear tests. James Hahn (University of California at San Diego) studied Yapese medical pluralism and ethnomedical theory.

20. The US Public Health Service (USPHS) prepared a Proposal for Pacific Trust Territory Health Care Programs, dated May 1, 1968, which argued for the transfer from the Secretary of the Interior to the Secretary of Health, Education, and Welfare (Peck 1968, 1).

21. This document also lists "several tentative studies . . . in various stages of early planning" including nutrition studies aimed at critical periods such as pregnancy and weaning when traditional practices may cause transient but severe protein deficiency; studies in alcoholism; studies in suicide; practical studies in correlating nutritional practices with agricultural and fishing practices; and the "development of a select atoll community as a 'laboratory' for studying optimum health practice within an optimum subsistence economy" (Peck 1968, 11–12).

22. "Since 1976, the USTTPI has participated in the U.S. National Health Planning and Resources Development Program funded by Public Law 93–641. Five-year comprehensive health plans have been developed for each district of the USTTPI. These district plans are synthesized into a territorial health plan" (Tabrah 1982, 6).

23. The development of health services and facilities in Micronesia according to a rigidly American model has been noted anecdotally by observers (e.g., Manhard 1979, 13–14). Lacking, however, is an adequate sociological analysis of the ways that linkages to American health service bureaucracies have shaped health service concepts and priorities in Micronesia, and how the linked bureaucracies serve each others' interests. But see Albert "Britt" Robillard (1987, 235ff) on "loosely joined networks" of mental health service development in Micronesia and the United States.

24. These figures are estimates based on incomplete available information. I am very grateful to Roylinne Wada of the University of Hawai'i School of Public Health for her help in compiling data on US federal funding to the University of Hawai'i professional schools for Pacific Islander health-related programs.

25. Senator Daniel Inouye, first elected to the 86th Congress in 1959, has been the single individual most responsible for health-related US congressional legislation on behalf of the US Pacific Islands jurisdictions. The University of Hawai'i health professional schools, founded in 1960, have thus been in a very advantageous position. The University of Hawai'i is also the only American university with organizational linkages (through an office in its School of Public Health) with the Pacific Islands Health Officers Association, which includes all the US-affiliated jurisdictions.

CHAPTER ELEVEN

Anthropology and the Law in the Trust Territory of the Pacific Islands

Edward C. King

THIS CHAPTER REVIEWS some of the very first reported opinions of the US Trust Territory of the Pacific Islands (USTTPI) High Court and assesses the impact of anthropologists on the development of the USTTPI judicial system in Micronesia. As one trained in the law and not in anthropology, I focus on how the USTTPI judicial and legal systems drew on and related to anthropology, rather than on how anthropologists acted toward these systems in the trust territory.

I begin by acknowledging some truths gleaned from my own personal experience. The work of anthropologists obviously played a role in shaping the USTTPI legal system and the legal principles that system produced. In addition, anthropologists and their work have continuously exerted significant influence on the activities of those involved in the legal systems of Micronesia. Although each advocate or judge would have had a different experience, mine, nevertheless, may serve as an example. Even before my entry into the Micronesian scene in 1972, I had read Ward H. Goodenough's book, *Cooperation in Change* (1963). I was impressed then and have continued to be impressed with his message that anyone planning to introduce change designed to affect or assist one aspect of a social or cultural system must do so cautiously. This caution comes from an understanding that such attempts at change may often have unanticipated and deleterious impact on other aspects of the cultural system.

Legal decisions of the USTTPI High Court are compiled in an eight-volume set known as the *Trust Territory Reports* (TTR). Those decisions, which constituted the "common law" of the former trust territory, are laced with references to anthropological studies and reports.

The first expert witness with whom I worked, when I was with Micronesian Legal Services Corporation, was an anthropologist, Robert C. Kiste. In 1972, we drew on his expertise to help demonstrate to the federal court in Hawai'i the impact on the people of Enewetak of the momentous disruptions that had been visited on them and their home atoll through the actions of their trustee nation. The people of Enewetak were moved from their own atoll to Ujelang, so that Enewetak could be subjected to nuclear testing in the late 1940s. My work with Kiste, however, was triggered by a later series of highly explosive but non-nuclear tests on Enewetak, known as the Pacific Cratering Experiments (PACE). The PACE program was conducted by the US Air Force in 1972 even as the Enewetakese were visiting the atoll as part of the preparations for their eventual return (see Kiste 1976).[1]

Anthropologists continued to be an influence on and a resource for my work as chief justice of the Federated States of Micronesia (FSM) from 1981 through 1992. During that time, I tried to keep Goodenough's admonitions in mind and attempted to insure that the FSM Supreme Court would not unwittingly become an agent of unnecessary social change. I also had the opportunity to study the ideas and approaches of several anthropologists, such as Glenn Petersen, Patricia Parker King, Eve Pinsker, and Suzanne Falgout, and my thinking was often stimulated by discussions with them. Of direct and particular use to me was some of the final work of the late Daniel Hughes, as he and a constitutional scholar, Stanley Laughlin, studied the reactions of FSM citizens and leaders to some of the key decisions of the FSM Supreme Court.

In contrast to my personal experiences, it is my impression that anthropologists had less of an impact on the legal system, and on USTTPI policies generally, than often is assumed to be the case. It appears that anthropologists were not involved in planning the original form and mission of the judicial system. Further, systemic problems made it awkward for the court to draw on anthropologists for guidance in decision making concerning Micronesian customs and traditions.

THE COURT AND THE ANTHROPOLOGISTS

It is readily obvious, at least in retrospect, that when the United States, a massive, modern nation, assumed the mantle of guardianship over the people of the much smaller, isolated, and traditional societies of Micronesia, there was great potential for harm and disruption to the Micronesian peoples. This is particularly apparent when one recognizes that the United States was setting out not only to "foster the development of such political institutions as are suited to the trust territory" and to promote the "economic," "social," and "educational" advancement of the inhabitants (UNTS Art 6, § 1, 2, 3, 4), but also had undertaken "to ensure that the trust territory shall play its part, in accordance with the Charter of the United Nations, in the maintenance of international peace and security" (UNTS Art 5).

In light of these commitments of the United States, it surely is understandable, even predictable, that the work of the trustee nation would begin with careful anthropological studies of the societies to be protected and "advanced" under the trusteeship. Indeed it could be contended that a careful anthropological study, aimed at assuring that the actions of the trustee nation would be carried out with sensitivity and foresight, was an essential duty of the trustee nation.

That establishment of the USTTPI judiciary needed anthropological knowledge and assistance is especially evident. When a "modern" society takes unto itself the awesome responsibility of establishing a dispute resolution system for traditional societies, ideally the work should be heavily influenced by an understanding of the principles and procedures traditionally employed by members of those societies.

Anthropologists presumably could have been helpful in developing information about such questions as whether or not existing (in the 1940s) indigenous Micronesian dispute resolution mechanisms should be encouraged or supplanted; whether traditional (those prior to any of the colonial governments) dispute resolution mechanisms could or should be restored; whether criminal punishment should be characterized by alternative forms of discipline rather than confinement; or whether use of traditional symbols, building design, or even procedures by the judiciary might enhance the comfort and familiarity litigants could feel toward the court.

I have found no white paper or policy analysis indicating that the court took advantage of the presence of anthropologists in an effort to determine answers to these questions. There is also no confirmation that the court worked with anthropologists or even directly asked itself or others fundamental operational questions such as how judges should relate to traditional leaders, either in court or elsewhere. One can also suppose that the court would or should have wished to consult the thinking of anthropologists concerning fundamental policy questions, such as whether the legal system should move

Judge Edward P. Furber and unidentified Micronesian, date and place
unknown. Trust Territory Archives
(Photo 3209.3), Pacific Collection,
University of Hawai'i Library.

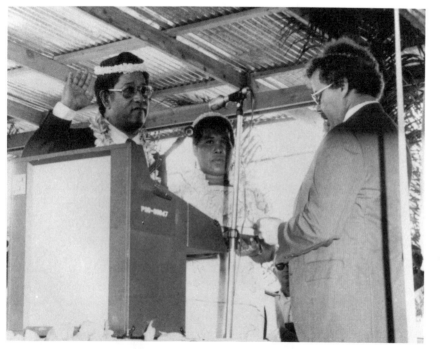

Judge Ed King
swearing in Tosiwo
Nakayama for his
second term as
president,
Federated States
of Micronesia.
Mrs. Miter
Nakayama observ-
ing. Pohnpei, 1983.
Trust Territory
Archives (Photo
3530.01), Pacific
Collection,
University of
Hawai'i Library.

1993 Conference. Left to right: *Ed King,*
Francis Hezel, William Alkire,
William Vitarelli. Photograph by
Carolyn Yacoe.

toward individual ownership of land or whether the clan or shared group
nature of traditional ownership should be emphasized.

In the USTTPI Archives there are records of meetings and exchanges of
correspondence between Chief Justice Edward P. Furber and various anthropologists during the 1950s. However, these suggest that the court's discussions
with anthropologists focused on the details of particular points of law and,
sometimes, on procedures, but not on the more fundamental questions, such
as the role of the court and how disputes should be resolved in the Micronesian cultures. I have found nothing reflecting consideration of the kinds of
questions mentioned above.

There could be several explanations for the absence of any indication that
these basic questions were being considered by the judiciary, working in consultation with anthropologists, when the court was in its formative stage. One
possibility is that the new judges were given marching orders at the very
outset, and were simply told that the court was to be based on an American

model. One would accept this explanation reluctantly, however, for it would reflect poorly on the bona fides and the competence of the trusteeship endeavor. Given the importance of the court in shaping the future of the people and societies of the trust territory, a decision in Washington, before there had been an opportunity for dialogue between judicial officials and anthropologists, would imply that the heavy commitment to anthropological studies may have been motivated by considerations other than a wish to provide Micronesians with the most appropriate structures of government.

On the other hand, it is also possible that officials in Washington did assume that anthropologists would be helpful to the judicial branch, but did not appreciate the realities of separation of powers in a remote colonial government. As it was, however, it appears that neither the anthropologists nor anyone else who was assigned to the executive branch thought that they should work with the judiciary branch in any formal, structured way. An April 17, 1956, letter from USTTPI Chief Justice Furber to Staff Anthropologist John E. deYoung bemoaned the situation. After noting his desire that anthropologists devote one-third of their time to court activities, Judge Furber added:

> To be really satisfactory . . . any assistance the anthropologists give, as friend of the court in particular cases, should involve regular attendance at court throughout a case, with the same regularity expected of counsel. This means that while such a case is on trial, their court attendance, and preparation for it, would take at least three-quarters of their time and quite possibly nearly all of it.

It is clear that the court never had sufficient leverage to obtain that kind of commitment by anthropologists to judicial activities. This shows the structural and institutional problems that were compounded by the fact that anthropologists were not assigned directly to work with the court.

Finally, and perhaps most significant, is the fact that in the earliest decisions found in the *Trust Territory Reports*, Judge Furber is identified as a district judge rather than as chief justice.[2] The year was 1951. This suggests that in its earliest days, the court may have lacked the leadership necessary to bring about any consideration of the fundamental questions referred to above.[3] Yet there also is no indication that the court later questioned in any fundamental way its own role or mission.

Whatever the reason may have been, it appears that the court undertook and carried out its work on the assumption that it should conduct itself as much as possible as an American court, and that the procedures employed in and basic values applied by courts in the United States would be the model for the USTTPI court system.

This suggests, then, that anthropologists originally played no significant role in defining the mission of the USTTPI judiciary. The framework was fixed and only interstitial work remained. Although many important details would be added to the framework through decision making over the years, much of the opportunity for creativity and insightful new directions had been lost at the outset. It could be that the court decided that it should not attempt to respond fully to values and goals that already existed among the peoples of the trust territory. Inherent in the concept of a trusteeship is a belief that the "ward" societies are not yet equipped to be self-governing and that the trustee nation should guide the ward in developing the proper institutions for self-government.

However, in embracing the American model the court ostensibly committed itself to procedural notions of fairness that are basic to the American system and to the common law system of decision making. This commitment, coupled with the necessity that the court respond to notions of fairness relating to customary institutions and rights in Micronesia, with which the judges were not intimately familiar, created for the court the dilemma of how to use anthropologists' information.

Under the American system, a court asked to rule on issues of unfamiliar custom would be required to entertain evidence as to the custom and would then make and explain a finding based on that evidence. However, in the context in which the USTTPI court operated, such a procedure presented major problems and almost certainly would have been unworkable. In the first place, for the court to have required evidence as to all the points of custom with which it was unfamiliar or on which it had not previously ruled, would have been unwieldy, particularly given the paucity of advocates trained in the American system. More than that, this procedure inevitably would have eroded the credibility of the court, pointing up the court's lack of familiarity with matters of everyday knowledge to most Micronesians.

Even had the court embarked on such an effort, it may well have proven unworkable. Evidence would have had to come from one of two sources, either anthropologists or Micronesian expert witnesses. As discussed below, anthropologists resisted the court's efforts to enlist their assistance as expert witnesses. Major reliance on indigenous witnesses, many of whom surely would have been traditional titleholders, would have placed the court in the very delicate situation of finding for or against witnesses who were "explaining" custom to the court.

The dilemma in turn gave rise to a paradox. While the court did not exhibit creativity in assessing its mission at the outset, it was forced to become creative as a matter of self-protection. In its conscientious efforts to reach fair decisions consistent with local values, the court had to create new approaches so that it could obtain and consider information that was unavailable under the American model.

This led, I suggest, to a panoply of devices, adopted in good faith, but which were disingenuous and inevitably undermined the credibility and integrity of the court. This is not the place for a comprehensive analysis of how these self-protective devices were employed throughout the entire period of the court's existence. Yet the court's difficulty in resolving the evidentiary and procedural dilemma emerged immediately. The following review of some of the court's earliest decisions is illustrative of the general problem and the basic protective devices the court employed.

From the very beginning the USTTPI High Court frequently cited anthropological reports in the course of its opinions. In Volume 1 of the *Trust Territory Reports,* at least thirteen cases include citations of anthropological studies. The rate of citation is even greater in subsequent volumes. The very first reported cases reveal the anthropological nature of the issues that were brought before the court. A review of all the reports persuades the reader that the greatest challenge to and novelty of the court's effort lay in addressing issues of customary law.

The first case in Volume 1 of the *Trust Territory Reports,* (*Kilara v Alexander,* 1 TTR 3 [Ponape 1951]), was decided on January 31, 1951, by Judge Furber, who is listed as "district judge" (UNTS Art 5). This case is representative of one of the ways the court responded to the necessity that it rule on issues of custom beyond the personal knowledge of the judge and without having adequate evidence before it. The method employed was simply to state rules as though no issue existed.

The plaintiffs, Kilara and several other Pohnpeians, claimed ownership of the land in question. The opinion does not indicate the theory on which the plaintiffs based their claim. In a tersely written, three-page opinion, the court simply held that the defendant, Tomuas, was adopted by the previous landowner, Alexander; that Tomuas was the eldest son when Alexander died about 1940; and that he therefore inherited the land.

The ambivalence of the court in addressing issues of custom is also foreshadowed in this first case. Necessary to the decision is the court's holding that Tomuas had been adopted by Alexander. Since this is identified as a "finding of fact," there must have been a dispute as to whether adoption had occurred. It is therefore significant that the court offers no explanation as to how this finding was made. The court does not say what steps were deemed necessary under Pohnpeian law or custom to establish that an adoption had taken place. There is no mention of any anthropologist or anthropological report, nor is there any indication as to what evidence the court had considered.

If the court had felt free to openly discuss anthropological and other fundamental considerations, it surely had an opportunity to do so in this case. Instead, this first opinion reveals a certain reluctance to acknowledge that it was confronting issues of first impression with which it was unfamiliar. The *Kilara* decision represents one of the ways the court could respond to the dilemma in which it found itself. The court simply made pronouncements as to both custom and law, almost as though the rulings were foreordained, admitting of no doubt or discussion.

The court's second reported case, decided five months later, on May 31, 1951, is a slightly more complex version of this same tendency. In *Plus v Pretrik*, 1 TTR 7 (Ponape 1951), District Judge Furber enforced the agreement of the decedent, Eukenio, that if the parents of the plaintiff, Dieko Plus, would agree to permit the decedent to have custody of Dieko and their other children, Eukenio would permit Dieko, the eldest child, to inherit the land Eukenio occupied. The children apparently lived with Eukenio, but sometime before his death he "attempt[ed] to will" the land to another person, Pretrik. After Eukenio died, Dieko brought this case to claim the land.

The court began by saying that under the German land documents, Dieko was not within the list of relatives entitled to inherit from Eukenio and that any gift to him would have to be with permission of the Nanmwarki or the German colonial governor. The court then added, without explanation, that "the gift by Eukenio to Pretrik would require this same permission or determination" (1 TTR at 9).[4] Therefore, the court concluded, "there is a vacancy in the legal title."

Although the court did not say so in its opinion, a vacancy in title is unknown to American law. This situation, then, plainly called for judicial creativity, which the court readily provided by explaining that until the authorities approved transfer of the title, "the right of possession and use of the land is controlled by the worth of the different claims to it." Here, too, the court pronounced these "rules" as though they preexisted, demanding specified court action. One almost has to pinch oneself to recall that, under American law, there are no rules designed to evaluate "the worth of the different claims" to land when there is a vacancy in title. Despite his assured rendering of "rules," Judge Furber clearly was breaking new ground or, perhaps more aptly stated in Micronesian terms, sailing into unknown waters.

But the court sailed on, supplying another proposition to evaluate the "worth of the different claims." "This in turn depends," the court opined, "in a case like the present one, in large part upon the agreements and conduct of those who formerly owned it or now claim it, or those through whom they claim" (1 TTR at 10). Eukenio, having "received the benefit" of his agreement concerning the agreement to give future land rights in exchange for immediate custodial rights, "was thereby prevented from himself taking any action which would have legal effect, to defeat this agreement, without either obtaining the consent of the plaintiff or complying with the requirements of the law for transfer of the legal title." Thus his attempt to will the land to Pretrik was without legal effect.

Observations about the dubious nature of the rule,[5] and its future application,[6] are only peripheral to our concerns. The important point is that we have no idea where this rule came from.

Obviously, this was not a case amenable to application of the standard rules of American law. For one thing, Americans tend to frown on contractual arrangements whereby custody over children is bartered in exchange for land rights. Secondly, the standard American approach would have been to scrutinize Eukenio's will, or, as the court called it, his "attempt to will." A properly executed will would prevail over his oral, unexecuted agreement to convey land, and his prior representations that the land would descend to Dieko by inheritance.[7]

On the other hand, there is no indication that the court was drawing on anything said or learned by anthropologists in reaching its conclusion, even though it almost certainly was.

The point here is procedural, not substantive. Surely, most Americans and most Micronesians would agree that Dieko should have received the land, since his family had fulfilled their part of the agreement by permitting Eukenio to raise the children. The justice of the result seems even more certain when one recognizes that, for reasons not clear in the opinion, Pretrik was held to be entitled to "the rest of the land in question in this action" (1 TTR at 10).

Whatever we may think of the outcome, though, several observations are in order. First, the opinion is written in such a style as to imply that some pre-existing force compelled the court's decision. The court does not speak of what the controlling rule "could" or "should" be, but says directly what the law "is." Yet, as already explained, there was no controlling precedent or rule of law, and the court was fashioning its own rule. The court's decision seems to be "result-oriented" in the sense that it was an effort to do what the court thought right rather than to seek and apply preexisting rules, or even new rules that would then be applied to other cases in the future. In more orthodox legal language, this was an attempt to "do equity" rather than to apply rules of law.

There is something quite attractive about this, of course. There is no reason to doubt that the court was acting with the purest of motives and surely none among us would argue that the USTTPI court should have attempted to resolve all the disputes that came before it by rigidly applying principles of law borrowed from the United States.

Yet the procedural concern remains an important one. After all, judges were assigned to the court presumably because they had been trained in the law. If the goal was not to apply existing law but instead to create new rules aimed at responding to the exigencies of Micronesian cultures, the court should have had help, and the parties to the litigation should have known what was happening. At a minimum, the court should have had the opportunity to consult openly and fully with anthropologists and Micronesian sources to assure that its rulings would be an appropriate response to Micronesian realities and values.

In truth, these kinds of consultations probably took place off to the side and went unrecorded. Yet, such surreptitious consultations introduce great risks for a court purporting to serve as a model of American-style justice. Ex parte communications erode the integrity of the American judicial process, undermining the fundamental precept that all parties are to be aware of all the evidence the court is considering.

Obtaining information through nonevidentiary sources leads inevitably to judicial disingenuousness. The *Plus* opinion is written in such a way as to suggest that the court was applying preexisting rules of law, when in fact it was engaging in result-oriented rationalization aimed at producing what the particular judge thought to be a good result.

The third reported case arose in Yap and was issued on September 18, 1951. *Filimew v Pong*, 1 TTR 11 (Yap 1951) was also an action seeking determination of land ownership and use rights. The Faniifinimaday clan had given use rights to one Rutmag. On Rutmag's death, a question arose over ownership of the land. The court's key conclusion of law was:

> Neither the fact that the Faniifinimaday Clan permitted the use-rights in the land in question to be exercised for many years by Rutmag who was not himself a member of the clan although his father was a member,

nor the fact that the clan has not held any meeting for some years and
has no active leader, nor the fact that a number of members of the clan
have moved away from Tamiil, nor the combination of these facts,
deprives the clan of its ownership of the land in question. (1 TTR at 12)

The court therefore held that ownership of the land remained in the clan and
that use rights would be determined by "a meeting of the . . . clan in accordance with Yapese custom" (1 TTR at 12–13).

In this decision, too, the first case that arose in Yap, the court presented its
holdings as though they were simply foregone and inescapable conclusions.
There is no indication of consultation with anthropologists, of reliance on
anthropological writings, or of evidence adduced during a trial of the case.
We are given no idea as to how the court came to possess the knowledge of
Yapese custom that ostensibly is reflected in the findings of fact and conclusions of law.

The first *Trust Territory Reports* decision concerning a dispute in the Marshall Islands is another example of the court's disinclination to discuss the
challenges it confronted and the options open to it (*Levi v Kumtak*, 1 TTR 36
[Marshall Islands 1953]). This opinion, written by Associate Justice James R.
Nichols, discusses at length the history leading to the division of Majuro
between two *iroij lablab* 'high chiefs,' and concludes that a decision made in
approximately 1925 "not to have any iroij lablab for Jebrik's side was undoubtedly a departure from Marshallese custom" (1 TTR at 40). Because the court
saw this as a "clear determination by the authority then administering the
Marshall Islands," it refused to grant plaintiffs' request for recognition of an
iroij lablab for "Jebrik's side" of the atoll.

Although historical events on Majuro and their ramifications are discussed
at some length in the opinion, no mention is made of how the court came to
possess such extensive knowledge of the "civil war" that took place in Majuro,
the subsequent actions of the Japanese government, or the impact of these on
the traditional rights of people bearing titles such as *iroij* 'chief,' *alab* 'lineage
head,' and *dri jerbal* 'worker.' Here again, the court seems to have been forced
to obtain knowledge on an extrajudicial basis, but chose to ignore normal
judicial evidentiary requirements.

A defendant in the *Levi* case, just discussed, did not like the trial court's
decision, and appealed to the appellate division of the high court. The opinion
written by Chief Justice Furber in response to that appeal exemplifies another
approach that seems to have been adopted to finesse the dilemma in which

the court found itself. In *Jatios v Levi*, 1 TTR 578 (Appellate 1954), the court also described the relevant custom and history at some length. On completion of this discussion, the court added the following observation:

> For a very helpful detailed anthropological study of this whole matter of Marshallese land ownership, see "Land Tenure of the Marshall Islands" by J. E. Tobin, issued by the Pacific Science Board as Atoll Research Bulletin No. 11. A discussion of it, with particular reference to Majuro, by another scientist will be found in the section on "Land, Tenure and Lineage," beginning at page 160, in "Majuro, a Village in the Marshall Islands," by Alexander Spoehr, published by the Chicago Natural History Museum as Volume 39 of Fieldiana: Anthropology. (1 TTR at 582 [Appellate 1954])

Note that the court did not acknowledge having used or learned from these anthropological reports. Rather, Chief Justice Furber mentioned the references quite casually, almost as an aside. The implication seemed to be that the court already knew everything in these studies, and was merely commending them as something that the casual reader who happened to be browsing through the *Trust Territory Reports* might find of interest. Of course, this citation also provided a hint to the reader that the court actually did obtain the information it was relating from these publications, although the court did not acknowledge this directly. The citation serves as a reference for people today who may wonder exactly how Chief Justice Furber got his information.

This exemplifies another method the court seems to have adopted in response to the fact that it was forced to rely on information it received outside of normal evidentiary procedures.

The first citation of an anthropological report in a USTTPI High Court case occurred on December 23, 1952 (*Petiele v Max*, 1 TTR 26 [Ponape 1952]). Chief Justice Furber took judicial notice that "issuance of title documents in the name of one person with the understanding that some other person should have the beneficial ownership [i.e., the right to use, or benefit from] for his life, was common on Ponape and not considered necessarily contrary to public policy." As the basis for this statement, he cited John L. Fischer's "Anthropological Report CAU [Civil Affairs Unit] Ponape, Eastern Caroline Islands, dated 5 June, 1951, on 'Contemporary Ponapean Land Tenure.' "

Thus, after the death of Kalio the court upheld his agreement with Max that "the land should belong to Max for his lifetime" (1 TTR at 27). Accordingly, the plaintiff, Petiele, Kalio's adopted daughter, was entitled to rely on her agreement with Max that she could be in possession of the land so long as Max remained alive.

Although *Petiele* is the first case that cited an anthropological report as the basis for a finding or conclusion, it nonetheless reflected the court's continued unwillingness to acknowledge the extent of its dependence on anthropologists, and to state clearly how it acquired the knowledge of Micronesian cultures necessary to its decision making.

After citing Fischer as grounds for taking judicial notice of the point mentioned above—that it was not unusual in Pohnpei for some person other than the titleholder to have beneficial ownership of the land for life—the court then directly took judicial notice of a separate matter. Without explaining any basis for doing so, the court simply said: "The court takes judicial notice . . . that under Ponapean customary law a legally adopted child was considered to be a legal child and furthermore that the Japanese authorities in construing this provision considered that it did not prohibit inheritance by an adopted child even though the deceased had at the time of his death a brother living" (1 TTR at 29).

This interlacing of reliance on anthropological reports to resolve some issues of custom and tradition, with unexplained and unsupported assertions of the applicable customary principle in other circumstances, was also to become characteristic of the court's approach to issues of an anthropological nature.

ANTHROPOLOGISTS AS SOURCES OF INFORMATION

Plainly, anthropologists were the primary source potentially available to the court for information concerning customs and traditions of the peoples of the former US Trust Territory of the Pacific Islands. After the early citations referred to above, the USTTPI reports contain many citations of anthropological studies in support of the court's findings. In cases arising in Pohnpei proper, for example, Fischer's writings are cited frequently.[8] His report, "Native Land Tenure in the Truk District" (Fischer 1958b) also is relied on with some frequency for cases arising in Chuuk. The high water mark was reached on June 30, 1958, when Chief Justice Furber issued three opinions concerning land rights on Wééné (Moen) Island, in each of which he cited and relied on Fischer's report.[9]

Although many other anthropological reports were cited through the years with some frequency by the USTTPI High Court, the Fischer report on Chuuk holds the distinction of being the anthropological work cited most frequently by courts in Micronesia.

Perusal of the citations indicates that Francis B. Mahoney's paper on Yapese land ownership and inheritance customs (1958) was most frequently cited in opinions concerning disputes in Yap,[10] and Homer G. Barnett's "Birth, Marriage and Death in Palauan Society" (1949, 100–155) took the prize for Palauan cases.[11] Alex Spoehr's two Fieldiana: Anthropology monographs on Majuro and Saipan seem to be the most frequently cited anthropological sources for those islands (1949a, 1954).

Even with these frequent citations of cases, however, the high court decisions retained the patterns discussed above, sometimes simply stating propositions without citation, other times referring to anthropological works as an aside but not stating squarely how the court had relied on the report, and in still other instances interlacing citations with simple assertions of custom or law.

The cases discussed here demonstrate that from the very beginning the court had difficulty in explaining how it considered and decided questions of custom and tradition. Given the complexity of the task and the absence of advocates trained in the adversarial system the court was establishing, it is to be expected that such difficulties would occur. However, it should be recognized that this difficulty was intimately linked to and compounded by the reluctance of anthropologists to serve as expert witnesses, and the court's failure to openly acknowledge and respond to the unusual problems it faced in considering issues of custom.

Materials in the USTTPI Archives indicate that judicial figures and anthropologists met to discuss issues of mutual interest and attempted to cooperate.[12] A memorandum reflecting the first anthropological conference, held in Palau in September 1952, speaks of a "mutually helpful liaison between the anthropologist and the Judicial Department" which was "tending to become more firm in most districts." The unidentified writer emphasizes, at page 3, the importance to "usefulness of anthropology in the future," of "developing rapport with departments outside Internal Affairs." The memo then adds, "In particular it was suggested that Staff Anthropologist and the Chief Justice put on record their concurrence on the value of anthropological research in promoting the ends of justice among the native populations of the Territory."

Yet it is also clear that the two groups had different perspectives and priorities. A summary of a district anthropological conference held in February 1957 reveals Chief Justice Furber's efforts to persuade anthropologists that they should be willing to "commit themselves" by testifying in court regarding local customs. The summary, in transcript form, shows responses of "Fran,"[13] saying that anthropologists have always been willing to provide information "privately." "Saul"[14] suggests that the problem could be solved by asking anthropologists in advance to "write memos regarding the case in question." Judge Furber's response was that secret material is of "no account," and that to be helpful, the material must "be public."

It is understandable that anthropologists would have been reluctant to serve as witnesses in the trust territory. The development of a relationship of trust between anthropologist and informant is crucial to anthropological work. An anthropologist who testifies publicly about information and attributes this information to a particular informant surely cannot expect that person or many others to share confidences in the future. Of course, few experts in any field, and especially those working in the social sciences, would relish having advocates questioning them in open court in an effort to raise doubts over the accuracy of their expertise.

As a general proposition, though, with a few carefully circumscribed exceptions, the public interest in assuring fair trials and accurate judicial decisions is held to outweigh the other side of the scale, which is the public interest in encouraging particular kinds of communications. Normally, any person who has knowledge that could be helpful in deciding a dispute before the courts may be required to testify.

In the US Trust Territory of the Pacific Islands, however, the reluctance of anthropologists to testify was given unusual import.[15] High Commissioner D. H. Nucker issued Executive Order no. 48 on January 24, 1955, inserting in the Trust Territory Code an "anthropologists' privilege."[16]

To understand the difficulties the unavailability of anthropologists placed on the court, recall that, with few exceptions, the adversarial system the court sought to employ contemplated that any findings of fact, including information about social reality, must be based on sworn testimony in court. Scientific testimony involves description of the witness's educational background, data, and reasoning. Under the American model which the court had selected, the adversary is given the opportunity to cross-examine the witness and to challenge the offered opinion or theory.

Information contained in learned articles and reports such as those produced by anthropologists who had worked in Micronesia is considered hearsay and cannot be admitted into evidence except through the testimony of the author, or in connection with cross-examination of another expert witness (Cleary 1984, §321). Of course, generally published material is rarely adequate anyway to resolve a dispute. In most cases, some variation of the published information is presented and resolution of the dispute calls for interpolation and the exercise of judgment and discretion.

Nor is taking of judicial notice of anthropological information easily reconcilable with American evidentiary requirements. Information crucial to resolution of a dispute is not likely to meet the requirements that permit the court to take "judicial notice," that is, to accept as true information that has not been submitted as evidence. The normal American judicial standards are that information accepted through judicial notice must either be known by all in the community or be a scientific fact about which there can be no reasonable dispute (Cleary 1984, §332).

If the parties agree that a particular point of custom is indisputably true, this may be entered into evidence in the American system through stipulation. However, if there is a dispute as to the proffered opinion, the point may almost never be established through judicial notice. The undesirability of taking judicial notice is especially marked when the trier of fact is a non-Micronesian judge, who may not be assumed to be personally familiar with the information nor with its significance within the community.

Thus a court employing American evidentiary practices normally can find the existence of an item of anthropological information only on the basis of testimonial evidence presented in court. Under that system, the trial court in its opinion normally indicates the findings or conclusions that it is drawing from the testimony. If the trial court cannot point to evidence in the record supporting the findings, the decision will be set aside on appeal.

These are not merely technical guidelines in the American system but are held to be matters of fundamental fairness, of "due process" in the constitutional vernacular. These evidentiary principles are calculated to assure that a party contesting a particular assertion of fact will have the opportunity to challenge the proponent's basis for asserting the information to be true. These evidentiary requirements, then, are basic to the American system of justice.

To ask the USTTPI High Court to deal intelligently and fairly with issues of custom and tradition by drawing on information obtained by anthropologists, but without calling on anthropologists to testify, was to demand that the court disregard its assumption, and betray its implied promise, that it was to conduct itself essentially as though it were functioning in the United States.

Unfortunately, the court seems never to have acknowledged this problem publicly nor to have attempted to fashion publicly a special rule or procedure for addressing issues of custom. Instead, its effort to appear to employ the American system while departing in a fundamental way from that system on issues of custom and tradition caused the court to adopt devices that can only be seen as disingenuous. Because the court on a daily basis faced issues of custom and tradition, the impact of these skewed approaches was pervasive.

The court was fundamentally eroded as an institution. The damage was not limited to procedural or evidentiary questions concerning custom. The court easily slipped into the practice of creating new rules of substantive law without acknowledging that it was doing so. The *Plus* case is one example of this, as is the *Wasisang* case discussed below.

POLICY DECISIONS

The USTTPI High Court and other USTTPI and military officials made many decisions during the trusteeship. I am unaware of any documentation of the degree of involvement of anthropologists in these decisions. Yet these decisions were certain to have tremendous impact on the people involved, and to affect generally the legal rights of the wards of the trust. It seems that anthropologists have played a role in addressing the issues.

One example of the kind of profound policy issue may be found in the court's very first opinion, *Kilara v Alexander*. As discussed above, that case turned on a question of adoption. Predictably, however, that initial case contained a momentous holding:

> The land law, as far as private ownership is concerned, as stated in the standard form of German title document issued in Ponape is still in effect outside of any changes that may have been made by the German authorities during their regime, the Japanese Authorities during their regime, or the American Authorities since the American occupation. (*Kilara v Alexander*, 1 TTR 3, 5 [Ponape 1951])

No explanation is given for this holding, which nonetheless had enormous implications of an anthropological nature. This very first decision committed the court to uphold as controlling and supreme only the actions of the colonial authorities and erased the potential importance of custom and tradition as a direct source of Pohnpeian land law. That this decision was made with no discussion implies that the court saw no possible alternatives. This case, therefore, may also dramatically illustrate the difficulties that flowed from the phenomenon discussed above, the fact that anthropologists and the court did not work closely together in the formative days of the court system.

Another example of the adoption of a critically important policy without apparent consideration of anthropological implications is the fourth case in the *Trust Territory Reports, Wasisang v Trust Territory*, 1 TTR 14 (Palau 1952). This case, decided on May 26, 1952, was a landmark decision, but a setback for many individual Micronesians in that it established a principle of law that was applied numerous times to their detriment. The case also needs to be considered here because it shows the court to be making an important policy decision while professing to be bound by preexisting rules.

Mr. Wasisang brought his case in an attempt to regain land in Palau that had been taken from his father by the Japanese administration around 1918. The land had been taken, the court found, "as part of the punishment imposed upon [the plaintiff's father] as one of the leaders of the Modeknei [Palauan religion] movement which the Japanese Government had made illegal and was endeavoring to stamp out" (1 TTR at 15).

Wasisang brought his suit against the USTTPI government, which had received the land as successor to the Japanese administration. The court began its analysis by suggesting that in the eyes of the law, the taking of property to punish a person for his religious beliefs was not "legally wrong."

> Whether any act was legally wrong should be decided according to the law as it was at the time the act was done. This is the rule, except when it is changed by some express provision in the law. On this basis, the plaintiff, Wasisang, has not shown that any wrong was done him or those through whom he claims. (1 TTR at 16)

Again, there is no statement of the authority on which this rule of law is based, so we cannot be certain what the court had in mind. Assuming that the court considered itself to be drawing on principles of international law as applied in the United States, however, it surely would have been difficult for the court to find support for its statement of law. Reference to "the time" when the act in question took place seems to suggest that the successor government would uphold the acts of its predecessor if those acts were legal at that time according to the predecessor government. This is flatly contrary to the message conveyed by the war crimes convictions of German and Japanese officers and soldiers. Those trials confirmed the principle that officials and soldiers may be held liable for fundamental violations of human rights even if the unacceptable conduct for which they were punished was not only encouraged but demanded of them by their own government at the time they acted.

Under general legal principles relating to comity among nations, the actions of the Japanese administration in taking the property of Wasisang's father would not be approved or given legal effect by American courts if those actions were contrary to fundamental American policies or principles. There can be little doubt that the taking of land to punish a person for his religious affiliations would have been regarded even in 1918 as offensive to fundamental American notions of justice, since any such action is prohibited by the Bill of Rights, specifically the First Amendment to the United States Constitution.

The court did not cite any authority for the statement of law mentioned above. Indeed, up to that time, the court had not in any of its reported opinions cited any authority, either legal or anthropological, to explain or support any of its holdings. It is, therefore, significant that the court in *Wasisang* did for the first time cite an authority, *American Jurisprudence,* in support of one proposition. The court relied on that legal encyclopedia in holding that the USTTPI government had no obligation to right the wrongs of its predecessor government. The court began its discussion of this issue by saying:

> So far as property rights are concerned, the present government of the Trust Territory of the Pacific Islands is in a position like that of a succeeding sovereign taking over the government of land conquered by it or ceded to it by another nation. The rights and obligations of such a succeeding sovereign are explained in general terms in Volume 30 of American Jurisprudence, pages 202 to 207, in paragraphs 44 to 47 of the article on "International Law." (1 TTR at 16)

It is true that the United States played a critical military role in wresting control of Micronesia from the Japanese government. Yet, it is strange that the USTTPI government in 1952 would have defined its relationship to Micronesia as that of a conquering nation. In theory and in fact, the United States had conquered Japan, not Micronesia. More to the point, by the time the *Wasisang* decision was issued, the role of the United States for some five years had been that of a trustee, sworn to protect the people of Micronesia against the loss of their lands and resources. Reliance on the law governing conquering nations, or nations to which lands had been ceded, to determine their own governmental obligations reflects badly on USTTPI officials and their understanding of their fiduciary duties. The court then went on to say:

> The present administration is entitled to rely upon and respect the official acts of the Japanese administration of these islands and is not required as a matter of right to correct wrongs which the former administration may have done, except in those cases where the wrong occurred so near the time of the change of administration that there was no opportunity for it to be corrected through the courts or other agencies of the former administration. . . . The general rule is that it is not a

proper function of the courts of the present administration to right wrongs which may have for many years before been persisted in by the former administration. (1 TTR at 16)

Thus, Wasisang's claim was denied and the USTTPI government retained title to the land wrongfully taken from his family.

It has been contended forcefully that neither *American Jurisprudence* nor any other legal authority justified this "prior wrongs doctrine" (see Olsen 1976). In addition, the suggestion that the passage of time should justify governmental retention of the property is hard to accept. Since the Japanese government had already taken the property wrongfully and forcefully to punish Wasisang's father for his religious beliefs, it is difficult to imagine how he could have obtained redress while the Japanese government remained in power. One also wonders whether anthropologists, if consulted on a question such as this, would have agreed that the lapse of time in asserting land rights denoted the same kind of acquiescence in Micronesian cultures as it may have signified in the United States and other western cultures.

Nonetheless, the prior wrongs doctrine became a central legal tenet of the USTTPI High Court and was invoked on numerous occasions to deny claims of Micronesians that the USTTPI government should be required to return land wrongfully taken by a predecessor government.[17]

In the course of the trusteeship, justices of the court and other officials necessarily made many other decisions that had profound impact on Micronesians and their way of life. These included, for example, the assertion of defenses such as sovereign immunity and the statute of limitations, to supplement the prior wrongs doctrine as a governmental shield against otherwise meritorious claims of Micronesians;[18] and refusals to regard provisions in the Trusteeship Agreement as judicially enforceable by Micronesians,[19] a posture maintained by the USTTPI High Court even after the federal courts had ruled otherwise.[20] Indefinite land use agreements were employed to permit the government to obtain or retain possession of land owned by beneficiaries of the trust. Policy letter P-1, calling for review of Japanese acquisitions of land after March 27, 1935, was applied by USTTPI officials grudgingly. The government claimed tidelands areas that under Micronesian custom were owned by clans.[21] The government adopted a land registration system permitting land to be registered in the name of one person, which may tend to erode the more communal interests in land under custom.

In the early years of this unique, "strategic" trusteeship, the primary concern of the United States was to do what was deemed necessary to "ensure that the trust territory shall play its part, in accordance with the charter of the United Nations, in the maintenance of international peace and security" (UNTS Art 5). We may therefore ask whether the primary motivation in sending anthropologists to Micronesia in those years was to learn how the administration might most efficiently obtain control over land that it desired in order to carry out its strategic obligations. One wonders, for example, to what extent consultation with anthropologists was a factor in obtaining for the United States the "permission" of the peoples of Bikini, Enewetak, and Kwajalein to use these areas for military purposes.

While we do not know the extent to which knowledge obtained by anthropologists was used as a tool by military administrators in obtaining land from Micronesians, it does seem that any knowledge by anthropologists of the importance of land to Micronesians and their social systems did not deter military and USTTPI officials from using numerous devices to obtain land rights from Micronesians.

CONCLUSIONS

This scrutiny of the earliest decisions of the USTTPI High Court obviously is not a comprehensive review of the activities either of the court, or of anthropologists in Micronesia, or of the relationship between the court and the anthropologists. Yet these early cases do reveal tendencies that remained characteristic of the court. Primary among these was a failure to come squarely to terms with the relationship between the court and anthropologists, and the circumstances under which the court considered anthropological information in its decision-making role.

The USTTPI High Court needed and sought the assistance of anthropologists. Especially in the early days when there apparently were few qualified advocates, the court must have felt almost entirely dependent on information from anthropologists. Without that information the court would not have been equipped to resolve the issues coming before it.

Anthropologists did supply useful information which was relied on by the court. Yet, as I have attempted to demonstrate, the relationship between the court and anthropologists ultimately contributed to unfair procedures, and court decisions that were of questionable substantive quality and poorly explained. Thus we find the court sometimes relying on anthropologists for a particular item of anthropological information, at other times saying that it was taking judicial notice of such information, and at still other times simply stating as true some anthropological concept.

The court's pragmatic and expeditious acceptance of anthropological conclusions without a coherent judicial policy, and even without open acknowledgment of the core principles at stake, both reflected and contributed to a lack of clarity in vision. It was only a short step from the fuzziness of exposition employed in the court's explanation of its anthropological rulings to an easy setting aside of substantive rights of Micronesians without judicial acknowledgment of the policy decisions it was making in so doing. We see in the early decisions, most notably in *Wasisang*, a willingness on the part of the court to pronounce dubious rules of law without careful analysis.

Finally, the array of policy decisions noted here, viewed together, suggest a general atmosphere of little regard for the fiduciary obligations of the trustee and legal rights of Micronesians. It is difficult to reconcile these policies, and the attitude they seem to reflect, with the sensitivity and concern that I have seen in the anthropologists I have known. The question that looms is whether anthropologists were involved in these key decisions. If they were not, the conclusion would seem to be that the commitment to anthropological studies was not to assure sensitivity to the interests and values of Micronesians. If anthropologists were involved in these more critical decisions, a review of the thinking behind adoption of the policies might provide an interesting and stimulating topic for further research.

NOTES

1. The litigation resulted in a ruling that US military officials acting in the US Trust Territory of the Pacific Islands were subject to the *National Environmental Policy Act* (42 USC § 4321 et seq). The PACE project was "voluntarily" abandoned as a result of the lawsuit (*People of Enewetak v Laird*, 353 F Supp 811 [District of Hawai'i 1973]).

2. See *Kilara v Alexander*, 1 TTR 3 (Ponape 1951) and *Plus v Pretrik*, 1 TTR 7 (Ponape 1951), discussed later. As with much in the early US Trust Territory of the Pacific Islands days, there is some ambiguity here. The foreword of Volume 1 of the *Trust Territory Reports*, at page vii, lists Edward P. Furber as having been chief justice from 1948 through 1968. Since the volume was published in 1969, and the opinions identifying Judge Furber as a district judge were written contemporaneously with the events, it appears that the designations in the opinions are likely correct.

3. Furber, a naval officer, served as a judge during the US naval administration of Micronesia as early as 1947 (Ward Goodenough, personal communication 1993). Goodenough speculates that there was an easy administrative transition from the US Navy

to the Department of the Interior and that the judiciary did not recognize that transition as calling for careful planning or fresh thinking.

4. This was an application of the holding in the first case, *Kilara,* that the German land documents remained controlling in Pohnpei (see below).

5. The opinion suggests that, despite the agreement, Eukenio's will would have been given legal effect if he had obtained the permission of the Nanmwarki. This could effectively strip the rule of any utility. Even assuming the rule were to be taken seriously, the court did not say which "agreements and conduct" should control. Is conduct relevant in absence of an agreement? But when is there an "agreement"? By definition, the rule would apply only when there is no legally enforceable agreement.

6. The apparent "rule" was crafted in such a way as to leave the court with almost unfettered discretion. Limitation of it to "a case like the present one" seemed calculated to enable the court to apply another rule in a later case on the ground that the later case is not "like" *Plus.* Similarly, the phrase, "in large part," suggests that the court could focus on other, unidentified considerations in a future case.

7. Compare with *Irons v Mailo,* 3 TTR 194 (Truk 1966). (The court relied on Fischer [1958b, 207] to indicate that a deathbed will supersedes any previous will, written or otherwise, even without the consent of or notice to the persons whom he has previously designated to receive his land.)

8. It is perhaps ironic that Fischer's work in Pohnpei often was cited to demonstrate powers asserted by the previous Japanese and German administrations. The translation of Japanese land lease forms used in Pohnpei was often cited to establish the retained power of the government to approve or disapprove any transfer of the leasehold rights to others. See *Mikelina v Simon,* 1 TTR 153, 154 (Ponape 1954) (permission of the Japanese administration required to effect transfer to new leaseholder upon death of original lessee); *Idingel v Mada,* 1 TTR 164, 166 (1954) (same); *Aknes v Weli,* 1 TTR 323, 324–325 (Ponape 1957) (for "history of the general practice of the Japanese Administration as to making government land on Pohnpei available to individuals"). See also *Protestant Mission v Trust Territory,* 3 TTR 26, 31 (Ponape 1965) (citing *Land Tenure Patterns* [deYoung 1958] for the proposition that "it was widely known on Ponape that all property from high-water mark out was considered to belong to the German Government."); and *Sehpin v Atta,* 4 TTR 33, 36 (Ponape 1968) ("The Ponapean text of the German land code provides that an illegitimate child may be legitimatized by the subsequent marriage of its biological parents. It is not known whether this provision was taken from Ponapean custom or not. . . . Where no further action is taken by the father an illegitimate child has very low status as an heir.")

9. *Santer v Onita,* 1 TTR 439, 440 (Truk 1958); *Kilion v Cheche,* 1 TTR 442 (Truk 1958); *Nusia v Sak,* 1 TTR 446 (Truk 1958).

10. See, e.g., *Duguwen v Dogned,* 1 TTR 223 (Yap 1955); *Kenul v Tamangin,* 2 TTR 648, 651 (Appellate 1964); *Moolang v Toruuan,* 3 TTR 219, 221 (Yap 1966).

11. *Orak v Ngiraukloi*, 1 TTR 454, 456 (Palau 1958); *Ngeskesuk v Moleul*, 2 TTR 188, 191 (Palau 1961); *Adelbai v Ngirchoteot*, 3 TTR 619, 625 (Appellate 1968).

12. I am indebted to Suzanne Falgout for bringing to my attention and providing copies of these items relating to the relationship between anthropologists and the USTTPI legal system.

13. I surmise this to be Francis Mahoney.

14. Saul Riesenberg.

15. The existence of such a privilege could be interpreted not only as recognition of the value of communications to an anthropologist, but also as devaluation of the importance of justice in the US Trust Territory of the Pacific Islands.

16. The Code provision, 7 TTC § 2 (1970), said: "Conversations held with an anthropologist in conference in his professional character shall be privileged. No statement made in such a conversation nor the substance thereof, shall be divulged without the consent of the person making it, nor shall the identity of any person making such a statement on any particular subject be divulged without his consent, except as provided herein. This privilege, however, shall not extend to the professional opinions or conclusions of an anthropologist even though they may be based in whole or in part on such conversations . . ."

17. See, e.g., *Christopher v Trust Territory*, 1 TTR 150, 151 (Ponape 1954) ("No matter how harsh the action of the German Government in confiscating all rights in this land may seem, . . . whether it was legal must be decided according to the law at the time it happened."); *Catholic Mission v Trust Territory*, 2 TTR 251 (Yap 1961); *Martin v Trust Territory*, 1 TTR 481 (Palau 1958). See also *Urrimech v Trust Territory*, 1 TTR 546 (Palau 1958) (Toomin, J.) and *Sechesuch v Trust Territory*, 2 TTR 458 (Palau 1963).

18. *Trust Territory v Camacho*, 7 TTR 273 (Appellate 1982); *Crisostimo v Trust Territory*, 7 TTR 375 (Appellate 1976).

19. *Alig v Trust Territory*, 3 TTR 601, 616 (Appellate 1966).

20. In *People of Saipan v Department of the Interior*, 502 F2d 90 (9th Circuit 1974), the United States Court of Appeals for the Ninth Circuit held the trusteeship agreement to be the constitutional document of Micronesia and a source of judicially enforceable rights. Two years later, in *Trust Territory v Lopez*, 7 TTR 449, 453–454 (Appellate 1976), the USTTPI High Court, "with all due respect to the majority of the court in *People of Saipan*," held that "*Alig* prevails" and "the trusteeship agreement does not create a trust capable of enforcement through the courts."

21. *Simiron v Trust Territory*, 8 TTR 615 (Appellate 1988).

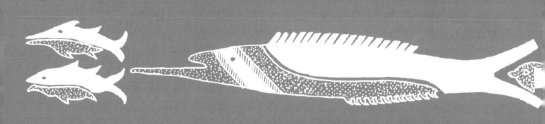

CHAPTER TWELVE

Ripples from a Micronesian Sea

Mac Marshall

WORLD WAR II WAS a pivotal event—perhaps *the* pivotal event—in modern Pacific history. Both directly and indirectly the war turned the Pacific upside down. New colonial relationships were established; new forms of transportation and communication grew rapidly after the war, building on the airfields and harbor facilities constructed as part of the war effort; and the war stimulated new migrations to towns in the islands and to countries beyond. New ideas, new social relationships, and new experiences born of the war and its aftermath wove Pacific peoples ever more tightly into the global system.

The war also strongly affected the discipline of anthropology in the United States; following World War II "everything in the anthropology field had changed direction and it lacked its old coherence" (Hall 1992, 159). This was especially true for Micronesia, which had been one of the major theaters of fighting in the western Pacific. Some anthropologists gave attention to Micronesia during the war in the preparation of background materials, while others served directly in military campaigns in the islands. For many, such wartime experiences proved decisive in leading them subsequently to conduct research there. This was particularly the case for those anthropologists involved in the United States Commercial Company (USCC) and the Coordinated Investigation of Micronesian Anthropology (CIMA), which are described by Robert C. Kiste and Suzanne Falgout (chap. 1).

My goal in this chapter is to evaluate the anthropological studies completed by American researchers in Micronesia from 1945 to 1997, as these studies are situated within the major shifts that have occurred in American anthropology over the past half century. I begin by examining the backgrounds and personal and institutional connections among researchers involved in the USCC, CIMA, and other projects in Micronesia—especially those who had significant impact on the discipline, on the American colonial administration, and (perhaps less apparently) on the Micronesians themselves. I then discuss the consequences of their research for anthropological theory and practice, for our ethnographic understanding of Micronesia, and for the growth and development of anthropology—especially Pacific anthropology—in the United States.

Kiste and Falgout also explain the background of the Scientific Investigation of Micronesia (SIM), the US Trust Territory of the Pacific Islands (USTTPI) applied anthropology program, the Tri-Institutional Pacific Program (TRIPP), and the Comparative Study of Cultural Change and Stability in Displaced Communities in the Pacific (DCPP), so this information is not repeated here. Over the entire period under investigation there has been considerable overlap in the key personalities and personnel who organized and participated in these different projects, which will be noted in this chapter.

To examine and evaluate the "ripples" that have emanated from these major anthropological projects in Micronesia, the discussion must be located within two historical frames: first, the geopolitical situation in the western Pacific in the prewar and immediate postwar years, and second, the history of ideas in anthropology over this same period of time.

HISTORICAL FRAMES

In the mid-1930s Great Britain, France, Japan, the Netherlands, Australia, and New Zealand formed the dominant colonial presence in Oceania. The United States controlled Hawai'i, American Samoa, and Guam, with Japan firmly ensconced in the rest of the Marianas, the Carolines, and the Marshall Islands (see Howe, Kiste, and Lal 1994). Most Pacific anthropologists in the preceding half century came from the three major European powers, plus Australia and New Zealand.[1] Before the beginning of World War II, most studies in cultural anthropology had taken place in Melanesia and Polynesia, and only seventeen American cultural anthropologists had conducted research in the Pacific region (other than Hawai'i).[2]

A few numbers will give some idea of the scale of the CIMA project relative to the prior involvement of American anthropologists in the Pacific Islands. This undertaking included twenty-five American cultural anthropologists, and two American physical anthropologists, along with three American linguists (see appendix 1A for a full listing of all CIMA participants). *Thus the number of cultural anthropologists involved in the Coordinated Investigation of Micronesian Anthropology was one and one-half times that of all American cultural anthropologists who had worked in Oceania other than Hawai'i before 1941 (twenty-five versus seventeen).* When the additional cultural anthropologists who participated in the USCC and SIM projects in the immediate postwar years are added to these (see below and appendix 1), the impact of anthropology in Micronesia at that time becomes even more impressive.

Before World War II, American cultural anthropology was a very small academic discipline located in a few major universities and several large research museums. Its dominant tone had been set by Franz Boas and the many prominent students he trained at Columbia University who went on to found or staff notable anthropology departments around the country. In Great Britain, by contrast, prewar anthropology had developed as a kind of comparative sociology of nonwestern peoples. A. R. Radcliffe-Brown emerged as a dominant figure in this social anthropology tradition, comparable to Boas in the United States in his influence on the discipline and on a whole generation of students. Radcliffe-Brown came to the University of Chicago in 1931 and remained there until 1937 (Kuklick 1991, 314), "converting" many American students and scholars in the process (among them, Frederick Eggan; see below). Similarly, from 1939 to 1942 Bronislaw Malinowski—another proponent of social anthropology—taught at Yale (Kuklick 1991, 316), where he, too, exercised considerable influence on American anthropology. Part of the postwar anthropological research in Micronesia traces its roots directly to either American cultural anthropology or British social anthropology (see figures 1 and 3).

While these two traditions differed in many ways in the late 1930s, the most prominent difference was the rise of culture and personality studies in the United States. This development derived from the intellectual excitement generated by Freud, and from efforts by American scholars to incorporate Freudian concepts and ideas into their scholarly work (see Black, chap. 7). Employed initially by some of Boas' students, particularly Margaret Mead and Ruth Benedict, culture and personality studies had entered the intellectual mainstream of American anthropology by 1941. One more prewar anthropological development in the United States was the rise of applied anthropology. As Kiste and Falgout discuss, American applied anthropology of the time grew from the heavy focus on Native Americans and from the involvement of some anthropologists with the Bureau of Indian Affairs (BIA). According to Murray Wax (1995), this research had a "revolutionary impact," embodied a set of "reformist goals" concerning the education of Indian youngsters, and contributed to the agenda of the "group of mavericks" who founded the Society for Applied Anthropology in 1941. Wax noted that Laura Thompson and Alice Joseph were part of this BIA involvement. One might well assume, then, that some such reformist goals animated Thompson's research on Guam in the late 1930s, particularly in those aspects that were critical of the naval administration (see Petersen, chap. 5); these same ideas may have carried over as well into the CIMA-sponsored research that Joseph completed on Saipan with her colleague, Veronica F. Murray (see Marshall, chap. 4; Rubinstein, chap. 10).

FIRST STIRRINGS OF AMERICAN ANTHROPOLOGY IN MICRONESIA: THE USCC SURVEY

The United States Commercial Company survey was organized and directed by Douglas L. Oliver of Harvard University.[3] Although he did not conduct anthropological fieldwork in Micronesia, Oliver wrote the final USCC report (1951) and his efforts produced one of the first major "ripples from a Micronesian sea." While employed by Harvard's Peabody Museum, Oliver oversaw a USCC economic survey research team comprised of three anthropologists, William Bascom, Edward T. Hall, and Leonard E. Mason, and a sociologist, John Useem. Indicative of the overlap among major anthropological research projects in Micronesia, USCC participants Oliver, Useem, and Mason all were also involved in CIMA projects, in one way or another. Bascom and Hall had little further to do with Micronesia once their assignment was finished. They had completed their doctorates (under the direction of Melville J. Herskovits and Ralph Linton, respectively) some years before they joined the economic survey. Bascom was one of the few American anthropologists touched by the Pacific during or after the war who did not "succumb" to the islands' lure. Instead, after writing up his Pohnpei material (e.g., Bascom 1946), he devoted the rest of his life to a distinguished career in African research. Having served in the army during the war, Hall enrolled in a postdoctoral program in sociology at Columbia, where he "realized that my predilection was clearly toward what was later to be known as applied anthropology" (Hall 1992, 160). Perhaps it was in following this predilection that Hall accepted the assignment to work as part of the USCC team after Useem recommended him (1992, 161). However, like Bascom, he wrote only a very few things about his Micronesia experiences in Chuuk before going on to other matters.

A sociologist by training, John Useem did postdoctoral study at Columbia in 1943–1944 while working as a social analyst at the Office of Indian Affairs, and then served in the navy in the islands of Yap and Palau toward the end of the war. In fact, he was in the third wave of assault troops to come ashore on Angaur, where he and his team of military government personnel were responsible for the civilian inhabitants caught in the midst of that battlefield (George 1995, 319). (One other member of that navy team, Francis Mahoney, had a speaking knowledge of Japanese, subsequently returned with Useem to Palau under CIMA auspices [George 1995, 323], and later served as a district anthropologist there and in Yap [see appendix 1C].) Although his background was in sociology, Useem served in the late 1940s as regional vice president of the Society for Applied Anthropology, one of many positions held during his distinguished career. It is Glenn Petersen's considered opinion that Useem's early work presaged many later important issues in the politics of Micronesia (see chap. 5).

The USCC team member who has exercised the greatest influence on Micronesian anthropology is Leonard Mason. He began graduate study at Yale before the war and started to work with Cornelius Osgood, studying the Swampy Cree in Canada (Mason 1967c). His Micronesia involvement grew directly from his wartime work with George Peter Murdock and others in Washington after Mason was recruited to join the Cross-Cultural Survey. This experience for him—as for so many others—shifted his research focus permanently to the Pacific. One result was that in 1947 Mason assumed a full-time position as chair of the department of anthropology at the University of Hawai'i;[4] another result was that he subsequently wrote a dissertation at Yale under Murdock's direction (Mason 1954), grounded in research with the Bikini Islanders who had been permanently affected by the selection of their atoll for atomic and nuclear weapons tests.

Mason is one of the deans of Micronesian anthropology, and his personal influence on at least two generations of younger anthropologists who have worked in Micronesia has been significant. While this was most dramatic for his former students (e.g., William Alkire and Jack Tobin), it was also true for many others, especially those who worked in the Marshall Islands (e.g., Robert Kiste, Nancy Pollock, and Michael Rynkiewich). Mason made facilities (including his home) available to young scholars as they passed through Honolulu en route to and from the field; assisted them with academic and other contacts; and all the while has continued to be actively involved in his own research in both the former US Trust Territory of the Pacific Islands and, later, Kiribati (e.g., Mason 1985b). Mason taught many of the contemporary leaders

1993 Conference. Left: *Jerome Feldman,
art historian, Hawai'i Pacific University;* right: *Leonard Mason. Photograph
by Carolyn Yacoe.*

of the new Micronesian nations while they were students at the University of
Hawai'i, and has consulted on many different projects—academic and applied
—over the years. He has made central contributions to cultural ecology and
ecological anthropology in the region (see Alkire, chap. 3), to applied anthropology (see Kiste and Falgout, chap. 1; Hezel, chap. 9), and to studies of Micronesian arts (see Nero, chap. 8).

On balance, some very sound ethnography resulted from the USCC survey,
representing the first English language material on Micronesian cultures
other than Thompson's prewar Guam study. Of the four men involved in the
economic survey, only Mason became a Micronesianist, although over the
years Oliver chaired the doctoral committees of four students who did their
fieldwork in Micronesia (William Stevens, Ann Fischer, Nancy Pollock, and
Maria Teresa del Valle).

THE CIMA WAVE

The Coordinated Investigation of Micronesian Anthropology washed over the discipline, and transformed the anthropology of Micronesia in its turn (see appendix 3 for one example). Both the initial CIMA wave and the subsequent ripples such as the Scientific Investigation of Micronesia continue to affect Pacific anthropology and anthropological theory to the present day. As Kiste and Falgout indicate, a total of forty-one researchers carried out CIMA studies between July 1947 and January 1949 (see appendix 1A). Murdock of Yale University was both mastermind behind and overall director of the CIMA project, although Oliver also played an important role (see, e.g., Bashkow 1991, 182). Most significantly, the "emergent network of academic veterans of the war agencies," led by Murdock and including Clellan S. Ford, Margaret Mead, Ralph Linton, Cora Du Bois, Fred Eggan, and Lauriston Sharp, gained the upper hand over a competing group with "an alternative vision" consisting of men such as Herbert Gregory, E. S. C. Handy, and Felix Keesing (Bashkow 1991, 182, 183). Concerning the importance of these personal connections for the Coordinated Investigation of Micronesian Anthropology, two of Eggan's students (William Lessa and Alex Spoehr) were CIMA participants, Ford chaired a CIMA dissertation (Frank LeBar), and Sharp was an undergraduate professor of two more CIMA researchers (Ward Goodenough and David Schneider).[5]

At the project's inauguration, eight of the twenty-five CIMA cultural anthropologists and one of the three physical anthropologists held a doctoral degree.[6] Nine of the remaining cultural anthropologists and the two other physical anthropologists completed their PhDs, all but two based on CIMA research (see appendixes 1A and 2A).[7] Despite the prominence of women like Ruth Benedict and Margaret Mead in American anthropology, women played a very minor role in CIMA projects (see appendix 1A). It is not clear whether this reflected the "old boy" networks of the day, or whether there simply were no women interested in participating. Other than Alice Joseph and Veronica Murray (neither of whom was an anthropologist by training) who were sent to the Marianas, the only woman in a CIMA study was Margaret Chave who went to Majuro. She completed a master's degree, and married anthropologist Lloyd Fallers, but did not go on to work professionally in anthropology. Perhaps one indication of why so few women were CIMA participants can be found in Schneider's assertion that his wife was not allowed to accompany him to Yap because Murdock "had set the policy: no wives" (Handler 1995, 86–87). In any case, the lack of women continued in the SIM program, with Ann

Fischer the only female participant, and no women were involved in the Displaced Communities in the Pacific Project. With two exceptions (Ann Fischer in 1957, and Jane Hainline Underwood's PhD in physical anthropology in 1964), no woman earned a Micronesia doctorate until Nancy Pollock in 1970. Since then, more than one-third of the PhDs based on Micronesian research have been awarded to women (see appendix 2A).

The eight cultural anthropologists with previous PhD training who participated in CIMA research were Homer G. Barnett, Sir Peter H. Buck, Edwin G. Burrows, Kenneth P. Emory,[8] William Lessa, George P. Murdock, Alex Spoehr, and Joseph Weckler. Burrows and Emory were among the few American anthropologists to have done prewar research in Oceania (both in Polynesia), and Buck (a New Zealand Māori) had also conducted research there before the war. Of these eight, Barnett, Murdock, and Spoehr especially continued to influence Pacific anthropology by training a number of doctoral students who worked in Micronesia and elsewhere in Oceania (see figures 1, 2, and 3).

Homer G. Barnett completed a doctorate at Berkeley under Franz Boas' first graduate student, A. L. Kroeber, and joined the faculty at the University of Oregon in 1939.

> During 1944–1946 he served as anthropologist with the Bureau of American Ethnology and concurrently as research associate with the Ethnogeographic Board, engaged in providing background information on peoples and places where the war was being prosecuted. His assigned focus was Oceania; and independently he drew up plans for a postwar study of the Palau Islanders and their experiences under a succession of colonial administrations. When, at war's end, he returned to Oregon, that project was incorporated in the Coordinated Investigation of Micronesian Anthropology. (Stern 1987, 702)

Thus, a wartime assignment sparked Barnett's interest in Micronesia, and this played out in several ways.

First, he succeeded his old graduate school chum Philip Drucker as staff anthropologist for the USTTPI government from 1951 to 1953, during which time he was also "a member of the Research Council of the South Pacific Commission," and after which he became a part-time advisor to the governor-general of Netherlands New Guinea (Stern 1987, 702). Second, having published *Palauan Society* in 1949, Barnett followed with his major theoretical formulation, *Innovation, The Basis of Cultural Change* (1953), and with a signal contribution to applied anthropology, *Anthropology in Administration* (1956).

Both of these works were heavily informed by his Micronesia and other Pacific experiences. Third, Barnett conceptualized the Displaced Communities in the Pacific Project and obtained National Science Foundation funding for it. Both his own students from Oregon and several from other institutions participated in this comparative study of the changes experienced by members of the twelve study communities. Among many other DCPP outcomes were three dissertations based on studies in Micronesia (Kiste 1967; Knudson 1970; Lieber 1968b). Beyond his writings Barnett wielded considerable influence on the wider discipline, as is indicated in tables 1 and 2.

George Peter Murdock's contributions to anthropology are legion, and while they go well beyond Micronesia they are also intimately connected to the area, particularly via his role in the Coordinated Investigation of Micronesian Anthropology (see Kiste and Falgout, chap. 1). In the mid-1930s, he began to develop his famous cross-cultural approach to a science of society based on a worldwide sample of reasonably independent cases. This theoretical position subsequently was strongly influenced by a cross-disciplinary group of scholars who met weekly at the Institute of Human Relations at Yale: anthropologists Clellan S. Ford, Bronislaw Malinowski, Edward Sapir, John Whiting, and Clark Wissler, and psychologists John Dollard, Arnold Gesell, Clark Hull, Neal Miller, and Robert Yerkes (J. Whiting 1986, 683–684). This seminar illustrates yet again the willingness of anthropologists in the 1930s and 1940s to entertain ideas from psychology.

Along with this intellectual engagement Murdock had already founded the Cross-Cultural Survey (CCS), and the first edition of the *Outline of Cultural Materials* had appeared in 1938. It was the CCS materials on which Murdock and colleagues drew during World War II to produce a set of civil affairs handbooks for Micronesia, Okinawa, and Taiwan, and it was out of Murdock's wartime contacts and experiences in the navy that the CIMA idea developed (see Kiste and Falgout, chap. 1). Building on all of this, Murdock played a pivotal role in founding the Human Relations Area Files (HRAF) in 1949, from which he eventually produced the World Ethnographic Sample and the *Ethnographic Atlas* (see appendix 3). In addition, he held many offices in professional organizations and received a host of honors for his work (see tables 1 and 2).

Closely related to the CCS and HRAF projects, Murdock's major theoretical work, *Social Structure,* was published in 1949, and in the mid-1960s he was instrumental in establishing the Society for Cross-Cultural Research. Throughout this time Murdock served as dissertation supervisor for a distinguished series of Pacific anthropologists, three of whom completed their degrees based on

Table 1 Major Honors Bestowed on American Anthropologists Who Conducted Post–World War II Research in Micronesia

	W. Goodenough	Spiro	Spoehr	Murdock	Barnett	Schneider	Emory	J. Fischer	Lessa
Fellow, NAS[1]	X	X	X	X					
Fellow, AAA&S[2]	X	X							
Fellow, CASBS[3]	X	X				X		X	
Honorary Fellow, ASAO	X		X		X		X		X
Guggenheim Fellowship		X				X			
Herbert E. Gregory Medal[4]				X			X		
Fellow, APS[5]	X								
Viking Fund Medal				X					
Huxley Medal, RAI[6]				X					
Wilbur Lucius Cross Medal				X					
Hawai'i Governor's Medal							X		
Charles Reed Bishop Award[7]			X						
Morgan Lecturer, U. Rochester	X								

| Distinguished Service Award, AAA[8] | X |
| Malinowski Award[9] | X |

[1] National Academy of Science
[2] American Academy of Arts & Sciences
[3] Center for the Advanced Study of the Behavioral Sciences, Palo Alto, California
[4] Awarded by the Pacific Science Congress
[5] American Philosophical Society
[6] Awarded by the Royal Anthropological Institute of Great Britain and Ireland
[7] Awarded by the Bernice Pauahi Bishop Museum, Honolulu, Hawai'i
[8] American Anthropological Association
[9] Awarded by the Society for Applied Anthropology

Table 2 Significant Offices Held in Professional Societies Other than ASAO by American Anthropologists Who Conducted Post–World War II Research in Micronesia

	Murdock	Spoehr	W. Goodenough	Spiro	Barnett	Schneider	J. Fischer	Weckler	Lessa	Riesenberg
President, AAA[1]	X	X								
President, AES[2]	X		X	X						
President, SfAA[3]	X		X		X					
President, SPA[4]				X	X					
President, SCA[5]						X				
President, SAS[6]							X			
President, SWAS[7]								X		
President, ASW[8]										X
Vice-Pres., AFS[9]									X	
Section H, AAAS[10]			X							
Executive Board, AAA						X	X			
Executive Board, AES							X			

Executive Board, AAAS X

Executive Board, SSRC[11] X X

Secretary, AAA X

[1] American Anthropological Association
[2] American Ethnological Society
[3] Society for Applied Anthropology
[4] Society for Psychological Anthropology
[5] Society for Cultural Anthropology
[6] Southern Anthropological Society
[7] Southwestern Anthropological Society
[8] Anthropological Society of Washington
[9] American Folklore Society
[10] American Association for the Advancement of Science
[11] Social Science Research Council

fieldwork in Micronesia and who subsequently have helped shape the direction of research there (Thomas Gladwin, Ward Goodenough, and Leonard Mason; see figure 2).

Alex Spoehr was Fred Eggan's first graduate student at the University of Chicago, completing a PhD there in 1940. Immediately thereafter he became assistant curator of American ethnology and archaeology at the Field Museum, where he remained until he entered the navy in 1942. His wartime service as an intelligence officer and a navigator on Military Air Rescue Service flying boats in the Pacific developed his anthropological interest in that part of the world (Engle 1992; Krauss 1992; Sutlive 1993). At one point he was stationed at Majuro Atoll in the Marshall Islands. Consequently, when he returned to the Field Museum in 1946, it was as curator of Oceanic ethnology. With this new-found interest he was chosen as both a CIMA participant (on Majuro) and a SIM researcher (on Saipan, Tinian, and Rota, Mariana Islands), and he prepared monographs of enduring importance on each of these experiences (Spoehr 1949a, 1954, 1957).

Spoehr has been described as "a rare individual who combined credentials as a scholar and scientist with abilities to lead centers of research through periods of change" (*Honolulu Star-Bulletin,* June 16, 1992), and it was in the next two phases of his career that he demonstrated this knack. Spoehr took over as director of the Bishop Museum in January 1953, and restored it "to a research and teaching institution of world renown" (Sutlive 1993, 45).[9] During the nine years that he directed the museum he also received a Presidential appointment as a US Commissioner to the South Pacific Commission, and he worked with fellow CIMA researchers Mason and Murdock to administer the Tri-Institutional Pacific Program (TRIPP). After two years as East-West Center chancellor, Spoehr moved to the University of Pittsburgh in 1964, joining Murdock who had gone there from Yale in 1960. Spoehr was "a major figure in the study of the societies of the Pacific" (Sutlive 1993, 45), and the man's stature in the discipline is reflected in the numerous honors and awards he received (see tables 1 and 2).

As an undergraduate William Lessa attended Harvard, where a course in human evolution from Earnest A. Hooten convinced him that he wanted to be an anthropologist. When Lessa graduated, Hooten hired him to work in his statistical laboratory, and later recommended him for a research position in physical anthropology at Columbia-Presbyterian Medical Center in New York under the supervision of Harry L. Shapiro of the American Museum of Natural History. Shapiro invited Lessa to conduct an anthropometric research project

*Alex Spoehr as navy officer stationed
at Majuro, Marshall Islands, 1943.
Photograph courtesy of Hardy Spoehr.*

in Honolulu, and from 1930 to 1932, as a research associate at the University of Hawai'i, Lessa measured the Chinese-Hawaiian population. Following this, he was sent to Kwangtung, China, to measure the relatives of those whom he had studied in Hawai'i.

Appropriately for one who eventually studied under Eggan at the University of Chicago (see figure 3), Lessa participated in a seminar at Yale during summer 1934, where "the participants were mostly administrators in colonial and administrative circles in nations throughout the world, and the binding force was A. R. Radcliffe-Brown and his daily lectures in social anthropology" (Lessa n.d., 7). It was at this time that Lessa "became truly conscious of a field of anthropology not dominated by human biology" (n.d., 7).[10]

Unlike most of the others who worked in Micronesia after the war, Lessa's wartime experiences had been in the European theater, and at Eggan's urging, these formed the basis for his doctoral dissertation in 1947.[11] Eggan's friendship with Murdock was instrumental in his students, Lessa and Spoehr, being accepted for the CIMA project, and by the end of 1947 Lessa was on Ulithi. He made two trips there under CIMA auspices, in between which he took up a tenure-track faculty position at the University of California, Los Angeles, where he remained for the duration of his academic career. Lessa played an active role in the discipline (see tables 1 and 2) and chaired the doctoral committees of two Oceanists (Walter Tiffany and Sharon Tiffany).

Lessa produced an abundant body of published material for Ulithi, covering a very wide range of data from folktales to projective tests (e.g., Lessa 1961; Lessa and Spiegelman 1954), and from demography to social organization (Lessa 1950a, 1955; Lessa and Myers 1962). Late in his career he turned his attention to Micronesian history and wrote a delightful and informative book on Sir Francis Drake's voyages to Micronesia (Lessa 1975).

Joseph Weckler also received a doctorate from the University of Chicago shortly before World War II with a library dissertation on ritual status in Polynesia, although he had completed fieldwork in a Spanish-American community in New Mexico at about the same time (Hoijer 1964). From 1941–1943 Weckler served as associate curator of ethnology at the US National Museum in Washington, D.C.; he then joined the Office of Inter-American Affairs, and soon thereafter was a field representative for the American Council on Race Relations (1943–1945). Eggan was a member of his doctoral committee, and this may account for Weckler's CIMA involvement, although it is also likely that he had contact with Murdock and others in Washington during the war years. Weckler became chair of the department of anthropology at the University of Southern California when the war was over and remained in that position until his untimely death in 1963 (Hoijer 1964). He wrote relatively little on his 1947 CIMA research on Mokil before he died, but the hour-long 16 mm color documentary film he, Conrad Bentzen, and Melvin Sloan made while there is one of the finest examples available for showing what life is like on a coral atoll.

After serving in the army in World War I, Edwin G. Burrows went to Honolulu in the 1920s before he began graduate study and had "a successful career in journalism which included the city editorship of the *Honolulu Advertiser*" (J. H. Barnett 1959, 97). Burrows worked at the Bishop Museum from 1931 to 1934, conducted fieldwork on Uvea and Futuna in western Polynesia in 1932 (Burrows 1970), taught as a visiting lecturer at the University of Hawai'i in 1936, and finished a doctorate in anthropology from Yale in 1937 (at age 46). In 1939 Burrows joined the faculty of the University of Connecticut, where he taught for the remainder of his career, interrupted only by a two-year period in the Military Intelligence Division of the War Department General Staff in Washington, D.C. Once more, wartime experiences and contacts led to Micronesia when hostilities ceased. Burrows' two books based on his Ifaluk research have become classics of Micronesian anthropology (Burrows 1963; Burrows and Spiro 1953), and Karen Nero sees him as someone who "offered theoretical perspectives well ahead of his time" (chap. 8, p. 255), and whose contributions still have not received the attention they deserve.

Kenneth Emory was hired by Herbert Gregory as assistant ethnologist for the Bishop Museum in January 1920. He studied under Kroeber at Berkeley in spring 1921, and then finished a master's degree at Harvard under Roland Dixon in 1923 (Krauss 1988, 401). Partially on this basis he was promoted to ethnologist at the Museum, a post he filled from 1924 to 1948. During his long, distinguished career in Pacific ethnology and archaeology, primarily in Polynesia, Emory did research in Hawai'i, the Society Islands, the Tuamotus, Mangareva, and—during World War II—on Espiritu Santo in Vanuatu. Emory taught island survival courses during the war and wrote a small guide book on the same subject as chief instructor to over 150,000 students at the Armed Forces Special Ranger and Combat School on Hawai'i (Danielsson 1967). Having begun his doctorate at Yale in 1940, he returned in 1945 and received a PhD in 1946 based on work he had completed years before in eastern Polynesia.

Emory had begun discussions with Murdock and Oliver as early as November 1944 about a planned exploration of Micronesia once the fighting ended (Krauss 1988, 405). As a Polynesianist, it was only appropriate that he was chosen to work in 1947 with his fellow Polynesianist (and Polynesian!) colleague, Sir Peter H. Buck, in the CIMA study on the Polynesian outlier of Kapingamarangi, where he later returned alone under SIM auspices. Among other accolades for his work (see table 1), Emory was honored with a major Festschrift volume (Highland et al. 1967).

Nine anthropology PhDs were based on CIMA research,[12] and three were awarded to SIM researchers (see appendix 2A). Collectively, these anthropologists have left a notable mark on the discipline through their writings, via the Oceania and other graduate students they have trained, and through the positions and offices they have held in universities, museums, government agencies, and academic associations (see tables 1–3, figures 1–4 and discussion below).[13]

One way to gauge the immediate effect of the Coordinated Investigation of Micronesian Anthropology and the Scientific Investigation of Micronesia is to calculate the proportion of all anthropology doctoral degrees awarded by universities in the United States that derived from these two projects. A recent study has been published that provides the number of anthropology PhDs granted by year for the 1948–1994 period (Givens and Jablonski 1995). Using those figures, plus those in appendix 2A, for the six years between 1949 and 1954 inclusive, 6 percent of all anthropology doctorates awarded in the United States derived from CIMA and SIM research.[14]

The three CIMA and SIM researchers who have been most prominent in the discipline writ large are Goodenough, Schneider, and Melford E. "Mel" Spiro. Each has exercised a profound influence on anthropological theory, particularly through their many writings on kinship and social organization (see Marshall, chap. 4), in psychological anthropology (see Black, chap. 7), and in the anthropology of religion.[15] These influences will be discussed in more detail in the concluding section to this chapter.

Ward Goodenough's work "has had a substantial impact on modern cultural anthropology" (Caughey and Marshall 1989, 1), especially in three areas: cognitive anthropology; "culture as a distinct, ideational, nonbehavioral construct"; and in "representations of cultural diversity and sharing, culture change, and the relationship of social psychological considerations to systems of knowledge" (Caughey and Marshall 1989, 6). Not only has Goodenough played a central role in the development of cognitive anthropology (e.g., Goodenough 1951, 1956c, 1965b, 1967), but he has also written extensively on language and linguistics (e.g., Goodenough 1957b, 1981b; Goodenough and Sugita 1980, 1990). No less important, and reinforcing the contributions anthropology in Micronesia has made to the development of applied anthropology in the United

States, he has also described very clearly some of the ways anthropological theory bears on the applications of anthropology to practical problems (Good-enough 1963). For many years Goodenough chaired the HRAF Board of Directors; he was editor of the _American Anthropologist_ from 1966 to 1970, and also a member of the editorial board of _Science_ in the late 1970s. More recently he has been honored by a Festschrift volume (Marshall and Caughey 1989), and his many other accomplishments are listed in tables 1 and 2.

Richard Handler wrote that he decided to gather the information for his recent book _Schneider on Schneider_ because "it seemed to me that, like [Clifford] Geertz, Schneider had been a key figure in defining the direction American anthropology had taken in the 1960s and 1970s" (1995, 1). Indeed, David Schneider became a major proponent of symbolic anthropology as a theoretical approach to cultural anthropology (see especially Dolgin, Kemnitzer, and Schneider 1977; Schneider 1968). He "was a leader in the revitalization of the culture concept," and his "work on American kinship transformed the anthropological study of kinship in contemporary Western societies" (Handler and McKinnon 1995, 39). Reviewing kinship studies in the late twentieth century, Michael Peletz referred to Schneider's monograph on American kinship "as an exemplar of an interpretive anthropology, pioneered under the tutelage of Talcott Parsons and centered on symbols and meanings" (1995, 346). In terms of the lasting effects of Schneider's work, however, perhaps most importantly, "his critique of the assumptions of earlier kinship studies opened the door for feminist scholars exploring the intersections among kinship, sex, gender and power that had been problematized, but left largely unexamined, in his work" (1995, 346). Based on Schneider's efforts to extend his analysis of kinship to nationality and religion (e.g., Schneider 1969b), other scholars "instigated a series of studies on those topics and their connection to gender, race, language and class" (1995, 346).

Schneider played a vital role in anthropology, nationally and internationally. He served as an associate editor of the _American Anthropologist_ from 1956 to 1959, and during the late 1960s, acting behind the scenes, he helped focus and organize the Association for Social Anthropology in Oceania (ASAO) in its formative stages. In more recent years he was involved directly in the establishment of the Society for Cultural Anthropology and its lively journal, _Cultural Anthropology_. It is thus fitting that his final publication has appeared posthumously in that society's journal (Schneider 1997). As befits a person of his stature, he held significant office and received numerous academic honors during his career (see tables 1 and 2).

No less impressive than Goodenough's and Schneider's contributions are those Mel Spiro has made to psychological anthropology, the anthropology of religion, and kinship and family studies. Spiro's generalist approach to anthropology reflects that of his mentor, A. I. Hallowell. Following his CIMA work on Ifaluk, Spiro subsequently conducted field research in Israel, Burma, and Thailand, with a particular concentration on Israel and Burma. While he remains the most widely known and cited neo-Freudian in anthropology, Spiro's studies of religion—especially Buddhism (Spiro 1966a, 1971, 1984)—are equally prominent. His role as a leading theoretician in the philosophy of social science, and a major voice for a scientific anthropology based on a sophisticated positivism, has been recognized in the numerous honors he has received and offices he has held (see tables 1 and 2). After teaching at Washington University, University of Connecticut (with Burrows), the University of Washington, and the University of Chicago (with Schneider), Spiro founded the department of anthropology at the University of California, San Diego, in 1968. That department has become widely known for the excellent training it provides in psychological anthropology and Oceanic studies, in no small part because of the hires Spiro made with this in mind. Spiro was also a founder of the Society for Psychological Anthropology and helped launch two journals, *Ethos* and *Cultural Anthropology*. In addition he has served as an associate editor of the *American Anthropologist* and of *Ethos*, among many other editorial positions.

Goodenough and Schneider played a central role in the growth of Pacific anthropology in the United States in the postwar period via their mentorship of numerous graduate students, many of whom went on to mentor still others and to make their own important contributions to the discipline (see figures 2 and 4).[16] Spiro's impact on Pacific anthropology has been less dramatic in this regard (although he supervised two students who completed dissertations based on fieldwork in Fiji and Papua New Guinea), but he has had many PhD students who have worked in other parts of the world.

Other CIMA and SIM PhDs also have made notable contributions to the wider discipline (see tables 1 and 2), as a few highlights will indicate. Saul Riesenberg advised the government of American Samoa during 1955–1956 (Rubinstein 1995, 196), taught in the anthropology department at the University of Hawai'i from 1949 to 1957, and then spent the remainder of his career at the Museum of Natural History, Smithsonian Institution, where "he served as Director of the Cultural Anthropology Division, Chair of the Anthropology Department, and Curator of Pacific Ethnology" (Rubinstein 1995, 196). In this last capacity he oversaw installation of the permanent exhibition in the Pacific Hall.

As is made clear in Peter Black's account (chap. 7), Thomas Gladwin wrote books and articles from his Micronesia research that helped shape and define the field of psychological anthropology in the postwar era. Particularly prominent in this regard were two books: *Truk: Man in Paradise* (Gladwin and Sarason 1953) about Romónum, Chuuk; and *East Is a Big Bird* (Gladwin 1970) about Puluwat. Following his CIMA study, Gladwin remained in Micronesia to work as a native affairs officer for the US Navy Civil Administration in Chuuk in the late 1940s. Near the end of his career, while on the faculty of the University of Hawai'i, he joined others in the emotionally wrenching questioning of anthropology's role in colonial administration that crested during the Vietnam conflict (see Petersen, chap. 5).

Arthur Vidich was in the US Marine Corps from 1942–1946, serving on Guam, Saipan, and later in Japan. Once again, wartime experiences shaped academic directions. After earning a master's degree at the University of Wisconsin, Vidich finished a doctorate in cultural anthropology in the department of social relations at Harvard based on his CIMA-derived Palauan material. His subsequent career has moved strongly in the direction of sociology, but perhaps more properly should be seen as presaging much of the work now conducted in the United States by anthropologists (e.g., Vidich and Bensman 1958; see also Vidich 1995). A prolific author, Vidich has held positions in the American Sociological Association and was honored by the Eastern Sociological Society. He has also held a host of editorial appointments for publications that cut across a broad range of the social sciences (e.g., *The International Journal of Politics, Culture and Society*).

For many years Frank LeBar worked for the Human Relations Area Files in New Haven, founded by his CIMA mentor, Murdock. His major work on the material culture of Chuuk (LeBar 1964) was followed by a very comprehensive and widely consulted volume on Southeast Asia published by the Human Relations Area Files (LeBar 1972).

Ann Fischer completed a dissertation on child training in Chuuk at Radcliffe College in 1957, following a year of SIM-funded research (in 1949) and three additional years' residence on Pohnpei. After being part of John Whiting's famous Six Cultures Project, conducting a study of child rearing in a New England town during 1954–1955 (Halpern 1973), Ann and John L. "Jack" Fischer moved to Tulane University where Ann became involved in anthropology, public health, and social work. Program chair of the 1969 annual meeting of the American Anthropological Association, and (with Jack Fischer) reviews editor of the *American Anthropologist* shortly before her untimely death from cancer at age 52, Ann Fischer made meaningful contributions to psychological anthropology, applied anthropology, and medical anthropology (see Rubinstein, chap. 10).

Jack Tobin served as the only district anthropologist in the Marshall Islands during the USTTPI government (from 1950 to 1958), and he later worked there as a community development advisor from 1967 to 1974. He first went to the Marshalls in 1950, accompanying Mason to Arno as part of the SIM Coral Atoll Project. After many years in the islands, he completed a dissertation at Berkeley, drawing on research material he had gathered on Enewetak, the other community forced to relocate to accommodate US atomic and nuclear weapons tests on their atoll.

TRIPP AND THE USTTPI APPLIED ANTHROPOLOGISTS

Like the Scientific Investigation of Micronesia, the Tri-Institutional Pacific Program (TRIPP) was not limited to Micronesia, and only one person, Roland Force, earned an anthropology PhD based on TRIPP-sponsored research in that region. Working under Felix Keesing at Stanford, Force was in Palau from the end of 1954 until April 1956. In the revised and published version of his dissertation, he acknowledged "a very special debt of gratitude to Dr. Alexander Spoehr . . . for his sustaining guidance and inspiration" (1960, 7), and this comment foreshadowed an interesting aspect of Force's career. After Spoehr left the Field Museum to become director of the Bishop Museum in 1953, Force eventually replaced him at the Field; after Spoehr left the Bishop Museum to become East-West Center chancellor, Force replaced him once again, this time as director of the Bishop Museum.[17] Many years later, on Spoehr's death, Force was quoted as saying that "Spoehr greatly influenced his career as an anthropologist, sending him into the Pacific after graduate [course] work, and later recommending him as curator of Oceanic archaeology and ethnology at the Field Museum in Chicago" (Krauss 1992).

In the entire history of the applied anthropology effort in the USTTPI there were five staff anthropologists and eleven district anthropologists (including Gladwin as a native affairs officer for the navy; see appendix 1C and Kiste and Falgout, chap. 1). Six of the latter eventually completed PhDs.[18]

Other than Gladwin (see above), Jack Fischer was the most visible of the applied anthropologists to the wider discipline. Fischer spent a year in Chuuk (where he met and married Ann), working as district anthropologist, before moving to Pohnpei for another three years in a similar capacity. He "pio-

Roland and Maryanne
Force visiting old friends
in Mengellang Village,
Babeldaop, Palau,
September 1994.
Photograph by
Robert Kiste.

neered a new style of applied anthropology," and helped open up Micronesia further as a research area to American scholars (Marshall and Ward 1987, 134). But his contributions to academic anthropology were of even greater import: "He was an accomplished linguist, a keen student of social organization, a pains- taking folklorist, an advocate for psychological anthropology, and a major fig- ure in Pacific ethnography" (1987, 135). While he also conducted research in New England and Japan, "it will be Fischer's continued interest in and major contributions to the anthropology of Micronesia for which he will be most remembered. His survey of what was then known of the anthropology of the Eastern Caroline Islands (1957), his debate with Goodenough over the classifi- cation of residence in village censuses (1958), and his edited and translated presentation of a valuable Pohnpeian manuscript history (1977) must be counted among his most significant contributions" (Marshall and Ward 1987, 135). Also important was Fischer's documentation in Chuuk of what we today call intracultural variation by demonstrating that the descriptions of Romónum Island by the Yale CIMA team did not hold for all of Chuuk

Lagoon, let alone for the surrounding atolls. This close attention to context and detail was developed into what Fischer (1968) termed "microethnology" in the comparisons he made between Chuuk and Pohnpei, which began with his doctoral dissertation. Fischer also supervised two Micronesia anthropology PhDs (Marksbury 1979; R. Ward 1977).

Robert McKnight was a district anthropologist in Palau and Yap from 1958 to 1963, and in the process earned a PhD from Ohio State University in 1960. He later became USTTPI community development officer from 1963 to 1965, and actively copublished with his Micronesian assistants, anticipating by many years what has become a trend in contemporary anthropology (see Nero, chap. 8).

Frank Mahony served in various applied anthropology positions in Pohnpei and especially Chuuk for many years, gaining an enviable mastery of the Chuuk language while doing so. This linguistic facility enabled him to explore the intricacies of the Chuuk ethnomedical system in his PhD dissertation, completed in 1970 at Stanford (see Rubinstein, chap. 10). Soon thereafter, Mason brought Mahony to join the anthropology faculty at the University of Hawai'i, from whence Mahony moved to a post with the South Pacific Commission before he died.

None of the other five USTTPI applied anthropologists finished a doctoral degree. Shigeru Kaneshiro did some graduate study in anthropology at the University of Hawai'i's department of anthropology before working as district anthropologist in Yap and later on Saipan. Harry Uyehara was involved in the USCC survey and CIMA and SIM studies before he became an applied anthropologist in Palau, and he obtained a master's degree based on a household study of Arno as part of the SIM research there. Francis Mahoney (not to be confused with Frank Mahony) had been in Palau at the end of the war as a navy interpreter (George 1995), returned as a member of the CIMA team to Palau led by Useem, and then stayed on in an applied role. Years afterward he did contract-funded applied research in Micronesia, authoring an important study on alcohol in the islands (Mahoney 1974; see Hezel, chap. 9). Robert Solenberger earned a master's degree under Goodenough, worked in applied roles in the former Marianas District of the trust territory, and eventually joined the faculty of Bloomsburg State College (now Bloomsburg University) in Pennsylvania. Other than his applied work in Micronesia, Al Whiting's anthropology career was mostly in museums, although he taught at the College of Guam in 1954.

MICRONESIANISTS' ACADEMIC LINEAGES

Through this plethora of programs and the many different anthropologists who were involved in them, the CIMA and SIM research in Micronesia has greatly influenced the growth of Pacific anthropology in the United States in the postwar era. It has also had a pronounced effect on the wider discipline, a matter to which I will return in the concluding section. Most anthropologists who organized and participated in CIMA and SIM projects had academic careers in the United States, and as they fanned out across the country they mentored students who themselves ventured out to the Pacific (both to Micronesia and elsewhere) to conduct their own research. It is far beyond the scope of this chapter to detail all of these connections; instead, I sketch how the ripples from a Micronesian sea have spread out across the anthropology of Oceania, particularly during the past thirty years, by examining the "academic pedigrees" and "lineages" of four major CIMA figures.[19] The four pedigrees derive from some of the major figures of the discipline: Barnett is linked to Franz Boas via Kroeber; Murdock is linked to William Graham Sumner via Keller; Schneider is linked to Alfred M. Tozzer via Kluckhohn; and Spoehr is linked to A. R. Radcliffe-Brown via Eggan. The lineages of these four researchers are sketched and examined by discussing their "descendants" who completed doctoral research in Oceania. The lineages do not include PhD students who worked elsewhere in the world. Nevertheless, a reminder that these scholars have had many such students provides further testimony to the wide impact on the discipline of the postwar Micronesia effort.

Homer G. Barnett trained ten Oceania doctoral students at the University of Oregon in the 1960s and 1970s, only partially as a result of the Displaced Communities in the Pacific Project (see figure 1). Two other Pacific anthropologists trained at Oregon (Craig Severance 1976, Piis-Emwar, Mortlocks, Chuuk; and Rebecca Stephenson 1976, Atiu, Cook Islands) were heavily influenced by Barnett during their graduate education, but he was not their dissertation advisor because he had retired by the time they finished. Moreover, two students who received their doctorates from other universities were also included in Barnett's DCPP research: Michael D. Lieber (Pittsburgh 1968, Kapingamarangi and Porakiet), and Henry P. Lundsgaarde (Wisconsin 1966, Kiribati).[20]

Barnett's students have made their mark as well. The entire group hold or have held faculty appointments at US colleges and universities, several in major departments, although Kiste is the only one to have chaired doctoral students

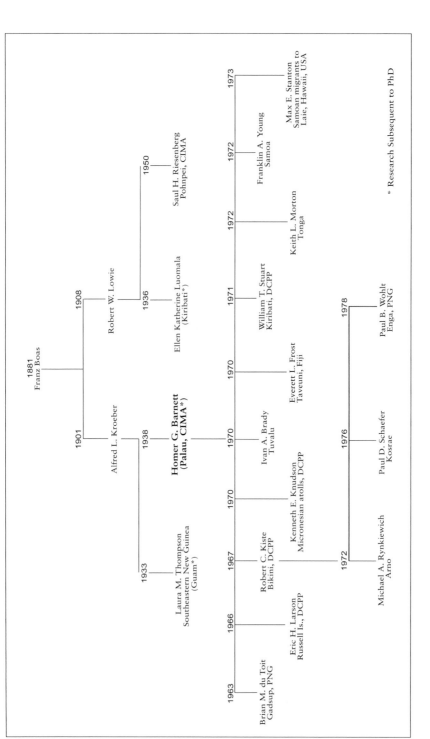

Figure 1. Homer G. Barnett's Academic Lineage, Showing Dates of PhD Dissertations and Locations of Doctoral Research in Oceania

Table 3 ASAO Offices Held by American Anthropologists Who Conducted Post–World War II Research in Micronesia

	Chair, Executive Committee	Member, Executive Committee[1]	Newsletter Editor	Secretary	Program Chair[2]	Series Editor
V. Carroll	X	X			X	X
M. Marshall	X	X	X		X	X
M. Lieber	X	X			X	
J. Fischer	X	X				
L. Poyer	X	X				
K. Nero	X	X				
R. Kiste		X	X	X	X	
R. McKnight		X				
D. Hughes		X				
J. Nason			X	X		
P. Dahlquist			X			
R. Marksbury			X			
R. Ward			X			
S. Falgout				X		
J. Flinn				X		
L. Mason					X	
L. Mayo					X	
L. Carucci					X	

[1] In addition, Leslie B. Marshall, whose background is in physiology and biophysics but who has done extensive research in Micronesia, served on and chaired the executive committee.

[2] The office of Program Chair was later converted to the office of Annual Meeting Coordinator.

to completion (see figure 1). Ivan Brady and Kiste, in particular, have played important roles in the development of the Association for Social Anthropology in Oceania (regarding Kiste, see table 3). Brady chaired the ASAO executive committee, edited ASAO Monograph No. 4, and was the first editor of the ASAO Occasional Papers Series (now ASAO Special Publications). He also served as book reviews editor for the *American Anthropologist* from 1978 to 1985, holds a distinguished teaching professorship at State University of New York, Oswego, and was president of the Society for Humanistic Anthropology in 1996–1998. Kiste became director of the Pacific Islands Program (later renamed

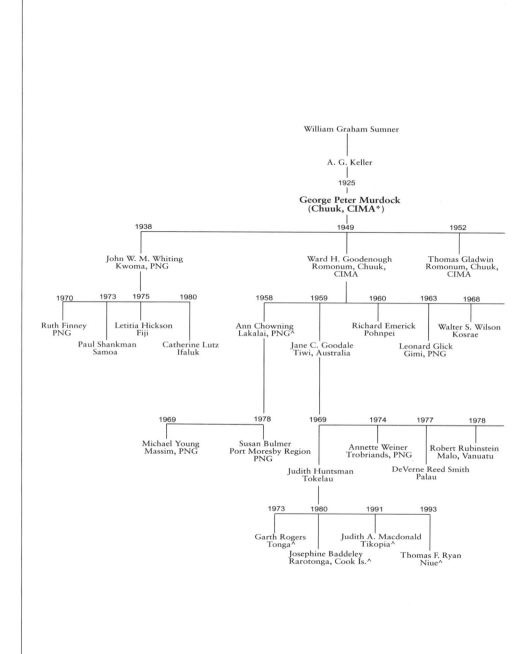

*Figure 2. George Peter Murdock's
Academic Lineage, Showing Dates of
PhD Dissertations and Locations of
Doctoral Research in Oceania*

1954   1958

Leonard E. Mason   Melvin L. Ember
Bikini, SIM   Samoa

1970 1972 1974 1977 1977 1979 1981 1983 1985 1990

Anne Salmond   Harold G. Levine   Elizabeth Dickie   James Flanagan   Elizabeth Faithorne
Maori, NZ   Kafe, PNG   Malo, Vanuatu^   Wovan, PNG   Kafe, PNG

John L. Caughey Stuart Berde Anna Meigs Jay Noricks Patricia Parker
Wuumaan, Chuuk Misima, PNG Hua, PNG Tuvalu Weene, Chuuk

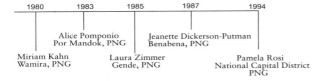

1980 1983 1985 1987 1994

Alice Pomponio   Jeanette Dickerson-Putman
Por Mandok, PNG   Benabena, PNG

Miriam Kahn Laura Zimmer Pamela Rosi
Wamira, PNG Gende, PNG National Capital District
PNG

* Research Subsequent to PhD   ^ Co-chair

the Center for Pacific Islands Studies [CPIS]) at the University of Hawai'i in 1978, and turned that into a thriving enterprise that offers a master's degree in Pacific Islands studies, and publishes the Pacific Islands Monograph Series, founded and edited by Kiste. He was also instrumental in founding a major regional journal, *The Contemporary Pacific,* which is edited and published by the University of Hawai'i Press.

A second Micronesianist who has left a long lineage in Pacific anthropology is George P. Murdock, and this lineage becomes especially rich because it includes Murdock's student Goodenough, who has chaired fifteen Oceania dissertations at the University of Pennsylvania, and Goodenough's student, Jane Goodale, who has chaired nine such dissertations at Bryn Mawr College (see figure 2). This group of CIMA "descendants" has left its mark in a multitude of ways. Ann Chowning chaired the department at Barnard; was a senior research fellow at the Australian National University; taught at the University of Papua New Guinea, where she served as dean of the faculty of arts; and from 1977 until her retirement in 1995, she served as professor and chair of the department of anthropology at Victoria University of Wellington, New Zealand. A professor at the University of Auckland, Anne Salmond has recently been knighted, and she has won a host of other honors for her research and writings about the New Zealand Māori. Most of Goodenough's other students have held academic appointments in the United States. James Flanagan has served as ASAO newsletter editor and executive committee member and has chaired his department at the University of Southern Mississippi, and Anna Meigs is director of the Women's and Gender Studies Program at Macalester College. Patricia Parker, along with her husband, Thomas King, has contributed to the archaeology of Chuuk (King and Parker 1984), and works for the National Park Service, in which capacity she has played a central role in directing research on historical preservation in Micronesia.

In addition to having chaired both her department at Bryn Mawr and the ASAO executive committee, Goodale has directed the dissertations of an active and distinguished set of doctoral students, one of whom (DeVerne Smith) worked in Micronesia (see figure 2). Two of Goodale's students became especially prominent in the discipline. Judith Huntsman has taught at the University of Auckland for many years, published extensively on Tokelau and Tokelau migrants to New Zealand, and edited *The Journal of the Polynesian Society.* Annette Weiner was internationally recognized for her work on gender and exchange in the Trobriands and elsewhere in Oceania, and served as president of the American Anthropological Association, chair of her department at New York University, and also as a dean there.

The third academic lineage of a Micronesianist to be discussed is that of Alex Spoehr during the years that he taught at the University of Pittsburgh (see figure 3). Spoehr's "descendants," while relatively few in number, have nevertheless made an impact in Pacific anthropology. Michael Lieber has been heavily involved in ASAO administration in several capacities (see table 3): he also cofounded the ASAONET Oceanic Anthropology Discussion Group, and edited ASAO Monograph No. 5. Richard Scaglion chaired the ASAO executive committee and also serves on the editorial board of *Ethnology*. Sherwood "Woody" Lingenfelter is the provost at Biola University. Both Scaglion and William Wormsley have engaged in significant applied anthropology projects in Papua New Guinea, following a tradition established by Spoehr and others in the CIMA contingent. All of these men have published important ethnographic works, and Scaglion has chaired two Oceania doctoral committees at Pittsburgh.

The final Micronesianist whose lineage is examined here is David M. Schneider, who chaired ten Oceania doctoral dissertations while at the University of Chicago (see figure 4). Many of Schneider's students, and students of his students, have authored highly acclaimed books about the Pacific. This lineage also has had a pivotal and continuing central role in the establishment and maintenance of the Association for Social Anthropology in Oceania. Vern Carroll played perhaps the most active role in the association's early history (see table 3), and edited ASAO Monographs Nos. 1 and 3. But in addition to Carroll, many other "descendants" of Schneider have been centrally involved in ASAO administration. Martin Silverman served on the fifth and sixth ASAO executive committees. James Nason, Mac Marshall, and Lin Poyer all have been heavily involved in ASAO governance (table 3), and Marshall was also volume editor of ASAO Monograph No. 8. Julia Hecht was ASAO secretary, Bradd Shore and Lamont "Monty" Lindstrom served on the executive committee, and Lindstrom is ASAO special publications editor and editor of ASAO Monograph No. 11. Silverman (University of British Columbia), Shore (Emory University), Marshall (University of Iowa), and Roy Wagner (University of Virginia) have all chaired their departments; Wagner has mentored five Oceania PhDs, and Margaret Mackenzie and Vern Carroll have supervised three each.

There have been seventy-eight dissertations in sociocultural anthropology completed in Micronesia by American researchers since World War II, and twenty-two of these are represented in figures 1–4. Barnett has four Micronesia "descendants," Murdock has nine, Spoehr two, and Schneider eight. But the CIMA and SIM programs have affected the doctoral committees of Micronesia anthropologists in other ways as well. For example, Mason and Schneider

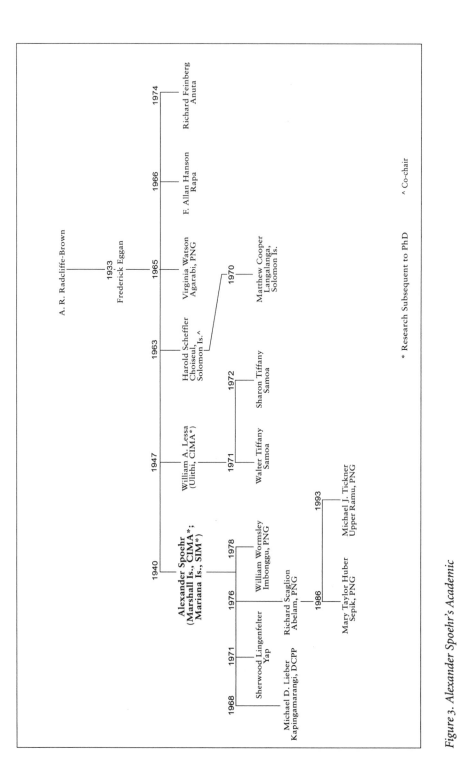

Figure 3. Alexander Spoehr's Academic
Lineage, Showing Dates of PhD Disser-
tations and Locations of Doctoral
Research in Oceania

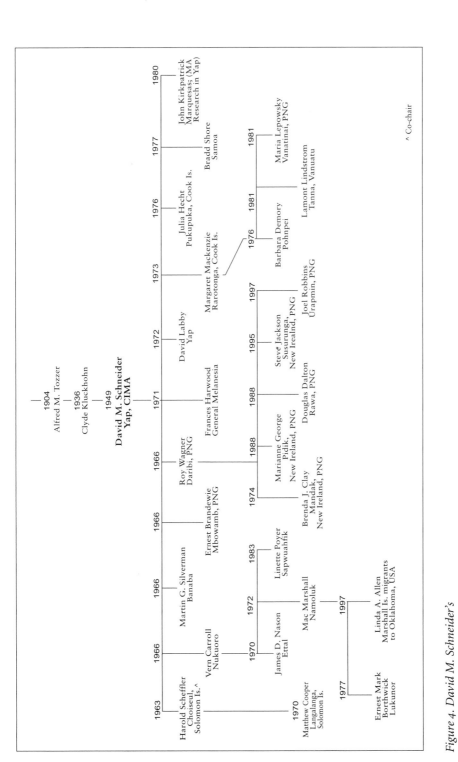

Figure 4. David M. Schneider's
Academic Lineage, Showing Dates of
PhD Dissertations and Locations of
Doctoral Research in Oceania

Table 4 Oceania PhDs Completed by "Descendants" of Barnett, Murdock, Schneider, and Spoehr, through 1997

	Micronesia	Polynesia	Melanesia	Total
Barnett	5	4	4	13
Murdock	9	9	21[a]	39
Schneider	10[b]	3	12	25
Spoehr	2[c]	0	4	6
Total	26	16	41	83

[a] Includes Jane Goodale (Tiwi, Melville Island, Australia).
[b] Includes Vern Carroll's study of Nukuoro and Linda Allen's study of a Marshallese migrant community in the United States.
[c] Includes Michael D. Lieber's study of Kapingamarangi.

each served on four such committees as a member other than chair, and Murdock did so on one. CIMA geographer Neal Bowers served on Nancy Pollock's PhD committee, and SIM nutritionist Mary Murai served on the doctoral committees of Barbara Demory and Peter Steager.

Yet another way to calculate the "staying power" of CIMA influence on Micronesian anthropology is to look at particular "lines of descent" in figures 1–4. Barnett supervised Kiste, who in turn oversaw Michael Rynkiewich and Paul Schaefer. Murdock supervised Goodenough, who chaired doctoral committees for John Caughey, Richard Emerick, Patricia Parker, and Walter "Scott" Wilson, and whose non-Micronesianist student, Goodale, served as DeVerne Smith's committee chair. Schneider supervised Carroll, who had three Micronesia PhD students: Nason, Poyer, and Marshall. Marshall oversaw Ernest "Mark" Borthwick's dissertation, served on Charles Reafsnyder's doctoral committee, and supervised Linda Allen's PhD study of Marshallese migrants to the United States.

Recall that only seventeen American anthropologists had conducted research in Oceania outside of Hawai'i before World War II (see note 2). Table 4 provides a partial measure of CIMA impact on Pacific anthropology as a whole, showing that eighty-three "descendants" of Barnett, Murdock, Spoehr, and Schneider have completed Oceania dissertations. Since one of these (John W. M. Whiting) did his dissertation before the war, and two (Linda A. Allen and Max E. Stanton) conducted fieldwork with Pacific Islands migrants to the United States, this leaves eighty non-Hawai'i-based Oceania dissertations completed by "descendants" of these four men between 1949 and 1997. Table 4 also shows that these four CIMA researchers' "descendants" worked in all three Pacific regions, with the number of Melanesia dissertations approximately equal to those from Micronesia and Polynesia combined. More ripples from a Micronesian sea.

CONCLUSIONS

The discussion above has demonstrated that World War II was a defining moment for Micronesian anthropology: the war concentrated the attention of American anthropologists on these islands and led many of them to carry out research there once hostilities ended. The war also produced experiences and created personal connections that led to the series of team projects beginning with the USCC economic survey and ending with the DCPP research approximately twenty years later. More fundamentally, the war turned American anthropology upside down and set it on a new course. Part of this course, as noted above and by Kiste and Falgout (chap. 1), was to accentuate more scientific and applied approaches in sociocultural anthropology.

Over the half century since World War II, American anthropology in Micronesia has continued in these scientific and applied directions. In a recent deconstruction of the term "positivism" as it has been used in anthropology of the 1990s, Paul Roscoe noted that positivism has mistakenly been identified with science, and that many participants in the current debate have ignored "the interpretive manner in which natural science is actually practiced" (1995, 497). He concluded that the hermeneutic methods of the natural sciences are applicable to the study of human culture and society.

The research done by American anthropologists in Micronesia since World War II discussed in this volume illustrates this natural science aspect of the discipline in a variety of ways outlined below. This is particularly true for the numerous instances in Micronesian anthropology where successive scholars have built on one another's work. "Cultural anthropology has tended to problematize such cases as the 'Rashomon effect,' but they might better be represented as normal science. Were it usual for several noncollaborating field-workers (rather than just one) simultaneously to study a community, their subsequent public scrutiny of one another's constructions would make fully apparent the scientific nature of the interpretive method" (Roscoe 1995, 498). Postwar American anthropology in Micronesia has been normal science in this sense. While in most cases field-workers have worked in the same communities not simultaneously but successively and steadily, in doing so they have scrutinized, criticized, corroborated, and refined our collective knowledge of Micronesian culture and society.

The Coordinated Investigation of Micronesian Anthropology was the launching pad for this endeavor. In several island areas in Micronesia the research completed by CIMA workers has been built on rigorously and resolutely by subsequent generations of scholars. Burrows and Spiro on Ifaluk were succeeded by Catherine Lutz, and then by Paul Turke; Buck and Emory on Kapingamarangi were followed by Lieber. After Mason on Bikini and Enewetak came Kiste and Tobin, who were followed in turn by Laurence Carucci. But the four island areas of CIMA involvement where such normal science has particularly flourished are Chuuk, Palau, Pohnpei, and Yap.

Chuuk was studied by the Yale CIMA team of Murdock, Goodenough, Gladwin, and LeBar, who were followed shortly by Ann Fischer (SIM), Gladwin, Jack Fischer, and Frank Mahony (in applied roles), and Marc Swartz (regarding Swartz, see Marshall, chap. 4). Goodenough and Gladwin returned to carry out further research in Chuuk in the 1960s and 1970s, by which time a new set of researchers had come to the islands of Chuuk State. Caughey, Marshall, Nason, and Steager in the late 1960s and early 1970s were followed by Borthwick, Severance, Mary Thomas, and John Thomas later in the 1970s, while Marshall did research in a second community in Chuuk State. The 1980s witnessed work by Juliana Flinn, Robert "Bruce" Larson, Marshall, Parker, Reafsnyder, and Don Rubinstein; Flinn, Edward D. "Ted" Lowe, and Marshall have all conducted fieldwork there since 1990. Similar networks of scholars rooted in the CIMA investigations of fifty years ago can be constructed for Palau, Pohnpei, and Yap, but perhaps the point has been made (see appendixes 2A, 2B, and 2C in this regard).

Without a doubt, the areas in which this normal science research tradition in Micronesia has most affected anthropological theory are psychological anthropology, cognitive anthropology, kinship and social organization, and the anthropology of religion. Black states that research in Micronesia has made major contributions to psychological anthropology and "has greatly enriched the subdiscipline" (chap. 7, p. 228). These contributions include the terrain "where cognitive anthropology, psychology, and linguistics overlap, especially in studies of emotion" (chap. 7, p. 229). Moreover, Black argues that ethnopsychology "which has largely replaced culture and personality, developed out of the cognitive turn in cultural anthropology which itself had at least some roots in culture and personality studies. Much of this story played itself

1993 Conference.
Mac Marshall,
Karen Peacock.
Photograph by
Carolyn Yacoe.

out in Micronesia" (chap. 7, p. 239); most visible in this regard was the work of two CIMA researchers—Spiro on Ifaluk and Gladwin in Chuuk. In addition, according to Black, "the emergence of the ethnopsychological perspective" (chap. 7, p. 244), exemplified by Lutz's 1988 study of Ifaluk emotion, builds on the pioneering work of Goodenough and Gladwin.

Black also credits Goodenough and Gladwin with helping to set the stage for "the rise of cognitive anthropology," particularly via their writings on "a spectacular, nonwestern, nonliterate, intellectual edifice": the indigenous navigation system *(etak)* of the Carolinians (chap. 7, p. 241; see Gladwin 1970; Goodenough 1953; Goodenough and Thomas 1987; cf. D'Andrade 1995, 152–158). This serious attention to "the knowledges and practices of non-Western peoples" by Gladwin and Goodenough, among others, has been labeled part of the legacy of Malinowski's view of science (Gonzalez, Nader, and Ou 1995, 867). But Goodenough's contributions to "the rise of cognitive anthropology" grow as much from his writings on the componential analysis of kinship terms as they do from those on the Carolinian star compass (Marshall, chap. 4; see Goodenough 1964, 1965a, 1965b, 1967). This provides a bridge to considering the influence of studies of kinship and social organization in Micronesia on anthropological theory.

The major forces in this area are the writings of Schneider on the one hand

and Goodenough on the other. As the careers of these two men unfolded, their approaches to the study of kinship diverged. Schneider turned toward the symbols and meanings encoded in kinship systems while Goodenough concentrated on their formal, logical (cognitive) properties. Both were advocates for emic analysis, but beyond that they took very different paths (see, for example, Goodenough 1965b; Schneider 1965a). Not only was the work of Schneider and Goodenough at the core of many of the theoretical debates that swirled through American cultural anthropology between the 1950s and the 1970s, but when anthropological attention began to turn to other arenas for theoretical sport, Schneider wrote the epitaph to the entire enterprise (1984).

Although not as strongly associated with kinship studies as Schneider and Goodenough, Spiro has also made very significant anthropological contributions in this area. While Spiro's Ifaluk research produced such gems as "A Typology of Functional Analysis" (1953b), it can be argued that his Micronesia experiences laid the groundwork for his later studies of the kibbutz in Israel (1956, 1958, 1979a) and the work he did in Burma (1977). Interspersed among these books is a series of important articles and chapters (e.g., 1954a, 1961a, 1963, 1965b).

Another area of kinship research in Micronesia that has had important theoretical repercussions is the focus on siblingship (see Marshall, chap. 4), something Peletz emphasized in a recent review: "The suggestion that we take siblingship, as opposed to, say, parent-child relations, as our point of departure is far more radical than it might initially appear. The proposal is that first we concentrate our analytical gaze on relations among the living (rather than links between the living and the dead and/or the unborn); and that, second, we zero in on bonds among individuals of the same relative generation—which, of course, constitute 'key' ('core') social relations in all societies" (1995, 350). Peletz went on to argue that greater attention to the study of siblingship would allow us to "reorient and revitalize the study of kinship" (1995, 350).

CIMA researchers have been extremely visible in the anthropology of religion since the war. Lessa was senior editor (with Evon Z. Vogt) of the most widely used textbook in this field, *Reader in Comparative Religion: An Anthropological Approach* (1958), a volume that has gone through four editions. This work built in part on Lessa's studies of Ulithian religion and cosmology. Schneider (1969b) tried to extend the kind of analysis he advocated for kinship to religion, and both Goodenough and Spiro made important contributions to the study of religion.

In a series of papers on religion covering more than twenty years, Goodenough's work has built mainly on his Chuuk material (1966b, 1974b, 1981a,

1986, 1988a). Spiro's contributions to the anthropology of religion, by contrast, began with Ifaluk (1961b, 1965a) but then expanded into intensive study of supernaturalism and Buddhism in Asia (1966b, 1967, 1968, 1971, 1984), and subsequently to more general publications (1966a, 1969, 1979b, 1982).

Postwar anthropological research has greatly increased our ethnographic data base for Micronesia—indeed, this may be the single greatest contribution of all this work taken together, because it allows for the pursuit of normal science as discussed above. For example, Petersen (chap. 5) notes the wealth of ethnographic detail on Micronesian political systems that has been published, research that consistently reveals the connections among descent, seniority, land, nurturance, chieftainship, and demonstrated individual competence. While he discovered no major theoretical contributions to political anthropology from the Micronesia work, he noted the use of this ethnographic material for several important comparative articles that yielded synthetic insights (e.g., Mason 1959a; Peoples 1992).

Rich ethnographic data also come to the fore in Nero's (chap. 8) focus on the works of three CIMA anthropologists—Burrows, LeBar, and Lessa. She sees these as important contributions to the study of Micronesian arts, although only Burrows' *Flower in My Ear* (1963) is singled out as a major theoretical contribution that, ironically, has been overlooked. Nero notes that the interactive nature of art in society and the study of performance, both of which have become important in contemporary anthropology of art research, are presaged in the ethnographic research done on the arts in Micronesia, but again not acknowledged in the discipline.

The ethnographic work by Lessa that Nero discusses is his focus on the verbal arts of Ulithi, particularly folktales (Lessa 1961, 1962b, 1966b, 1980). While Lessa's collection of such materials is perhaps the largest for any single Micronesian society, others have gathered and published folkloric material of enduring value to the discipline—particularly in more recent years as such oral material has become lost. This includes contributions by Jack Fischer (e.g., 1959b; Fischer and Swartz 1960), Spiro (1951b), Rufino Mauricio (1992), and Nero (1992a).

Like Petersen and Nero, William Alkire (chap. 3) concludes that no major theoretical contributions to cultural ecology and ecological anthropology have derived from Micronesian research, but that much excellent ethnographic information has been gathered in the islands that can be put to good purpose. In his own work, Alkire has been exemplary in doing just that (e.g., Alkire 1960, 1977, 1978).

In chapter 6, Poyer suggests that studies in Micronesia have enriched the anthropological theory informing ethnicity and identity. She notes how concepts of community, psychological theories of identity, and ethnic boundaries were dealt with by Micronesianists in works by Brady (1976), Carroll (1970a, 1975a), Goodenough (1951, 1963, 1965a), and Lieber (1977a), and shows how this work connects "with developing cultural, interpretive, political, economic, and critical perspectives in anthropological theory" (Poyer, chap. 6, p. 219).

The wartime and postwar reorientation of sociocultural anthropology toward more practical concerns is most visible in the applied anthropology program during the 1950s and 1960s in the US Trust Territory of the Pacific Islands (see Kiste and Falgout, chap. 1). In terms of the overall development of the discipline, particularly in its greatest area of current job growth, research in Micronesia has been central to matters of anthropological application and practice. It is no accident that USCC/CIMA researchers Murdock, Barnett, Goodenough, Oliver, and Useem all held elective office in the Society for Applied Anthropology (see table 2). But while Barnett's influential book, *Anthropology in Administration* (1956), illustrated applied anthropology in colonial settings, other ways of applying anthropology have come to the fore in subsequent years.

The book that captures this shift is Goodenough's *Cooperation in Change* (1963). As Edward C. King (chap. 11) notes, it was widely read outside of anthropology, and one of the places where it had considerable influence was the Peace Corps. The impact of Goodenough's book on the Peace Corps and other development and assistance efforts globally goes beyond our concerns here. But it is pertinent to note that Goodenough and several other anthropologists took an active role in training the hundreds of Peace Corps Volunteers who went to Micronesia beginning in 1966. Among the other anthropologists involved in this effort were Alkire, Jack and Ann Fischer, Roland and Maryanne Force, Kaneshiro, Kiste, Mahoney, Mahony, Mason, McKnight, Schneider, and Tobin. At least as important, several prominent researchers came into Micronesian anthropology after first serving as Peace Corps Volunteers in the islands (e.g., Black, James Carucci, Flinn, Reafsnyder, Philip Ritter, and Severance). Poyer (chap. 6) and Hezel (chap. 9) discuss how some anthropologists in more recent years have conducted research on "social problems" with both applied and academic aspects. It is likely that work of this sort will continue to grow in Micronesia.

Beyond such theoretical and applied contributions, a number of anthropologists who have worked in Micronesia over the past half century have helped shape the course of the discipline through important leadership positions they occupied, and academic societies and journals they helped create. For example, nineteen have chaired their departments,[21] another seven have held higher administrative jobs at their universities,[22] six have held curatorial positions at major museums,[23] and four have directed leading museums in the United States.[24] Micronesianist sociocultural anthropologists have been centrally involved in the establishment of six professional journals: *Cultural Anthropology* (Schneider and Spiro), *Ethnology* (Murdock), *Ethos* (Spiro), *ISLA* (Rubinstein), *Micronesica* (W. S. Wilson), and *The Contemporary Pacific* (Kiste), and have had a major hand in founding four professional organizations: Association for Anthropology in Micronesia (Mason), Association for Social Anthropology in Oceania (Carroll and Schneider), Society for Cross-Cultural Research (Murdock). and the Society for Cultural Anthropology (Schneider and Spiro).

Without question, however, the place on the professional landscape of contemporary American anthropology where Micronesianists have left their greatest mark has been the Association for Social Anthropology in Oceania. No single individual played a greater role in the establishment and early success of the organization than Vern Carroll. After the first three years, during which it had no formal governance, Carroll served as the first chair of the executive committee, almost single-handedly launched the ASAO Monograph Series, and was monograph series editor until 1974. He was also the first ASAO annual meeting coordinator, serving from 1979 until 1985. However, Carroll was far from the only Micronesianist to have been deeply involved in the ASAO governance (see table 3). Besides ASAO offices, six of the fifteen ASAO Monographs published from 1970 to 1995 were edited by Micronesianists.

The CIMA, SIM, and other programs in Micronesia in the decade following World War II not only produced an incremental growth in our knowledge about Micronesian society and culture, but these endeavors created a splash of such magnitude that the ripples continue to move across the discipline today. Those who participated in these programs had a major hand in redirecting postwar anthropology in America, contributed importantly to anthropological theory and method, trained subsequent generations of Oceanists who spread to Melanesia and Polynesia as well as Micronesia, and assumed major leadership positions that have helped shape the course of American anthropology over the past half century. Such are the ripples from a Micronesian sea.

NOTES

Special thanks to the following individuals who provided me with information that I have incorporated into this chapter: Suzanne Calpestri, Ann Chen, Ann Chowning, Suzanne Falgout, Maradel Gale, Ruth Goodenough, Ward Goodenough, Rebecca Grow, Richard Handler, Alan Howard, Robert Kiste, William Lessa, Nancy Lurie, Jeff Marck, Leonard Mason, Eugene Ogan, Richard Scaglion, Virginia Smyers, Beverly Sperring, Mary Tugaoen, and Arthur Vidich. I also have benefited from critical readings of an earlier draft by Ward Goodenough, Terry Hays, June Helm, Lin Poyer, Margery Wolf, and particularly by Peter Black, Robert Kiste, and Don Rubinstein.

1. Of course, before the strong German colonial presence in Oceania ended at the outbreak of World War I, German researchers also conducted extensive studies in the islands.

2. There were about 300 members of the American Anthropological Association at that time, and the annual meetings typically attracted no more than 100. Using the 2,123 biographical sketches available in the *International Directory of Anthropologists* (Herskovits 1950), I found there were 689 American anthropologists at the end of the 1940s. (For purposes of this analysis "Americans" are defined as those who were US born [including Puerto Rico, Guam, and what was then the Territory of Hawai'i] who were not specifically listed as citizens of another country, and those listed as US nationals who were resident abroad.) Of these American anthropologists (in all four fields), 56 (approximately 8 percent) had conducted research in Oceania *outside of Hawai'i* before 1941, but only 17 (thus about 2 percent of all American anthropologists alive in the late 1940s) had conducted *cultural* anthropological research in Oceania before the advent of World War II. These included several very prominent figures in American anthropology (see Kiste and Falgout, chap. 1, note 1). Of them, Burrows, Emory, Ford, Felix Keesing, Oliver, Thompson, and John Whiting were all involved with postwar anthropology in Micronesia, either as researchers or dissertation supervisors (see below).

3. While at Harvard, Oliver organized significant expeditions to the Society Islands in the late 1950s, and (with W. W. Howells and Albert Damon) to the Solomon Islands and Bougainville in the mid-1960s, which trained numerous PhD students. He assumed a joint appointment between Harvard and the University of Hawai'i from 1969 to 1973, and then taught full-time at Hawai'i until 1978.

4. Hawai'i's department of anthropology and sociology was built by Felix Keesing beginning in the mid-1930s. Keesing subsequently chaired the combined department of sociology and anthropology at Stanford in 1948, and became the first chair of the department of anthropology there after the two disciplines separated in 1956 (Siegel and Spindler 1962). Mason taught and influenced numerous students at the University of Hawai'i, many of whom went on to earn doctorates elsewhere (because Hawai'i did not then offer the PhD), and who have had distinguished careers in Pacific anthropol-

ogy (e.g., William Alkire, William Davenport, Ben Finney, Eugene Ogan, and Henry Rutz). Mason played a major role in hiring fellow CIMA researchers Samuel H. Elbert, Thomas Gladwin, and Saul Riesenberg in Hawaiʻi's anthropology department, and likewise, Mason helped bring Frank Mahony (a former USTTPI applied anthropologist) to the department after Mahony finished his PhD. Elbert later moved to the department of linguistics when that was founded.

5. Schneider also wrote a master's thesis under Sharp at Cornell, using some of Sharp's Yir Yoront material (Handler 1995, 69).

6. These numbers include Sir Peter H. Buck, director of the B. P. Bishop Museum in Honolulu, who was a citizen of New Zealand, and Rupert Murrill, a Canadian physical anthropologist from the American Museum of Natural History.

7. Murrill published several papers on his CIMA-based studies on Pohnpei, but he wrote a dissertation based on data from Puerto Rico (Eugene Ogan, personal communication 1995). Similarly, Robert Ritzenthaler was a CIMA participant on Palau, but wrote his dissertation at Columbia University based on Chippewa material (Lurie 1981 and personal communication 1995).

8. While Emory is remembered primarily as an archaeologist, he completed at least as much cultural anthropology in Oceania as he did archaeology (see Highland et al. 1967). In particular, his CIMA and SIM research resulted in a major ethnographic study of Kapingamarangi (Emory 1965).

9. Spoehr presided over construction of the planetarium and the Hall of Pacific Life at the Bishop Museum, and founded the Bishop Museum Association. So beloved was he that when he left the museum in 1962 to become the first chancellor of the newly established East-West Center, Kaʻupena Wong composed the "Alika Spoehr Hula" in his honor (Engle 1992).

10. Lessa returned to Hawaiʻi during the Depression and eventually became involved in labor organizing and helped unionize the Honolulu waterfront. On the recommendation of Chicago graduate John Embree, then teaching at the University of Hawaiʻi, Lessa selected the University of Chicago for graduate study. After he completed his PhD comprehensive examination he taught as an instructor at Brooklyn College in the fall of 1941. When the war broke out in December his draft number came up almost immediately, and he entered the army.

11. They have since been published (Lessa 1985).

12. One was by a physical anthropologist, Edward E. Hunt, Jr. In a recent tribute to his memory, Marcha Flint and Leslie Sue Lieberman extol his virtues as a teacher and "as one of the last of the generalists in human biology and physical anthropology" (1995, 423). These former students note that he was a pioneer in the application of statistics to biological anthropology, and that "he was one of the originators of the field now labeled medical anthropology, particularly applied medical anthropology" (1995, 423; see Rubinstein, chap. 10). Moreover, as part of his legacy to the profession, he was a cofounder of the Dental Anthropology Association.

13. Those who wrote anthropology dissertations from their CIMA studies were Thomas Gladwin, Ward Goodenough, Edward E. Hunt, Jr., Frank LeBar, Saul Riesenberg, David Schneider, Mel Spiro, William Stevens, and Arthur Vidich (see appendix 2A). To these can be added three more who finished the doctorate using SIM research: Ann Fischer, Leonard Mason and Jack Tobin (see appendix 1B). Showing further the overlap among major research programs in Micronesia, Gladwin, Riesenberg, and Tobin all served as applied anthropologists in the islands, and Goodenough worked as a SIM researcher on Onotoa in Kiribati.

14. Twelve percent (2/17) of the degrees awarded in 1949 were CIMA-based, as were close to one-fifth of the degrees awarded the following year (4/22 or 18 percent). By 1951, the proportion of such degrees began to decline to 1/35 or 3 percent, and the drop continued in 1952 (1/51 or 2 percent), 1953 (1/37 or 3 percent), and rose again in 1954 (2/33 or 6 percent). The last CIMA/SIM-based dissertation was defended in 1957, in which year it was 1/48 or 2 percent of the total.

15. For examples of this work on kinship and social organization see Goodenough (1951, 1955, 1956b, 1965a, 1965b); Homans and Schneider (1955); Schneider (1953, 1962, 1965a, 1965b, 1968, 1969a, 1972, 1976, 1981, 1984); Schneider and Cottrell (1975); Schneider and Gough (1961); Schneider and Homans (1955); Schneider and Smith (1973); and Spiro (1956, 1958, 1977). For material on psychological anthropology see Spiro (1951a, 1953a, 1954b, 1955, 1961a, 1962, 1978, 1992, 1993), and for illustrations of their contributions to the anthropology of religion see Goodenough (1966b, 1974b, 1981b, 1986, 1988a); Schneider (1969b); and Spiro (1965a, 1966a, 1966b, 1967, 1968, 1969, 1971, 1979b, 1982, 1984).

16. Interestingly, Goodenough and Schneider became lifelong friends while both were undergraduates at Cornell. They met in the spring of 1938 when both were nineteen years old, and together took their first class in cultural anthropology, taught by Lauriston Sharp (Goodenough, personal communication 1995).

Because Eggan and Schneider cochaired Harold Scheffler's dissertation (Scheffler 1965, ix), Scheffler and his doctoral student, Matthew Cooper, appear in both figure 3 and figure 4.

17. Force was third in a line of anthropologists who succeeded one another as directors of the Bishop Museum, after Peter Buck and Alex Spoehr. Marking the reduced role played by museums as loci of anthropological research today, the present director of the Bishop Museum is not an anthropologist.

18. Richard Emerick served both as a district anthropologist and, later, as assistant staff anthropologist. While he did not publish much of his Micronesia material, he had a distinguished career as a teacher at Bowdoin College, and he then founded and chaired the department of anthropology at the University of Maine, Orono, before his recent retirement.

19. By "academic pedigree" and "lineage" I refer to the specific links between dissertation advisor and student. I recognize that these differ from "intellectual genealo-

gies" (whose ideas a student found most influential to her work), and I am cognizant that claims based on academic pedigrees or lineages must be suitably modest. Nonetheless, I believe that these links do provide one way to demonstrate the interconnections among anthropologists who have worked in Oceania, and to show that many of these connections are a direct consequence of the postwar efflorescence of anthropology in Micronesia.

20. Lundsgaarde was recommended to Barnett for the Displaced Communities in the Pacific Project by his dissertation supervisor, William Elmendorf, who had been Barnett's classmate at Berkeley (Henry P. Lundsgaarde, personal communication 1996).

21. In alphabetical order with the institution following their names, these are: Barnett (Oregon), Burrows (Connecticut), Emerick (Maine-Orono), Emory (Bishop Museum), Goodenough (Pennsylvania), Hall (Denver), Daniel Hughes (Ohio State), Kenneth Knudson (Nevada-Reno), Marshall (Iowa), Mason (Hawai'i-Mānoa), McKnight (CSU-Hayward), Murdock (Yale), Oliver (Harvard), Riesenberg (Smithsonian), Schneider (Chicago), Severance (Hawai'i-Hilo), Spiro (California-San Diego), Vidich (New School), and Weckler (Southern California).

22. These are: Kiste (director, Center for Pacific Islands Studies, University of Hawai'i), Lingenfelter (provost, Biola University), Marksbury (associate dean, Tulane University), Larry Mayo (associate dean, DePaul University), Nason (associate dean and director of the American Indian Studies Program, University of Washington), Rubinstein (director, Micronesian Area Research Center, University of Guam), and Allan H. Smith (vice president, Washington State University).

23. These are: Emory (Bishop Museum), Force (Chicago Museum of Natural History), Nason (Thomas Burke Washington State Museum), Riesenberg (Smithsonian Institution), Spoehr (Chicago Museum of Natural History), and Weckler (US National Museum).

24. Murdock, Spoehr, and Force at the Bishop Museum and Force at the Museum of the American Indian, Heye Foundation, in New York.

CHAPTER THIRTEEN

A Half Century in Retrospect

Robert C. Kiste

THE NOTION OF MICRONESIA

The notion of "Micronesia" is problematic. Prior to the dissolution of the US Trust Territory of the Pacific Islands (USTTPI), Americans familiar with the Pacific, including anthropologists who worked in the area, commonly referred to the trust territory as Micronesia. These two terms were often used interchangeably, and occasionally Guam was also included when Micronesia was the referent. Sometimes both Guam and the trust territory were labeled "American Micronesia." Because they were outside the American sphere of influence, Nauru and Kiribati were routinely ignored when the word Micronesia was used, even though they are part of the geographical culture area known as Micronesia.

Concerning the culture area, David Hanlon (chap. 2) suggests that the very idea of Micronesia is nothing but a figment of the ethnographer's imagination. For him, it is a foreign imposition, unwarranted by the "ethnographic facts," and he notes that at least until recent times, it had no meaning for the island peoples themselves. In his survey of prehistory in the northwest tropical Pacific, archaeologist Paul Rainbird took a position similar to Hanlon's: "There is no cohesive 'Micronesian culture', the area in question is marked not only by its geographic diversity, but by its obvious connections with places external to the conceptual construct reified by a line on the map" (1994, 296). Finally, concerning indigenous perceptions and with reference to the three culture areas into which the Pacific is usually divided, Felix Keesing observed a half century ago: "The names given here are obviously scientific labels. They have as yet little if any meaning to the people concerned. Most of the islanders still living within very local horizons speak of themselves by their district, tribal, or village names" (1945, 9).

While Hanlon, Rainbird, and others would abandon the notion of Micronesia as a culture area, it seems certain that Keesing would have argued that culture areas have some empirical reality based on the "ethnographic facts." It may be inferred from the above quotation that Keesing believed the culture area concept useful for scientific purposes, and Suzanne Falgout and I (chap. 1) discuss his conviction about the scientific nature of anthropology. That the culture area concept still has its advocates is shown by a recent article in *Current Anthropology*, "Regions Based on Social Structure," in which the authors advanced new statistical methodologies with the intent of providing a more empirical basis for delineating regional areas (Burton, Moore, Whiting, and Romney 1996).

At the 1993 conference on which this volume is based, Ward H. Goodenough responded to Hanlon with the observation that several factors give the islands of Micronesia (in the broadest sense) a certain cohesiveness. He noted that a linguistic connectedness is found throughout most of the area, and it seems certain that his reference was to those languages that are classified as "Nuclear Micronesian." With the exception of the westernmost three, (Chamorro, Yapese, and Palauan), the two Polynesian outliers, and perhaps Nauruan, they are the languages of Micronesia. They are a dozen or so in number, and they are historically related. Goodenough also argued that there were "interactive spheres" that linked Micronesians prior to European times, by which he presumably meant connections through interisland voyaging. There was two-way voyaging within the Caroline Islands and between the Carolinian atolls and the Marianas. Carolinians assisted the Yapese with their voyages to and from Palau. Marshallese navigators roamed throughout their own archipelago, the Eastern Carolines, Nauru, and Kiribati. Goodenough also suggested that the "interactive spheres" did not regularly include parts of Polynesia and Melanesia. Many of Goodenough's points were reiterated by Kenneth Rehg in a 1995 article entitled "The Significance of Linguistic Interaction Spheres in Reconstructing Micronesian Prehistory."

Six chapters (3 through 8) of this volume focus primarily on ethnological matters, and the authors of the four most relevant to this discussion all come down on Goodenough's side of the argument. William Alkire (chap. 3) argues that there are certain major uniformities as well as minor contrasts in the ways that Micronesians have adapted to their environments. He posits that "a universal conceptual unity inalienably ties people (kin groups) to land (their estates) in Micronesia" and goes on to list several attributes that are common if not universal to Micronesian systems of land tenure (p. 86). Concerning "interactive spheres," Alkire discusses the *sawei* system that linked Yap to atolls to the east and comments on more limited regional networks. He also suggests that three contrasting adaptive types—isolates, clusters, and complexes—are common to the region.

Mac Marshall (chap. 4) and Glenn Petersen (chap. 5) advance somewhat similar arguments. Drawing on Marilyn Strathern's work in highland New Guinea, Marshall suggests that there are "partial connections" among Micronesian societies. Such connections consist of a set of social and cultural themes drawn from a pool of common ideas. The pool is dynamic and ever changing as its elements variously combine and recombine. This common pool of ideas provides a conventional cultural repertoire that is itself a framework of "Micronesian-ness." Marshall suggests that it is found throughout the Caroline Islands and the Marshalls, but not the contemporary Marianas. He identifies certain other exceptions, the Polynesian outliers of Kapingamarangi and Nukuoro being the most obvious. Contact with Polynesia also accounts for the cultural differences that distinguish Kiribati from the Marshalls and Carolines.

Petersen writes of "shared Micronesian political patterns" and indicates that the Coordinated Investigation of Micronesian Anthropology (CIMA) research of the late 1940s "preserved a marvelous record of some very fundamental similarities in Micronesian sociopolitical organization" (p. 166). At the conference, he spoke of "shared principles that focus around matriliny."

Necessarily, Marshall and Petersen analyze many of the same elements of kinship and social organization that reflect the centrality of matrilineal descent. Throughout much of the region, matrilineages are landholding corporations. Aggregations of lineages make up larger exogamous clans. Principles of rank and seniority permeate the entire social order. The interdependence of siblings reflects the centrality of matriliny and is also manifest in patterns of fictive kinship. Marshall recalls that Joseph Weckler, one of the CIMA participants, referred to the "matrilineal sea" in Micronesia.

Karen Nero (chap. 8) notes that in contrast to the rest of the Pacific, the visual arts of Micronesia are not highly developed. Indeed, they absolutely pale when compared to the flamboyant masks and sculpture that flourish in Melanesia. The paucity of the visual arts initially led researchers to puzzle over the "absence of art" in Micronesia. Nero notes Edwin G. Burrows' reflection that "there seemed to be so little that could be called art." However, Burrows later realized that the area of the greatest aesthetic creativity and appreciation was to be found in the performing arts, and this insight eventually led him to a surprisingly contemporary definition of art that was not appreciated at the time. In short, Nero suggests that the art forms of Micronesia have a distinctive character of their own.

All of this does not invalidate Hanlon's basic point. The culture area notion is an abstraction derived from an attempt by anthropologists to make sense of and bring order to their ethnographic data. The data themselves, be they called culture elements, traits, complexes, or something else, are the categories that anthropologists have found useful for purposes of ethnographic description and analysis.

The epistemological predilections of different researchers introduce subjective dimensions to the debate, and in the last analysis, the real issue may be whether or not the culture area concept is useful for understanding the region, or, as Hanlon suggests, is but an invention of outsiders that may obscure understanding and sometimes mask their hidden agendas. But while it is necessary to recognize that the culture area is an abstraction and its boundaries are at best fuzzy and arbitrary, it is quite another thing to dismiss the concept as being without any substance and utility. In an earlier article, Hanlon noted: "There certainly do exist historical linkages among the different island groups of the area that hopefully will become clearer through future research and investigation" (1989, 2). Indeed, and as noted above, linguistic evidence as well as the ethnographic record point to the conclusion that the variations of matriliny among the Nuclear Micronesian–speaking societies have common origins. The chapters by Alkire, Marshall, and Petersen indicate that controlled comparisons of such closely related societies have improved the quality of ethnographic observation, description, and analysis in most of Micronesia over the past half century. The relationships of the three westernmost island groups to the rest of the area remain problematic. It appears that they may have more direct origins from Southeast Asia, and, as Hanlon suggested, hopefully their histories and relations with the rest of Micronesia will become clearer with further investigation.

A MATTER OF IDENTITY

The culture area notion has had other consequences. Lin Poyer (chap. 6) comments that European intervention in the Pacific produced "new sensibili-

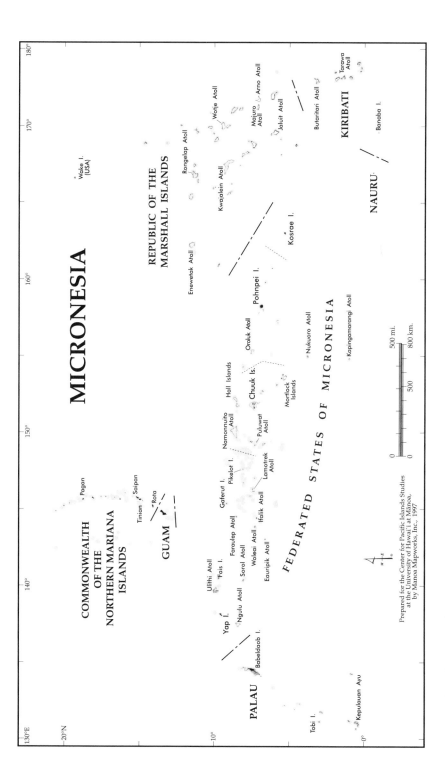

Map 4. Political Entities of Micronesia, 1997

ties about islander vs. non-islander identities, and about differences among islanders" (p. 199). Such processes continued well after colonial regimes were in place, and at about the time that the US Trust Territory of the Pacific Islands came into being in 1947, the establishment of the first major regional organization set in motion new forces that added yet other dimensions to island identities.

At the end of World War II, there was little or no shared identity among Pacific peoples. On the contrary, as Epeli Hau'ofa has pointed out, the colonial powers had introduced colonial divisions that isolated Pacific Islanders from one another (1993, 7). Most of Micronesia was a case in point. After World War I, when Japan replaced Germany in what would become the League of Nations Mandated Territory, the islands became closely tied to Japan, and there was almost no interaction with the rest of the Pacific. Beginning some twenty years earlier, Guam had become a protected enclave of the US Navy, and by and large, its people also had little contact with other Pacific Islanders. Even the short stretch of water that separates Guam from the rest of the Marianas proved an impenetrable barrier, one that continues to have consequences today.

To a large extent, the isolation of American Micronesia continued during the first two decades after World War II. As discussed in chapter 1, the American policy of strategic denial restricted access to both Guam and the trust territory, and during that era, most Micronesians had neither the means nor the reasons to journey far from home. Thus, for nearly a half century (from roughly 1914 to the early 1960s), the people of the trust territory had little contact with other Pacific peoples, and the isolation of the Guamanians was of even longer duration (from the beginning of US Navy rule in 1898 to the early 1960s). Both peoples also remained outside the mainstream of events that signaled the beginnings of Pacific regionalism.

As also discussed in chapter 1, the South Pacific Commission (spc) was founded in 1947 by the region's six colonial powers. Each appointed two commissioners to the spc body of twelve members. A secretariat headed by a secretary-general was created to carry out the commission's work. From the outset the founders gave at least lip service to the involvement of Pacific Islanders in spc affairs. American Samoa was included in the area served by the commission in 1947, but Guam and the trust territory were not included until the responsibility for their administration was transferred to the Department of Interior in 1951 (T. R. Smith 1972, 64).

The first opportunity for direct islander involvement in the South Pacific

Commission came with the first South Pacific Conference in 1950. The conference was held every three years until 1965 and annually from 1967. Initially, it was only an advisory body. Nonetheless, the first conference was a turning point in Pacific affairs. For the first time in history, islanders from most of the region met on a face-to-face basis. Political scientist Greg Fry has observed: "The conference is an aspect of the SPC which stands out as having influenced the development of Islander awareness of the region, and other Islanders within it" (1979, 66–67). A pan-Pacific identity, that of Pacific Islander, was born, and the Micronesians under American rule were not invited to the party.

Guam and the US Trust Territory of the Pacific Islands became involved in the process of sorting out regional identities when they began to participate in the SPC conferences in 1953. One of the clearer boundaries of the time was that between islanders and non-islanders. The commission was dominated by males of European descent; the twelve commissioners and the secretary-general held all real authority and were accorded respect and deference. There was no ambiguity about the order of the day. With only an advisory capacity, Pacific Islanders were subordinate.

While contact among the islanders helped give shape to a new Pacific identity, it also heightened sensibilities about their differences. Polynesians had long thought of themselves as superior to Melanesians, and much of their exalted self-image derived from their own experience with Europeans. From their earliest contact with Pacific peoples, Europeans had preferred the larger and lighter-skinned Polynesians and had admired much of their culture and chiefly social organization. With the exceptions of the Chamorros of the Marianas, the Polynesians were also the first to be converted to Christianity, and their own sense of superiority was enhanced when they were used as missionaries to spread the gospel in Melanesia. Micronesians were peripheral to these events south of the equator, but Hawaiians played an important role in the missionization of eastern Micronesia.

Later, the process of decolonization also had an impact on island identities, and the Polynesians' sense of their own superiority was enhanced when they led the way. In 1962, Western Samoa was the first Pacific state to achieve independence, and in the following decade, five other countries became independent or self-governing states in free association with their former colonial power. Three of these were Polynesian (the Cook Islands [1965], Tonga [1970], and Niue [1974]) and one was Micronesian (Nauru [1968]). The fifth was Fiji (1970), which occupies an intermediate position on the borderline between Polynesia and Melanesia.

The next decade saw independence come to most of Melanesia: Papua New Guinea (1975), Solomon Islands (1978), and Vanuatu (1980). They were joined by the small Polynesian state of Tuvalu (1978) and Kiribati, the second Micronesian country to gain independence (1979). In the same decade, the Northern Marianas was the first to break away from the trust territory, but in contrast to political changes elsewhere, it opted for closer integration with the United States as the Commonwealth of the Northern Marianas Islands (CNMI).

The decolonization of the Pacific was well into its third decade before any part of the trust territory became self-governing. The Republic of the Marshall Islands (RMI) and the Federated States of Micronesia (FSM) became self-governing states freely associated with the United States in 1986. Palau did not follow suit until 1994, more than thirty years after Western Samoa became a sovereign nation.

Progress in decolonization was accompanied by further developments in Pacific regionalism, and once again, Polynesia led the way. When the South Pacific Commission was slow to respond to the needs and aspirations of the newly independent and self-governing states, they invited Australia and New Zealand to join them in founding of the South Pacific Forum (SPF) in 1971. The charter members were the Cook Islands, Fiji, Nauru, Tonga, and Western Samoa as well as the two metropolitan powers. Within short order, the South Pacific Forum emerged as the most influential of the regional organizations, and additional members were added as they gained independence. Most importantly, the independent Melanesian states became Forum members in the decade of the 1970s.

Thus, for well over two decades, the Micronesians of the trust territory lagged behind other Pacific nations with regard to regional affairs. During the 1960s, 1970s, and well into the 1980s, they were preoccupied with negotiations with the United States over their own future political status. Washington, D.C. was simply of greater importance than their regional neighbors and organizations. However, they were beneficiaries of the programs of the South Pacific Commission and participated in its conferences. They were involved in the indigenization of the commission during the late 1970s and early 1980s and witnessed the transfer of authority from European to Pacific hands. Nonetheless, they participated as representatives of the US Trust Territory of the Pacific Islands, an entity to which they had no commitment and were working hard to dissolve. Significant change for the Micronesians occurred with free association. Forum membership came within a year after their new political status and marked recognition that they had gained control over much of their own affairs.

Partly from participation in regional activities, some islanders from Guam and the trust territory acquired an identity as both Pacific Islanders and Micronesians. Within regional affairs, small states are sometimes organized in opposition to larger ones. In other instances, the culture areas come into play. For example, there is an unwritten rule that the offices of the secretaries-general of the South Pacific Commission and the South Pacific Forum should rotate among Melanesians, Micronesians, and Polynesians. Some equitable distribution of other positions, programs, and resources is also expected.

In 1986, the prime ministers of Papua New Guinea, the Solomons, and Vanuatu formed the Melanesian Spearhead group (Henningham 1992, 195–196). They have a strong sense of brotherhood with the Kanaks (indigenous people) of New Caledonia, and they began to meet before the South Pacific Forum's annual meetings to agree on their own priorities. In response, the king of Tonga attempted to organize a Polynesian Community group, but he was unsuccessful, and little more has been heard of the matter.

The Micronesians have been the last to attempt to a regional association of their own. On the initiative and invitation of the governor of Guam, the heads of government of all seven Micronesian entities met on Guam in January 1996. The presidents and governors of the Commonwealth of the Northern Marianas, the Federated States of Micronesia, Guam, Kiribati, Nauru, Palau, and the Republic of the Marshall Islands make for a strange mixture of political partners, but nonetheless, in the following April, they met again in Honolulu to form the Council of Micronesian Chief Executives. Its charter has a long list of objectives, but the immediate focus is on matters of trade and transportation. While the council is new, it met again in 1997 and 1998, and such an assemblage of Micronesian leaders is without precedent in the history of the region.

Coinciding with developments at the regional level, Poyer (chap. 6) and Petersen (chap. 5) point out that there were deliberate efforts by the American administration to foster a Micronesian identity within the trust territory. These included initiatives in education, the creation of a Micronesian anthem and flag, and last but not least, the Congress of Micronesia. Whatever their private sentiments in their negotiations with the United States over future political status, islanders have employed the banner of Micronesian-ness to promote solidarity and define the boundary between "them" and "us." And there is no doubt that some came to see themselves as Micronesians who were committed to a unified Micronesian state (Heine 1974).

However, a Micronesian identity has remained elusive at best and has never been strong enough to sustain any real unity. Micronesian identities remain multiple, layered, and contextual, and as in Keesing's day, the strongest and most enduring identities for most islanders are at local levels—a particular island, an island district, or a village. Those who have any strong sense of being a Pacific Islander or a Micronesian are in the minority, and in nearly all instances they have had significant experiences abroad. Many have attended an American college or university or received other training in the United States. They form an island elite and enjoy positions in government, education, health and medicine, and less commonly, the private sector. A privileged few have found positions on the staffs of the regional organizations.

Micronesian identities have a sliding quality. Local identities are employed at home and in traditional settings. More inclusive categories come into play in nontraditional contexts and as islanders move further away from their home base. In Honolulu, an individual from the Marshalls may identify himself as a Marshall Islander or a Micronesian. In other contexts and on the US mainland, these identities might have little meaning, and the same person may well don the persona of Pacific Islander (cf. Hereniko 1994).

Within Micronesia today, identities above the local level appear to have coalesced along the lines of the polities that have emerged from the former trust territory. Palauans and Marshallese now tend to identify with their new nationalities, and the notion of being Micronesian is becoming somewhat linked with citizenship in the Federated States of Micronesia. However, FSM unity is fragile, and stronger loyalties are found at the level of that nation's four constituent states and subdivisions within those states. Concerning issues of national identity and nation building, the Federated States has problems that are similar to those of the Melanesian states. For historical reasons, the Chamorros of Guam and the Northern Marianas have generally not identified themselves as Micronesians, and they themselves remain divided over issues that go back to the events of World War II.

A MATTER OF SCALE

In any sense of the term, Micronesia is at once both large and small. With regard to overall dimensions, it covers a vast ocean area of several million square miles. Otherwise, Micronesia is aptly named. In terms of total land area, the number of languages and cultures, and the size of its population, Micronesia in even its most inclusive sense is smaller than some Melanesian islands, and it is the smallest of the region's three culture areas.

By definition, American Micronesia is smaller still. According to mid-1995 estimates, the population of Guam, the Northern Marianas, and the three freely associated states was about 382,900, slightly less than 6 percent of the Pacific region's 6,583,800 people (SPC 1995). The number is a dramatic increase over the immediate postwar figure of about 100,000 (US Department of the Navy 1948; _Pacific Islands Yearbook_ 1950).

Both the size and location of American Micronesia have had major consequences for its people and partly account for the unique colonial history that sets it outside the experience of the rest of the Pacific. Following precedents established by Germany and Japan, the United States divided the trust territory into a small number of districts under a centralized authority for administrative purposes. Appointed by the president, the high commissioner was the chief executive officer. His staff included the directors of education, health, and so on; the chief justice; and during the 1950s, the staff anthropologist. District administrators were also directly under the authority of the high commissioner, and they had their counterparts to the high commissioner's staff, that is, there were directors of education, health, and other departments at the district level. The chain of command was simple and direct. Decisions made in far off Washington, D.C. went to the high commissioner, and directives from the Office of the High Commissioner went straight to the districts for implementation. The consequences could be direct, immediate, and have an impact on the entire territory.

Once the islands came under American rule, individuals and institutions in Hawai'i played a major role in the affairs of Guam and the US Trust Territory of the Pacific Islands. The USTTPI Office of the High Commissioner was located in Honolulu until 1954 when it was moved to Guam, and subsequently to Saipan in 1962 (Hezel 1995, 284–300). Officials from Washington passed through Honolulu en route to Micronesia. Until the late 1960s, the only commercial flights to the trust territory went through Guam, so it, too, was a transit point for travelers to the territory.

The first Micronesians to receive tertiary education attended the universities of Guam and Hawai'i. Patients requiring medical care unavailable in the islands were treated at the navy facilities on Guam or at Tripler Army Hospital in Honolulu. Scores of specialists at the two universities and federal agencies with offices in Guam and Honolulu have served as consultants on island affairs. Today, the Commonwealth of the Northern Mariana Islands and the three freely associated states have liaison offices in Honolulu.

As evidenced by several chapters in this volume, two University of Hawai'i professors, anthropologist Leonard E. Mason and political scientist Norman

Meller, have been particularly identified with Micronesia, and at an earlier time they had considerable influence in the region. Both have conducted extensive research in and have devoted most of their careers to the area.

Mason and Meller have had a unique place in the history of Micronesia because of the area's relatively small scale, their own research interests, the strategic location of Hawai'i, and the single colonial administration of most of postwar Micronesia. No other social scientists have played a comparable role in either of the other two culture areas of Oceania. Both men were instrumental in the development of Pacific Islands studies at the University of Hawai'i. Mason founded the Pacific Islands Studies Program (since 1986, the Center for Pacific Islands Studies) in 1950, and served as its director for most of the next fifteen years. Meller then succeeded him and directed the program for much of the following decade. In many respects, the 1993 conference and this volume derive from foundations they laid over the quarter century that they nurtured Pacific Islands studies at the university.

THE APPLICATION OF ANTHROPOLOGY

As discussed in chapter 1, American anthropological research in Micronesia was launched as an exercise in applied social science, and in a sense, it had two beginnings. The first was Laura Thompson's groundbreaking work on Guam in the late 1930s; the second was the applied, wartime effort that began at Yale and was followed by the United States Commercial Company (USCC), CIMA, and Scientific Investigation of Micronesia (SIM) projects, and the use of applied anthropologists at the levels of both the Office of the High Commissioner and the several districts.

The Marianas were treated differently from the beginning. The Chamorro people had been colonized longer than any other Pacific people (almost three hundred years). Much of their indigenous culture was long gone, and they, particularly the people of Guam, were among the most westernized of all Pacific Islanders. Apparently because of her criticism of the military government, the navy denied Thompson permission to return to Guam after World War II (Thompson 1947, vii). At the same time, the CIMA planners evidently believed that anthropological research was not warranted in the Northern Marianas; it was the only USTTPI district to have no anthropologist as part of its CIMA team. Chamorros may have been seen as too acculturated, too westernized, to merit anthropological investigation, or perhaps the people of Saipan were considered a pathological case. Alice Joseph and Veronica Murray, the

CIMA researchers on the island, were physicians, and as Don Rubinstein (chap. 10) points out, they administered intelligence tests and personality tests and collected psychiatric case histories. Alex Spoehr was the first anthropologist to conduct research in the Marianas when he worked on Saipan as part of the SIM project (Spoehr 1954).

In his conference paper, "Reclaiming Culture and History from a History of Culture in Guam," Vicente Diaz commented on how Guam has been treated as a special case: "For all intents and purposes, Guam for anthropologists is but a transit point to and from culture in Micronesia," and "indeed, with few exceptions, anthropologists have systematically overlooked the Chamorros, especially of Guam, in their search for culture in Micronesia" (Diaz 1993). Diaz suggested that anthropologists have misunderstood Guam, but he agreed with Thompson that, three hundred years of colonial rule notwithstanding, there are important continuities in Chamorro culture and society. Diaz has a point in that anthropologists did not "rediscover" Guam until the late 1970s. For example, the first doctoral dissertation in sociocultural anthropology based on research with the Chamorros of Guam was in 1978, and a cluster of five appeared between 1978 and 1984 (see appendix 2C). The Northern Mariana Islands, however, are even more of a case in point. Aside from Spoehr's work on Saipan, they have indeed been neglected and are represented by only a single dissertation, a study of land tenure on Rota (J. Smith 1972).

A significant historical point is often overlooked. While anthropologists were employed early in the US administration, an American agenda had been initiated before anthropologists appeared on the scene, and it was not informed by anthropological advice. In the very immediate postwar years, and with little or no deliberation, the navy administration introduced education, health, and political programs and a legal system and institutions based on American models. Although the initial efforts were modest at best, there was no serious consideration of alternatives. A course of action was simply set in motion on the assumption that the American way of doing things would somehow be appropriate.

Once the American agenda was in place, different courses of development followed in the various program areas. In the political arena and education, anthropologists were involved in a dialogue about how and, to some extent, what should be introduced and at what pace. However, they had little involvement in health and medicine, and with the judiciary, anthropology was employed in ways never intended.

Petersen (chap. 5) discusses the introduction of American political institu-

1993 Conference. Left:
David Hanlon; right:
*Vicente Diaz. Photograph
by Carolyn Yacoe.*

1993 Conference. Left:
Suzanne Falgout; right:
*Glenn Petersen. Photo-
graph by Carolyn Yacoe.*

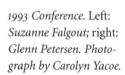

1993 Conference. Left: *William Alkire;*
right: *Robert Kiste. Photograph by*
Carolyn Yacoe.

tions in the US Trust Territory of the Pacific Islands, and only a few additional
comments are required. As part of their brief, CIMA researchers investigated
forms of governance, and because of American initiatives, democracy was very
much on their minds. As one reads their work today, one is struck by their
preoccupation with democracy and the subjectivity of their accounts. Some
were caught up in the euphoria that followed the war's end and the triumph
of the Allies over totalitarianism. In spite of his insistence on the neutrality of
the anthropologists, Staff Anthropologist Homer G. Barnett was committed
to the introduction of elected officials and representative councils. In contrast,
John "Jack" Fischer thought traditional institutions "were probably much more
democratic" than reports suggested (1957a, 185). As Nero (chap. 8) points out,
Burrows went so far as to place "emphasis on the truly democratic nature of
Micronesian art" (p. 265).

Today, American-style political institutions as modified by islanders have
taken hold at every level of Micronesian society, from local municipalities to
the national governments of the three freely associated states and the CNMI
government. These introduced institutions have proliferated into large, expen-

sive, and redundant bureaucracies. The ultimate example is Palau. In addition to their national government, the 16,000 people of Palau are divided into sixteen separate states, each with its own legislature, judicial, and executive branches.

Turning to education, in her conference paper, "Dick and Jane Meet Emi and Tamag: Culture and the Classroom," Karen Peacock (1993) discussed anthropology's involvement with educational programs in the US Trust Territory of the Pacific Islands. She noted that rudimentary schools were established as early as 1944 by the navy. Islanders with little formal education and a limited command of English were processed through brief teacher training programs. Eventually, intermediate schools were established in each district. The government sponsored one high school, and a second, Xavier High School, was a Jesuit institution.

In 1948, an Advisory Committee on Education that included anthropologists Kenneth P. Emory from the Bishop Museum, Leonard Mason, and other educators in Hawai'i, agreed with official policy that instruction was to be both in the vernacular and in English. The committee went a step further, however, and recommended that instruction in the first few years be in the vernacular, with English gradually phased in as a second language in later years. When the US Department of the Interior replaced the navy administration in 1951, Robert "Bob" Gibson became the first civilian director of education. He had had cross-cultural experience in education, and he further emphasized instruction in the local languages and advocated culturally relevant education that included large elements of island culture, history, and geography.

In retrospect, such policy positions had few tangible results, and it could not have been otherwise. Given the financial constraints of the era, little was possible in the way of significant program development. As most teachers had only a limited control of English themselves, most instruction was necessarily in the vernacular. Further, for teachers in communities far from the district centers, ruminations about educational philosophy at the level of the Office of the High Commissioner had little meaning.

In any event, Gibson's approach was eventually challenged by Micronesians who demanded English instruction for their children. Both Gibson and his policies fell out of favor with the administration in the early 1960s when the decision was made in Washington, D.C. to "do something about Micronesia" and the massive flow of dollars to the islands began. The first new initiative in education was an accelerated English program launched in 1963.

Gibson was appalled at what he called the "hurry up boys from Washington," and he retired in 1964.

As Peacock (1993) noted: "During the 1960s Micronesia underwent a virtual Americanization of educational development." High schools were established in each district, and education became Micronesia's largest single industry (Hezel 1979). In the 1970s and 1980s, hundreds of Micronesian students attended American colleges and universities. Ironically, during the same period, bilingual education became something of a fad in the United States, and abundant federal funds were also made available to export bilingual education to Micronesia. The Pacific and Asian Linguistics Institute (PALI) was founded at the University of Hawai'i, and a sizable volume of material in the vernacular languages was produced. But this initiative came from Washington, not from Micronesia, and not from anthropologists. After Gibson's departure, anthropologists had little involvement with education in Micronesia.

Rubinstein (chap. 10) and Edward C. King (chap. 11) discuss some of the reasons that anthropology had little influence on the development of the health care and legal systems in the trust territory, and Rubinstein also includes some observations on Guam. CIMA researchers investigated matters of depopulation and diet. Depopulation on Yap had been a source of some anxiety as far back as Japanese times, and nutrition was of widespread concern immediately after the war. Otherwise, decisions concerning the practice of medicine and health care delivery were always in the hands of health professionals. Guam had had long experience with American hospitals and health care, and Micronesians from elsewhere were trained at the school for medical practitioners that opened on Guam in early 1946. New hospitals in the several USTTPI districts laid the foundation for American medicine in the trust territory before the CIMA researchers came on the scene. Similarly, Goodenough recalled at the 1993 conference that the American judicial system was already functioning in Chuuk before he and the rest of the Yale CIMA team arrived in 1947. (Also see Richard 1957a, 623–629; 1957b, 316–321; 1957c, 84–90).

In contrast to the lengthy debate about appropriate education in the US Trust Territory of the Pacific Islands, in the fields of both health and law there was little or no appreciation that indigenous knowledge and practices might somehow have been useful and integrated into the American approaches. Micronesian concepts of health and medicine were ridiculed as so much mumbo jumbo that might well be harmful if not dangerous enough to be outlawed to protect public safety. In the judicial arena, indigenous notions about wrongful behavior, dispute resolution, and punishment were not so denigrated; rather, they were simply ignored.

King (chap. 11) laments that there was never any dialogue between anthropologists and the judiciary in regard to fundamental questions about the nature and role of the courts in Micronesia, that is, appropriate forms of judicial proceedings for the islands, the relationship between the courts and island leaders, and the manner in which customary law should be understood and interpreted. Instead, King observes that the court launched "its work on the assumption that it should conduct itself as much as possible as an American court" which suggests that "anthropologists originally played no significant role in defining the mission of the USTTPI judiciary" (pp. 366, 367).

At the most practical and basic level, anthropologists and the courts had different expectations. The judiciary urgently wanted anthropologists to be more active in the judicial process, including the provision of courtroom testimony. While anthropologists were willing to offer advice in private, they declined to take sides in public or reveal information that might betray the confidentiality of informants. As one consequence, the courts used "creative means" to offer anthropological work as evidence. King believes and regrets that in the process the courts compromised their own integrity.

Anthropologists and the judiciary never arrived at a working relationship, and in light of what was asked of the anthropologists, it is difficult to see how the results could have been otherwise. King is probably correct that a productive dialogue might have been possible at the very outset, before the judiciary was launched as a basically American system in the trust territory. Given this historical context, it is somehow fitting that legal anthropology has been almost totally neglected in Micronesia.

Rubinstein (chap. 10) discusses health-related research by anthropologists on Guam and in the US Trust Territory of the Pacific Islands since the 1960s. A solid body of work has focused on those matters that were of concern to the CIMA program: population, diet, and nutrition. New ground has also been broken. A small but promising body of literature on the use and abuse of tobacco, alcohol, and other psychoactive substances has appeared. Significant inquiry has been made into the etiology and ecology of certain diseases, particularly on Guam.

Research on the indigenous medicines of Micronesia, however, remained neglected until the 1970s when Frank Mahony and Roger Ward completed their doctoral dissertations. It seems plausible to suggest that both were at least partly inspired by the applied anthropology of the 1950s. Ward was a student of Jack

Fischer's at Tulane, and Mahony and Fischer were district anthropologists on both Chuuk and Pohnpei. Mahony's dissertation examined the theoretical underpinnings of the Chuukese medical system (1970), while Ward's concerned the indigenous medicine of Pohnpei (1977). Rubinstein considers the two works as centerpieces in the ethnomedicine of Micronesia. Unfortunately, neither has been published, and there has been no subsequent work of significance in ethnomedicine. In fact, after the 1970s, general medical anthropological research in the area declined.

Ironically, at the very time medical anthropology was declining in Micronesia, it was expanding elsewhere to become the largest topical subfield in the discipline. Coinciding with these developments within anthropology, and thanks to an influx of federal dollars, Micronesian health services in concert with federal health agencies became a major growth industry. Agencies in Washington, D.C. competed for control over programs in the islands. Within the trust territory, health services created research opportunities for American universities, and schools of public health garnered most of the action.

As in the past, the University of Hawai'i was uniquely positioned to take advantage of the opportunity, which involved an estimated $40 million in grants and contracts over a period of three decades. But the field was dominated by the school of public health. Rubinstein indicates: "Perhaps over 95 percent of all American university-based health research and training projects for Micronesia have been carried out at the University of Hawai'i through its schools of medicine, nursing, and public health." While those schools had the capacity to respond to research and training programs, Rubinstein notes that the dominance of the University of Hawai'i also reflected the "health professional schools' close relationship with congressional leaders and policy makers in Washington . . . and with the health service leadership in Micronesia" (p. 354).

A recent assessment of higher education in Hawai'i (Yount 1995, 237–241) corroborates Rubinstein's historical sketch, but matters of academic turf were also involved. The keepers of informal history on the Mānoa campus of the University of Hawai'i today recall that the power brokers within the school of public health viewed others in the university as unwelcome interlopers. At the same time, the department of anthropology felt no compelling reason to collaborate with public health. Since Mason's retirement in 1969, the department was without a Micronesian specialist, and none of its faculty has had a serious interest in the area. However, medical anthropology remained an option within the graduate program. The department had its own federal funds for training and research, but there was no strong commitment to the Pacific Islands. It is difficult to disagree with Rubinstein's assessment that this was "a missed opportunity for medical anthropology" (p. 355).

The era of applied anthropology in the US Trust Territory of the Pacific Islands ended about 1960 when the last of the district anthropologists were phased out and the Americanization of Micronesia began in earnest. Subsequently, and as noted in chapter 1, individual anthropologists have occasionally engaged in applied activities, but they have been exceptions. Others have hoped that their endeavors might have beneficial applications. For example, in his dissertation on the elderly on one of the Chuuk State atolls, Mark Borthwick noted that he had shared the results of his work with appropriate USTTPI agencies "in the hope they will assist American and Micronesian policy-makers in implementing . . . culturally meaningful old age assistance programs" (1977, 13). Another case is unique. In response to a request from the magistrate of Rull municipality on Yap, the Peace Corps recruited an anthropologist to record customs and traditions before they disappeared from both practice and memory. Richard Marksbury's 1979 dissertation was the result.

The most extensive use of anthropology for applied purposes today is found not in the endeavors of professional anthropologists, but in the efforts of Jesuit priest, educator, and scholar, Francis X. Hezel. A self-taught scholar who has helped to pioneer work on Micronesian history (1983, 1995), Hezel began his career in Micronesia as an educator in 1963. Out of a concern over social issues and problems, he helped to found the Micronesian Seminar in 1972 and became its first director, a position he again occupies today. Dedicated to community education, the Micronesian Seminar examines, researches, and sponsors debate on issues of importance to the peoples of Micronesia. Hezel (chap. 9) discusses his long association with anthropologists and the influence that their discipline has had on his work and that of the Micronesian Seminar. Acknowledging that notions drawn from western sociology have largely been discarded as inadequate for understanding the dynamics of contemporary Micronesian societies, Hezel traces how anthropological concepts and perspectives have helped to provide a better understanding of a wide variety of issues: youth delinquency, alcohol use and abuse, teen suicide, child and spouse abuse, and the changing structure and organization of family life. The Micronesian Seminar's occasional publication, *The Micronesian Counselor*, discusses social problems and is a valuable record of issues of contemporary concern.

FUNDING AND RESEARCH TRENDS

Marshall (chap. 12) reviews the development of American anthropology in Micronesia and the contributions it has made to the discipline. The discussion here places anthropology into a larger context, with particular concern for the funding of anthropological research and the training of its practitioners. From the perspective of funding, the half century of American anthropology's involvement in Micronesia may be divided into three periods. In the first, the US Navy was the primary source of funding and other support for anthropology, both pure research and applied; in addition to the USCC, CIMA, and SIM reports, eleven of the first thirteen PhD dissertations by American anthropologists in Micronesia were derived from navy-sponsored research. The second period coincided with and benefited from the generous outlay of federal funds that accompanied the immediate post-Sputnik years and the launching of the Great Society during the Johnson administration. The third period covers more recent times, which have witnessed a marked decline in federal support for social programs and basic research.

The number of PhDs earned in any given decade provides one measure of anthropological output. Between 1949 and 1997, a total of seventy-eight doctorates in sociocultural anthropology have been based on research in Micronesia (see table 5). In 1949, Ward Goodenough and David M. Schneider completed their dissertations at Yale and Harvard. Considering the impact they were to have on the discipline (see Marshall, chap. 12), it is appropriate that Goodenough and Schneider were the very first to emerge as new PhDs from American anthropology's engagement with Micronesia. Eleven doctorates were produced in the next decade (see appendix 2A and table 5). Nine of the eleven were by anthropologists who were involved in USCC, CIMA, or SIM projects or had served as district anthropologists. A tenth was by Roland Force, whose research was sponsored by the Tri-Institutional Pacific Project (TRIPP), and the last was by Marc Swartz who had other funding. Of the eleven, Ann Fischer was the first woman to earn a PhD in anthropology based on Micronesian research.

Nine more doctorates in sociocultural anthropology were produced in the 1960s, seven of these having connections to the work of the 1940s and 1950s. Richard Emerick, Robert McKnight, and Jack Tobin were the last of the district anthropologists to complete their doctorates. (Emerick was also a student of Goodenough's.) Vern Carroll, Robert C. Kiste, Michael D. Lieber, and Walter

Table 5 Doctorates in Sociocultural Anthropology by Decade and Gender, 1949–1997

Decade	Male	Female	Total
1940s	2	0	2
1950s	10	1	11
1960s	9	0	9
1970s	25	9	34
1980s	9	8	17
1990s	0	5	5
Totals	55	23	78

"Scott" Wilson earned their PhDs under the guidance of Schneider, Barnett, Spoehr, and Goodenough, respectively. Three of these mentors were founders of the "academic lineages" discussed by Marshall (chap. 12), and Goodenough was second only to George Peter Murdock in his line. William Alkire and Daniel Hughes were the first to complete doctorates with advisors who had no connections to Micronesia. Alkire took his master's degree with Mason at the University of Hawai'i, but Hawai'i had no doctoral program at the time, so he moved to the University of Illinois to study cultural ecology with Julian Steward. Hughes was a teacher in Micronesia along with his fellow Jesuits, and then pursued his graduate work at Catholic University where there were no Pacific specialists.

The 1960s were important for other reasons. A combination of events had enormous consequences for both Micronesia and anthropology in Micronesia. In response to the launching of Sputnik by the Soviet Union in 1957, the National Defense Education Act was passed by the US Congress to support graduate education in the sciences, including anthropology. The 1960s were a prosperous time, and the nation's mood was expansive and forward looking. The Act foreshadowed a vast array of educational and social programs that were the core of President Johnson's Great Society initiative and its ambitious goal to eliminate poverty and raise standards of living in the United States and its territories. Much of the Americanization of Micronesia was a product of that initiative. The guidelines for the funding of research in the medical and health sciences were sufficiently broad and flexible to include basic research in anthropology (with the exception of archaeology), and National Science Foundation funding for anthropology was at an all-time high. The Americanization of Micronesia was federally financed, and social and cultural change in Micronesia became a favorite (but not prescribed) topic of anthropological research supported by federal funds.

There was an explosion of anthropological fieldwork in Micronesia when students of CIMA participants began sending their own students to the field. In the 1970s, thirty-four dissertations were completed, more than the total of twenty-two that had been produced prior to the 1970s, and certain to far outnumber those produced in the 1980s and 1990s. As the availability of federal funds began to decline in the late 1970s, a downward trend was experienced in the number of dissertations produced, and this has continued. The seventeen dissertations of the 1980s were exactly one-half of those produced during the previous decade. Only five sociocultural dissertations have appeared so far during the 1990s although a half dozen or so are in progress.

The research explosion in the 1970s also brought the first significant number of women researchers to Micronesian sociocultural anthropology. More than a decade lapsed between Ann Fischer's 1957 dissertation and Nancy Pollock's 1970 work on the Marshalls. The number of female researchers has increased proportionately ever since. Nine of the thirty-four dissertations in the 1970s were by women, and in the 1980s eight of seventeen dissertations were by female anthropologists. All five dissertations completed so far in the 1990s are by women.

Concerning the topics of research, the seventy-eight sociocultural dissertations may be divided into two broad categories. Thirty (38 percent of the total) focus largely on traditional ethnographic concerns or topics of primarily academic interest. A second and larger category involves forty-eight dissertations (62 percent) that focus on or evidence a major interest in sociocultural change. These two categories may be subdivided according to certain topics and subject matter. The divisions are rough, and they could not be otherwise. Dissertations in anthropology are not easily tucked away into neat pigeonholes. However, certain overall trends may be identified.

The thirty dissertations on traditional ethnographic topics fall into several small clusters. Goodenough (1949) and Schneider (1949) were the first to write dissertations focused on kinship and social organization of a particular society and culture, and five others (Swartz 1958; Carroll 1966; Marshall 1972a; D. Smith 1977; J. Thomas 1978) subsequently followed suit. General ethnographies that attempt to be holistic in coverage are seldom written by anthropologists today, and only two (Riesenberg 1950; W. S. Wilson 1968), separated by almost twenty years, appear among the dissertations discussed here.

Two related topics are each represented by three dissertations. As Peter Black (chap. 7) points out, early works by Melford E. Spiro (1950b) and Thomas Gladwin (1952) got psychological anthropology off to a good start and were influential in their time, but three decades elapsed before another work appeared in that subfield (Lutz 1980). Related to the work in psychological anthropology, three dissertations have concerned enculturation. In a sequence somewhat opposite that of psychological anthropology, one early work (A. Fischer 1957) was followed by two others (Rubinstein 1979; M. Thomas 1978) after a twenty-year interval.

As several chapters of this volume indicate, the subfields of cultural ecology, ethnomedicine, and art have been relatively neglected in Micronesia. Each is represented by only two dissertations that appeared within a relatively short time of each other. Cultural ecology (Alkire 1965b; Knudson 1970) was followed by ethnomedicine (Mahony 1970; Ward 1977). After Burrows' pioneering work, art was not a topic of exploration until dissertations by Earl Jernigan (1973) and Marvin Montvel-Cohen (1982).

Land tenure received considerable attention from the district anthropologists of the 1950s, especially via the volume edited by John deYoung (1958). Subsequently, most studies of land tenure have focused on change, and only two are primarily concerned with traditional systems (Lieber 1968b; Parker 1985). Folklore and material culture have also been neglected topics, and each is represented by a single work (J. Fischer 1954 and LeBar 1951, respectively). Five other dissertations deal with such academic topics as ritual cycles, indigenous systems of knowledge, and symbolic anthropology (L. Carucci 1980; Caughey 1970; Falgout 1984; Labby 1972; Parmentier 1981).

In the second major group, forty-eight dissertations focus on aspects of sociocultural change. In one way or another, eleven are concerned with matters related to urban or peri-urban life and processes of urbanization. As noted in the above discussion about the Marianas, five of these (del Valle 1978; Poehlman 1979; Muñoz 1979; Jorgensen 1984; Mayo 1984) focus on Guam. Three others (Alexander 1978; Flinn 1982; Reafsnyder 1984) are concerned with the movement of people to urban areas in Micronesia, and two more (Snyder 1976; Larson 1989) examine university students, their aspirations, and their role in contemporary Micronesian societies. One dissertation is a study of a Marshallese community in the United States (Allen 1997).

Political change is the subject of nine dissertations. Palau has received the most attention in this regard with four (Vidich 1953; R. Force 1958; Epstein 1986; L. Wilson 1993), and Pohnpei comes in second with three (Hughes 1968; Petersen 1977; Evans 1988). Yap is represented by a single work (Lingenfelter 1971), and one dissertation deals with political change in the Federated States of Micronesia (Pinsker 1997). Political change has not been a dissertation topic in Chuuk, Kosrae, the Marshalls, the Northern Marianas, or Guam.

The remaining twenty-eight dissertations form no logical cluster and may be divided among a half dozen topical areas. Four are concerned with relocation and resettlement programs: the Bikinians (Mason 1954; Kiste 1967), and the Enewetak (Tobin 1967) communities in the Marshalls, and a resettlement program on Pohnpei (Emerick 1960). Five provide analyses of changing systems of land tenure in Chuuk (Nason 1970), the Marshalls (Rynkiewich 1972a), Rota in the Northern Marianas (J. Smith 1972), Yap (Marksbury 1979), and Palau (McCutcheon 1981). Two others examine the consequences of depopulation on Yap (Stevens 1950) and repopulation of Kosrae (Ritter 1978). Reminiscent of the CIMA era, five investigate issues pertaining to food, diet, and nutrition in Chuuk State (Steager 1972; Severance 1976), the Marshalls (Pollock 1970), and on Pohnpei (Dahlquist 1972; Demory 1976).

Three dissertations describe societies that have undergone major transformations and have achieved new forms of social and cultural integration: Kosrae (Schaefer 1976), Tobi (Black 1977), and Ngatik (Poyer 1983). The remaining nine cover a wide range of topics, from the experience of the elderly on Guam (Torsch 1996) and an atoll community in Chuuk State (Borthwick 1977) to the changing role of women on contemporary Pohnpei (Kihleng 1996). (Also see McKnight 1960; Price 1975, M. Force 1976; Peoples 1977; Abe 1986; Nero 1987.)[1]

The seventy-eight dissertations discussed above represent a substantial contribution to the ethnographic record, and in the preceding chapter, Marshall describes other contributions that the authors of these dissertations have made to their discipline. Before turning to a consideration of future directions in Micronesian anthropology, a few related items warrant attention.

Several questions may be asked about the implications and impact of anthropological research in Micronesia for and on the subfield of sociocultural anthropology. There is the question of how research in Micronesia has influenced and shaped the theoretical and conceptual frameworks of those who have worked in the area. This question is particularly interesting in regard to Goodenough and Schneider, the two Micronesia specialists who have made the greatest contributions to anthropological theory. Both believe that their research in Micronesia was of little, if any, significance for the development of their theoretical perspectives.

Ward Goodenough reported that he had arrived at his linguistic model for describing the grammar of a culture prior to his fieldwork in 1947 (see Preface to *Property, Kin, and Community on Truk* [Goodenough 1951, 9–13]), and that the actual field site in which he conducted research was of little or no relevance (personal communication 1996). Nonetheless, it may be suggested that Goodenough's research on Chuuk made him aware of the problems inherent in the structure of matriliny. This may have enabled him to see the implications of the cognatic descent system that he later encountered in Kiribati, which resulted in his article, "A Problem in Malayo-Polynesian Social Organization" (1955).

In a series of interviews published posthumously, David Schneider claimed that his work on Yap had no significant influence on his later thought (Handler 1995, 206–216). However, he went to Yap with an interest in culture and personality (Bashkow 1991), only to come away with what was to become his lifelong interest in kinship. That interest, focused initially on Yapese kinship, resulted in his publications on double descent (Schneider 1962, 1980) and his collaboration with Kathleen Gough in their comparative analysis of matriliny (Schneider and Gough 1961). While Schneider's theoretical contributions to the discipline may not all have been directly influenced by his work in Micronesia, it seems certain that the major subject of his work derived from his experience on Yap. For example, Schneider's last major work on kinship, *A Critique of the Study of Kinship* (1984), was based mainly on his Yapese material. Although he appears to contradict himself later, Schneider at one point went so far as to suggest that fieldwork itself may not be essential for the training of anthropologists (Handler 1995, 204–217). Most anthropologists would disagree and might argue as well that the fieldwork experience enables one to be a critical reader of ethnography. This latter point was not addressed by Schneider.

Concerning the impact of the published work on Micronesia on the larger discipline, Alkire (chap. 3) expresses disappointment and believes that Micronesia has been somewhat neglected. He refers to "this seeming disciplinary neglect" and notes: "Micronesian research of any kind is rarely mentioned in introductory texts or cited by disciplinary colleagues" (p. 103). In appendix 3, " 'The Tiny Islands': A Comparable Impact on the Larger Discipline?,"

Terence Hays analyzes the published record and suggests that Alkire's assessment may be a bit too bleak.

As an indicator of Micronesia's impact on anthropology, Hays employs the frequency with which Micronesian sources are cited in comparison with other areas of Oceania. He uses two measures: (1) the number of Micronesian cases that have been included in worldwide data bases, standard samples, and holocultural comparative studies, and (2) the citation of Micronesian societies in introductory texts. For Hays, the estimated precontact population size and the number of indigenous languages provides an indicator of the "ethnographic size" of an area, and he observes that judging by these two variables, but not geographic size, Micronesia is the smallest area of Oceania.

With regard to the first measure, Hays reviews the Human Relations Area Files (HRAF) project and the results of the World Ethnographic Sample, the Ethnographic Atlas, the Standard Cross-Cultural Sample, the Atlas of World Cultures, and the Encyclopedia of World Cultures. He concludes that the use of Micronesian cases "by comparative researchers appears to be entirely reasonable given its status as the 'ethnographically smallest' " area in the region (pp. 511, 512), and "when one considers the small 'ethnographic size' of the 'tiny islands,' they could be said to be *over*-represented" (p. 510). In addition to the role that he played in Micronesia, George P. Murdock was instrumental in the development of the HRAF project and was a major proponent of holocultural comparative studies, and it would be surprising if Micronesia were not reasonably well represented in such work.

Turning to citations in introductory texts, Hays suggests that there is no reason to expect a representative sampling of societies. Nonetheless, in terms of the total number of societies cited, the Pacific ranks low in the number of references, and appropriate to its small ethnographic size, Micronesia is the least cited of the three island regions.

Hays gives three reasons why societies are selected for examples in introductory textbooks: personal bias, mimicry, and salience. The personal preference of authors would not produce a systematic bias across a large number of texts and is probably the least significant of the three. Mimicry and salience are much more important.

Mimicry is evident in the topical organization of textbooks, and regarding the selection of societies to be used as examples, Hays reports that "an initial appearance in a textbook almost guarantees later ones" (p. 507) The case must be a good choice in the first place, and the "salience" of a given example is crucial. Examples of the most primitive and most pristine are favored. The exotic illustrates diversity and may communicate lessons about cultural relativity. Hays observes that many popular examples have what has been referred to as "cultural flash." The most frequently cited cases from Oceania today include "the Trobriand Island *kula* ring; Arapesh, Mundugumor, and Tchambuli alleged variations on sex roles; the postwar 'cargo cults' of Manus; Siuai as the *locus classicus* of the 'big man' concept; and Samoans' 'stress-free adolescence' " (p. 508). Research on all but one of these seven societies was conducted before World War II, and Hays notes that five are associated with Margaret Mead. One might add that the names of other well-known Pacific anthropologists— Bronislaw Malinowski and Douglas L. Oliver—are attached to the other two.

This raises an issue discussed by Hays that was previously considered in chapters 1 and 3. Polynesia and Melanesia were well established in the ethnographic literature long before there was a significant English-language literature on Micronesia. Although the number of case studies was relatively few, several anthropological classics on Polynesian and Melanesian societies were part of anthropology's culture before the American initiative was launched in Micronesia. Given the tendency for mimicry, it is not surprising that Micronesian societies have not been cited more frequently in introductory texts.

Timing and salience also have had consequences. By the time American anthropologists reached Micronesia, all Micronesians had experienced decades (and in the case of the Marianas, centuries) of colonial rule and missionization. Micronesian societies had lost most of whatever exotic qualities they might have had, and by no stretch of the imagination could they have been said to represent pristine societies, untarnished by what Hezel (1983) has called that "first taint of civilization." Micronesia's "cultural flash" had dimmed.

Further, it may be suggested that Micronesia was upstaged. As Alkire (chap. 3) points out, shortly after American fieldwork began in Micronesia, Pacific research interests shifted to the "new frontier" of interior New Guinea. The societies of the New Guinea highlands were more conducive to the ecological anthropology that emerged at the time, and they represented the anthropological dream of relatively "untouched" populations. There has been much anthropological mythmaking about the pristine qualities of New Guinea (Ogan 1996), but even so, European contact with the highlands was recent, and they represented the newly discovered and the exotic. They had "cultural flash." Hays reports that textbooks reflected this turn of events. In the 1960s, New Guinea alone (for the purposes of his analysis, Hays treats

New Guinea and island Melanesia as two areas) surpassed Polynesia in the number of citations in introductory textbooks, and it has remained in first place ever since.

The holocultural research and the textbooks discussed above are largely, if not solely, American enterprises, and some comment is required about the impact of Micronesian research outside of American academia. In my own experience, I have become well aware that my colleagues in Australia and New Zealand who also specialize in the Pacific have little familiarity with Micronesia. Alkire reports similar experiences during his quarter century of residence and work in Canada.

Part of the reason for this state of affairs was suggested in a book review some thirty years ago in the *American Anthropologist*. In that review, Evon Z. Vogt opined that there was a "continuing intellectual parochialism of certain conservative traditions in British social anthropology" and that scholars working within those traditions neglected work in American anthropology, whereas the reverse was not true. (While Vogt was primarily concerned with anthropology as practiced in the United Kingdom, I would expand his observations to include the British Commonwealth as a whole, thus including Australia and New Zealand.) With some good humor, Vogt wrote: "My good friend and older colleague, Professor Evans-Pritchard, once told me (with a twinkle in his eye) that he never reads books 'by Americans, Sociologists, or Women.' " Vogt went on to comment that he was afraid that sometimes Evans-Pritchard's students and younger colleagues miss the twinkle in his eye when "he makes such delightfully preposterous statements!" (Vogt 1965, 555). While times have changed since Vogt's writing, even a cursory examination of library collections in Australia and New Zealand today reveals a woeful lack of Micronesian materials, and colleagues confirm that interest in the smallest of the Pacific's culture areas is largely absent in both countries.

Another important factor that helps to account for the lack of interest in American Micronesia among researchers outside the United States is found in the origins of the American administration of Micronesia. The security restrictions that prevailed until the early 1960s prevented all foreign researchers and discouraged many American anthropologists from working in American Micronesia, and many of the former came to view Micronesia as an exclusively American conclave. This perception continues to the present day. One New Zealand colleague recently commented that he was familiar with the work of Goodenough and Schneider, but that Micronesia is of little interest down under because non-American researchers have been excluded.[2] Alkire ends his own observations, however, on a more optimistic note when he comments that perceptions seem to be changing; he points to the increasing number of Japanese scholars (as well as the occasional Australian) who have recently worked in Micronesia.

FUTURE DIRECTIONS

When the anthropological initiative was launched in Micronesia in the 1940s, traditional ethnographic topics were the main areas of interest and research, and no one anticipated that over one-half of all doctoral dissertations would eventually focus on issues pertaining to social and cultural change. After more than a half century, American Micronesia is now one of the most studied of all world areas. While much work has been done, the chapters of this volume and the above discussion of doctoral dissertations both reveal a number of areas that have been neglected and suggest some topics for future research. A few warrant further comment.

Peacock's discussion (1993) of education serves as a reminder that the impact of Micronesia's largest industry has been relatively ignored. Going beyond the immediate concerns of King's discussion (chap. 11), the almost total absence of legal anthropology calls for both explanation and research. Rubinstein (chap. 10) notes that ethnomedicine has largely been neglected, and other areas relating to health and medicine cry out for attention; many of these are related to urbanization and migration and are discussed below. Nero (chap. 8) offers numerous suggestions for research in the visual and performing arts. While Marshall (chap. 12) reviews contributions to the study of indigenous Micronesian religions, our knowledge of this important area is woefully inadequate, and much of what once existed is no longer recoverable. However, contemporary religious life, the indigenization of Christianity, and the proliferation of Protestant denominations and other new faiths in recent years offer potentially exciting areas for future work.

Urbanization and migration are the primary engines of change in Micronesia today. Islanders leave rural areas and outer islands for urban centers in their own states and nations, and many move on to Guam, Saipan, Hawai'i, and the US mainland. Related to urbanization generally, Hezel (chap. 9) suggests the need for studies of changes in family structure, gender relations, and relations between generations. Related to both urbanization and greater involvement in a money economy, studies of the increased reliance on imported foodstuffs and chronic disease are long overdue. This would continue the old research interest in diet and nutrition and add the more recent emergence of the diseases of modernization (e.g., heart disease, stroke, non–insulin-dependent diabetes, and some cancers) that are tied to changed diet and a decline in physical fitness.

The outward migration of Micronesians suggests a host of topics for research, and there are many parallels with the experience of American Samoans and their movements to Hawai'i and other US destinations, and the citizens of the two freely associated states of the Cook Islands and Niue and their movements to and from New Zealand. Questions of identity become paramount, and a variety of issues are involved. What are the relationships of migrants to those who remain at home? To what extent is migration circular or one-way and permanent? Does the vernacular language persist past the first generation of migrants? Related to migration and identity questions is the increase in interethnic or interlanguage marriages among Micronesians. What is the ethnicity of the offspring of such unions? What is their relationship to their parents' home communities?

Guam, and to a lesser extent Saipan, provide extremely interesting venues for studies of interethnic relations among different Micronesian populations and various categories of "others." For example, Guam now has large resident communities from different language and culture areas of the Philippines, Taiwan, Hong Kong, South Korea, Japan, the United States, Palau, and the Federated States of Micronesia, particularly Chuuk. A host of fascinating social science questions might be explored in this context. Guam today is reminiscent of the Hawai'i of a few decades ago, and is still small enough to be researched with anthropological methodologies.

Interesting questions remain on the home front. While urbanization enjoys high visibility, the number of Micronesians who live on the outer islands today is about the same as in the years immediately after World War II. There are important differences from the past, however. Those who live on the outer islands now constitute a minority of the overall population, and the demographic structure of the outlying communities is radically different from times past. Communities have been depleted of the middle-aged and young adults who have been attracted to urban life, and those who remain at home are predominantly older adults with some of their grandchildren. Such communities must adjust to their new circumstances, and it seems likely that patterns of land use and tenure are being affected.

There are other issues concerning land tenure. Since the beginning of the American era, the judicial system has increasingly intervened in matters pertaining to the inheritance and use of land, and new patterns are emerging. There is also the issue of the land rights of all individuals related and connected to those Micronesians who have left, married, and had children elsewhere. Economic development has increased pressures for the privatization of landholdings as both indigenous and foreign entrepreneurs demand secure right, if not title, to land. All attempts at economic development—tourism, fishing industries, commercial agriculture, and so on—offer opportunities for research.

Lastly, as table 5 reveals, of the seventy-eight dissertations in sociocultural anthropology, twenty have been completed by women. Of these, only five have concerned women's roles or feminist perspectives and issues (A. Fischer 1957; M. Thomas 1978; Poehlman 1979; L. Wilson 1993; Kihleng 1996). Essentially, the ethnography of women by women is missing from the ethnographic record in Micronesia, and much work remains to be done in this area.

CLOSING THE CIRCLE

In some respects, American anthropology's involvement in Micronesia has come full circle. The first two doctorates in sociocultural anthropology were earned by males in 1949, both on the traditional topics of kinship and social organization. In contrast, the five doctorates earned in the 1990s were by women, and two focused on feminist issues and women's roles.

Developments in Micronesian anthropology have also reflected larger events and trends in the United States. Anthropology's optimistic alliance with the navy and other federal agencies in the immediate postwar years was reversed and replaced by mutual distrust and hostility in the wake of American involvement in Southeast Asia during the 1960s and much of the 1970s. The intense feelings associated with the Vietnam era have long since subsided, but America's reluctance to decolonize and the long, tortuous negotiations that led to self-government in Micronesia have done little to restore confidence in the United States when American strategic interests are at stake.

Funds for training and research in Micronesia have largely been subject to the priorities and whims of Washington, D.C. Largely financed by the US

Navy, the initial research effort of the late 1940s was without precedent in the history of the discipline. The 1950s were generally lean years, but anthropology in Micronesia (and elsewhere) grew rapidly with the generous availability of federal funds for graduate education and scientific research in the 1960s and much of the 1970s. As discussed, federal and other support has subsequently eroded, and the 1990s have witnessed a retrenchment previously unknown to the anthropologists who joined university faculties as new PhDs in the 1960s and 1970s. To a large extent, the production of doctorates in sociocultural anthropology in Micronesia as depicted in table 5 reflects the ups and downs in funding for training and research over the last fifty years, and the rapid decline in the number of new doctorates in the 1980s and 1990s speaks for itself. There is no expectation that the trend will be reversed in the near future.

Much of American Micronesia faces uncertain times. The Compacts of Free Association for the Federated States of Micronesia and the Republic of the Marshall Islands will expire in the year 2001. Negotiations about the future relationship between the United States and these two Micronesian states are not scheduled to begin until 1999, and anxieties are building in both countries. While the relationship of free association will probably be extended or renewed, Micronesia's decreased strategic value in the post–Cold War era and the economic retrenchment in Washington, D.C. indicate that funding for the island nations will be far less generous in the future. Inevitably that lessened economic support from the United States will result in uncomfortable times in the islands. There will be fewer employment opportunities in both the public and private sectors and reduced government services in such important areas as education and health care. Such conditions may well serve as "push factors" to encourage a far greater number of Micronesians to exercise their option to migrate to the Northern Marianas, Guam, and United States. That trend has already been set in motion and may be accelerated. Micronesians may well repeat the experience of American Samoans. When the US Navy withdrew from Pago Pago in the early 1950s, the economy of American Sāmoa was dealt a severe blow. The exodus of American Samoans began, and today more Samoans live abroad than remain at home. The number of Micronesians living abroad will dramatically increase early in the next century, and Linda Allen's dissertation (1997) on a Marshallese community in Oklahoma may portend the focus of future studies.

NOTES

Critiques of earlier drafts of this chapter by Bill Alkire, Terence Hays, Fran Hezel, Mac Marshall, Karen Nero, Eugene Ogan, Lin Poyer, and Don Rubinstein were helpful and much appreciated.

1. While sociocultural anthropology is the focus of this volume, it is appropriate to comment briefly on the twenty PhD dissertations that have been completed in anthropology's three other subfields. Twelve have been in archaeology, and Fred Reinman's work in 1965 was the first of those. An interim of almost two decades followed before the next archaeology dissertation appeared, and between 1983 and 1996, eleven more were completed. Again federal funding accounted for this sudden burst of activity. Beginning in the early 1980s, the Office for Historic Preservation provided support for a wide range of activity that was broadly defined to include archaeology.

Of the eleven dissertations after Reinman's, eight were by students of William Ayres, University of Oregon, and George Gumerman, Southern Illinois University at Carbondale. Ayres took his own doctorate (based on Easter Island research) at Tulane, where he had connections with Jack and Ann Fischer. Gumerman had no previous connection with Micronesia. All five of Ayres' students conducted research on Pohnpei: Robert Bryson (1989); Larry Goodwin (1983); Alan Haun (1984); Osamu Kataoka (1996); and Rufino Mauricio (1993). Mauricio is from Pohnpei, and he is the first Micronesian to earn a PhD in anthropology. Gumerman's three students worked on Palau: William Masse (1989); David Snyder (1989); and James Carucci (1992). The other three archaeology dissertations were completed at other institutions: Joyce Bath's dissertation at the University of Hawai'i was on Pohnpei and Kosrae (1984); a Brown University student, Takeshi Ueki, did research on Kosrae (1984); and Laurie Lucking's dissertation at the University of Minnesota represented another research effort on Palau (1984).

Seven of the above dissertations were based on materials from Pohnpei and Kosrae that have the monumental architectural sites of Nan Madol and Lelu. Palau is also of archaeological interest for several reasons. Babelthuap, the largest island in Palau, has extensive terraces, other large earthen works, and extensive surface accumulations of prehistoric pottery. Other features link Palau with New Guinea and Southeast Asia, particularly the Philippines and Indonesia. It is not surprising that Pohnpei and Palau have attracted the most interest from archaeologists.

Physical anthropology is represented by six dissertations. Four of these (Hunt 1950; Hainline 1964; Levin 1976; and Turke 1985) have focused on issues concerning demography and fertility. A fifth examined Parkinson's disease on Guam (Rossman 1978), and the sixth was a primatological study of macaques on the island of Angaur in Palau (Farslow 1987).

The remaining two dissertations were in anthropological linguistics. One concerned with the sociosemantics of the language of Kosrae (Vesper 1976), and the other dealt with honorific speech on Pohnpei (Keating 1994).

2. Ironically, three of the CIMA researchers were not Americans. As noted elsewhere, Sir Peter H. Buck was a New Zealander of Māori descent, Rupert Murrill was a Canadian, and Arthur Capell was from Australia.

American Anthropologists in Micronesia Research Projects and Positions

A. Participants in the Coordinated Investigation of Micronesian Anthropology (CIMA)

Research Location	Participant	Home Institution	Discipline
Federated States of Micronesia			
Chuuk State			
Romónum Island	George Peter Murdock	Yale University	sociocultural anthropology
	Thomas Gladwin	Yale University	sociocultural anthropology
	Ward H. Goodenough	Yale University	sociocultural anthropology
	Frank LeBar	Yale University	sociocultural anthropology
	Isidore Dyen	Yale University	linguistics
	Clarence Wong	Yale University and Harvard University	botany
Lukunor Atoll, Mortlock Islands (Nomoi)	Jerome Rauch	Columbia University	sociocultural anthropology
	Burt Tolerton	Columbia University	sociocultural anthropology
Pohnpei State			
Pohnpei Island	Saul Riesenberg	University of California, Berkeley	sociocultural anthropology
	Paul Garvin	Indiana University	linguistics
	Rupert Murrill	American Museum of Natural History	physical anthropology
Mokil Atoll	Joseph Weckler	University of Southern California	sociocultural anthropology
	Conrad Bentzen	University of Southern California	film-making
	Raymond Murphy	Clark University	geography

Research Location	Participant	Home Institution	Discipline
Kapingamarangi Atoll	Peter H. Buck	Bernice P. Bishop Museum	sociocultural anthropology
	Kenneth P. Emory	Bernice P. Bishop Museum	sociocultural anthropology
	Samuel Elbert	Bernice P. Bishop Museum	linguistics
Kosrae State			
Kosrae Island	James L. Lewis	University of Pennsylvania	sociocultural anthropology
Yap State			
All Islands	Isidore Dyen	Yale University	linguistics
	Clarence Wong	Yale University and Harvard University	botany
Yap Islands	Edward E. Hunt, Jr.	Harvard University	physical anthropology
	Nathaniel Kidder	Harvard University	sociology (demography)
	David M. Schneider	Harvard University	sociocultural anthropology
	William D. Stevens	Harvard University	sociocultural anthropology
Ulithi Atoll	William A. Lessa	University of Chicago	sociocultural anthropology
Ifaluk Atoll	Edwin Grant Burrows	University of Connecticut	sociocultural anthropology
	Melford E. Spiro	Northwestern University	sociocultural anthropology
Republic of Belau			
Palau Islands	Homer G. Barnett	University of Oregon	sociocultural anthropology
	Arthur Capell	University of Sydney	linguistics
	Francis Mahoney	University of Wisconsin	sociocultural anthropology
	Allen Murphy	University of Oregon	sociocultural anthropology
	Robert Ritzenthaler	Milwaukee Public Museum	sociocultural anthropology
	John Useem	University of Wisconsin	sociology

Research Location	Participant	Home Institution	Discipline
	Harry Uyehara	University of Wisconsin	sociocultural anthropology
	Arthur Vidich	University of Wisconsin	sociocultural anthropology
Republic of the Marshall Islands			
Majuro Atoll	Margaret Chave	University of Hawai'i	sociocultural anthropology
	Alex Spoehr	Field Museum of Natural History	sociocultural anthropology
Guam			
Guam Island	William W. Greulich	Stanford University	physical anthropology
	Mildred L. Greulich	Stanford University	physical anthropology
Commonwealth of the Northern Mariana Islands			
Saipan	Alice Joseph	Institute of Ethnic Relations	psychiatry and sociocultural anthropology
	Veronica F. Murray	Institute of Ethnic Relations	psychiatry
Saipan, Tinian, and Rota Islands	Neal Bowers	University of Michigan	geography
	Rohma Bowers	University of Michigan	geography

B. Anthropological Participants in the Scientific Investigation of Micronesia (SIM)

Research Location	Participant	Home Institution
Federated States of Micronesia		
Chuuk State		
Romónum Island	Ann Fischer	Radcliffe College
Pohnpei State		
Kapingamarangi Atoll	Kenneth P. Emory	Bernice P. Bishop Museum

Research Location	Participant	Home Institution
Yap State		
Ifaluk Atoll	Edwin Grant Burrows	University of Connecticut
Republic of the Marshall Islands		
Arno Atoll	Leonard E. Mason	University of Hawaiʻi
	Harry Uyehara	University of Hawaiʻi
	Jack Tobin	University of Hawaiʻi
Bikini Atoll	Leonard E. Mason	University of Hawaiʻi
Commonwealth of the Northern Mariana Islands		
Saipan, Tinian, and Rota Islands	Alex Spoehr	Field Museum of Natural History

Ward H. Goodenough was also a SIM participant on Onotoa Atoll, Kiribati.

C. USTTPI Staff, District, and Assistant Anthropologists

USTTPI Staff Anthropologists

December 1949–June 1951	Philip Drucker	US Navy Civil Administration
1951–1953	Homer G. Barnett	beginning Department of the Interior administration
1953–1954	Saul Riesenberg	
1954–1955	Allan Smith	
1955–1961	John deYoung	
1957–1958	Richard Emerick	Assistant Staff Anthropologist

USTTPI District Anthropologists

Marshall Islands District	1950–1958	Jack Tobin	
Palau District	March 1949–March 1950	Harry Uyehara	Anthropological Field Consultant[1]
	June 1950–June 1951	Shigeru Kaneshiro	Anthropological Field Consultant[1]
	1951–1954	Francis Mahoney	
	1958–1963	Robert McKnight	
Ponape District	September 1950–June 1951	Jack Fischer	Anthropological Field Consultant[1]

	1951–1953	Jack Fischer	Internal Affairs Officer[2]
	1952–1954	Alfred Whiting	
	1955–1956	Richard Emerick	
	1957–1960	Frank Mahony	
Saipan District	1951–1952	Robert Solenberger	
Truk District	1948–1951	Thomas Gladwin	Anthropological Field Consultant and Native Affairs Officer during navy period[2]
	March 1949–June 1950	Jack Fischer	Anthropological Field Consultant[1]
	September 1950– June 1951	Frank Mahony	Anthropological Field Consultant[1]
	1952–1957	Frank Mahony	
Yap District	September 1950– June 1951	Francis Mahoney	
	1951–1957	Shigeru Kaneshiro	

Assistant Anthropologists (years of service unknown)

Marshall Islands District	Tion Bikajle
Palau District	M. Emesiochl
	Adalbert Obak
Ponape District	Pensile Lawrence
	Gustave Weilbacher
Yap District	Francis Defngin

Sources: Cattell 1949; Jaque Cattell Press 1968; Daniel and Shirley Peacock, personal communication 1997; Richard 1957c; University of Hawai'i Micronesian Program 1966–1969; USTTPI 1957.

[1] The district anthropologists were initially known as anthropological field consultants.
[2] Jack Fischer and Thomas Gladwin served in applied capacities other than district anthropologists in Ponape and Truk districts.

D. Micronesia Participants in the Displaced Communities in the Pacific Project (DCPP)

Research Location or Responsibility	Participant	Home Institution
Project Director	Homer G. Barnett	University of Oregon
General Micronesia	Kenneth Knudson	University of Oregon
Kapingamarangi Atoll and Porakiet, Pohnpei	Michael D. Lieber	University of Pittsburgh
Bikini Atoll and Kili Island, Marshall Islands	Robert C. Kiste	University of Oregon

APPENDIX 2

Micronesia Anthropology Dissertations Accepted by US Universities, 1949–1997

A. Dissertations by Decade

Decade	Name	Year	Dissertation Site	Institution	Subfield	Chair	Committee[1]
1940s	W. Goodenough	1949	Chuuk[2]	Yale	cultural	G. P. Murdock	
	D. Schneider	1949	Yap[2]	Harvard	cultural	C. Kluckhohn	
1950s	A. Fischer	1957	Chuuk[3]	Radcliffe	cultural	D. Oliver	
	J. Fischer[4]	1954	Chuuk, Pohnpei	Harvard	cultural	R. Brown	D. Schneider
	R. Force	1958	Palau[5]	Stanford	cultural	F. Keesing	
	T. Gladwin[6]	1952	Chuuk[2]	Yale	cultural	G. P. Murdock	
	E. Hunt, Jr.	1950	Yap[2]	Harvard	physical	S. Garn	
	F. LeBar	1951	Chuuk[2]	Yale	cultural	C. S. Ford	
	L. Mason	1954	Bikini migrants[3,7]	Yale	cultural	G. P. Murdock	
	S. Riesenberg	1950	Pohnpei[2]	UC Berkeley	cultural	R. Lowie	E. Gifford
	M. Spiro	1950	Ifaluk[2]	Northwestern	cultural	A. I. Hallowell	
	W. Stevens	1950	Yap[2]	Harvard	cultural	D. Oliver	
	M. Swartz	1958	Chuuk	Harvard	cultural	W. Caudill	J. Fischer
	A. Vidich	1953	Palau[2]	Harvard	cultural	B. Moore	D. Schneider
1960s	W. Alkire	1965	Lamotrek	Illinois	cultural	J. Steward	
	V. Carroll	1966	Nukuoro	Chicago	cultural	D. Schneider	
	R. Emerick[4]	1960	Pohnpei	Pennsylvania	cultural	W. Goodenough	
	D. Hughes	1968	Pohnpei	Catholic U	cultural	J. Ingersoll	
	R. Kiste	1967	Bikini migrants[8]	Oregon	cultural	H. G. Barnett	
	M. Lieber	1968	Kapingamarangi[8]	Pittsburgh	cultural	A. Spoehr	G. P. Murdock
	R. McKnight[4]	1960	Palau	Ohio State	cultural	L. Estel	
	F. Reinman	1965	Guam	UCLA	archaeology	C. Meighan	

Decade	Name	Year	Dissertation	Institution Site	Subfield	Chair	Committee[1]
	J. Tobin[4]	1967	Enewetak[3]	UC Berkeley	cultural	E. Colson	
	J. Hainline Underwood	1964	Micronesia	UCLA	physical	J. Birdsell	
	W. S. Wilson	1968	Kosrae	Pennsylvania	cultural	W. Goodenough	
1970s	W. Alexander	1978	Ebeye, Lib	New School for Social Research	cultural	M. Harner and S. Diamond	
	P. Black	1977	Tobi	UC San Diego	cultural	F. G. Bailey	
	E. M. Borthwick	1977	Lukunor	Iowa	cultural	M. Marshall	
	J. Caughey	1970	Chuuk	Pennsylvania	cultural	W. Goodenough	
	P. Dahlquist	1972	Pohnpei	Ohio State	cultural	D. Hughes	
	M. T. del Valle	1978	Guam	Hawai'i	cultural	D. Oliver	L. Mason, D. Topping
	B. Demory	1976	Pohnpei	UC Berkeley	cultural	M. Mackenzie	M. Murai
	M. Force	1976	Palau	Walden	cultural	D. Oliver	
	E. Jernigan	1973	Palau	Arizona	cultural	K. Basso	J. Underwood
	K. Knudson	1970	Micronesia[8]	Oregon	cultural	H. G. Barnett	
	D. Labby	1972	Yap	Chicago	cultural	D. Schneider	
	M. Levin	1976	Eauripik	Michigan	physical	F. Livingstone	
	S. Lingenfelter	1971	Yap	Pittsburgh	cultural	A. Spoehr	
	F. Mahony[4]	1970	Chuuk	Stanford	cultural	C. Barnett	
	R. Marksbury	1979	Yap	Tulane	cultural	J. Fischer	
	M. Marshall	1972	Namoluk	U Washington	cultural	V. Carroll	
	F. Muñoz	1979	Guam	UCLA	cultural	A. Katz	
	J. Nason	1970	Ettal	U Washington	cultural	V. Carroll	
	J. Peoples	1977	Kosrae	UC Davis	cultural	H. Rutz	
	G. Petersen	1977	Pohnpei	Columbia	cultural	D. Boyd	
	J. Poehlman	1979	Guam	Minnesota	cultural	F. Miller	
	N. Pollock	1970	Namu	Hawai'i	cultural	D. Oliver	F. Mahony, N. Bowers

Decade	Name	Year	Dissertation	Institution Site	Subfield	Chair	Committee[1]
	S. Price	1975	Yap	Washington State	cultural	R. Ferrell	A. Smith
	P. Ritter	1978	Kosrae	Stanford	cultural	C. Frake	
	D. Rossman	1978	Guam	Michigan	physical	F. Livingstone, C. Singh	
	D. Rubinstein	1979	Fais	Stanford	cultural	C. Frake	
	M. Rynkiewich	1972	Arno	Minnesota	cultural	R. Kiste	
	P. Schaefer	1976	Kosrae	Minnesota	cultural	R. Kiste	
	C. Severance	1976	Piis-Emwar	Oregon	cultural	R. Tonkinson	
	D. R. Smith	1977	Palau	Bryn Mawr	cultural	J. Goodale	
	J. J. Smith	1972	Rota	Arizona	cultural	K. Basso	J. Underwood
	J. Snyder	1976	Micronesia	UC Santa Barbara	cultural	T. Harding	
	P. Steager	1972	Puluwat	UC Berkeley	cultural	J. Anderson	M. Murai
	J. Thomas	1978	Namonuito	Hawai'i	cultural	A. Dewey	L. Mason
	M. Thomas	1978	Namonuito	Hawai'i	cultural	A. Dewey	L. Mason
	E. Vesper	1976	Kosrae	Missouri	anthropological linguistics	P. Gardner	
	R. Ward	1977	Pohnpei	Tulane	cultural	J. Fischer	
1980s	G. Abe	1986	Micronesia	Kansas	cultural	F. Moos	
	J. Bath	1984	Kosrae, Pohnpei	Hawai'i	archaeology	P. B. Griffin	R. Kiste
	R. Bryson	1989	Pohnpei	Oregon	archaeology	W. Ayres	
	L. Carucci	1980	Enewetak	Chicago	cultural	M. Sahlins	D. Schneider
	J. Epstein	1986	Palau	Hawai'i	cultural	A. Dewey	
	M. Evans	1988	Pohnpei	Florida	cultural	H. R. Bernard	
	S. Falgout	1984	Pohnpei	Oregon	cultural	R. Chaney	W. Ayres
	D. Farslow	1987	Palau	Ohio State	physical	F. Poirier	
	J. Flinn	1982	Pulap	Stanford	cultural	B. Siegel	
	L. Goodwin	1983	Pohnpei	Oregon	archaeology	W. Ayres	
	A. Haun	1984	Pohnpei	Oregon	archaeology	W. Ayres	
	M. Jorgensen	1984	Guam	Texas	cultural	R. Bauman	
	R. B. Larson	1989	Chuuk	Hawai'i	cultural	J. Linnekin	L. Mason

Decade	Name	Year	Disser-tation	Institution Site	Subfield	Chair	Committee[1]
	L. Lucking	1984	Palau	Minnesota	archae-ology	E. Johnson	
	C. Lutz	1980	Ifaluk	Harvard	cultural	J. Whiting	
	W. Masse	1989	Palau	So. Illinois Carbondale	archae-ology	G. Gumerman	
	L. Mayo	1984	Guam	UC Berkeley	cultural	W. Shack	
	M. McCutcheon	1981	Palau	Arizona	cultural	J. Officer	J. Under-wood
	M. Montvel-Cohen	1982	Yap	So. Illinois Carbondale	cultural	J. Maring	G. Gumer-man
	K. Nero	1987	Palau	UC Berkeley	cultural	N. Graburn	
	P. Parker	1985	Chuuk	Pennsyl-vania	cultural	W. Goodenough	
	R. Parmen-tier	1981	Palau	Chicago	cultural	M. Sahlins	D. Schneider
	L. Poyer	1983	Ngatik, Sapwuah-fik	Michigan	cultural	V. Carroll	
	C. Reafsnyder	1984	Chuuk	Indiana	cultural	M. Kendall	M. Marshall
	D. Snyder	1989	Palau	So. Illinois Carbondale	archae-ology	G. Gumerman	
	P. Turke	1985	Ifaluk, Yap	North-western	physical	W. Irons	
	T. Ueki	1984	Kosrae	Brown	archae-ology	D. Anderson	
1990s	L. Allen	1997	Marshall Is. migrants	Iowa	cultural	M. Marshall	L. Carucci
	J. Carucci	1992	Palau	So. Illinois Carbondale	archae-ology	G. Gumerman	
	O. Kataoka	1996	Pohnpei	Oregon	archae-ology	W. Ayres	
	E. Keating	1994	Pohnpei	UCLA	anthro-pological linguistics	A. Duranti	
	K. Kihleng	1996	Pohnpei	Hawai'i	cultural	J. Linnekin	
	R. Mauricio	1993	Pohnpei	Oregon	archae-ology	W. Ayres	
	E. Pinsker	1997	FSM general	Chicago	cultural	John Comaroff	

Decade	Name	Year	Disser-tation	Institution Site	Subfield	Chair	Committee[1]
	V. Torsch	1996	Guam	Oklahoma	cultural	B. Harris	
	L. Wilson	1993	Palau	U Mass Amherst	cultural	J. Urla	
ABD	G. Alcalay		Marshall Is.	New School for Social Research			
	J. Egan		Yap	UC Irvine			
	J. Hahn		Yap	UC San Diego			
	J. Hess		Marshall Is.	UC Irvine			
	J. Wendel		Xavier High School graduates	Rochester			

[1]Committee members who have done research in Micronesia
[2]CIMA-based
[3]SIM-based
[4]District Anthropologist
[5]TRIPP-based
[6]Native Affairs Officer
[7]USCC-based
[8]DCPP-based

B. Dissertations by University

University of Oregon

Kiste, Robert C.	1967
Knudson, Kenneth E.	1970
Severance, Craig J.	1976
Goodwin, Larry A.	1983
Falgout, Suzanne	1984
Haun, Alan E.	1984
Bryson, Robert U.	1989
Maurįcio, Rufino	1993
Kataoka, Osamu	1996

Harvard University/Radcliffe College

Schneider, David M.	1949
Stevens, William D.	1950
Hunt, Edward E., Jr.	1950
Vidich, Arthur J.	1953
Fischer, John L.	1954
Fischer, Ann M.	1957
Swartz, Marc J.	1958
Lutz, Catherine	1980

University of Hawai'i

Pollock, Nancy J.	1970
del Valle, Maria Teresa	1978
Thomas, John B.	1978
Thomas, Mary D.	1978
Bath, Joyce	1984
Epstein, Joshua L.	1986
Larson, Robert Bruce	1989
Kihleng, Kimberlee	1996

University of California, Berkeley

Riesenberg, Saul H.	1950
Tobin, Jack A.	1967
Steager, Peter W.	1972
Demory, Barbara	1976
Mayo, Larry W.	1984
Nero, Karen L.	1987

Stanford University

Force, Roland W.	1958
Mahony, Frank J.	1970
Ritter, Philip L.	1978
Rubinstein, Donald H.	1979
Flinn, Juliana B.	1982

University of Chicago

Carroll, Vern	1966
Labby, David	1972
Carucci, Laurence M.	1980
Parmentier, Richard J.	1981
Pinsker, Eve	1997

Yale University

Goodenough, Ward H.	1949
LeBar, Frank M.	1951
Gladwin, Thomas	1952
Mason, Leonard E.	1954

University of Pennsylvania

Emerick, Richard G.	1960
Wilson, Walter Scott	1968
Caughey, John L.	1979
Parker, Patricia L.	1985

University of California, Los Angeles

Underwood, Jane Hainline	1964
Reinman, Fred M.	1965
Muñoz, Faye Untalan	1979
Keating, Elizabeth	1994

University of Minnesota

Rynkiewich, Michael	1972
Schaefer, Paul D.	1976

Poehlman, Joanne	1979
Lucking, Laurie J.	1984

Southern Illinois University, Carbondale

Montvel-Cohen, Marvin	1982
Masse, William B.	1989
Snyder, David	1989
Carucci, James	1992

Ohio State University

McKnight, Robert	1960
Dahlquist, Paul D.	1972
Farslow, Daniel	1987

University of Arizona

Smith, James Jerome	1972
Jernigan, Earl W.	1973
McCutcheon, Mary S.	1981

University of Michigan

Levin, Michael	1976
Rossman, David L.	1978
Poyer, Linette	1983

Northwestern University

Spiro, Melford E.	1950
Turke, Paul W.	1985

University of Pittsburgh

Lieber, Michael D.	1968
Lingenfelter, Sherwood	1971

University of Washington

Nason, James D.	1970
Marshall, Mac	1972

Tulane University

Ward, Roger L.	1977
Marksbury, Richard	1979

University of Iowa

Borthwick, Ernest Mark	1977
Allen, Linda A.	1997

University of Illinois, Urbana
Alkire, William H.   1965

Catholic University
Hughes, Daniel T.   1968

Washington State University
Price, Samuel T.   1975

University of California, Santa Barbara
Snyder, Jacqueline M.   1976

University of Missouri
Vesper, Ethel R.   1976

Walden University
Force, Maryanne T.   1976

Bryn Mawr College
Smith, DeVerne Reed   1977

Columbia University
Petersen, Glenn T.   1977

University of California, Davis
Peoples, James G.   1977

University of California, San Diego
Black, Peter W.   1977

New School for Social Research
Alexander, William J.   1978

Brown University
Ueki, Takeshi   1984

Indiana University
Reafsnyder, Charles B.   1984

University of Texas, Austin
Jorgensen, Marilyn A.   1984

University of Kansas
Abe, Goh   1986

University of Florida
Evans, Michael   1988

University of Massachusetts, Amherst
Wilson, Lynn B.   1993

University of Oklahoma
Torsch, Vicki L.   1996

C. Dissertations by Island Area and Subfield

Federated States of Micronesia (60 dissertations)
Chuuk State (19 dissertations)
Sociocultural Anthropology

Goodenough, Ward H.	1949	Chuuk Lagoon		
LeBar, Frank	1951	Chuuk Lagoon		
Gladwin, Thomas	1952	Chuuk Lagoon		
Fischer, John L.	1954	Chuuk Lagoon[1]		
Fischer, Ann M.	1957	Chuuk Lagoon		
Swartz, Marc J.	1958	Chuuk Lagoon		
Caughey, John L.	1970	Chuuk Lagoon		
Mahony, Frank			1970	Chuuk Lagoon
Nason, James D.			1970	Mortlocks
Marshall, Mac			1972	Mortlocks
Steager, Peter			1972	Westerns
Severance, Craig J.			1976	Mortlocks
Borthwick, Ernest Mark			1977	Mortlocks
Thomas, John B.			1978	Namonuito

[1]Comparative study of Chuuk and Pohnpei.

Thomas, Mary D.   1978 Namonuito
Flinn, Juliana   1982 Westerns
Reafsnyder, Charles   1984 Mortlocks
Parker, Patricia   1985 Chuuk Lagoon
Larson, Robert Bruce   1989 Chuuk Lagoon

No dissertations in archaeology, biological anthropology, or anthropological linguistics have been completed in Chuuk State.

Pohnpei State (21 dissertations)
Sociocultural Anthropology

Riesenberg, Saul H.   1950 Pohnpei
Emerick, Richard   1960 Pohnpei
Carroll, Vern   1966 Nukuoro
Hughes, Daniel T.   1968 Pohnpei
Lieber, Michael D.   1968 Kapinga-
                               marangi
Dahlquist, Paul   1972 Pohnpei
Demory, Barbara   1976 Pohnpei
Petersen, Glenn   1977 Pohnpei
Ward, Roger   1977 Pohnpei
Poyer, Linette   1983 Ngatik;
                               Sapwuahfik
Falgout, Suzanne   1984 Pohnpei
Evans, Michael   1988 Pohnpei
Kihleng, Kimberlee   1996 Pohnpei
Pinsker, Eve   1997 FSM general

Archaeology

Goodwin, Larry A.   1983 Pohnpei
Haun, Alan E.   1984 Pohnpei
Bath, Joyce   1984 Pohnpei[2]
Bryson, Robert U.   1989 Pohnpei
Mauricio, Rufino   1993 Pohnpei
Kataoka, Osamu   1996 Pohnpei

Anthropological Linguistics

Keating, Elizabeth   1994 Pohnpei

No dissertations in biological anthropology have been completed in Pohnpei State.

[2]Comparative study of Pohnpei and Kosrae.

Yap State (14 dissertations)
Sociocultural Anthropology

Schneider, David M.   1949 Yap
Stevens, William D.   1950 Yap
Spiro, Melford E.   1950 Ifaluk
Alkire, William H.   1965 Lamotrek
Lingenfelter,   1971 Yap
  Sherwood
Labby, David   1972 Yap
Price, Samuel   1975 Yap
Marksbury, Richard   1979 Yap
Rubinstein, Donald H.   1979 Fais
Lutz, Catherine   1980 Ifaluk
Montvel-Cohen,   1982 Yap
  Marvin

Biological Anthropology

Hunt, Edward E., Jr.   1950 Yap
Levin, Michael   1976 Eauripik
Turke, Paul   1985 Yap and Ifaluk

No dissertations in archaeology or anthropological linguistics have been completed in Yap State.

Kosrae State (6 dissertations)
Sociocultural Anthropology

Wilson, Walter Scott   1968
Schaefer, Paul D.   1976
Peoples, James   1977
Ritter, Philip   1978

Archaeology

Ueki, Takeshi   1984

Anthropological Linguistics

Vesper, Ethel   1976

No dissertations in biological anthropology have been completed in Kosrae State.

Republic of Palau (17 dissertations)

Sociocultural Anthropology

Vidich, Arthur J.	1953	Palau
Force, Roland	1958	Palau
McKnight, Robert	1960	Palau
Jernigan, Earl W.	1973	Palau
Force, Maryanne	1976	Palau
Black, Peter W.	1977	Tobi
Smith, DeVerne Reed	1977	Palau
McCutcheon, Mary	1981	Palau
Parmentier, Richard	1981	Palau
Epstein, Joshua	1986	Palau
Nero, Karen L.	1987	Palau
Wilson, Lynn	1993	Palau

Archaeology

Lucking, Laurie J.	1984	Palau
Masse, William B.	1989	Palau
Snyder, David	1989	Palau
Carucci, James	1992	Palau

Biological Anthropology

Farslow, Daniel	1987	Angaur macaques

No dissertations in linguistic anthropology have been completed in Palau.

Republic of the Marshall Islands (8 dissertations)

Sociocultural Anthropology

Mason, Leonard E.	1954	Bikini
Kiste, Robert C.	1967	Bikini
Tobin, Jack A.	1967	Enewetak
Pollock, Nancy J.	1970	Namu
Rynkiewich, Michael	1972	Arno
Alexander, William	1978	Ebeye, Lib
Carucci, Laurence M.	1980	Enewetak
Allen, Linda A.	1997	Marshall Islands migrants to United States

No dissertations in archaeology, biological anthropology, or anthropological linguistics have been completed in the Marshall Islands.

Guam (7 dissertations)

Sociocultural Anthropology

del Valle, Maria Teresa	1978	
Muñoz, Faye Untalan	1979	
Poehlman, Joanne	1979	
Jorgensen, Marilyn A.	1984	
Mayo, Larry W.	1984	
Torsch, Vicki L.	1978	

Biological Anthropology

Rossman, David L.	1978

No dissertations in archaeology or anthropological linguistics have been completed in Guam.

General Micronesia (5 dissertations)

Sociocultural Anthropology

Knudson, Kenneth	1970
Snyder, Jacqueline M.	1976
Abe, Goh	1986

Archaeology

Reinman, Fred	1965

Biological Anthropology

Hainline, Jane [Underwood]	1964

No dissertations in anthropological linguistics have been completed on material from Micronesia generally.

Commonwealth of the Northern Mariana Islands (CNMI) (1 dissertation)

Sociocultural Anthropology

Smith, James Jerome	1972	Rota

No dissertations in archaeology, biological anthropology, or anthropological linguistics have been completed in the Northern Marianas.

Subfield	Dissertations	Years
Sociocultural Anthropology	78	1949–1997
Archaeology	12	1965–1996
Biological Anthropology	6	1951–1987
Anthropological Linguistics	2	1976–1994
Total	98	

The "Tiny Islands":

A Comparable Impact on the Larger Discipline?

Terence E. Hays

Despite increasing topical specialization within our discipline, in many respects cultural anthropology continues to be organized geographically. Through regional associations and journals, institutional staffing priorities, and numerous other means, the *place* where research is conducted becomes a significant dimension of the work itself. While, in principle, ethnography concerning *any* people is grist for the comparative mill and theory building, for a variety of reasons some peoples have become so well known that they have entered a kind of "Anthropological Hall of Fame"—one thinks immediately of the Kwakiutl potlatch, Nayar "marriage," and the Trobrianders' *kula* exchange as obvious candidates. To the extent that these institutions have become classics in the world ethnographic catalog, one could say that the studies (and authors) that yielded our knowledge of them have had a substantial impact on the discipline. But to ask what has been the overall impact of ethnography conducted in a particular geographical region, such as Micronesia, is to pose a question to which no single measure is likely to produce a complete answer.

So far as Oceania is concerned, I was recently faced with a related task: selection of the societies for which summary descriptions would be included in a volume for the *Encyclopedia of World Cultures* (Hays 1991). The guidelines I was given by the general editor were apparently straightforward: within imposed space limits, to choose those cases that are the best described in the ethnographic literature, most often used in holocultural (worldwide) comparative studies, and most often cited in the general literature. Rather than trust my own judgment on the first point, I determined which Oceania cases had been considered by others to be sufficiently well described to be included in standard databases or samples, namely, the Human Relations Area Files, the World Ethnographic Sample, the Ethnographic Atlas, the Standard Cross-Cultural Sample, and the *Atlas of World Cultures*. With respect to holocultural studies, I examined one hundred ninety-eight published studies and recorded each Oceania society identified as having been used. Finally, viewing "the general literature" as impossible to survey, I examined the indexes of one hundred twelve introductory anthropology textbooks published between 1940 and

1990, recording each Oceania society mentioned by name and, presumably, referred to or discussed in the text.

The results of these searches now can be used to explore the question of the "overall impact" of ethnographic research in Micronesia, using two measures: (1) the extent to which Micronesian cases have been included in worldwide databases and standard samples, and used in holocultural studies which, through the testing of specific hypotheses, play a major role in theory building; and (2) the frequency with which Micronesian societies have been cited and discussed in introductory anthropology textbooks—such mentions and uses being considered not only to have an impact on students' general knowledge of the world but also to indicate which societies in the world are judged by professional anthropologists (the textbook authors themselves and those whose work they have surveyed) as particularly salient or notable. Given the focus of this volume, and the fact that the bulk of the ethnographic research conducted in Micronesia has taken place since the beginning of World War II, the time focus here is from the mid 1940s to 1990. Because most of the material used in this appendix is drawn from earlier literature in Micronesia, the place names here reflect the spellings of the time.

DATABASES, STANDARD SAMPLES, AND HOLOCULTURAL STUDIES

When researchers conduct holocultural studies to test hypotheses, one of their primary concerns is that the sample they use is "representative," that is, that the full range of human variation is taken into account and that the cases used can be considered to be reasonably independent of each other. The inclusion of any particular society, Micronesian or otherwise, depends then on its suitability on these grounds (e.g., not including two different communities on Pohnpei) but also, of course, on researchers' judgments that the case is well described in the ethnographic literature, that is, that reliable information is available for a wide range of variables.

Over the past six decades, the compilation of databases (such as the Human Relations Area Files, the Ethnographic Atlas, and the *Atlas of World Cultures*) has made the tasks of identifying and learning about the best-described societies of the world much easier, whether the user is interested in hypothesis testing or any other kind of research. In addition to the production of such databases, several attempts have been made to construct standard samples (sometimes including coded data for the cases) for the use of holocultural researchers, lessening the chances that the results of one study are not compara-

Table 1 Oceania Cases in Databases and Standard Samples

NUMBER OF CASES

	HRAF	WES	EA	SCCS	AWC	EWC
Australia	4	10	13	2	9	17
New Guinea	5	14	45	5	20	69
Melanesia	6	15	28	6	14	29
Polynesia	6	19	22	4	15	22
Micronesia	4	11	17	5	12	14
All Oceania	25	69	125	22	70	151

PERCENTAGE OF CASES

	HRAF	WES	EA	SCCS	AWC	EWC
Australia	16.0	14.5	10.4	9.1	12.9	11.3
New Guinea	20.0	20.3	36.0	22.7	28.6	45.7
Melanesia	24.0	21.7	22.4	27.3	20.0	19.2
Polynesia	24.0	27.5	17.6	18.2	21.4	14.6
Micronesia	16.0	15.9	13.6	22.7	17.1	9.3

ble to those of another due to the use of different samples. This process has not resulted in any particular sample being universally adopted, but some (the World Ethnographic Sample and the Standard Cross-Cultural Sample) have been much more widely used than others. In table 1, Oceania cases incorporated in the most widely used databases and standardized samples are compared with respect to areal representation.

Human Relations Area Files

Since their inception as the "Cross-Cultural Survey" in 1937 at Yale University under the direction of George Peter Murdock, the Human Relations Area Files (HRAF) have had as their primary goal to provide systematically organized source material on selected societies of the world, with the selection based largely on breadth and quality of information available (Lagacé 1974). As of 1974, about three hundred cases had been incorporated in the main (paper) files (not significantly expanded since then), with twenty-five representing

Oceania. As reflected in tables 1 and 2, four Micronesian cases have been included: Marshalls (especially Arno, Bikinians, and Majuro); Truk (now Chuuk); Woleai (especially Ifaluk); and Yap. While this number may appear small, it is the same as that for Australia and not significantly smaller than those for other parts of Oceania (table 1).

This near parity is inconsistent with the relative sizes and internal diversity of the five regions of Oceania (though consistent with HRAF purposes). Whether measured in terms of estimated precontact population size or numbers of indigenous languages spoken, there are considerable disparities to be found within Oceania (as here delimited). New Guinea (here taken to exclude the Bismarck Archipelago), with perhaps 2,000,000 people speaking as many as 850 languages, is gigantic compared to the others: Melanesia (including the Bismarck Archipelago, Solomon Islands, Polynesian outliers located in the Solomons, Vanuatu, New Caledonia, and the Loyalty Islands), with a population of perhaps 500,000 and 250 languages; Australia, with about 200 languages spoken aboriginally by 300,000 people; Polynesia (including Fiji), whose Melanesia-sized population of 500,000 spoke only 21 or 22 languages (excluding Polynesian outliers); and Micronesia (including Kapingamarangi), the smallest area, with about 180,000 people and only about a dozen languages (see table 12).

Of course, not all societies of Oceania have been studied and described by ethnographers, so not all would have been available for inclusion in the Human Relations Area Files during the period of case selection (primarily the 1930s to the 1950s), even if proportional representation had been an explicit goal. For example, even at the time of this writing only about 200 of New Guinea's 850 language groups are represented by substantial ethnographic coverage in the literature, and this number was probably no higher than 50 as of 1950. At that time also, well-described Melanesian cases numbered perhaps 30; ethnographically known Aboriginal Australia consisted of maybe 20 cases; Polynesia about the same; and Micronesia somewhat fewer. Such limitations on information available are fairly clearly seen with respect to the Micronesian societies included as HRAF cases. For the Marshalls, nearly half of the 21 sources listed in the *Hraf Source Bibliography* (HRAF 1969) are from prewar German researchers, with postwar research by Leonard E. Mason, Alex Spoehr, and Jack Tobin constituting significant additions. The results of postwar research by American anthropologists are most dramatically evident in the case of Truk, with the work of Ann Fischer, John "Jack" Fischer, Thomas Gladwin, Ward H. Goodenough, Frank LeBar, Seymour Sarason, and Marc Swartz providing the

vast majority of the 24 sources used. By contrast, the work of Edwin G. Burrows and Melford E. Spiro on Ifaluk was used for the Woleai case, but prewar
German sources overwhelmingly dominate the 41-item bibliography. For Yap,
David M. Schneider's publications account for 4 of the 14 sources used, the remainder consisting largely of German prewar publications and assorted minor
sources.

World Ethnographic Sample

As the Human Relations Area Files were developing in the 1950s, Murdock
proposed (1957, 664) what he called the "World Ethnographic Sample" (WES)
—"a carefully selected sample of all the cultures known to history and ethnography," which was, unlike the HRAF database, "specifically designed to be as
representative as possible of the entire known range of cultural variation."
The sample included 565 societies, of which 69 were from Oceania: 10 Australian, 14 from New Guinea, 18 Melanesian, 16 Polynesian, and 11 Micronesian
(Chamorro [Saipan]; Gilbertese [Onotoa]; Ifaluk; Kapingamarangi; Kusaians;
Marshallese [Bikini]; Nauruans; Palauans; Ponapeans; Trukese; and Yapese).
The number of societies for each area within Oceania increased substantially
over those in the HRAF database, with the total number almost tripling. But
the proportions of cases remained much the same (see table 1). Though Murdock provided no bibliography with the World Ethnographic Sample, it is
clear from his subsequent publications that the postwar boom in Micronesian
ethnographic research made many more societies eligible for inclusion as
"well described."

Ethnographic Atlas

With Murdock's move to the University of Pittsburgh, he began producing
the "Ethnographic Atlas" (EA). Appearing in regular installments in the journal _Ethnology_, the Atlas was intended to provide coding systems and codes—
which could then be used as laborsaving devices for holocultural researchers
—covering a wide range of variables for most of the well-described societies
of the world. When Murdock initiated this series, he presented "a geographical classification of the peoples of the world," (_Ethnology_ 1962, 113), derived
almost completely from his earlier World Ethnographic Sample. It included a
total of 100 societies, "representing a fairly even distribution throughout the
world" (1962, 113). This sample was said to differ "substantially from those

previously used in cross-cultural studies" (1962, 113), and the initial intent was to include in later installments "the societies which they have assessed" (1962, 114). For Oceania, 12 societies were included: 1 Australian, 3 from New Guinea, 4 Melanesian, 2 Polynesian, and 2 Micronesian (Palauans and Trukese).

In 1967, Murdock compiled all of the installments published to that point under the title *Ethnographic Atlas: A Summary* (Murdock 1967). The number of societies had increased to 862, including 100 from Oceania: 9 Australian, 34 for New Guinea, 20 Melanesian, 21 Polynesian, and 16 from Micronesia (Bikinians; Carolinians of Saipan; Chamorro [Saipan]; Gilbertese [Onotoa]; Kapingamarangi; Kusaians; Makin; Marshallese [Majuro]; Nauruans; Nomoians [Mortlockese]; Palauans; Ponapeans; Trukese; Ulithians; Woleaians [Ifaluk]; and Yapese). Additional supplements appeared in *Ethnology* until 1971, bringing the total number to 1,264 societies, with 25 additions for Oceania: 4 Australian, 11 from New Guinea, 8 Melanesian, 1 Polynesian, and 1 Micronesian (Lamotrek); also, Jaluit was added as a second focus for the Marshallese case. Thus, in its entirety the Ethnographic Atlas included 125 Oceania cases, with 17 of these from Micronesia.

The increase in the number of Oceania cases compared to the World Ethnographic Sample was substantial—almost double—but much of this was due to expansion of the representation of New Guinea and Melanesia, though Micronesian cases increased by about 50 percent. Not only does this reflect the 1960s influx of researchers working in these areas, but, by design, coverage in the Ethnographic Atlas attempted to approximate the variable cultural diversity of Oceania regions. In fact, Micronesia, with 13.6 percent of the Oceania cases, might be said to be overrepresented (see table 1).

Standard Cross-Cultural Sample

The Ethnographic Atlas proved foundational to what is probably the most widely used sample in holocultural studies since 1969, the "Standard Cross-Cultural Sample" (sccs) which Murdock and Douglas White (1969) drew from the Atlas. Intended as "a representative sample of the world's known and well-described cultures, 186 in number" (1969, 329), 22 Oceania cases are included: 2 Australian, 5 from New Guinea, 6 Melanesian, 4 Polynesian, and 5 Micronesian (Gilbertese [Makin and Butaritari]; Marshallese [Jaluit]; Palauans; Trukese; and Yapese). Despite the avowed concern with representativeness, these proportions are puzzling, with Micronesian cases equaling in number those from New Guinea.

Atlas of World Cultures

A later attempt at winnowing down the Ethnographic Atlas was Murdock's 1981 _Atlas of World Cultures_ (awc). Though not widely used as a sample per se by holocultural researchers, the _Atlas of World Cultures_ includes 563 societies that "presumably number the majority of those whose cultures are most fully described in the ethnographic literature," chosen to represent comparably large and culturally diverse geographical regions (Murdock 1981, 3). Oceania is represented by 70 cases: 9 Australian, 20 from New Guinea, 14 Melanesian, 15 Polynesian, and 12 Micronesian. With respect to size and content, Oceania's inclusion in the _Atlas of World Cultures_ resembles its presence in the World Ethnographic Sample more than that in the Ethnographic Atlas, but its proportional representation is different yet again (see table 1). So far as Micronesia is concerned, the work of American researchers is used to about the same degree as prewar German sources: Chamorros of Saipan (Joseph and Murray, Spoehr); Kapingamarangi (Eilers, Emory); Kusaians (Sarfert); Lamotrek (Alkire); Majuro (Mason, Spoehr); Makin (Lambert, Maude); Nauruans (Hambruch, Wedgwood); Palauans (Keate, Barnett); Ponapeans (Hambruch, Riesenberg); Trukese (Gladwin and Sarason, Goodenough); Woleaians (Ifaluk) (Burrows and Spiro); and Yapese (Müller, Schneider).

Encyclopedia of World Cultures

After identifying the most commonly occurring cases in these diverse sources, but seeking proportional representation in terms of the diversity within each "culture area," I selected 151 societies for inclusion in the Oceania volume of the _Encyclopedia of World Cultures_ (Hays 1991): 17 from Australia, 69 from New Guinea, 29 from Melanesia, 22 from Polynesia, and 14 from Micronesia (Belau [Palau]; Bikini; Chamorros; Kapingamarangi; Kiribati [Gilberts]; Kosrae [Kusaie]; Marshall Islands; Nauru; Nomoi [Mortlock Islands]; Pohnpei [Ponape]; Chuuk [Truk]; Ulithi; Woleai; and Yap).

So far as most (but not all) holocultural studies are concerned, the impact our knowledge about any particular society will have on our general understanding of humanity is dependent not only on its having been well described in the literature, but also on its having been selected for inclusion in databases and standard samples. As we have seen, how many and which Micronesian cases have been so selected has varied, and not simply incrementally over time (see table 2 for a summary). Just as some societies have been added to later or

Table 2 Micronesian Cases in Databases and Standard Samples

Cases (Total 18)	HRAF 4	WES 11	EA 17	SCCS 5	AWC 12
Marshalls (Bikini)	+	+ (B)	+ (B)		
Truk	+	+	+	+	+
Woleai (Ifaluk)	+	+	+		+
Yap	+	+	+	+	+
Chamorros (Saipan)		+	+		+
Gilbertese (Onotoa)		+	+		
Kapingamarangi		+	+		+
Kusaians		+	+		+
Nauruans		+	+		+
Palauans		+	+	+	+
Ponapeans		+	+		+
Carolinians of Saipan			+		
Lamotrek			+		+
Makin			+		+
Marshallese (Jaluit, Majuro)			+	+ (J)	+ (M)
Nomoians			+		
Ulithians			+		
Gilbertese (Makin, Butiritari)				+	

larger samples, others have been dropped (without explanation). Thus, the use of specific societies in any particular study depends, at first, on which (if any) database or standard sample is employed. This point must be kept in mind when trying to find and interpret patterns in the fate of Micronesian societies in holocultural studies.

In my survey of holocultural studies, focusing on those published since the end of World War II, I examined the listing provided in David Levinson and Martin Malone's critical review of cross-cultural research (1980), comprehensive up through about 1979. Searching area libraries available to me, I then perused a total of 198 studies, recording every Oceania case indicated by name as having been employed (i.e., for which sufficient data were found by the

Table 3 Oceania Cases Used in Holocultural Studies, 1949–1979

	Societies	Uses	Studies	% of Studies
Australia	25	224	112	72.7
New Guinea	46	481	127	82.5
Melanesia	29	435	120	78.0
Polynesia	23	466	137	89.0
Micronesia	21	271	115	74.7
All Oceania	144	1877	154	

investigator to retain the case in the sample used). In 44 instances, cases used were not identified other than by citing HRAF, WES, EA, SCCS, or whatever had been the source of the sample. This left a total of 154 published holocultural studies that appeared during the time period 1949–1979 and that used named Oceania cases. Frequencies of use by area are listed in table 3.

As can be seen there, the sheer number of societies used does not necessarily correspond to frequency of use; for example, at least one society from Polynesia was used in 89.0 percent of the holocultural studies, while New Guinea—with twice as many total societies—appeared in somewhat fewer studies (82.5 percent). Third in frequency of use is Melanesia (78.0 percent), with Micronesia (74.7 percent) and Australia (72.7 percent) not far behind. While one might expect use frequencies to correspond closely to occurrences in databases or standard samples, such seems not to be the case, reflecting, at least in part, the fact that some researchers devise their own samples. It is interesting to note, for example, that in the holocultural studies examined, New Guinea is represented by a substantially larger number of different cases than is any of the other three areas, but this was strikingly true only for the EA database (cf. table 1). Moreover, with respect to Micronesia, if one examines uses over time (see table 4), there is no simple incremental pattern related to increased inclusion in databases and standardized samples.

If one supposes that studies published in the 1950s drew largely on the HRAF database, then the Micronesian cases included there (frequency of use italicized in table 4) might be expected to be the most likely ones used. However, the "Marshalls" (identified in studies as either Bikini, Jaluit, Majuro, or Marshall Islands) were used in only 2 out of the 10 studies examined, Truk also in 2, and Yap in only 1, while Woleai (including Ifaluk) was not used at all. With the publication of the World Ethnographic Survey in 1957, holocultural

Table 4 Micronesian Cases in Holocultural Studies (by Decade)

Cases	1940s	1950s	1960s	1970s	Total
Cases	2	7	76	69	154
Bikini	0	0	1	2	3
Carolinians of Saipan	0	0	0	0	0
Chamorros	0	3	13	6	22
Gilbert Islands	0	0	3	8	11
Ifaluk	0	0	29	8	37
Jaluit	0	0	0	1	1
Kapingamarangi	0	0	1	0	1
Kusaie	0	0	0	2	2
Lamotrek	0	0	1	0	1
Majuro	0	0	1	4	5
Makin	0	0	0	4	4
Marshall Islands	1	2	22	21	46
Nauru	1	1	3	1	6
Nomoi	0	0	1	1	2
Onotoa	0	0	1	1	2
Palau	0	0	3	5	8
Ponape	0	0	3	5	8
Saipan	0	0	1	0	1
Truk	1	2	18	26	47
Ulithi	0	1	12	3	16
Woleai	0	0	11	3	14
Yap	0	1	8	17	26
All Micronesia	3	10	137	125	271
"Gilberts"[a]	0	0	4	13	17
"Marshalls"[b]	1	2	24	28	55
"Saipan"[c]	0	3	14	6	23
"Woleai"[d]	0	0	41	11	52

Underscored use frequencies reflect the differential availability of cases across the decades considered. For holocultural researchers in the 1950s, only HRAF Micronesian cases were available to be used, i.e., Marshall Islands (including Bikini and Majuro for more specific emphasis), Truk, Woleai (including Ifaluk), and Yap. By the 1960s, these were supplemented with WES cases, and in the 1970s these two resources were further complemented with EA and SCCS cases.

[a]Gilbert Islands, Makin, and Onotoa
[b]Bikini, Jaluit, Majuro, and Marshall Islands
[c]Carolinians of Saipan and Chamorros
[d]Ifaluk and Woleai

studies published in the 1960s understandably include new WES cases (see the use frequencies in italics, table 4). Some of these appear with considerable frequency, for example, "Woleai" (including Ifaluk and Woleai) occurs in 41 out of 154 studies examined, while others, included earlier in the Human Relations Area Files, substantially increase in use, for example, the "Marshalls," Truk, and Yap. Other new cases, however, show only modest use (e.g., Nauru, Palau, and Ponape), and Kusaie was not used at all. And finally, in the 1970s researchers had two new databases and samples available, with the Ethnographic Atlas adding six new cases, and the Standard Cross-Cultural Sample a new focus (Makin and Butaritari) for the "Gilberts" (identified as the Gilbert Islands, Makin, and Onotoa). The "Gilberts," Truk, and Yap show sizeable increases in use, while the "Marshalls" only slightly increased in frequency, and some cases ("Saipan" [including Carolinians as well as Chamorros there] and "Woleai") decreased considerably as choices of holocultural researchers.

A further indication that use in holocultural studies is not simply a reflection of occurrence in databases or standard samples can be seen in the fact that for any given Oceania region some societies have been used considerably more than have others. Table 5 lists the most often used societies by area, indicating, for example, that 8 out of 29 Melanesian societies account for 85.1 percent of the uses of cases from that area, and that Sāmoa was used in 59.7 percent of the studies, compared to 89.0 percent for Polynesian societies as a whole (cf. table 3). In this regard it is notable that the most often used Micronesian societies—Truk and the "Marshalls"—show considerably lower frequencies of use (30.5 percent and 35.7 percent, respectively) than is true for their analogues in any other Oceania region. This may (and probably does) reflect less thorough coverage of these societies in the literature, that is, information is available to researchers on substantially fewer variables than for other Oceania cases. But it also is possible that some kind of bias is present, a conclusion that is nearly inescapable when introductory textbooks are examined.

INTRODUCTORY TEXTBOOKS

Authors of introductory textbooks in cultural anthropology rarely, if ever, state their criteria for selecting particular societies for illustrative material or "mini case studies." When maps are provided to indicate cases highlighted in the text (e.g., endpapers in Peoples and Bailey 1994), at least non-European areas of the world appear to be represented, though not evenly so. When one considers the _purpose_ of such textbooks—presumably, to present and illustrate

Table 5 Oceania Societies Most Often Used in Holocultural Studies

Australia (25 Societies)	No. of Studies	% of Studies (Total 154)	% of Uses of Australia Cases (Total 224)
Murngin	68	44.2	30.4
Aranda (Arunta)	62	40.3	27.7
Tiwi	26	16.9	11.6
			69.7

New Guinea (46 Societies)	No. of Studies	% of Studies (Total 154)	% of Uses of New Guinea Cases (Total 481)
Trobriand Is.	87	56.5	18.1
Kwoma	56	36.4	11.6
Wogeo	47	30.5	9.8
Arapesh	41	26.6	8.5
Kapauku	37	24.0	7.7
Orokaiva	35	22.7	7.3
D'Entrecasteaux Is.	30	19.5	6.2
Kiwai	25	16.2	5.2
			74.4

Melanesia (29 Societies)	No. of Studies	% of Studies (Total 154)	% of Uses of Melanesia Cases (Total 435)
Tikopia	83	53.9	19.1
Lesu	73	47.4	16.8
Buka (Kurtatchi)	62	40.3	14.3
Manus	55	35.7	12.6
Ontong Java	34	22.1	7.8
Buin (Siuai)	24	15.6	5.5
Malekula (Seniang)	23	14.9	5.3
Malaita	16	10.4	3.7
			85.1

Table 5 *(Continued)*

Polynesia (23 Societies)	No. of Studies	% of Studies (Total 154)	% of Uses of Polynesian Cases (Total 466)
Sāmoa	92	59.7	19.7
Māori	68	44.2	14.6
Marquesas Is.	68	44.2	14.6
Pukapuka	60	39.0	12.9
Lau	46	29.9	9.9
Fiji	21	13.6	<u>4.5</u>
			76.2

Micronesia (22 Societies)	No. of Studies	% of Studies (Total 154)	% of Uses of Micronesia Cases (Total 271)
Truk	47	30.5	17.3
Marshall Islands	46	29.9	17.0
Ifaluk	37	24.0	13.7
Yap	26	16.9	9.6
Chamorros	22	14.3	8.1
Palau	16	10.4	5.9
Ulithi	16	10.4	<u>5.9</u>
			77.5

Micronesia (incl. Combined Cases)	No. of Studies	% of Studies (Total 154)	% of Uses of Micronesia Cases
"Marshalls"[a]	55	35.7	20.3
"Woleai"[b]	52	33.8	19.2
Truk	47	30.5	17.3
Yap	26	16.9	9.6
Chamorros	22	14.3	8.1
"Gilberts"[c]	17	11.0	6.3
Palau	16	10.4	5.9
Ulithi	16	10.4	<u>5.9</u>
			92.6

[a]Bikini, Jaluit, Majuro, and Marshall Islands
[b]Ifaluk, Lamotrek, and Woleai
[c]Gilbert Islands, Makin, and Onotoa

basic concepts of the discipline and major "findings," rather than a compendium of world ethnography—representative sampling would not be expected, in contrast to the purposes of worldwide databases, standard samples, and holocultural studies, as discussed above.

Disproportionate attention to some cases, resulting in differential impact on students' awareness of the world's peoples and the fruits of ethnographers' labors, might be expected to occur in relation to at least three factors: *personal bias, mimicry,* and variable *cultural "salience."* Probably the least significant of the three is personal bias. It is understandable that an author might privilege his or her own field site, or those of mentors and colleagues, but this should not produce systematic bias across large numbers of texts, given the wide range of areal specializations among authors. On the other hand, there is the potential of systematic bias across time to the extent that authors of new texts mimic their predecessors, as they obviously do in terms of topical organization. It is a rare textbook that does not present its chapters around "institutions," with language treated early in the book, and change, modernization, or "applied anthropology" closing the work. If this also occurs with regard to selection of illustrative cases, then skewed representation of different regions or specific societies—whatever the original reason(s) might have been—would be expected to continue over time. Among the likely reasons for case selection in textbooks, whether they are prototypic "classics" which have appeared in numerous editions or innovative attempts at originality, is the "salience" of a given case: the author's perception of it as an especially apt illustration of a particular concept or phenomenon, or perhaps merely an exceptionally "colorful" one. Here, despite anthropologists' continual denial of the accuracy of laypersons' views of our discipline, the matter of "exoticism" undoubtedly enters into consideration. If among the overall objectives of an introductory course in cultural anthropology are to impress on students the diversity to be found among the world's peoples, and to communicate lessons about "cultural relativity," then the exotic is surely given high priority. (A cursory examination of almost any introductory textbook reveals very few references or significant attention to European communities.) While data are not available for all of the world's regions and societies as they are represented in introductory textbooks, such data are available for Oceania. We can examine them to gain a sense of the impact of Micronesian ethnography on the principal way in which we present our discipline to the general public in the form of beginning students.

Using collections belonging to colleagues and my local area libraries, I

Table 6 Oceania Cases in Introductory Cultural Anthropology Textbooks, 1940–1990

	No. of Societies	No. of Citations	Average No. of Citations per Textbook
Australia	23	212	1.9
New Guinea	66	548	4.9
Melanesia	28	181	1.6
Polynesia	19	285	2.5
Micronesia	15	95	0.8
All Oceania	151	1321	11.8

Table 7 Oceania Cases in Introductory Cultural Anthropology Textbooks, 1940–1990 (by Decade)

TOTAL CITATIONS

Decade (No. of Textbooks)	1940s (4)	1950s (10)	1960s (16)	1970s (52)	1980s (30)	Total (112)
Australia	6	30	23	94	59	212
New Guinea	18	26	48	247	209	548
Melanesia	10	21	29	74	47	181
Polynesia	23	34	38	108	82	285
Micronesia	6	7	14	43	25	95
All Oceania	63	118	152	566	422	1321

AVERAGE NUMBER OF CITATIONS PER TEXTBOOK

Decade (No. of Textbooks)	1940s (4)	1950s (10)	1960s (16)	1970s (52)	1980s (30)	Total (112)
Australia	1.5	3.0	1.4	1.8	2.0	1.9
New Guinea	4.5	2.6	3.0	4.8	7.0	4.9
Melanesia	2.5	2.1	1.8	1.4	1.6	1.6
Polynesia	5.8	3.4	2.4	2.1	2.7	2.5
Micronesia	1.5	0.7	0.9	0.8	0.8	0.8
All Oceania	15.8	11.8	9.5	10.9	14.1	11.8

examined one hundred twelve introductory cultural anthropology textbooks published during the period 1940–1990. Assuming that their indexes (and occasional maps) reflected their contents with reasonable accuracy, I recorded every Oceania society listed by name and organized these data by region (as delimited above). The overall results are presented by region and decade in tables 6 and 7.

As can be seen in table 6, for the time period 1940–1990 an average introductory cultural anthropology textbook contained about 12 references to societies of Oceania, including a total of 151 different peoples. (Given the fact that only one of the one hundred twelve textbooks was published before the end of World War II [Lowie 1940], the authors can be presumed [although variably so] to have had access to the results of postwar ethnographic research.) A wide range of variation can be seen with respect to the use of information from different regions within Oceania. So far as the total number of societies cited is concerned, more than twice as many peoples of New Guinea are represented (66) as for Melanesia (28); in third place is Australia (23), followed by Polynesia (19) and, by the same margin, Micronesia (15). Interestingly, while proportional representation is not an explicitly stated objective of textbook authors, this ranking parallels that of the relative size and ethnolinguistic diversity of the five regions, as was also true for the numbers of societies included in holocultural studies (cf. table 3). However, with respect to numbers of citations of those societies, we find a different ranking, as was also true for holocultural studies. In the latter, while New Guinea cases were used more than those from other regions (481 uses), Polynesia was a close second (466), then Melanesia (435), followed—with a substantial gap—by Micronesia (271), and Australian cases were the least used (224). With the textbooks (table 6), we find a different pattern. Again, New Guinea "wins," with 548 citations, but second place is held (distantly) by Polynesia (285), followed by Australia (212), then Melanesia (181), and Micronesia, at only half of Melanesia's citations with 95. Thus, in both holocultural studies and introductory textbooks, numbers of uses and citations do not simply reflect the relative cultural diversity of regions.

Table 7 indicates that relative citations of Oceania cases have not held to a constant pattern over time, although there is considerable consistency beginning with the 1960s. In the few textbooks (4) from the 1940s, Polynesian societies were cited more often (23 instances) than those of any other Oceania region, although New Guinea was not far behind (18), Melanesia was cited substantially less often (10), and Australia tied with Micronesia (6 each). A radically different pattern emerged in the 1950s, with "first place" going to Polynesia (34 citations), followed fairly closely by Australia (30), then (by the same margin) New Guinea (26) and Melanesia (21), with Micronesia in "last place," with only one-third (7) as many citations as Melanesia. Textbooks published beginning in 1960 established a new pattern, but one that has held almost constant for thirty years: New Guinea rose to "first place" (48 citations), followed by Polynesia (38), Melanesia (29), Australia (23) and, considerably lower though with twice as many citations as in the previous decade, Micronesia (14). With the 1970s, Melanesia and Australia reversed their positions in the ranking, yielding an order the same as that for all time periods taken together: New Guinea, Polynesia, Australia, Melanesia, and—always with strikingly lower frequencies than any other region—Micronesia.

There is no question that postwar ethnographic research in Oceania dramatically increased our knowledge of that area, but this is not reflected in textbooks equally for all regions. Substantial prewar research had been conducted by Anglophone field-workers in Australia, New Guinea, Melanesia, and Polynesia, and German researchers produced massive amounts of data for Micronesia. The fact that the vast bulk of information about Micronesia was published in German may well account for its fate in prewar textbooks, although there are few of them to examine, and my findings regarding them should not be overinterpreted. In table 8 one can see that in the 1920s and 1930s taken as a whole, New Guinea *societies* cited are the most numerous (14), followed fairly closely by Polynesia (10), Australia and Melanesia (7 each), and Micronesia (3). As we have seen in other analyses, the order shifts somewhat when number of *citations* is considered: Polynesia is the most cited region (34 instances), followed by Australia (19), then closely by New Guinea (17), with Melanesia achieving about one-half that frequency (9), and Micronesia with less than half of Melanesia (4). Put another way, table 8 shows that if one picked up, at random, a textbook from this period, at least 4 Polynesian societies would be mentioned, 2 each for Australia and New Guinea, and 1 from Melanesia, while there was a fifty-fifty chance that Micronesia would not be mentioned at all.

With regard to regional rankings, this prewar pattern is in fact identical to that of the textbooks from the 1950s, and deviates only slightly from that of the 1940s (cf. tables 7 and 8). One could argue that, so far as usage in textbooks is concerned, the major consequence of the postwar "boom" in ethnographic research in Oceania (apart from the substantial increase overall in numbers of societies that became ethnographically known) was the "ascen-

Table 8 Oceania Societies in Prewar Introductory Textbooks

SOCIETIES CITED IN ALL TEXTBOOKS

Region	No. of Societies	1920s (3 Textbooks)	1930s (5 Textbooks)	Total (8 Textbooks)
Australia	7	9	10	19
New Guinea	14	12	5	17
Melanesia	7	4	5	9
Polynesia	10	13	21	34
Micronesia	3	3	1	4
All Oceania	41	41	42	83

AVERAGE NUMBER OF SOCIETIES CITED PER TEXTBOOK

Region	No. of Societies	1920s (3 Textbooks)	1930s (5 Textbooks)	Total (8 Textbooks)
Australia	7	3.0	2.0	2.4
New Guinea	14	4.0	1.0	2.1
Melanesia	7	1.3	1.0	1.1
Polynesia	10	4.3	4.2	4.3
Micronesia	3	1.0	0.2	0.5
All Oceania	41	13.7	8.4	10.4

dancy" of New Guinea over Polynesia; the relative neglect of Micronesia seems to be the one constant over seven decades.

A different way of assessing the impact of postwar research on textbook usage of the ethnographic information it produced—and one that yields a very different conclusion—is to examine *which* societies have been cited, and when, as is presented for Micronesia in tables 9 and 10.

During the postwar period, three Micronesian societies have accounted for more than half of the Micronesia textbook citations: Truk, by far the leader with 25.3 percent of all uses of Micronesian cases, followed by the Gilbert Islands and Yap, with equal records, 14.7 percent each (table 9). Only one of these—the Gilbert Islands—was also used by prewar authors, who cited it in two out of eight textbooks, the other cases cited being the Caroline Islands and Palau, with one citation each (see table 10). While Palau continued to be

Table 9 Micronesian Cases in Introductory Textbooks, 1940–1990

Society	No. of Cases	% of Texts (Total 112)	% of All Micronesian Cases (Total 95)
Truk	24	21.4	25.3
Gilbert Is.	14	12.5	14.7
Yap	14	12.5	14.7
subtotal			54.7
Palau	8	7.1	8.4
Ponape	8	7.1	8.4
Bikini	6	5.4	6.3
Ulithi	6	5.4	6.3
Ifaluk	3	2.7	3.2
Kapingamarangi	3	2.7	3.2
Nukuoro	3	2.7	3.2
Marshall Is.	2	1.8	2.1
Caroline Is.	1	0.9	1.1
Kosrae	1	0.9	1.1
Marianas Is.	1	0.9	1.1
Puluwat	1	0.9	1.1

used in postwar texts (especially in the 1970s), the Caroline Islands, as such, virtually dropped out of textbooks after the war, being cited only once, in the 1950s. Moreover, postwar citations of the Gilbert Islands and Palau overwhelmingly have drawn on postwar ethnographic research, rather than the sources used in prewar textbooks, as did those for Truk and Yap. The implication of these figures is that, with respect to the specific Micronesian cases used, postwar textbooks, being based almost entirely on postwar ethnography, are very different in content from the prewar ones.

This situation contrasts markedly with that of some other regions of Oceania, as can be seen by examining the cases most frequently cited over time (see table 11). For Australia, prewar ethnographic research was the basis for the continual citations of three out of the five most frequently cited cases, with the Tiwi and Yir Yoront emerging more recently (in the 1960s and 1950s, respectively). New Guinea presents a more complex picture, with the more recently studied Tsembaga Maring, Kapauku, Dani, and Gururumba becom-

Table 10 Micronesian Societies Cited in Introductory Textbooks (by Decade)

Decade (No. of Textbooks)	1920s (3)	1930s (5)	1940s (4)	1950s (10)	1960s (16)	1970s (52)	1980s (30)	Total (112)
Bikini	0	0	2	0	2	2	0	6
Caroline Is.	1	0	0	1	0	0	0	2
Gilbert Is.	1	1	1	0	2	10	1	16
Ifaluk	0	0	0	0	0	0	3	3
Kapingamarangi	0	0	0	0	0	2	1	3
Kosrae	0	0	0	0	0	0	1	1
Marianas Is.	0	0	0	1	0	0	0	1
Marshall Is.	0	0	0	2	0	0	0	2
Nukuoro	0	0	0	0	0	2	1	3
Palau	1	0	0	1	1	5	1	9
Ponape	0	0	1	0	2	0	5	8
Puluwat	0	0	0	0	0	1	0	1
Truk	0	0	0	0	2	15	7	24
Ulithi	0	0	0	0	2	4	0	6
Yap	0	0	2	2	3	2	5	14
All Micronesia	3	1	6	7	14	43	25	99

ing prominent in textbooks especially in the 1970s, while the top three cases—the Trobriand Islands, Arapesh, and Dobu (as well as Tchambuli)—represent continuing usage of prewar ethnography. Melanesia is alone among Oceania regions in that none of the four most often cited was mentioned in prewar textbooks (perhaps surprisingly so in the case of Tikopia, which did not begin to be used by authors until the 1950s, despite Raymond Firth's prewar research there). The exact opposite is found with Polynesia, with all six leading societies being the most cited in both prewar and postwar textbooks. Thus the differential impact of postwar ethnographic research in various regions can be seen again, with Melanesia and Micronesia as striking examples of regions where the impact has been the greatest in terms of contemporary representations of Oceania.

Returning to the factors that might account for the observed patterns in textbook authors' use of examples from Oceania, it would seem that *personal bias* on the part of authors is unlikely to have been a major factor. Of the one hundred twelve textbooks (including multiple editions) surveyed, sixteen (14.3

Table 11 Oceania Societies Most Frequently Cited in Introductory Textbooks

Decade (No. of Textbooks)	1920s (3)	1930s (5)	1940s (4)	1950s (10)	1960s (16)	1970s (52)	1980s (30)	Total (112)
Australia								
Aranda	3	3	1	8	7	18	8	48
Tiwi	0	0	0	0	4	25	12	41
Tasmanians	2	3	2	6	4	5	6	28
Yir Yoront	0	0	0	1	2	13	9	25
Murngin	0	1	1	3	0	9	6	20
New Guinea								
Trobriand Is.	2	2	4	9	16	48	28	109
Arapesh	0	1	3	3	5	23	15	49
Dobu	0	1	3	4	8	14	12	41
Tsembaga Maring	0	0	0	0	0	20	19	39
Kapauku	0	0	0	0	2	23	13	38
Tchambuli	0	1	0	0	0	14	12	27
Dani	0	0	0	0	0	12	12	24
Gururumba	0	0	0	0	1	13	10	24
Melanesia								
Manus	0	0	1	4	9	24	20	48
Tikopia	0	0	0	4	7	14	13	38
Siuai	0	0	0	2	2	10	6	20
Lesu	0	0	3	2	1	6	5	18
Polynesia								
Sāmoa	1	3	3	6	11	29	19	72
Māori	1	4	4	7	9	17	12	54
Hawai'i	2	3	3	3	3	20	15	49
Marquesas Is.	1	3	3	5	4	14	6	36
Fiji	3	3	2	6	4	4	7	29
Tahiti	1	3	2	2	0	6	6	16
Micronesia								
Truk	0	0	0	0	2	15	7	24
Gilbert Is.	1	1	1	0	2	10	1	16
Yap	0	0	2	2	3	2	5	14

percent) were authored or coauthored by individuals who have conducted ethnographic research in Oceania. As we have seen (table 6), in terms of both number of societies referred to and number of citations, New Guinea is by far the most widely used region of Oceania, yet only two textbooks were (co)authored by anthropologists who have done fieldwork there (and that not extensively), Abraham Rosman and Paula Rubel (1981, 1989). The second most frequently cited region (in terms of number of citations, but not in number of societies cited) is Polynesia, which also was the field region for three authors, who have produced seven textbooks: Lowell Holmes (1965; Holmes and Parris 1981), Michael Howard (1986, 1989b; Howard and McKim 1983), and Felix Keesing (1958; R. Keesing and F. Keesing 1971). While two of these three (Holmes and F. Keesing) have worked in Sāmoa, the most frequently cited Polynesian society, it should be noted that Margaret Mead's ethnography accounts for the vast majority of these citations. The third highest number of citations is for Australian societies, the locale for fieldwork by two authors of four textbooks: Michael Howard (1986, 1989; Howard and McKim 1983) and Ralph Pidding-ton (1950). Fourth-ranked in number of citations is Melanesia, with four text-books produced by Melanesian field-workers: Roger Keesing (1976; R. Keesing and F. Keesing 1971), and Abraham Rosman and Paula Rubel (1981, 1989). Finally, two authors with two textbooks—identical to the record for New Guinea, the most-cited region—conducted fieldwork in the least often cited region, Micronesia: James Peoples (Peoples and Bailey 1988) and Marc Swartz (Swartz and Jordan 1976). While personal bias might be argued in the case of the text by Peoples—the *sole* citation of Kosrae, where he conducted fieldwork —the same cannot account for the citations of Truk, Swartz's field site, which entered the textbook literature prior to his textbook and has been cited in many more (see table 11). But for any single decade, or taking all time periods into consideration, the number of textbooks in which citations of any Oceania region appear considerably exceeds that of texts authored by individuals who have done ethnographic research there (see table 7). Thus personal bias seems an unlikely explanation for the patterns described.

Mimicry, on the other hand, seems a likely factor for inclusion of cases, once they have entered the textbook literature. There are societies that have been used as illustrations once or twice, and then disappeared from textbooks (as is also true for databases, standard samples, and holocultural studies—for Micronesian examples, see table 2), but these are uncommon, except when one compares prewar and postwar textbooks. For example, the Kamilaroi of Australia were cited in two prewar textbooks, but none after the war; New

Guinea examples are numerous, including Kiwai, Koita, and Mekeo; for Melanesia, postwar disappearances include the Loyalty Islands and Tanna; Rarotonga of Polynesia has not been cited since the 1920s; and for Micronesia, the Caroline Islands as such have been cited only once since the 1920s. There also are cases that have been cited only once in postwar texts (e.g., Puluwat; see table 10), but again this pattern is rare. For the great majority of cases, an initial appearance in a textbook almost guarantees later ones (and not simply in new editions by the same author), though sometimes erratically and never in a simple cumulative pattern (see table 10 for Micronesian examples). We should not be surprised if cases chosen as good illustrations by one author are adopted by at least some others.

The question remains of how a society is chosen in the first place, if personal bias is likely in very few instances. Here the factor of _cultural "salience"_ undoubtedly is operative, although it is the factor most resistant to easy definition or discovery. With regard to databases, standard samples, and holocultural studies, inclusion of cases is based largely on the issue of completeness of information available for a wide range of variables. It is to be expected, then, that the Oceania societies most often used in holocultural studies (see table 5) are ones with sizeable bodies of ethnographic literature, but, impressionistically at least, this is not the case with textbook citations. To take a New Guinea example, Ian Hogbin produced eighteen articles and two books describing Wogeo society, which has been included in the HRAF, WES, EA, and AWC databases (though not in the SCCS) and has been used in 30.5 percent of the 154 holocultural studies surveyed. However, Wogeo has been cited in only 5 (4.4 percent) of the introductory textbooks examined. When one examines the Oceania cases most frequently cited in textbooks, certainly there are some—for example, the overall leader, the Trobriand Islands, cited in 107 (97.3 percent) of the textbooks—for which the body of ethnographic literature available is immense. But there also are cases like the Yir Yoront, cited in 25 (22.3 percent) of the textbooks seemingly on the basis of one journal article (Sharp 1952). The Yir Yoront, of course, have become a "classic" illustration of the wide ramifications that can occur with a technological change, supporting the common claim in introductory courses that societies must be understood as systems of interrelated customs, institutions, and so on.

Without conducting a content analysis of the textbooks and identifying what concept or point is being illustrated by each case selected, an argument for cultural "salience" can be little more than speculation. Nevertheless, a cursory examination of the most frequently cited societies of Oceania (table 11) suggests the workings of such a factor in at least some cases. The list is studded with "classics," including the Tiwis' curious marriage system; the Tasmanians' extinction; the Trobriand Island *kula* ring; Arapesh, Mundugumor, and Tchambuli alleged variations on sex roles; the postwar "cargo cults" of Manus; Siuai as the *locus classicus* of the "big man" concept; Samoans' "stress-free adolescence." These are instances of what a colleague has called "cultural flash." If Micronesian societies have the lowest citation rates in textbooks of any region of Oceania, and even the most frequently cited Micronesian cases compare fairly poorly to those of other regions, it may be that they are being "upstaged" in this regard.

CONCLUSIONS

Ethnographic field research can have an impact on the larger discipline in a variety of ways, both directly and indirectly, and many diverse measures (e.g., citation analyses for specific ethnographic works or reprinting of articles or book excerpts in anthologies) could be used to assess it for a particular case or region. Only two types of measures have been used here: the use of Oceania cases in databases, standard samples, and holocultural studies; and citations of societies of Oceania in introductory cultural anthropology textbooks. Given the very different purposes of these forms by which the results of fieldwork become known to and used by others, we might not expect consistency among them and, indeed, quite different patterns have emerged, including some surprises.

Subdividing Oceania into five regions (as delimited above), there are striking differences among them in estimated population sizes at contact and numbers of languages spoken aboriginally (see table 12). In both respects, though not in terms of sheer geographical size, the "tiny" islands of Micronesia constitute the smallest of the five regions. Polynesia is next, with more than twice the population of Micronesia and nearly twice as many languages. While the estimated contact population of Aboriginal Australia was substantially smaller than that of Polynesia, the number of languages in the former region was larger, almost by a factor of ten. Melanesia was considerably larger than Australia in terms of both population and linguistic diversity but, like the others, it was dwarfed by New Guinea, with more than ten times the population of Micronesia and seventy times the number of languages.

So far as our purposes are concerned, a region's size at contact in these terms is probably less relevant than its "size" in terms of our ethnographic

Table 12 Oceania Regions by Size and Diversity

Region	Population at Contact	Number of Languages	"Ethnographic Size"
New Guinea	2,000,000	850	200
Melanesia	500,000	250	30
Australia	300,000	200	20
Polynesia	500,000	22	22
Micronesia	180,000	12	12

knowledge. Such knowledge, of course, has grown over time, and especially during the postwar years, but to varying degrees in various parts of Oceania. At the time of this writing, assuming a general correspondence between languages and cultures, both Micronesia and Polynesia could be said to be fairly fully described in the literature, while this is much less true for the other three regions. In table 12, the five regions of Oceania are listed in order of these various terms, including the "ethnographic size" of each—the number of well-described societies speaking different languages (rough estimates). It can be seen that in focusing on the ethnographic size of each region, their rank orders do not change materially, except that Australia and Polynesia reverse positions by a slight margin.

In the first column of table 13, the five regions are listed in order of ethnographic size, an order that is not exactly duplicated in *any* of the databases or standard samples (with "matches" indicated by underscoring), including those (marked with an asterisk) that purport to be representative of the cultural diversity of different regions of the world (cf. table 1). Two points are worth noting regarding New Guinea: (1) Not until the Ethnographic Atlas began to appear in the 1960s did cases included from New Guinea become more numerous than those from the other regions. This doubtless reflects our increasing knowledge from postwar field research, although New Guinea's ascendancy has not been consistent (it was slightly outranked by Melanesia in the Standard Cross-Cultural Sample). (2) In *none* of the databases or standard samples is New Guinea represented proportionally, considering the huge differences in ethnographic sizes.

With respect to the other four regions, one might expect no simple ordering pattern to recur, given that numerical differences in their ethnographic sizes are slight. However, it should be noted that Melanesia's ethnographic

Table 13 Oceania Cases Used in Databases and Standard Samples
(in Rank Order)

Ethnographic Size		HRAF		WES*	
New Guinea	(200)	Melanesia	(6)	Melanesia	(18)
Melanesia	(30)	Polynesia	(6)	Polynesia	(16)
Polynesia	(22)	New Guinea	(5)	New Guinea	(14)
Australia	(20)	Australia	(4)	Micronesia	(11)
Micronesia	(12)	Micronesia	(4)	Australia	(10)

EA		SCCS*		AWC*	
New Guinea	(45)	Melanesia	(6)	New Guinea	(20)
Melanesia	(28)	New Guinea	(5)	Polynesia	(15)
Polynesia	(22)	Micronesia	(5)	Melanesia	(14)
Micronesia	(17)	Polynesia	(4)	Micronesia	(12)
Australia	(13)	Australia	(2)	Australia	(9)

size is more than twice that of Micronesia. It may be understandable, then, that Micronesia does not outrank Melanesia in any of the databases or standard samples. But Micronesia has a higher ranking than Australia in all cases except for the HRAF database, where the two areas are tied; and Micronesia even outranks Polynesia in the Standard Cross-Cultural Sample, where it achieves parity with New Guinea! On the whole, when one considers the small ethnographic size of "the tiny islands," they could be said to be *over-represented* (if not quite "looming large") in databases and standard samples.

Since holocultural researchers have tended to draw on these samples and databases, the rank orders achieved by examining holocultural studies published in the period 1949–1979 might be expected to resemble those just discussed, and they do, although not at first glance. Table 14 shows the results of my analyses of one hundred fifty-four holocultural studies, using the totals from table 3. So far as the numbers of *societies* used at all in the studies is concerned, the rank order of the five regions is almost exactly the same as that based on their ethnographic sizes (with the order inverted for Australia and Polynesia, whose scores are very close) although, as with the databases and standard samples, the differential use of New Guinea cases is not as great as might be expected. However, this order is not repeated when it comes to the

Table 14 Oceania Cases Used in Holocultural Studies, 1949–1979
(in Rank Order)

Ethnographic Size		Societies		Uses		Studies	
New Guinea	(200)	New Guinea	(46)	New Guinea	(481)	Polynesia	(137)
Melanesia	(30)	Melanesia	(29)	Polynesia	(466)	New Guinea	(127)
Polynesia	(22)	Australia	(25)	Melanesia	(435)	Melanesia	(120)
Australia	(20)	Polynesia	(23)	Micronesia	(271)	Micronesia	(115)
Micronesia	(12)	Micronesia	(21)	Australia	(224)	Australia	(112)

numbers of _uses_ of cases (with some cases used much more often than others; cf. table 5) or the numbers of _holocultural studies_ in which cases have been used. New Guinea maintains its supremacy in the first regard but is exceeded by Polynesia in the second. Micronesia shows a similar pattern to that previously discussed, in that while the number of societies used is the lowest of all regions of Oceania (reflecting its ethnographic size), Micronesian cases have been used more often and in a larger number of holocultural studies than Australian ones.

Explaining the patterns found with regard to databases, standard samples, and holocultural studies is not a simple matter. In all of these endeavors, scholars have chosen to include those cases deemed by them to be well described in the ethnographic literature. Given this fact, and the burgeoning of field research in Oceania following World War II, resulting in nearly complete "coverage" of Micronesia, Polynesia, and most of Melanesia, one might expect the more recent databases and standard samples to reflect the ethnographic sizes of the five regions more closely than they do. Yet this is only true of the Ethnographic Atlas, with such anomalies as Micronesia's parity with New Guinea in the Standard Cross-Cultural Survey and Polynesia's slight margin over Melanesia in the _Atlas of World Cultures_ standing out as particularly curious divergencies. Some kind of bias would seem to be operative in holocultural studies, again with respect to Polynesia, cases from which have been used more often and in more studies than might be expected given its ethnographic size. With respect to the "top three" regions, however, differences in use scores tend to be small, so there would seem to be no evidence of a gross bias in case selection, even if it does not simply follow proportional representation in the literature. So far as Micronesia is concerned, its use by comparative researchers appears to be entirely reasonable given its status as the "ethno-

Table 15 Oceania Societies Cited in Introductory Textbooks, 1940–1990 (in Rank Order)

Ethnographic Size	1940s		1950s		1960s	
New Guinea (200)	Polynesia	(23)	Polynesia	(34)	New Guinea	(48)
Melanesia (30)	New Guinea	(18)	Australia	(30)	Polynesia	(38)
Polynesia (22)	Melanesia	(10)	New Guinea	(26)	Melanesia	(29)
Australia (20)	Australia	(6)	Melanesia	(21)	Australia	(23)
Micronesia (12)	Micronesia	(6)	Micronesia	(7)	Micronesia	(14)

1970s		1980s		Totals	
New Guinea	(247)	New Guinea	(209)	New Guinea	(548)
Polynesia	(108)	Polynesia	(82)	Polynesia	(285)
Australia	(94)	Australia	(59)	Australia	(212)
Melanesia	(74)	Melanesia	(47)	Melanesia	(181)
Micronesia	(43)	Micronesia	(25)	Micronesia	(95)

graphically smallest" of the five regions. If any bias is to be suspected, it would seem to be operating against Australia, whose ethnographic size is two-thirds greater than that of Micronesia, yet Micronesia outranks it in every instance except the Human Relations Area Files, that is, in all databases, standard samples, and holocultural studies that have drawn extensively on postwar research results.

When we turn to the one hundred twelve introductory textbooks surveyed, we should not expect ethnographic size to be predictive of citation frequency to the same degree as when geographic representativeness is a major goal, and indeed it is not, although it may seem that way so far as Micronesia is concerned. As shown in table 15, Micronesian societies have been the least cited for Oceania consistently over five decades since World War II. While this accords with Micronesia's ethnographic size, other matches (underscored in the table) are few, with New Guinea rising to the top only beginning in the 1960s. Melanesia, the second "largest" region, has never risen above third place in citations, and overall ranks second to last; Polynesia yielded first place to New Guinea eventually, but has remained in second place since then; and Australia has followed no consistent pattern.

When the most frequently cited societies are considered (cf. table 11), a curious pattern seems to emerge. First, one notes that the sheer number of different textbooks (including multiple editions) has grown phenomenally since World War II, as of course has the number of ethnographic studies. One might expect, then, that postwar texts would take advantage of the more recent literature and that citations from postwar research would then account for a large percentage of the overall citations. But this is true only for three of the five Oceania regions. So far as the most frequently cited societies are concerned, two of the societies studied after the war (Tiwi and Yir Yoront) account for 31.1 percent of the total Australian citations (compare societal totals from table 11 with regional totals in table 7); in Melanesia, two postwar ethnographies (Manus and Siuai) account for 37.6 percent of the Melanesian citations; and two for Micronesia (Truk and Yap) account for 40.0 percent of the total citations for that region. By contrast, New Guinea and Polynesia—the two most cited regions—are very different. Four New Guinea societies studied after the war (Tsembaga Maring, Kapauku, Dani, and Gururumba) account for only 22.8 percent of the total New Guinea citations, and it would appear that Polynesian citations derive almost entirely from *pre*-war research.

It is possible, then, that New Guinea and Polynesia have "pride of place" when textbook authors choose examples from Oceania because the ethnographic literature for at least some of their peoples has been available for so long, with the attendant likelihood that authors would have studied them in graduate school or otherwise have long familiarity with them. However, if selection of examples were simply a function of the availablity of literature, one might expect the other three regions to have "caught up" more than they have done, especially since the 1970s and 1980s saw the publication of more than twice as many textbooks (82) as the previous five decades combined (38). It seems, then, that inertia and mimicry are likely to be responsible for much of the dominance of New Guinea and Polynesian citations.

It is difficult to escape, though, the conclusion that "cultural flash" has also been a major factor. In my survey of one hundred twelve textbooks, I found that one hundred fifty-one societies of Oceania have been cited, but of these only six account for more than one-fourth (25.4 percent) of all citations: the Trobriand Islands (109); Arapesh (49), Mundugumor (30), and Tchambuli (27) (or 106 for these New Guinea societies); Sāmoa (72); and Manus (48). While not all of these citations necessarily refer to the *kula,* "sex and temperament," "stress-free adolescence," or "cargo cults," these certainly are "classic" topics and cases. (Is it insignificant that five of these six societies are associated with Margaret Mead?) To be sure, such phenomena as Aranda totemism, extinct

Tasmanians, Siuai "big men," and Hawaiian and Māori cognatic descent are "classics," too, and they have competed well in the field of textbook writing. But for most of Oceania, and apparently especially so for Micronesia, only occasionally have the islands—whether "tiny" or large—captured the attention of authors and entered the mental worlds of our students.

References

Abe, Goh
1986 A comparative analysis of social change in Micronesia under Japan and the United States with special reference to Palau. PhD dissertation, University of Kansas.

Aberle, David F.
1961 Matrilineal descent in cross-cultural perspective. In *Matrilineal Kinship*, edited by David M. Schneider and Kathleen Gough, pp. 655–730. Berkeley: University of California Press.

Adams, Marie Jeanne
1969 *System and Meaning in East Sumba Textile Design: A Study in Traditional Indonesian Art.* Southeast Asia Studies Cultural Report Series 16. New Haven, Conn.: Yale University Press.
1973 Structural aspects of village art. *American Anthropologist* 75 (1): 265–279.

Adelbai, Sam
1985 Palauan story boards: The art of visual narrative. In *Story Board: Narrative in the Visual Arts.* An exhibition sponsored by the Institute of Culture and Communication art exploration series. East-West Center, Honolulu.

Adelbai, Sam, and Phyllis Koontz
1989 The storyboards of Ngiraibuuch. *Guam & Micronesia Glimpses* 29 (2): 24–29.

Akimichi, Tomoya
1979 Fish, image, and space (sakana, image, and kukan). *Kikan Jinrui Gaku* 12 (2): 3–46.
1981 Bad fish or good fish: Ethnoicthyology of the Satawalese. *Bulletin of the National Museum of Ethnology* (Osaka) 6 (1): 66–133.
1985 Island orientation and the perception of sea areas in Satawal, Central Caroline Islands. *Bulletin of the National Museum of Ethnology* (Osaka) 9 (4):651–709.
1986 Conservation of the sea: Satawal, Micronesia. In *Traditional Fishing in the Pacific,* edited by Atholl Anderson, pp. 15–33. Pacific Anthropological Records no. 37, Report no. 2. Honolulu: Department of Anthropology, Bernice P. Bishop Museum.
1987 Classification and contexts: Food categories in Satawalese culture. In *Cultural Uniformity and Diversity in Micronesia,* edited by Iwao Ushijima and Ken-ichi Sudo, pp. 255–277. Senri Ethnological Studies no. 21. Osaka: National Museum of Ethnology.

Alcalay, Glenn

1992   The United States anthropologist in Micronesia: Toward a counter-hegemonic study of sapiens. In *Confronting the Margaret Mead Legacy: Scholarship, Empire, and the South Pacific,* edited by Lenora Foerstel and Angela Gilliam, pp. 173–203. Philadelphia, Pa.: Temple University Press.

Alexander, William J.

1978   Wage labor, urbanization and culture change in the Marshall Islands: The Ebeye case. PhD dissertation, New School for Social Research.

Alkire, William H.

1960   Cultural adaptation in the Caroline Islands. *Journal of the Polynesian Society* 69 (2): 123–150.

1965a *Lamotrek Atoll and Inter-Island Socioeconomic Ties.* Illinois Studies in Anthropology no. 5. Urbana: University of Illinois Press. Reprinted 1989. Prospect Heights, Ill.: Waveland Press.

1965b Lamotrek Atoll and inter-island socioeconomic ties. PhD dissertation, University of Illinois, Urbana.

1968   An atoll environment and ethnogeography. *Geographica* (Kuala Lumpur) 4:54–59.

1970   Systems of measurement on Woleai Atoll, Caroline Islands. *Anthropos* 65:1–73.

1972a Population dynamics of Woleai and Lamotrek atolls. Paper read at the Conference on Pacific Atoll Populations, East-West Center Population Institute, December 27–30, Honolulu, Hawai'i. Copy on file in the Hawaiian and Pacific Collection, University of Hawai'i, Mānoa.

1972b Concepts of order in Southeast Asia and Micronesia. *Comparative Studies in Society and History* 14 (4): 484–493.

1974a Land tenure in the Woleai. In *Land Tenure in Oceania,* edited by Henry P. Lundsgaarde. Asao Monograph no. 2, pp. 39–69. Honolulu: University of Hawai'i Press.

1974b Native classification of flora on Woleai Atoll. *Micronesica* 10 (1): 1–5.

1977   *An Introduction to the Peoples and Cultures of Micronesia.* 2d ed. Menlo Park, Ca.: Cummings Publishing Company. First published 1972.

1978   *Coral Islanders.* Arlington Heights, Ill.: AHM Publishing Company.

1980   Technical knowledge and the evolution of political systems in the Central and Western Caroline Islands of Micronesia. *Canadian Journal of Anthropology* 1 (2): 229–237.

1981   Traditional exchange systems and modern political developments in the Yap district of Micronesia. In *Persistence and Exchange,* edited by Roland W. Force and Brenda Bishop, pp. 15–23. Honolulu: Pacific Science Association.

1982   The traditional classification and treatment of illness on Woleai and Lamotrek, Caroline Islands, Micronesia. *Culture* 2 (1): 29–41.

1984a Central Carolinian oral narratives: Indigenous migration theories and principles of order and rank. *Pacific Studies* 7 (2): 1–14.

1984b The Carolinians of Saipan and the Commonwealth of the Northern Mariana Islands. *Pacific Affairs* 57 (2): 270–283.

1987   Cultural dimensions of resource definition and use in Micronesia. In *Integrated Renewable Resource Management for US Insular Areas.* US Congress, Office of Technology Assessment, vol. II, pt. A, The Setting for Resource Development, pp. 107–150. Springfield, Va.: US Dept. of Commerce, National Technical Information Service.

1988   Evolution and structure in Micronesia. Paper read at the 12th International Congress of Anthropological and Ethnological Sciences, July 18, Zagreb, Yugoslavia.

1989a   See 1965a.

1989b   Land, sea, gender, and ghosts on Woleai-Lamotrek. In *Culture, Kin, and Cognition in Oceania: Essays in Honor of Ward H. Goodenough,* edited by Mac Marshall and John L. Caughey. American Anthropological Association Special Publication no. 25, pp. 79–94. Washington, D.C.: American Anthropological Association.

1993a   Marine exploitation on Woleai and Lamotrek Atolls, Micronesia: Conservation, redistribution, and reciprocity. In *Culture and Environment: A Fragile Coexistence,* edited by R. W. Jamieson et al., pp. 431–436. Calgary, Alberta: University of Calgary Archaeological Association.

1993b   Madrich: Outer islanders on Yap. *Pacific Studies* 16 (2): 31–66.

Alland, Alexander
1966   Medical anthropology and the study of biological and cultural adaptation. *American Anthropologist* 68 (1): 40–51.

Allen, Linda A.
1997   Enid "Atoll": A Marshallese migrant community in the midwestern United States. PhD dissertation, University of Iowa.

Alpert, Elmer A.
1946   Nutrition and Dietary Patterns of Micronesia. US Commercial Company's Economic Survey of Micronesia, Report no. 18. Honolulu: US Commercial Company. Mimeographed.

Aoyagi, Machiko
1982   The geographical recognition of Palauan people with reference to the four directions. In *Islanders and Their Outside World: A Report of the Cultural Anthropological Research in the Caroline Islands of Micronesia, 1980–1981,* edited by Machiko Aoyagi, pp. 3–33. Tokyo: St. Paul's (Rikkyo) University, Committee for Micronesian Research.

Appadurai, Arjun
1986   Introduction: Commodities and the politics of value. In *The Social Life of Things: Commodities in Cultural Perspective,* edited by Arjun Appadurai, pp. 3–63. Cambridge: Cambridge University Press.

Arnold, Arthur, Donald C. Edgren, and Vincent S. Paladino
1953   Amyotrophic lateral sclerosis: Fifty cases observed on Guam. *Journal of Nervous and Mental Disease* 117 (2): 135–139.

Asakawa, Shigeo

1980 Building process of Wuut, men's house in Tol Island, Truk. *Kikan Zinruigaku* 11 (3): 112–175.

Ashman, C. Michael

1970 The second annual Micronesia Arts Festival awards. *Micronesian Reporter* 18 (2): 21–29.

Athens, J. Stephen

1980a Nan Madol: Ponape's spectacular ruins. *Glimpses of Micronesia and the Western Pacific* 20 (3): 58–61.

1980b Pottery from Nan Madol, Ponape, Eastern Caroline Islands. *Journal of the Polynesian Society* 89 (1): 95–99.

Aveni, Anthony F.

1981 Tropical archeoastronomy. *Science* 213:161–171.

Avruch, Kevin

1990 Melford Spiro and the scientific study of culture. In *Personality and the Cultural Construction of Society,* edited by David Jordan and Marc J. Swartz, pp. 15–59. Tuscaloosa: University of Alabama Press.

Ayres, William S.

1990 Prehistoric food production in Micronesia. In *Pacific Production Systems: Approaches to Economic Prehistory, Papers from a Symposium at the XV Pacific Science Congress, Dunedin, New Zealand, 1983,* edited by Douglas E. Yen and J. M. J. Mummery, pp. 211–227. Canberra: Department of Prehistory, Research School of Pacific Studies, The Australian National University.

Ayres, William S., Alan Haun, and Craig J. Severance

1981 Ponape archaeological survey: 1978 research. *Micronesian Archaeological Survey Reports* no. 4. Saipan: Trust Territory Historic Preservation Office.

Bailey, C. R. Kim

1978 Traditional Ponapean music: Classification and description. Master's thesis, University of Hawai‘i, Mānoa.

1985 Acculturation and change in Ponapean dances. In *Dance as Cultural Heritage,* vol. 2, edited by Betty True Jones, pp. 122–130. New York: Congress on Research in Dance.

Baird, J. Henry

1954 The Guam Museum. *Journal of the Polynesian Society* 63 (3 & 4): 253–254.

Baker, Frances S., and Joshua Tanaka

1973 *Art and Craft: Teaching Guide.* Saipan: Mariana District Department of Education.

Bargatzky, Thomas

1984 Culture, environment, and the ills of adaptationism. *Current Anthropology* 25 (4): 399–415.

Barizo, Jerry

1979a Portfolio: The Palau Museum. Preserving Palau's past for the future. *New Pacific* 4 (1): 28–31.

1979b Portfolio: The storyboards of Palau. *New Pacific* 4 (6): 34–36.

Barnabas, Seberiano J., and Francis X. Hezel

1993 The changing Pohnpeian family. *Micronesian Counselor,* Occasional Papers no. 12. Kolonia, Pohnpei, FSM: Micronesian Seminar.

Barnett, Homer G.

1949 *Palauan Society, A Study of Contemporary Native Life in the Palau Islands.* CIMA Report no. 20. Also published 1949. Eugene: Department of Anthropology, University of Oregon.

1951 Proposal to South Pacific Commission, Project S.12. Copy in the personal files of Karen L. Nero.

1953 *Innovation: The Basis of Cultural Change.* New York: McGraw-Hill.

1956 *Anthropology in Administration.* Evanston, Ill.: Row, Peterson and Company.

1960 *Being a Palauan.* Case Studies in Cultural Anthropology. New York: Holt, Rinehart & Winston.

1979 *Being a Palauan: Fieldwork Edition.* New York: Holt, Rinehart & Winston.

n.d.a American-Micronesian Relations. Trust Territory Archives, roll #575, frame #0102, document number 10031. Copy on file in the Hawaiian and Pacific Collection, University of Hawai'i, Mānoa.

n.d.b CIMA Interim Report. Copy on file in the National Anthropological Archives, Smithsonian Institution.

Barnett, James H.

1959 Obituary. Edwin Grant Burrows. *American Anthropologist* 61 (1): 97–98.

Barnouw, Victor

1985 *Culture and Personality.* 4th ed. Homewood, Ill.: Dorsey.

Barrau, Jacques

1961 *Subsistence Agriculture in Polynesia and Micronesia.* Bernice P. Bishop Museum Bulletin no. 223. Honolulu: Bishop Museum Press.

1965 L'humide et le sec: An essay on ethnobiological adaptation to contrastive environments in the Indo-Pacific area. *Journal of the Polynesian Society* 74 (3): 329–346.

Barringer, Herbert R., Robert W. Gardner, and Michael J. Levin

1993 *Asians and Pacific Islanders in the United States.* New York: Russell Sage Foundation.

Bascom, William R.

1946 *Ponape: A Pacific Economy in Transition.* US Commercial Company's Economic Survey of Micronesia, Report no. 8. Honolulu: US Commercial Company. Mimeographed. Reprinted 1965. University of California Anthropological Records no. 22. Berkeley: University of California Press.

1948 Ponapean prestige economy. *Southwestern Journal of Anthropology* 4 (3): 211–221.

1949 Subsistence farming on Ponape. *New Zealand Geographer* 5 (2): 115–129.

1965 See 1946.

Bashkow, Ira

1991 The dynamics of rapport in a colonial situation: David Schneider's fieldwork on the islands of Yap. In *Colonial Situations: Essays on the Contextualization of Ethnographic Knowledge,* edited by George W. Stocking, Jr. History of Anthropology, vol. 7, pp. 170–242. Madison: University of Wisconsin Press.

Basilius, Bonifacio

1973 Turning liabilities into assets. *Micronesian Reporter* 21 (4): 25–29.

Bastian, Adolph

1899 *Die Mikronesischen Colonien aus Ethnologischen Gesichtspunkten.* Berlin: A. Asher.

Bates, Marston, and Donald P. Abbott

1958 *Coral Island, Portrait of an Atoll.* New York: Charles Scribner's Sons.

Bateson, Gregory

1958 *Naven.* 2d ed. Stanford, Ca.: Stanford University Press. First published 1936.

1961 (ed.) *Perceval's Narrative: A Patient's Account of his Psychosis, 1830–1832.* Reprint. Stanford, Ca.: Stanford University Press.

Bath, Joyce E.

1984 A tale of two cities: An evaluation of political evolution in the Eastern Caroline Islands of Micronesia since AD 1000. PhD dissertation, University of Hawai'i.

Bath, Joyce, and J. Stephen Athens

1990 Prehistoric social complexity on Pohnpei: The *saudeleur* to *nahnmwarki* transformation. In *Recent Advances in Micronesian Archaeology,* edited by Rosalind L. Hunter-Anderson. *Micronesica* Supplement no. 2: 275-290.

Baty-Smith, Gregoria

1989 Hanging up a dance. *Guam & Micronesia Glimpses* 29 (3): 15–17.

Bayliss-Smith, Tim

1974 Constraints on population growth: The case of the Polynesian outlier atolls in the precontact period. *Human Ecology* 2 (4): 259–295.

1982 *The Ecology of Agricultural Systems.* Cambridge: Cambridge University Press.

1990 Atoll production systems: Fish and fishing on Ontong Java Atoll, Solomon Islands. In *Pacific Production Systems: Approaches to Economic Prehistory, Papers from a Symposium at the XV Pacific Science Congress, Dunedin, New Zealand, 1983,* edited by Douglas E. Yen and J. M. J. Mummery, pp. 57–69. Canberra: Dept. of Prehistory, Research School of Pacific Studies, The Australian National University.

Beasley, Harry G.

1914 Inlaid bowl and stand from the Pelews. *Man,* o.s., 14:334.

Becker, Maxine

1993 Establishment of navy health services on Guam, 1889–1919. Copy on file in Micronesian Health Archives, College of Nursing and Allied Health, University of Guam.

Bee, Robert L.

1974 *Patterns and Processes: An Introduction to Anthropological Strategies for the Study of Change.* New York: The Free Press.

Belau National Museum

1989 *Kle Belau:* Palau through the eyes of Rechucher Charlie Gibbons. Videorecording. Koror: Belau National Museum.

Benedict, Ruth

1934 *Patterns of Culture.* Boston and New York: Houghton Mifflin.

1946 *The Chrysanthemum and the Sword: Patterns of Japanese Culture.* New York: Houghton Mifflin.

Bennett, John W.

1976 *The Ecological Transition: Cultural Anthropology and Human Adaptation.* New York: Pergamon.

Bennett, Linda A., and Paul W. Cook, Jr.

1990 Drug studies. In *Medical Anthropology: A Handbook of Theory and Method,* edited by Thomas M. Johnson and Carolyn F. Sargent, pp. 230–247. New York: Greenwood Press.

Bentzen, Conrad

1949 *Land and Livelihood on Mokil, An Atoll in the Eastern Carolines,* pt. 2. CIMA Report no. 25. Washington, D.C.: Pacific Science Board, National Research Council.

Berg, Mark L.

1988 'The wandering life among unreliable islanders': The Hamburg Südsee-Expedition in Micronesia. *Journal of Pacific History* 23 (1): 95–101.

Bernart, Luelen

1977 *The Book of Luelen: A Ponapean Manuscript History,* translated and edited by John L. Fischer, Saul H. Riesenberg, and Marjorie G. Whiting. Pacific History Series no. 8. 2 vols. Canberra: Australian National University Press, and Honolulu: University Press of Hawai'i.

Betzig, Laura L.

1988a Mothering on Ifaluk. *Mothering* 47:28–31.

1988b Redistribution: Equity or exploitation? In *Human Reproductive Behaviour: A Darwinian Perspective,* edited by Laura L. Betzig, Monique Borgerhoff Mulder, and Paul W. Turke, pp. 49–63. Cambridge: Cambridge University Press.

1988c Adoption by rank on Ifaluk. *American Anthropologist* 90 (1): 121–129.

Betzig, Laura L., Alisa Harrigan, and Paul W. Turke
1989   Childcare on Ifaluk. *Zeitschrift für Ethnologie* 114:161–177.

Betzig, Laura L., Monique Borgerhoff Mulder, and Paul W. Turke (eds.)
1988   *Human Reproductive Behaviour: A Darwinian Perspective.* Cambridge: Cambridge University Press.

Betzig, Laura L., and Paul W. Turke
1986a Food sharing on Ifaluk. *Current Anthropology* 27 (4): 397–400.
1986b Parental investment by sex on Ifaluk. *Ethology and Sociobiology* 7:29–37.

Betzig, Laura L., and Santus Wichimai
1991   A not so perfect peace: A history of conflict on Ifaluk. *Oceania* 61 (3): 240–256.

Bhabha, Homi K.
1990   The other question: Difference, discrimination and the discourse of colonialism. In *Out There: Marginalization and Contemporary Culture,* edited by Richard Ferguson, Martha Gever, Trinh T. Minh-ha, and Cornel West, pp. 71–87. New York: The New Museum of Contemporary Art.

Bidney, David
1949   Toward a psychocultural definition of the concept of personality. In *Culture and Personality,* edited by Stansfeld Sargent and Marian W. Smith, pp. 31–55. New York: Viking Fund.

Biersack, Aletta
1991   Introduction. In *Clio in Oceania: Toward a Historical Anthropology,* edited by Aletta Biersack, pp. 1–36. Washington, D.C.: Smithsonian Institution Press.

Black, Peter W.
1968   Notes on medical plants of Tobi. Fieldnotes on file in RFK Memorial Library, University of Guam.
1977   Neo-Tobian culture: Modern life on a Micronesian atoll. PhD dissertation, University of California, San Diego.
1978   The teachings of Father Marino: Christianity on Tobi Atoll. In *Mission, Church, and Sect in Oceania,* edited by James A. Boutilier, Daniel T. Hughes and Sharon W. Tiffany. Asao Monograph no. 6, pp. 307–354. Ann Arbor: University of Michigan Press.
1984   The anthropology of tobacco use: Tobian data and theoretical issues. *Journal of Anthropological Research* 40 (4): 475–503.
1985   Ghosts, gossip and suicide: Meaning and action in Tobian folk psychology. In *Person, Self, and Experience: Exploring Pacific Ethnopsychologies,* edited by Geoffrey M. White and John T. Kirkpatrick, pp. 245–300. Berkeley: University of California Press.
1994   The domestication of Catholicism on Tobi. *Pacific Studies* 17 (1): 1–28.
n.d.   Bibliography of Psychological Anthropology and Related Studies in Micronesia. Copy in author's personal files.

Bloch, Maurice
1974 Symbols, song, dance, and features of articulation: Is religion an extreme form of traditional authority? *European Journal of Sociology* 15:55–81.

Boas, Franz
1940 *Race, Language and Culture.* New York: Macmillan.
1955 *Primitive Art.* New York: Dover. First published 1927.

Bock, Philip
1988 *Rethinking Psychological Anthropology: Continuity and Change in the Study of Human Action.* New York: W. H. Freeman.

Bodrogi, Tibor
1959 *Oceanian Art.* Budapest: Corvina.

Boeberitz, Bob, and Johannes Ngiraibuuch
1969 The first annual Micronesia Arts Festival awards. *Micronesian Reporter* 17 (3): 21–29.

Boggs, Stephen T. (ed.)
1969 *The Truk Report: A Report on Field Training in Truk.* Honolulu: Department of Anthropology, University of Hawai‘i.

Borofsky, Robert (ed.)
1993 *Assessing Cultural Anthropology.* New York: McGraw-Hill.

Borthwick, Ernest Mark
1977 Aging and social change on Lukunor Atoll. PhD dissertation, University of Iowa.

Borthwick, Ernest Mark, and Jun Takayama
1977 Pottery from Fefan Island, Truk, Caroline Islands. *Journal of the Polynesian Society* 86 (2): 271.

Bothmer, Judith
1988 Pandanus and breadfruit: Traditional uses in Arno. *Guam & Micronesia Glimpses* 28 (1): 14–21.

Bowen, Robert N. (compiler)
1963 Bibliography of the Coordinated Investigation of Micronesian Anthropology (CIMA). Honolulu: Pacific Scientific Information Center, Bernice P. Bishop Museum. Mimeographed.

Bowers, Neal M.
1950 Problems of resettlement on Saipan, Tinian, and Rota, Mariana Islands. PhD dissertation, University of Michigan. Published 1950. CIMA Report no. 31. Washington, D.C.: Pacific Science Board, National Research Council.

Brady, Ivan A. (ed.)
1976 *Transactions in Kinship: Adoption and Fosterage in Oceania.* ASAO Monograph no. 4. Honolulu: University of Hawai‘i Press.

Brake, Brian, James McNeish, and David Simmons
1980   *The Art of the Pacific.* New York: Harry Abrams.

Brandt, John H.
1963   By *dunung* and *bouj:* Water movements, stick charts and magic help natives stay on course. *Natural History* 72 (7): 26–29.

Brantlinger, Patrick
1988   *Rule of Darkness: British Literature and Imperialism.* Ithaca, N. Y.: Cornell University Press.

Brooks, Jean
1988   Ours is the dance: A source and demonstration of power on the island of Yap in the Caroline Islands of Micronesia. Master's thesis, University of Victoria, Canada.

Brown, Peter J., and Marcia C. Inhorn
1990   Disease, ecology, and human behavior. In *Medical Anthropology: A Handbook of Theory and Method,* edited by Thomas M. Johnson and Carolyn F. Sargent, pp. 187–214. New York: Greenwood Press.

Browning, Mary A.
1970   Micronesian heritage. *Dance Perspectives* no. 43. New York: Dance Perspectives Foundation.
1972   *Walab im medo:* Canoes and navigation in the Marshalls. *Oceans* 5 (1): 25–37.

Bruner, Jerome
1990   *Acts of Meaning.* Cambridge, Mass.: Harvard University Press.

Bryan, Edwin H., Jr.
1937   Notes on the ancient culture of Guam: Pottery. *Guam Recorder* 14 (4): 12–13.
1967   Reconstruction begins. Hour Glass Special, May 19. Kwajalein, Marshall Islands. Reprinted as article #22 in *Life in Micronesia,* distributed by Micronesian Handicraft Shop, Box 448, APO, San Francisco, Ca.
1978   *Stick charts from the Marshall Islands.* Honolulu: Bishop Museum Press.

Bryson, Robert U.
1989   Ceramic and spatial archaeology at Nan Madol, Pohnpei. PhD dissertation, University of Oregon.

Buck, Sir Peter H. (Te Rangi Hiroa)
1927   *The Material Culture of the Cook Islands (Aitutaki).* New Plymouth, New Zealand: Thomas Avery & Sons Ltd.
1930   *Samoan Material Culture.* Bernice P. Bishop Museum Bulletin no. 75. Honolulu: Bishop Museum Press.

Buhler, Alfred, Terry Barrow, and Charles P. Mountford
1962   *The Art of the South Sea Islands, including Australia and New Zealand.* New York: Crown Publishers.

Bulatao, Jaime

1969   Westernization and the split-level personality in the Filipino. In _Mental Health Research in Asia and the Pacific,_ edited by William Caudill and Tsung-yi Lin, pp. 296–305. Honolulu: East-West Center Press.

Burrows, Edwin Grant

1938   _Western Polynesia: A Study in Cultural Differentiation. Etnologiska Studier_ 7:1–192. Reprinted 1970. Dunedin, New Zealand: University of Otago, University Book Shop Ltd.

1958   Music on Ifaluk Atoll in the Caroline Islands. _Ethnomusicology_ 2 (1): 9–22.

1963   _Flower in My Ear: Art and Ethos of Ifaluk Atoll._ University of Washington Publications in Anthropology, vol. 14. Seattle: University of Washington Press.

1970   Songs of Ifaluk. Copy on file in the Bernice P. Bishop Museum Library, Honolulu, Hawai'i.

Burrows, Edwin Grant, and Melford E. Spiro

1953   _An Atoll Culture, Ethnography of Ifaluk in the Central Carolines._ Behavior Science Monographs. New Haven, Conn.: Human Relations Area Files Press. CIMA Reports no. 16 and no. 18. 2d ed. 1957. New Haven, Conn.: Human Relations Area Files Press. Reprinted 1970. Westport, Conn.: Greenwood Press.

1957   See 1953.

1970   See 1953.

Burton-Bradley, Sir Burton B.

1968   _Mixed-Race Society in Port Moresby._ New Guinea Research Bulletin no. 23. Canberra: Australian National University.

Burton, Michael L., Carmella C. Moore, John W. M. Whiting, and A. Kimball Romney

1996   Regions based on social structure. _Current Anthropology_ 37 (1): 87–123.

Capelle, Alfred

1978   _Pelok Ilo Meto Ekauwotata._ Majuro, Marshall Islands: Marshall Islands Department of Education. Novel in Marshallese.

Carneiro, Robert

1970   A theory of the origin of the state. _Science_ 169:733–738.

Carr, E. H.

1961   _What Is History?_ New York: Vintage Books.

1964   _The Twenty Years' Crisis._ New York: Harper.

Carrier, James G. (ed.)

1992   _History and Tradition in Melanesian Anthropology._ Berkeley: University of California Press.

Carroll, Vern

1966 Nukuoro kinship. PhD dissertation, University of Chicago.

1968 Nukuoro kinship terms. Paper read at the 67th Annual Meeting of the American Anthropological Association, November 21–24, Seattle, Washington.

1970a (ed.) *Adoption in Eastern Oceania.* Asao Monograph no. 1. Honolulu: University of Hawai'i Press.

1970b Adoption on Nukuoro. In *Adoption in Eastern Oceania,* edited by Vern Carroll. Asao Monograph no. 1, pp. 121–157. Honolulu: University of Hawai'i Press.

1975a (ed.) *Pacific Atoll Populations.* Asao Monograph no. 3. Honolulu: University Press of Hawai'i.

1975b The demography of communities. In *Pacific Atoll Populations,* edited by Vern Carroll. Asao Monograph no. 3, pp. 3–19. Honolulu: University Press of Hawai'i.

Carsten, Janet

1995 Children in between: Fosterage and the process of kinship on Pulau Langkawi, Malaysia. *Man* 26 (3): 425–443.

Carucci, James

1992 Cultural and natural patterning in prehistoric marine foodshell from Palau, Micronesia. PhD dissertation, Southern Illinois University, Carbondale.

Carucci, Laurence Marshall

1980 The renewal of life: A ritual encounter in the Marshall Islands. PhD dissertation, University of Chicago.

1987 *Kijen emaan ilo baat:* Methods and meanings of smoking in Marshallese society. In *Drugs in Western Pacific Societies: Relations of Substance,* edited by Lamont Lindstrom. Asao Monograph no. 11, pp. 51–71. Lanham, Md.: University Press of America.

1988 Joking with gender on Ujelang Atoll. Paper read at the 17th Annual Meeting of the Association for Social Anthropology in Oceania, February 16–20, Savannah, Georgia.

1989 The source of the force in Marshallese cosmology. In *The Pacific Theater: Island Representations of World War II,* edited by Geoffrey M. White and Lamont Lindstrom. Pacific Islands Monograph Series no. 8, pp. 73–96. Honolulu: University of Hawai'i Press.

1990 Negotiations of violence in the Marshallese household. *Pacific Studies* 13 (3): 93–113. In *Domestic Violence in Oceania,* edited by Dorothy A. Counts. Special Issues of *Pacific Studies* 13 (3): 93–113.

Cattell, Jaques (ed.)

1949 *American Men of Science, A Biographical Directory.* 8th ed. Lancaster, Pa.: The Science Press.

Caudill, William

1953 Applied anthropology in medicine. In *Anthropology Today: An Encyclopedic Inventory,* edited by Alfred L. Kroeber, pp. 771–806. Chicago: University of Chicago Press.

Caughey, John L.

1970 Cultural values in a Micronesian society. PhD dissertation, University of Pennsylvania.

1977 *Fáánakkar: Cultural Values in a Micronesian Society.* University of Pennsylvania Publications in Anthropology no. 2. Philadelphia: Department of Anthropology, University of Pennsylvania.

Caughey, John L., and Mac Marshall

1989 Introduction. In *Culture, Kin, and Cognition in Oceania: Essays in Honor of Ward H. Goodenough,* edited by Mac Marshall and John L. Caughey. American Anthropological Association Special Publication no. 25, pp. 1–16. Washington, D.C.: American Anthropological Association.

Cawte, John

1974 *Medicine is the Law: Studies in Psychiatric Anthropology of Australian Aboriginal Societies.* Honolulu: University Press of Hawai‘i.

Chave, Margaret E.

1950 The changing position of mixed-bloods in the Marshall Islands. Master's thesis, University of Chicago. Published 1950. CIMA Report no. 7. Washington, D.C.: Pacific Science Board, National Research Council.

Chrisman, Noel J., and Thomas M. Johnson

1990 Clinically applied anthropology. In *Medical Anthropology: A Handbook of Theory and Method,* edited by Thomas M. Johnson and Carolyn F. Sargent, pp. 93–113. New York: Greenwood Press.

Clarke, William C.

1966 From extensive to intensive shifting cultivation: A succession from New Guinea. *Ethnology* 5 (4): 347–359.

1971 *Place and People: An Ecology of a New Guinean Community.* Canberra: Australian National University Press.

Cleary, Edward W.

1984 *McCormick on Evidence.* 3d ed. St. Paul, Minn.: West Publishing Company.

Clifford, James

1988 *The Predicament of Culture: Twentieth Century Ethnography, Literature and Art.* Cambridge, Mass.: Harvard University Press.

1990 Collecting art and culture. In *Out There: Marginalization and Contemporary Cultures,* edited by Richard Ferguson, Martha Gever, Trinh Minh-ha, and Cornel West, pp. 141–169. New York: The New Museum of Contemporary Art.

Cohen, Yehudi A.

1974 *Man in Adaptation: The Cultural Present.* 2d ed. Chicago: Aldine.

Cohn, Bernard S.

1987 An anthropologist among the historians: A field study. In *An Anthropologist Among the Historians and other Essays,* by Bernard S. Cohn, pp. 1–17. New Delhi: Oxford University Press.

Cole, Michael, John Gay, Joseph A. Glick, and Donald W. Sharp

1971 *The Cultural Context of Learning and Thinking: An Exploration in Experimental Anthropology.* New York: Basic Books.

Comaroff, Jean, and John Comaroff

1991 *Revelation and Revolution: Christianity, Colonialism, and Consciousness in South Africa.* Vol. 1. Chicago: University of Chicago Press.

1992 *Ethnography and the Historical Imagination.* Boulder, Colo.: Westview Press.

Connell, John

1983 *Migration, Employment, and Development in the South Pacific.* Country Report no. 8: Marshall Islands. Noumea, New Caledonia: South Pacific Commission.

1986 Population, migration, and problems of atoll development in the South Pacific. *Pacific Studies* 9 (2): 41–58.

Coote, Jeremy, and Anthony Shelton

1992 Introduction. In *Anthropology, Art, and Aesthetics,* edited by Jeremy Coote and Anthony Shelton, pp. 1–11. Oxford: Clarendon Press.

Corbin, George A.

1988 *Native Arts of North America, Africa, and the South Pacific.* New York: Harper & Row.

Cordy, Ross

1980 Social stratification in Micronesia. Manuscript. Trust Territory of the Pacific Islands Historic Preservation Office, Saipan. Copy in the personal files of William H. Alkire.

1983 Social stratification in the Mariana Islands. *Oceania* 53 (3): 272–276.

1986 Relationships between the extent of social stratification and population in Micronesian polities at the time of European contact. *American Anthropologist* 88 (1): 136–142.

1993 *The Lelu Stone Ruins.* Asian and Pacific Archaeology Series no. 10. Honolulu: Social Science Research Institute, University of Hawai'i.

Coyne, Terry

1984 The effects of urbanisation and western diet on the health of Pacific Island populations. *South Pacific Commission Technical Paper* no. 186, edited by Jacqui Badcock and Richard Taylor. Noumea, New Caledonia: South Pacific Commission.

Craddock, Gerald, and Elfriede Craddock

1967 *Palau Museum Guide.* Koror: Department of Community Development.

Craib, John L.

1981 Settlement on Ulithi Atoll, Western Caroline Islands. *Asian Perspectives* 24 (1): 47–55.

Croce, Benedetto

1923   *History, Its Theory and Practice,* translated by Douglas Ainslie. New York: Harcourt, Brace & Co.

Crocombe, Marjorie Tuainekore, Ron Crocombe, Kauraka Kauraka, and
Makiuti Tongia (eds.)

1992   *Te Rau Maire: Poems and Stories of the Pacific.* Rarotonga, Cook Islands: Tauranga Vananga (Ministry of Cultural Development); Suva: The Institute of Pacific Studies and the South Pacific Creative Arts Society; Wellington: The Cook Islands Studies, University of Victoria; and Auckland: The Centre for Pacific Studies, University of Auckland.

Cronk, Lee

1991   Human behavioral ecology. *Annual Review of Anthropology* 20:25–53.

D'Andrade, Roy G.

1987   Folk model of the mind. In *Cultural Models of Language and Thought,* edited by Dorothy Holland and Naomi Quinn, pp. 112–148. Cambridge: Cambridge University Press.

1995   *The Development of Cognitive Anthropology.* Cambridge: Cambridge University Press.

D'Andrade, Roy G., Eugene A. Hammel, D. L. Adkins, and C. K. McDaniel

1975   Academic opportunity in anthropology 1974–90. *American Anthropologist* 77 (4): 753–773.

Dahlquist, Paul

1972   *Kohdo mwenge:* The food complex in a changing Ponapean community. PhD dissertation, Ohio State University.

Damas, David

1979   Double descent in the Eastern Carolines. *Journal of the Polynesian Society* 88 (2): 177–198.

1981   The *keinek* of Pingelap and patrilineal descent. *Journal of the Polynesian Society* 90 (1): 117–122.

1983   Demography and kinship as variables of adoption in the Carolines. *American Ethnologist* 10 (2): 328–344.

1986   Residential group types, virilocality, and migration: The Pingelap case. *Ethnology* 25 (4): 241–255.

1994   *Bountiful Island: A Study of Land Tenure on a Micronesian Atoll.* Waterloo, Ontario: Wilfred Laurier University Press.

Damm, Hans

1935   Inseln um Truk: Polowat, Hok und Satowal. Vol. II, B, 6, pt. 2, *Ergebnisse der Südsee-Expedition, 1908–1910,* edited by Georg Thilenius. Hamburg: Friederichsen, de Gruyter.

1938   Zentralkarolinen: Ifaluk, Aurepik, Faraulip, Sorol, Mogemog. Vol. II, B, 10, pt. 2, *Ergebnisse der Südsee-Expedition, 1908–1910,* edited by Georg Thilenius. Hamburg: Friederichsen, de Gruyter.

Danielsson, Bengt
1967   Kia ora Keneti. In *Polynesian Culture History: Essays in Honor of Kenneth P. Emory*, edited by Genevieve Highland et al. Bernice P. Bishop Museum Special Publication no. 56, pp. 1–36. Honolulu: Bishop Museum Press.

Dark, Philip J. C.
1993   The future of Pacific arts: A matter of style? In *Artistic Heritage in a Changing Pacific*, edited by Philip. J. C. Dark and Roger G. Rose, pp. 206–222. Honolulu: University of Hawai'i Press.

Davenport, William H.
1960   Marshall Islands navigation charts. *Imago Mundi* 15:19–26.
1964   Marshall Islands cartography. *Expedition* 6 (4): 10–13.
1986   Two kinds of value in the Eastern Solomon Islands. In *The Social Life of Things: Commodities in Cultural Perspective*, edited by Arjun Appadurai, pp. 95–109. Cambridge: Cambridge University Press.

Davidson, Janet M.
1968   A wooden image from Nukuoro in the Auckland Museum. *Journal of the Polynesian Society* 77 (1): 77–79.
1971   *Archaeology on Nukuoro Atoll: A Polynesian Outlier in the Eastern Caroline Islands*. Bulletin of the Auckland Institute and Museum no. 9. Auckland, New Zealand.

Dean, Beth
1976   *Three Dances of Oceania*. Sydney: Sydney Opera House Trust.

Dean, Judy
1983   Artistic stops. *Glimpses of Micronesia* 23 (1): 44–47.

de Beauclair, Inez
1960   Notes on Pottery of Yap, Micronesia. *Journal of East Asian Studies* 9 (2 & 3): 64–67.
1962a Ken-pai: A glass bracelet from Yap. *Asian Perspectives* 5 (1): 113–115.
1962b Addenda to "Ken-pai": A glass bracelet from Yap. *Asian Perspectives* 6 (2): 232–235.
1963   Some ancient beads of Yap and Palau. *Journal of the Polynesian Society* 72 (1): 1–10.
1966   On pottery in Micronesia, Palauan lamps and Mediterranean lamps in the Far East. *Bulletin of the Institute of Ethnology, Academia Sinica* 21:197–214.

de Brum, Raymond
1961   The Marshallese 'sticks.' *Micronesian Reporter* 9 (3): 27.

Defngin, Francis
1964   Yam cultivation practices and beliefs in Yap. In *Yam Cultivation in the Trust Territory*, edited by John deYoung. Anthropological Working Papers no. 4, pp. 38–65. Guam: Office of the Staff Anthropologist, Trust Territory of the Pacific Islands.
1966   The nature and scope of customary land rights of the Yapese community. Saipan: Trust Territory of the Pacific Islands. Mimeographed. Copy in the personal files of William H. Alkire.

del Valle, Maria Teresa
1978 Social and cultural change in the community of Umatac, Southern Guam. PhD dissertation, University of Hawai'i.

Demory, Barbara G.
1976 An illusion of surplus: The effect of status rivalry upon family food consumption. PhD dissertation, University of California, Berkeley.

de Munck, Victor C.
1993 The dialectics and norms of self interest: Reciprocity among cross-siblings in a Sri Lankan Muslim community. In *Siblings in South Asia,* edited by Charles W. Nuckolls, pp. 143–162. New York: The Guilford Press.

Dengokl, Yukiwo, John Libyan, John Mori, Fred Primo, and Vincent Sebastian
1975 High School Drop-Outs. Xavier High School Town Study Project, Chuuk. Copy on file in the Micronesian Seminar Library, Kolonia, Pohnpei, FSM.

Dening, Greg
1978 Review of *Marists and Melanesians* by Hugh Laracy. *New Zealand Journal of History* 12:82.
1980 *Islands and Beaches; Discourse on a Silent Land, Marquesas, 1774–1880.* Honolulu: University Press of Hawai'i.
1988 *The Bounty: An Ethnographic History.* Melbourne University History Monograph Series no. 1. Melbourne: Department of History, University of Melbourne.

Devereux, George
1951 *Reality and Dream: Psychotherapy of a Plains Indian.* New York: International Universities Press.

deYoung, John (ed.)
1958 *Land Tenure Patterns: Trust Territory of the Pacific Islands.* Vol. 1. Guam: Office of the Staff Anthropologist, Trust Territory of the Pacific Islands.
1961 *Notes on the Present Regulations and Practices of Harvesting Sea Turtle and Sea Turtle Eggs in the Trust Territory of the Pacific Islands.* 2d ed. Anthropological Working Paper no. 1. Guam: Office of the Staff Anthropologist, Trust Territory of the Pacific Islands.

Diaz, Vicente M.
1992 Pious sites: Chamorro cultural history at the crossroads of church and state. *ISLA: A Journal of Micronesian Studies* 1 (1): 91–112.
1993 Reclaiming culture and history from a history of culture in Guam. Paper read at the American Anthropology and Micronesia Conference, October 20–23, Honolulu, Hawai'i.
1994 Simply Chamorro: Telling tales of demise and survival in Guam. *The Contemporary Pacific* 6 (1): 29–58.

Divine, David
1950 *The King of Fassarai.* New York: Macmillan.

Dobbin, Jay

1992   Hysteria and possession on Chuuk. Paper read at the 20th Annual Meeting of the Association for Social Anthropology in Oceania, February 19–23, New Orleans, Louisiana.

n.d.   Articulating ambiguity: Possession trance on Chuuk. Manuscript. Copy in author's personal files.

Dolgin, Janet, Luis Kemnitzer, and David M. Schneider (eds.)

1977   *Symbolic Anthropology: A Reader in the Study of Symbols and Meanings.* New York: Columbia University Press.

Dominy, Michele

1990   Maori sovereignty: A feminist invention of tradition. In *Cultural Identity and Ethnicity in the Pacific,* edited by Jocelyn Linnekin and Lin Poyer, pp. 237–257. Honolulu: University of Hawai'i Press.

Doran, Edwin, Jr.

1961   *Land Tenure in the Pacific: A Symposium of the 10th Pacific Science Congress. Atoll Research Bulletin* no. 85. Washington, D.C.: Smithsonian Institution.

Dressler, William W., Ellen Gruenbaum, Carole E. Hill, and Ann McElroy

1993   Separate commentaries on "A proposed curriculum for the third decade of medical anthropology training." *Anthropology Newsletter* (American Anthropological Association) 34 (September): 41–42.

Drucker, Philip

1950   The ex-Bikini inhabitants of Kili Island. Typewritten Report to the High Commissioner, Trust Territory of the Pacific Islands, A 11, ser. 580, July 12. Copy on file in the Hawaiian and Pacific Collection, Hamilton Library, University of Hawai'i, Mānoa.

Du Bois, Cora

1944   *The People of Alor: A Social-Psychological Study of an East Indian Island.* Minneapolis: University of Minnesota Press.

Eggan, Frederick

1972   Lewis Henry Morgan's *Systems:* A reevaluation. In *Kinship Studies in the Morgan Centennial Year,* edited by Priscilla Reining, pp. 1–16. Washington, D.C.: The Anthropological Society of Washington.

Eilers, Anneliese

1934a   Inseln um Ponape: Kapingamarangi, Nukuor, Ngatik, Mokil, Pingelap. Vol. II, B, 8, *Ergebnisse der Südsee-Expedition, 1908–1910,* edited by Georg Thilenius. Hamburg: Friederichsen, de Gruyter.

1934b   Westkarolinen: Songosor, Pur, Merir. Vol. II, B, 9, pt. 1, *Ergebnisse der Südsee-Expedition, 1908–1910,* edited by Georg Thilenius. Hamburg: Friederichsen, de Gruyter.

1936   Westkarolinen: Tobi und Ngulu. Vol. II, B, 8, *Ergebnisse der Südsee-Expedition, 1908–1910,* edited by Georg Thilenius. Hamburg: Friederichsen, de Gruyter.

Embree, John

1946a Micronesia. The navy and democracy. *Far Eastern Survey* 15 (11): 161–164.

1946b Report on field trip to Micronesia, December 14, 1945–January 5, 1946. Copy on file in the Hawaiian and Pacific Collection, Hamilton Library, University of Hawai'i, Mānoa.

1949 American military government. In *Social Structure: Essays Presented to A. R. Radcliffe-Brown,* edited by Meyer Fortes, pp. 207–225. London: Oxford University Press.

1950 Letter to the editor: A note on ethnocentrism in anthropology. *American Anthropologist* 52 (3): 430–432.

Emerick, Richard G.

1960 Homesteading on Ponape: A study and analysis of a resettlement program of the US Trust Territory government in Micronesia. PhD dissertation, University of Pennsylvania.

Emory, Kenneth P.

1940 Tuamotuan concepts of creation. *Journal of the Polynesian Society* 49 (1): 69–136.

1965 *Kapingamarangi: Social and Religious Life of a Polynesian Atoll.* Bernice P. Bishop Museum Bulletin no. 228. Honolulu: Bishop Museum Press.

1975 *Material Culture of the Tuamotu Archipelago.* Pacific Anthropological Records no. 22. Honolulu: Department of Anthropology, Bernice P. Bishop Museum.

Engle, Murry

1992 Spoehr, first EWC chancellor, dies. *Honolulu Star-Bulletin,* June 13, 1992.

Enloe, Cynthia

1989 *Bananas, Beaches, and Bases.* Berkeley: University of California Press.

Epstein, Joshua L.

1986 Dependency and affluence as challenges to national development in Palau. PhD dissertation, University of Hawai'i.

Erickson, Mark

1989 Incest avoidance and familial bonding. *Journal of Anthropological Research* 45 (3): 267–291.

Ethnology

1962 Ethnographic atlas. *Ethnology* 1 (1): 113–134.

Evans, Michael

1988 Political development in Micronesia: A view from the island of Pohnpei. PhD dissertation, University of Florida.

Evans-Pritchard, E. E.

1940 *The Nuer.* Oxford: Clarendon Press.

1962 *Social Anthropology and Other Essays.* New York: The Free Press of Glencoe.

Ezekiel, Ymesei

1962   *Some Songs of Palau.* Song Book Series 1. Saipan: Education Department, Trust Territory of the Pacific Islands.

1963   *Some Songs of Palau.* Song Book Series 2. Saipan: Education Department, Trust Territory of the Pacific Islands.

Fabrega, Horatio

1989   The self and schizophrenia: A cultural perspective. *Schizophrenia Bulletin* 15:277–290.

Falanruw, Marjorie V. C.

1971   Conservation in Micronesia. *Atoll Research Bulletin* no. 148:18–20. Washington, D.C.: Smithsonian Institution.

Falgout, Suzanne

1984   Persons and knowledge in Ponape. PhD dissertation, University of Oregon.

1989   From passive pawns to political strategists: Wartime lessons for the people of Pohnpei. In *The Pacific Theater: Island Representations of World War II,* edited by Geoffrey M. White and Lamont Lindstrom. Pacific Islands Monograph Series no. 8, pp. 279–297. Honolulu: University of Hawai'i Press.

1990   American anthropologists: Keeping Micronesian traditions in trust. Paper read at the 19th Annual Meeting of the Association for Social Anthropology in Oceania, March 21–25, Kaua'i, Hawai'i. Copy in author's personal files.

1993   Tying the knot in Pohnpei. In *The Business of Marriage: Transformations in Oceanic Matrimony,* edited by Richard A. Marksbury. AsAO Monograph no. 14, pp. 127–148. Pittsburgh, Pa.: University of Pittsburgh Press.

1995   Americans in paradise: Custom, democracy, and anthropology in postwar Micronesia. In *Politics of Culture in the Pacific,* edited by Richard Feinberg and Laura Zimmer-Tamakoshi, pp. 99–111. Special issue of *Ethnology* 34 (2).

Falgout, Suzanne, and Paula Levin (eds.)

1992   *Transforming Knowledge: Western Schooling in the Pacific.* Theme issue of *Anthropology and Education Quarterly* 23:3–82.

Farslow, Daniel

1987   The behavior and ecology of the long-tailed macaque *(Macaca fascicularis)* on Angaur Island, Palau, Micronesia. PhD dissertation, Ohio State University.

Feldman, Jerome, and Donald H. Rubinstein

1986   *The Art of Micronesia.* Honolulu: The University of Hawai'i Art Gallery.

Finney, Ben R.

1979   *Hokule'a: The Way to Tahiti.* New York: Dodd, Mead.

Firth, Sir Raymond

1936   *Art and Life in New Guinea.* London: The Studio Ltd.

Firth, Stewart

1987   *Nuclear Playground.* Honolulu: University of Hawai'i Press.

1989   Sovereignty and independence in the contemporary Pacific. *The Contemporary Pacific* 1 (1 & 2): 75–96.

Fischer, Ann M.
1957   The role of the Trukese mother and its effect on child training. PhD dissertation, Radcliffe College.

Fischer, John L.
1951   Letter to the editor: Applied anthropology and the administration. *American Anthropologist* 53 (1): 133–134.
1954   Language and folktale in Truk and Ponape: A study in cultural integration. PhD dissertation, Harvard University.
1955   Avunculocal residence on Losap. *American Anthropologist* 57 (5): 1025–1032.
1957a *The Eastern Carolines,* by John L. Fisher with the assistance of Ann M. Fischer. Hraf Behavior Science Monograph. New Haven, Conn.: Human Relations Area Files Press. Reprinted 1970. New Haven, Conn.: Human Relations Area Files Press.
1957b Totemism on Truk and Ponape. *American Anthropologist* 59 (2): 250–265.
1958a The classification of residence in censuses. *American Anthropologist* 60 (3): 508–517.
1958b Native land tenure in the Truk District. In *Land Tenure Patterns: Trust Territory of the Pacific Islands,* edited by John deYoung, pp. 165–215. Guam: Office of the Staff Anthropologist, Trust Territory of the Pacific Islands.
1959a Reply to Raulet. *American Anthropologist* 61 (4): 679–681.
1959b Meter in Eastern Carolinian oral literature. *Journal of American Folklore* 72 (283): 47–52.
1961   Art styles as cultural cognitive maps. *American Anthropologist* 63 (1): 79–93.
1968   Microethnology: Small-scale comparative studies (with appendix consisting of Totemism in Truk and Ponape, 1957). In *Introduction to Cultural Anthropology, Essays in the Scope and Methods of the Science of Man,* edited by James A. Clifton, pp. 374–401. New York: Houghton and Mifflin.
1970a Adoption on Ponape. In *Adoption in Eastern Oceania,* edited by Vern Carroll. Asao Monograph no. 1, pp. 292–313. Honolulu: University of Hawai'i Press.
1970b See 1957a.
1974   The role of the traditional chiefs on Ponape in the American period. In *Political Development in Micronesia,* edited by Daniel T. Hughes and Sherwood G. Lingenfelter, pp. 166–177. Columbus: Ohio State University Press.
1979   Government anthropologists in the Trust Territory of Micronesia. In *The Uses of Anthropology,* edited by Walter Goldschmit. American Anthropological Association Special Publication no. 11, pp. 238–252. Washington, D.C.: American Anthropological Association.
n.d.   Fieldnotes of John L. Fischer. 3 vols. Collection on file in the archives of the Bernice P. Bishop Museum, Honolulu, Hawai'i.

Fischer, John L., Ann M. Fischer, and Frank Mahony
1959   Totemism and allergy. *International Journal of Social Psychiatry* 5 (1): 33–40.

Fischer, John L., and Marc J. Swartz
1960 Socio-psychological aspects of some Trukese and Ponapean love songs. *Journal of American Folklore* 73 (289): 218–224.

Fischer, John L., Roger Ward, and Martha Ward
1976 Ponapean conceptions of incest. *Journal of the Polynesian Society* 85 (2): 199–207.

Flinn, Juliana
1982 Migration and inter-island ties: A case study of Pulap, Caroline Islands. PhD dissertation, Stanford University.
1985a Kinship, gender, and aging on Pulap, Caroline Islands. In *Aging and Its Transformations,* edited by Dorothy Counts and David Counts. ASAO Monograph no. 10, pp. 66–82. Lanham, Md.: University Press of America.
1985b Adoption and migration from Pulap, Caroline Islands. *Ethnology* 24 (2): 95–104.
1987 Pregnancy and motherhood among Micronesian students in the United States. In *Encounters in Biomedicine: Case Studies in Medical Anthropology,* edited by Hans A. Baer, pp. 119–146. New York: Gordon and Breach.
1990 We still have our customs: Being Pulapese in Truk. In *Cultural Identity and Ethnicity in the Pacific,* edited by Jocelyn Linnekin and Lin Poyer, pp. 103–126. Honolulu: University of Hawai‘i Press.
1992a *Diplomas and Thatch Houses: Asserting Tradition in a Changing Micronesia.* Ann Arbor: University of Michigan Press.
1992b Transmitting traditional values in new schools: Elementary education on Pulap Atoll. In *Transforming Knowledge: Western Schooling in the Pacific,* edited by Suzanne Falgout and Paula Levin. Theme issue of *Anthropology and Education Quarterly* 23: 44–58.
1992c Pulapese dance: Asserting identity and tradition in modern contexts. *Pacific Studies* 15 (4): 57–66.

Flint, Marcha, and Leslie Sue Lieberman
1995 A special tribute to Edward Eyre Hunt, Jr. *American Journal of Human Biology* 7 (4): 423.

Force, Maryanne T.
1976 The persistence of precolonial exchange patterns in Palau: A study of cultural continuities. PhD dissertation, Walden University.

Force, Roland W.
1958 Leadership and cultural change in Palau. PhD dissertation, Stanford University.
1960 *Leadership and Cultural Change in Palau.* Fieldiana: Anthropology, vol. 50. Chicago: Chicago Natural History Museum.

Force, Roland W., and Maryanne T. Force
1959 Palauan money: Some preliminary comments on material and origins. *Journal of the Polynesian Society* 68 (1): 40–44.

1965 Political change in Micronesia. In *Induced Political Change in the Pacific: A Symposium,* edited by Roland W. Force, pp. 1–16. Honolulu: Bishop Museum Press.

1972 *Just One House: A Description and Analysis of Kinship in the Palau Islands.* Bernice P. Bishop Museum Bulletin no. 235. Honolulu: Bishop Museum Press.

Forge, Anthony
1973 *Primitive Art and Society.* New York: Oxford University Press.

Fortes, Meyer
1969 *Kinship and the Social Order: The Legacy of Lewis Henry Morgan.* Chicago: Aldine.
1976 Foreword. In *Social Anthropology and Medicine,* edited by Joseph B. Loudon. ASA Monograph no. 13, pp. ix–xx. London: Academic Press.

Fosberg, F. Raymond (ed.)
1963 *Man's Place in the Island Ecosystem.* Honolulu: Bishop Museum Press.

Foster, George M.
1969 *Applied Anthropology.* Boston: Little, Brown & Co.

Foster, George M., and Barbara Gallatin Anderson
1978 *Medical Anthropology.* New York: John Wiley & Sons.

Foucault, Michel
1979 *Discipline and Punish: The Birth of the Prison,* translated by Alan M. Sheridan. New York: Vintage Books.
1980 *Power/Knowledge: Selected Interviews and Other Writings, 1972–1977,* edited by Colin Gordon; translated by Colin Gordon et al. New York: Pantheon Books.

Fox, Morris G.
1971 *Strengthening the Contribution of Social Services to the Development of the Trust Territory of the Pacific Islands.* Noumea, New Caledonia: South Pacific Commission.

Frake, Charles O.
1961 The diagnosis of disease among the Subanun of Mindinao. *American Anthropologist* 63 (1): 113–132.
1962 Cultural ecology and ethnography. *American Anthropologist* 64 (1): 53–59.
1985 Cognitive maps of time and tide among medieval seafarers. *Man* 20 (2): 254–270.

Freire, Paulo
1970 *Pedagogy of the Oppressed.* New York: Herder and Herder.

Frijda, Nico H.
1987 *The Emotions.* Cambridge: Cambridge University Press.

Fry, G. E.
1979 South Pacific regionalism: The development of an indigenous commitment. Master's thesis, Australian National University.

FSM, Federated States of Micronesia

1989   *The 1987/88 National Nutrition Survey of the Federated States of Micronesia.* A Summary Report Prepared for the Government and the Department of Human Resources, Federated States of Micronesia. 88 pp. Palikir, Pohnpei: Department of Human Resources, Federated States of Micronesia.

1991   *Second National Development Plan, 1992–1996.* Palikir, Pohnpei: Office of Planning and Statistics, Government of the Federated States of Micronesia.

Fujimura, Keiko, and William H. Alkire

1984   Archaeological test excavations on Faraulep, Woleai and Lamotrek in the Caroline Islands of Micronesia. In *Caroline Islands Archaeology, Investigations on Fefan, Faraulep, Woleai and Lamotrek,* edited by Yosihiko H. Sinoto. Report no. 2 in Pacific Anthropological Records no. 35. Honolulu: Department of Anthropology, Bernice P. Bishop Museum.

Gale, Roger W.

1973   Anthropological colonialism in Micronesia. *Association for Anthropology in Micronesia Newsletter* 2 (1): 2–19.

1979   *The Americanization of Micronesia: A Study of the Consolidation of US Rule in the Pacific.* Washington, D.C.: University Press of America.

Garruto, Ralph M.

1981   Disease patterns of isolated groups. In *Biocultural Aspects of Disease,* edited by Henry R. Rothschild, pp. 557–597. New York: Academic Press.

1985   Elemental insults provoking neuronal degeneration: The suspected etiology of high incidence amyotrophic lateral sclerosis and parkinsonism-dementia of Guam. In *Senile Dementia of the Alzheimer's Type: Proceedings of the Fifth Tarbox Symposium,* pp. 319–336. Neurology and Neurobiology, vol. 18. New York: Alan R. Liss.

1987   Neurotoxicity of trace and essential elements: Factors provoking the high incidence of motor neuron disease, parkinsonism and dementia in the western Pacific. In *Motor Neuron Disease,* edited by M. Gourie-Devi, pp. 73–82. Proceedings of the International Symposium on Motor Neuron Disease, Bangalore, October 29–30, 1984. New Delhi: Oxford and IBH Publishing Group.

1991   Pacific paradigms of environmentally-induced neurological disorders: Clinical, epidemiological, and molecular perspectives. *NeuroToxicology* 12:347–378.

Garruto, Ralph M., and D. Carleton Gajdusek

1984   Pacific cultures: A paradigm for the study of late-onset neurological disorders. In *Risk Factors for Senility,* edited by Henry R. Rothschild, pp. 74–89. New York: Oxford University Press.

1985   Factors provoking the high incidence of amyotrophic lateral sclerosis and parkinsonism-dementia of Guam: Deposition and distribution of toxic metals and essential minerals in the central nervous system. In *Normal Aging, Alzheimer's Disease and Senile Dementia. Aspects on Etiology, Pathogenesis, Diagnosis and Treatment,* edited by C. G. Gottfries, pp. 69–82. Bruxelles: Editions de L'Université de Bruxelles.

Garruto, Ralph M., D. Carleton Gajdusek, and Kwang-Ming Chen
1980　Amyotrophic lateral sclerosis among Chamorro migrants from Guam. *Annals of Neurology* 8 (6): 612–619.

Garruto, Ralph M., and Richard Yanagihara
1991　Amyotrophic lateral sclerosis in the Mariana Islands. *Handbook of Clinical Neurology* 15 (59): 253–271.

Garruto, Ralph M., Richard Yanagihara, Doreen M. Arion, Catherine Ann Daum, and D. Carleton Gajdusek
1983　*Bibliography of Amyotrophic Lateral Sclerosis and Parkinsonism-Dementia of Guam.* Bethesda, Md.: US Department of Health and Human Services, Public Health Service, National Institutes of Health. NIH Publication no. 83–2622.

Garruto, Ralph M., Richard Yanagihara, and D. Carleton Gajdusek
1985　Disappearance of high incidence of amyotrophic lateral sclerosis and parkinsonism-dementia on Guam. *Neurology* 35 (2): 193–198.

Gathercole, Peter, Adrienne L. Kaeppler, and Douglas Newton
1979　*The Art of the Pacific Islands.* Washington, D.C.: National Gallery of Art.

Geertz, Clifford
1963　*Agricultural Involution.* Berkeley: University of California Press.

Gell, Alfred
1985　How to read a map: Remarks on the practical logic of navigation. *Man* 20 (2): 271–286.
1992　The technology of enchantment and the enchantment of technology. In *Anthropology, Art, and Aesthetics,* edited by Jeremy Coote and Anthony Shelton, pp. 40–63. Oxford: Clarendon Press.

George, Karen R.
1995　Through a glass darkly: Palau's passage through war, 1944–1945. *ISLA: A Journal of Micronesian Studies* 3 (2): 313–337.

Gewertz, Deborah B., and Frederick Errington
1991　*Twisted Histories, Altered Contexts: Representing the Chambri in a World System.* Cambridge: Cambridge University Press.

Gifford, Edward W., and Delila S. Gifford
1959　*Archaeological Excavations in Yap.* Anthropological Records 18 (2): 149-224. Berkeley: University of California Press.

Gilbert, Jean
1993　Commentary on "A proposed curriculum for the third decade of medical anthropology training." *Anthropology Newsletter* (American Anthropological Association) 34 (October): 21.

Gillespie, Jennifer
1977 Integration of the movement patterns of traditional dances and daily activities in Ponape. Master's thesis, University of California, Los Angeles.

Givens, David B., and Timothy Jablonski
1995 1995 survey of anthropology PhDs. In *American Anthropological Association 1995–96 Guide,* pp. 306–317. Arlington, Va.: American Anthropological Association.

Gladwin, Thomas
1950 Civil administration on Truk, A rejoinder. *Human Organization* 9 (4): 15–24.
1952 Personality and development on Truk. PhD dissertation, Yale University.
1954 Anthropology and administration in the Trust Territory of the Pacific Islands. Trust Territory Archives, roll #0106, frame #0003, document #01687. Copy on file in the Hawaiian and Pacific Collection, Hamilton Library, University of Hawaiʻi, Mānoa.
1956 Anthropology and administration in the Trust Territory of the Pacific Islands. In *Some Uses of Anthropology: Theoretical and Applied,* pp. 58–65. Washington, D.C.: The Anthropological Society of Washington.
1958 Canoe travel in the Truk area: Technology and its psychological correlates. *American Anthropologist* 60 (5): 893–899.
1960 The need: Better ways of teaching children to think. In *Freeing Capacity to Learn,* edited by Alexander Frazier, pp. 23–29. Washington Association for Supervision and Curriculum Development. Washington, D.C.: National Education Association.
1961 Oceania. In *Psychological Anthropology: Approaches to Culture and Personality,* edited by Francis L. K. Hsu, pp. 135–171. Homewood, Ill.: Dorsey Press.
1964 Culture and logical process. In *Explorations in Cultural Anthropology: Essays in Honor of G. P. Murdock,* edited by Ward H. Goodenough, pp. 167–177. New York: McGraw-Hill.
1970 *East Is a Big Bird: Navigation and Logic on Puluwat Atoll.* Cambridge, Mass.: Harvard University Press.
n.d. Micronesian Independence: The Essential Elements. Copy on file in the Hawaiian and Pacific Collection, University of Hawaiʻi, Mānoa.

Gladwin, Thomas, and Seymour B. Sarason
1953 *Truk: Man in Paradise.* Viking Fund Publications in Anthropology no. 20. New York: Wenner-Gren Foundation for Anthropological Research, Inc.

Glassner, Martin
1993 *Political Geography.* New York: John Wiley.

Glenn, Thelma H.
1975 The Guam Museum. *South Pacific Bulletin* 25 (1): 28–30.

Goetzfridt, Nicholas J.
1992 *Indigenous Navigation and Voyaging in the Pacific: A Reference Guide.* New York: Greenwood Press.

Goetzfridt, Nicholas J., and William L. Wuerch (compilers)
1989   *Micronesia 1975–1987: A Social Science Bibliography.* Bibliographies and Indexes in Anthropology no. 5. New York: Greenwood Press.

Gonzalez, Roberto J., Laura Nader, and C. Jay Ou
1995   Between Two Poles: Bronislaw Malinowski, Ludwik Fleck, and the anthropology of science. *Current Anthropology* 36 (5): 866–869.

Goodenough, Ruth Gallagher
1970   Adoption on Romónum, Truk. In *Adoption in Eastern Oceania,* edited by Vern Carroll. Asao Monograph no. 1, pp. 314–340. Honolulu: University of Hawaiʻi Press.

Goodenough, Ward H.
1949   A grammar of social interaction. PhD dissertation, Yale University.
1951   *Property, Kin, and Community on Truk.* Yale University Publications in Anthropology no. 46. New Haven, Conn.: Department of Anthropology, Yale University. Reprinted 1978. Hamden, Conn.: Archon Books.
1953   *Native Astronomy in the Central Carolines.* University of Pennsylvania Museum Monographs. Philadelphia: University of Pennsylvania.
1955   A problem in Malayo-Polynesian social organization. *American Anthropologist* 57 (1): 71–83.
1956a Malayo-Polynesian land tenure: Reply [to Frake]. *American Anthropologist* 58 (1): 173–176.
1956b Residence rules. *Southwestern Journal of Anthropology* 12 (1): 22–37.
1956c Componential analysis and the study of meaning. *Language* 32 (1): 195–216.
1957a Oceania and the problem of controls in the study of cultural and human evolution. *Journal of the Polynesian Society* 66 (2): 146–155.
1957b Cultural anthropology and linguistics. In *Report of the Seventh Annual Round Table Meeting on Linguistics and Language Study,* edited by Paul L. Garvin. Georgetown University Monograph Series on Language and Linguistics 9:167–173. Washington, D.C.: Georgetown University.
1963   *Cooperation in Change: An Anthropological Approach to Community Development.* New York: Russell Sage Foundation.
1964   Property and language on Truk: Some methodological considerations. In *Language in Culture and Society: A Reader in Linguistics and Anthropology,* edited by Dell Hymes, pp. 185–188. New York: Harper & Row.
1965a Rethinking 'status' and 'role': Toward a general model of the cultural organization of social relationships. In *The Relevance of Models for Social Anthropology,* edited by Michael Banton. Asa Monograph no. 1, pp. 1–24. London: Tavistock Publications.
1965b Yankee kinship terminology: A problem in componential analysis. In *Formal Semantic Analysis,* edited by Eugene Hammel. Special Publication, *American Anthropologist* 67 (5), pt. 2: 259–287.
1966a Notes on Truk's place names. *Micronesica* 2 (2): 95–129.
1966b Human purpose in life. *Zygon, Journal of Religion and Science* 1 (3): 217–229.

1967   Componential analysis. *Science* 156:1203–1209.

1968   Arts and crafts in Truk. *Expedition* 11 (1): 13–15.

1970   *Description and Comparison in Cultural Anthropology.* Chicago: Aldine.

1974a   Changing social organization on Romónum, Truk, 1947–1965. In *Social Organization and the Applications of Anthropology: Essays in Honor of Lauriston Sharp,* edited by Robert J. Smith, pp. 62–93. Ithaca, N. Y.: Cornell University Press.

1974b   Toward an anthropologically useful definition of religion. In *Changing Perspectives in the Scientific Study of Religion,* edited by Alan W. Eister, pp. 165–184. New York: John Wiley & Sons.

1981a   On describing religion in Truk: An anthropological dilemma. *Proceedings of the American Philosophical Society* 125 (6): 411–415.

1981b   *Culture, Language, and Society.* 2d ed. Menlo Park, Ca.: Benjamin Cummings Publishing Co., Inc. First published 1971.

1986   Sky world and this world: The place of *Kachaw* in Micronesian cosmology. *American Anthropologist* 88 (3): 551–568.

1988a   Self-maintenance as a religious concern. *Zygon, Journal of Religion and Science* 23 (2): 117–128.

1988b   *Waasééna* 'Drift Voyager.' *Anthropology and Humanism Quarterly* 13 (1): 26–27.

1993   Toward a working theory of culture. In *Assessing Cultural Anthropology,* edited by Robert Borofsky, pp. 262–275. New York: McGraw-Hill.

n.d.   A terminal illness in Truk. Manuscript. Copy in author's personal files.

Goodenough, Ward H., and Hiroshi Sugita

1980   *Trukese-English Dictionary.* Memoirs of the American Philosophical Society, vol. 141. Philadelphia: American Philosophical Society.

1990   *Trukese-English Dictionary. Supplementary Volume: English-Trukese and Index of Trukese Word Roots.* Memoirs of the American Philosophical Society, vol. 141S. Philadelphia: American Philosophical Society.

Goodenough, Ward H., and Stephen D. Thomas

1987   Traditional navigation in the Western Pacific. *Expedition* 29:3–14.

Goodwin, Larry A.

1983   Change is continuity: The maritime and subsistence economics of Ponape, Micronesia. PhD dissertation, University of Oregon.

Goody, Jack (ed.)

1973   *The Character of Kinship.* Cambridge: Cambridge University Press.

Gordon, Maura Mechaet

1979   A time to laugh, a time to dance. *Glimpses of Micronesia and the Western Pacific* 19 (1): 80–82.

Gorenflo, Lawrence J., and Michael J. Levin

1989   The demographic evolution of Ebeye. *Pacific Studies* 12 (3): 91–128.

1991 Regional demographic change in Yap State, Federated States of Micronesia. *Pacific Studies* 14 (3): 97–145.

1994 The evolution of regional demography in the Marshall Islands. *Pacific Studies* 17 (1): 93–158.

Gould, Stephen Jay

1983 *Hen's Teeth and Horse's Toes.* New York: W. W. Norton.

1986 Archetype and adaptation. *Natural History* 95 (10): 16–27.

Graburn, Nelson H.

1976 Introduction: Arts of the fourth world. In *Ethnic and Tourist Arts,* edited by Nelson H. Graburn, pp. 1–32. Berkeley: University of California Press.

1979 New directions in contemporary arts. In *Exploring the Visual Art of Oceania: Australia, Melanesia, Micronesia, and Polynesia,* edited by Sidney M. Mead, pp. 354–362. Honolulu: The University Press of Hawai'i.

Gramsci, Antonio

1971 *Prison Notebooks,* translated by Quintin Hoare and Geoffrey Noel-Smith. New York: International Publishers.

Green, Roger C.

1979 Early Lapita art from Polynesia and Island Melanesia: Continuities in ceramic, bark-cloth, and tattoo decorations. In *Exploring the Visual Art of Oceania: Australia, Melanesia, Micronesia, and Polynesia,* edited by Sidney M. Mead, pp. 13–31. Honolulu: The University Press of Hawai'i.

Griffing, Robert P., Jr.

1951a An exhibition of Micronesian art and life. *Paradise of the Pacific* 63 (5): 13, 16.

1951b Life and Art in Micronesia. *Honolulu Academy of Arts News Bulletin and Calendar* 13 (5): 2–5.

Grollig, Francis X., SJ, and Harold B. Haley (eds.)

1976 *Medical Anthropology.* The Hague: Mouton.

Guam Recorder

1939 Aggag weaving. *Guam Recorder* 16 (7): 281, 307.

Guemple, Lee

1979 *Inuit Adoption.* National Museum of Man Mercury Series, Canadian Ethnology Service Paper no. 47. Ottawa: National Museum of Canada.

Guiart, Jean

1963 *The Arts of the South Pacific.* New York: Golden Press.

Haddon, Alfred C.

1894 *The Decorative Art of British New Guinea.* Cunningham Memoir 10. Dublin: Royal Irish Academy.

1905 Tatuing at Huia, British New Guinea. *Man,* o.s., 5:86–87.

1912   *Reports of the Cambridge Anthropological Expedition to Torres Straits: Arts and Crafts,*
       vol. 4. Cambridge: Cambridge University Press.

Haddon, Alfred C., and James Hornell
1936   *Canoes of Oceania.* Bernice P. Bishop Museum Special Publication no. 27. Honolulu:
       Bishop Museum Press. Reprinted 1975. Honolulu: Bishop Museum Press.

Hage, Per, and Frank Harary
1983   *Structural Models in Anthropology.* Cambridge Studies in Social Anthropology no. 46.
       Cambridge: Cambridge University Press.
1991   *Exchange in Oceania: A Graph Theoretic Analysis.* Oxford Studies in Social and Cul-
       tural Anthropology. New York: Clarendon Press.

Hainline, Jane (Underwood)
1964   Human ecology in Micronesia: Determinants of population size, structure and
       dynamics. PhD dissertation, University of California, Los Angeles.
1965   Culture and biological adaptation. Population and environment in Micronesia. *Ameri-
       can Anthropologist* 67 (5), pt. 1: 1174–1197.

Hall, Edward T., Jr.
1950a Military government on Truk. *Human Organization* 9 (2): 25–30.
1950b A reply [to Gladwin 1950]. *Human Organization* 9 (4): 24.
1992   *An Anthropology of Everyday Life: An Autobiography.* New York: Doubleday Anchor
       Books.

Hall, Edward T., Jr., and Karl J. Pelzer
1946   The Economy of the Truk Islands, An Anthropological and Economic Survey. In US
       Commercial Company's Economic Survey of Micronesia, Report no. 17. Honolulu:
       US Commercial Company. Mimeographed.

Hallowell, Alfred Irving
1956   The Rorschach technique in personality and culture studies. In *Developments in the
       Rorschach Technique,* vol. 2, edited by Bruno Klopfer, pp. 458–545. New York:
       Harcourt, Brace and World.

Halpern, Katherine Spencer
1973   Obituary. Ann Fischer (1919–1971). *American Anthropologist* 75 (1): 292–294.

Hambruch, Paul
1932/1936 Ponape. 3 vols. *Ergebnisse der Südsee Expedition, 1908–1910,* edited by Georg
       Thilenius. Vol. II, B, 7. Hamburg: Friederichsen, de Gruyter (vol. I) and 1936 (vols.
       II and III).

Hambruch, Paul, and Anneliese Eilers
1936   Ponape. Vol. II, B, 7, pt. 2, *Ergebnisse der Südsee-Expedition, 1908–1910,* edited by
       Georg Thilenius. Hamburg: Friederichsen, de Gruyter.

Handler, Richard (ed.)

1995   *Schneider on Schneider: The Conversion of the Jews and Other Anthropological Stories. David M. Schneider as Told to Richard Handler.* Durham, N. C.: Duke University Press.

Handler, Richard, and Susan McKinnon

1995   Obituary. David M. Schneider. *Anthropology Newsletter* (American Anthropological Association) 36 (9): 39.

Handy, Edward S. Craighill

1930   *History and Culture of the Society Islands.* Bernice P. Bishop Museum Bulletin no. 79. Honolulu: Bishop Museum Press.

Hanlon, David

1984   God versus gods: First years of the Micronesian Mission on Ponape, 1852–1859. *Journal of Pacific History* 19 (1): 41–59.

1988   *Upon a Stone Altar: A History of the Island of Pohnpei to 1890.* Honolulu: University of Hawai'i Press.

1989   Micronesia: Writing and rewriting the histories of a nonentity. *Pacific Studies* 12 (2): 1–21.

1992a Sorcery, 'savage memories,' and the edge of commensurability for history in the Pacific. In *Pacific Islands History: Journeys and Transformations,* edited by Brij V. Lal, pp. 107–128. Canberra: Journal of Pacific History.

1992b The path back to Pohnsakar: Luelen Bernart, his book, and the practice of history on Pohnpei. *ISLA: A Journal of Micronesian Studies* 1 (1): 13–36.

1994   Remaking Micronesia: A reflection on the cultural and strategic politics of economic development in American Micronesia, 1945–1968. In *Dangerous Liaisons: Essays in Honour of Greg Dening,* edited by Donna Merwick. Melbourne University History Monograph Series no. 19, pp. 135–156. Melbourne: Department of History, University of Melbourne.

Hanson, F. Allan

1989   The making of the Maori: Culture invention and its logic. *American Anthropologist* 91 (4): 890–902.

Hanson, F. Allan, and Louise Hanson

1984   *The Art of Oceania: A Bibliography.* Boston: G. K. Hall.

Hardesty, Donald L.

1977   *Ecological Anthropology.* New York: Wiley.

Harris, Marvin

1979   *Cultural Materialism: The Struggle for a Science of Culture.* New York: Random House.

Harui-Walsh, Eulalia

1984   Changes in the lifestyle of women in Ulithi, Micronesia. In *Micronesia as Strategic Colony: The Impact of US Policy on Micronesian Health and Culture,* edited by Catherine Lutz, pp. 81–88. Cambridge, Mass.: Cultural Survival.

Hasan, Khwaja A.

1978   What is medical anthropology? In *Health and the Human Condition: Perspectives on Medical Anthropology,* edited by Michael H. Logan and Edward E. Hunt, Jr., pp. 17–23. North Scituate, Mass.: Duxbury Press.

Hasebe, Kotondo

1942   Manifestations of chagrin among Micronesians. *Zinruigaku Zassi* 57 (659). In Japanese; translated in Cross-Cultural Survey Files.

Hashiura, Yasuo

1940   The customs and manners of childbirth and infant care among the South Sea Islanders. *Japanese Journal of Ethnology* 6:36–46.

Hatanaka, Sachiko (compiler)

1979   *A Bibliography of Micronesia Compiled from Japanese Publication, 1915–1945.* Tokyo: Research Institute for Oriental Cultures, Gakushuin University.

Haun, Alan E.

1984   Prehistoric subsistence, population, and sociopolitical evolution on Ponape, Micronesia. PhD dissertation, University of Oregon.

Hauʻofa, Epeli

1993   Our sea of islands. In *Rediscovering Our Sea of Islands,* edited by Eric Waddell, Vijay Naidu, and Epeli Hauʻofa, pp. 2–16. Suva: School of Social and Economic Development, University of the South Pacific.

Hays, Terence E. (ed.)

1991   Oceania. *Encyclopedia of World Cultures,* vol. 2. Boston, Mass.: G. K. Hall & Co.

Hazlehurst, Kayleen M.

1993   *Political Expression and Ethnicity: Statecraft and Mobilization in the Maori World.* Westport, Conn.: Praeger.

Heider, Karl G.

1972   Environment, subsistence, and society. *Annual Review of Anthropology* 1:207–226.

1988   The Rashomon effect: When ethnographers disagree. *American Anthropologist* 90 (1): 73–81.

Heine, Carl

1970   Micronesia: Unification and the coming of self-government. In *The Politics of Melanesia,* edited by Marian W. Ward, pp. 193–206. Canberra: Australian National University Press.

1974   *Micronesia at the Crossroads.* Honolulu: University Press of Hawaiʻi.

Helfman, Gene S., and John E. Randall

1973   Palauan fish names. *Pacific Science* 27 (2): 136–153.

Henning, Theodore F.

1961   *Buritis in Paradise: The Revealing Story of a Dedicated Teacher's Conflicts with Officialdom in the Trust Territories of the Pacific Islands.* New York: Greenwich Book Publishers.

Henningham, Stephen

1992   *France and the South Pacific: A Contemporary History.* Honolulu: University of Hawai‘i Press.

Henrickson, Paul R.

1968   Two forms of primitive art in Micronesia. *Micronesica* 4 (1): 39–48.

Hereniko, Vilsoni

1994   Representations of cultural identities. In *Tides of History: the Pacific Islands in the Twentieth Century,* edited by Kerry R. Howe, Robert C. Kiste, and Brij V. Lal. Pp. 406-434. Honolulu: University of Hawai‘i Press.

Herskovits, Melville J.

1930   The culture areas of Africa. *Africa* 3:59–77.

1950   (ed.) *International Directory of Anthropologists.* 3d ed. Washington, D.C.: Committee on International Relations in Anthropology, National Research Council.

Hezel, Francis X.

1976   Micronesia's hanging spree. *Micronesian Reporter* 24 (4): 8–13.

1977   Micronesia's youth today: A report on the Conference on Youth held in Kolonia, Ponape, April 20–24. Truk: Micronesian Seminar. Copy on file in the Hawaiian and Pacific Collection, Hamilton Library, University of Hawai‘i, Mānoa.

1979   The education explosion in Truk. *Pacific Studies* 2 (2): 167–185.

1981   Youth drinking in Micronesia. A report on the Working Seminar on Alcohol Use and Abuse Among Micronesian Youth held in Kolonia, Ponape, November 12–14. Truk: Micronesian Seminar.

1983   *The First Taint of Civilization: A History of the Caroline and Marshall Islands in Pre-Colonial Days 1521–1885.* Pacific Islands Monograph Series no. 1. Honolulu: University of Hawai‘i Press.

1984   Cultural patterns in Trukese suicide. *Ethnology* 23 (3): 193–206.

1985a Trukese suicide. In *Culture, Youth and Suicide in the Pacific: Papers from An East-West Center Conference,* edited by Francis X. Hezel, Donald H. Rubinstein, and Geoffrey M. White, pp. 112–124. Working Paper Series, Pacific Islands Studies Program. Honolulu: University of Hawai‘i.

1985b A report on child abuse and neglect in Truk. Manuscript. Copy on file in the Micronesian Seminar Library, Kolonia, Pohnpei, FSM.

1987a Truk suicide epidemic and social change. *Human Organization* 46 (4): 283–296.

1987b In search of the social roots of mental health pathology in Micronesia. In *Contemporary Issues in Mental Health Research in the Pacific Islands,* edited by Albert B.

Robillard and Anthony J. Marsella, pp. 12–31. Honolulu: Social Science Research Institute, University of Hawai'i.

1988   New directions in Pacific history: A practitioner's critical view. *Pacific Studies* 11 (3): 101–110.

1989   Suicide and the Micronesian family. *The Contemporary Pacific* 1 (1): 43–74.

1991   *The Catholic Church in Palau.* Koror: Catholic Media Center.

1992   The expensive taste for modernity: Caroline and Marshall Islands. In *Social Change in the Pacific Islands,* edited by Albert B. Robillard, pp. 203–219. London: Kegan Paul International.

1993   Spirit possession in Chuuk: A socio-cultural interpretation. *Micronesian Counselor,* Occasional Papers no. 11. Kolonia, Pohnpei, FSM: Micronesian Seminar.

1995   *Strangers in their Own Land: A Century of Colonial Rule in the Caroline and Marshall Islands.* Pacific Islands Monograph Series no. 13. Honolulu: University of Hawai'i Press.

Hezel, Francis X., and A. Michael Wylie.

1992   Schizophrenia and chronic mental illness in Micronesia: An epidemiological survey. *ISLA: A Journal of Micronesian Studies* 1 (2): 329–354.

Highland, Genevieve, Roland W. Force, Alan Howard, Marion Kelly, and Yoshihiko Sinoto (eds.)

1967   *Polynesian Culture History: Essays in Honor of Kenneth P. Emory.* Bernice P. Bishop Museum Special Publication no. 56. Honolulu: Bishop Museum Press.

Hijikata Hisakatsu

1941   Education and sex training of children on Satawal Island in comparison with Palau. *East Asian Review* 4:239–261.

1993   *Collective Works of Hijikata Hisakatsu: Society and Life of Palau.* Vol. 1, edited by Endo Hisashi. Tokyo: The Sasakawa Peace Foundation.

1995   *Collective Works of Hijikata Hisakatsu: Gods and Religion of Palau.* Vol. 2, edited by Endo Hisashi. Tokyo: The Sasakawa Peace Foundation.

Hines, Neal O.

1952   The secret of the Marshallese sticks. *Pacific Discovery* 5 (5): 18–23.

1962   *Proving Ground: An Account of the Radiobiological Studies in the Pacific, 1946–1961.* Seattle: University of Washington Press.

Hirano, Asao, Leonard T. Kurland, Robert S. Krooth, and Simmons Lessell

1961   Parkinsonism-dementia complex, an endemic disease on the island of Guam. I. Clinical Features. *Brain* 84 (4): 642–661.

Hirano, Asao, Nathan Malamud, and Leonard T. Kurland

1961   Parkinsonism-dementia complex, an endemic disease on the island of Guam. II. Pathological features. *Brain* 84 (4): 662–679.

Hobson, Sandra Vitarelli

1970   Ceramicist's odyssey of clay: The Palau islands. *Craft Horizons* 30:16–17.

Hoijer, Harry
1964 Obituary. Joseph Edwin Weckler, Jr. *American Anthropologist* 66 (6), pt. 1: 1348–1350.

Holmes, Lowell D.
1965 *Anthropology: An Introduction.* New York: The Ronald Press.

Holmes, Lowell D., and Wayne Parris
1981 *Anthropology: An Introduction.* 3d ed. New York: John Wiley.

Homans, George, and David M. Schneider
1955 *Marriage, Authority and Final Causes.* Glencoe, Ill.: Free Press.

Honigmann, John
1973 Personality in culture. In *Main Currents in Cultural Anthropology,* edited by Raoul Naroll and Frada Naroll, pp. 217–245. New York: Appleton-Century-Crofts.

Horizon
1979 *Pacific Expressions* (National Gallery of Art Exhibition). *Horizon* 22 (1): 6.

Howard, Alan
1990 Cultural paradigms, history, and the search for identity in Oceania. In *Cultural Identity and Ethnicity in the Pacific,* edited by Jocelyn Linnekin and Lin Poyer, pp. 259–279. Honolulu: University of Hawai‘i Press.

Howard, Michael C.
1986 *Contemporary Cultural Anthropology.* 2d ed. Boston: Little, Brown.
1989a *Ethnicity and Nation-Building in the Pacific.* Tokyo: United Nations University.
1989b *Contemporary Cultural Anthropology.* 3d ed. Glenview, Ill.: Scott, Foresman.

Howard, Michael C., and Patrick C. McKim
1983 *Contemporary Cultural Anthropology.* Boston: Little, Brown.

Howe, Kerry R., Robert C. Kiste, and Brij V. Lal (eds.)
1994 *Tides of History: The Pacific Islands in the Twentieth Century.* Honolulu: University of Hawai‘i Press.

Hughes, Daniel T.
1968 Democracy in a traditional society: A role analysis of the political system of Ponape. PhD dissertation, Catholic University.
1969a Conflict and harmony: Roles of councilman and section chief on Ponape. *Oceania* 40 (1): 32–41.
1969b Reciprocal influence of traditional and democratic leadership roles on Ponape. *Ethnology* 8 (3): 278–291.
1969c Democracy in a traditional society: Two hypotheses on role. *American Anthropologist* 71 (1): 36–45.
1970 *Political Conflict and Harmony on Ponape.* New Haven, Conn.: HRAFlex Books.
1972 Integration of the role of territorial congressman into Ponapean society. *Oceania* 43 (2): 140–152.

1974   Obstacles to the integration of the district legislature into Ponapean society. In *Political Development in Micronesia,* edited by Daniel T. Hughes and Sherwood G. Lingenfelter, pp. 93–109. Columbus: Ohio State University Press.
1982   Continuity of indigenous Ponapean social structure and stratification. *Oceania* 53 (1): 5–18.

Hughes, Daniel T., and Stanley K. Laughlin, Jr.
1982   Key elements in the evolving political culture of the Federated States of Micronesia. *Pacific Studies* 6 (1): 71–84.

Hughes, Daniel T., and Sherwood G. Lingenfelter (eds.)
1974   *Political Development in Micronesia.* Columbus: Ohio State University Press.

HRAF, Human Relations Area Files
1969   *HRAF Source Bibliography.* New Haven, Conn.: Human Relations Area Files, Inc.

Hunt, Edward E., Jr.
1950   Studies in physical anthropology in Micronesia. PhD dissertation, Harvard University.
1978   Ecological frameworks and hypothesis testing in medical anthropology. In *Health and the Human Condition: Perspectives on Medical Anthropology,* edited by Michael H. Logan and Edward E. Hunt, Jr., pp. 84–100. North Scituate, Mass.: Duxbury Press.

Hunt, Edward E., Jr., Nathaniel R. Kidder, and David M. Schneider
1954   The depopulation of Yap. *Human Biology* 26 (1): 21–51.

Hunt, Edward E., Jr., Nathaniel R. Kidder, David M. Schneider, and William D. Stevens
1949   *The Micronesians of Yap and Their Depopulation. Report of the Peabody Museum Expedition to Yap Island, Micronesia, 1947–1948.* Cambridge, Mass.: Peabody Museum, Harvard University. Also published 1949. CIMA Report no. 24. Washington D.C.: Pacific Science Board, National Research Council.

Hunt, Edward E., Jr., William A. Lessa, and Arobati Hicking
1965   The sex ratio of live births in three Pacific Island populations (Yap, Samoa and New Guinea). *Human Biology* 37 (2): 148–155.

Hunt, Lynn (ed.)
1989   *The New Cultural History.* Berkeley: University of California Press.

Hunt, Robert
1967   *Personalities and Cultures: Readings in Psychological Anthropology.* Garden City, N. Y.: Natural History Press.

Hunter-Anderson, Rosalind L.
1982   *Yapese Settlement Patterns: An Ethnoarchaeological Approach.* Agaña, Guam: Pacific Studies Institute.
1990   (ed.) *Recent Advances in Micronesian Archaeology.* Selected Papers from the Micronesian Archaeology Conference, September 9–12, 1987. *Micronesica* Supplement no. 2. Mangilao, Guam: University of Guam Press.

Hunter-Anderson, Rosalind L., and Michael W. Graves

1990   Coming from where? An introduction to recent advances in Micronesian archaeol-
       ogy. In *Recent Advances in Micronesian Archaeology,* edited by Rosalind L. Hunter-
       Anderson. *Micronesica* Supplement no. 2: 5–16.

Hunter-Anderson, Rosalind L., and Yigal Zan

1985   Where's the fish?, or, what limited the size of aboriginal populations in small tropical
       high islands? *Journal of the Polynesian Society* 94 (1): 61–65.

Huntsman, Judith, and Mervyn McLean (eds.)

1976   *Incest Prohibitions in Micronesia and Polynesia.* Special issue of *Journal of the Polyne-
       sian Society* 85 (2): 149–298.

Hutchins, Edward

1980   *Conceptual Structures of Caroline Island Navigation.* Center for Human Information
       Processing Report 93. La Jolla, Ca.: University of California, San Diego.

1983   Understanding Micronesian navigation. In *Mental Models,* edited by Dedre Gentner
       and Albert L. Stevens, pp. 191–226. Hillsdale, N. J.: Lawrence Erlbaum Associates.

Hutchins, Edward, and G. Hinton

1984   Why the islands move. *Perception* 13:629–632.

Ishimori, Shuzo

1987   Song and cosmology on Satawal. *Senri Ethnological Studies* 21:241–253.

Iwata, Junko

1985   An anthropological study of Yapese music. Bachelor's thesis, Osaka College of Music.

1988   YADAM [Yap Archives of Dance and Music] Handbook. Version 1, 1988–03–28. Osaka,
       Japan.

Jaques Cattell Press, The (ed.)

1968   *American Men of Science, A Biographical Directory: The Social and Behavioral Sciences.*
       11th ed. New York: R. R. Bowker.

Jensen, Gordon, and Anthony H. Polloi

1984   Health and life-style of longevous Palauans: Implications for development theory.
       International Journal of Aging and Human Development 19 (4): 271–285.

1988   The very old of Palau: Health and mental state. *Age and Aging* 17 (4): 220–226.

Jernigan, Earl W.

1973   *Lochukle:* A Palauan art tradition. PhD dissertation, University of Arizona.

Jochim, Michael A.

1981   *Strategies for Survival: Cultural Behavior in an Ecological Context.* New York: Aca-
       demic Press.

Johannes, Robert E.

1981   *Words of the Lagoon: Fishing and Marine Lore in the Palau District of Micronesia.*
       Berkeley: University of California Press.

1985 The role of marine resource tenure systems (TURFs) in sustainable nearshore marine resource development and management in US-affiliated tropical Pacific Islands. Manuscript prepared for Office of Technology Assessment, US Congress. Copy available from US Department of Commerce, National Technical Information Service, Springfield, VA 22161.

Johnson, Allen
1982 Nonreductionist cultural ecology. In *Culture and Ecology,* edited by John G. Kennedy and Robert B. Edgerton. American Anthropological Association Special Publication no. 15, pp. 18–25. Washington, D.C.: American Anthropological Association.

Johnson, Giff
1984 *Collision Course at Kwajalein: Marshall Islanders in the Shadow of the Bomb.* Honolulu: Pacific Resource Center.

Johnson, James B.
1969 *Land Ownership in the Northern Mariana Islands: An Outline History.* Saipan: Division of Land Management, US Trust Territory of the Pacific Islands.

Johnson, Thomas M., and Carolyn F. Sargent (eds.)
1990 *Medical Anthropology: A Handbook of Theory and Method.* New York: Greenwood Press.

Jolly, Margaret
1992 Specters of inauthenticity. *The Contemporary Pacific* 4 (1): 49–72.

Jopling, Carol F. (ed.)
1971 *Art and Aesthetics in Primitive Societies: A Critical Anthology.* New York: Dutton.

Jorgensen, Marilyn A.
1984 Expressive manifestations of Santa Marian Camalin as key symbol in Guamanian culture. PhD dissertation, University of Texas.

Joseph, Alice, and Veronica F. Murray
1951 *Chamorros and Carolinians of Saipan: Personality Studies.* CIMA Report no. 12. Washington, D.C.: Pacific Science Board, National Research Council. Published 1951. Cambridge, Mass.: Harvard University Press. Reprinted 1971. Westport, Conn.: Greenwood Press.

Joseph, Alice, Rosamond B. Spicer, and Jane Chesky
1949 *The Desert People: A Study of the Papago Indians.* Chicago: University of Chicago Press.

Joseph, Suad
1994 Brother/sister relationships: Connectivity, love, and power in the reproduction of patriarchy in Lebanon. *American Ethnologist* 21 (1): 50–73.

Kaeppler, Adrienne L.

1965   Decorative arts in the Marshall Islands. In *Life in Micronesia*, edited by Edwin H. Bryan Jr., pp. 164–172. Honolulu: Pacific Scientific Information Center, Bernice P. Bishop Museum.

1978   Melody, drone and decoration: Underlying structures and surface manifestations in Tongan art and society. In *Art in Society*, edited by Michael Greenhalgh and Vincent Megaw, pp. 261–274. London: Duckworth.

Kaeser, Lothar

1977   Der Begriff "Seele" bei den Insulanern von Truk. PhD dissertation, Albert Ludwigs-Universität, Freiberg.

1989   *Die Besiedlung Mikronesiens: Eine Ethnologisch-Linguistische Untersuchung.* Berlin: Dietrich Reimer Verlag.

Kaplan, Bernice

1961   Cross-cultural use of projective techniques. In *Psychological Anthropology*, edited by Francis L. K. Hsu, pp. 235–254. Homewood, Ill.: Dorsey.

Kardiner, Abraham

1939   *The Individual and Society*. New York: Columbia University Press.

Karig, Walter

1948   *The Fortunate Islands. A Pacific Interlude; An Account of the Pleasant Lands and People in the United States Trust Territory of the Pacific.* New York: Rinehart & Co.

Kataoka, Osamu

1996   Prehistoric and historic faunal utilization in Pohnpei: An ecological and ethno-archaeological understanding. PhD dissertation, University of Oregon.

Kauders, Frank R., James P. MacMurray, and Kenric W. Hammond

1982   Male predominance among Palauan schizophrenics. *International Journal of Social Psychology* 28 (2): 97–102.

Keate, George

1788   *An Account of the Pelew Islands . . . from the Journals and Communications of Captain Henry Wilson, 1783.* London: G. Nichol.

Keating, Elizabeth

1994   Power sharing: Language, rank, gender and social space in Pohnpei, Micronesia. PhD dissertation, University of California, Los Angeles.

Keegan, William F., and Morgan D. Maclachlan

1989   The evolution of avunculocal chiefdoms: A reconstruction of Taino kinship and politics. *American Anthropologist* 91 (3): 613–630.

Keene, Dennis T. P.

1992   Kokan: Youthful Female Runaways in the Marshalls. *Micronesian Counselor*, Occasional Paper no. 8. Kolonia, Pohnpei, FSM: Micronesian Seminar.

Keesing, Felix M.

1945   Applied anthropology in colonial administration. In *The Science of Man in the World Crisis,* edited by Ralph Linton, pp. 373–398. New York: Columbia University Press.

1947   Administration in Pacific Islands. *Far Eastern Survey* 16 (6): 61–65.

1949   Experiments in training overseas administrators. *Human Organization* 8:20–22.

1958   *Cultural Anthropology: The Science of Custom.* New York: Holt, Rinehart & Winston.

Keesing, Felix M., and Marie M. Keesing

1956   *Elite Communication in Samoa.* Stanford, Ca.: Stanford University Press.

Keesing, Roger M.

1972   Simple models of complexity: The lure of kinship. In *Kinship Studies in the Morgan Centennial Year,* edited by Priscilla Reining, pp. 17–31. Washington, D.C.: The Anthropological Society of Washington.

1976   *Cultural Anthropology: A Contemporary Perspective.* New York: Holt, Rinehart & Winston.

1991   Reply to Trask. *The Contemporary Pacific* 3 (1): 168–171.

1992   *Custom and Confrontation: The Kwaio Struggle for Cultural Autonomy.* Chicago: University of Chicago Press.

Keesing, Roger M., and Margaret Jolly

1992   Epilogue. In *History and Tradition in Melanesian Anthropology,* edited by James G. Carrier, pp. 224–243. Berkeley: University of California Press.

Keesing, Roger M,. and Felix M. Keesing

1971   *New Perspectives in Cultural Anthropology.* New York: Holt, Rinehart & Winston.

Keesing, Roger M., and Robert Tonkinson (eds.)

1982   *Reinventing Traditional Culture: The Politics of Kastom in Island Melanesia.* Special issue of *Mankind* 13 (4): 297–399.

Keller, Janet D.

1988   Woven world: Neotraditional symbols of unity in Vanuatu. *Mankind* 18 (1): 1–13.

Kennard, Edward A., and Gordon Macgregor

1953   Applied anthropology in government: United States. In *Anthropology Today,* edited by Alfred L. Kroeber, pp. 832–840. Chicago: University of Chicago Press.

Kennedy, Raymond F.

1972   Musics of Oceania. In *Music in World Cultures,* edited by Malcolm E. Bessom, pp. 43–48. Washington, D.C.: Music Educators National Conference.

1980a   Chamorro music and dance. In *The New Grove Dictionary of Music and Musicians.* 6th ed. Vol. 12, edited by Stanley Sadie, pp. 277–278. London: Macmillan.

1980b   Ponape. In *The New Grove Dictionary of Music and Musicians.* 6th ed. Vol. 12, edited by Stanley Sadie, pp. 273–274. London: Macmillan.

Kenney, Michael
1976 *Youth in Micronesia in the 1970's: The Impact of Changing Family, Employment and Justice Systems.* Report on Youth Development Research Conducted Under Law Enforcement Assistance Administration, US Department of Justice. Saipan: Trust Territory Printing Office.

Kent, George
1992 Children's survival in the Pacific Islands. In *Social Change in the Pacific Islands,* edited by Albert B. Robillard, pp. 414–427. New York: Kegan Paul International.

Kesolei, Katharine (ed.)
1971 *Palauan Legends,* vol. 1. Koror: Palau Community Action Agency.
1975 *Palauan Legends,* vol. 2. Koror: Palau Community Action Agency.

Kihleng, Kimberlee
1996 Women in exchange: Negotiated relations, practice, and the constitution of female power in processes of cultural reproduction and change in Pohnpei, Micronesia. PhD dissertation, University of Hawai'i.

Kim, Dai You, and Francis Defngin
1960 Taro cultivation in Yap. In *Taro Cultivation, Practices and Beliefs,* pt. 1 *(The Western Carolines),* edited by John deYoung. Anthropological Working Papers no. 6, pp. 48–68. Guam: Office of the Staff Anthropologist, Trust Territory of the Pacific Islands.

King, Thomas, and Patricia L. Parker
1984 *Pisekin Nóómw Nóón Tonaachaw, Archaeology in the Tonaachaw Historic District, Moen Island.* Micronesia Archaeological Survey Report no. 18. Occasional Paper no. 3. Carbondale, Ill.: Southern Illinois University, Carbondale, Center for Archaeological Investigations.

Kirkpatrick, John T., and Charles R. Broder
1976 Adoption and parenthood on Yap. In *Transactions in Kinship: Adoption and Fosterage in Oceania,* edited by Ivan A. Brady. Asao Monograph no. 4, pp. 200–227. Honolulu: University of Hawai'i Press.

Kiste, Robert C.
1967 Changing patterns of land tenure and social organization among the ex-Bikini Marshallese. PhD dissertation, University of Oregon.
1968 *Kili Island: A Study of the Relocation of the Ex-Bikini Marshallese.* Eugene: Department of Anthropology, University of Oregon.
1974 *The Bikinians: A Study in Forced Migration.* Menlo Park, Ca.: Cummings Publishing Co.
1976 The people of Enewetak Atoll vs. the US Department of Defense. In *Ethics and Anthropology: Dilemmas in Fieldwork,* edited by Michael A. Rynkiewich and James P. Spradley, pp. 61-80. New York: John Wiley & Sons.

1983   The policies that hid a non-policy. *Pacific Islands Monthly* 54 (10): 37-40.

1985   Identity and relocation: The Bikini case. In *Mobility and Identity in the Island Pacific,* edited by Murray Chapman, pp. 116–138. Special issue of *Pacific Viewpoint* 26 (1).

1986   Termination of the US trusteeship in Micronesia. *Journal of Pacific History* 21 (3): 127–138.

1987   History of the people of Enewetak Atoll. In *The Ecosystem: Environments, Biotas, and Processes,* edited by Dennis M. Devaney, Ernst S. Reese, Beatrice L. Burch, and Philip Helfrich. Vol. 1, *The Natural History of Enewetak Atoll,* pp. 17–25. Washington, D.C.: Office of Scientific and Technical Information, US Department of Energy.

1993   New political statuses in American Micronesia. In *Contemporary Pacific Societies: Studies in Development and Change,* edited by Victoria S. Lockwood, Thomas G. Harding and Ben J. Wallace, pp. 67–80. Englewood Cliffs, N. J.: Prentice-Hall.

1994   Overview of the Pacific with a Micronesia/Palau focus. Paper read at the international conference, "The War in Palau: Fifty Years of Change," September, Koror, Palau. Copy in author's personal files.

Kiste, Robert C., and Michael A. Rynkiewich

1976   Incest and exogamy: A comparative study of two Marshall Island populations. *Journal of the Polynesian Society* 85 (2): 209–226.

Kitayama, Shinobu, and Hazel Rose Markus (eds.)

1994   *Emotion and Culture: Empirical Studies of Mutual Influence.* Washington, D.C.: American Psychological Association.

Kluge, Paul Frederick

1969   This quarter's worth. *Micronesian Reporter* 17 (3): 1.

1991   *The Edge of Paradise.* New York: Random House.

Knudson, Kenneth E.

1970   Resource fluctuation, productivity, and social organization on Micronesian coral islands. PhD dissertation, University of Oregon.

1990   Social complexity on Truk and in the Marianas: Lack of correspondence between anthropological models and historical evidence. In *Recent Advances in Micronesian Archaeology,* edited by Rosalind L. Hunter-Anderson. *Micronesica* Supplement no. 2: 117–124.

Kobayashi, Shigeki

1978   The structure and house constructing processes in Yap Island. *Bulletin of the Museum of Little World* 2.

Koerner, Donald R.

1952   Amyotrophic lateral sclerosis on Guam: A clinical study and review of the literature. *Annals of Internal Medicine* 37 (6): 1204–1220.

Kopytoff, Igor

1986 The cultural biography of things: Commoditization as process. In *The Social Life of Things: Commodities in Cultural Perspective,* edited by Arjun Appadurai, pp. 64–91. Cambridge: Cambridge University Press.

Krämer, Augustin

1919 Palau. Vol. II, B, 3, pt. 2, *Ergebnisse der Südsee-Expedition, 1908–1910,* edited by Georg Thilenius. Hamburg: Friederichsen, de Gruyter.

1926 Palau. Vol. II, B, 3, pt. 3, *Ergebnisse der Südsee-Expedition, 1908–1910,* edited by Georg Thilenius. Hamburg: Friederichsen, de Gruyter.

1929 Palau. Vol. II, B, 3, pt. 5, *Ergebnisse der Südsee-Expedition, 1908–1910,* edited by Georg Thilenius. Hamburg: Friederichsen, de Gruyter.

1932 Truk. Vol. II, B, 5, *Ergebnisse der Südsee-Expedition, 1908–1910,* edited by Georg Thilenius. Hamburg: Friederichsen, de Gruyter.

1935 Inseln um Truk (Centralkarolinen ost): Lukunor-Inseln und Namoluk; Losap und Nama; Lemarafat, Namonuito oder Onoun; Pollap-Tamatam. Vol. II, B, 1, pt. 1, *Ergebnisse der Südsee-Expedition, 1908–1910,* edited by Georg Thilenius. Hamburg: Friederichsen, de Gruyter.

1937 Zentralkarolinen: Lamotrek-Gruppe, Oleai, Feis. Vol. II, B, 10, pt. 1, *Ergebnisse der Südsee-Expedition, 1908–1910,* edited by Georg Thilenius. Hamburg: Friederichsen, de Gruyter.

Krämer, Augustin, and Hans Nevermann

1938 Ralik-Ratik (Marshall-Inseln). Vol. II, B, 11, *Ergebnisse der Südsee-Expedition, 1908–1910,* edited by Georg Thilenius. Hamburg: Friederichsen, de Gruyter.

Krauss, Bob

1988 *Keneti: South Seas Adventures of Kenneth Emory.* Honolulu: University of Hawai'i Press.

1992 Famed anthropologist A. Spoehr, 78, dies. *The Honolulu Advertiser,* June 13.

Krech III, Shepard

1991 The state of ethnohistory. *Annual Review of Anthropology* 20:345–375.

Kroeber, Alfred L.

1939 *Cultural and Natural Areas of Native North America.* University of California Publications in American Archaeology and Ethnology no. 38. Berkeley: University of California Press.

Kubary, Johan Stanislaus

1873 *Bericht ber Meinen Aufenthalt in Palau.* Hamburg: Godeffroy Journal.

Kuklick, Henrika

1991 *The Savage Within: The Social History of British Anthropology, 1885–1945.* Cambridge: Cambridge University Press.

Kurashina, Hiro, and Russell N. Clayshulte
1983   Site formation processes and cultural sequence of Tarague, Guam. *Bulletin of the Indo-Pacific Prehistory Association* no. 4. Canberra: Australian National University.

Labby, David
1972   The anthropology of others: An analysis of the traditional ideology of Yap, Western Caroline Islands. PhD dissertation, University of Chicago.
1976a   *The Demystification of Yap: Dialectics of Culture on a Micronesian Island.* Chicago: University of Chicago Press.
1976b   Incest as cannibalism: The Yapese analysis. *Journal of the Polynesian Society* 85 (2): 171–179.

Lagacé, Robert O.
1974   *Nature and Use of the Hraf Files: A Research and Teaching Guide.* New Haven, Conn.: Human Relations Area Files, Inc.

Lal, Brij V. (ed.)
1986   *Politics in Fiji: Studies in Contemporary History.* Sydney: Allen & Unwin.

Landy, David (ed.)
1977   *Culture, Disease, and Healing: Studies in Medical Anthropology.* New York: Macmillan.

Larcom, Joan
1990   Custom by decree: Legitimation crisis in Vanuatu. In *Cultural Identity and Ethnicity in the Pacific,* edited by Jocelyn Linnekin and Lin Poyer, pp. 175–190. Honolulu: University of Hawaiʻi Press.

Larsen, Otto N.
1992   *Milestones and Millstones: Social Science Funding at the National Science Foundation, 1945–1991.* New Brunswick, N. J.: Transaction Publishers.

Larson, Robert Bruce
1987   Marijuana in Truk. In *Drugs in Western Pacific Societies: Relations of Substance,* edited by Lamont Lindstrom. Asao Monograph no. 11, pp. 219–230. Lanham, Md.: University Press of America.
1989   Sojourning and personhood: College students return to Truk, Federated States of Micronesia. PhD dissertation, University of Hawaiʻi.

Last, Murray
1990   Professionalization of indigenous healers. In *Medical Anthropology: A Handbook of Theory and Method,* edited by Thomas M. Johnson and Carolyn F. Sargent, pp. 349–366. New York: Greenwood Press.

Lawrence, Pensile, Masao Kinser Hadley, and Robert K. McKnight
1964   Breadfruit cultivation practices and beliefs in Ponape. In *Breadfruit Cultivation Practices and Beliefs in the Trust Territory of the Pacific Islands,* edited by John deYoung.

Anthropological Working Papers nos. 7 & 8 (rev.), pp. 42–64. Saipan: Trust Territory of the Pacific Islands.

Leach, Edmund
1965   _Political Systems of Highland Burma._ Boston: Beacon Press.

Leach, Foss, and Graeme Ward
1981   _Archaeology on Kapingamarangi Atoll: A Polynesian Outlier in the Eastern Caroline Islands._ University of Otago Studies in Prehistoric Anthropology no. 16. Dunedin, New Zealand: Department of Anthropology, University of Otago.

Leatherman, Thomas L., Alan H. Goodman, and R. Brooke Thomas
1993   On seeking common ground between medical ecology and critical medical anthropology. _Medical Anthropology Quarterly_ 7 (2): 202–207.

Leavitt, Gregory C.
1989   Disappearance of the incest taboo: A cross-cultural test of general evolutionary hypotheses. _American Anthropologist_ 91 (1): 116–131.
1990   Sociobiological explanations of incest avoidance: A critical review of evidential claims. _American Anthropologist_ 92 (4): 971–993.

LeBar, Frank
1951   Trukese material culture: A study in analytical method. PhD dissertation, Yale University.
1964   _The Material Culture of Truk._ Yale University Publications in Anthropology no. 68. New Haven, Conn.: Yale University Press.
1972   _Ethnic Groups of Insular Southeast Asia._ New Haven, Conn.: Human Relations Area Files Press.

Lebra, Takie S.
1989   Adoption among the hereditary elite of Japan: Status preservation through mobility. _Ethnology_ 28 (3): 185–218.

Lebra, William P.
1982   Shaman-client interchange in Okinawa: Performative stages in shamanic therapy. In _Cultural Conceptions of Mental Health and Therapy,_ edited by Anthony J. Marsella and Geoffrey M. White, pp. 303–315. Dordrecht: D. Reidel.

Leenhardt, Maurice
1950   _Arts of the Oceanic Peoples._ London: Thames & Hudson.

Le Geyt, Linda M.
1986   Hand fans of Micronesia. Master's thesis, Asian and Pacific Art History, University of Hawai'i, Mānoa.

Leibowitz, Arnold H.
1989   _Defining Status: A Comprehensive Analysis of United States Territorial Relations._ Dordrecht: Kluwer/Academic Publications.

Leighton, Alexander H.

1945 *The Governing of Men.* Princeton, N. J.: Princeton University Press.

1949 *Human Relations in a Changing World.* New York: E. P. Dutton.

Lessa, William A.

1950a *The Ethnology of Ulithi Atoll.* CIMA Report no. 28. Washington, D.C.: Pacific Science Board, National Research Council.

1950b The place of Ulithi in the Yap empire. *Human Organization* 9 (1): 16–18.

1950c Ulithi and the outer native world. *American Anthropologist* 52 (1): 27–52.

1955 Depopulation on Ulithi. *Human Biology* 27 (3): 161–183.

1956 Myth and blackmail in the Western Carolines. *Journal of the Polynesian Society* 65 (1): 66–74.

1961 *Tales from Ulithi Atoll: A Comparative Study in Oceanic Folklore.* University of California Publications, Folklore Studies no. 13. Berkeley: University of California Press.

1962a An evaluation of early descriptions of Carolinian culture. *Ethnohistory* 9 (4): 313–403.

1962b The decreasing power of myth on Ulithi. *Journal of American Folklore* 75 (296): 153–159.

1964 The social effects of typhoon Ophelia (1960) on Ulithi. *Micronesica* 1 (1 & 2): 1–47.

1966a *Ulithi: A Micronesian Design for Living.* Case Studies in Cultural Anthropology. New York: Holt, Rinehart & Winston.

1966b Discoverer-of-the-sun, mythology as a reflection of culture. *Journal of American Folklore* 79 (311): 3–51.

1975 *Drake's Island of Thieves: Ethnological Sleuthing.* Honolulu: University Press of Hawai'i.

1980 *More Tales from Ulithi Atoll: A Content Analysis.* Folklore and Mythology Studies no. 32. Berkeley: University of California Press.

1983 Sea turtles and ritual: Conservation in the Caroline Islands. In *The Fishing Culture of the World, Studies in Ethnology, Cultural Ecology and Folklore,* edited by Bela Gunda, pp. 1183–1201. Budapest: Akademiai Kiado, Publishing House of the Hungarian Academy of Sciences.

1985 *Spearhead Governatore: Remembrances of the Campaign in Italy.* Malibu, Ca.: Undena Publications.

n.d. Autobiographical notes: Professor William A. Lessa. Manuscript. Copy in the personal files of Mac Marshall.

Lessa, William A., and George C. Myers

1962 Population dynamics of an atoll community. *Population Studies* 15 (3): 244–257.

Lessa, William A., and Marvin Spiegelman

1954 *Ulithian Personality as Seen Through Ethnological Materials and Thematic Test Analysis.* University of California Publications in Culture and Society, vol. 2, no. 5, pp. 243–301. Berkeley: University of California Press.

Lessa, William A., and Evon Z. Vogt (eds.)

1958 *Reader in Comparative Religion: An Anthropological Approach.* Evanston, Ill.: Row, Peterson.

Lévi-Strauss, Claude
1963 *Structural Anthropology,* translated by Claire Jacobson and Brooke Grundfest Schoepf. New York: Basic Books.
1970 *Tristes Tropiques,* translated by John Russell. New York: Atheneum. First published 1955.

Levin, Michael J.
1976 Eauripik population structure. PhD dissertation, University of Michigan.

Levin, Michael J., and Larry J. Gorenflo
1994 Demographic controls and shifting adaptive constraints on Eauripik Atoll. *ISLA: A Journal of Micronesia Studies* 2 (1): 103–145.

LeVine, Robert A.
1973 *Culture, Behavior, and Personality.* Chicago: Aldine.

Levinson, David, and Martin J. Malone
1980 *Toward Explaining Human Culture: A Critical Review of the Findings of Worldwide Cross-Cultural Research.* New Haven, Conn.: Human Relations Area Files Press.

Lewis, David
1971 A return voyage between Puluwat and Saipan using Micronesian navigational techniques. *Journal of the Polynesian Society* 80 (4): 437–448.
1973 *We, the Navigators: The Ancient Art of Landfinding in the Pacific.* Honolulu: University Press of Hawai‘i.

Lieber, Michael D.
1968a *Porakiet: A Kapingamarangi Colony on Ponape.* Eugene: Department of Anthropology, University of Oregon.
1968b The nature of the relationship between kinship and land tenure on Kapingamarangi Atoll. PhD dissertation, University of Pittsburgh.
1970 Adoption on Kapingamarangi. In *Adoption in Eastern Oceania,* edited by Vern Carroll. ASAO Monograph no. 1, pp. 158–205. Honolulu: University of Hawai‘i Press.
1974 Land tenure on Kapingamarangi. In *Land Tenure in Oceania,* edited by Henry P. Lundsgaarde. ASAO Monograph no. 2, pp. 70–99. Honolulu: University Press of Hawai‘i.
1977a (ed.) *Exiles and Migrants in Oceania.* ASAO Monograph no. 5. Honolulu: University Press of Hawai‘i.
1977b Conclusion: The resettled community in its context. In *Exiles and Migrants in Oceania,* edited by Michael D. Lieber. ASAO Monograph no. 5, pp. 342–387. Honolulu: University Press of Hawai‘i.
1977c The processes of change in two Kapingamarangi communities. In *Exiles and Migrants in Oceania,* edited by Michael D. Lieber. ASAO Monograph no. 5, pp. 35–67. Honolulu: University Press of Hawai‘i.
1979 Kapingamarangi: Land history. Research report for the Ponape Historic Preservation Committee. Manuscript. Copy in the personal files of William H. Alkire.

1984   Strange feast: Negotiating identities on Ponape. *Journal of the Polynesian Society* 93 (2): 141–189.

1990   Lamarckian definitions of identity on Kapingamarangi and Pohnpei. In *Cultural Identity and Ethnicity in the Pacific*, edited by Jocelyn Linnekin and Lin Poyer, pp. 71–101. Honolulu: University of Hawai'i Press.

Lieber, Michael D., and Esther B. Lieber

1987   Social and demographic aspects of a leprosy epidemic on a Polynesian atoll: Implications of a pattern. *International Journal of Leprosy* 55:468–480.

Lindenbaum, Shirley

1979   *Kuru Sorcery: Disease and Danger in the New Guinea Highlands.* Palo Alto, Ca.: Mayfield Publishing Co.

Lindsmith, Alfred R., and Anselm A. Strauss

1950   A critique of culture and personality writings. *American Sociological Review* 15 (5): 587–600.

Lindstrom, Lamont, and Geoffrey M. White

1993   Singing history: Island songs from the Pacific war. In *Artistic Heritage in a Changing Pacific*, edited by Philip J. Dark and Roger G. Rose, pp. 185–196. Honolulu: University of Hawai'i Press.

Lingenfelter, Sherwood G.

1971   Social structure and political change in Yap. PhD dissertation, University of Pittsburgh.

1974   Administrative officials, Peace Corps lawyers, and directed change on Yap. In *Political Development in Micronesia*, edited by Daniel T. Hughes and Sherwood G. Lingenfelter, pp. 54–71. Columbus: Ohio State University Press.

1975   *Yap: Political Leadership and Culture Change in an Island Society.* Honolulu: University Press of Hawai'i.

1993   Courtship and marriage on Yap: Budweiser, U-drives, and rock guitars. In *The Business of Marriage: Transformations in Oceanic Matrimony*, edited by Richard A. Marksbury. Asao Monograph no. 14, pp. 149–174. Pittsburgh, Pa.: University of Pittsburgh Press.

Linnekin, Jocelyn

1983   Defining tradition: Variations on the Hawaiian identity. *American Ethnologist* 10 (2): 241–252.

1990   The politics of culture in the Pacific. In *Cultural Identity and Ethnicity in the Pacific*, edited by Jocelyn Linnekin and Lin Poyer, pp. 149–173. Honolulu: University of Hawai'i Press.

Linnekin, Jocelyn, and Lin Poyer

1990a (eds.) *Cultural Identity and Ethnicity in the Pacific.* Honolulu: University of Hawai'i Press.

1990b Introduction. In *Cultural Identity and Ethnicity in the Pacific,* edited by Jocelyn Linnekin and Lin Poyer, pp. 1–16. Honolulu: University of Hawai'i Press.

Linton, Ralph

1923 *The Material Culture of the Marquesas Islands.* Bernard Dominick Expedition Publication 5, Memoirs of the Bernice P. Bishop Museum, vol. 8, no. 5. Honolulu: Bishop Museum Press.

1925 *Archaeology of the Marquesas Islands.* Bernice P. Bishop Museum Bulletin no. 23. Honolulu: Bishop Museum Press.

1926 *Ethnology of Polynesia and Micronesia.* Chicago: Field Museum of Natural History.

Linton, Ralph, and Paul S. Wingert

1946 *Arts of the South Seas.* New York: Museum of Modern Art.

Lips, Julius E.

1937 *The Savage Hits Back, or the White Man Through Native Eyes.* London: Lowat Dickson.

Lockhart, Bill

1983a Living art: Palau's story tellers. *Glimpses of Micronesia* 23 (3): 68–71.

1983b The storyboard of Palau. *School Arts* 82 (5): 37–39.

1985 *The Art of Palau.* Catalog for an exhibition at Texas Tech University, March–April. Lubbock, Tex.: Publications Bureau.

Logan, Michael H., and Edward E. Hunt, Jr. (eds.)

1978 *Health and the Human Condition: Perspectives on Medical Anthropology.* North Scituate, Mass.: Duxbury Press.

Loudon, Joseph B. (ed.)

1976 *Social Anthropology and Medicine.* Asa Monograph no. 13. London: Academic Press.

Lowie, Robert H.

1921 *Primitive Society.* London: Routledge & Kegan Paul.

1940 *An Introduction to Cultural Anthropology.* New and enl. ed. New York: Rinehart & Co.

Lucking, Laurie J.

1984 Archaeological investigation of prehistoric Palauan terraces. PhD dissertation, University of Minnesota.

Lundsgaarde, Henry P.

1966 *Cultural Adaptation in the Southern Gilbert Islands.* Eugene: Department of Anthropology, University of Oregon.

Lurie, Nancy Oestreich

1981 Obituary. Robert Eugene Ritzenthaler (1911–1980). *American Anthropologist* 83 (3): 607–611.

Lutz, Catherine

1980 Emotion words and emotional development on Ifaluk Atoll. PhD dissertation, Harvard University.

1981a Goals, events and understanding: Towards a formal model of Ifaluk emotion theory. Paper read at the 80th Annual Meeting of the American Anthropological Association, December 2–6, Los Angeles, California. Copy in the personal files of Peter W. Black.

1981b Situation based emotion frames and the cultural construction of emotions. In *Proceedings of the Third Annual Conference of the Cognitive Science Society,* August 19–21, Berkeley, California, pp. 84–89.

1982a Ifaluk ethnopsychology: The undivided self and interpersonal interpretation. Paper read at the 11th Annual Meeting of the Association for Social Anthropology in Oceania, February 25–28, Hilton Head, South Carolina. Copy in the personal files of Peter W. Black.

1982b The domain of emotion words on Ifaluk. *American Ethnologist* 9 (1): 113–128.

1983a Culture and consciousness: A problem in the anthropology of knowledge. Revised version of an address delivered at the 6th Houston Symposium, "Self and Consciousness," April 4–5, Houston, Texas. Copy in the personal files of Peter W. Black.

1983b Parental goals, ethnopsychology, and the development of emotional meaning. *Ethos* 11 (4): 246–262.

1984a (ed.) *Micronesia as Strategic Colony: The Impact of US Policy on Micronesian Health and Culture.* Cultural Survival Occasional Paper no. 12. Cambridge, Mass.: Cultural Survival.

1984b Violence and anger: A comparative interpretation of Ifaluk and American ethnopsychologies. Paper read at the 13th Annual Meeting of the Association for Social Anthropology in Oceania, February 29–March 3, Moloka'i, Hawai'i. Copy in the personal files of Peter W. Black.

1985   Ethnopsychology compared to what? Explaining behavior and consciousness among the Ifaluk. In *Person, Self and Experience: Exploring Pacific Ethnopsychologies,* edited by Geoffrey M. White and John T. Kirkpatrick, pp. 35–79. Berkeley: University of California Press.

1987   Goals, events and understanding in Ifaluk emotion theory. In *Cultural Models in Language and Thought,* edited by Dorothy Holland and Naomi Quinn, pp. 290–312. Cambridge: Cambridge University Press.

1988   *Unnatural Emotions: Everyday Sentiments on a Micronesian Atoll and Their Challenge to Western Theory.* Chicago: University of Chicago Press.

Lutz, Catherine, and Robert A. LeVine

1983   Culture and intelligence in infancy: An ethnopsychological view. In *Origins of Intelligence: Infancy and Early Childhood,* edited by Michael Lewis. 2d ed, pp. 1–28. New York: Plenum Press.

Macgregor, Gordon

1955   Anthropology in government: United States. In *Yearbook in Anthropology 1955,* edited by William L. Thomas, Jr., pp. 421–433. New York: Wenner-Gren Foundation for Anthropological Research.

MacKenzie, J. Boyd, and Tion Bikajle
1960   Breadfruit cultivation practices and beliefs in the Marshall Islands. Anthropological Working Papers no. 8. Guam: Office of the Staff Anthropologist, Trust Territory of the Pacific Islands. Reprinted 1964 in *Breadfruit Cultivation Practices and Beliefs in the Trust Territory of the Pacific Islands,* edited by John deYoung, pp. 1–15. Saipan: Trust Territory of the Pacific Islands.

MacMillan, Howard G.
1947   Rehabilitation for the Marshallese natives of Rongerik. Kwajalein: Marshall Islands. Typescript. Copy in the personal files of William H. Alkire.

Mahoney, Francis B.
1958   Land tenure patterns on Yap Island. In *Land Tenure Patterns: Trust Territory of the Pacific Islands,* edited by John deYoung, pp. 252–287. Guam: Office of the Staff Anthropologist, Trust Territory of the Pacific Islands.
1974   *Social and Cultural Factors Relating to the Cause and Control of Alcohol Abuse Among Micronesian Youth.* Prepared for the Government of the Trust Territory of the Pacific Islands under Contract: TT 174–8 with James R. Leonard Associates, Inc., Washington, D.C.

Mahony, Frank J.
1959   Anthropology and public health. *South Pacific Commission Quarterly Bulletin* 9 (4): 54–59.
1970   A Trukese theory of medicine. PhD dissertation, Stanford University.

Mahony, Frank J., and Pensile Lawrence
1964   Ponapean yam cultivation. In *Yam Cultivation in the Trust Territory,* edited by John deYoung. Anthropological Working Papers no. 4, pp. 1–13. Guam: Office of the Staff Anthropologist, Trust Territory of the Pacific Islands.

Maitland, Frederic W.
1936   *Selected Essays,* edited by Gaillard T. Lapsley, Percy H. Winfield, and H. D. Hazeltine. Cambridge: The University Press.

Malinowski, Bronislaw
1922   *Argonauts of the Western Pacific.* London: Routledge.
1929   Practical anthropology. *Africa* 2 (1): 22–38.
1930   The rationalization of anthropology and administration. *Africa* 3 (4): 405–430.

Manhard, Philip W.
1979   *The United States and Micronesia in Free Association: A Chance to do Better?* National Security Affairs Monograph Series 79–4. Washington, D.C.: National Defense University Research Directorate.

Maquet, Jacques
1971   Introduction. *Aesthetic Anthropology,* by Jacques Maquet. Addison-Wesley Module in Anthropology. Reading, Mass.: Addison-Wesley.

1986 *The Aesthetic Experience: An Anthropologist Looks at the Visual Arts.* New Haven, Conn.: Yale University Press.

Marcus, Mariano
1991 Child abuse and neglect in Micronesia. *Micronesian Counselor,* Occasional Papers no. 2. Kolonia, Pohnpei, FSM: Micronesian Seminar.

Marksbury, Richard A.
1979 Land tenure and modernization in the Yap Islands. PhD dissertation, Tulane University.
1993 (ed.) *The Business of Marriage: Transformations in Oceanic Matrimony.* Asao Monograph no. 14. Pittsburgh, Pa.: University of Pittsburgh Press.

Marshall, Leslie B.
1993 Disease ecologies of Australia and Oceania. In *The Cambridge World History of Human Disease,* edited by Kenneth F. Kiple, pp. 482–496. Cambridge: Cambridge University Press.

Marshall, Leslie B., and Mac Marshall
1979 Breasts, bottles and babies: Historical changes in infant feeding practices in a Micronesian village. *Ecology of Food and Nutrition* 8 (4): 241–249.
1980 Infant feeding and infant illness in a Micronesian village. *Social Science & Medicine* 14B:33–38.
1982 Education of women and family size in two Micronesian communities. *Micronesica* 18 (1): 1–21.

Marshall, Mac
1972a The structure of solidarity and alliance on Namoluk Atoll. PhD dissertation, University of Washington.
1972b Of cats and rats and *Toxoplasma gondii* at Namoluk. *Micronesian Reporter* 20 (2): 30–31.
1975a The natural history of Namoluk Atoll, Eastern Caroline Islands. *Atoll Research Bulletin* no. 189. Washington, D.C.: The Smithsonian Institution.
1975b Changing patterns of marriage and migration on Namoluk Atoll. In *Pacific Atoll Populations,* edited by Vern Carroll. Asao Monograph no. 3, pp. 160–211. Honolulu: University Press of Hawai‘i.
1976a Solidarity or sterility? Adoption and fosterage on Namoluk Atoll. In *Transactions in Kinship: Adoption and Fosterage in Oceania,* edited by Ivan A. Brady. Asao Monograph no. 4, pp. 28–50. Honolulu: University of Hawai‘i Press.
1976b Incest and endogamy on Namoluk Atoll. *Journal of the Polynesian Society* 85 (2): 181–197.
1977 The nature of nurture. *American Ethnologist* 4 (4): 643–662.
1978 The riddle of the Hawaiian Crow. Paper read at the 7th Annual Meeting of the Association for Social Anthropology in Oceania, February 15–19, Asilomar, California.
1979a *Weekend Warriors: Alcohol in a Micronesian Culture.* Palo Alto, Ca.: Mayfield Publishing Company.

1979b Natural and unnatural disaster in the Mortlock Islands of Micronesia. *Human Organization* 35 (3): 265–272.

1979c Education and depopulation on a Micronesian atoll. *Micronesica* 15 (1 & 2): 1–11.

1981a Sibling sets as building blocks in Greater Trukese Society. In *Siblingship in Oceania: Studies in the Meaning of Kin Relations,* edited by Mac Marshall. Asao Monograph no. 8, pp. 201–224. Ann Arbor: University of Michigan Press.

1981b (ed.) *Siblingship in Oceania: Studies in the Meaning of Kin Relations.* Asao Monograph no. 8. Ann Arbor: University of Michigan Press.

1981c Tobacco use and abuse in Micronesia: A preliminary discussion. *Journal of Studies on Alcohol* 42 (9): 885–893.

1982 (ed.) *Through a Glass Darkly: Beer and Modernization in Papua New Guinea.* Iaser Monograph no. 18. Boroko, Papua New Guinea: Institute for Applied Social and Economic Research.

1987 An overview of drugs in Oceania. In *Drugs in Western Pacific Societies: Relations of Substance,* edited by Lamont Lindstrom. Asao Monograph no. 11, pp. 13–49. Lanham, Md.: University Press of America.

1989 Rashomon in reverse: Ethnographic agreement in Truk. In *Culture, Kin, and Cognition in Oceania: Essays in Honor of Ward H. Goodenough,* edited by Mac Marshall and John L. Caughey. American Anthropological Association Special Publication no. 25, pp. 95–106. Washington, D.C.: American Anthropological Association.

1990a Combining insights from epidemiological and ethnographic data to investigate substance use in Truk, Federated States of Micronesia. *British Journal of Addiction* 85 (11): 1457–1468.

1990b "Problem deflation" and the ethnographic record: Interpretation and introspection in anthropological studies of alcohol. *Journal of Substance Abuse* 2 (3): 353–367.

1991a Beverage alcohol and other psychoactive substance use by young people in Chuuk, Federated States of Micronesia (Eastern Caroline Islands). *Contemporary Drug Problems* 18 (2): 331–371.

1991b The second fatal impact: Cigarette smoking, chronic disease, and the epidemiological transition in Oceania. *Social Science & Medicine* 33 (12): 1327–1342.

1993a Background briefing paper. Prepared for FSM/WHO Joint Conference on Alcohol-Related and Drug-Related Problems in Micronesia, August 9–12, Kolonia, Pohnpei, FSM. Copy on file in the RFK Memorial Library, University of Guam.

1993b A Pacific haze: Alcohol and drugs in Oceania. In *Contemporary Pacific Societies: Studies in Development and Change,* edited by Victoria S. Lockwood, Thomas G. Harding, and Ben J. Wallace, pp. 260–272. Englewood Cliffs, N. J.: Prentice Hall.

Marshall, Mac, and John L. Caughey (eds.)

1989 *Culture, Kin, and Cognition in Oceania: Essays in Honor of Ward H. Goodenough.* American Anthropological Association Special Publication no. 25. Washington, D.C.: American Anthropological Association.

Marshall, Mac, and Leslie B. Marshall

1975 Opening Pandora's bottle: Reconstructing Micronesians' early contacts with alcoholic beverages. *Journal of the Polynesian Society* 84 (4): 441–465.

1976 Holy and unholy spirits: The effects of missionization on alcohol use in Eastern Micronesia. *Journal of Pacific History* 11 (3 & 4): 135–166.

1990 *Silent Voices Speak: Women and Prohibition in Truk.* Belmont, Ca.: Wadsworth Publishing Company.

Marshall, Mac, and James D. Nason (compilers)

1975 *Micronesia 1944–1974: A Bibliography of Anthropological and Related Source Materials.* New Haven, Conn.: Human Relations Area Files Press.

Marshall, Mac, and Martha Ward

1987 Obituary. John (Jack) Fischer. *American Anthropologist* 89 (1): 134–136.

Marshall, Mac, Rocky Sexton, and Lee Insko

1994 Inhalant abuse in the Pacific Islands: Gasoline sniffing in Chuuk, Federated States of Micronesia. *Pacific Studies* 17 (2): 23–37.

Marvich, Detta, and Betsy Robb

1980 Different drums: A celebration of Pacific arts. *Glimpses of Micronesia and the Western Pacific* 20 (4): 24–31.

Mason, Leonard E.

1946 The Economic Organization of the Marshall Islanders. In US Commercial Company's Economic Survey of Micronesia, Report no. 9. Honolulu: US Commercial Company. Mimeographed.

1947 Economic and Human Resources: Marshall Islands. In US Commercial Company's Economic Survey of Micronesia, Report no. 8. Honolulu: US Commercial Company. Mimeographed.

1950 The Bikinians: A transplanted population. *Human Organization* 9 (1): 5–15.

1951 Marshalls, Gilberts, Ocean Island, and Nauru. In *Geography of the Pacific,* edited by Otis W. Freeman, pp. 270–297. New York: John Wiley & Sons.

1952 Anthropology-geography study of Arno Atoll, Marshall Islands. *Atoll Research Bulletin* no. 10. Washington, D.C.: The Smithsonian Institution.

1953 Anthropology in American Micronesia: A progress report. *Clearinghouse Bulletin of Research in Human Organization* 2 (3): 1–5.

1954 Relocation of the Bikini Marshallese: A study in group migration. PhD dissertation, Yale University.

1957 Ecologic change and culture pattern in the resettlement of Bikini Marshallese. In *Cultural Stability and Cultural Change,* edited by Verne F. Ray. Proceedings of the 1957 Annual Spring Meeting of the American Ethnological Society, pp. 1–6. Seattle: University of Washington Press.

1958a Habitat and social change on Kili Island. Abstract. *Proceedings of the Hawaiian Academy of Science, 1957–1958,* pp. 21–22.

1958b Kili community in transition. _South Pacific Commission Quarterly Bulletin_ 8 (2): 32–35, 46.

1959a Suprafamilial authority and economic process. _Humanités,-Cahiers de l'Institut de Science Économique Appliquée,_ no. 96, ser. 5, 1:87–118. Paris: I.S.E.A. Reprinted 1968. In _Peoples and Cultures of the Pacific,_ edited by Andrew P. Vayda, pp. 299-329. Garden City, N. Y.: Natural History Press.

1959b Micronesian cultures. _Encyclopedia of World Art_ 9:918–930.

1964 Micronesian cultures. _Encyclopedia of World Art_ 9:915–930.

1967a (ed.) _The Laura Report. A Field Report of Training and Research in Majuro Atoll, Marshall Islands._ Honolulu: Department of Anthropology, University of Hawai'i.

1967b Research problems and ethics in Micronesia. A survey undertaken for the Committee on Research Problems and Ethics, American Anthropological Association, Ralph L. Beals, Chairman. Special issue of _Micronesian Program Bulletin._ Copy on file in the Hawaiian and Pacific Collection, Hamilton Library, University of Hawai'i, Mānoa.

1967c _The Swampy Cree: A Study in Acculturation._ National Museum of Canada Anthropological Paper no. 13. Ottawa: National Museum of Canada.

1968 See 1959a.

1969a Anthropological research in Micronesia, 1954–1968. _Anthropologica,_ n.s., 11 (1): 85–115.

1969b Popular participation in the development of Trust Territory self-government. In _Political Modernization of Micronesia, A Symposium._ Santa Cruz, Ca.: Center for South Pacific Studies, University of California, Santa Cruz. n.p.

1973 The anthropological presence in American Micronesia. _Association for Anthropology in Micronesia Newsletter_ 2 (1): 19–31.

1974 Unity and disunity in Micronesia: Internal problems and future status. In _Political Development in Micronesia,_ edited by Daniel T. Hughes and Sherwood G. Lingenfelter, pp. 203–262. Columbus: Ohio State University Press.

1975 The many faces of Micronesia: District center and outer island culture. _Pacific Asian Studies_ (University of Guam) 1 (1): 5–37.

1977 An introduction to land tenure practice for archeologists engaged in field research in the Marshall Islands. Micronesian Archaeological Survey, Historic Preservation Program, Trust Territory of the Pacific Islands. Copy in the personal files of William H. Alkire.

1985a Applied anthropology in the TTPI. In _History of the US Trust Territory of the Pacific Islands,_ edited by Karen Knudson. Working Paper Series, Pacific Islands Studies Program, pp. 31–56. Honolulu: Center for Asian and Pacific Studies, University of Hawai'i.

1985b (ed.) _Kiribati: A Changing Atoll Culture._ Suva, Fiji: Institute of Pacific Studies, University of the South Pacific.

Mason, Leonard E., Jack A. Tobin, and Gerald Wade

1950 Anthropology-geography study of Arno Atoll, Marshall Islands. SIM Report no. 7. Reprinted 1952. _Atoll Research Bulletin_ no. 10. Washington, D.C.: The Smithsonian Institution.

Mason, Leonard E., and Harry Uyehara

1953   A quantitative study of certain aspects of the man-land relationship in Marshallese economy at Arno Island. In *Handbook for Atoll Research,* edited by F. Raymond Fosberg and Marie-Helene Sachet. *Atoll Research Bulletin* no. 17:116–121. Washington, D.C.: The Smithsonian Institution.

Masse, William B.

1989   The archaeology and ecology of fishing in the Belau Islands, Micronesia. PhD dissertation, Southern Illinois University, Carbondale.

Mauricio, Rufino

1992   A history of Pohnpei history or *Poadoapoad:* Description and explanation of recorded oral traditions. In *Pacific History: Papers from the 8th Pacific History Association Conference,* edited by Donald H. Rubinstein, pp. 351–380. Mangilao: University of Guam and the Micronesian Area Research Center.

1993   Ideological bases for power and leadership on Pohnpei, Micronesia: Perspectives from archaeology and oral history. PhD dissertation, University of Oregon.

Mayo, Larry W.

1984   Occupations and Chamorro social status: A study of urbanization in Guam. PhD dissertation, University of California, Berkeley.

McBean, Angus

1976   *Handicrafts in the South Seas: An Illustrated Guide for Buyers.* Noumea, New Caledonia: South Pacific Commission.

McCoy, Michael

1973   A renaissance in Carolinian-Marianas voyaging. *Journal of the Polynesian Society* 82 (4): 355–365.

1974   Man and turtle in the Central Carolines. *Micronesica* 10 (2): 207–222.

McCutcheon, Mary S.

1981   Resource exploitation and the tenure of land and sea in Palau. PhD dissertation, University of Arizona.

McElroy, Ann, and Patricia K. Townsend

1979   *Medical Anthropology in Ecological Perspective.* North Scituate, Mass.: Duxbury Press.

1989   *Medical Anthropology in Ecological Perspective.* 2d ed. Boulder, Colo.: Westview Press.

McGrath, William A., and Walter Scott Wilson

1971   The Marshall, Caroline and Marianas Islands: Too many foreign precedents. In *Land Tenure in the Pacific,* edited by Ron Crocombe, pp. 172–191. London: Oxford University Press.

McKnight, Robert K.

1960   Competition in Palau. PhD dissertation, Ohio State University.

1962   Palauan handicraft. Koror: Palau Museum.

1964a Handicrafts of the Trust Territory of the Pacific Islands. *South Pacific Bulletin* 14 (2): 37–40.

1964b *Orachl's Drawings: Palauan Rock Paintings.* Micronesian Research Working Paper no. 1. Saipan: Literature Production Center, Trust Territory of the Pacific Islands.

1964c Shell inlay: Art of Palau. *Micronesian Reporter* 12 (2): 10–14.

1964d Traditional Nan-Madol jewelry reconstructed. *Micronesian Reporter* 12 (6): 8–9.

1967 Palauan story boards. *Lore* 17 (3): 83–88.

1974 Rigid models and ridiculous boundaries: Political development and practice in Palau, circa 1955–1964. In *Political Development in Micronesia,* edited by Daniel T. Hughes and Sherwood G. Lingenfelter, pp. 37–53. Columbus: Ohio State University Press.

1977 Commas in microcosm: The movement of Southwest Islanders to Palau, Micronesia. In *Exiles and Migrants in Oceania,* edited by Michael D. Lieber. Asao Monograph no. 5, pp. 10–33. Honolulu: University of Hawai'i Press.

McKnight, Robert K., and Adalbert Obak

1964 Yam cultivation in the Palau District. In *Yam Cultivation in the Trust Territory,* edited by John deYoung. Anthropological Working Papers no. 4, pp. 14–37. Guam: Office of the Staff Anthropologist, Trust Territory of the Pacific Islands.

McKnight, Robert K., Adalbert Obak, and M. Emesiochl

1960 Breadfruit cultivation practices and beliefs in Palau. Anthropological Working Papers no. 7. Guam: Office of the Staff Anthropologist, Trust Territory of the Pacific Islands. Reprinted 1964 in *Breadfruit Cultivation Practices and Beliefs in the Trust Territory of the Pacific Islands,* edited by John deYoung, pp. 16–41. Saipan: Trust Territory of the Pacific Islands.

McLean, Mervyn

1977 *An Annotated Bibliography of Oceanic Music and Dance.* Polynesian Society Memoir no. 41. Wellington, New Zealand: The Polynesian Society.

1981 *Supplement: An Annotated Bibliography of Oceanic Music and Dance.* Auckland, New Zealand: The Polynesian Society.

McMakin, Patrick D.

1975 The suruhanos: Traditional curers on the island of Guam. Master's thesis, University of Guam.

1978 The suruhanos: Traditional curers on the island of Guam. *Micronesica* 14 (1): 13–68.

McMakin, Patrick D., and Philip H. Moore

1977 *A Guide to the Medicinal Plants of Guam.* Agaña, Guam: Coastal Management Section, Bureau of Planning.

Mead, Margaret

1928 *Coming of Age in Samoa: A Psychological Study of Primitive Youth for Western Civilization.* New York: W. Morrow & Co.

1935 *Sex and Temperament in Three Primitive Societies.* New York: W. Morrow & Co.

1972   Changing styles of anthropological work. *Annual Review of Anthropology* 2:1–26.
1979   Anthropological contributions to national policies during and immediately after World War II. In *The Uses of Anthropology,* edited by Walter Goldschmidt. American Anthropological Association Special Publication no. 11, pp. 145–157. Washington, D.C.: American Anthropological Association.

Meller, Norman
1965   Political change in the Pacific. *Asian Survey* 5 (5): 245–254.
1967   Districting a new legislature in Micronesia. *Asian Survey* 7 (7): 457–468.
1969   *The Congress of Micronesia.* Honolulu: University of Hawai'i Press.
1970   Indigenous leadership in the Trust Territory of the Pacific Islands. In *Development Administration in Asia,* edited by Edward Weidner, pp. 309–335. Durham, N. C.: Duke University Press.
1985   *Constitutionalism in Micronesia.* Lā'ie, Hawai'i: Institute for Polynesian Studies, Brigham Young University, Hawai'i Campus.

Merrill, Elmer D.
1943   Emergency food plants and poisonous plants of the islands of the Pacific. War Department Technical Manual 10–420. Washington, D.C.: US Government Printing Office.

Michal, Edward J.
1993   Protected states: The political status of the Federated States of Micronesia and the Republic of the Marshall Islands. *The Contemporary Pacific* 5 (2): 303–332.

Micronesian Reporter
1956   Palau Museum celebrates first birthday. *Micronesian Reporter* 4 (3): 12–14.
1958   The story about love sticks. *Micronesian Reporter* 6 (2): 7.
1959   The first Palau art show. *Micronesian Reporter* 7 (5): 18–19.
1960   Trust Territory economic fair. *Micronesian Reporter* 8 (6): 1–4.

Micronesian Seminar
1995   *Micronesian Seminar Voices of Pohnpei, II.* Kolonia, Pohnpei, FSM: Micronesian Seminar.

Miller, Edward
1991   *War Plan Orange.* Annapolis, Md.: US Naval Institute Press.

Millis, Walter
1989   *The Martial Spirit.* Chicago: Elephant. First published 1931.

Mitchell, Roger E.
1975   The Palauan storyboard: The evolution of a folk art style. *Midwestern Journal of Language and Folklore* 1 (2): 41–51.

Miura, Momoshige, and Masashi Murakami
1967   Psychiatric research in Micronesia. *Psychologica* 19 (3–4): 159–165.

Modell, Judith S.

1994 *Kinship with Strangers: Adoption and Interpretations of Kinship in American Culture.* Berkeley: University of California Press.

Monmaney, Terence

1990 This obscure malady. *The New Yorker* October 29: 85–113.

Montvel-Cohen, Marvin

1970a *Notes on Micronesian Art: A Working Paper in Conjunction with the First Micronesian Art Exhibition at the University of Guam, April 1969.* Micronesian Working Papers no. 1. Agaña: Gallery of Art, University of Guam.

1970b *Canoes in Micronesia.* Micronesian Working Papers no. 2. Agaña: Gallery of Art, University of Guam.

1982 Craft and context on Yap (Caroline Islands). PhD dissertation, Southern Illinois University, Carbondale.

1988 Micronesian artifacts exhibited. *Guam & Micronesia Glimpses* 28 (1): 30–31.

Moore, Anne

1974 Those who cure. *Glimpses of Guam* 14:157–160.

Moore, John H.

1988 The dialects of Cheyenne kinship: Variability and change. *Ethnology* 27 (3): 253–269.

Moran, Emilio F.

1979 *Human Adaptability: An Introduction to Ecological Anthropology.* North Scituate, Mass.: Duxbury Press.

Morei, Elicita

1992 Belau, Be Brave. In *Te Rau Maire: Poems and Stories of the Pacific,* edited by Marjorie T. Crocombe, Ron Crocombe, Kauraka Kauraka, and Makiuti Tongia, p. 4. Rarotonga, Cook Islands: Tauranga Vananga (Ministry of Cultural Development); Suva: The Institute of Pacific Studies and the South Pacific Creative Arts Society; Wellington: The Cook Islands Studies, University of Victoria; and Auckland: The Centre for Pacific Studies, University of Auckland.

Morgan, William N.

1988 *Prehistoric Architecture in Micronesia.* Austin: University of Texas Press.

Morsy, Soheir

1990 Political economy in medical anthropology. In *Medical Anthropology: A Handbook of Theory and Method,* edited by Thomas M. Johnson and Carolyn F. Sargent, pp. 26–46. New York: Greenwood Press.

Morton, Newton E.

1973 Population structure of Micronesia. In *Methods and Theories of Anthropological Genetics,* edited by Michael H. Crawford and Peter L. Workman, pp. 333–366. Albuquerque: University of New Mexico Press.

Mulford, Judith H.

1980 Lava lavas of the Western Caroline Islands. Master's thesis, California State University, Northridge.

1991 *Decorative Marshallese Baskets.* Los Angeles: Wonder Publications.

Müller, Wilhelm

1917 Yap. Vol. II, B, 2, *Ergebnisse der Südsee-Expedition, 1908–1910,* edited by Georg Thilenius. Hamburg: Friederichsen, de Gruyter.

Mumford, Edward Philpot, and John Luther Mohr

1943 Background to post-war reconstruction. Pt. 1. Preliminary report on parasitic and other infectious diseases of the Japanese Mandated Islands and Guam. *American Journal of Tropical Medicine* 23:381–400.

Muñoz, Faye Untalan

1979 An exploratory study of island migration: Chamorros of Guam. PhD dissertation, University of California, Los Angeles.

Murai, Mary

1954 Nutrition study in Micronesia. *Atoll Research Bulletin* no. 27. Washington D.C.: The Smithsonian Institution.

Murai, Mary, Florence Pen, and Carey P. Miller

1958 *Some Tropical South Pacific Island Foods: Description, History, Use, Composition, and Nutritive Value.* Honolulu: University of Hawai'i Press. Reprinted 1970. Honolulu: University of Hawai'i Press.

Murdock, George Peter

1948a How shall we administer our Pacific Trust Territory? Address to the Society for Applied Anthropology, May. Copy on file in the Hawaiian and Pacific Collection, Hamilton Library, University of Hawai'i, Mānoa.

1948b New light on the peoples of Micronesia. *Science* 108 (2808): 423–425.

1948c Anthropology in Micronesia. *Transactions of the New York Academy of Sciences* 11 (1): 9–16. Reprinted 1965. In *Culture and Society, Twenty-Four Essays,* by George P. Murdock, pp. 237–248. Pittsburgh, Pa.: University of Pittsburgh Press.

1949 *Social Structure.* New York: Macmillan Co.

1951 Foreword. In *Property, Kin, and Community on Truk,* by Ward H. Goodenough. Yale University Publications in Anthropology no. 46, pp. 5–8. New Haven, Conn.: Department of Anthropology, Yale University.

1957 World ethnographic sample. *American Anthropologist* 59 (4): 664–687.

1965 See 1948c.

1967 *Ethnographic Atlas: A Summary.* Pittsburgh, Pa.: University of Pittsburgh Press.

1981 *Atlas of World Cultures.* Pittsburgh, Pa.: University of Pittsburgh Press.

Murdock, George Peter, Clellan S. Ford, Alfred E. Hudson, Raymond Kennedy, Leo W. Simmons, and John W. M. Whiting

1938 *Outline of Cultural Materials.* New Haven, Conn.: Cross-Cultural Survey, Institute of Human Relations, Yale University.

Murdock, George Peter, and Douglas R. White

1969   Standard cross-cultural sample. *Ethnology* 8 (4): 329–369.

Murphy, Raymond E.

1948   Landownership on a Micronesian atoll. *The Geographical Review* 38 (4): 598–614.

1949   'High' and 'low' islands in the Eastern Carolines. *The Geographical Review* 39 (3): 425–439.

1950   The economic geography of a Micronesian atoll. *Annals of the Association of American Geographers,* 40 (1): 58–83.

Murphy, Robert F.

1967   Culture change. In *Biennial Review of Anthropology 1967,* edited by Bernard J. Siegel and Alan R. Beals, pp. 1–45. Stanford, Ca.: Stanford University Press.

Nakamura, Motoe

1977   House and family in Pulusuk Island, Micronesia. *Bulletin of the National Museum of Ethnology* 2–3:565–589.

Nakayama, Masao, and Frederick L. Ramp

1974   Micronesian Navigation, Island Empires and Traditional Concepts of Ownership of the Sea. Saipan: Congress of Micronesia. Copy on file in the Federated States of Micronesia Congressional Library, Palikir, Pohnpei, FSM.

Nason, James D.

1967   Ecological aspects of cultural stability and culture change in Micronesia. Master's thesis, University of Washington.

1970   Clan and copra: Modernization on Etal Island, Eastern Caroline Islands. PhD dissertation, University of Washington.

1974   Political change: An outer island perspective. In *Political Development in Micronesia,* edited by Daniel T. Hughes and Sherwood G. Lingenfelter, pp. 119–142. Columbus: Ohio State University Press.

1975   The strength of the land: Community perception of population on Etal. In *Pacific Atoll Populations,* edited by Vern Carroll. Asao Monograph no. 3, pp. 117–159. Honolulu: The University Press of Hawai'i.

1984   Tourism, handicrafts, and ethnic identity in Micronesia. *Annals of Tourism Research* 11 (3): 421–449.

Nathan Associates, Inc., Robert R.

1966   *Economic Development for Micronesia,* pt. 1. Washington, D.C.: Robert R. Nathan Associates, Inc.

Neas, Maynard

1961   Land ownership patterns in the Marshall Islands. In *Land Tenure in the Pacific: A Symposium of the 10th Pacific Science Congress. Atoll Research Bulletin* no. 85:17–23. Washington, D.C.: The Smithsonian Institution.

Neisser, Ulric

1976   *Cognition and Reality.* San Francisco, Ca.: W. H. Freeman.

Nelson, Ginny Guzman (ed.)

1994   *Island Art at the Guam Hilton.* Agaña, Guam: Guam Hilton.

Nero, Karen L.

1987   *A Cherecher a Lokelii:* Beads of history of Koror, Palau, 1783–1983. PhD dissertation, University of California, Berkeley.

1989   Time of famine, time of transformation: Hell in the Pacific, Palau. In *The Pacific Theater: Island Representations of World War II,* edited by Geoffrey M. White and Lamont Lindstrom. Pacific Islands Monograph Series no. 8, pp. 117–147. Honolulu: University of Hawai'i Press.

1990   The hidden pain: Drunkenness and domestic violence in Palau. *Pacific Studies* 13 (3): 63–92.

1992a The breadfruit tree story: Mythological transformations in Palauan politics. *Pacific Studies* 15 (4): 235–260.

1992b (ed.) *The Arts and Politics.* Special issue of *Pacific Studies* 15 (4).

1992c Introduction: Challenging communications in the contemporary Pacific. *Pacific Studies* 15 (4): 1–12.

1992d Cross-cultural performances: A Palauan hoax? *ISLA: A Journal of Micronesian Studies* 1 (1): 37–72.

Nero, Karen L., and Nelson H. Graburn

1981   The institutional context of the art of Oceania with special reference to Micronesia. *Kroeber Anthropological Society Papers* 57–58:147–159.

Netting, Robert McC.

1974   Agrarian ecology. *Annual Review of Anthropology* 3:21–56.

1986   *Cultural Ecology.* 2d ed. Prospect Heights, Ill.: Waveland Press, Inc.

Nevin, David

1977   *The American Touch in Micronesia.* New York: W. W. Norton & Company.

Niering, William A.

1956   Bioecology of Kapingamarangi Atoll, Eastern Caroline Islands: Terrestrial aspects. *Atoll Research Bulletin* no. 49. Washington, D.C.: The Smithsonian Institution.

Nuckolls, Charles W.

1993a An introduction to the cross-cultural study of sibling relations. In *Siblings in South Asia,* edited by Charles W. Nuckolls, pp. 19–41. New York: The Guilford Press.

1993b (ed.) *Siblings in South Asia.* New York: The Guilford Press.

1996   Spiro and Lutz on Ifaluk: Toward a synthesis of cultural cognition and depth psychology. *Ethos* 24:695–717.

Nurge, Ethel

1978   Anthropological perspective for medical students. In *Health and the Human Condition: Perspectives on Medical Anthropology,* edited by Michael H. Logan and Edward E. Hunt, Jr., pp. 388–400. North Scituate, Mass.: Duxbury Press.

Obak, Adalbert, and Robert K. McKnight
1964 The Palauan kite. _Micronesian Reporter_ 12 (7): 10–14.
1966 _Palauan Proverbs._ Micronesian Research Working Paper no. 2. Saipan: Publications Office, Trust Territory of the Pacific Islands.
1969 Kadam, the Palauan kite. _Lore_ 19 (2): 49–57.

Obeyesekere, Gananath
1990 _The Work of Culture: Symbolic Transformation in Psychoanalysis and Anthropology._ Chicago: University of Chicago Press.

O'Connor, Carol
1989 Woodcarver Jose Aguon. _Guam & Micronesia Glimpses_ 29 (3): 21–23.

Odum, Howard T.
1971 _Environment, Power, and Society._ New York: Wiley.

Ogan, Eugene
1996 The (re)making of modern New Guinea. _Reviews in Anthropology_ 25 (2): 95–106.

Olesen, Virginia L.
1978 Convergences and divergences: Anthropology and sociology in health care. In _Health and the Human Condition: Perspectives on Medical Anthropology,_ edited by Michael H. Logan and Edward E. Hunt, Jr., pp. 11–17. North Scituate, Mass.: Duxbury Press.

Oliver, Douglas L.
1951 _Planning Micronesia's Future: A Summary of the United States Commercial Company's Economic Survey of Micronesia, 1946._ Cambridge, Mass.: Harvard University Press. Reprinted 1971. Honolulu: University of Hawai'i Press.
1955 _A Solomon Island Society: Kinship and Leadership Among the Siuai of Bougainville._ Cambridge, Mass.: Harvard University Press.
1961 _The Pacific Islands._ Rev. ed. Honolulu: The University Press of Hawai'i.
1971 See 1951.

Olsen, Dennis F.
1976 Piercing Micronesia's colonial veil: Enewetak v. Laird and Saipan v. Department of Interior. _Columbia Journal of Transnational Law_ 15 (3): 473–495.

Oneisom, Innocente
1994 The changing family in Chuuk. _Micronesian Counselor,_ Occasional Papers no. 14. Kolonia, Pohnpei, FSM: Micronesian Seminar.

Opie, Ellen
1991 Parenting difficulties in the Republic of the Marshall Islands: Towards the prevention of child maltreatment. San Francisco: Department of Health and Human Services, Public Health Service, Region IX. Copy on file in the Micronesian Seminar Library, Kolonia, Pohnpei, FSM.

Orlove, Benjamin S.

1980   Ecological anthropology. *Annual Review of Anthropology* 9:235–273.

Ortner, Sherry B.

1974   On 'key symbols.' *American Anthropologist* 75 (5): 1338–1346.

Osborne, Douglas

1966   *The Archaeology of the Palau Islands.* Bernice P. Bishop Museum Bulletin no. 230. Honolulu: Bishop Museum Press.

Otten, Charlotte M. (ed.)

1971   *Anthropology and Art: Readings in Cross-Cultural Aesthetics.* New York: Holt, Rinehart & Winston.

Owen, Hera Ware

1972   The art of Charlie Gibbons. *Micronesian Reporter* 20 (3): 24–27.

1974   A museum in Micronesia. *South Pacific Bulletin* 24 (1): 19–22.

1978   Palau Museum guide to the museum buildings, the cultural objects there contained, and supplemental information. Koror: Palau Museum.

Pacific Islands Yearbook

1950   *Pacific Islands Yearbook,* edited and compiled by R. W. Robson. 6th ed. Sydney: Pacific Publications.

Packard, Vance O.

1957   *The Hidden Persuaders.* New York: D. McKay Co.

1959   *The Status Seekers: An Exploration of Class Behavior in America and the Hidden Barriers that Affect You, Your Community, Your Future.* New York: D. McKay Co.

Palafox, Neal A.

1991   Malnutrition in the Republic of the Marshall Islands. Manuscript. Copy on file in RFK Memorial Library, University of Guam.

Palau Community Action Agency

1976–1978   *Palau Community History of Palau.* Vols. 1–3. Koror: Palau Community Action Agency.

Palau Museum

1973   Tie-Beam stories: Brief explanations from Palau Museum Bai, *Bai ra Ngesechel ar Cherchar,* Traditional Men's Meeting House. Koror: Palau Museum Publications.

1976   Today's art in Palau: The October 1976 exhibition: Drawing, painting, pottery, sculpture, weaving by artists residing in Palau. Koror: Palau Museum.

Parker, Patricia Lee

1985   Land tenure in Trukese society, 1850–1980. PhD dissertation, University of Pennsylvania.

Parmentier, Richard J.

1981　The sacred remains: An historical ethnography of Ngeremlengui, Palau. PhD dissertation, University of Chicago.

1984　House affiliation systems in Belau. *American Ethnologist* 11 (4): 656–676.

1987　*The Sacred Remains: Myth, History and Polity in Belau.* Chicago: University of Chicago Press.

Partridge, William L., and Elizabeth M. Eddy

1978　The development of applied anthropology in America. In *Applied Anthropology in America,* edited by Elizabeth M. Eddy and William L. Partridge, pp. 3–45. New York: Columbia University Press.

Paul, Benjamin

1963　Anthropological perspectives on medicine and public health. *Annals of the American Academy of Political and Social Science* 346:34–43.

Peacock, Karen

1993　Dick and Jane meet Emi and Tamag: Culture and the classroom. Paper read at the American Anthropology and Micronesia Conference, October 20–23, Honolulu, Hawai'i. Copy on file in the Hawaiian and Pacific Collection, University of Hawai'i, Mānoa.

Peattie, Mark R.

1988　*Nan'yo: The Rise and Fall of the Japanese in Micronesia, 1885–1945.* Pacific Islands Monograph Series no. 4. Honolulu: University of Hawai'i Press.

Peck, William M.

1968　Critique of PHS proposal for their administration of Trust Territory Health Services. Manuscript. Copy on file in the Hawaiian and Pacific Collection, University of Hawai'i, Mānoa.

1982　*I Speak the Beginning: An Anthology of Surviving Poetry of the Northern Mariana Islands.* Saipan: Commonwealth Council for Arts and Culture.

Peel, John D. Y.

1993　Review essay of *Clio in Oceania: Toward a Historical Anthropology and Culture Through Time: Anthropological Approaches,* Aletta Biersack (ed.). *History and Theory* 32 (1): 162–178.

Peletz, Michael G.

1995　Kinship studies in late twentieth-century anthropology. *Annual Review of Anthropology* 24:343–372.

Peoples, James

1977　Deculturation and dependence in a Micronesian community. PhD dissertation, University of California, Davis.

1985   *Island in Trust: Culture Change and Dependence in a Micronesian Economy.* Boulder, Colo.: Westview Press.

1992   Political evolution in Micronesia. *Ethnology* 32 (1): 1–17.

Peoples, James, and Garrick Bailey

1988   Humanity: An Introduction to Cultural Anthropology. St. Paul, Minn.: West Publishing Co.

Petersen, Glenn

1971   American anthropology and the colonial experience in Micronesia. Manuscript. Copy in author's personal files.

1977   Ponapean agriculture and economy: Politics, prestige and problems of commercialization in the Eastern Caroline Islands. PhD dissertation, Columbia University.

1979   External politics, internal economics and Ponapean social formation. *American Ethnologist* 6 (1): 25–40.

1982a Ponapean matriliny: Production, exchange, and the ties that bind. *American Ethnologist* 9 (1): 129–144.

1982b *One Man Cannot Rule a Thousand: Fission in a Ponapean Chiefdom.* Ann Arbor: University of Michigan Press.

1984   The Ponapean culture of resistance. *Radical History Review* 28–30:347–366.

1985   A cultural analysis of the Ponapean vote for independence in the 1983 plebiscite. *Pacific Studies* 9 (1): 83–96.

1986a Redistribution in a Micronesian commercial economy. *Oceania* 57 (2): 83–98.

1986b Decentralisation and Micronesian federalism. *South Pacific Forum Working Papers* no. 5. Suva, Fiji: University of the South Pacific.

1989   Pohnpei ethnicity and Micronesian nation-building. In *Ethnicity and Nation-Building in the Pacific,* edited by Michael Howard, pp. 285–308. Tokyo: The United Nations University.

1990a *Lost in the Weeds: Theme and Variation in Pohnpei Political Mythology.* Occasional Paper no. 25. Honolulu: Center for Pacific Islands Studies, University of Hawai'i.

1990b The small-republic argument in Micronesia. *Philosophical Forum* 21:393–411.

1990c Some overlooked complexities in the study of Pohnpei social complexity. In *Recent Advances in Micronesian Archaeology,* edited by Rosalind L. Hunter-Anderson. *Micronesica* Supplement no. 2:137–151.

1992a Off-the-shelf tradition. In *Pacific History,* edited by Donald H. Rubinstein, pp. 201–211. Mangilao: University of Guam Press.

1992b Dancing defiance: The politics of Pohnpeian dance performances. *Pacific Studies* 15 (4): 13–28.

1992c Some Pohnpei strategies for economic survival. In *Contemporary Pacific Societies: Studies in Development and Change,* edited by Victoria S. Lockwood, Thomas G. Harding, and Ben J. Wallace, pp. 185–196. Englewood Cliffs, N. J.: Prentice-Hall.

1993a *Kanengamah* and Pohnpei's politics of concealment. *American Anthropologist* 95 (2): 334–352.

1993b On cross-cutting and contradictory hierarchies. Paper read at the 13th International Congress of Anthropological and Ethnological Sciences, July 29–August 5, Mexico City, Mexico.

1993c Ethnicity and interests at the 1990 Federated States of Micronesia constitutional convention. In *Regime Change and Regime Maintenance in Asia and the Pacific*. Discussion Paper no. 12, pp. 1–74. Canberra: Department of Political and Social Change, The Australian National University.

1994 The Federated States of Micronesia's 1990 Constitutional Convention: Calm before the storm? *The Contemporary Pacific* 6 (2): 337–369.

n.d. Chieftainship and the evolution of power: A Micronesian case. Manuscript. Copy in the personal files of William H. Alkire.

Petrosian-Husa, Carmen

1994 Lavalava: Eine ethnologische Übersicht der Technologie des Webens bei den *rei metau* auf den Outer Islands von Yap in Mikronesien. Dissertation zur Erlangen des Doktorgrades der Philosophie an der Grand- und Integrativwissenschaftlichen fakultät der Universität Wien.

Phillips, Leslie, and Juris Draguns

1969 Some issues in intercultural research on psychopathology. In *Mental Health Research in Asia and the Pacific,* edited by William Caudill and Tsung-yi Lin, pp. 21–32. Honolulu: East-West Center Press.

Piddington, Ralph

1950 *An Introduction to Social Anthropology.* New York: Frederick A. Praeger.

1958 Review of *Anthropology in Administration* by Homer Barnett. *Journal of the Polynesian Society* 67 (4): 427–429.

Pinsker, Eve C.

1992 Celebrations of government: Dance performance and legitimacy in the Federated States of Micronesia. *Pacific Studies* 15 (4): 29–56.

1997 Point of order, point of change: Nation, culture, and community in the Federated States of Micronesia. PhD dissertation, University of Chicago.

Pirie, Peter

1972 The effects of treponematosis and gonorrhea on the populations of the Pacific Islands. *Human Biology in Oceania* 1:187–206.

Pitt-Rivers, George H.

1927 *The Clash of Culture and the Contact of Races: Depopulation of the Pacific and the Government of Subject Races.* London: G. Routledge.

Pobutsky, Ann Marie G.

1982 Suruhanas: A profile of traditional women healers in the village of Umatac, Guam. In *Umatac by the Sea: A Village in Transition,* edited by Rebecca A. Stephenson and Hiro Kurashina, pp. 18–28. Mangilao, Guam: Micronesian Area Research Center.

1983   Suruhanas: Women herbalists of Guam. Senior thesis report, University of Guam. Copy on file in RFK Memorial Library, University of Guam.

Poehlman, Joanne
1979   Culture change and identity among Chamorro women of Guam. PhD dissertation, University of Minnesota.

Pollock, Nancy J.
1970   Breadfruit and breadwinning on Namu Atoll, Marshall Islands. PhD dissertation, University of Hawai'i.
1973   Breadfruit or rice: Dietary choice on a Micronesian atoll. *Ecology of Food and Nutrition* 2 (1): 1–9.
1974   Land tenure and land usage on Namu Atoll. In *Land Tenure in Oceania,* edited by Henry P. Lundsgaarde. Asao Monograph no. 2, pp. 100–129. Honolulu: University Press of Hawai'i.
1975   The risks of dietary change: A Pacific atoll example. In *Maritime Adaptations of the Pacific,* edited by Richard W. Casteel and George I. Quimby. World Anthropology Series, pp. 255–264. The Hague: Mouton.
1986   Food habits in Guam over 500 years. *Pacific Viewpoint* 27 (2): 120–143.
1992   *These Roots Remain: Food Habits in Islands of the Central and Eastern Pacific since Western Contact.* Lā'ie, Hawai'i: The Institute for Polynesian Studies, Brigham Young University, Hawai'i Campus.

Pollock, Nancy J., Jean M. Laloulel, and Newton E. Morton
1972   Kinship and inbreeding on Namu Atoll (Marshall Islands). *Human Biology* 44 (3): 459–474.

Pomponio, Alice
1992   *Seagulls Don't Fly into the Bush: Cultural Identity and Development in Melanesia.* Belmont, Ca.: Wadsworth Publishing Co.

Poort, W. A.
1975   *The Dance in the Pacific: A Comparative and Critical Survey of Dancing in Polynesia, Micronesia and Indonesia.* Katwijk, Netherlands: Van der Lee Press.

Powdermaker, Hortense
1933   *Life in Lesu: The Study of a Melanesian Society in New Ireland.* London: Williams & Norgate.

Poyer, Lin
1983   The Ngatik massacre: History and identity on a Micronesia atoll. PhD dissertation, University of Michigan.
1984   The Ngatik massacre: Documentary and oral traditional accounts. *Journal of Pacific History,* 20 (1): 4–22.
1988a Maintaining "otherness": Sapwuahfik cultural identity. *American Ethnologist* 15 (3): 472–485.

1988b History, identity, and Christian evangelism: The Sapwuahfik massacre. *Ethnohistory* 35 (3): 209–233.

1989 Echoes of massacre: Recollections of World War II on Sapwuahfik (Ngatik Atoll). In *The Pacific Theater: Island Representations of World War II,* edited by Geoffrey M. White and Lamont Lindstrom. Pacific Islands Monograph Series no. 8, pp. 97–115. Honolulu: University of Hawaiʻi Press.

1990 Being Sapwuahfik: Cultural and ethnic identity in a Micronesian society. In *Cultural Identity and Ethnicity in the Pacific,* edited by Jocelyn Linnekin and Lin Poyer, pp. 127–147. Honolulu: University of Hawaiʻi Press.

1991 Maintaining egalitarianism: Social equality on a Micronesian atoll. In *Between Bands and States,* edited by Susan A. Gregg. Occasional Paper no. 9, pp. 359–375. Carbondale, Ill.: Center for Archaeological Investigations, Southern Illinois University, Carbondale.

1992 Defining history across cultures: Islander and outsider contrasts. *ISLA: A Journal of Micronesian Studies* 1 (1): 73–89.

1993 *The Ngatik Massacre: History and Identity on a Micronesian Atoll.* Washington, D.C.: Smithsonian Institution Press.

Pratt, Fletcher

1948 *The Marines' War: An Account of the Struggle for the Pacific From Both American and Japanese Accounts.* New York: William Sloane & Associates, Inc.

Pratt, Mary Louise

1992 *Imperial Eyes: Travel Writing and Transculturation.* London: Routledge.

Price, Christine

1979 *Made in the South Pacific: Arts of the Sea People.* London: The Bodley Head.

Price, Samuel T.

1975 The transformation of Yap: Causes and consequences of socio-economic change in Micronesia. PhD dissertation, Washington State University.

Pugh, Judy F.

1993 Brothers' lives: Kinship and ethnopsychology in North India. In *Siblings in South Asia,* edited by Charles W. Nuckolls, pp. 219–234. New York: The Guilford Press.

Pulsford, Robert L., and John Cawte

1972 *Health in a Developing Country: Principles of Medical Anthropology in Melanesia.* Milton, Queensland: Jacaranda Press.

Quig, Agnes

1987 History of the Pacific Islands Studies Program at the University of Hawaii, 1950–1986. Honolulu: Working Paper Series, Pacific Islands Studies Program, University of Hawaii.

Radcliffe-Brown, A. R.

1952 *Structure and Function in Primitive Society: Essays and Addresses.* London: Cohen and West.

Rainbird, Paul
1994   Prehistory in the northwest tropical Pacific: The Caroline, Mariana, and Marshall Islands. *Journal of World Prehistory* 8 (3): 293–349.

Ramarui, David
1976   Education in Micronesia: Its past, present, and future. *Micronesian Reporter* 24 (1): 9–20.
1980   *The Palauan Arts.* Palau: Omnibus Program for Social Studies and Cultural Heritage.

Ramarui, Hermana
1984   *Palauan Perspectives: A Poetry Book.* Koror. Copy in the Hawaiian and Pacific Collection, Hamilton Library, University of Hawai'i, Mānoa.

Ramon, Derson
1975   A photo album of the Palau Museum. *Micronesian Reporter* 23 (3): 21–26.

Ranney, Austin, and Howard R. Penniman
1985   *Democracy in the Islands: The Micronesian Plebiscites of 1983.* Washington, D.C.: American Enterprise Institute for Public Policy Research.

Rappaport, Roy A.
1968   *Pigs for the Ancestors: Ritual in the Ecology of a New Guinea People.* New Haven, Conn.: Yale University Press.
1971   The flow of energy in an agricultural society. *Scientific American* 225 (3): 116–132.

Raulet, Harry M.
1959   A note on Fischer's residence typology. *American Anthropologist* 61 (1): 108–112.

Reafsnyder, Charles B.
1984   Emergent ethnic identity in an urban migrant community in Truk State, Federated States of Micronesia. PhD dissertation, Indiana University.

Redfield, Robert, Ralph Linton, and Melville J. Herskovits
1936   Memorandum for the study of acculturation. *American Anthropologist* 38 (1): 149–152.

Rehg, Kenneth L.
1995   The significance of linguistic interaction spheres in reconstructing Micronesian prehistory. *Oceanic Linguistics* 34 (2): 305–326.

Rehuher, Faustina K. (ed.)
1980   *Belau Art Exhibition.* Koror: Palau Museum.
1993   *Bai. Imuul 1.* Koror: Belau National Museum.

Reinman, Fred M.
1965   Maritime adaptation: An aspect of oceanic economy. PhD dissertation, University of California, Los Angeles.
1967   *Fishing: An Aspect of Oceanic Economy. An Archaeological Approach.* Fieldiana: Anthropology, vol. 54 (2): 95–208. Chicago: Field Museum of Natural History.

Richard, Dorothy E.

1957a *US Naval Administration of the Trust Territory of the Pacific Islands,* vol. 1, *The War-time Military Government Period 1942–1945.* Washington, D.C.: Office of the Chief of Naval Operations.

1957b *US Naval Administration of the Trust Territory of the Pacific Islands,* vol. 2, *The Post-war Military Government Era 1945–1947.* Washington, D.C.: Office of the Chief of Naval Operations.

1957c *US Naval Administration of the Trust Territory of the Pacific Islands,* vol. 3, *The Trusteeship Period 1947–1951.* Washington, D.C.: Office of the Chief of Naval Operations.

Richards, Audrey I.

1950 Some types of family structure amongst the Central Bantu. In *African Systems of Kinship and Marriage,* edited by A. R. Radcliffe-Brown and Daryll Forde, pp. 207–251. London: Oxford University Press.

Riesenberg, Saul H.

1948 Magic and medicine in Ponape. *Southwestern Journal of Anthropology* 4 (4): 406–429.

1950 The cultural position of Ponape in Oceania. PhD dissertation, University of California, Berkeley.

1968 *The Native Polity of Ponape.* Smithsonian Contributions to Anthropology, vol. 10. Washington, D.C.: Smithsonian Institution Press.

1972 The organization of navigational knowledge on Puluwat. *Journal of the Polynesian Society* 81 (1): 19–56.

Riesenberg, Saul H., and A. H. Gayton

1952 Caroline Island belt weaving. *Southwestern Journal of Anthropology* 8 (3): 342–375.

Riesman, David

1950 *The Lonely Crowd: A Study of the Changing American Character.* New Haven, Conn.: Yale University Press.

Ritter, Philip L.

1978 The repopulation of Kosrae: Population and social organization on a Micronesian high island. PhD dissertation, Stanford University.

1978–1979 Kosraen circulation, out-marriage, and migration. *Anthropological Forum* 4 (3 & 4): 352–374.

1980 Social organization, incest, and fertility in a Kosraean village. *American Ethnologist* 7 (4): 759–773.

1981 Adoption on Kosrae Island: Solidarity and sterility. *Ethnology* 20 (1): 45–61.

Ritzenthaler, Robert E.

1949 *Native Money of Palau.* CIMA Report no. 27. Washington, D.C.: Pacific Science Board, National Research Council. Published 1954. Publications in Anthropology no. 1. Milwaukee, Wisc.: Milwaukee Public Museum.

1954 See 1949.

Rivers, William H. R.

1924   *Medicine, Magic, and Religion.* The Fitz Patrick Lectures delivered before the Royal College of Physicians of London in 1915 and 1916. London: Kegan Paul, Trench, Trubner & Co.

RMI, Republic of the Marshall Islands

1984   *Five-Year Comprehensive Health Plan 1983–1988.* Saipan and Majuro: Trust Territory Health Planning and Development Agency, and the Republic of the Marshall Islands Office of Health Planning.

1989   Statement of the Honorable Oscar de Brum, Chief Secretary, Government of the Republic of the Marshall Islands. Submitted to the United States House of Representatives, Committee on Appropriations, Subcommittee on Interior and Related Agencies, in respect to the fiscal year 1990 budget. April 20.

1990   Situation analysis of the Marshallese child. Technical Report, Supplement to the National Population Policy Document. Majuro, Marshall Islands: Republic of the Marshall Islands Office of Planning and Statistics.

1991   National nutrition survey: *Ij yokwe mour e ao.* Technical Report. Majuro, Marshall Islands: Ministry of Health Services, Republic of the Marshall Islands.

Robbins, Robert

1969   Political future of Micronesia and the timing of self-determination. In *Political Modernization of Micronesia, A Symposium.* Santa Cruz, Ca.: Center for South Pacific Studies, University of California, Santa Cruz. n.p.

Robillard, Albert B.

1987   Mental health services in Micronesia: A history. In *Contemporary Issues in Mental Health Research in the Pacific Islands,* edited by Albert B. Robillard and Anthony J. Marsella, pp. 215–244. Honolulu: Social Science Research Institute, University of Hawai‘i.

Robinson, David

1983   The decorative motifs of Palauan clubhouses. In *Art and Artists of Oceania,* edited by Sidney M. Mead and Bernie Kernot, pp. 162–178. Palmerston North, New Zealand: The Dunmore Press.

Rodgers-Johnson, Pamela, Ralph M. Garruto, Richard Yanagihara, Kwang-Ming Chen, D. Carleton Gajdusek, and Clarence J. Gibbs, Jr.

1986   Amyotrophic lateral sclerosis and parkinsonism-dementia on Guam: A 30-year evaluation of clinical and neuropathologic trends. *Neurology* 36:7–13.

Romanucci-Ross, Lola, Daniel E. Moerman, and Laurence R. Tancredi (eds.)

1991   *The Anthropology of Medicine: From Culture to Method.* 2d ed. New York: Bergin & Garvey.

Roscoe, Paul B.

1994   Amity and aggression: A symbolic theory of incest. *Man* 29 (1): 49–76.

1995 The perils of 'positivism' in cultural anthropology. *American Anthropologist* 97 (3): 492–504.

Rose, Steven
1983 And zebra stripes and chocolate bars. *The New York Times Book Review,* May 8: 3, 22.

Rosman, Abraham, and Paula G. Rubel
1981 *The Tapestry of Culture: An Introduction to Cultural Anthropology.* Glenview, Ill.: Scott, Foresman.
1989 *The Tapestry of Culture: An Introduction to Cultural Anthropology.* 3d ed. New York: Random House.

Rossman, David L.
1978 Increased fertility among amyotrophic lateral sclerosis and parkinsonism-dementia complex cases on the island of Guam. PhD dissertation, University of Michigan.

Rubel, Arthur J., and Michael R. Hass
1990 Ethnomedicine. In *Medical Anthropology: A Handbook of Theory and Method,* edited by Thomas M. Johnson and Carolyn F. Sargent, pp. 115–131. New York: Greenwood Press.

Rubin, William (ed.)
1984 *'Primitivism' in 20th Century Art: Affinity of the Tribal and Modern.* New York: Museum of Modern Art.

Rubinstein, Donald H.
1978 Adoption on Fais Island: An ethnography of childhood. Paper read at the 77th Annual Meeting of the American Anthropological Association, November 14–18, Los Angeles, California.
1979 An ethnography of Micronesian childhood: Contexts of socialization of Fais Island. PhD dissertation, Stanford University.
1980a Suicide in Micronesia: Transactions in anger and guilt. Paper read at the 79th Annual Meeting of the American Anthropological Association, December 3–7, Washington, D.C.
1980b Social Aspects of Juvenile Delinquency in Micronesia: Conference Report for the Micronesian Seminar and Justice Improvement Commission. Mangilao, Guam: Micronesian Area Research Center, University of Guam.
1981 Micronesian suicides: Anomic or epidemic? Colloquium presentation, March 11, Department of Anthropology, University of Hawai'i, Mānoa. Copy on file in the Micronesian Seminar Library, Kolonia, Pohnpei, FSM.
1983 Epidemic suicide among Micronesian adolescents. *Social Science & Medicine* 17 (10): 657–665.
1984 Self-righteous anger, soft talk, and *amwúnúmwún* suicides of young men: The ambivalent ethos of gentleness and violence in Truk. Paper read at the 83rd Annual Meeting of the American Anthropological Association, November 15–18, Denver, Colorado. Copy on file in the Micronesian Seminar Library, Kolonia, Pohnpei, FSM.

1985 Suicide in Micronesia. In *Culture, Youth and Suicide in the Pacific: Papers from An East-West Center Conference,* edited by Francis X. Hezel, Donald H. Rubinstein, and Geoffrey M. White. Working Paper Series, pp. 88–111. Honolulu: Pacific Islands Studies Program, University of Hawai‘i.

1986 Fabric arts and traditions. In *The Art of Micronesia,* by Jerome Feldman and Donald H. Rubinstein, pp. 45–66. Honolulu: University of Hawai‘i Art Gallery.

1987 The social fabric: Micronesian textile patterns as an embodiment of social order. In *Mirror and Metaphor: Material and Social Constructions of Reality,* edited by Daniel W. Ingersoll, Jr., and Gordon Bronitsky, pp. 64–82. Lanham, Md.: University Press of America.

1992a *Power and Enchantment: Ritual Textiles from the Islands.* Catalog for an exhibit August 6–October 9, ISLA Gallery, University of Guam.

1992b Suicide in Micronesia and Samoa: A critique of explanations. *Pacific Studies* 15 (1): 51–75.

1995 In Memoriam. Saul Herbert Riesenberg (1912–1994). *ISLA: A Journal of Micronesian Studies* 3 (1): 195–197.

n.d. "And We Remain, Suffering": A wartime song from Fais Island. Copy in the personal files of Karen L. Nero.

Rubinstein, Donald H., and Michael J. Levin

1992 Micronesian migration to Guam: Social and economic characteristics. *Asian and Pacific Migration Journal* 1 (2): 350–385.

Ruddle, Kenneth, and Tomoya Akimichi (eds.)

1984 *Maritime Institutions in the Western Pacific.* Senri Ethnological Studies no. 17. Osaka: National Museum of Ethnology.

Rynkiewich, Michael A.

1972a Land tenure among Arno Marshallese. PhD dissertation, University of Minnesota.

1972b Demography and social structure on Arno Atoll. Paper read at the Conference on Pacific Atoll Populations, East-West Center Population Institute, December 27–30, Honolulu, Hawai‘i.

1974 The ossification of local politics: The impact of colonialism on a Marshall Islands atoll. In *Political Development in Micronesia,* edited by Daniel T. Hughes and Sherwood G. Lingenfelter, pp. 143–165. Columbus: Ohio State University Press.

1976 Adoption and land tenure among Arno Marshallese. In *Transactions in Kinship: Adoption and Fosterage in Oceania,* edited by Ivan A. Brady. Asao Monograph no. 4, pp. 93–119. Honolulu: University of Hawai‘i Press.

1984 Matrilineal kinship: Coming home to Bokelab. In *Conformity and Conflict: Readings in Cultural Anthropology,* edited by James P. Spradley and David W. McCurdy. 5th ed, pp. 110–122. Boston: Little, Brown & Co.

Sahlins, Marshall D.

1958 *Social Stratification in Polynesia.* American Ethnological Society Monograph no. 29. Seattle: University of Washington Press.

1981   *Historical Metaphors and Mythical Realities: Structure in the Early History of the Sand-wich Islands Kingdom.* Asao Special Publication no. 1. Ann Arbor: University of Michigan Press.

1985   *Islands of History.* Chicago: University of Chicago Press.

Sahlins, Marshall D., and Elman R. Service
1960   *Evolution and Culture.* Ann Arbor: University of Michigan Press.

Said, Edward
1979   *Orientalism.* New York: Vintage Books.

Sarfert, Ernst G.
1919   Kusae. Vol. II, B, 4, pt. 1, *Ergebnisse der Südsee Expedition 1908–1910,* edited by Georg Thilenius. Hamburg: Friederichsen, de Gruyter.

Sargent, S. Stansfeld, and Marian W. Smith (eds.)
1949   *Culture and Personality. Proceedings of an Interdisciplinary Conference, November 7 and 8, 1947.* New York: Viking Fund.

Schaefer, Paul D.
1976   Confess therefore your sins: Status and sins on Kusaie. PhD dissertation, University of Minnesota.

Schechner, Richard, and Willa Appel (eds.)
1990   *By Means of Performance: Intercultural Studies of Theatre and Ritual.* Cambridge: Cambridge University Press.

Scheffler, Harold
1965   *Choiseul Island Social Structure.* Berkeley: University of California Press.

Schensul, Stephen L.
1993   A proposed curriculum for the third decade of medical anthropology training. *Anthropology Newsletter* (American Anthropological Association) 34 (May): 15–16.

Schleip, Dietrich
n.d.   A glance on Augustin Krämer. Manuscript. Copy in the personal files of Robert C. Kiste.

Schmidt, Lynn Woodworth
1974   An investigation into the origin of a prehistoric Palauan rock art style. Master's thesis, California State University, Long Beach.

Schneider, David M.
1949   The kinship system and village organization of Yap, West Caroline Islands, Micronesia: A structural and functional account. PhD dissertation, Harvard University.

1953   Yap kinship terminology and kin groups. *American Anthropologist* 55 (2): 215–236.

1955   Abortion and depopulation on a Pacific island. In *Health, Culture, and Community: Case Studies of Public Reactions to Health Programs,* edited by Benjamin D. Paul and Walter B. Miller, pp. 211–235. New York: Russell Sage Foundation.

1957a Typhoons on Yap. *Human Organization* 16 (2): 10–15.

1957b Political organization, supernatural sanctions, and the punishment for incest on Yap. *American Anthropologist* 59 (5): 791–800.

1961a The distinctive features of matrilineal descent groups. In *Matrilineal Kinship*, edited by David M. Schneider and Kathleen Gough, pp. 1–29. Berkeley: University of California Press.

1961b Truk. In *Matrilineal Kinship*, edited by David M. Schneider and Kathleen Gough, pp. 202–233. Berkeley: University of California Press.

1962 Double descent on Yap. *Journal of the Polynesian Society* 71 (1): 1–24.

1965a American kin terms and terms for kinsmen: A critique of Goodenough's componential analysis of Yankee kinship terminology. In *Formal Semantic Analysis*, edited by Eugene A. Hammel. Special issue of *American Anthropologist* 67 (5), pt. 2: 288–308.

1965b Some muddles in the models: Or, how the system really works. In *The Relevance of Models for Social Anthropology*, edited by Michael Banton. ASA Monograph no. 1, pp. 25–85. London: Tavistock Publications.

1968 *American Kinship: A Cultural Account.* Englewood Cliffs, N. J.: Prentice-Hall.

1969a A re-analysis of the kinship system of Yap in the light of Dumont's statement. Paper read at a Wenner-Gren Foundation symposium, August 23–September 1, Burg Wartenstein, Austria. Copy in the personal files of Mac Marshall.

1969b Kinship, nationality and religion in American culture: Toward a definition of kinship. In *Forms of Symbolic Action,* edited by Robert F. Spencer. Proceedings of the 1969 Annual Spring Meeting of the American Ethnological Society, pp. 116–125. Seattle: University of Washington Press.

1972 What is kinship all about? In *Kinship Studies in the Morgan Centennial Year*, edited by Priscilla Reining, pp. 32–63. Washington, D.C.: Anthropological Society of Washington.

1976 Notes toward a theory of culture. In *Meaning in Anthropology*, edited by Keith Basso and Henry Selby, pp. 197–220. Albuquerque: University of New Mexico Press.

1980 Is there really double descent in Pingelap?: On Damas 1979 (88 [2]: 177–198). *Journal of the Polynesian Society* 89 (4): 525–528.

1981 Conclusions. In *Siblingship in Oceania: Studies in the Meaning of Kin Relations*, edited by Mac Marshall. ASAO Monograph no. 8, pp. 389–404. Ann Arbor: University of Michigan Press.

1984 *A Critique of the Study of Kinship.* Ann Arbor: University of Michigan Press.

1997 The power of culture: Notes on some aspects of gay and lesbian kinship in America today. *Cultural Anthropology* 12 (2): 270–274.

Schneider, David M., and Calvert B. Cottrell

1975 *The American Kin Universe: A Genealogical Study.* Chicago: University of Chicago Press.

Schneider, David M., and Kathleen Gough (eds.)

1961 *Matrilineal Kinship.* Berkeley: University of California Press.

Schneider, David M., and George Homans

1955 Kinship terminology and the American kinship system. *American Anthropologist* 57 (6), pt. 1: 1194–1208.

Schneider, David M., and Raymond T. Smith

1973 *Class Differences and Sex Roles in American Kinship and Family Structure.* Englewood Cliffs, N. J.: Prentice-Hall.

Schwalbenberg, Henry M.

1984 The plebiscite on the future political status of the Federated States of Micronesia: Factionalism, separatism, and sovereignty. *Journal of Pacific History* 19 (3): 172–184.

Schwartz, Theodore

1992 Anthropology and psychology: An unrequited relationship. In *New Directions in Psychological Anthropology,* edited by Theodore Schwartz, Geoffrey M. White, and Catherine Lutz, pp. 324–349. Cambridge: Cambridge University Press.

Schwartz, Theodore, Geoffrey M. White, and Catherine Lutz (eds.)

1992 *New Directions in Psychological Anthropology.* Cambridge: Cambridge University Press.

Schweizer, Thomas

1989 Changing perspectives in anthropological primary and secondary analysis. *Kolner Zeitschrift für Soziologie und Sozialpsychologie* 41:465–482. In German.

Science

1993 Anthropology: Nature-culture battleground. *Science* 261:1800–1802.

Scotch, Norman A.

1963 Medical anthropology. In *Biennial Review of Anthropology 1963,* edited by Bernard H. Siegel, pp. 30–68. Stanford, Ca.: Stanford University Press.

Semper, Karl

1982 *The Palau Islands in the Pacific Ocean,* translated by Mark L. Berg. Agaña, Guam: University of Guam, Micronesian Area Research Center. First published 1873.

Sengebau, Valentine N.

1976 Muddy fingers and fingerprints. *Micronesian Reporter* 24 (1): 38–39.

Sengebau, Valentine N., Paul Frederick Kluge, Carolyn Osborne, Douglas Osborne, and Hera W. Owen

1969 *Palau Museum Bai (Bai ra Ngesechel ar Cherchar).* Koror: Palau Museum.

Severance, Craig J.

1976 Land, food and fish: Strategy and transaction on a Micronesian atoll. PhD dissertation, University of Oregon.

1979 Marine resources study. In *Settlement and Subsistence on Ponape,* edited by William S. Ayres, Alan E. Haun, and Craig J. Severance. Ponape Archaeological Survey Interim Report 78–2. Eugene: Department of Anthropology, University of Oregon.

1980 Food for Piis: Interests, linkages and the impact of federal feeding programs on a peripheral atoll. Paper read at the 9th Annual Meeting of the Association for Social Anthropology in Oceania, February 26–March 2, Galveston, Texas.

Sharp, Lauriston
1952 Steel axes for Stone-Age Australians. *Human Organization* 11 (2): 17–22.

Sharpe, Henry S.
1986 Darwin and sociobiology: A reply to Turke. *American Anthropologist* 88 (1): 155–156.

Shaver, Phillip R., Shelley Wu, and Judith C. Schwartz
1992 Cross-cultural similarities and differences in emotion and its representation. In *Emotion. Review of Personality and Psychology,* vol. 13, edited by Margaret S. Clark, pp. 175–212. Newbury Park, Ca.: Sage Publications.

Shewman, Richard D.
1981 Ethnic institutions and identity: Palau migrants on Guam. *Micronesica* 17 (1 & 2): 29–46.
1983 *Coordinator's Manual for Local Juvenile Justice Planning Workshops.* Prepared for TTPI Attorney General's Office. Saipan: Trust Territory of the Pacific Islands Printing Office.
1984 *Community Based Planning in Micronesia: Phase II. A Manual for Conducting Workshops.* Saipan: Trust Territory of the Pacific Islands Printing Office.
1992 Neglect, physical abuse, and sexual molestation in Palau. *Micronesian Counselor,* Occasional Papers no. 7. Kolonia, Pohnpei, FSM: Micronesian Seminar.

Shimizu, Akitoshi
1982 Chiefdom and the spatial classification of the life-world: Everyday life, subsistence and the political system on Ponape. In *Islanders and their Outside World: A Report of the Cultural Anthropological Research in the Caroline Islands of Micronesia, 1980–1981,* edited by Machiko Aoyagi, pp. 35–76. Tokyo: Committee for Micronesian Research, St. Paul's (Rikkyo) University.
1991 On the notion of kinship. *Man* 26 (3): 377–403.

Shweder, Richard A.
1984 Preview: A colloquy of culture theorists. In *Culture Theory: Essays on Mind, Self and Emotion,* edited by Richard Shweder and Robert A. LeVine, pp. 1–24. Cambridge: Cambridge University Press.
1990 Cultural psychology: What is it? In *Cultural Psychology: Essays on Comparative Human Development,* edited by James W. Stigler, Richard A. Shweder, and Gilbert H. Herdt, pp. 1–43. Cambridge: Cambridge University Press.

Shweder, Richard A., and Robert A. LeVine (eds.)
1984 *Culture Theory: Essays on Mind, Self and Emotion.* Cambridge: Cambridge University Press.

Siegel, Bernard J., and George D. Spindler
1962 Obituary. Felix Maxwell Keesing. *American Anthropologist* 64 (2): 351–355.

Silverman, Martin G.
1971 *Disconcerting Issue: Meaning and Struggle in a Resettled Pacific Community.* Chicago: University of Chicago Press.

Simmons, David R.
1970 Palau cave paintings on Aulong Island. *Records of the Auckland Institute and Museum* 7:171–173.

Singer, Merrill
1986 Developing a critical perspective in medical anthropology. *Medical Anthropology Quarterly,* o.s., 17 (5): 128–129.
1989a The coming of age of critical medical anthropology. *Social Science & Medicine* 28 (11): 1193–1203.
1989b The limitations of medical ecology: The concept of adaptation in the context of social stratification and social transformation. *Medical Anthropology* 10 (4): 223–234.
1993 A rejoinder to Wiley's critique of critical medical anthropology. *Medical Anthropology Quarterly,* n.s., 7 (2): 185–191.

Skinner, Mark E.
n.d. Contemporary Micronesian Literature: A Preliminary Bibliography. Pacific Business Center Program, University of Hawai'i, Mānoa.

Smith, Alfred G., and John P. Kennedy
1960 The extension of incest taboos in the Woleai, Micronesia. *American Anthropologist* 62 (4): 643–647.

Smith, DeVerne Reed
1975 The Palauan storyboards: From traditional architecture to airport art. *Expedition* 18: 2–17.
1977 The ties that bind: Exchange and transactions in kinsmen in Palau. PhD dissertation, Bryn Mawr College.
1981 Palauan siblingship: A study in structural complementarity. In *Siblingship in Oceania: Studies in the Meaning of Kin Relations,* edited by Mac Marshall. ASAO Monograph no. 8, pp. 225–273. Ann Arbor: University of Michigan Press.
1983 *Palauan Social Structure.* New Brunswick, N. J.: Rutgers University Press.

Smith, Frances McReynolds (ed.)
1972 *Micronesian Realities: Political and Economic.* Seminar Series no. 2. Santa Cruz, Ca.: Center for South Pacific Studies, University of California, Santa Cruz.

Smith, J. Jerome
1972 Intergenerational land transactions on Rota, Mariana Islands: A study of ethnographic theory. PhD dissertation, University of Arizona.
1974 Land tenure on Rota, Mariana Islands. *Micronesica* 10 (2): 223–236.

1976   Rotanese fosterage: Counterexample of an Oceanic pattern. In *Transactions in Kinship: Adoption and Fosterage in Oceania,* edited by Ivan A. Brady. Asao Monograph no. 4, pp. 247–270. Honolulu: University of Hawai'i Press.

Smith, Marian W. (ed.)
1961   *The Artist in Tribal Society: Proceedings of a Symposium Held at the Royal Anthropological Institute.* London: Routledge & Kegan Paul.

Smith, Thomas R.
1972   *The South Pacific Commission: An Analysis after Twenty-five Years.* Published for the New Zealand Institute of International Affairs by Price Milburn & Co. Ltd., Wellington.

Smith, Woodruff
1991   *Politics and the Sciences of Culture in Germany 1840–1920.* Oxford: Oxford University Press.

Snyder, David
1989   Towards chronometric models for Palauan prehistory: Ceramic attributes. PhD dissertation, Southern Illinois University, Carbondale.

Snyder, Jacqueline M.
1976   The role of education in affecting changes in attitudes and values toward strategies of elite selection: Micronesia under an American administration. PhD dissertation, University of California, Santa Barbara.

SONA, School of Naval Administration
1948   *Handbook on the Trust Territory of the Pacific Islands. A Handbook for Use in Training and Administration.* Prepared at the School of Naval Administration, Hoover Institute, Stanford University. Washington, D.C.: Navy Department, Office of the Chief of Naval Operations.

Sonoda, K.
1938   The personality and development of boys on Ponape as evaluated by blood type and location of whorls of hair on the head. *Collected Medical Treatises on the South Seas* 4:50-57. (In Japanese, translated in Cross-Cultural Survey Files.)

Souder-Jaffery, Laura
1992   *Daughters of the Island: Contemporary Chamorro Women Organizers of Guam.* 2d ed. Lanham, Md.: University Press of America.

SPC, South Pacific Commission
1993   *Statistical Bulletin.* Noumea, New Caledonia.
1995   *Population Statistics.* Noumea, New Caledonia.

Spicer, Edward H. (ed.)
1952   *Human Problems in Technological Change: A Casebook.* New York: Russell Sage Foundation.

Spicer, Edward H., Asael T. Hansen, Katherine Luomala, and Marvin K. Opler

1969 *Impounded People: Japanese-Americans in the Relocation Centers.* Tucson: University of Arizona Press.

Spiro, Melford E.

1950a A psychotic personality in the South Seas. *Psychiatry* 13 (2): 189–204.

1950b The problem of aggression in a South Sea culture. PhD dissertation, Northwestern University.

1951a Culture and personality: The natural history of a false dichotomy. *Psychiatry* 14 (1): 19–46.

1951b Some Ifaluk myths and folktales. *Journal of American Folklore* 64 (253): 289–302.

1952 Ghosts, Ifaluk, and teleological functionalism. *American Anthropologist* 54 (4): 497–503.

1953a Ghosts: An anthropological inquiry into learning and perception. *Journal of Abnormal and Social Psychology* 43 (3): 376–382.

1953b A typology of functional analysis. *Explorations* 1:84–95.

1954a Is the family universal? *American Anthropologist* 56 (5), pt. 1: 839–846.

1954b Human nature in its psychological dimensions. *American Anthropologist* 56 (1): 19–31.

1955 Comments on the use of projective tests. *American Anthropologist* 57 (2), pt. 1: 256–258.

1956 *Kibbutz: Venture in Utopia.* Cambridge, Mass.: Harvard University Press.

1958 *Children of the Kibbutz.* Cambridge, Mass.: Harvard University Press.

1959 Cultural heritage, personal tensions, and mental illness in a South Sea culture. In *Culture and Mental Health,* edited by Marvin K. Opler, pp. 141–171. New York: Macmillan.

1961a Social systems, personality and functional analysis. In *Studying Personality Cross-Culturally,* edited by Bert Kaplan, pp. 93–127. Evanston, Ill.: Harper & Row.

1961b Sorcery, evil spirits and functional analysis. *American Anthropologist* 63 (4): 820–824.

1962 Culture and personality: An overview and a suggested reorientation. In *Psychological Anthropology,* edited by Francis L. K. Hsu. Homewood, Ill.: Dorsey Press.

1963 Causes, function, and cross-cousin marriage: An essay in anthropological explanation. *Journal of the Royal Anthropological Institute* 94:30–43.

1965a Religious systems as culturally constituted defense mechanisms. In *Context and Meaning in Cultural Anthropology: Essays in Honor of A. I. Hallowell,* edited by Melford E. Spiro, pp. 100–113. Glencoe, Ill.: Free Press.

1965b A typology of social structure and the patterning of social institutions. *American Anthropologist* 67 (5), pt. 1: 1097–1119.

1966a Religion: Problems of definition and explanation. In *Anthropological Approaches to the Study of Religion,* edited by Michael Banton. ASA Monograph no. 3, pp. 85–126. London: Tavistock Publications.

1966b Buddhism and economic action in Burma. *American Anthropologist* 68 (5): 1163–1173.

1967 *Burmese Supernaturalism: A Study in the Explanation and Resolution of Suffering.*
      Englewood Cliffs, N. J.: Prentice-Hall.
1968 Religion, personality and behavior in Burma. *American Anthropologist* 70 (2): 359–
      363.
1969 Religious symbols and social behavior. *Proceedings of the American Philosophical
      Society* 113:341–350.
1971 *Buddhism and Society: A Great Tradition and its Burmese Vicissitudes.* New York:
      Harper & Row.
1977 *Kinship and Marriage in Burma.* Berkeley: University of California Press.
1978 Culture and human nature. In *The Making of Psychological Anthropology,* edited by
      George Spindler, pp. 330-360. Berkeley: University of California Press.
1979a *Gender and Culture: Kibbutz Women Revisited.* Durham, N. C.: Duke University
      Press.
1979b Symbolism and functionalism in the anthropological study of religion. In *Science of
      Religion: Studies in Methodology,* edited by Lauri Honko. Hague: Mouton.
1982 *Oedipus in the Trobriands: The Making of a Scientific Myth.* Chicago: University of
      Chicago Press.
1984 Images of man, nature, and the supernatural in the Buddhist schema of salvation. In
      Images of Man: Studies in Religion and Anthropology. Lectures by distinguished visit-
      ing scholars at Wake Forest University, edited by J. William Angel and E. Pendleton
      Banks. Macon, Ga.: Mercer University Press.
1992 The primary process revisited. *Psychoanalytic Study of Society* 17:171–180.
1993 Tropes, defenses and unconscious mental representation: Some critical reflections
      on the primary process. *Psychoanalysis and Contemporary Thought* 16:155–196.

Spoehr, Alexander
1949a *Majuro, a Village in the Marshall Islands.* Fieldiana: Anthropology, vol. 39. Chicago:
      Chicago Natural History Museum.
1949b The generation type kinship system in the Marshall and Gilbert Islands. *Southwest-
      ern Journal of Anthropology* 5 (2): 107–116.
1951 Anthropology and the Trust Territory: A summary of recent researches. *Clearing-
      house Bulletin of Research in Human Organization* 1 (2): 1–3.
1953 Anthropology and coral atoll field research. *Atoll Research Bulletin* no. 17: 109–110.
      Washington, D.C.: The Smithsonian Institution.
1954 *Saipan: The Ethnology of a War-Devastated Island.* Fieldiana: Anthropology, vol. 41.
      Chicago: Chicago Natural History Museum.
1956 Cultural differences in the interpretation of natural resources. In *Man's Role in
      Changing the Face of the Earth,* edited by William L. Thomas, pp. 93–102. Chicago:
      University of Chicago Press.
1957 *Marianas Prehistory; Archaeological Survey and Excavations on Saipan, Tinian and
      Rota.* Fieldiana: Anthropology, vol. 48. Chicago: Chicago Natural History Museum.
1966 (compiler) *Bibliography of the Tri-Institutional Pacific Program, 1953–1964 (TRIPP).*
      Honolulu: Pacific Scientific Information Center, Bernice P. Bishop Museum.

Steager, Peter William

1972 Food in its social context on Puluwat, Eastern Caroline Islands. PhD dissertation, University of California, Berkeley.

1979 Where does art begin on Puluwat? In *Exploring the Visual Art of Oceania: Australia, Melanesia, Micronesia, and Polynesia,* edited by Sidney M. Mead, pp. 342–353. Honolulu: The University Press of Hawai'i.

Stephens, William N.

1963 *The Family in Cross-Cultural Perspective.* New York: Holt, Rinehart & Winston.

Stephenson, F. A.

1971 Talafofo cave writing. *Guam Recorder,* n.s., 1 (1): 10–11.

Stephenson, Rebecca Ann

1987 A comparison of freshwater use customs on Ulithi Atoll with those of selected other Micronesian atolls. In *Water, Land and People: Selected Studies in Fresh Water Resources,* edited by Rebecca A. Stephenson, pp. 107–126. Guam: University of Guam, Water and Energy Research Institute and the Micronesian Area Research Center.

Stern, Theodore

1987 Obituary. Homer Garner Barnett (1906–1985). *American Anthropologist* 89 (3): 701–703.

Stevens, William D.

1950 A study of depopulation on Yap Island. PhD dissertation, Harvard University.

Steward, Julian H.

1946–1950 (ed.) *Handbook of South American Indians.* Bureau of American Ethnology, Bulletin 143, vols. 1–6. Washington, D.C.: Bureau of American Ethnology.

1955 *Theory of Culture Change.* Urbana: University of Illinois Press.

1968 Ecology: II. Cultural ecology. In *International Encyclopedia of the Social Sciences,* edited by David Sills, 4:337–344. New York: Macmillan and Free Press.

Stigler, James W., Richard A. Shweder, and Gilbert H. Herdt (eds.)

1990 *Cultural Psychology: Essays on Comparative Human Development.* Cambridge: Cambridge University Press.

Stocking, George W.

1985 (ed.) *Objects and Others: Essays on Museums and Material Culture.* History of Anthropology, vol. 3. Madison: University of Wisconsin Press.

1992 *The Ethnographer's Magic and Other Essays in the History of Anthropology.* Madison: University of Wisconsin Press.

Stone, Earl L., Jr.

1951 The agriculture of Arno Atoll, Marshall Islands. *Atoll Research Bulletin* no. 6. Washington, D.C.: The Smithsonian Institution.

Strathern, Marilyn

1990   Artefacts of history: Events and the interpretation of images. In *Culture and History in the Pacific,* edited by Jukka Siikala, pp. 25–44. Transactions of the Finnish Anthropological Society, 27, Anna-Leena Siikala, general editor. Helsinki: Finnish Anthropological Society.

1991   *Partial Connections.* Asao Special Publication no. 3. Savage, Md.: Rowman & Littlefield.

Sturtevant, William C.

1964   Studies in ethnoscience. In *Transcultural Studies in Cognition,* edited by A. Kimball Romney and Roy G. D'Andrade. Special Publication, *American Anthropologist* 66 (3), pt. 2: 99–131.

Sudo, Ken-ichi

1980a Canoe house of Satawal Island. *Kikan Jinruigaku* 11 (3): 177–182.

1980b Comment on Asakawa's paper: Building process of *wuut,* men's house in Tol Island, Truk. *Kikan Jinruigaku* 11 (3): 177–182.

1984   Social organization and types of sea tenure in Micronesia. In *Maritime Institutions in the Western Pacific,* edited by Kenneth Ruddle and Tomoya Akimichi. Senri Ethnological Studies no. 17, pp. 203–230. Osaka: National Museum of Ethnology.

1985   Avoidance behavior and kin category in Satawalese society. *Man and Culture in Oceania* 1:1–26.

1987   Nurturing in matrilineal society: A case study of Satawal Island. In *Cultural Uniformity and Diversity in Micronesia,* edited by Iwao Ushijima and Ken-ichi Sudo. Senri Ethnological Studies no. 21, pp. 87–106. Osaka: National Museum of Ethnology.

Sugito, Shigenobu

1982a Traditional knowledge and techniques of building on Elato Atoll, Caroline Islands, Micronesia. *Bulletin of the National Museum of Ethnology* 7:349–415.

1982b Women's loinclothes on Elato Atoll, Caroline Islands, Micronesia. *Kikan Minzokugaku* 9:74–82.

1987   Construction techniques and traditional architectural knowledge on Elato Atoll, Caroline Islands. *Senri Ethnological Studies* 21:279–320.

Sutlive, Vinson H., Jr.

1993   Obituary of Alexander Spoehr. *Anthropology Newsletter* (American Anthropological Association) 34 (October): 45.

Swartz, Marc J.

1958   The social organization of behavior: Relations among kinsmen on Romónum, Truk. PhD dissertation, Harvard University.

1959   Leadership and status conflict on Romónum, Truk. *Southwestern Journal of Anthropology* 15 (2): 213–218.

1960   Situational determinants of kinship terminology. *Southwestern Journal of Anthropology* 16 (4): 393–397.

1962 Recruiting labor for fissionary descent lines on Romónum, Truk. _Southwestern Journal of Anthropology_ 18 (4): 351–364.

1965 Personality and structure: Political acquiesence in Truk. In _Induced Political Change in the Pacific: A Symposium,_ edited by Roland W. Force, pp. 17–39. Honolulu: Bishop Museum Press.

Swartz, Marc J., and David K. Jordan

1976 _Anthropology: Perspective on Humanity._ New York: John Wiley.

Tabrah, Frank L.

1982 _Medical Manual for the Pacific Islands. A Brief Manual of Health Care Precepts Appropriate to Micronesia._ Honolulu: John Burns School of Medicine, University of Hawai'i.

Tanabe, Satoru

1980 Music and dancing in the Marshall and Caroline Islands. _Japanese Journal of Ethnology_ 1 (2): 18.

Tapsell, Paul

1997 The flight of Pareraututu: An investigation of tribal taonga through the eyes of Te Arawa. _Journal of the Polynesian Society_ 106 (4): 323–374.

Tatar, Elizabeth

1985 _Call of the Morning Bird: Chants and Songs of Palau, Yap, and Ponape, Collected by Iwakichi Muranushi, 1936,_ compiled and edited by Elizabeth Tatar; translated by Maria Ikelau Otto and Vincent Anselm Parren. Honolulu: Department of Anthropology, Bernice P. Bishop Museum.

Taylor, Richard, Nancy Davis Lewis, and Sue Levy

1989 Societies in transition: Mortality patterns in Pacific Island populations. _International Journal of Epidemiology_ 18:634–646.

Tenorio, Froilan Cruz

1989 _1988 Annual Report._ Washington, D.C.: Office of the Resident Representative to the United States of America for the Northern Mariana Islands.

Thaman, Randolph R.

1985 Pacific Islands' health and nutrition: Trends and areas for action. Report prepared as background material for the 2d Pacific Islands Conference, August, Pacific Islands Development Program, East-West Center, Honolulu, Hawai'i. Copy on file in the RFK Memorial Library, University of Guam.

Thilenius, Georg (ed.)

1914–1938 _Ergebnisse der Südsee-Expedition, 1908–1910,_ pt. 2, B Mikronesien, 12 vols. in 25 parts. Hamburg: Friederichsen, de Gruyter.

Thomas, Frank R.

1993 Successes and failures on atolls: A review of prehistoric adaptations and contemporary lessons. In _Culture and Environment: A Fragile Coexistence,_ edited by Ross W.

Jamieson, Sylvia Abonyi, and Neil A. Mirau, pp. 423–430. Calgary, Alberta: University of Calgary Archaeological Association.

Thomas, John B.
1977   "Consanguinity" and filiation on Namonuito Atoll. *Journal of the Polynesian Society* 86 (4): 513–519.
1978   Adoption, filiation, and matrilineal descent on Namonuito Atoll, Caroline Islands. PhD dissertation, University of Hawai'i.
1980   The Namonuito solution to the "matrilineal puzzle." *American Ethnologist* 7 (1): 172–177.

Thomas, Mary D.
1978   Transmitting culture to children on Namonuito Atoll, Caroline Islands. PhD dissertation, University of Hawai'i.

Thomas, Nicholas
1990   Sanitation and seeing: The creation of state power in early colonial Fiji. *Comparative Studies in Society and History* 32:149–170.
1991   *Entangled Objects: Exchange, Material Culture, and Colonialism in the Pacific.* Cambridge, Mass.: Harvard University Press.
1994   *Colonialism's Culture: Travel, Literature and Government.* Princeton, N. J.: Princeton University Press.
1995   *Oceanic Art.* London: Thames & Hudson.

Thomas, William L. (ed.)
1956   *Man's Role in Changing the Face of the Earth.* Chicago: University of Chicago Press.

Thompson, Laura
1941   *Guam and Its People: A Study of Cultural Change and Colonial Education.* New York: Institute of Pacific Relations. Reprinted 1947. 3d Rev. ed. Princeton, N. J.: Princeton University Press.
1944   Guam: Study in military government. *Far Eastern Survey* 13 (16): 149–154.
1946   Crisis on Guam. *Far Eastern Quarterly* 7 (1): 5–11.
1947   See 1941.
1957   Dance around the world: The South Pacific islands. *Dance Magazine* 31:28–35.
1987   Talking stones. *Glimpses of Guam & Micronesia* 27 (4): 16–21.
1991   *Beyond the Dream: A Search for Meaning.* Marc Monograph Series no. 2. Mangilao: Micronesian Area Research Center, University of Guam.

Thompson, Laura, and Alice Joseph
1944   *The Hopi Way.* Chicago: University of Chicago Press.

Thurnwald, Richard
1913   Ethno-psychologisch Studien an Südseevolkern auf dem Bismarck-Archipel und den Salomo-Inseln. Beihefte zur Zeitschrift für angewandte psychologie und psychologishe sammelforschung, vol. 6. Leipzig: J. A. Barth.

Tiesler, Friedrich-Karl
1981 Hausbalken von den Palau-Inseln, Mikronesien. *Kleine Beiträge* (Dresden) 4:2–8.

Tobin, Jack A.
1952 Land tenure in the Marshall Islands. *Atoll Research Bulletin* no. 11. Washington, D.C.: Pacific Science Board, The Smithsonian Institution.
1954a Ebeye village: An atypical Marshallese community. Mimeographed. Copy on file in the Hawaiian and Pacific Collection, Hamilton Library, University of Hawai'i, Mānoa.
1954b Kili Journal: August 28 to September 18. Report to the Office of the District Administrator, Marshalls District, Trust Territory of the Pacific Islands, Serial IA–120. Majuro: Trust Territory of the Pacific Islands.
1955 Special Field Study: Ujilan Atoll. Report of the District Anthropologist, Marshalls District, Serial AD–779. Majuro: Trust Territory of the Pacific Islands. Copy in the personal files of William H. Alkire.
1967 The resettlement of the Eniwetak people: A study of a displaced community in the Marshall Islands. PhD dissertation, University of California, Berkeley.

Todd, Harry F., Jr., and Julio L. Ruffini (eds.)
1979 *Teaching Medical Anthropology: Model Courses for Graduate and Undergraduate Instruction.* Society for Medical Anthropology Special Publication no. 1. Washington, D.C.: Society for Medical Anthropology.

Tolerton, Burt, and Jerome Rauch
1949 *Social Organization, Land Tenure and Subsistence Economy of Lukunor, Nomoi Islands.* CIMA Report no. 26. Washington, D.C.: Pacific Science Board, National Research Council.

Torsch, Vicki L.
1996 The elderly experience among the Chamorros of Guam. PhD dissertation, University of Oklahoma.

Trask, Haunani-Kay
1991 Natives and anthropologists: The colonial struggle. *The Contemporary Pacific* 3 (1): 159–167.

Truk District
1957 Sixth Annual Conference of Island Magistrates, July 23–25. Proceedings. Copy on file in the Hawaiian and Pacific Collection, Hamilton Library, University of Hawai'i, Mānoa.

TTR, Trust Territory Reports
1969 *Trust Territory Reports.* Vol. 1, 1951–1958. Orford, N. H.: Equity Publishing Corporation.

Turke, Paul W.
1985 Fertility determinants on Ifaluk and Yap: Tests of economic and Darwinian hypotheses. PhD dissertation, Northwestern University.
1986 Darwin didn't know about genes. *American Anthropologist* 88 (1): 156–157.

Turke, Paul W., and Laura L. Betzig
1985   Those who can do: Wealth, status and reproductive success on Ifaluk. *Ethology and Sociobiology* 6 (2): 79–87.

Turner, Victor
1986   *The Anthropology of Performance.* New York: PAJ Publications.

Tylor, Edward B.
1909   *Anthropology.* New York: D. Appleton & Company.
1958   *Primitive Society.* New York: Harper & Row. First published 1871.

Uag, Raphael, and Frank Molinski
1969a The legendary history of Yap. *Micronesian Reporter* 17 (2): 33–35.
1969b The legendary history of Yap. *Micronesian Reporter* 17 (3): 30–33.

Udui, Elizabeth
1966   Palauan craftsmen produce many beautiful forms of art. *Micronesian Reporter* 14 (2): 14–15.
1971   Handicraft produced in Micronesia. Saipan: Office of Tourism/Economic Development, Trust Territory of the Pacific Islands.
1979   Micronesian Handicrafts. Saipan: Bureau of Resources, Trust Territory of the Pacific Islands.

Udui, Kaleb
1972   America's dilemmas in carrying out its international trusteeship obligations in Micronesia. In *Micronesian Realities: Political and Economic,* edited by Francis M. Smith. Seminar Series no. 2, pp. 1–20. Santa Cruz, Ca.: Center for South Pacific Studies, University of California, Santa Cruz.

Ueki, Takeshi
1984   Processes of increasing social complexity on Kosrae, Micronesia. PhD dissertation, Brown University.

Underwood, Jane (née Hainline)
1969   Preliminary investigations of demographic features and ecological variables of a Micronesian island population. *Micronesica* 5 (1): 1–24.
1973   The demography of a myth: Abortion in Yap. *Human Biology in Oceania* 2 (2): 115–127.
1992   Birth seasonality and the etiology of neurodegenerative diseases in the native population of Guam. *American Journal of Human Biology* 4 (3): 373–379.

Underwood, Robert
1985a Guahutaotaotano: A Chamorro stage presentation. *Glimpses of Micronesia* 25:31–32.
1985b Excursions into inauthenticity: The Chamorros of Guam. *Pacific Viewpoint* 26: 160–184.
1987   Saying No (A Poem). In *Chamorro Self-Determination: The Right of a People,* edited by Laura Souder-Jaffery and Robert A. Underwood, p. 149. Mangilao: Chamorro Studies Association and MARC, University of Guam.

University of Guam Gallery of Art
1973   Charles Gibbons: Visions of old Palau. *Micronesian Working Papers* no. 4. Agaña: Gallery of Art, University of Guam.

University of Hawai'i
1984   An evaluation of federal support to health systems of the Pacific insular jurisdiction of the US. Pt. 3. Appendices. A report by the University of Hawai'i Schools of Medicine, Nursing and Public Health, prepared for Public Health Services, Department of Health and Human Services. Honolulu: University of Hawai'i. Copy on file in the Hawaiian and Pacific Collection, Hamilton Library, University of Hawai'i, Mānoa.

University of Hawai'i Micronesian Program
1966–1969   *Bulletin.* Honolulu: Department of Anthropology, University of Hawai'i.

UNTS, United Nations Treaty Series
1947   United Nations and United States of America. Trusteeship for Former Japanese Mandated Islands, approved by the Security Council of the United Nations at Lake Success, NY, April 2; approved by the President of the United States July 18; entered into force July 18. 8 UNTS 189 (61 Stat. 3301; TIAS 16665; Bevans 12:951).

US Army, Office of the Surgeon General
1944   Medical and sanitary data on the Caroline Islands. *War Department Technical Bulletin* TB MED 50 (May 31): 1–19.

US Department of the Navy
1948   *Trust Territory of the Pacific Islands, 1947/48.* Washington, D.C.: US Department of the Navy.

US Naval Medical Center
1948   School of medical practitioners. Bulletin. Guam. 6 pp. Copy on file in the Hawaiian and Pacific Collection, Hamilton Library, University of Hawai'i, Mānoa.
1949   School of medical practitioners. Bulletin. Guam. 13 pp. Copy on file in the Hawaiian and Pacific Collection, Hamilton Library, University of Hawai'i, Mānoa.

US Navy, Office of the Chief of Naval Operations
1943   *Military Government Handbook: Marshall Islands.* Washington, D.C.: Office of the Chief of Naval Operations.
1944a   *Civil Affairs Handbook: West Caroline Islands.* Washington, D.C.: Office of the Chief of Naval Operations.
1944b   *Civil Affairs Handbook: East Caroline Islands.* Washington, D.C.: Office of the Chief of Naval Operations.
1944c   *Civil Affairs Handbook: Mandated Mariana Islands.* Washington, D.C.: Office of the Chief of Naval Operations.
1944d   *Civil Affairs Handbook: Marshall Islands Statistical Supplement.* Washington, D.C.: Office of the Chief of Naval Operations.

US Navy, Pacific Fleet and Pacific Ocean Areas
1945   Naval Government Plan, Pacific Island Area, Medical Department. Typescript.

US Senate, Committee on Energy and Natural Resources
1984   Hearing to Approve the Compact of Free Association, May 24. Washington, D.C.:
       Government Printing Office.

US Survey Mission to the Trust Territory of the Pacific Islands
1962   Report (commonly referred to as the Solomon Report). Unpublished confidential
       report to the President, Washington, D.C. Copy on file in the Hawaiian and Pacific
       Collection, Hamilton Library, University of Hawai'i, Mānoa.

Useem, John
1945a The American pattern of military government in the Pacific. *American Journal of
       Sociology* 51 (2): 93–102.
1945b Governing the occupied areas of the South Pacific: War time lessons and peace time
       proposals. *Applied Anthropology* 4 (3): 1–10.
1945c The changing structure of a Micronesian society. *American Anthropologist* 47 (4):
       567–588.
1946a Americans as governors of natives in the Pacific. *Journal of Social Issues* 2 (3): 39–49.
1946b Military government on Saipan and Tinian. *Applied Anthropology* 5 (1): 1–39.
1946c Report on Yap and Palau, and the lesser islands of the Western Carolines. US
       Commercial Company's Economic Survey of Micronesia, Report no. 6. Honolulu:
       US Commercial Company. Mimeographed.
1947   Applied anthropology in Micronesia. *Applied Anthropology* 6 (4): 1–14.
1948   Institutions of Micronesia. *Far Eastern Survey* 17 (2): 22–25.
1950   Structure of power in Palau. *Social Forces* 29 (2): 141–148.
1952   Democracy in process: The development of democratic leadership in the Microne-
       sian Islands. In *Human Problems in Technological Change,* edited by Edward H.
       Spicer, pp. 261–280. New York: Russell Sage Foundation.

Ushijima, Iwao
1982   The control of reefs and lagoons: Some aspects of the political structure of Ulithi
       Atoll. In *Islanders and their Outside World: A Report of the Cultural Anthropological
       Research in the Caroline Islands of Micronesia in 1980–1981,* edited by Machiko Aoyagi,
       pp. 35–76. Tokyo: St. Paul's (Rikkyo) University, Committee for Micronesian
       Research.
1987   A reinterpretation of the *sawai* overseas exchange system of the Caroline Islands. In
       *Cultural Adaptation to Atolls in Micronesia and West Polynesia: A Report of the
       Cultural Anthropological Research in Caroline, Marshall and Ellice Islands,* edited by
       Eikichi Ishikawa, pp. 55–79. Tokyo: Committee for Micronesian Research, Tokyo
       Metropolitan University.
1990   (ed.) *Anthropological Research on the Atoll Cultures of Micronesia, 1988.* Tsukuba:
       Committee for Micronesian Research, University of Tsukuba.

USTTPI, United States Trust Territory of the Pacific Islands

1957 *Anthropology Newsletter.* Agaña, Guam: Office of the Staff Anthropologist.

1976 *FY 1977 State Plan for Delinquency Prevention in the Trust Territory of the Pacific Islands.* Saipan: Trust Territory Printing Office.

USTTPI Archives

1950–1960 Meetings, reports, and miscellaneous information on the Trust Territory, re. anthropologists' chron. file, 1950–1960. In USTTPI Microfilmed Archives, eleven folders, roll #0551, frame #0000, document #9290. Honolulu: Hamilton Library, University of Hawai'i, Mānoa.

1952 First TT Anthropologists' Conference held in Koror, Palau, on September 4–12, 1952, to acquaint district anthropologists with problems in districts other than their own. In USTTPI Microfilmed Archives, one folder, roll #0106, starting at frame #0049, document #1698. Honolulu: Hamilton Library, University of Hawai'i, Mānoa.

1952–1959 Assignments, classifications and definitions of the function of the Trust Territory anthropologists and their place in government, 1952–1959. In USTTPI Microfilmed Archives, one folder, roll #0106, frame #0055, document #0172. Honolulu: Hamilton Library, University of Hawai'i, Mānoa.

1953 Dialogues between the anthropologists of the TTPI during their conference in 1953 regarding Micronesian problems, relations and culture. In USTTPI Microfilmed Archives, one folder, roll #0108, frame #0006, document #1691. Honolulu: Hamilton Library, University of Hawai'i, Mānoa.

1955 Executive Order no. 48, 1/24/1955. Unpublished records of the US Trust Territory.

1957 Anthropology Conference, January 21–25, 1957. Unpublished records of the US Trust Territory. Copy on file in the Hawaiian and Pacific Collection, Hamilton Library, University of Hawai'i, Mānoa.

Van Cleve, Ruth G.

1974 *The Office of Territorial Affairs.* New York and Washington: Praeger Publishers.

Vayda, Andrew P. (ed.)

1969 *Environment and Cultural Behavior.* American Museum Sourcebooks in Anthropology. Garden City, N. Y.: Natural History Press.

Vayda, Andrew P., and Bonnie J. McCay

1975 New directions in ecology and ecological anthropology. *Annual Review of Anthropology* 5:293–306.

Vayda, Andrew P., and Roy A. Rappaport

1963 Island cultures. In *Man's Place in the Island Ecosystem,* edited by F. Raymond Fosberg, pp. 133–142. Honolulu: Bishop Museum Press.

1968 Ecology, cultural and noncultural. In *Introduction to Cultural Anthropology, Essays in the Scope and Method of the Science of Man,* edited by James A. Clifton, pp. 477–497. New York: Houghton Mifflin.

Vesper, Ethel R.

1976   Structural and sociosemantics of Kusaien. PhD dissertation, University of Missouri.

Vidich, Arthur J.

1949   *Political Factionalism in Palau: Its Rise and Development.* Cima Report no. 23. Washington D.C.: Pacific Science Board, National Research Council.

1953   The political impact of colonial administration. PhD dissertation, Harvard University.

1995   *The New Middle Classes: Lifestyles and Status Claims and Political Orientations.* New York: Macmillan.

Vidich, Arthur J., and Joseph Bensman

1958   *Small Town in Mass Society; Class, Power, and Religion in a Rural Community.* Princeton, N.J.: Princeton University Press.

Vincent, Joan

1990   *Anthropology and Politics.* Tucson: University of Arizona Press.

Vitarelli, Margo

1986   Handicrafts industry development and renewable resource management for US-affiliated Pacific Islands. Prepared for Office of Technology Assessment, Congress of the United States, Washington, D.C. Copy on file in the Hawaiian and Pacific Collection, Hamilton Library, University of Hawai'i, Mānoa.

Vogt, Evon Z.

1965   Review of *Other Cultures: Aims, Methods and Achievements in Social Anthropology* by John Beattie. *American Anthropologist* 67 (2): 554–555.

Wallace, Anthony F. C.

1970   *Culture and Personality.* 2d ed. New York: Random House.

1993   *The Long Bitter Trail.* New York: Hill & Wang.

Wallace, Gordon D.

1969   Serologic and epidemiologic observations on toxoplasmosis on three Pacific atolls. *American Journal of Epidemiology* 90 (2): 103–111.

Wallace, Gordon D., Leslie B. Marshall, and Mac Marshall

1972   Cats, rats, and toxoplasmosis on a small Pacific island. *American Journal of Epidemiology* 95 (5): 475–482.

Walleser, Sixtus

1979   *Dance Songs of Yap,* translated by B. M. Langscheidt. Jamestown, N.C.: Pacificana.

Ward, Martha C.

1989   *Nest in the Wind: Adventures in Anthropology on a Tropical Island.* Prospect Heights, Ill.: Waveland Press.

Ward, Roger L.

1977   Curing on Ponape: A medical ethnography. PhD dissertation, Tulane University.

Washington Pacific Report

1986   Reagan signs compact into law. *Washington Pacific Report* 4 (8): 1–2.

Watson, James B.

1990   Other people do other things: Lamarckian identities in Kainantu Subdistrict, Papua New Guinea. In *Cultural Identity and Ethnicity in the Pacific,* edited by Jocelyn Linnekin and Lin Poyer, pp. 17–41. Honolulu: University of Hawaiʻi Press.

Wax, Murray L.

1995   Notes on the past and toward the future. *Society for Applied Anthropology Newsletter* 6 (2): 3–4.

Wax, Rosalie H.

1971   *Doing Fieldwork: Warnings and Advice.* Chicago: University of Chicago Press.

Webb, George

1975   A comparative study of the traditional houses in the Caroline Islands. *Journal of Geography* 74 (2): 87–103.

Weckler, Joseph E.

1949   *Land and Livelihood on Mokil, An Atoll in the Eastern Carolines,* pt. 1. Cima Report no. 11. Washington, D.C.: Pacific Science Board, National Research Council.

1953   Adoption on Mokil. *American Anthropologist* 55 (4): 555–568.

Wees, Marshall Paul, and Francis Beauchesne Thornton

1950   *King-Doctor of Ulithi: The True Story of the Wartime Experiences of Marshall Paul Wees as Related to Francis Beauchesne Thornton.* New York: Macmillan.

Weiner, Annette B.

1976   *Women of Value, Men of Renown.* Austin: University of Texas Press.

1980   Stability in banana leaves: Colonization and women in Kiriwina, Trobriand Islands. In *Women and Colonization: Anthropological Perspectives,* edited by Mona Etienne and Eleanor Leacock, pp. 270–293. New York: Bergin & Garvey.

1992   *Inalienable Possessions: The Paradox of Keeping-While-Giving.* Berkeley: University of California Press.

Weiner, Annette B., and Jane Schneider (eds.)

1989   *Cloth and Human Experience.* Washington, D.C.: Smithsonian Institution Press.

Weisner, Thomas S.

1993   Overview: Sibling similarity and difference in different cultures. In *Siblings in South Asia,* edited by Charles W. Nuckolls, pp. 1–17. New York: The Guilford Press.

Weiss, Kenneth M.

1976   Demographic theory and anthropological inference. *Annual Review of Anthropology* 5:351–381.

Welborn, Sonoko, and Judith Bothmer
1977   Lava-Lava. *Glimpses of Micronesia* 17 (3): 23–25.

Wells, Marjorie D.
1982   *Micronesian Handicraft Book of the Trust Territory of the Pacific Islands.* New York: Carlton Press.

Wendt, Albert
1983   Contemporary arts in Oceania. In *Art and Artists of Oceania,* edited by Sidney M. Mead and Bernie Kernot, pp. 198–209. Palmerston North, New Zealand: The Dunmore Press.

White, Geoffrey M.
1991   *Identity Through History: Living Stories in a Solomon Islands Society.* Cambridge: Cambridge University Press.

White, Geoffrey M., and Anthony J. Marsella
1982   Introduction: Cultural conceptions in mental health research and practice. In *Cultural Conceptions of Mental Health and Therapy,* edited by Anthony J. Marsella and Geoffrey M. White, pp. 3–38. Dordrecht: D. Reidel.

White, Leslie
1949   *The Science of Culture.* New York: Farar Straus.
1959   *The Evolution of Culture.* New York: McGraw-Hill.

Whiting, John W. M.
1941   *Becoming a Kwoma.* New Haven, Conn.: Yale University Press.
1986   Obituary. George Peter Murdock (1897–1985). *American Anthropologist* 88 (3): 682–686.
n.d.   Fieldnotes. On file in the Smithsonian Institution Library.

Whiting, Marjorie Grant
1963   Toxicity of cycads. *Economic Botany* 17 (4): 270–302.

Whyte, William Foote
1956   *The Organization Man.* New York: Simon and Schuster.

Wiens, Harold
1962   *Atoll Environment and Ecology.* New Haven, Conn.: Yale University Press.

Wierzbicka, Anna
1994   Emotion, language and cultural script. In *Emotion and Culture: Empirical Studies of Mutual Influence,* edited by Shinobu Kitayama and Hazel Rose Markus, pp. 133–196. Washington, D.C.: American Psychological Association.

Wiley, Andrea
1992   Adaptation and the biocultural paradigm in medical anthropology: A critical review. *Medical Anthropology Quarterly* 6 (3): 216–236.

1993 Evolution, adaptation, and the role of biocultural medical anthropology. *Medical Anthropology Quarterly* 7 (2): 192–199.

Wiliander, Hans
1972 Economic realities of independence. In *Micronesian Realities: Political and Economic,* edited by Francis M. Smith. Seminar Series no. 2, pp. 21–29. Santa Cruz, Ca.: Center for South Pacific Studies, University of California, Santa Cruz.

Williams, Brackette F.
1995 Classification systems revisited: Kinship, caste, race, and nationality as the flow of blood and the spread of rights. In *Naturalizing Power: Essays in Feminist Cultural Analysis,* edited by Sylvia Yanagisako and Carol Delaney, pp. 201–236. New York: Routledge.

Williamson, Ian, and Michael D. Sabath
1982 Island population, land area, and climate: A case study of the Marshall Islands. *Human Ecology* 10 (1): 71–84.
1984 Small population instability and island settlement patterns. *Human Ecology* 12 (1): 21–34.

Wilson, Lynn B.
1993 Speaking to power: Gender, politics, and discourse in the context of United States military priorities in Belau, Western Micronesia. PhD dissertation, University of Massachusetts, Amherst.

Wilson, Walter Scott
1968 Land, activity, and social organization of Lelu, Kusaie. PhD dissertation, University of Pennsylvania.
1976 Household, land, and adoption on Kusaie. In *Transactions in Kinship: Adoption and Fosterage in Oceania,* edited by Ivan A. Brady. Asao Monograph no. 4, pp. 81–92. Honolulu: University of Hawai'i Press.

Wolf, Arthur P.
1993 Westermarck recidivus. *Annual Review of Anthropology* 22:157–175.

Wolf, Eric R.
1982 *Europe and the People without History.* Berkeley: University of California Press.

Workman, Ann M., Linda Cruz-Ortiz, and Debbie Kaminga-Quinata
1994 Use of traditional medicine and healers on Guam. In *Science of Pacific Island Peoples,* vol. 3, *Fauna, Flora, Food, and Medicine,* edited by John Morrison, Paul Geraghty, and Linda Crowl, pp. 210–233. Suva, Fiji: Institute of Pacific Studies, University of the South Pacific.

Worth, Robert M., James T. Douglas, Carol Murry, Jeanne Windsor, Michael D. Lieber, and Esther Lieber
1984 A "virgin-soil" leprosy epidemic in a Polynesian population. Abstract. *International Journal of Leprosy and Other Mycobacterial Diseases* 52 (4): 740.

Yamaguchi, Osamu
1967   The music of Palau: An ethnomusicological study of the classical tradition. Master's thesis, University of Hawai'i.
1968   The taxonomy of music in Palau. *Journal of the Society for Ethnomusicology* 12 (3): 345–351.
1969   [Music in Ancient Palau.] *Ongaku-gaku* 15 (13): 39–48. In Japanese.
1973   Music as behavior in ancient Palau. *Ongaku no Tomo Sha* 1973:547–568.
1980   Palau. In *The New Grove Dictionary of Music and Musicians.* 6th ed. Vol. 12, edited by Stanley Sadie, pp. 272–273. London: Macmillan.
1985   *An Anthology of Song Texts of Belau, Micronesia: Ethnomusicological Documentation from the Fieldwork in 1965–1966.* Osaka: Osaka Daigaku Bungakubu. In English, Japanese, and Palauan.
1993   *Uta no naka no syokuminti* (Colonialism reflected in songs). *Kindai Nippon to syokuminti* (Modern Japan and its colonies), edited by Oe Sinobu et al. 7:137–156. Iwanami Series. In Japanese.

Yatar, Maria Santos
1992   With the First Canoe: Traditional Tatu of Micronesia. Video.

Yen, Douglas E.
1990   Environment, agriculture and the colonisation of the Pacific. In *Pacific Production Systems: Approaches to Economic Prehistory, Papers from a Symposium at the XV Pacific Science Congress, Dunedin, New Zealand, 1983,* edited by Douglas E. Yen and J. M. J. Mummery, pp. 258–277. Canberra: Department of Prehistory, Research School of Pacific Studies, The Australian National University.

Yoffee, Michael L.
1979   The economics of handicrafts in Micronesia. *Micronesian Reporter* 27 (3): 26–31.

Yount, David
1995   *Who Runs the University? The Politics of Higher Education in Hawaii, 1985–1992.* Honolulu: University of Hawai'i Press.

Contributors

William H. Alkire, PhD, University of Illinois, 1965. Professor, Department of Anthropology, University of Victoria, Canada.

Peter W. Black, PhD, University of California, San Diego, 1977. Professor, Department of Sociology and Anthropology, George Mason University.

Suzanne Falgout, PhD, University of Oregon, 1984. Associate Professor, Division of Social Sciences, University of Hawai'i, West O'ahu.

David L. Hanlon, PhD, University of Hawai'i, 1984. Professor, Department of History, University of Hawai'i.

Terence E. Hays, PhD, University of Washington, 1974. Professor, Department of Anthropology and Geography, Rhode Island College.

Francis X. Hezel, SJ, Doctor of Humane Letters, Fordham University, 1994. Director, Micronesian Seminar.

Edward C. King, JD, Indiana University, 1964. Arbitrator, Hawai'i Supreme Court Appellate Mediation Program; Chief Justice Emeritus, Federated States of Micronesia.

Robert C. Kiste, PhD, University of Oregon, 1967. Professor and Director, Center for Pacific Islands Studies, University of Hawai'i.

Mac Marshall, PhD, University of Washington, 1972. Professor, Department of Anthropology, University of Iowa.

Karen L. Nero, PhD, University of California, Berkeley, 1987. Senior Lecturer, Department of Anthropology, University of Auckland.

Glenn Petersen, PhD, Columbia University, 1977. Professor, Department of Sociology and Anthropology, Baruch College, City University of New York.

Lin Poyer, PhD, University of Michigan, 1983. Associate Professor, Department of Anthropology, University of Wyoming.

Donald H. Rubinstein, PhD, Stanford, 1979. Professor, Micronesian Area Research Center, University of Guam.

Subject Index

A large number of government agencies and universities are frequently mentioned throughout the text. Index entries are limited to those institutions most relevant to this analysis of American anthropology in Micronesia. With the exception of American Samoa, island groups outside Micronesia are not indexed separately. See more generic entries concerning comparisons and research in Melanesia and Polynesia.

Name Index